Praise for
Unequal Schools, Unequal Chances

"Professor Fernando Reimers has assembled a highly important volume on the relationships between poverty, inequality, and educational opportunity in six countries in the Americas. Thus he and his colleagues advance our understanding of the growing gap between the educationally and economically privileged and the educationally and economically poor in our hemisphere. We are also challenged to promote the kinds of policies and practices that will guarantee for every child the fundamental right to an education, and contribute to making a better life possible for all peoples in the Americas."

—*Johnnetta B. Cole, Presidential Professor of Anthropology, Women's Studies and African American Studies, Emory University*

"Amid repeated calls for education reform in the Americas, increasing attention has been given to the relationship between education and social equity. This book presents a comprehensive account of educational policies and practices to improve the possibilities of learning for poor children throughout the Hemisphere. This powerful compilation of refreshing contributions represents an insightful guide for policymakers and school managers of all educational levels. It is particularly valuable for those who are committed to fostering educational opportunity and social equity in this new age of globalization."

—*Cesar Gaviria, Secretary General, Organization of American States; Former President of Colombia*

"This is an extremely useful book to understand the causes and effects of educational inequality in the countries of the Americas. It is a significant contribution to the educational policy debate at the beginning of the new century and to our collective search for social justice."

—*Ricardo Lagos, President of Chile; Former Minister of Education*

"Despite all of the prominent reforms of the last decades, educational inequalities persist in the Americas and have gotten worse in some cases. These inequalities challenge the most fundamental premises of democracy and pose threats to economic competitiveness, and political stability. This book provides a penetrating analysis of the extent and causes of educational inequality in the Americas and an array of provocative solutions in a highly readable format."

—*Henry M. Levin, William Heard Kilpatrick Professor of Economics and Education, Teachers College, Columbia University*

"This book offers a critical review of alternative approaches to the crux of educational planning: the complex relationship between education and poverty. The book is an invaluable tool for decision-makers."

—*Pablo Latapí, Centro de Estudios sobre la Universidad, Universidad Nacional Autónoma de Mexico*

"Education matters a great deal in the fight against poverty and inequality. This book presents well-crafted research that substantiates much that the IDB has been defending and doing."

—*Enrique V. Iglesias, President, InterAmerican Development Bank*

"Fernando Reimers' *Unequal Schools, Unequal Chances* is insightful and timely. His leadership in the field of education policy and his deep appreciation of Latin America have combined to produce a first-rate collection that raises profoundly important questions about education and equity. Scholars, policymakers, and reformers will find this collection illuminating, challenging, highly readable, and instructive. In short, an outstanding contribution."

—*Susan C. Bourque, Esther Booth Wiley Professor of Government, Smith College*

"This is an admirable and very important book. In an era when the policy discourse regarding education is full of terms, and policy goals, like 'quality,' 'global competitiveness,' 'efficiency,' and 'standards' it is highly useful to have a major new book which focuses our attention back onto a now almost absent policy goal: EQUALITY. The book brings together analyses of recent empirical work regarding educational inequality in the Americas, presented by many of the outstanding educational researchers/policy analysts in the hemisphere. A particular merit of the book is the comprehensiveness and depth of the analysis. It treats potential reduction of educational (and life) inequality not simply as a technical, 'what works,' issue (although it deals very well with that issue), but as a profoundly and inherently political issue, in which the interests of the already powerful and well-placed are deeply invested. This book is a major advance in our understanding of educational inequality, and not only in the Americas. It should be very widely read. I rate it as a 'must read.'"

—*Joseph P. Farrell, Professor and Head, Comparative, International and Development Education Centre, Ontario, Institute for Studies in Education of the University of Toronto*

"As the Latin American educational policy community searches for politically viable, cost-effective solutions to the alarming inequity of educational achievement, this book makes an extremely important contribution to framing the debate."

—*John W. Swope, S.J., Executive Director, Secretariat for the Church in Latin America, National Conference of Catholic Bishops of the United States*

"*Unequal Schools, Unequal Chances* challenges the widely held belief that expanding the educational system by itself equalizes opportunity and earnings. It shows that in both a rich, well-educated country such as the United States and in the developing countries of Latin America, governments will have to implement policies that specifically address inequality in order to reduce it. Hopefully, policymakers throughout the hemisphere will read this book with the attention it deserves."

—*Martin Carnoy, Professor of Education and Economics, Stanford University*

"A strategic book for those concerned with education reform in Latin America where current education systems widen the social inequalities because of their low quality, equity, and relevancy of the education for the children of the poor. This book contributes many practical proposals to make education a key to empowerment, security and new ways of overcoming poverty."

—*Xabier Gorostiaga, S.J., Executive Secretary of AUSJAL (Association of the Latin American Universities Entrusted to the Society of Jesus)*

"This volume is indispensable reading for those researchers, policymakers, and practitioners interested in the issues of poverty, educational opportunity, and social inequality in the Americas. Particularly useful is the book's focus on those policy interventions that promise to overcome past inequities in schooling and society and improve the life chances of the most discriminated against students. Ultimately, *Unequal Schools, Unequal Chances* addresses the question of what education best serves the future well being of all children in the region."

—*Robert Arnove, Professor of International and Comparative Education, Indiana University; President, Comparative and International Education Society*

"The fight against poverty is foremost on UNESCO's agenda. Education is a critical tool in this respect and in achieving globalization with a human face. We need to continuously expand our knowledge and understanding of how and under what circumstances education can best promote positive development for the poor and excluded. And we need policymakers to transform such newly gained knowledge into concrete action in favor of the poor. Therefore, UNESCO welcomes this rich collection of case studies on *Unequal Schools, Unequal Chances*. UNESCO hopes it can assist in forging the much-needed link between scholarship and policymaking, not only in Latin America but in other continents as well."

—*Koïchiro Matsuura, Director-General, UNESCO*

Unequal Schools, Unequal Chances:
The Challenges to Equal Opportunity in the Americas

Edited by
Fernando Reimers

Published by
Harvard University
David Rockefeller Center for Latin American Studies

DISTRIBUTED BY
HARVARD UNIVERSITY PRESS
CAMBRIDGE, MASSACHUSETTS
LONDON, ENGLAND

A catalogue record for this book is available from the Library of Congress in
Washington, D.C.: Control No. 00-136541

ISBN 0-674-00375-6

Cover Photo: Escuela Nezahualcoyotl, Chalco, Mexico. [Jose C. Gonzalez]

To the memory of my mother, Angeles Arias,
who taught me about justice, courage, and love

Contents

Chapter 15

Chapter 16

Acknowledgments

This manuscript is the result of two years of collaboration among twenty-one colleagues studying six different countries in the Americas. Early in 1998 I invited a group of colleagues who had worked for multiple years studying issues of equality of opportunity to join me on this research project. By design, many of these colleagues are academics who have spent considerable periods of their lives as practitioners, either as direct advisers to policymakers, as policymakers themselves, or as managers of education programs. One of them is a former secretary of education; several have been deputy secretaries; and many have been advisers to presidents, secretaries of education, legislatures, and international development organizations on matters of education policy. Many of them have also been university faculty and researchers of education processes and policy with an established record of scholarship in the study of education policy and inequality. The team assembled to undertake this study thus included actors as well as students of education policy reform processes.

My purpose in bringing together this team was to produce a book from the vantage point of those who had learned up close what it takes to change the direction of national education systems and who had confronted, many of them firsthand, the successes and the disappointments of trying to change the reality of school practice through policy reform. My purpose in creating this opportunity for dialogue across national boundaries was to get us to push one another's thinking, to reexamine our deeply held assumptions, about the universality of what we each knew of the potential of education policy to reform schools and ultimately to change society.

The contributors to the book were invited to write chapters addressing questions about the educational opportunities of low-income children—about policies to improve those opportunities. They were asked to support their arguments with systematic analysis of empirical evidence and to attempt to elucidate the nature of the relationship among education, poverty, and inequality: What are the causal processes involved? What is the direction of causation? How does the education system reproduce social inequality? How does education provide opportunities for social mobility? What do we know about implementing policies to improve equity? No uniform outline or structure was imposed to try to answer these questions, although authors received a conceptual framework presented in Chapter 4. Each author was asked to highlight an aspect of these questions from his or her particular vantage point.

I apologize to those of you who think I have abused the usual prerogatives of an editor in authoring four lengthy chapters in this book. My purpose was to set this study in context, both in terms of the larger social and economic changes that make this research timely and in terms of the preexisting body of research to which this book hopes to contribute. Chapter 4 provides a conceptual framework for this study and advances a number of theoretical propositions that are examined in light of empirical evidence from Latin America.

I commented on all chapter drafts and all authors met at a seminar at Harvard in June 1999 to present and discuss each other's work. At that seminar, various members of the Harvard faculty provided additional feedback and critical questions on the chapters.

After the seminar, the authors redrafted their chapters with an eye to strengthening the unity and coherence of the final manuscript. I then made revisions to the chapters, with the help of several graduate students and copyeditors, to put together the final text. After all chapters were finalized, I wrote a concluding chapter which benefited from the critical feedback of my collaborators.

My co-authors in writing the different chapters of this book are only the most visible part of what has been truly a collaborative venture which benefited much from the support and guidance of many good friends and colleagues. I beg forgiveness to those I accidentally omit in mentioning those who stand most distinctly in my mind.

I want to express my appreciation to the David Rockefeller Center for Latin American Studies at Harvard for the financial support with the international seminar of June 1999 and to the Mexico office of the Ford Foundation which provided support to some of the participants. I especially thank my friend Steve Reifenberg, executive director of the Center, for his ongoing support of my research interests on the topics covered in this book. I thank Debra-Lee Hagopian for her efficient handling of the logistics of the seminar. I am grateful to the anonymous reviewer of the manuscript and to the publications committee of the Center, chaired by Professor Marcelo Suarez-Orozco, who made valuable recommendations to rewrite sections of the book. My gratitude also to June Erlick, director of publications of the Center and a perfect editorial director. Her skilled guidance helped to bring this project to completion. I thank Jacquie Commanday and her colleagues at Commanday Publishing Services for their good work in the production of this book. The sharp and critical minds and eyes of Jacquie Commanday and Angela Hoover Morrison in the final copyediting greatly improved the readability of the text.

On a personal level, my colleagues Noel McGinn, Richard Murnane, and Gary Orfield have generously and patiently educated me as we have talked many times about sections of what I have written here and elsewhere and about my larger interests in the topics covered in this book. I am also indebted to several of my graduate students for their valuable assistance in translating chapters and for translating during the seminar. My thanks to Laura Ascencio-Medina, Allison Borden, Andrea Broda, Claire Brown, Maria Martiniello, David Rash, Valeria Rocha, and Claudia Uribe. My gratitude also to the students who took my course on education, poverty, and inequality in Latin America in the fall of 1999 and who used and commented on a draft of this manuscript, particularly Nathalia Jaramillo and Rachel Kline, both of whom helped edit the final draft. I also thank Susan Kenyon for help in editing my own chapters.

I am also very appreciative of the help provided by my colleagues at Harvard for participating in the seminar, commenting on the manuscripts, and revising their commentary after the authors had turned in the final version of their chapter. I thank John Coatsworth, Sue Grant-Lewis, Emily Hannum, Noel McGinn, Richard Murnane, Terry Tivnan, and Lewis Tyler for their insights and time. I appreciate the generosity of Susie Fitzhugh, Jose C. Gonzalez, Arnaldo Guevara, Gregorio Marrero, Miriam Molina, Robert Myers, Joaquin Jardi of CONAFE, Carlos Cortes of Diario AZ, Ellen Tolmie, and Nicole Toutounji of UNICEF in providing photos that say so much about the promise of education in the Americas. Kelly McMurray distinguished the cover with her talent for design. My thanks also to those who so generously agreed to write endorsements for the book; their voices remind us that the issues discussed in this volume call for serious concerted efforts to improve schools where improvement is most needed.

Many of my colleagues and students at the Harvard Graduate School of Education have stimulated and supported through conversation, collaboration, or with their example my interest on the topics discussed in this book. I am grateful to have been part of this community at a time of reflection and learning about these issues. At Harvard I learned much from conversation with my colleagues Mary-Jo Bane, Merilee Grindle, and Gary Orfield and from our regular guests and participants at the inter-faculty seminar on education and poverty in the Americas in 1990–2000.

My biggest debt of gratitude is to my wife, Eleonora Villegas-Reimers, for her good spirit and constant support when our travels take us uphill and along difficult paths and specifically for all the extra work she did during the final months of completion of this manuscript, allowing me to have the necessary time to finish.

My late mother, Angeles Arias, with whom I talked about this project many times, taught me much of what I know about how to live and make choices. With the permission of my co-authors I have dedicated this book to her as an imperfect recognition of my gratitude.

One Sunday afternoon, working on the last stages of this book, I tried to explain to my sons, Tomas and Pablo, what I was doing. As we looked at pictures I had taken in Latin America of children in rural schools, my son Tomas asked, "Why don't some of these children have shoes?" "Because their parents have little money," I replied, to which he responded, "And why don't their parents have money?" "Because they couldn't go to school." My hope is that the many voices in this book can help us improve upon the reasoning of this conversation and perhaps contribute to improving the unfairness a four-year-old can see in the images of child poverty in the Americas.

Fernando Reimers
Cambridge, Massachusetts
Fall 2000

Unequal Schools, Unequal Chances:

The Challenges to Equal Opportunity in the Americas

A girl sits at her desk at the Calle Larga Escuela Nueva (New School) in the rural district of Barcelona, Colombia.
[UNICEF/90-0024/Ellen Tolmie (Colombia)]

1

What Can We Learn from Studying Educational Opportunity in the Americas and Why Should We Care?[1]

Fernando Reimers
Harvard Graduate School of Education

At the age of nine, Rosa, who lives with her family in a semirural village in a Latin American country, is still in the second grade. Like her oldest brother, now almost eleven, Rosa spent two years in first grade. At the time it seemed that most of her classmates did too. Some things seemed easier to understand the second time around, especially as Rosa could not go to school every day in first grade because she helped around her house, was ill sometimes, or took care of her younger siblings when her mother was ill. But sometimes Rosa was bored in her second round of first grade and wished she could be among her friends who were then in second grade. Nonetheless, now in second grade, Rosa likes to go to school, she likes her teacher and her friends, and she enjoys looking at the colorful pictures in her textbooks which the government provides her. Her brother, who is still in school, sometimes helps her with homework, though most days the teacher assigns no homework.

Rosa's teacher says that things are better now because the government is helping with some of the materials they use and because the teacher goes to talk with other teachers from time to time "to learn new ways to teach." An aluminum sheet painted in bright colors is posted outside the school. Rosa knows that the sign is a good thing because since it came up, early last year, more people from the city have come to her school. Last year some men came in suits and ties in big cars; they visited classrooms and talked to Rosa's teacher. Some of the parents also came that day. They posed next to the tin sign as someone took many pictures of them. Another time other men came with boxes of notebooks and pencils which the teachers distributed. Another time there was no class because the teachers had to travel to bring in boxes with beautiful posters with letters, numbers, and pictures of other places. All these good things started to happen since the sign came up, so Rosa thinks that sign, which says something about a government office, is a good thing. Rosa has heard from her teacher that the government will give her parents money if she goes to secondary school after she finishes the sixth grade. Her parents think this must be another government program, like when they came to give money to those who did not have work. Rosa doesn't know; the sixth grade seems so far away.

Hundreds of miles away from Rosa's village a group of people meet with the president-elect. They are the transition team of a government that has just been elected in the country. The president has brought together people who until recently barely knew one another. Their task is to fine-tune the details of the strategy of the new government that will take office in three months. They are also to initiate conversations with the senior government officials of the administration. Some will undoubtedly form the new Cabinet, but it is unclear yet who will be chosen. This group talks about education. The president-elect made poverty reduction a salient theme in his campaign. He thinks education should help deliver on that electoral promise. He'd like to be able to increase federal spending on education and expects his transition team will help him figure out how. Some argue for deepening the kinds of programs the current government has implemented to improve the quality of schools attended by low-income children. Others argue against this; they believe the state uses, and possibly misuses, funds that should be directly channeled to communities and civil society. Some argue for an expanded program of scholarships. Others argue for less intervention directly in the education sector and more in areas likely to increase employment and community organization.

The decisions made by this team in these discussions will likely impact the educational opportunities of Rosa and her two youngest siblings. Rosa's family has not been well educated; her mother finished fifth grade of primary school and her father went to school for only five years, but it appears to Rosa and her oldest brother that he may have finished only third grade because he did not go to school too regularly and he repeated grades a couple of times.

This book has been written on the assumption that the decisions made by this team, and others who care about the future of children like Rosa, may be more effective if they are informed by what is known about the relationship between poverty and educational opportunity, in Rosa's country and elsewhere in the hemisphere. Unfortunately, not enough is known that would allow policymakers to make error-free choices. By the standards of rigorous social science, too little is known to be of much help in informing these kinds of choices. Much of what has been written is advocacy rather than careful evaluation of the impact of programs or of the tradeoffs between alternative courses of action. Much of the existing research is based on poor designs and does not allow for the establishment of cause-and-effect relationships or for the adequate control over the likely effect of other factors, not included in the studies. An academic review of the existing stock of knowledge could go on indefinitely about the methodological weaknesses of what has been done and about the need to improve the methodological sophistication of future studies.

While further methodological savvy is needed if we are to advance our understanding of the ways to help children like Rosa stay and succeed in school, Rosa and her friends go to school now. They will be too old to be in school by the time better studies may be available. It is also unlikely that future studies will be much better if they ignore what has already been done. Those who are meeting in the capital city today will make choices now that will be of great consequence to Rosa. They may decide to stop government funding for quality improvement programs that paid for the notebooks she has received because there is not sufficient evidence that they have the desired impact. They may decide instead to discontinue the scholarship program to increase the percentage of girls who go on to secondary education because it is not clear whether the apparent growth in enrollments at that level are the result of the program, or of the programs to improve quality in rural schools, or maybe even of other programs to transfer cash to poor families.

Elected government officials and those working with them need to make policy choices with the best knowledge that is available to them. Stating that the existing knowledge is not very good is of little use in choosing among alternative courses of action. This book has been written to take stock of what we know that might be helpful in understanding how to expand the educational opportunities of children like Rosa today at the beginning of the twenty-first century. I expect that with time some of what is presented here will be superseded by knowledge generated by better research. I also hope that this stock-taking exercise might help inform what kind of knowledge is needed and how to go about generating it. I make explicit recommendations in this regard at the conclusion of this volume.

While I believe that all children have the same rights and advocate for equality of educational opportunity for all children, I have tried in this book to present arguments that are based on evidence, which can be independently verified by others regardless of whether or not we hold similar values. The validity of the conclusions reached by me and my colleagues should rest on the evidence presented in this book. I have tried to recognize the limits of such evidence. In assessing the knowledge generated by the studies I review in my chapters in this book, I have tried to concentrate on the evidence provided and to think about the ways in which the methods and designs used to obtain and analyze the evidence might have influenced the findings reported. My goal is to understand how education reproduces social stratification and to look at policies that intend to make educational opportunity more equitable.

The chapters in this book help us think about the following questions: Is it possible to attain equality of educational opportunity in highly unequal societies? How much of this can be accomplished with educational interventions? Is it possible to make education systems more egalitarian, at least to counter the inertia that leads them to reproduce initial inequalities? These questions are central to advance our understanding of the links between education and society, but they are especially pressing to inform the policy choices that will shape the future of the children of this vast region of hope.

The basic theme of this book is that there are deep inequalities in educational opportunities in the Americas for children of different social backgrounds. Even as the countries of the hemisphere have made gains in expanding access to education at all levels, when everybody gains but nonschool resources become more unequal in society, inequality is stubbornly persistent and the educational requirements for accessing the jobs that matter to improve life opportunities may be raised.

A basic paradox of both the United States and Latin America is the presence of growing levels of educational opportunity and attainment along with growing levels of income inequality and very severe, persistant poverty. Some look at this pattern and the sharp link with educational attainment and argue that education can overcome inequality and that, since all groups strongly desire education, the key is raising the quantity and quality of educational inputs and standards.

Recognizing the importance of education to attain greater social equity, this book takes issue with the view that overall expansion and improvement will accomplish this goal. Given that there are many mechanisms that will tend to preserve educational inequality even as general levels rise and that the economic and educational inequalities and other advantages of middle- and upper-class families are so powerful, some combination of social and economic policy and explicitly redistributive educational policy is necessary to produce greater educational equity on a large scale, which would, in turn, tend to produce still greater economic and social equality.

The chapters in this book provide evidence on three topics: (1) the extent and persistence of educational inequality, (2) the factors that are associated with different levels of achievement across groups of children, and (3) the kinds of policies and programs that have been implemented to foster greater educational equality and the impact of those programs on access to education and learning. The evidence is very solid on documenting the extent and persistence of educational inequality. That knowledge alone is valuable to policymakers who intend to influence schools even if it does not show what to do to solve the problem. Recognizing the extent and persistence of inequality is fundamental to addressing inequality as a policy priority. As will be discussed in this book, only recently have policies been designed explicitly with this policy objective, particularly in Latin America.

Parts of this book also show that students from particular types of backgrounds attending different types of schools have different patterns of achievement. Much of the research on school effectiveness is of this kind. This kind of knowledge is limited in that it does not tell us what will happen if particular policies are pursued, but it does suggest hypotheses as to which factors might be important in accounting for the differences described in the first group of studies.

Finally, the book describes what has been attempted. This kind of knowledge is helpful so that those who try to improve equity do not have to reinvent the wheel in generating alternatives, although it still tells us too little about the costs and effects of alternatives. The evidence is weakest on the impact of policies on access and learning. In discussing existing policies, implementation emerges as a significant topic to explain why impact appears to be so modest. The limited evidence that exists suggests that it is easier to reduce some kinds of inequalities (in access, in educational inputs) than others (in teacher practices, in learning outcomes). This knowledge is valuable for suggesting what can be reasonably expected from interventions, such as the ones recently tried in Latin America, as well as which areas need further research-based knowledge. When strong evaluations of compensatory policies become available, evaluations with adequate estimates of what would have happened in the absence of the policy intervention, they should receive the greatest attention in discussing alternative options. Those evaluations are still few and far between and choices must still be made in the absence of such knowledge.

In compiling evidence from a number of different countries in the hemisphere, I do not imply that what works in one context will work in another. The conditions of education systems differ between countries in too many ways. But examining evidence comparatively can suggest hypotheses of what might work or at least be considered in trying to expand educational opportunity, until further knowledge or evidence disconfirms its applicability. Like the research that highlights factors associated with differences in the academic results of students who experience different interventions, the comparative analysis of what has and has not worked across contexts might suggest plausible courses of action, with appropriate adjustments for known differences between contexts.

In Chapter 4, I present a conceptual framework to think about how to foster equality. I use this framework to review the existing evidence on the role of educational interventions in fostering educational opportunity. I use this framework again in Chapter 16 to review the chapters in this book and conclude that the efforts to generalize a unique model of education to all social groups are misguided and that furthering equity will require promoting diverse modalities to reach groups that are currently excluded. In thinking through some of the policy implications of the evidence reviewed in this book, I depart from the data; I try to take perspective of the larger issues at stake and to fill in the blanks not solved by sound studies with judgment and imagination.

The rest of this chapter provides a justification for this volume as well as a summary of each chapter and highlights the major contributions of each author to the basic argument of the book. I do not belabor the methodological strengths and weaknesses of each chapter, but do acknowledge their limits to inform causal inferences.

PURPOSE OF THIS BOOK

Educational opportunity is a prerequisite to improving one's chances in life. While other factors influence social opportunity, the cognitive and social skills that are gained in educational institutions are the foundation upon which people can build their future well-being. This book examines the learning opportunities of the children of the poor and the role of education policy in expanding those chances. These are subjects of practical and theoretical significance. The chapters of this book take up the study of educational opportunity in several countries of the Americas at the end of the twentieth century.

The pragmatic value of this book rests in the persisting, and arguably growing, challenges to equal educational opportunity in the hemisphere. While policy discourse in the Americas during the last half-century has advocated equal educational opportunity, persisting access and quality divides in education mirror social inequalities of origin and contribute to reproducing social stratification. Conditions have recently changed in ways that make equal opportunity an even more important, yet difficult goal to attain than in the past. We still know relatively little about the conditions that provide opportunity and about which interventions can close the learning gaps between children of different social backgrounds. For this reason we need to take stock of what we do know, both about the educational chances of the children of the poor and about the effects of policy interventions to expand those chances.

The integrating forces that operate in several countries in the hemisphere justify studying this topic in a sample of countries of the Americas. As a result of the forces of globalization, greater migratory flows, and advances in communications, the countries of this hemisphere are increasingly integrated. Poverty and inequality also unite the countries of this hemisphere. Therefore, an exploration of challenges to educational opportunity in several countries of the Americas is useful and timely. In addition, as already mentioned, examining the constraints to equality comparatively and taking stock of what is known about factors related to inequality and about the policies that have been tried to reverse it might generate hypotheses to explain and intervene in inequality and to further understand what determines it that are more robust than those generated within a narrow context.[2]

The past ten years have been characterized by a globalization of the world economy, along with an increase in income and social inequality within and between nations (Szekely and Hilgert 1999). Social exclusion follows growing inequality as those with the least schooling among the poor find it increasingly difficult to participate in social and economic processes in this new, knowledge-based economy. Unless the reduction of inequality becomes an explicit focus of policy in the coming years, a number of social divides will emerge and deepen. But such political focus and determination require knowledge of what is to be done to level the educational playing field—hence the practicality of analyzing the conditions that make the field uneven and evaluating the consequences of efforts to ameliorate opportunities for the poor.

In spite of the remarkable achievements and increases in standards of living in this hemisphere during the last fifty years, poverty is on the rise or is not diminishing as fast as it did prior to 1980. In the United States, in spite of remarkable economic performance in recent years, poverty rates have barely changed—one in every five youngsters is still poor, compared with one in seven in the 1970s. The number of people living in extreme circumstances of poverty has actually increased from 13.9 million in 1995 to 14.6 million in 1997 (Gergen 1999). In Latin America the number of people living below the poverty line increased from 136 million in 1980 to 204 million in 1997, representing 40 percent of the population (CEPAL 1999). It is apparent, as discussed in several chapters of this book, that the forces unleashed by globalization will give greater advantages to those who have more education. Unless deliberate efforts are made to increase the educational qualifications of children of the poor and to reduce educational inequality, the gap in opportunity between those who are educationally and economically privileged and those who are not will only increase.

Several scholars have documented the crucial role of education in reducing inequality. Londono (1996), for example, examining long-term trends for the region, concludes that the systematic underinvestment in human capital is at the root of the income inequalities in Latin America. Birdsall (1998) concurs with this assessment. A recent report of the InterAmerican Development Bank (1999) points to educational inequality as one of the determinants of income inequality in Latin America.

Some have argued that the policy commitment to equity and public education may be diminishing. This trend has particularly dire implications for equity since education is becoming increasingly vital in the transforming global economy. Torres and Puiggros (1997) explain that equity has shifted to a secondary position in the agenda of financially pressed states. In their view the state has retrenched from the pedagogical utopia of public education. Arnove, Franz, Mollis, and Torres (1999) make similar claims as they argue that the introduction of market-based education policies in the 1990s eroded the equity gains made in previous decades. David Post (1999) documents a worsening of educational opportunities for adolescents as a result of globalization in Mexico.

There are several excellent books that provide an overview of the key education issues facing a number of countries in Latin America (Puryear and Brunner 1995; Randall and Anderson 1999; Torres and Puiggros 1997), some of which discuss the constraints to equity in education. However, none of them specifically sets out to investigate the status of equality of educational opportunity or the impact of interventions aimed at improving opportunity, nor do they focus on the Americas as a region. The purpose of this book is to present a current account of the status of educational opportunity for low-income groups in the Americas. The goal is to offer various frameworks to conceptualize the dynamics of educational inequality at the micro level and to discuss, based on empirical evidence, the short- and long-term impact of various policy efforts aimed at expanding the learning chances of the children of the poor. In taking stock of where we are, we also hope to advance the understanding of questions and issues that merit further systematic inquiry.

STRUCTURE OF THE BOOK

The objective of this book is to unveil some of the intricacies and paradoxes in the links among education, poverty, and inequality in the Americas. Our[3] objective is as much to answer some of the central questions arising from this topic as it is to raise new questions. By taking stock of where we are and what we know, we hope to stimulate further thinking and research on this subject.

In planning this book I strove for a balance between chapters offering a regional perspective and chapters focusing, in depth, on the study of specific countries. In selecting countries I tried to cover a wide range, while also representing countries through which it was possible to document and follow policies deliberately aimed at increasing equality of educational opportunity. My original goal was to have at least two perspectives on each of the countries analyzed, but I achieved this goal for only three of the six countries discussed in the book. Further, it was not possible for all authors contacted to contribute to this book. Therefore, some countries I intended to include in this volume are unfortunately not represented. In terms of topics, authors were encouraged to look at the links among poverty and inequality and various educational outcomes, processes, and inputs; achievement differences; and, where possible, learning. They were also encouraged to look at the access to different levels of schooling and at progression from one level to another. The aim was to characterize existing relationships to try to discern the extent to which the dynamics of education serve to reproduce the larger social structure or, where the dynamics foster social change, to look at explicit policies, programs, and outcomes to make educational opportunity more equitable.

This book covers Argentina, Chile, Colombia, Mexico, Peru, and the United States, with two chapters that address Latin America as a region. The 474 million people living in these countries represent 61 percent of the people in the Americas; for the countries of Latin America included in the study, they represent 41 percent of the people in that region. Perhaps most important from the point of view of the objectives of this book, these countries represent a wide range of policy efforts over time which have resulted in different degrees of equity in these societies. For instance, the likelihood that twenty- to twenty-five-year-olds in Argentina's wealthiest 10 percent of households have completed primary education is 10 percent greater than the likelihood that their counterparts in the poorest 40 percent have completed this level. It is 30 percent more likely in Chile, 50 percent more likely in Mexico, and 60 percent more likely in Peru.[4] The likelihood of completing secondary school for the same age group is four times greater for the richest 10 percent than for the poorest 40 percent in Argentina, two times greater in Chile, seven times greater in Mexico, and two times greater in

Peru. Education and income inequality appear to be related in varied ways, or to different degrees, in the countries represented in this book.

The idea that all people should be educated is at least 150 years old in the Americas. The idea itself can be traced to the establishment of the Prussian state in the mid-eighteenth century.[5] Several modern states of the nineteenth century adopted legislation that embraced compulsory primary education following the example of the Prussian state. In the United States, Horace Mann (1891), proponent of the "common school," argued in the mid-nineteenth century that education could be the "great equalizer . . . the balance wheel of the social machinery." Domingo Sarmiento, a friend of Mann who lived for some time in Massachusetts, made the case for the development of public education and the common school in Argentina, Chile, and Paraguay in the latter part of nineteenth century. These ideas spread to the rest of South America at the beginning of the twentieth century through the works of José Pedro Varela in Uruguay and José Vasconcelos in Mexico. Following these early influences, the countries of this hemisphere expanded access to education at all levels continuously during the twentieth century. Countries like Argentina and the United States started this expansion in the nineteenth century. Others such as Costa Rica followed soon after, and still others did so in the middle of the twentieth century as part of political projects of consolidation of democracy (Venezuela) or of socialism (Cuba, Peru). Educational opportunity thus came to be perceived, in the collective consciousness of many in the Americas in the middle of the twentieth century, both as a fundamental human right, as ratified in the Universal Declaration of Human Rights in 1948 (United Nations 1949), and as a gateway to social opportunity.

The struggle to achieve equality of educational opportunity in the Americas since the declaration of human rights, however, has a mixed record. In the United States, there are still children who study in schools highly segregated by race (mostly as a function of residential segregation), even though this is illegal. The chances of U.S. citizens of Hispanic descent completing a secondary education are still significantly lower than those of any other ethnic group. In Latin America, schools are also highly segregated by the socioeconomic background of children. The educational chances of indigenous children, of those living in rural areas, and of the poor are significantly lower than those of other children.

Obviously, the expansion of access to different levels of education in all countries of the hemisphere allowed the incorporation of new social groups in schools. Where access to a particular level of education is universal, that level of educational attainment can no longer be used to reproduce social stratification. But as we will see in this book, the countries of the Americas are too far from having achieved universal access to all levels of education. The key question then becomes, who moves on through the system? To the extent the education system selects some students to move on to higher levels, which will then form the basis of further social stratification, to what extent is this selection a function of merit and student effort as opposed to social inequality of origin?

These questions are not new. As described earlier, they were central concerns to education policy reform initiatives during the 1950s and 1960s in several countries of the hemisphere, particularly the United States. The questions were also central to educational research and theory in different traditions, including structural-functionalism, conflict theory, and the new sociology of education.[6] These interpretive approaches try to explain the degree to which schools are autonomous from society, their reproductive functions, and their potential to change social inequality and structure. All of these frameworks were developed to explain the relationship between education and social structure in societies where universalization of primary education and significant expansion of secondary education had been consolidated many decades prior to these writings. Thus, while the authors' interest was in explaining the dynamic relationship between two dynamic social processes (education and social stratification), they studied education systems that exhibited, at the time of their writings, considerably less dynamism in terms of expansion than that experienced by education systems in the Americas at any other time during the twentieth century.

Nor have the key questions posed above been fully answered. It is difficult to resolve these questions because they are complex. It is even more difficult to make education systems more equitable because education is a contested terrain. Education policies reflect different views of what is desirable in life as well as competition of interests among different groups. Beginning in the mid-1970s, a new set of priorities began to influence education policy discourse around the world. The new priorities valued the development of individual, national, and global competitiveness more than the achievement of equal opportunity. In education, this translated into a greater priority accorded to quality than to access and equity.

As a result of the new education priorities, policymakers have initiated reforms during the past twenty years that aim to achieve a better link between the products of the education system and the needs of the economy and that seek to achieve efficiency gains in the management and delivery of education. It is thus that the twentieth century concluded with much of the education debate occupied by questions about minimum standards, testing, decentralization and management, vouchers and privatization, and discussions about what kind of education is suitable for what kind of economy.[7] Of course, the questions about the extent to which education systems around the world are providing equal educational opportunity to all children also occupy a place in the education debate. These are questions to which many different groups in different societies, and several of the United Nations Organizations, particularly UNDP, UNICEF, and UNESCO, consistently return.

The World Conference on Education for All, held in Jomtien, Thailand, was largely about achieving equal educational opportunity at the basic level. The two influential education policy frameworks produced by UNESCO over the past twenty years, the Faure report and the Delors report, are also fundamentally about equality of educational opportunity. The hemispheric presidential summit which took place in Santiago in March 1998 agreed that education was the most important area for hemispheric initiative and explicitly linked its priority to reducing poverty in the hemisphere.

But reports, conferences, and policy frameworks are only part of the education landscape in the Americas as the century concludes. We need to take stock of where we are in terms of what happens as poor children enroll in school, or fail to do so, as they try to learn, as some of them drop out, as some proceed to the next levels. We need to assess the effects of policy interventions designed to improve equity.

Again, the purpose of this book is to portray the relationship among education, poverty, and inequality in this hemisphere at the end of the twentieth century and to discuss the effect of policies implemented to increase the educational opportunities of poor children. Poverty and inequality are not the same thing. It is possible to reduce inequality without influencing poverty, and it is possible to reduce poverty without influencing inequality.[8] It is important to advance our understanding of these concepts and of their dynamic relationships. How does poverty relate to educational poverty; how do both of them relate to education and social inequality? How is this relationship influenced by the degree of educational expansion, by the rate of growth of the education system, and by other social and economic forces at work in different societies? How does the relationship between education inequality and poverty and between social class of origin and educational attainment change over time?

The portrait presented by the chapters of this book is, like any undertaking of its kind, inevitably limited. It is limited because not all countries of the hemisphere are represented and because the emphases of the different authors of this book vary, from those who focus primarily on financing policies, to those who look at broad policy reforms, to those who look at specific programs and projects to expand educational opportunity, to those who do not look at any program or policy at all. Most of the chapters focus on the meso level, discussing the institutional dynamics of education and inequality, with some inroads to the micro level, examining the role of school and household influences and interactions. A few have references to macro-level influences in the form of competing forces in shaping state performance. This collection is limited, like any exercise in social analysis, by the particular perspectives adopted by the authors to analyze the subject. The knowledge offered by these chapters is also limited by the methods used to generate it, which do not allow us to establish causation. The studies examining empirical evidence do describe the extent and nature of inequalities, and the factors associated with them, but they do not shed light on what causes inequality or on the impact of particular interventions to address them. None of the chapters discusses true experiments with randomized assignments of students to treatment groups. Only two studies use multiple regression in an attempt to isolate the effect of interventions from other factors that might likely cause the observed effects, but given the selection effects, even multiple regression is limited to establish causality. For all these limitations, my hope is that this book will contribute to the much-needed debate and stock taking on education, poverty, and inequality in the Americas at the end of the twentieth century. The portrait that emerges from the following pages is informative in what it details but also in what it omits. It informs our perspective with facts and explanations as well as with the questions that still remain unanswered.

SUMMARY OF THE CHAPTERS

Chapter 2, "Perspectives in the Study of Educational Opportunity," situates this volume historically in the context of research previously conducted. My attempt has not been to select studies based on methodological sophistication or adequacy, but to highlight the main lines of thinking that have characterized this field over the last decades. I believe this previous work, with its strengths and limitations, has influenced current education policy and research and is therefore the historical foundation on which this volume is situated. I highlight which questions have been addressed by extant research and which questions remain unanswered.

Chapter 3 by Charles Willie, "Excellence, Equity, and Diversity in Education," discusses several key foundational concepts to the study of educational opportunity. He argues for the centrality of equity as a goal of education policy and for the importance of targeted efforts to reach disadvantaged groups in order to attain equality of educational opportunity. He discusses schools as social institutions where the composition of the school is a critical factor in explaining opportunity for students of different racial and socioeconomic background. From an analysis of evidence collected in a recent study in Charleston, South Carolina, Willie concludes that achieving racial and socioeconomic diversity in the composition of the student body is an effective way to maximize equality of educational opportunity.

Willie's chapter contributes to setting the stage for the rest of the book, elaborating several key themes: Why equity and diversity are important, not just for social reasons, but for educational and pedagogical reasons as well. The chapter shows, at the same time, that change is possible, but slow and difficult to achieve. The evidence of how educational expansion in the United States signified large gains in educational attainment for minority groups is indicative of the importance of policy choices. The persistence of inequality, however, also reminds us of the fact that the task of achieving equality of educational opportunity is far from complete in the United States.

Willie's chapter also signals the importance of identifying critical points of intervention to further equality. Willie focuses on the importance of the social context of schools and the mix of students, and he demonstrates how it matters for the learning opportunities of different students. The study does not unravel the specific mechanisms by which integrated schools lead to higher levels of achievement for poor and black students and to the lowest gaps in educational attainment among all groups. One can hypothesize that the causal links might involve direct effects of peer groups, bringing the different social capital brought in by all students to bear on the education of each member of a class. Links might involve indirect effects as well, leading to different instructional processes and routines experienced in integrated schools. But this study shows the power of parsimony in explanation, as the findings tie in with a very specific policy instrument—desegregation.

These findings, alas, point also to the role of social forces in resisting the best intentions of policy reform. That half of the black students in this county attend schools that are highly segregated, forty-seven years after the Supreme Court of the United States ruled that segregated schools were illegal, is a humbling reminder of the limits of policy reform in affecting school change. A likely counterfactual scenario is that in the absence of such policy intervention a situation of educational apartheid would be prevalent. A logical question stemming from these findings is to know what it would take, and how much longer, to integrate the segregated environments in which half of the black student population and one-tenth of the white student population go to school even now. The chapter inspires another question for reflection about the social purpose of schools. What can students learn about others, about valuing differences, in schools that limit their opportunities to meet and interact with those who are different?

In Chapter 4, "Educational Opportunity and Policy in Latin America," I present an overview of the relationship among education, poverty, and inequality. After discussing the high levels of poverty and inequality in Latin America, the chapter compares the education profiles of the poor and the non-poor which define essentially two populations within each country, with 25 percent of those living in urban areas having twice as many years of schooling as the poorest 25 percent. In the chapter, I propose a five-step ladder of educational opportunity, progressing from the opportunity to enroll in first grade to the opportunity that the skills learned in school might afford all graduates the same life chances. Most of the emphasis of education policy in the region concentrates on the first level of opportunity, and I argue it is this misguided understanding of educational opportunity that explains, in part, the limited educational opportunities for poor children in the region. The information analyzed in the chapter shows that social inequality of origin significantly influences the probability of repeating a grade and of completing primary school, as well as transition rates to secondary school and participation at high school and university levels.

Unequal access to preschool by different income groups is the first and most important divider in the education system. Most of the chapters in this book will reiterate this theme; as countries in the region have succeeded at universalizing access to primary education, inequalities have been pushed to earlier grades (preschool) and to later grades. It is thus that the children of the poor are not as likely to enter school or as ready to learn as their non-poor counterparts, and it is thus that most of them will not make it to the end of primary education. The discussion of unequal school inputs shows that the education system reproduces social inequality, by providing substandard learning environments to low-income children.

From Willie's discussion, and from the five-step model of educational opportunity, it follows that unequal treatment is necessary to compensate for social inequalities. Chapter 4 notes that many low-income children do not even have learning environments equivalent to those raised in higher-income homes. The last argument, regarding the lack of compensatory policies, follows from the model of equality espoused earlier: Not enough is being done to affirm the educational opportunities of low-income children, which would call for more than equal treatment. The discourse of affirmative action is, I argue, relatively recent in the region; it appears timidly at the beginning of the 1990s in calls for "positive discrimination." Many of the policies and programs carried out since are discussed in this book. Chapter 4 raises a question that will stay with us as we read through subsequent chapters: Are these efforts enough? How much affirmative action is necessary to overcome the deep social inequalities characterizing Latin America? Chapter 5 begins to discuss some of the efforts under way in this regard.

In Chapter 5, "Educating the Poor in Latin America and the Caribbean: Examples of Compensatory Education," Donald Winkler offers a framework to classify approaches to improving educational opportunity for poor children. He then reviews a number of ongoing programs in the region and discusses what is known about their impact. The chapter adds an important theme to this book: the need for systematic evaluation of ongoing actions to expand educational opportunity. Winkler shows that there is a wide range of actions to expand educational opportunity under way already and that, to an extent, these actions show that it is possible to ameliorate conditions for the education of poor children, particularly in terms of access. His conclusion, assessing the existing evidence about the impact of these programs, is "to neither rejoice unduly in the successes nor to despair excessively in the failures." Winkler's search for evidence of impact in the areas of quality alludes to a central theme of the book, to which several authors will return: Should the purpose of compensatory education be to enable poor students to do just as well as the other students (even if this means only bringing them at par with relatively low levels of student achievement), or should it be to improve quality beyond what other students are achieving? There is no easy answer to this question because it is apparent that in a changing social and economic context, schools should do more to help students opt for better social opportunities. The chapters by the Schiefelbeins (8) and Orfield (15) particularly address the question of the relevancy of specific knowledge to help disadvantaged groups change their position in the social structure.

Argentina, one of the first countries in the hemisphere to adopt legislation to provide universal primary education, is the context in which Ines Aguerrondo studies the question "Can education measure up to poverty?" in Chapter 6. Aguerrondo's answer to this question is multifaceted. On the one hand, she argues that, indeed, educational expansion in Argentina gave new social groups additional educational opportunities. She shows that education matters for social opportunity. Those few Argentineans who have not been to school cannot read; those who have been to school even a few years are more likely to be literate. She argues that without literacy all kinds of opportunities for social participation are foregone. She also shows that completing primary school helps to obtain credit to buy housing, increases the likelihood of obtaining adequate health coverage, and is associated with better health practices and care for children. This constitutes part of her two-pronged explanation of the relationship between education and poverty: Those with less education are more likely to be poor because of their lack of education.

At the same time, poverty leads to lower educational opportunities. For all the early achievements of Argentina's education system, it still today segregates students by social class of origin. The main gateways, Aguerrondo argues, are preschool and university education. But in primary education there are also important quality cleavages that separate students of different social groups. It is thus that Aguerrondo talks about three types of educational marginalization: marginalization through total exclusion (no access), marginalization through early exclusion (no completion), and marginalization through inclusion (tracks of different quality). The chapter systematically examines evidence to explore these three forms of marginalization facing the poor in Argentina today. We see how while there are still differences between the poor and the non-poor in primary completion rates, the main differences are in completion rates at secondary or higher education.

Chapter 6 is central to the book for two reasons. First, Aguerrondo illustrates the pervasiveness of educational inequality even in a society with more than a century of espoused commitment to equal educational opportunity. Second, the chapter shows that it is indeed possible to expand educational opportunity for new social groups as a result of policy choices—policy and priorities do clearly matter. The Social Action Plan illustrates a new generation of education reforms initiated in Latin America that attempt to reconstruct the meaning of equality of opportunity, from equal opportunity to enroll in school to providing more resources to the most vulnerable members of society. Other chapters in the book explore similar policies. Whether this latest generation of equity reforms will truly close social gaps is a question that the chapter leaves unanswered.

Chapters 7 and 8 discuss recent policy reform efforts in Chile aimed at overcoming educational inequality. They reach different conclusions, highlighting some of the difficulties implicit in the analysis of compensatory policies. The core of the disparate conclusions is in the standard used to gauge success. One point of view would argue that reforms that help low-income children learn more and that close the gap with the non-poor are successful. Another point of view would argue that equating outcomes with those of the non-poor is a very low standard, as the education that the non-poor receive is of low quality too, and therefore not pertinent to help low-income children improve their life chances. This brings back the question of what kind of education is relevant to help poor children aspire to a better life.

In Chapter 7, "Educational Policies and Equity in Chile," Juan Eduardo García-Huidobro presents and discusses the results of the major education policy initiatives undertaken in Chile since the arrival of democratic government in 1990. The chapter discusses the content of two specific targeted programs: the 900 Schools Program and the Rural Primary Education Program. The 900 Schools Program was the first visible action of the democratic government, initially intended to improve the infrastructure of 10 percent of all schools (those attended by the poorest students). From an emphasis on improving physical infrastructure and providing teaching materials, the program gradually shifted to emphasizing teacher education and training supervisors to focus more on pedagogical matters. The program also ran learning workshops for those children who were not performing at grade level. The Rural Primary Education Program targeted isolated, small rural schools and emphasized providing opportunities for teachers to discuss pedagogical challenges and innovative approaches with other teachers, along with providing instructional materials and teaching guides.

The significance of Chapter 7 to this volume lies in that it demonstrates that it is possible to address equality of educational opportunity through public policy choices. García-Huidobro suggests that it is possible to narrow the gap between the poorest students and their non-poor counterparts as a result of a series of rather modest interventions in a relatively short period of time. This chapter, with the others preceding it, emphasizes the importance of focusing on learning and not just on access to school. The chapter also suggests further questions to the understanding of the topic of equality: How much is required to compensate for unequal initial conditions facing children of different social backgrounds, and how long will it take to overcome these learning gaps? The next chapter develops some of these questions even further, anchoring the analysis of equity gaps not on how much different groups learn, but on what they learn and the extent to which that knowledge is pertinent to help them advance their chances in life.

Chapter 8, "Education and Poverty in Chile: Affirmative Action in the 1990s," presents a less sanguine perspective on the impact of the reforms undertaken to improve equity during the last ten years. Ernesto and Paulina Schiefelbein argue that while these reforms have indeed shown a modest impact on student achievement levels in test scores, these levels are still very low for students in private schools and that a substantial gap remains between them and students in public schools.

The authors contend that the main shortcomings of the reforms that have been implemented are that they do not prepare school graduates for lifelong learning, adaptation to change, application of knowledge to new situations, adoption of new methods, organization of new tasks, openness to new ideas, taking initiative, accepting responsibility, and ongoing training in how to use critical thinking skills. They point out that the second main reason students drop out of school, after economic hardship, is that they find what they are studying irrelevant to their lives. The authors conclude that the 20 percent increase in student achievement over a decade should also be assessed against the doubling of the education budget over the same period. In discussing the potential impact of the programs that have been funded, the Schiefelbeins argue that they are traditional and have failed to address teaching approaches and therefore missed an opportunity to prepare graduates for the demands of the twenty-first century.

Chapter 8 brings up a very important purpose of this book. In attempting to improve equality in educational opportunity, should the emphasis be on overcoming past inequities or in preparing all students for the future? Is closing the gap in learning outcomes between the poor and the non-poor sufficient when neither of them is being helped by schools to develop skills that will be valued in the new economy of the twenty-first century? And, if the aim should be to improve equity with an eye toward the future, rather than to the past, who knows what the future will require? What are the skills that should be central as criteria to evaluate the success of policy reform? It is in this regard that an equity and excellence perspective might come together. In Chapter 15, Gary Orfield returns to some of these questions as he discusses the record of U.S. equity reforms.

In Chapter 9, "Equity and Education in Colombia," Alfredo Sarmiento offers a comprehensive case study examining the relationship among education, poverty, and equity in Colombia and discusses the changes in educational opportunity over the past several decades. The chapter examines the main policy interventions implemented by Colombia in an attempt to equalize educational opportunities. A fundamental area of reform has been in the financing of education. The constitutional reform of 1991 attempted to reconcile multiple agendas with regard to education. Regarding financing, the main changes were aimed at securing a steady and predictable resource base for education and at favoring the poor in allocating resources. The financing formula to allocate education resources to departments and municipalities is based on population and relative poverty of the region, as well as administrative and fiscal efficiency. Begun in 1995, there is also a compensation fund to specifically target poor students. In the chapter, Sarmiento discusses the limitations of this policy reform, particularly regarding the tradeoffs between multiple objectives, the bureaucratic inertia that has hampered the transformation of the role of the federal ministry, and the inadequacy of management instruments. He argues that education is a long-term investment and that the impact of policy changes can be appropriately evaluated only over the long term. He shows that private financing of education accounts for almost as much as public spending (4.2 percent of GDP versus 5.7 percent of GDP). This suggests that even progressive criteria in allocating public expenditures will be balanced by the regressive nature of private expenditures, where those who have more can spend more in the education of their children.

Chapter 9 highlights the central themes of this book: the pervasiveness of inequality, how social and income inequality is related to educational inequality, and how educational inequality is growing. But the chapter also points out that it is possible to change policy priorities in the form of more progressive financing of education and in the form of support to new programs of positive discrimination. While the result of these changes should be assessed in the long term, short-term available evidence suggests that it is possible to obtain effects, in the form of more progressive allocations of education expenditures and in the form of increased learning gains for low-income children in rural schools. Are these changes enough to overcome the social inequalities that are pervasive in Colombia and in other Latin American countries? The chapter does not answer this question but argues that making education a more progressive force for social inclusion is preferable, for all in the region, to the alternatives.

In Chapter 10, "Poverty and Education in Mexico, 1984–1996," Teresa Bracho examines the relationship between educational attainment of household heads and relative poverty at different points during this period. The chapter concludes by examining why educational participation is disproportionately lower for children in the poorer households. Policies to achieve universal primary enrollment during the past ten years have had a noticeable impact on the poorest segments of society, but at the same time the gap between rich and poor has moved up and now applies to participation in secondary and higher education.

Chapter 10 also describes the relationship between educational attainment and income in Mexico and how that relationship has evolved during a period of important economic reforms intended to further integrate Mexico into the world's economy. The chapter shows that it is possible to narrow the gaps in educational participation among income groups in relatively short periods of time, as shown in the incorporation of primary school age children who were still out of school during the last ten years as a result of deliberate policy initiatives. As universal access is gained at the primary level, the main distinction between income groups becomes higher levels of education, most notably postsecondary and higher education. The chapter also shows the persistence of basic patterns of inequality between regions and between indigenous and nonindigenous groups, in spite of almost a century of education reforms. Is the persistence of these forms of exclusion an indication of insufficient priority accorded to overcoming them? Is it a sign of the complexity of overcoming them? Does it signal the failure of education reform to address these forms of exclusion?

In Chapter 11, 'The Schooling Situation of Children in Highly Underprivileged Rural Localities in Mexico," Patricia Muñiz examines the impact of sociodemographic variables in school attendance in highly disadvantaged rural communities. The chapter examines evidence from the 1995 national census and from a special household survey conducted between 1996 and 1998 in the most disadvantaged rural communities in Mexico designed to monitor implementation of the Education, Health, and Nutrition Program (Progresa), a supply-oriented intervention to improve the living conditions of the poor. This survey covered 35 percent of the communities with less than 5,000 people and 48 percent of the total number of the most underprivileged locations. Muñiz selected a sample of 100,000 households for analysis. Within this sample she classified households as poor and non-poor. Since these households are all located in highly disadvantaged communities, the divide is between relative degrees of poverty, separating the extremely poor from those who are less poor. It should be noted that only communities in which there was ready access to a school were selected, so the chapter does not compare the households surveyed with those located in extremely isolated communities or with those located in not-disadvantaged communities. The focus of the analysis is on children who, because of their age, should be enrolled in compulsory schooling (six to sixteen).

Chapter 11 contributes to our understanding of the fact that school participation is the result of multifaceted social processes, which include decisions made at home by parents and children as they face alternative options for use of their time. The analysis takes for granted the presence of a school where the child can participate and assumes equivalent quality among schools. It therefore also assumes that the decisions made by households are independent of the conditions children encounter in school.

Chapter 12, "Education and Indian Peoples in Mexico: An Example of Policy Failure," by Sylvia Schmelkes discusses the deep educational cleavages separating indigenous children from their mestizo and white counterparts in Mexico. Schmelkes discusses what is perhaps one of the oldest taboos in education policy in Latin America: the racism that is at the root of the limited educational and social opportunities facing Indian children. Almost 7 million culturally Indian Mexicans—those who speak an Indian language—account for over 6 percent of the total population of the country. They are disproportionately poor, living in the poorest regions, and are concentrated in nine of the thirty-two states. Because of lower life expectancy and greater fertility, a great many of them, two in five, are children under fifteen years of age. These children have the lowest educational attainment, as evidenced in a recent national survey to establish the extent to which Mexican children achieved the intended curriculum standards in different grades in primary education. The percentage of Indian children who meet the curriculum standards is comparable only to those who meet the standards in courses offered in marginalized rural communities, and lower than the numbers meeting the standard in rural and urban public and private schools.

Chapter 12 explores some themes that are central to this book. It documents the unequal opportunities and outcomes for children of different ethnic and cultural backgrounds. It suggests that where there are high levels of initial inequality, and lower social opportunities for members of racial minorities, extending access to a single model of school is not sufficient to achieve equality of outcomes. The most obvious expression of this limitation concerns the language of instruction. Offering Indian children access to schools taught exclusively in Spanish in first grade is a way to lead them to early school failure. The chapter also suggests the importance of implementation of policy as one of the key arenas where conflicting views on education policy are resolved. It is unclear whether the recent decentralization reforms in Mexico will help further progress in educational opportunities for indigenous groups or whether they will set them back. The local forms and sources of racial discrimination may be accentuated now that the federal government has relinquished responsibility for basic education to the states without keeping any explicit responsibility for furthering racial equality.

An underlying theme of Chapter 12 is the extent to which struggles for equal educational opportunity are political struggles, among different groups in society with competing views on whose interests should be advanced through education and at what cost. From the chapter, one can conclude that indigenous people in Mexico, and perhaps in the rest of the hemisphere, have been marginalized by an education system that gives them limited opportunities only at the price of giving up their indigenous identity. To what extent these historical trends can and will be reversed in the coming decades is still very much an open question, the answer to which will be revealed only as people in this region, primarily the nonindigenous, begin to appreciate and value cultural diversity not as a threat but as a source of richness and as indigenous communities gain a greater voice in shaping collective priorities.

In Chapter 13, "Function and Evaluation of a Compensatory Program Directed at the Poorest Mexican States: Chiapas, Guerrero, Hidalgo, and Oaxaca," Carlos Muñoz

Izquierdo and Raquel Ahuja Sanchez discuss the implementation and results of a five-year program to target school resources to disadvantaged children in the poorest Mexican states. The authors offer a rich and detailed description and analysis of the dynamics of implementation in the operation of the program and of the schools but then find large gaps between program theory and actual implementation. The program, as implemented, was different from the one intended.

Chapter 13 is important because it offers an empirically based evaluation of the implementation of a program to compensate for unequal educational opportunities. The results, unfortunately, are more revealing of the unequal educational conditions encountered by children of different socioeconomic backgrounds and of the difficulties in implementing this type of program than of any positive effects. It is possible that evaluating the impact of this type of program requires long lags—that we should not expect quick victories in overcoming the effects of long and sustained unequal educational and social conditions. It is also possible that some important effects should be assessed in domains other than academic achievement. Perhaps we should assess school retention and the development of self-esteem, attitudes, and social skills that can help low-income children stay in school and reach higher levels of education. An important finding of this study is the identification of the highly segregated nature of school systems in Mexico. We should ponder the implications of such segregation for the educational and social opportunities of low-income children and for the quality of education for all children. As discussed by Willie, we know that the composition of the peer group is an important influence in educational achievement in the United States and other contexts. Low-income children gain more from learning in diverse education settings. We can argue that in many ways all children gain from learning in diverse settings to the extent that such settings lead them to better appreciate fellow students from different social and ethnic backgrounds, laying the foundation for social cohesion amid cultural and socioeconomic diversity. Is this possible in school systems that channel students into compartmentalized streams reflecting their socioeconomic origins?

Muñoz Izquierdo and Ahuja Sanchez conclude by challenging the way compensatory programs are designed, with a priori assumptions about what will work to overcome the obstacles faced by all children. They argue, instead, for a bottom-up approach that starts at the root, in each type of school setting, identifying the problems and involving local actors in the identification of interventions and processes necessary to improve their school. Their challenge moves the search for effective interventions to foster equity away from "borrowing" magic bullets across contexts and away from production-function approaches, toward experimentation and bottom-up school improvement.

Chapter 14, "Education and Poverty in Peru," by Kin Bing Wu, Patricia Arregui, Pete Goldschmidt, Arturo Miranda, Suhas Parandekar, Jaime Saavedra, and Juan Pablo Silva, discusses the role of educational finance in fostering inequality. The authors point out that in Peru, one of the countries in the region with the greatest disparities in income distribution and high levels of poverty, access to education for children of different socioeconomic backgrounds is surprisingly equitable. Furthermore, most of the gains in expanding education were achieved during the last five decades when the average level of education of the population older than fifteen years increased from 1.9 years to 7.5 years and illiteracy rates dropped from 58 percent to 11 percent of the population. Policy reforms in the 1950s and 1960s brought this country from an average position in the region (in terms of its education indicators) to a level comparable to that of Argentina and Chile, which had had much longer and sustained commitments to education. What is even more remarkable is that this significant expansion of the education system was achieved at relatively low, and fluctuating, levels of public expenditures in education, currently at 3 percent of GDP. These levels were particularly low during the last twenty-seven years.

Wu and her colleagues discovered that private contributions to education amount to 2 percent of Peru's GDP, two-thirds of the total spent by the government on education. These contributions are made disproportionately by parents in upper-income groups, even for those who enrolled their children in public institutions. As a result, the amount of private resources spent on education reflects the high-income inequality of Peruvian society. A distribution of public resources that is neutral respective of income cannot counteract the unequal opportunities resulting from such differences in the contributions made by households. The poorest 20 percent of the population accounts for only 4 percent of the private expenditures in education, compared to the richest 20 percent, which accounts for 57 percent of these expenditures.

The authors discuss evidence that Peruvian parents, rich and poor, value education highly and that educational participation changes little as a result of differences in income. But some parents are more able to pay for school fees, education materials, and transportation costs; as a result, private expenditures mirror income inequality.

Chapter 14 contributes two principal points to the themes explored in this book. The first is the very real possibility of expanding access to education and significantly improving the levels of education of the population, including the poor, even in the context of high income inequality. The other theme discussed by the chapter relates to the limitations of government education expenditures as an instrument to achieve greater equality. Participation of the poor in a given education level only partially influences equity. Another influence stems from the actual amounts spent by the government for children attending different kinds of schools. A third, and a most significant influence in the chapter, stems from the financial contributions parents make to the education of their children. Perhaps these are the most visible expression of the differential contributions parents from different social groups can make to the education of their children. Even when all parents value education highly, the acute levels of economic and social inequality enable some parents to transfer more advantages to their children than others. This is a most significant undercurrent of resistance to equality of opportunity facing education systems in the hemisphere. Recognizing its significance is central to understanding the justification for affirmative action, positive discrimination, and compensatory policies. Several chapters have raised the question of the extent to which positive discrimination policies should be funded: How much is needed to achieve equality? A possible answer to this question would be: as much as is necessary to overcome the educational advantages of the children of the non-poor resulting from the greater resources available to their parents. In contexts such as Peru, where private contributions amount to two-thirds of public expenditures on education and are severely skewed toward the upper-income groups, public expenditures would have to be distributed in a reverse mirror image among income groups simply to make the total distribution of expenditures neutral.

Chapter 15, "Policy and Equity: Lessons of a Third of a Century of Educational Reforms in the United States," by Gary Orfield, reviews two distinct eras in U.S. education policy since mid-century. He claims that between 1960 and 1980 the emphasis of education policy was on equity issues and since the 1980s the emphasis has been on competition and standards. Orfield argues that there have been important setbacks in equity in the United States: "A number of inequalities are actually becoming worse. Policy-makers in other societies should look on any claims that the United States has found the path to major breakthroughs on education with considerable skepticism."

The chapter concludes by reviewing the lessons learned from policy reforms in the areas of language of instruction, compensatory education, and market-based reforms. Orfield argues that the U.S. experience documents the difference national leadership can make in setting an agenda aimed at improving the opportunities of low-income students and the importance of the federal role in a broad equity agenda because the poorer members of society tend to have less voice in local politics. Given the ongoing efforts to decentralize educational management in many countries of the hemisphere, this reminder of the potential role of the federal government is particularly significant.

Orfield speaks to several of the central themes of this book: the need to assess the impact of policy on equity over long periods of time; the compelling evidence that it is possible, through policy reform, to improve educational opportunity; and that it is equally possible to reverse these gains as a result of shifts in policy priorities. Orfield joins other authors in this volume who raise the question "What should schools teach poor children to help them gain greater opportunities?" He challenges the use of achievement tests because of their emphasis on short-term gains, poor links to social mobility, and omission of potential gains in other domains arguably more important for the social advancement of low-income children and for the contribution to a more democratic society. A theme this chapter illustrates is the importance of having a good base of research and evaluation-based knowledge to inform our analysis of policy alternatives in terms of their potential impact on equity.

Finally, Chapter 16, "Conclusions: Can Our Knowledge Change What Low-Income Children Learn," reprises some of the major themes of the book, highlights specific policy recommendations that emerge from the evidence examined, and suggests directions for further research.

NOTES

1. I appreciate the helpful feedback of Noel McGinn, Gary Orfield, and Richard Murnane to a draft of this chapter. As I have responded to their advice selectively and partially, at times disagreeing and ignoring consciously their suggestions, I alone am responsible for the ideas presented here.
2. The risks of inappropriately generalizing findings beyond the range of values studied in specific studies is quite obvious here. The systematic stock taking of regularities across contexts will illuminate what can be generalized and what cannot. There will be areas where it is not possible to examine regularities because there is no comparable research across contexts; this will be suggestive of potential future lines of inquiry.
3. I use the collective *we* to refer to the joint purpose of the contributors of the book. I use the pronoun *I* to describe my individual ideas or purposes.
4. See Chapter 4 in this book for more detail on the differences between the countries of the region.

5. See Green (1990). I am grateful to my colleagues Patricia Graham and Julie Reuben for their advice regarding the history of universal education.
6. For some of the major works in these traditions, see Bowles and Gintis (1976); Carnoy and Levin (1986); Durkheim (1956); and Weber (1947).
7. A good example of this kind of argumentation is the chapter on education policy options in the report of the InterAmerican Development Bank devoted to inequality in the Americas (1999).
8. Reducing poverty requires that some among the poor improve their income beyond the poverty line; this may happen even as the non-poor also increase their income, leaving inequality unchanged. In this case, poverty would be reduced, in an absolute sense, without affecting inequality. It is similarly possible to change inequality; for example, by changes in the relative share of income among groups above the poverty line, without affecting the percentage of the people living below the poverty line. In this case, inequality would be changed, without influencing poverty.

REFERENCES

Arnove, Robert, Stephen Franz, Marcela Mollis, and Carlos Alberto Torres. 1999. Education in Latin America at the end of the 1990s. In *Comparative Education: The Dialectic of the Global and the Local,* ed. R. Arnove and C. A. Torres, 305–328. Lanham, Md.: Rowman and Littlefield.

Birdsall, Nancy. 1998. The people's asset: Education in Latin America. Paper presented at the Thirtieth Anniversary Conference, Special Program for Urban and Regional Studies of Developing Areas. Cambridge, Mass.: Massachusetts Institute of Technology.

Bowles, Samuel, and Herbert Gintis. 1976. *Schooling in Capitalist America: Education and the Contradictions of Economic Life.* New York: Basic Books.

Carnoy, Martin, and Henry Levin. 1986. Educational reform and class conflict. *Journal of Education* 168(1): 35–46.

CEPAL (UN Economic Commission for Latin America). 1999. *Panorama Social 1998.* Santiago, Chile: United Nations.

Durkheim, Emile. 1956. *Education and Sociology.* Glencoe, Ill.: Free Press.

Gergen, David. 1999. *U.S. News and World Report* (July 16): 64.

Green, Andy. 1990. *Education and State Formation.* New York: St. Martin's Press.

InterAmerican Development Bank. 1999. *Facing up to Inequality in Latin America.* Washington, D.C.: InterAmerican Development Bank.

Londono, Juan Luis. 1996. *Poverty, Inequality, and Human Capital Development in Latin America, 1950–2025.* Washington, D.C.: World Bank.

Mann, Horace. 1891. *The Twelfth Annual Report.* New York: Dillingham.

Post, David. 1999. Globalization, national policy, and the distribution of educational opportunity for Mexican adolescents. Mimeograph. College Park, Penn.: Pennsylvania State University, Department of Education Policy Studies.

Puryear, Jeffrey, and José Joaquin Brunner, eds. 1995. *Educacion, Equidad y Competitividad Economica en las Americas.* Washington, D.C.: Organization of American States.

Randall, Laura, and Joan Anderson, eds. 1999. *Schooling for Success.* New York: Sharpe.

Szekely, Miguel, and Marianne Hilgert. 1999. The 1990s in Latin America: Another decade of persistent inequality. Mimeograph. Washington, D.C.: InterAmerican Development Bank.

Torres, Carlos Alberto, and Adriana Puiggros, eds. 1997. *Latin American Education. Comparative Perspectives.* Boulder, Colo.: Westview Press.

Weber, Max. 1947. *The Theory of Social and Economic Organization.* Glencoe, Ill.: Free Press.

Students meet in the morning outside the Gesu School in Philadelphia, Pennsylvania, before class begins.

2

Perspectives in the Study of Educational Opportunity

Fernando Reimers
Harvard Graduate School of Education

Research into the links among poverty, inequality, and education is not new. As topics of scientific inquiry in the sociology of education, these subjects are at least thirty years old. But much of the existing knowledge about how education and poverty relate was distilled from contexts rather different from the countries of the Americas today. For example, some of the earliest studies about education and social opportunity in the United States were conducted during the 1960s—a time when a series of progressive policies were just being launched and when there had not been sufficient time to assess policies' impact or sustainability (Coleman et al. 1966). In Europe during the 1970s, some of the seminal work on these relationships stemmed from the analysis of education systems that had been consolidated for many decades (Bernstein 1975; Bourdieu and Passeron 1977). In contrast to the European education systems of the 1960s and 1970s, the education systems in the Americas have expanded significantly during most of the twentieth century and access to education at all levels has increased to incorporate new social groups. As a result of this expansion, many of the children attending elementary and secondary education in the Americas exceed the level of educational attainment of their parents. Many teachers themselves gained higher levels of education and social status through professional opportunities than did their parents. Many of these teachers know from experience, and model for their students, how education can help improve individuals' opportunities in life.

Education reform has for many governments in the hemisphere been a central policy instrument in the effort to influence the distribution of social opportunities.[1] But in the unique and vastly changing educational and social landscape of this region, it is not enough to assume that the answers to old questions about social stratification and educational opportunity are necessarily still valid.

At the end of World War II, a number of educators in democratic countries proposed that it was only by ensuring equal educational opportunities that democracies could promote equal opportunities for all people.[2] In the United States achieving universal secondary education became a priority (Mirel 1999), as did expanding access to higher education (Freeland 1992). A number of education reforms in Europe around this time aimed at expanding educational opportunity to children of all social backgrounds. The 1944 Educational Act in England, for example, made secondary education universal and free (Husen 1972). The Swedish educator Torsten Husen argues that many education reforms in Europe during this era were guided by what he terms "a liberal conception of equality of educational opportunity consisting of expanding compulsory schooling and making it less differentiated (no tracks)" (Husen 1972, 42). In 1948, the Universal Declaration of Human Rights established that education was to be considered both a fundamental human right and a gateway to social opportunity. During the 1950s and 1960s education reforms around the world centered on fostering equity of access. The mismatch between the expectations for these early reforms to foster equal opportunity and their relative failure to meet those expectations stimulated systematic inquiry into three related subjects: the relationship between social inequality and educational inequality, the characteristics of effective schools, and the conditions that facilitated the improvement of schools.

Researchers tackled the relationship between social and educational inequality from a number of alternative conceptual frameworks, most notably from a conflict perspective and a functionalist perspective. The latter strand of this research seamlessly meshed with the research on characteristics of effective schools. At several junctures this research has also focused on the social distribution of characteristics of effective schools, but by and large, particularly in the research carried out in developing countries, the emphasis has been on identifying the factors that can boost quality for all children. The study of the implementation of educational change—or most typically the lack of implementation of intended change—opened yet a third strand of research: the links between policy and results—between policy output and policy outcomes. As with its distant cousin, the school effectiveness research, the school improvement research has neglected, particularly in recent decades, the mediating role of social inequality and poverty; however, a particular subfield has focused precisely on studying the implementation results of policies to expand the learning chances of low-income children. In what follows, I will provide a broad overview of these three strands of research, as they provide the contours of the intellectual landscape within which this book is situated.

EDUCATION AND INEQUALITY

In the United States, education reform was one of the basic pillars of the 1960s War on Poverty. Following the court battles to dismantle racial school segregation culminating in the Supreme Court ruling in *Brown v. Board of Education* in 1954, the federal government took on a new role to set policies aimed at fostering equal opportunity. In addition to specific interventions aimed at expanding the educational chances of children in poverty, including Title I, Head Start, and funding for low-income students to attend college, the government sponsored the first serious efforts to systematically study what factors constrained equality of educational opportunity.

James Coleman and colleagues (1966) produced a landmark study on this topic in 1966, laying the foundation for an intense debate about the extent to which schools could account for the unequal educational outcomes attained by the children of the poor and their non-poor counterparts. The findings of the Coleman report stimulated controversy and further research on the topic of what difference schools could make for low-income students. Christopher Jencks and colleagues (1972) conducted a major study of the determinants of inequality, which emphasized the importance of income redistribution but also of school funding in enabling children in low-income communities to learn. More recent studies in the United States have found that the impoverished conditions of schools attended by at-risk children make it highly unlikely that they will break out of the cycle of poverty (Kozol 1991; Kotlowitz 1991; Natriello et al. 1990).

In a review of the evolution of understandings of the concept of equality of educational opportunity over the last several decades, Farrell (1999) states that comparative evidence supported the view that "educational reforms aimed at increasing equality were very difficult to enact and implement successfully, and even when implemented reasonably well seldom had the intended effects on comparative life chances of the children of various social groups within and among nations." Although Farrell argues that the limited success stories reflect idiosyncracies of the contexts in which they were intended (e.g., Chile in the 1960s), he proposes that the impact of education on social mobility is greater when societies are "in the middle"—that is, when the modernization of the economy generates a large number of jobs for which educational attainment becomes the most effective passport.

A number of studies in several Latin American countries have pointed out the relationship between aggregate indicators of poverty—of regions or states—and school enrollment and completion rates.[3] Some have documented links between contextual poverty—of regions or microregions—and indicators of school quality, such as qualifications of teachers or instructional resources.[4] Other studies have established correlations between socioeconomic levels of students and school participation and student achievement in standardized tests.[5] For example, a study of fourth-grade students in sixteen schools in four countries in Latin America (Argentina, Brazil, Chile, and Mexico) found that socioeconomic characteristics of students explained about half of the variation in student scores in math and language tests. Poor students are significantly more likely to repeat (30 percent of the poor children have repeated, compared to 5 percent among the non-poor). This study found that in addition to the individual poverty of the child, neighborhood poverty significantly influences achievement through its association with poor conditions in schools and teaching (Randall and Anderson 1999).

Some researchers have consistently argued that the effects of schools are more significant than those of socioeconomic background in less industrialized countries. Consistent with this view, a recent study of factors associated with achievement in second-grade literacy tests in schools in northeastern Brazil found that socioeconomic and background factors explained only 10 percent of the variation in student outcomes (Fuller et al. 1999).

One of the first and best known longitudinal studies of the determinants of educational attainment and learning was conducted in Chile in the 1970s. It documented the importance of the effect of peer groups as well as the large contributions of school quality to learning and attainment (Schiefelbein and Farrell 1982).

A related but independent line of inquiry in the United States and Europe set out to examine the extent to which the education system served to reproduce social stratification. This line of inquiry centered on the study of average differences in achievement between students of different social backgrounds, concluding, by and large, that schools mirrored larger forces of social reproduction (Bowles and Gintis 1970; Bourdieu and Passeron 1970; Bernstein 1971). This literature primarily held implications for reform of the curriculum and of organization of instruction.

The question of what should be learned in school is important to understanding how education can change the position of low-income children in the social structure. One answer to this question would be that all children should attain the same standards. Uniformity of overall purpose, however, leads one to attend to the particular contexts and communities where children make meaning of such purposes. Recognizing the variability of such contexts, and the growing diversity of students, research has emphasized the role teachers and pedagogy play in ensuring success for all. The traditional graded school, with its expectation that all students should progress through the same curriculum at the same pace is inherently less responsive to the children who are less prepared by the time they begin school. As students "fail" to progress at the expected "average" rate, they are progressively more excluded from this frontal model of teaching (Gimeno-Sacristaan and Perez-Gomez 1992). It is only recently that scholars within the change perspective have pointed out the need to develop capacity among teachers and schools to enable them to be "responsive to diverse and changing student and community needs, interests, and concerns" (Darling Hammond 1998, 643). Research attentive to how to achieve equally high standards for all has focused on the role of pedagogy, teacher education, and community participation in shaping the interactions between teachers and students and in the degree of fit between the culture of the school and the culture of home and peers.[6] Reviews of teacher education in Latin America point out a significant disconnect between the curriculum of teacher training institutions and the realities faced by teachers in schools, particularly those serving disadvantaged populations (Villegas-Reimers 1998; Villegas-Reimers and Reimers 1996). A germane issue is whether tests are adequate instruments to assess the progress of schools in expanding the chances of low-income children.

Another line of critical inquiry that has studied the purposes and content of schooling as it relates to inequality looks at the extent to which the curriculum reflects the very oppressive conditions that account for the lower power and social status of disadvantaged groups in society. Following a normative and phenomenological epistemology, this line of reasoning argues that education can either oppress or liberate depending on whether it helps students understand the conditions that account for their position in the social structure and depending on whether it helps them act, individually and collectively, to transform that structure (Freire 1996; Giroux 1986; McLaren 1989).

The links between education and inequality as well as the result of the interaction of large social and institutional forces have been studied at a macro level. Torres and Puiggros (1997) argue that the crisis of public education in Latin America reflects a crisis of the state. The public education system played a mayor role in the consolidation of political systems in the late nineteenth and early twentieth centuries, but toward the end of the twentieth century, economic restructuring and the demands posed by economic integration called into question the role of public education. In an analysis of the origins of educational inequality in Brazil, Plank (1996) posits that it is the self-serving attitudes of bureaucrats and politicians that lies at the core of the systematic underinvestment in the schools attended by the children of the poor. The inequalities in the distribution of public resources across regions and across different social groups contribute to the political interests of decision makers. Therefore, they argue, it is the lack of voice of the poor in the political process that explains educational inequality.

Missing in much of the literature documenting the relationship between inequality and educational opportunity is a conceptual framework that simultaneously accounts for the influence of poverty on educational opportunity at the micro (school and classroom) level and that explains the role of school interventions to boost the learning chances of the children of the poor. The underlying conceptual framework of much of this research assumes that education reproduces larger social inequalities, and is therefore a more adequate explanation to account for average effects and for the lack of change, than it is an explanation for the variation of individual students and schools around the "average" levels of achievement of others in their "class." Few of these studies have focused on the question of the impact of policy interventions designed to alter the learning chances of the poor.[7]

EFFECTIVE SCHOOLS

The interest in schools as avenues of social opportunity and the interest in quality of education led to studies of the characteristics of schools that produced "learning." In the mid-1970s, Michael Rutter and colleagues (1979) in England conducted a study of twelve public schools serving disadvantaged students to investigate the effects of secondary schools on children. This study found that differences between schools explained a significant proportion of the differences between students' learning outcomes, attendance, behavior, and delinquency rates. It highlighted the role of academic emphasis, the nature of teacher-student interactions, the organization of instruction, feedback to students (rewards rather than punishment), and positive views about students in fostering student achievement.

The Rutter's study was followed by the Schools Matter longitudinal study; it looked at the effects of schools at the primary level using more sophisticated analytic methodologies (multilevel analysis). This study also concluded that schools mattered and that they were uneven in their effects. A synthesis of the results of these two studies, and of other related research, concluded that eleven factors are critical to schooling effectiveness: professional leadership, shared vision and goals, learning environment, concentration on teaching and learning, purposeful teaching, high expectations, positive reinforcement, monitoring progress, pupil responsibilities, partnerships with homes, and a learning organization (Sammons et al. 1995).

Researchers extending school effectiveness studies to diverse contexts or to different student populations concluded that characteristics of schools and teachers matter more to the most disadvantaged students. They also concluded that community, relationships of trust and interdependence, explained an important part of student success (Coleman and Hoffer 1987).

The publication of *A Nation at Risk* in 1983 signaled a shift in education research priorities, away from equity and toward quality and the competitiveness of U.S. graduates as compared to their international counterparts.[8] But this displacement of equality of educational opportunity from the center of the education research agenda was premature, as the problems of inequity had not yet been solved or sufficiently understood.

A study is focused on equity when socioeconomic background is used as a predictor variable to identify differences in levels of student achievement, in the distribution of educational resources, and in school conditions.[9] In other words, the focus on equity means explicit concern for the extent to which school resources and achievement vary by the socioeconomic status of students. In contrast, a study is focused on quality when the main purpose is to understand what school and teacher characteristics and practices are associated with levels of student achievement or with changes in such levels. When socioeconomic background is included in such studies it is used as a control factor.[10] During the 1970s and 1980s a number of studies on the determinants of school effects were conducted in industrialized and developing countries.[11] Most of these studies focused on identifying the factors that contributed to improving education quality for children, treating social background as a control factor or ignoring it altogether. In a review of 187 school effectiveness studies in the United States and of 97 studies in developing countries, Harbison and Hanushek (1992) conclude that educational inputs in developing countries have larger effects on student achievement than in industrialized countries. Reviews of school effectiveness studies in developing countries identify a number of important predictors of student achievement: the availability and use of textbooks and learning materials, the presence and use of school libraries, the presence of furniture and quality of school facilities, child nutrition programs, and school size (Fuller and Clark 1994).

Studies of the factors associated with student achievement conducted in several countries in Latin America confirm the importance of educational materials (Vaccaro 1994), especially when combined with teachers' professional development and with more individualized instructional approaches (McEwan 1998; Psacharopoulos et al. 1992). These studies also highlight the importance of instructional time, heavily influenced by student and teacher absenteeism (McGinn et al. 1992), of adequate lesson planning (Redondo Rojo 1997), and of teacher education and experience (Wolff et al. 1994). Two studies of factors associated with student achievement in the states of Puebla and Aguascalientes in Mexico found that, within type of school (urban, rural, indigenous), the most significant predictors of achievement levels relate to teacher characteristics (stability, desire to change profession, expectations about students, and gender) (Ruiz 1999; Schmelkes et al. 1997).

A recent review of school effectiveness studies in Latin America concludes that most of the research is dominated by first-generation input-output studies and that school effectiveness research proper arrived to the region only in the 1990s. "The input-output model predominates, and much less is known about processes and their relation to learning. It is certainly more difficult to operationalize processes such as classroom interaction, teaching style, student grouping, etc. [Another review of the literature] indicates that the studies deal mainly with the presence-absence of the factor, but that the quality of the factors involved has been much more difficult to take into account. Perhaps the quality of the factors is more important than their mere presence" (Schmelkes et al. 2000). This review concludes that too little is known in Latin America about how policy reform relates to teaching and school functioning.

A more recent and rare variety of school effectiveness study includes those that measure student achievement over several points in time (longitudinal). They use multi-level analysis methodologies to appropriately account for the fact that students are nested within organizational structures (classrooms and schools) that define several independent levels of effects on learning. Studies of school effectiveness have been extended to other contexts including a number of developing countries. In the 1980s a number of reviews of this research identified gaps in knowledge which prevented the formalization of theoretical propositions. One of the weaknesses of many of these studies is that they infer causality from the observed associations between school and teacher characteristics and achievement levels measured at one point in time. In fact, such cross-sectional studies could not adequately distinguish causal effects of school resources on student achievement from selection effects generated by the nonrandom assignment or self-selection of students to different schools and classrooms.

Recent reviews of the school effectiveness literature highlight the fact that more empirical work is needed in order to test a theory of education effects, particularly extending it to new contexts. "The literature on school effectiveness is now substantial. . . . There are, however, far fewer detailed empirical studies than there are critiques and commentaries. If the field is to flourish, more empirical work is needed" (Mortimore 1998, 96).

A recent review of school effectiveness research in developing countries identifies fifteen studies using multilevel analysis and concludes that such research has concentrated on quality improvement, rather than on examining equity issues: "Begun in the style of large-scale, quantitative research in industrialized countries, Third World studies continued in that tradition, but from a perspective that stressed efficiency rather than equity, taking as gospel that school mattered more than the home. While research in industrialized countries focused on how schooling could compensate for the inequalities inherent in students' backgrounds, the emphasis in developing countries was how to provide the best education for all with limited resources" (Riddell 1997, 187).

Notable in the reviews of school effectiveness research is the absence of information about how socioeconomic background of students and socioeconomic contexts of schools influence the distribution of educational resources.

POLICY REFORM, SCHOOL CHANGE, AND IMPROVEMENT

Relatively independent of the school effectiveness approach, another research tradition studied the problem of educational change. Drawing on phenomenological epistemology and on the study of implementation, this perspective focuses on understanding the factors that induce change at the school level.

While the school change and improvement literature refers to a "family" of studies which includes various "generations" with distinct emphases, including organizational theory and the sociological study of change, the role of the social background of students is notably absent as an object of study in this perspective (Fullan 1982; 1993). This is ironic since, in part, the school improvement tradition was based on the studies of implementation of educational change, many of which were investigating the implementation of programs launched during the Great Society precisely to expand educational and social opportunities to disadvantaged groups (Elmore 1976; Mazmanian and Sabatier 1989; Pressman and Wildavsky 1973). Beginning in the 1970s, these studies opened the implementation black box to discover that policy is as policy does—that street-level implementers had much discretion, particularly in loosely coupled organizations, and that much of what had been billed as educational change was merely cosmetic and failed to affect the "core" of education—interactions between teachers and students in the classroom (Gross et al. 1971; Sarason 1971). Researchers operating from the perspectives of school improvement, restructuring, and reculturing (Fink and Stoll 1998) of schools proposed that understanding the differences between schools where students achieved at high levels and those where they did not was insufficient to understanding how to get schools to change (Elmore 1982; Fullan 1982; Fullan 1993). The emphasis of the bulk of this research has been in understanding the dynamics of the change process, to the point that critics suggest that the purpose of change has been overshadowed by the fascination with change per se (Holmes 1998). Missing in much of the school improvement, and school effectiveness, research has been attention to the purposes of education, to the content of curriculum, as well as to the politics of educational change. These are critical aspects to understanding the relationship between education and inequality. "Until very recently, within the change field, there has been little attention to how systemic social inequalities and power imbalances do not just surround the school and its community as part of the change context, but permeate the politics of change within the school itself" (Hargreaves 1998, 291).

This lack of attention to the politics of change in the study of education and inequality is especially problematic for inequality is fundamentally about different voice and differential access to social opportunities by different groups in society. Attempts to change these dynamics are the very essence of politics. It is not just that the change process is political because schools are political organizations (Blasé 1998; Sarason 1990); it is that educational change to alter the social distribution of opportunities is the most political act of all. Oakes and colleagues (1998), studying the implementation of detracking in ten racially mixed schools, found that larger political and economic forces influence the micropolitics of school change. The assumptions and beliefs of administrators, teachers, and parents undergird the resistance to change. Policy reform is important in that it may expand the "zone of tolerance" for change. But change will be mediated by schools and local actors, and "mutual adaptation" may in the end not be favorable to equity as the most advantaged parents resist integration, which they perceive as detrimental to their children maintaining a position of privilege in an unequal society.

The study of the politics of changing educational equity is central to research on changing curriculum to better serve disadvantaged students and to research on specific programs to provide more learning opportunities and resources to those students. A distinct strand of research on the implementation of educational change includes the studies of compensatory policies. In this book I define *compensatory policies* as those that attempt significant redistribution of education resources and opportunities by redressing existing inequalities. These policies attempt to "compensate" the inequalities in school chances created by schools or social inequalities. In the United States, twenty-five years of federal funding for compensatory policies have supported the design and implementation of innovative programs and, more important, supported the study of their effects.[12] As a result of this support there is a wide range of programs available to schools and districts to improve the educational chances of low-income children: the National Diffusion Network, the Regional Educational Laboratories,

Chapter 1 Technical Assistance Centers, and Chapter 1 State Offices and Departments of Education.

A large national study using longitudinal data, the Prospects study, followed a 1988 congressional mandate for evaluation, along with smaller-scale studies of "promising programs," the Special Strategies study (Stringfield et al. 1998). The Special Strategies study sampled programs that aimed to restructure complete schools and provide services outside the regular classroom; it also sampled school programs that were developed externally as well as internally. The programs evaluated[13] include whole school restructuring programs such as the Comer School Development Program, Success for All, the Paidea Program, the Coalition of Essential Schools, Chapter 1 schoolwide projects, and extended-year schoolwide projects. It also evaluated interventions such as Reading Recovery, METRA/peer tutoring, computer-assisted instruction laboratories, and after-school and summer programs. The Special Strategies study concluded that at-risk students can achieve at levels that exceed current national averages. Students who began participation in these programs at well below the national average in reading comprehension levels increased their performance substantially to exceed those averages. "Given that the predominantly poor, overwhelmingly minority, initially low achieving students in these schools demonstrated reading comprehension levels near or above the national average by the end of grade three, there is good reason to believe that most children of poverty, when well educated, can achieve at similar levels. The current national average can be viewed as an achievable benchmark for schools serving America's children of poverty, when programs that have proven to be effective are well implemented" (Stringfield et al. 1998, 1325). There were modest gains in norm-referenced tests attributable to the programs evaluated. "[P]rograms concentrating scarce resources early in students' careers, before a pattern of failure could set in, were more successful than schools at which the intervention began later" (Stringfield et al. 1998, 1330). None of the secondary schools showed consistent academic gains and schools attempting whole school reform obtained greater gains than pull-out strategies.

This study also found substantial variability of implementation and effects across sites within each program type. The schools that obtained the greatest gains focused on initial and long-term implementation issues. Implementation was easier where there was commitment from the district, school administration, and faculty to the approach chosen.

The Special Strategies study found that the schools in which these programs operated faced many needs and that without the support of additional funding could not have undertaken these initiatives. "The importance of Chapter 1 funds for facilitating reform in schools serving high numbers of financially disadvantaged families could hardly be overstated. In particular, the Chapter 1 schoolwide project option often created an environment in which administrators and teachers firmly believed that long-term support would be provided for their reform efforts" (Stringfield et al. 1998, 1332).

Orfield and DeBray (2000) argue that Title I (formerly Chapter 1) has been undermined by disappointing findings about its impact. Amendments introduced in 1994 provided for more flexibility in implementing the program, allowing schools to use the funds for comprehensive reforms with limited oversight of the impact of such use on at-risk children. "The dollars can now be used for the entire school rather than focused on poor children and nobody is keeping track of what is being done and whether or not it is working" (Orfield and DeBray 2000). In a review of fourteen recent studies of program effects commissioned by the Harvard Civil Rights Project, the authors conclude that producing learning gains in concentrated poverty schools "takes hard work and long-term, institutional investment, and governmental commitment to accountability for the lowest performing students" (Orfield and DeBray 2000, 6). Decentralization of funding is not helpful. What is most relevant are structured interventions in core aspects of pedagogy: better prepared teachers, smaller classes, more socially integrated schools, focused educational interventions, and more demanding curricular materials (Orfield and DeBray 2000, 6). Their review also finds that neighborhood poverty exerts a powerful contextual influence on student achievement and can dilute the effects of compensatory policies.

Research that focuses specifically on the effects of compensatory policies finds modest impacts of these programs and attributes a key role to variability in the operation of programs as implemented. As mentioned, however, a distinguishing feature of much of the school improvement literature is the absence of explicit consideration of the mediating role of inequalities in the change process. As a result, we know little about the specifics of changing schools when the aim is to redress inequalities.

NOTES

1. Other influences in this expansion of educational opportunity include urbanization, improved health conditions, and better standards of living which have freed up time for more children to attend school.
2. Harvard University President James Bryant Conant proposed in the 1940s that equality of educational opportunity, along with meritocracy, made it possible for a democracy to provide equality of social opportunity to all individuals. Conant, of course, built on the idea that education could be the great equalizer, the "balance wheel of the social machinery," as Horace Mann had proposed a century earlier. The period between the two world wars placed renewed emphasis on this question as educators searched for the unique contributions that education could make to a democratic society, in the face of the challenges to the free world posed by communism and fascism. In 1942 Alonzo Myers, one of the first sociologists to address this topic in the United States, cast it as a moral imperative of democracy, calling for the expansion of educational opportunity throughout the free world as soon as hostilities ceased (Lemman 1995; Mann 1891; and Myers 1942).
3. See Aguerrondo (1993); Ezpeleta (1989); Braslavsky (1995); Ibarrola (1995); and Schwartzman, Ribeiro, and Goldbemberg (1995).
4. See Schmelkes et al. (1995) and Muñoz-Izquierdo (1979).
5. See Brunner and Cox (1995) and Rama (1991).
6. See Delpit (1988); Ogbu and Fordham (1986); Phelan et al. (1993); and Trueba (1988).
7. An exception are a few recent studies of the impact of compensatory education programs in Mexico and Chile. See Muñoz-Izquierdo et al. (1995) and Ezpeleta and Weiss (1994).
8. Ann Lieberman distinguishes four distinct "eras" in the study of educational change in the United States, marked by the following social events: World War II, the launching of *Sputnik,* the civil rights movement, and the conservative movement. The shift I am describing corresponds to the shift from the civil rights movement to the conservative movement. See Lieberman (1998). See also the chapter by Gary Orfield in this book.
9. The Coleman study is a classic in this tradition. More recent versions of this approach are the surveys produced by the Department of Education based on the National Assessment of

Educational Progress (NAEP) surveys, using cross-sectional data to describe the nature of educational inequalities across states and schools in the United States.

10. As will be explained later, a good part of the school effectiveness literature, particularly the early production function studies and most of those conducted in developing countries, either exclude socioeconomic background of students from the analysis or include it as a control in the regressions, where the main aim is primarily to identify the "effective inputs" to increase levels of achievement.

11. As mentioned, the Coleman study played a seminal role in this line of research, followed by the study of Christopher Jencks and collaborators of inequality and by the study of Michael Rutter in England of twelve public schools serving disadvantaged children (Jencks et al. 1972; Rutter et al. 1979).

12. In 1965 Title I of the Elementary and Secondary Education Act earmarked $1 billion to fund programs in schools serving large numbers of poor children. Title I grew to represent $8 billion in 2000. This program requires periodic reauthorization by Congress. Congress in turn has frequently supported research to inform the reauthorization of Title I.

13. These programs have different objectives—some focus on developing reading ability, others reasoning skills; consequently, program effectiveness is assessed by reference to the intended objectives of each program and is not compared across programs.

REFERENCES

Aguerrondo, Ines. 1993. *Escuela, Fracaso y Pobreza: Como Salir del Circulo Vicioso.* Washington, D.C.: Organization of American States.

Arnove, Robert, Stephen Franz, Marcela Mollis, and Carlos Alberto Torres. 1999. Education in Latin America at the end of the 1990s. In *Comparative Education: The Dialectic of the Global and the Local,* ed. Robert Arnove and Carlos Alberto Torres, 305–328. Lanham, Md.: Rowman and Littlefield.

Bernstein, Basil. 1971. *Class, Codes and Control,* vol. 1. London: Routledge and Kegan.

Bernstein, Basil. 1975. *Class, Codes and Control,* vol. 3. London: Routledge and Kegan.

Birdsall, Nancy. 1998. The people's asset: Education in Latin America. Paper presented at the Thirtieth Anniversary Conference. Special Program for Urban and Regional Studies of Developing Areas. Massachusetts Institute of Technology, Cambridge, Mass., October 30.

Blasé, Joseph. 1998. The micropolitics of educational change. In *International Handbook of Educational Change,* ed. Andy Hargreaves, Ann Lieberman, Michael Fullan, and David Hopkins, 544–557. Dordrecht, Netherlands: Kluwer Academic.

Bourdieu, Pierre, and Jean Claude Passeron. 1977. *Reproduction in Education, Society and Culture.* London: Sage.

Bowles, Samuel, and Herbert Gintis. 1976. *Schooling in Capitalist America: Education and the Contradictions of Economic Life.* New York: Basic Books.

Braslavsky, Cecilia. 1995. Transformaciones en curso en el sistema educativo Argentino. In *Educacion, Equidad y Competitividad Economica en las Americas,* ed. Jeffrey Puryear and José Joaquin Brunner, 7–50. Washington, D.C.: Organization of American States.

Brunner, José Joaquin, and Christian Cox. 1995. Dinamicas de transformacion en el sistema educacional de Chile. In *Educacion, Equidad y Competitividad Economica en las Americas,* ed. Jeffrey Puryear and José Joaquin Brunner, 101–152. Washington, D.C.: Organization of American States.

Carnoy, Martin, and Henry Levin. 1986. Educational reform and class conflict. *Journal of Education* 168(1): 35–46.

CEPAL (UN Economic Commission for Latin America). 1999. *Panorama Social 1998.* Santiago, Chile: United Nations.

Coleman, James, and Thomas Hoffer. 1987. *Public and Private High Schools.* New York: Basic Books.

Coleman, James, et al. 1966. *Equality of Educational Opportunity.* Washington, D.C.: U.S. Department of Education.

Darling Hammond, Linda. 1998. Policy and change: Getting beyond bureaucracy. In *International Handbook of Educational Change,* ed. Andy Hargreaves et al., 642–667. Dordrecht, Netherlands: Kluwer Academic.

Delpit, Lisa. 1988. Silenced dialogue: The power and pedagogy in educating other people's children. *Harvard Educational Review* 58(3): 280–298.

Elmore, Richard. 1976. Follow through planned variation. In *Social Program Implementation,* ed. Walter Williams and Richard Elmore, 101–123. New York: Academic Press.

Elmore, Richard. 1982. Backward mapping: Implementation research and policy decisions. In *Studying Implementation: Methodological and Administrative Issues,* ed. Walter Williams et al., 18–35. Chatham, N.J.: Chatham House.

Ezpeleta, Justa. 1989. *Escuelas y Maestros. Condiciones del Trabajo Docente en Argentina.* Chile: UNESCO.

Ezpeleta, Justa, and Eduardo Weiss. 1994. Programa para Abatir el rezago educativo. Mexico. Centro de Investigacion y Estudios Avanzados del Instituto Politecnico Nacional. Departamento de Investigaciones Educativas, Mexico (Center of Research and Advanced Studies of the Polytechnic National Institute. Department of Educational Research, Mexico).

Farrell, Joseph. 1999. Changing conceptions of equality of education. In *Comparative Education: The Dialectic of the Global and the Local,* ed. Robert Arnove and Carlos Alberto Torres, 149–177. Lanham, Md.: Rowman and Littlefield.

Fink, Dean, and Louise Stoll. 1998. Educational change: Easier said than done. In *International Handbook of Educational Change,* ed. Andy Hargreaves et al., 297–321. Dordrecht, Netherlands: Kluwer Academic.

Fordham, Signithia, and John U. Ogbu. 1986. Black students' school success: Coping with the burden of "acting white." *Urban Review* 18(3): 176–206.

Freeland, Richard. 1992. *Academia's Golden Age: Universities in Massachusetts 1945–1970.* New York: Oxford University Press.

Freire, Paulo. 1996. *Pedagogy of the Oppressed.* New York: Continuum.

Fullan, Michael. 1982. *The Meaning of Educational Change.* Toronto: OISE Press.

Fullan, Michael. 1993. *Change Forces: Probing the Depths of Educational Reform.* London: Falmer Press.

Fuller, Bruce, and Pamela Clark. 1994. Raising school effects while ignoring culture? Local conditions and the influence of classroom tools, rules and pedagogy. *Review of Education Research* 64(1): 119–157.

Fuller, Bruce, et al. 1999. How to raise children's early literacy? The influence of family, teacher, and classroom in Northeast Brazil. *Comparative Education Review* 43(1): 1–35.

Gergen, David. 1999. To have and have less: Don't look now but the gap between rich and poor is widening. *U.S. News and World Report* (July 26): 64.

Gimeno-Sacristaan, José. 1992. *Comprender y Transformar la Ensenanza.* Madrid: Morata.

Giroux, Henry. 1986. *Theory and Resistance in Education: A Pedagogy for the Opposition.* Westport, Conn.: Bergin and Rarvy.

Gross, Neil, Joseph Giacquinta, and Michael Bernstein. 1971. *Implementing Organizational Innovations.* New York: Basic Books.

Harbison, Ralph, and Eric Hanushek. 1992. *Educational Performance of the Poor: Lessons from Rural Northeast Brazil.* New York: Oxford University Press.

Hargreaves, Andy. 1998. Pushing the boundaries of educational change. In *International Handbook of Educational Change,* ed. Andy Hargreaves et al., 281–294. Dordrecht, Netherlands: Kluwer Academic.

Holmes, Mark. 1998. Change and tradition in education: The loss of community. In *International Handbook of Educational Change,* ed. Andy Hargreaves et al., 242–260. Dordrecht, Netherlands: Kluwer Academic.

Husen, Torsten. 1972. *Social Background and Educational Career.* Paris: OECD.

Ibarrola, Maria. 1995. Dinamicas de transformacion en el sistema educativo Mexicano. In *Educacion, Equidad y Competitividad Economica en las Americas,* ed. Jeffrey Puryear and José Joaquin Brunner, 253–287. Washington, D.C.: Organization of American States.

InterAmerican Development Bank. 1999. *Facing up to Inequality in Latin America.* Washington, D.C.: InterAmerican Development Bank.

Jencks, Christopher, et al. 1972. *Inequality: A Reassessment of the Effect of Family and Schooling in America.* New York: Basic Books.

Kotlowitz, Alex. 1991. *There Are No Children Here.* New York: Doubleday.

Kozol, Jonathan. 1991. *Savage Inequalities.* New York: Crown, HarperPerennial.

Lemman, Nicholas. 1995. The structure of success in America. *Atlantic Monthly* (August): 41–58.

Lieberman, Ann. 1998. The growth of educational change as a field of study: Understanding its roots and branches. In *International Handbook of Educational Change,* ed. Andy Hargreaves et al., 13–20. Dordrecht, Netherlands: Kluwer Academic.

Londono, Juan Luis. 1996. *Poverty, Inequality and Human Capital Formation in Latin America, 1950–2025.* Washington, D.C.: World Bank.

Mazmanian, Daniel, and Paul Sabatier. 1989. *Implementation and Public Policy.* New York: University Press of America.

McEwan, Patrick. 1998. The effectiveness of multigrade schools in Colombia. Mimeograph. Stanford University.

McGinn, Noel, et al. 1992. *Repeating in Primary School in Honduras.* Cambridge, Mass.: Bridges Research Report Series.

McLaren, Peter. 1989. *Life in Schools: An Introduction to Critical Pedagogy in the Foundations of Education.* New York: Longman.

Mirel, Jeffrey. 1999. *The Failed Promise of the American High School, 1890–1995.* New York: Teachers College Press.

Mortimore, Peter. 1998. The vital hour: Reflecting on research on schools and their effects. In *International Handbook of Educational Change,* ed. Andy Hargreaves et al., 85–98. Dordrecht, Netherlands: Kluwer Academic.

Muñoz-Izquierdo, Carlos, et al. 1979. El syndrome del atraso escolar y el abandono del sistema educativo. *Revista Latinoamericana de Estudios Educativos* IX(3): 1–60.

Muñoz-Izquierdo, Carlos, et al. 1995. Valoracion del impacto educativo de un programa compensatorio, orientado a abatir el rezago escolar en la educacion primaria. *Revista Latinoamericana de Estudios Educativos* XXV(4): 11–58.

Myers, Alonzo. 1942. The democratic ideal of equality of education and equality of opportunity. *Journal of Educational Sociology* 16(1): 3–14.

Myers, Robert. 1992. *The Twelve Who Survive.* New York: Routledge.

Myers, Robert. 2000. Primary school repetition and drop-out in two Mexican communities: A follow-up study. Mimeograph. Mexico City: World Bank.

Natriello, Gary, Edward McDill, and Aaron Pallas. 1990. *Schooling Disadvantaged Children: Racing against Catastrophe.* New York: Teachers College Press.

Oakes, Jeannie, Kevin Welner, Susan Yonezawa, and Ricky Allen. 1998. Norms and politics of equity-minded change: Researching the "zone of mediation." In *International Handbook of Educational Change,* ed. Andy Hargreaves et al., 952–975. Dordrecht, Netherlands: Kluwer Academic.

Orfield, Gary, and Elizabeth DeBray. 2000. Education for the poor: Lessons from new research on the U.S. program to aid concentrated poverty schools. Presented at the Conference on Poverty and Education in the Americas, Harvard University, Cambridge (May 3–4).

Phelan, Patricia, Ann Locke Davidson, and Hanh Cao Yu. 1993. Students' multiple worlds: Navigating the borders of family, peer, and school cultures. In *Renegotiating Cultural Diversity in American Schools,* ed. Patricia Phelan and Ann Locke Davidson. New York: Teachers College Press.

Plank, David. 1996. *The Means of Our Salvation: Public Education in Brazil, 1930–1995.* Boulder, Colo.: Westview Press.

Post, David. 1999. Globalization, national policy, and the distribution of educational opportunity for Mexican adolescents. Mimeograph. Pennsylvania State University, Department of Education Policy Studies.

Pressman, Jeffrey, and Aaron Wildavsky. 1973. *Implementation.* Berkeley, Calif.: University of California Press.

Psacharopoulos, George, Carlos Rojas, and Eduardo Velez. 1992. *Achievement Evaluation of Colombia's Escuela Nueva: Is Multigrade the Answer?* Washington, D.C.: World Bank.

Puryear, Jeffrey, and José Joaquin Brunner, eds. 1995. *Educacion, Equidad y Competitividad Economica en las Americas.* Washington, D.C.: Organization of American States.

Rama, German. 1991. *Que Aprenden y Quienes Aprenden en las Escuelas de Uruguay.* Montevideo: Comision Economica para America Latina.

Randall, Laura, and Joan Anderson. 1999. Factors affecting learning in poor and non-poor primary schools in Argentina, Brazil, Chile, and Mexico. Mimeograph.

Redondo Rojo, José. 1997. La dinamica escolar: De la diferencia a la desigualdad. *Revista de Psicologia de la Universidad de Chile* (6).

Riddell, Abby. 1997. Assessing designs for school effectiveness research and school improvement in developing countries. *Comparative Education Review* 41(2): 178–204.

Ruiz, Guadalupe. 1999. *Un Acercamiento a la Calidad de la Educacion Primaria en Aguascalientes desde la Perspectiva de la Efectividad Escolar.* Aguascalientes: Universidad Autonoma de Aguascalientes.

Rutter, Michael, Janet Ouston, and Peter Mortimer. 1979. *Fifteen Thousand Hours: Secondary Schools and Their Effects on Children.* London: Open Books.

Sammons, Pam, Joan Hillman, and Peter Mortimore. 1995. *Key Characteristics of Effective Schools: A Review of School Effectiveness Research.* London: Office for Standards in Education.

Sarason, Seymour. 1971. *The Culture of the School and the Problem of Change.* Boston: Allyn and Bacon.

Sarason, Seymour. 1990. *The Predictable Failure of Educational Reform.* San Francisco: Jossey-Bass.

Schiefelbein, Ernesto, and Joseph Farrell. 1982. *Eight Years of Their Lives.* Ottawa: IDRC.

Schmelkes, Sylvia, Carlos Muñoz-Izquierdo, and Raquel Ahuja. 2000. Teaching, schools and learning outcomes in Latin America. Presented at the Conference on Poverty and Education, Harvard University (May 3–4).

Schmelkes, Sylvia, Sonia Lavin, Francisco Martinez, and Carmen Noriega. 1997. *La Calidad de la Educacion Primaria. Un Estudio de Caso.* Mexico: Fondo de Cultura Economica.

Schwartzman, Simon, Eunice Ribeiro, and José Goldbemberg. 1995. A educacao no Brasil em uma perspectiva de transformacao. In *Educacion, Equidad y Competitividad Economica en las Americas,* ed. J. Puryear and J. Brunner, 51–100. Washington, D.C.: Organization of American States.

Stringfield, Sam, Mary Millsap, and Rebecca Herman. 1998. Using "promising programs" to improve educational processes and student outcomes. In *International Handbook of Educational Change,* ed. Andy Hargreaves et al., 1314–1338. Dordrecht, Netherlands: Kluwer Academic.

Szekely, Miguel, and Marianne Hilgert. 1999. The 1990s in Latin America: Another decade of persistent inequality. Mimeograph. Washington, D.C.: InterAmerican Development Bank.

Torres, Carlos Alberto, and Adriana Puiggros, eds. 1997. *Latin American Education: Comparative Perspectives.* Boulder, Colo.: Westview Press.

Trueba, Enrique. 1988. Peer socialization among minority students: A high school drop out prevention program. In *School and Society: Learning Content through Culture,* ed. Enrique Trueba and Concha Delgado-Gaitan, 201–217. New York: Praeger.

United Nations, General Assembly. 1949. *Universal Declaration of Human Rights.* Lake Success, N.Y.: United Nations.

Vaccaro, Liliana. 1994. Escuela efectiva y maestros creativos: Apuesta realista? *Pensamiento Educativo* 14(1).

Villegas-Reimers, Eleonora. 1998. *The Preparation of Teachers in Latin America: Challenges and Trends.* Washington D.C.: World Bank.

Villegas-Reimers, Eleonora, and Fernando Reimers. 1996. Where are 60 million teachers? The missing voice in educational reforms around the world. *Prospects* 26(3): 469–492.

Wolff, Larry, Ernesto Schiefelbein, and Julio Valenzuela. 1994. *Improving the Quality of Primary Education in Latin America: Towards the Twenty-First Century.* Washington, D.C.: World Bank.

Two students work together at a computer in the Hamilton Middle School in Seattle, Washington.
[© 2000 Susie Fitzhugh. All Rights Reserved.]

3

Excellence, Equity, and Diversity in Education

Charles V. Willie
Harvard Graduate School of Education

The United States has come close to achieving universal education at elementary and secondary school levels. "In . . . 1997, over four-fifths (82.1 percent) of all adults age 25 or older reported completing at least high school, a record high" (U.S. Census Bureau 1997, 1). By racial and ethnic groups, however, there is substantial inequality in the attainment of this level of education. Eighty-three percent of white adults twenty-five years and older have high school diplomas compared with only 54.7 percent of Hispanic adults of a similar age. Among black adults, the proportion of 74.9 percent is high but less than that for whites. However, among U.S. residents who identify as Asian or Pacific Islanders, the proportion of adults who have graduated from high school is 84.9 percent, the highest in the nation (U.S. Census Bureau 1997, 3).

In the past, the discrepancy in educational attainment between racial and ethnic groups was larger in the United States. In 1950, before the U.S. Supreme Court ruled that segregated education in the United States was illegal, about one-third (33.4 percent) of the adult population over twenty-five years of age had graduated from high school—35.5 percent of whites but only 13.2 percent of blacks and other nonwhite races of a similar age group. More whites (2.7 times as many) graduated than blacks and all other racial groups combined a half-century ago (U.S. Census Bureau 1960, 108). Today, after a remarkable increase in the percentage of all racial groups that have completed high school, the proportional difference in educational attainment for whites at this level of education is only 1.2 times greater than the proportion for blacks and other racial groups combined.

A half-century ago, less than a majority of adults in all racial groups in the United States had graduated from high school. At the close of the twentieth century, a majority of adults in all racial groups were high school graduates. Two things may be said about education during this half-century experience. First, when the level of attainment was low for all population groups in the United States, the discrepancy between racial groups in educational attainment was greater than it is today when all racial groups have a higher level of educational attainment (one could say, a rising tide raises all ships).

Second, despite the remarkable increase in education for all population groups, inequality remains between whites and people of color in the United States (which is to say, some things change and yet remain the same). Recognizing that inequality by race remains and that overcoming inequality helps all and harms none, the United States has struggled with several ways of dealing with the persisting problem of inequality.

AFFIRMATIVE ACTION

The popular label for efforts taken thus far is "affirmative action." It is a necessary and essential effort but one that is quite controversial because of the misguided belief held by some whites that affirmative action aimed at helping people of color harms whites. Affirmative action is based on the assumption that "if all artificial barriers to access to education were lifted and the effects of past discrimination overcome, blacks [and other nonwhite racial populations] would gain qualifications for positions in [education] that would approximate their position in the population at large" (Fleming et al. 1978, 7). John Fleming, Gerald Gill, and David Swinton call affirmative action "a peaceful strategy for making the transition to a fair and equitable society" (Fleming et al. 1978, 4).

From the executive branch of the U.S. federal government, orders have been issued regarding efforts that should be taken to end racial discrimination. Fleming, Gill, and Swinton state that the government had to take affirmative action and order other institutions in the United States to do the same because past federal, state, and local official policies were designed "to keep blacks in a state of ignorance during slavery and then ensure that the education finally extended would be of an inferior quality" (Fleming et al. 1978, xxi). In their book, *Black Wealth/White Wealth* (1995), Melvin Oliver and Thomas Shapiro state that "practically every circumstance of bias and discrimination against blacks [in the United States] has produced a circumstance and opportunity of positive gain for whites" (Oliver and Shapiro 1995, 95).

REMEDY AND PREVENTION

In the United States, we are tending toward a society in which the winner takes all and in which only our similarities are recognized as valid because of our developing "culture of intolerance" (Cohen 1998). Anthropologist Mark Cohen asserts that "many Americans seem to be moving toward increasing indifference to others. Intolerance, even outright hatred, of people who are 'different' is on the rise. This attitude . . . divides people who ought to be united and supports a variety of political agendas that do not address our real needs" (Cohen 1998, ix).

One political agenda that cultural intolerance does not support is knowing the difference between remedy and prevention:

> Remedy is a form of redress. Philosopher John Rawls states that the principle of redress is an important element in a theory of justice. It requires compensation for those who have lost out. The principle of redress . . . mitigates the effects of natural accidents and contingencies of history in awarding opportunities. . . . [T]he principle of redress is implemented by activating the principle of difference . . . that acknowledges the uniqueness of each unit of society . . . and attests to its validity (Willie 1994, 91).

Rawls states that "those who have been favored by nature, whoever they are, may gain from their good fortune only in terms that improve the situation of those who lost out" (Rawls 1971, 101–102). We improve the situation of those who did not luck out by way of remedy. In other words, our natural and cultivated talents should result in the well being of others because, according to Rawls, "no one deserves his [or her] greater natural capacity nor merits a more favorable starting place in society" (Rawls 1971, 100).

There is an important distinction between remedies and prevention. Remedies require person-specific or group-specific approaches that place individuals in the position they would have occupied if they had not experienced discrimination in gaining access to opportunities. Prevention, however, requires a universal approach that distributes common resources in ways that benefit all.

It is important for experts in social organizations to determine whether their efforts are designed to prevent or to remedy. Prevention is preparation to ward off harm. Remedy is preparation to overcome harm. Social action designed to remedy past wrongs is not effective when it uses universal methods. In contrast, social action designed to prevent wrongs in the future is not effective when it focuses on specific individuals or groups. In summary, to prevent, one uses a universal approach; to remedy, one uses a particularistic approach. For example, contemporary proposals on how to deal effectively with poverty are inappropriate when they recommend universal action as opposed to person-specific or group-specific action.

In his book *The Truly Disadvantaged* (1987), William Wilson stated his belief that the life chances of poor individuals, such as those found in inner city, underclass populations, can be improved "by emphasizing programs to which the more advantaged groups of all race and class backgrounds can positively relate" (Wilson 1987, 55). In this statement, Wilson rejects population-specific remedies. I have been critical of his recommendation because it seems not to distinguish between prevention and remedy. Prevention is appropriate for the future. But for individuals who suffer because they are poor today, remedy is necessary and essential now.

It is not our privilege to pick and choose whether to use universal, preventive means or particularistic, remedial means. The action-strategy used ought to be dictated by the requirements of the situation and not by the preferences of the action-agents. It is incumbent upon education professionals to share this insight with the society at large. Without such understanding, our action-strategies are likely to be arbitrary and capricious, not flexible enough to deal with the variety of needs that are presented in a society of pluralistic populations.

EQUITY AND EXCELLENCE

School reform efforts tend to be inadequate and insufficient when they attempt to achieve either excellent outcomes or equitable outcomes, one or the other but not both. Nearly two decades ago, the National Commission on Excellence in Education in the United States warned that the nation should not permit equity to yield to excellence or excellence to yield to equity. To favor either goal alone, according to the National Commission's report, could lead to mediocrity in our society, on the one hand, or the creation of an undemocratic elitism, on the other (National Commission on Excellence in Education 1983, 13). This discussion highlights the link between excellence and equity in education.

Academic attainment, of course, is an educational outcome that is associated with the presence or absence of excellence. Schools may be analyzed as opportunity systems that provide equitable or inequitable educational experiences for student groups. Equity pertains to groups and excellence pertains to individuals. Individuals aspire to achieve excellence, while groups strive to attain equity. These phenomena complement each other in educational planning. Lisbeth Schorr (1997, 258) agrees that school systems can and should be equitable in the distribution of educational opportunities. When educational opportunities are available to all according to their needs, equity is present. A school system that is equitable is truly unitary and fair.

THE CONTEXTUAL EFFECTS OF SCHOOLS

It is important to view schools as the context within which education takes place. The following discussion on contextual effects is based on my study of a county school system in Charleston, South Carolina, from 1997 to 1998 (Willie et al. 1998), as well as professional literature such as *Fifteen Thousand Hours* by Michael Rutter and associates (1979) and *People in Context* by George Stern (1970). According to George Stern, schools are "systems of pressures, practices and policies intended to influence the development of students toward the attainment of institutional objectives" (Stern 1970, 4). Michael Rutter and his associates found a "causal relationship between school process and children's progress" (Rutter et al. 1979, 180). Noting that children are quick to pick up other people's expectations about both their academic competence and their behavior, Rutter and his associates stated that the school process may foster enthusiasm and interest in learning, the ability to take on responsibility, and the adaptability to cope with changes (Rutter et al. 1979, 187).

In June 1997, the Charleston Planning Project in Charleston, South Carolina, formed a team of educational planners including José Alicea, Craig Mitchell, Michael Alves, and the author to conduct a study on educational services in the Charleston County Public Schools and to prepare a plan that, when implemented, would improve educational opportunities for all children. We were asked to identify and analyze barriers to quality education for students in all racial and ethnic groups at all socioeconomic levels.

The goals of the project included the following: (1) the school reform plan should seek to achieve both excellence and equity, (2) the plan should be comprehensive and achieve systematic change, and (3) each school should be recognized as a basic unit of the educational system.

To work toward these goals, the planners addressed culture-based structural problems such as racial isolation and integration and paid attention to development and achievement outcomes. To these ends, we focused on the school as a "holistic, complex, contextual description . . . of reality" (Lawrence-Lightfoot 1983, 13) that mediates the achievement behavior of individuals.

Our study of Charleston County schools is limited to elementary and middle schools. We wanted to analyze achievement scores of students in relation to racial and socioeconomic characteristics. Elementary schools include grades 1 through 5, and middle schools include grades 6, 7, and 8. The only socioeconomic indicator readily available was the eligibility or ineligibility of students to participate in the free and reduced-cost lunch program. Children who participated in this program were classified as low-income or poor. Because the reporting of these data on socioeconomic status is unreliable for secondary students, high schools were eliminated from this phase of the analysis.

Scores received by students on the Metropolitan Achievement Test (called MAT7) were used as an indicator of individual achievement. For the student body as a whole, the proportion of students scoring above the national norm in the United States on the MAT7 in each Charleston, South Carolina, school are reported. The MAT7 score used in this study is a composite that reflects achievement in reading, mathematics, language, science, and social studies.

Of the forty-four elementary schools in Charleston County, two-thirds had student bodies in which a majority of students scored *below* the national norm on MAT7. Also, two-thirds of sixteen middle schools in Charleston County had student bodies in which a majority of students scored *below* the national norm. MAT7 data were disaggregated and reported separately by schools for students in low-income and in nonlow-income families and for students in black and in white families. In the analysis of student achievement by schools, therefore, we were able to hold race and socioeconomic status constant.

By identifying each school as the contextual community for teaching and learning in public education, the data analyzed will show that variations in student achievement are substantially affected by variations in the characteristics of school communities.

The current distribution of students in Charleston County's sixty elementary and middle schools reveals substantial racial imbalance in the school system. There is a racial imbalance in nearly half of the elementary and middle schools (47 percent). Schools in which eight out of every ten students are members of a single racial group are classified as racially isolated or imbalanced schools. When the members of a single racial group in a school range from three to seven out of every ten students, such a school is classified as racially mixed.

Of the twenty-eight racially imbalanced schools in Charleston County, twenty-five are black-isolated schools but only five are white-isolated schools. Thus black students tend to experience the effects of racial isolation more frequently than white students; slightly more than half of the black students (52 percent) attend such schools, but only one out of ten white students attends a racially isolated school. The racial imbalance is extensive in black-isolated schools: nine out of every ten students (94%) are members of the same race. Blacks in these schools have little, if any, interaction with students in other racial groups.

It is fair to conclude that in Charleston County Public Schools white students tend to experience racial integration more frequently than black students. Eighty-four percent of white students in this school system are enrolled in racially mixed schools, but only 47 percent of black students are so enrolled. Thus a higher proportion of white students than black students enjoy the benefits of desegregated schools.

Schools in which 80 percent of the students receive free or reduced-cost lunches are classified as low-income schools. Schools in which less than one-fifth of the students are eligible for free and reduced-cost lunches are classified as high-income schools. Finally, schools in which low-income students range from three to seven students out of every ten are classified as middle-income (or socioeconomically mixed) schools. This classification of schools by socioeconomic status is flawed because information available for income gradations is only dichotomous, not trichotomous;

data are recorded for low-income and non-low-income status only. Thus high-income schools are so designated because of the presence of few low-income students—less than 20 percent. Most students who attend schools that are isolated from low-income children may come from high-income as well as middle-income families, although the probability is that most have parents with high incomes.

Taking into consideration this benign flaw, an analysis of the socioeconomic characteristics of Charleston County schools follows. Nearly half of the public schools (45 percent) may be classified as schools in which low-income students are concentrated. Slightly more than one-third (36 percent) of all elementary and middle school students attend these schools. Nine out of every ten students in low-income concentrated schools are poor.

In Charleston County Public Schools, 62 percent of all students attend racially mixed schools in which black and white students are almost equally balanced (10,339 blacks to 9,058 whites) and nearly half of all students (49 percent) attend middle-income (or socioeconomically mixed) schools that are more or less equally balanced between low-income and non-low-income students (7,417 low-income to 6,265 middle- and high-income students).

Because a fairly large proportion of low-income students and black students attend schools that are not racially or socioeconomically isolated, an opportunity is available to determine the contextual effects of these schools upon student outcomes compared with student outcomes in segregated schools. The achievement of students is analyzed for students who attend schools in and outside black ghettoes and low-income ghettoes. The MAT7 is used in this analysis. The Charleston County school system collects data on the proportion of students in each school scoring above the national norm on this achievement test. These were the only data readily available for determining the association, if any, between school contextual characteristics and student achievement.

The varying proportions of Charleston County students scoring above the national norm on the achievement test are 26 percent, 43 percent, and 82 percent in black-isolated schools, racially mixed schools, and white-isolated schools, respectively. The extreme ends of the distribution are interesting, since 80 percent or more of the students in schools at each end of the distribution are members of the same race. An overwhelming majority of students *do not* score above the national norm on the achievement test in black-isolated schools, but a majority of students *do* score above the national norm in white-isolated schools. These facts mean that black and white students who experience segregated education have radically different achievement levels.

The proportion of students scoring above the national norm ranges from 26 percent to 44 percent to 79 percent in low-income, middle-income, and high-income schools, respectively. The proportion of students scoring above the national norm in both distributions was lowest in black-isolated or low-income schools and highest in white-isolated or high-income schools.

In schools of varying racial composition (ranging from black-isolated to white-isolated), achievement scores have a different pattern from that mentioned above when the analysis is reported for black students and white students separately. White students perform their best in white-isolated schools; in these schools, 91 percent score above the national norm. This proportion is the highest for white students scoring above the national average in any of the three race-contextual school types. However, the highest proportion of black students scoring above the national norm is found in racially mixed schools, not in black-isolated schools. About one-third of black students (34 percent) in these kinds of schools score above the national norm.

Thus, among black students in Charleston County schools, the lowest proportion scoring above the national norm is found in black-isolated schools. This is a radical contrast from the achievement experience of the small proportion of white students who attend white-isolated schools in this county school system. Clearly, the white experience in Charleston County schools differs from the black experience.

These findings of different achievement patterns in different racial groups within a common school system indicate why equity and excellence must complement each other in systemic reform. While white students manifest their best academic achievement in racially isolated white schools, black students manifest their worst academic achievement in racially isolated black schools. Racially mixed schools in which blacks have their best academic achievement are second best for whites. Nevertheless, the proportion of white students whose achievement is above average in their second-best schools is substantially higher at 67 percent than the 34 percent of black students whose achievement is above average in these racially mixed schools.

We know based on the Charleston County experience that a school system that maintains racially isolated schools tends to harm the achievement of its subdominant students of power and help the achievement of its dominant students of power. One may recall that black students had their lowest score in nearly all-black schools, and white students had their highest score in nearly all-white schools. While it is good public policy to help all students, it is bad public policy to harm any students. To deal with these matters appropriately one must implement policies that promote both equity and excellence at the same time.

It is admirable and important to strive for excellence. However, the data indicate that excellence associated with schooling in white racially isolated schools is experienced by only 4 percent of all Charleston County students. By race, only 10 percent of white students and 1 percent of black students attend racially isolated white schools.

Also, data show that the highest proportion of all students in Charleston County attends racially mixed schools. Racially mixed schools not only accommodate the largest proportion of students in the school system; they also minimize the discrepancy in achievement between black and white students. The difference in achievement proportions between black students and white students is 33 percentage points in racially mixed schools and 61 percentage points in racially isolated white schools. Thus the search for excellence and equity requires that a school system like Charleston County increase the number of racially mixed schools that seem to help the system and not harm any group, since two-thirds of the white students who attend these schools have achievement scores that are above the national norm and this proportion is higher than that for any other racial group in the school system.

While it might seem that white students (91 percent of whom score above the national norm in nearly all-white schools) are asked to sacrifice their excellent performance by enrolling in racially mixed schools, this phenomenon should be placed in context; only one out of every ten white students attends schools that have the high achievement rates in Charleston, South Carolina. Thus a school system that is urged to create more racially mixed schools is urged to expand an educational opportunity that will do the greatest good for the greatest number of students. To increase the number of racially mixed schools is to increase opportunities that are helpful to students in all racial groups.

THE PURPOSE OF AFFIRMATIVE ACTION

The Charleston County Public Schools study clearly shows both the important impact of the racial context of schools on the achievement of minority students and the significant imbalances in the racial composition of schools that negatively affect black students. While, as mentioned earlier, the gap between the levels of educational attainment of whites and minorities has narrowed in the past fifty years, it is evident from this study that differences in educational opportunities are still glaring. Changes must take place within the context of schools to alter these inequities. However, the policy of affirmative action is a remedy that focuses on individuals that can help make up for the disadvantages many minorities suffer from in the educational system.

Through creating greater diversity in the contexts of work and education, affirmative action does not primarily benefit minorities themselves but society in general. Former president of Harvard University, Neil Rudenstine, said in *The President's Report* (1996) that "diversity is not an end in itself or a pleasant but dispensable accessory. It is the substance from which much human learning, understanding, and wisdom derive. It offers one of the most powerful ways of creating the intellectual energy and robustness that lead to greater knowledge, as well as tolerance and mutual respect that are so essential to the maintenance of our civil society" (Rudenstine 1996, 53). Educational institutions are truth-seeking agencies. And the truth is possible only in a diversified setting. Thus affirmative action is essential for the purpose of recruiting diverse voices and experiences that are essential in the self-correction that a truth-seeking institution requires.

REFERENCES

Bok, Derek. 1975. Harvard: Then, now and the future. *Harvard Today* 18(3): 4.
Bok, Derek. 1977. Welcome. *Black Law Journal* 4(2): 242–244.
Boston Globe. 1977. Kingman Brewster, Jr. (March 20): 2.
Cohen, Mark N. 1998. *Culture of Intolerance.* New Haven, Conn.: Yale University Press.
Fleming, John, Gerald R. Gill, and David Swinton. 1978. *The Case for Affirmative Action for Blacks in Higher Education.* Washington, D.C.: Howard University Press.
Lawrence-Lightfoot, Sara. 1983. *The Good High School.* New York: Basic Books.
National Commission on Excellence in Education. 1983. *A Nation at Risk.* Washington, D.C.: U.S. Government Printing Office.
Oliver, Melvin, and Thomas Shapiro. 1995. *Black Wealth/White Wealth.* New York: Routledge.
Rawls, John D. 1971. *A Theory of Justice.* Cambridge, Mass.: Harvard University Press.
Rudenstine, Neil. 1996. *The President's Report, 1993–1995.* Cambridge, Mass.: Harvard University Press.
Rutter, Michael, Janet Ouston, and Peter Mortimer. 1979. *Fifteen Thousand Hours.* Cambridge, Mass.: Harvard University Press.
Schorr, Lisbeth B. 1997. *Common Purpose.* New York: Doubleday.
Stern, George. 1970. *People in Context.* New York: Wiley.

U.S. Census Bureau. 1960. *Statistical Abstract of the United States.* Washington, D.C.: U.S. Government Printing Office.

U.S. Census Bureau. 1997. *Educational Attainment in the United States: March 1997.* Washington, D.C.: U.S. Department of Commerce (March): 1–7.

Willie, Charles V. 1994. *Theories of Human Social Action.* Dix Hills, N.Y.: General Hall.

Willie, Charles V., et al. 1998. *Equity and Excellence: A Plan for Educational Improvement of the Charleston County Public Schools.* Charleston, S.C.: Charleston Planning Project for Public Education.

Wilson, William J. 1987. *The Truly Disadvantaged.* Chicago: University of Chicago Press.

Commentary

Carlos Muñoz Izquierdo, Universidad Iberoamericana, Mexico City

Charles Willie's analysis of the changes during the latter half of the twentieth century in the proportion of the different ethnic groups that finish high school in the United States is very interesting. A conclusion derived from this analysis is that, while the expansion of the school system has allowed for an improvement in the distribution of educational opportunities among these groups, it has not been possible to completely eliminate the unequal patterns of distributions that were observable in 1950.

Indeed, while the proportion of the white population that finishes high school was multiplied by 2.33 during this last half-century, the corresponding factor for the rest of the ethnic groups was 4 or 5 (depending on the group). However, the proportion of whites that finishes high school (83%) is still 1.2 times higher than that of other ethnic groups. Therefore, Willie concludes his analysis saying that the growth of the educational system is similar to "a rising tide that rises all ships" but, on the other hand, "some things [have changed] and yet [remain] the same."

The similarities between the behavior of this phenomenon in the United States and the patterns in Mexico, a very different country, come to the forefront when analyzing these data. The reader is impressed by the contrast between schooling of the population in the two countries. While in the United States 82 percent of adults complete high school, in Mexico only 18.6 percent of those who enroll in primary school graduate. It is even more dramatic to observe that, while fifty years ago 13.2 percent of the black adult population had finished high school in the United States, in Mexico only 12.5 percent of those who had enrolled in primary school in the most underdeveloped region in Mexico are at present finishing high school.

STRATEGIES TO OVERCOME INEQUALITY

The author distinguishes between preventive and remedial strategies. From his point of view, preventive programs should be based on universal policies, while remedial programs should be based on strategies specifically designed for each of the groups in question.

From my point of view, Willie is right in distinguishing between these two strategies, if by "prevention" we understand acting against those structural factors—such as poverty, undernourishment, or insufficiency of resources destined to school systems—that do not allow for an equitable distribution of education. However, I ask myself if it would not be convenient for preventive programs directed at promoting family "educogenesis" (or the improvement of the psychoeducational conditions of children when they are first enrolled in primary school) also be implemented through differentiated strategies, in order to satisfy the requirements of the different populations (or social groups) at which these programs are targeted.

CONCEPTUAL MODEL, DESIGN OF THE STUDY, AND MAIN FINDINGS

Willie's study is based on a publication by George Stern in 1970 and on a research project published by Rutter and associates in 1979. These authors developed the theory on the contextual effects of schools, which, in the words of Lawrence-Lightfoot, predicts that "the school mediates the achievement behavior of individuals."

Based on this theory, Willie designed his study in a county in which, while many of the schools are racially unbalanced, a number of the schools are racially mixed. The main objective of his study was to observe if black students obtain better academic scores in the racially mixed schools than in schools where few white students are enrolled.

Among the findings of this study, the ones that I find especially relevant are as follows:

- There is a perfect rank-order correlation between the proportion of students who obtain scores above the national norm in the Metropolitan Achievement Test, on the one hand, and the racial composition of schools (and/or the socioeconomic origin of their students), on the other. This correlation can be clearly observed in the following table:

Percentage of Students Who Obtain Scores Above the National Norm in the Metropolitan Achievement Test

Racial Composition of Schools	Percentage	Students' Socioeconomic Status	Percentage
Black-isolated schools	26%	Low-income schools	26%
Racially mixed schools	43%	Middle-income schools	44%
White-isolated schools	82%	High-income schools	79%

- Contrary to what some authors suppose, excellence is not incompatible with equity. This statement is based on three arguments: (1) While racially mixed schools are the second-best option for whites, white students in racially mixed schools obtain scores that are higher than those of black students. Sixty-seven percent of white students obtain scores above the national norm, while only 34 percent of the black students scored that high. (2) Racially mixed schools minimize differences in the scores obtained by students of these two ethnic groups. In these more integrated schools, the difference between the two groups is 33 percent, while in racially isolated white schools, the difference is 61 percent. (3) Only 4 percent of the students in the county obtain excellent scores in racially isolated white schools. These students represent 10 percent of all white students and 1 percent of all black students.

George Stern stated that schools are "systems of pressures, practices and policies intended to influence the development of students towards the attainment of institutional objectives." Rutter and associates found "a causal relationship between school process and children's progress; [because] the school process may foster enthusiasm and interest in learning, the ability to take responsibility, and the adaptability to cope with changes." These findings are the basis for the study we are discussing. Willie's findings are totally compatible with the former ones.

Nevertheless, I ask myself if the evidence available is sufficient to confirm that these results are in fact due to the processes that Willie names "contextual effects of schools." This interrogation stems from the following sets of questions:

- Why do some black students have access to racially mixed schools and others only have access to black-isolated schools? Are there differences in family environments of both groups of students that could be associated with, for example, differences in the socioeconomic and cultural conditions of the areas where these students live? (I am referring, among other things, to the access of both groups of students to initial and preschool education, to health services, and to para-school centers that offer assistance to students who attend public schools.)
- Are teachers—and all other resources—in racially mixed schools equivalent to those in black-isolated schools? In other words, are teachers (and other resources) available in both types of schools totally interchangeable between them? For example, do teachers have the same academic background; do they belong to the same ethnic group?
- Do black students who attend racially mixed schools interact freely, spontaneously, and cooperatively with black students, or do black students improve their scores independently, by trying to reach the standards of the white students?

Finally, I would like to add a question related to the feasibility of implementing policies oriented toward increasing the number of racially mixed schools. Taking the geographic distribution of racially isolated schools into account, is it really feasible to increase the proportion of white students in the black-isolated schools or, on the contrary, is it possible to increase the proportion of black students in the racially isolated white schools?

A primary-school student works at the Andy Aparicio Fe y Alegria School in the La Vega neighborhood of Caracas, Venezuela.
[Miriam Molina]

4

Educational Opportunity and Policy in Latin America

Fernando Reimers
Harvard Graduate School of Education

To be able to make intelligent choices among policy alternatives, the team of presidential advisors interested in helping children like Rosa (see Chapter 1) stay in and benefit from school need a framework to organize their thinking about educational opportunity. This framework should help them answer questions such as the following: Why is Rosa enrolled in school while other children are not? Why did Rosa repeat first grade while children of the same age from wealthier families were significantly less likely to do so? How does the process of education work? How critical is early intervention and to what extent can experiences later in life compensate for poor educational environments early on? This chapter[1] provides a framework to think systematically about these issues and weaves the existing evidence in a story that explains why so many poor children fail in school in Latin America.

I contrast two models to think about educational opportunity, a stochastic model, which sees opportunity as a sequence of probabilities, and a cumulative model, which sees later opportunity as having the potential to remedy early deficiencies of school experiences. Which model one adopts to think about opportunity has significant consequences for how to think about compensatory policies. I define *compensatory policies* as those that try to significantly redistribute educational opportunities by targeting resources disproportionately to improve the educational environments of poor children, therefore compensating for prior neglect or social disadvantage. I argue that compensatory policies in the region are recent and that a stochastic model underlies their design, even though evidence is limited on whether effective compensation follows a probabilistic or a cumulative process.

Using empirical evidence I demonstrate that the poor have less access to preschool, secondary, and tertiary education; they also attend schools of lower quality where they are socially segregated. Poor parents have fewer resources to support the education of their children, and they have less financial, cultural, and social capital to transmit. Only policies that explicitly address inequality, with a major redistributive purpose, therefore, could make education an equalizing force in social opportunity. For most of the last century, education policy has not had this focus on reducing inequality. While access has improved for the poor, disparities remain in those levels that most matter for social mobility. The emphasis on overall educational expansion and quality improvement has done little to close the gap in education resources and conditions separating the poor and the non-poor. Recent policy rhetoric has begun to acknowledge this problem, but action trails rhetoric still. Given the significant disparities in the social circumstances of poor and non-poor children, it is unlikely that providing the poor with the same educational environments provided to the non-poor will close the gap. Future efforts should aim at developing alternative models of education that can effectively provide the opportunities to acquire in school the cultural and social capital that more privileged children acquire at home and in their communities.

In this chapter I discuss the educational opportunities of children of the poor in Latin America. Attempting to characterize a region that includes countries as different in size as El Salvador and Brazil, or as culturally diverse as Mexico and Uruguay, may reflect poor judgment, but that is the task undertaken here. What most defines Latin America is diversity and variability, both between and within countries. It is to one particular form of variability, the different educational chances that the poor and non-poor face in the region, that this chapter is devoted. My goal is to enhance our understanding of ways to make education systems more inclusive by identifying the regularities and the differences in these inequalities. In this chapter, Latin America refers to the Spanish-speaking independent countries of the American continent plus Brazil. These are former colonies of the Spanish and Portuguese empires that share an historical and institutional background and, most important, that address issues of education policy in regionally specific ways and where regional meetings play a role in influencing national education policies.

The people of Latin America receive on average six years of schooling (compared to 9.5 in OECD [Organization of Economic Cooperation and Development] countries). Of those of primary school age, 92 percent are enrolled in school; of those whose ages fall within the expected age for upper secondary school, however, only 32 percent are in school (the average figures for OECD countries are 98 percent enrolled in primary and 91 percent in upper secondary). Thirteen percent of Latin Americans declare themselves unable to read and write (OECD 1998).

What most defines the countries of Latin America is not the average level of schooling of the population or the dramatic educational expansion that characterizes the last century but rather the wide gap in educational attainment between the rich and the poor. Exploring the links among education, poverty, and inequality and understanding how it is that schools fail to provide equal educational opportunity to the children of the poor in the region are the purposes of this chapter.

This chapter has seven sections. The first three sections analyze empirical evidence to develop in detail some of the arguments advanced in Chapter 1. The first section characterizes the persistent levels of poverty and inequality in Latin America and argues that they are the roots of divided societies. The second section explains why equality of educational opportunity is the key to guaranteeing social opportunity in the region and discusses the two-way relationship between education and poverty. The third discusses the links between education and inequality examining the levels of educational attainment of the poor and their access to different levels of education. The next two sections use a theoretical framework to integrate evidence explaining why poor children have limited educational opportunities. The fourth section of the chapter presents a conceptual model to explain the dynamics of educational opportunity and uses empirical evidence to characterize the kinds of educational opportunities facing poor children in the countries of the region. The fifth explains the processes underlying the unequal educational chances faced by the poor, in terms of initial inequality outside school and in terms of characteristics of their schools and teachers. Finally, I discuss how education policy has addressed equality of opportunity. The sixth section reviews the role of education policy in the region in addressing equality of opportunity, characterizes the policy emphases of different periods, and analyzes the focus of recent policies and what we know about their results. The last section presents the conclusions of the chapter.

PERSISTENT POVERTY AND INEQUALITY IN LATIN AMERICA: THE NEED FOR REDISTRIBUTIVE POLICY

Latin America has the highest levels of income inequality in the world; at least one in three households and two in five persons live below the poverty line.[2] The number of people living below country-specific poverty lines in the region increased from 136 million in 1980 to 204 million in 1997. The number of extreme poor increased from 62 million to 90 million in the same period (CEPAL 1999). Further, the poor represented 35 percent of households in 1980, 41 percent in 1990, and 36 percent in 1997; the extreme poor represented 15 percent in 1980, 18 percent in 1990, and 15 percent in 1997 (CEPAL 1999). Poverty is more acute for indigenous people in the region. In Guatemala, for instance, 87 percent of indigenous households live below the poverty line and 61 percent live in extreme poverty. In Mexico, in predominantly indigenous municipalities, 80 percent of the population is poor. In Peru, 79 percent of indigenous people live in poverty (Psacharopoulos and Patrinos 1994, xviii). While the incidence of poverty decreased significantly from 1950 to 1980, it increased during the 1980s and at the end of the 1990s regained the levels of 1980.[3] During the last nineteen years the absolute number of people living in poverty has increased. Given predictions for low economic growth in the coming years, it is unlikely that these poverty levels will change significantly (CEPAL 1999). The problem is not just that it would take decades to halve current poverty levels at the current rates of decline of poverty incidence; it is also that changes in economic circumstances in the countries of the region make it unlikely that those who remain poor and socially marginalized will be able to benefit from the opportunities generated by the new economy. The social distance between them and other Latin American citizens will widen in the absence of deliberate and affirmative actions to deepen social inclusion.

This high incidence of poverty is particularly striking given that the region has the resources to lift a significant number of its population out of poverty. A quarter of national income is received by the wealthiest 5 percent of the population, while the poorest 30 percent of the population—those living below the poverty line—receive only 7.5 percent of all national income. By comparison, the corresponding figures for developed countries are 13 percent of income for the wealthiest 5 percent, and 13 percent of income for the poorest 30 percent. For countries in Southeast Asia, 16 percent of income goes to the wealthiest 5 percent and 12 percent to the poorest 30 percent. For the rest of Asia, 18 percent goes to the wealthiest and 12.5 percent to the poorest. In Africa, 24 percent of income goes to the wealthiest, while only 10 percent is held by the poorest (IDB 1998, 11).

Helping people get out of poverty is important for a number of reasons. The main reason is to preserve the basic human rights of all Latin Americans—their right to employment, to food and shelter, to an education for their children, and to make choices to improve their life chances. While poverty clearly has more dimensions than poverty of income, for those who cannot purchase the food necessary to meet the minimum caloric requirements to stay alive the constraints presented by income poverty are severe.[4] Another important reason to address poverty is to fully place the human potential of all Latin Americans, including the poor, at the service of the social, political, and economic development of the countries of the region. A third reason is that societies that exclude almost half their populations cannot count on much social cohesion. Social conflict is to be expected in nations where there are sharp social and economic disparities between those who enjoy the benefits of prosperity and modernity and those who live in poverty. The legitimacy of democracy and of the state in the region rests on the extent to which citizens perceive that democracy provides equality of social opportunity. Education is a fundamental gate to social opportunity and, therefore, essential to shrinking the opportunity gap between rich and poor.

EDUCATIONAL OPPORTUNITY: CAUSE AND EFFECT OF POVERTY

Educational opportunity and poverty are related in multiple ways. In some respects, poverty of the households in which children are raised "causes" children to have low educational opportunities. In turn, as the children of the poor develop insufficient skills and knowledge to gain access to jobs of high productivity, their low education levels "cause" poverty to be reproduced between generations. In what ways does poverty lead to reduced educational opportunities? What role do Latin American schools play in compensating for initial inequalities? What role do they play in reproducing initial inequalities? What difference does policy make? The focus of this chapter is on answering these questions.

It may be argued that equalizing educational opportunities is insufficient to reduce social stratification as the wealthy will find some other mechanism to pass on advantages to their children if the education system could be reformed so as to cease reproducing social inequalities.[5] In the absence of equality of educational opportunity, however, this argument is not a testable proposition. As a matter of sequencing in advancing our understanding of the relationship between educational and social stratification, the first step is to determine how poverty influences educational opportunity. The second step is to identify which options are most cost-effective and politically and administratively feasible to provide low-income children greater educational opportunities. The third step is to determine whether equal educational opportunity in fact yields greater social equity. This chapter is concerned with the first step in this sequence.

Reducing poverty and improving income distribution results from multifaceted economic and social processes, not just from improving education conditions. An important factor in the reduction of poverty incidence is an increase in economic productivity so that average per capita income can increase and so that the living conditions of all people, including the poor, can improve.[6] From this perspective, an avenue to reduce poverty is to foster economic growth. Growth and other processes associated with increases in national income, such as urbanization, expansion of basic infrastructure, and reduction in fertility rates, increase the incomes of many families so that the percentage living in poverty declines.[7] Much of the decline of poverty incidence between 1950 and 1980 was the result of these processes. Then, during the 1980s, the region experienced a debt crisis and slow or negative growth in most countries. Poverty increased between 1980 and 1990.[8]

Growth has resumed in most of the region since 1990, but poverty incidence has changed slowly in most countries, in part because growth rates have been modest. But even where growth rates have been significant, there has not been a consistent or significant decline of poverty incidence. Between 1990 and 1997, the average annual growth of the gross domestic product per capita exceeded 4 percent only in Argentina (4.3 percent) and Chile (6.9 percent). It was between 2 percent and 4 percent in Bolivia (2 percent), 2.5 percent in Colombia, 2.2 percent in the Dominican Republic, 3.3 percent in El Salvador, 3.7 percent in Panama, 2.7 percent in Peru, and 3.6 percent in Uruguay. It has been below 2 percent in the ten remaining countries and below 0.5 percent or negative in half of them (IDB 1998, 209). Only two of these countries showed significant rates of decline of poverty incidence between 1990 and 1997: Chile (9 percent) and Uruguay (10 percent). On the other hand, in a country with a high rate of growth, such as Argentina, poverty incidence declined only 3 percent in this period. Brazil and Panama, with modest rates of economic growth, exhibited declines of poverty of 6 percent and 4 percent, respectively, in this period. In most other countries, poverty incidence declined less than 2 percent or increased during the decade (CEPAL 1999). In the case of Argentina and in others, economic growth brought the creation of new jobs and increases in wages. In spite of this, open unemployment rates in urban areas more than doubled in Argentina (from 6 percent to 14.3 percent) and Brazil (from 4.5 percent to 8.1 percent) and increased in Colombia (from 10.6 percent to 12.1 percent), Ecuador (from 6.2 percent to 9.3 percent), Mexico (from 4.3 percent to 5.1 percent), Uruguay (from 9 percent to 11.4 percent), and Venezuela (from 9.8 percent to 10.7 percent) (CEPAL 1999, 80).

How can one explain the apparent paradox that economic growth alone has been insufficient during the last ten years to significantly reduce poverty in Latin America, and that unemployment can increase even as new jobs are being created as a result of growth? One explanation is that as a result of the economic changes implemented in the last wave of economic reforms in Latin America, growth is highly related to participation in the world economy. Much of this growth creates opportunities for high productivity occupations. Integration of Latin America into the world economy is increasing for Latin America the returns to the quality of labor—that is, to education. Private rates of return to higher education, for example, have increased in Argentina from 16.5 percent in 1986 to 26 percent in 1994, in Brazil from 19 percent in 1979 to 23 percent in 1995, and in Mexico from 10 percent in 1984 to 20 percent in 1994 (World Bank 1994, cited by Winkler 1999). As would be expected, as the number of graduates from lower levels of education increase, the economic advantages of attaining that level diminish. In this sense education as a gateway to social opportunity is a moving bar. This is critical to understanding the paradox that even as access to education has expanded, deep inequalities remain in those levels that matter the most for social mobility. For those who have lower levels of education, there are few prospects to enter high productivity employment and therefore to benefit significantly from knowledge-based economic growth. Furthermore, those with higher levels of education fare better during periods of economic restructuring, elimination of industries, and job dislocations. In Argentina, for example, between 1990 and 1997 unemployment increased from 1.1 percent to 3 percent for the wealthiest 25 percent of the population, but it increased from 17.3 percent to 31.9 percent for the poorest 25 percent. The key factor differentiating these groups is the average levels of education, at seven years of schooling for the poorest 25 percent and thirteen years of schooling for the wealthiest 25 percent (CEPAL 1999, 80, 294).

Reducing educational inequality and income inequality, in addition to sustaining economic growth, are therefore critical to helping a significant number of people in Latin America get out of poverty. Education and income inequality are related, as suggested by Table 4.1. Table 4.1 shows the values of several measures of educational inequality and of income inequality, as well as the ranking of each country within the region. The second column contains the ratio of the primary completion rate for the wealthiest 10 percent of the income distribution relative to the primary completion rate for the poorest 40 percent. In Argentina, for example, those in the wealthier group are only 10 percent more likely than the poorer 40 percent to have completed this level. This is the lowest difference for the region and therefore the ranking for Argentina in this index is 1, represented in the third column. In El Salvador, the wealthiest 10 percent of the population is three times more likely (ratio 4.2) to have completed primary education than the poorest 40 percent. This is the greatest gap in the region and the country obtains the highest ranking of inequality at 15.

Columns 4 and 5 present a similar set of indicators, referring to the completion of secondary education. The last four columns present Gini coefficients for education and for income, where lower values represent greater equality in the distribution of education or income, respectively.

Table 4.1 shows that countries that are more egalitarian in the distribution of education are also more egalitarian in the distribution of income. The table also suggests that there is greater equality in the distribution of education than in the distribution of income.

As would be expected, because they measure different aspects of the same construct, the Gini coefficient for education is related to the indices of inequality in completion of primary and secondary education. Countries with lower overall educational inequality (low Gini coefficients) also have lower inequality gaps in the probability of completing primary education between income groups. Inequality gaps in the completion of primary and secondary education are loosely related in that the countries with the larger gaps in the completion of primary education also have the larger gaps in the completion of secondary. However, there appears to be no relationship between the magnitude of the gaps in both levels. While the gap is always larger for secondary completion than for primary completion, it is between 50 percent and 100 percent greater in cases such as Bolivia, Chile, and El Salvador, and three or more times greater in cases such as Brazil, Costa Rica, Honduras, Mexico, and Paraguay.

TABLE 4.1

Educational Inequality and Income Inequality in Latin America

Country	Primary Completion Gap (Top Decile versus Bottom 40%)	Ranking Primary Completion Gap	Secondary Completion Gap (Top Decile versus Bottom 40%)	Ranking Secondary Completion Gap	Gini Coefficient* for Education	Ranking Gini Coefficient for Education	Gini Coefficient for Income	Ranking Gini Coefficient for Income
Argentina	1.1	1	4.2	8	0.229	1	0.48	5
Bolivia	1.1	2	1.6	1	0.457	14	0.53	7
Brazil	3.2	14	14.6	13	0.454	13	0.59	13
Chile	1.3	7	2.5	3	0.261	2	0.56	9
Colombia					0.378	11		
Costa Rica	1.4	8	6.2	9	0.318	7	0.46	3
Cuba								
Ecuador	1.2	6	3.8	7	0.377	10	0.57	11
El Salvador	4.2	15	8.4	12	0.524	16	0.51	6
Honduras	2.0	12	15.4	14	0.476	15		
Mexico	1.5	9	6.8	10	0.406	12	0.55	8
Nicaragua	2.3	13	8.2	11	0.532	17		
Panama	1.2	5	3.7	6	0.297	5	0.56	10
Paraguay	1.7	11	24.8	15	0.361	8	0.59	12
Peru	1.6	10	2.3	2	0.306	6	0.46	2
Dominican Republic					0.374	9		
Uruguay	1.1	3	3.0	4	0.268	3	0.43	1
Venezuela	1.2	4	3.6	5	0.294	4	0.47	4

*A Gini coefficient is a summary measure of inequality in the distribution of a resource such as education or income in the population. The closer the Gini coefficient is to zero, the greater the equality in the distribution of the resource. The closer the Gini coefficient is to one, the greater the inequality. Argentina has the most equal distribution of education, while Uruguay has the most equal distribution of income in Latin America.

Source: Completion gaps between income groups derived from IDB (1999). Education Gini coefficients are from Duryea and Szekely (1999). Income Gini coefficients are from UNDP (1998).

There is more inequality in the distribution of secondary education than in the distribution of primary education and greater variation between countries in inequality at the secondary level. The direction of causation is probably running both ways. Greater income equality makes it possible for children to attain similar levels of schooling, but at the same time, greater equality of educational attainment makes it possible to have less disparity in the distribution of income for each successive generation.

Several processes explain why education matters for the reduction of poverty and for the reduction of inequality. First, the cognitive and social skills and the credentials, which can be gained in school, expand the choices available to people. These skills and credentials increase the probability that people can become more productive and obtain better-paid jobs. They also increase the likelihood that individuals will adopt practices that lead to better health, and they may effectively influence the number of children in the family. In Latin America, the poor have significantly more children than their wealthier counterparts.[9] The wealthiest 10 percent have, on average, 1.4 children, while the poorer 30 percent have, on average, 3.3 children, which limits the resources available per child in each family and the options to seek employment in the formal sector for the mothers (IDB 1998, 57).[10]

Obviously, poverty and inequality cannot be eradicated solely by intervening in education. Higher levels of education, in themselves, will not generate more jobs with decent pay. These are a product of the choices countries, governments, and industries make about how to respond to the opportunities and constraints posed by participation in the international economy and of how international investors respond to the choices countries make. The "quality" of growth is critical as not all growth has the same impact on employment and wages. There are, however, interactions between the kinds of choices that are possible and the distribution of educational attainment of the labor force. It is difficult to set up highly productive export-oriented industries in places where people are poorly educated. It is noteworthy that the largest reductions in poverty in the last decade have occurred in Chile and Uruguay—countries with high average levels of schooling and higher levels of education for the poorest 25 percent of the population.

Because most inequality in Latin America stems from income inequality, reducing inequality would require reducing the gaps in income between the poor and the nonpoor. These gaps largely reflect the different educational characteristics of workers in different income groups. An analysis of the income gaps associated with education level, age, gender, location of residence (rural versus urban), type of employment, and economic sector found that the larger gaps in income in Latin America are associated with levels of education. On average, a graduate of primary school earns 50 percent more than a person who has never been to school; a secondary school graduate, 120 percent more; and a university graduate, 200 percent more (IDB 1998, 39). This gap varies by country, reflecting the educational structure of the population and the relative premium the labor market places on different levels of educational attainment.

There are several mechanisms through which inequality can be transmitted from one generation to the next. They include the size and composition of the family; the availability and utilization of resources available at home, which sustain health and cognitive development; and the support home environments can provide to school endeavors, including the amount of time available for children and parents to engage in school-related or supportive activities. One of the best predictors of schooling attainment in Latin America, and elsewhere in the world, is the level of education of the parents. The average level of schooling attained by fifteen-year-olds is directly related to the level of education of their mothers. There is an increase of one year of schooling on average from children whose mothers have zero to three years of schooling compared to those whose mothers have four to six years of schooling, and another year increase for children whose mothers have seven to twelve years of schooling.[11] Fostering equality of educational opportunity requires countering the mechanisms underlying the existing intergenerational transmission of inequality in educational achievement.

To sum up, education is a potentially promising avenue to social mobility and an important link in the reproduction of inequality. There is growing consensus in Latin America on the importance of education to reduce poverty as illustrated in a number of recent governmental declarations. In March 1998, the heads of state of the countries of the Americas agreed that education would be a key priority to reduce poverty in the region (OAS 1998). Several countries of the region have launched education reforms aimed at improving quality and equity during the past few years, which will be discussed later in this chapter. Most countries of the region increased education spending during the 1990s to recuperate the declines that took place in the 1980s (CEPAL 1999). Increasing education spending alone, however, is insufficient to foster educational opportunity. We need to understand the processes that constrain the learning chances of low-income children and to examine carefully the evidence on the impact of existing and new interventions so that more resources do indeed lead to greater educational chances. Furthermore, increasing overall spending to improve quality for all is unlikely to close the equity divides discussed in this chapter.

THE INFLUENCE OF EDUCATION ON INEQUALITY

There are very significant differences in the education profiles of the poor and the non-poor. On average, heads of household in the top decile have completed 11.3 years of schooling, the equivalent of a high school degree. This is seven years higher than the level of education of the heads of household in the poorest 30 percent of the population, who on average have not even completed a primary education (IDB 1998, 17). The education gaps between rich and poor are higher in the countries with the highest income inequality (more than eight years in Brazil, Mexico, El Salvador, and Panama) and lowest in the countries with the lowest income inequality in the region (Uruguay, Venezuela, and Peru) (IDB 1998, 17). Because the rates of return to higher education are rising as the Latin American economies integrate into the world economy, we can anticipate greater increases in inequality. From the perspective of reducing inequality, it is first necessary to reduce the education gaps between the poor and the non-poor.

Table 4.2 shows that people living in rural areas, where proportionately more people are poor, have significantly lower levels of education than those in urban areas. In urban areas, the lower income groups have significantly lower levels of schooling. In Brazil, for example, the poorest 25 percent in urban areas have completed less than four grades of schooling, compared to ten years of schooling for the wealthiest 25 percent. In most

TABLE 4.2

Average Number of Grades Completed by Income Group (Quartiles)

Country	Year	Urban Areas				Rural Areas			
		Q1	Q2	Q3	Q4	Q1	Q2	Q3	Q4
Brazil	1996	3.9	5.4	7.1	10.3	1.7	2.5	3.2	5.4
Colombia	1997	6.1	7.3	9.0	11.9	3.3	4.0	4.3	6.5
Costa Rica	1997	7.3	7.9	9.6	12.2	5.1	5.7	6.3	8.1
Chile	1996	8.2	9.5	10.8	13.1	5.5	6.1	6.2	7.7
El Salvador	1997	4.6	6.5	8.4	11.9	2.0	2.4	3.0	4.3
Honduras	1997	4.6	6.1	7.5	10.5	2.4	2.7	3.4	5.3
Nicaragua	1997	6.0	6.9	8.0	11.0				
Panama	1997	7.5	8.8	11.0	13.6	5.0	5.8	7.0	9.6
Paraguay	1996	6.2	7.6	9.4	12.1				
Dominican Republic	1997	6.4	7.4	8.5	10.4	3.3	4.4	5.0	6.1
Uruguay	1997	6.9	8.2	9.5	11.9				
Venezuela	1997	6.3	7.5	8.5	10.9				

Source: CEPAL (1999, 294).

countries of the region, in urban areas the average level of schooling of the wealthiest 25 percent is close to a complete secondary education (of twelve years).

There is limited information on the influence of race on educational opportunity. Existing evidence suggests, however, that indigenous groups (and blacks in Brazil) have fewer educational chances. For example, in Brazil, there are significant differences in the educational attainment of blacks and whites. Only one in four students attaining nine or more years of education is non-white (World Bank 2000, 25). Because racial discrimination is related to economic marginalization and to regional segregation, the independent effect of each of these factors (race, socioeconomic background, or place of residence) is hard to isolate. For practical purposes, however, this matters little as the net effect is that a person who is not white has fewer educational chances than a white person. The study of the racial distribution of educational opportunities has been largely omitted from scholarly analysis and policy debate in the region.

Indigenous groups suffer disproportionately from educational exclusion. In urban areas in Bolivia, for instance, the average level of schooling of the nonindigenous is 9.7 years; for indigenous people who speak Spanish, the average level of schooling is 6.5 years; and for the monolingual indigenous, the average is 0.4 years. Among the poor, only 3.5 percent of the nonindigenous have never been to school, while among the indigenous who also speak Spanish 12.9 percent have never been to school. By comparison, among the indigenous who do not speak Spanish, 81 percent has never been to school (Wood and Patrinos 1994, 62–63). In Guatemala, 60 percent of the indigenous have never been to school, compared to 25 percent for the rest of the population. Only 35 percent of the indigenous have had some primary education, compared to 55 percent for the rest of the population. In Mexico, those who live in predominantly indigenous municipalities also have lower education levels. The percentage of illiterate men is three times higher in municipalities where 40 percent of the population are indigenous than in municipalities where less than 10 percent are indigenous (43 percent versus 10 percent) (Panagides 1994, 141). In Peru, the average level of schooling of the indigenous is six years compared to eight years for the nonindigenous (Macisaac 1994, 178).

The gaps observed in the education profile of different income groups define essentially two different populations in each country. Twenty-five percent of the people living in urban areas have twice as much education as the poorest 25 percent in the same cities. These differences define not just two different levels of competency in basic reading and numeracy skills, but two different worldviews. For instance, in general, there is no serious emphasis on science education in Latin American primary schools. Most teaching of sciences occurs in secondary education. Therefore, the understanding of social and physical phenomena changes significantly as primary school graduates proceed through secondary school.

The main educational dividers for the younger groups are in the completion of secondary and higher education. Table 4.3 shows the relationship between income inequalities and educational inequalities among twenty- to twenty-five-year-olds—some of the youngest people who are beyond the expected age of graduation for high school, and therefore the most likely to have benefited from recent efforts to expand educational opportunity. The table shows that the lower-income groups are less likely to have completed primary and secondary education than their upper-income counterparts. For the primary education level, most of those in the upper decile have completed this level. There is wide variation among countries in the region in the percentage of the poor who have completed primary education. The educational equity gap (defined as the percentage increase in the likelihood to have completed primary for the upper decile relative to the bottom four deciles) ranges from 10 percent (in four countries) to 300 percent. Of these, there are only six countries where at least 80 percent among the poorest 40 percent have completed primary school.

At the secondary level, there is a greater educational gap between rich and poor, ranging from 60 percent (in urban Bolivia where the percentage of twenty- to twenty-five-year-olds in the top decile who have completed secondary school is 60 percent greater than the percentage who have completed this level among the poorest 40 percent) to 2,400 percent. In most countries, the likelihood that the top decile has completed secondary education is several times greater than the likelihood that the poorest 40 percent of the population have done so.

Because the gaps between rich and poor are greater for secondary education, and even greater for higher education, I conclude that these levels represent, at the moment, the key to the educational reproduction of inequality. However, our understanding of the social consequences of educational inequality should include both the factors that relate to social mobility and the factors that relate to social exclusion—two different, but mutually reinforcing social processes. The greatest social mobility for an individual is associated with completing the highest levels of education. Because so many people already have completed primary education, there is very little social mobility associated with completing this level. In many countries, having completed primary education makes no difference in the likelihood of being employed. However, those who have not completed this level are likely to be severely excluded from opportunities to participate in any meaningful way in labor markets or social and political organizations.

TABLE 4.3

Primary and Secondary Completion Rates by Income Group

Country	Bottom 40%	Top 10%	Gap 10%/40%	Decile 1	2	3	4	5	6	7	8	9	10	Total
Primary Completion Rates for 20–25-Year-Olds by Income Level														
Argentina	92	100	1.1	83	94	92	99	96	98	100	99	99	100	97
Bolivia	88	94	1.1	84	89	90	87	94	94	93	94	95	94	92
Brazil	30	95	3.2	19	24	33	43	48	57	67	76	85	95	57
Chile	76	96	1.3	67	75	77	84	85	89	91	94	95	96	86
Costa Rica	72	99	1.4	64	69	78	77	81	84	92	95	95	99	86
Ecuador	82	98	1.2	76	85	81	85	83	89	92	93	94	98	88
El Salvador	20	85	4.2	17	17	22	25	34	37	52	63	75	85	47
Honduras	44	87	2.0	39	48	41	46	53	58	71	76	87	87	64
Mexico	63	92	1.5	52	66	65	70	84	87	91	93	95	92	83
Nicaragua	40	90	2.3	31	31	44	53	57	62	53	75	82	90	60
Panama	84	99	1.2	75	82	89	89	93	95	96	97	98	99	92
Paraguay	56	93	1.7	49	62	51	60	64	72	75	85	90	93	74
Peru	58	95	1.6	53	52	56	71	75	78	85	90	91	95	78
Uruguay	92	99	1.1	88	94	92	95	97	98	99	98	99	99	96
Venezuela	78	97	1.2	76	79	79	79	89	91	91	94	96	97	88
Secondary Completion Rates for 20–25-Year-Olds by Income Level														
Argentina	22	92	4.2	13	17	27	31	42	51	54	65	68	92	50
Bolivia	52	83	1.6	51	48	55	52	59	60	60	64	65	83	61
Brazil	5	73	14.6	2	3	6	9	12	16	22	32	46	73	23
Chile	33	83	2.5	23	31	35	44	50	56	65	74	80	83	56
Costa Rica	11	70	6.2	10	10	11	14	13	18	29	42	44	70	30
Ecuador	19	73	3.8	14	15	18	29	26	33	40	46	49	73	36
El Salvador	8	69	8.4	8	6	10	9	14	15	27	35	47	69	27
Honduras	3	50	15.4	2	3	4	4	9	11	15	23	35	50	18
Mexico	10	70	6.8	4	9	12	16	18	26	32	39	53	70	32
Nicaragua	5	43	8.2	3	2	8	8	16	14	15	22	25	43	17
Panama	23	84	3.7	11	16	30	33	41	47	57	66	72	84	49
Paraguay	3	62	24.8	0	2	3	5	4	11	20	34	41	62	23
Peru	37	87	2.3	33	32	36	48	51	60	65	75	82	87	61
Uruguay	24	72	3.0	16	21	24	35	35	43	46	51	63	72	42
Venezuela	21	74	3.6	15	17	26	24	31	32	44	48	53	74	40

Source: Household surveys circa 1995 as reported in IDB (1998, 27). Data for Argentina refer to the Greater Buenos Aires; data for Bolivia and Uruguay are for urban areas only.

To sum up, within each Latin American country, one can effectively identify *two* countries from the educational standpoint: 30–40 percent of the population with very low levels of education, having completed sometimes just a second grade education, and 20 percent of the population with educational levels twice and three times higher. It is this inequality in educational attainment that is at the root of the high levels of inequality in the region and that indicates that it will be harder for the poor than for the rest of the population to benefit from the opportunities generated by economic growth, so long as the former do not have opportunities to increase their level of education. Most income inequality in Latin America stems from the large gaps in income between the 10 percent of the population with the highest incomes and the rest of the population. This group earns on average 160 percent more than the next highest 10 percent (ninth decile). In the United States, by comparison, the gap in income between these groups is 60 percent (IDB 1998, 2). What most clearly differentiates this group from the rest of the population is its higher levels of education.

THE LOW EDUCATIONAL OPPORTUNITIES OF THE CHILDREN OF THE POOR

The education systems of all countries in Latin America have expanded significantly over the last fifty years. Many new schools have been opened and many new teachers hired. The constitutions of all countries in the region state that education is a right of every citizen, and most children, including the children of the poor, enroll in first grade. As an illustration of how much the education profile of the population has changed in recent decades, in Mexico, for example, 40 percent of the students enrolled in sixth grade at this point exceed the education level of their parents.[12] In 1996 those who were twenty-five years old had attained nine years of schooling, on average, twice as much the level of school attainment of those fifty-five years old.[13] In two decades, the education system doubled the level of schooling attainment of the population, a significant achievement given population growth in excess of 3 percent per year between 1965 and 1980. In Brazil, between 1980 and 1996 the average level of schooling increased from 4 to 5.7, the percentage of students completing primary (fourth grade) increased from 50 percent to 75 percent, and the percentage completing secondary education increased from 17 percent to 25 percent (World Bank 2000).

Paradoxically, while the expansion of educational access incorporated new social groups into the education system, particularly into the lower levels of education, the disparities between different groups and regions have increased because the most advantaged groups have attained even higher levels of schooling. In Argentina, for example, during the last three decades the average level of schooling increased in all provinces. However, the gap between the provinces and the capital of Buenos Aires increased. In 1960, Buenos Aires was 1.4 years above the average level of schooling of 5.7, whereas in 1991, it was 2.5 years above the average of 8.8 years (Llach, Montoya, and Roldan 1999, 61). In Mexico, the standard deviation of schooling attainment is as large among twenty-five- and twenty-six-year-olds as among people over sixty.[14]

What is the root of the problem? How can one explain the paradox that in spite of equal opportunities there are unequal results in the education profiles of different income groups? If all children have the same opportunities to be educated, why is it that education of the parents is still a significant predictor of final educational attainment?

We can think of educational opportunity as the ascent between five different levels of opportunity.[15] Central to this understanding of opportunity is thinking about education, specifically about schooling, as a process that happens over time. The schooling experience is structured to engage learners during a period of their growth and development and to foster such growth and development in deliberate ways. Understood in this way, the process of education takes place alongside the development of learners; it is not a discrete act or a commodity that can be acquired or not. It is not useful to think of educational opportunity as something that one has or does not have, for different components of opportunity are meaningful at different stages of the schooling process. Rather, educational opportunity is a sequence of probabilities, a sequence of gates, so to speak, that a person can go through during her or his lifetime. For expository purposes, we can focus on a few of these gates and think of them as stages of opportunity, but there is really a continuum connecting them. Of course, at any particular point in the sequence of opportunity, one can assess whether a particular learner operates within conditions that allow her or him to be engaged in the schooling process in ways that foster cognitive growth and development. But such a snapshot has to be understood as just that—an assessment of a condition at a single point in time in an evolving process. The process of educational opportunity is time-dependent in the same way that the process of human development is time-dependent. We can productively think of "stages" of opportunity as distinct moments in a temporal sequence. This dynamic, time-dependent view of opportunity has crucial implications relating to what I believe to be essential aspects of this concept. For instance, a dynamic perspective suggests that educational opportunity at a point in time builds on opportunities from earlier points in time, though we have limited empirical evidence on the nature of these functional relationships. An implicit assumption of much education policy is that these linkages are deterministic (stochastic rather than cumulative). That is, that early opportunity determines later opportunities. Much of the emphasis of compensatory policies on early childhood education and primary education is built on that premise. Does that mean that children who have not had early opportunities are doomed to fail? Can teachers who engage learners at later stages of their development recoup the damage done by poor teachers in earlier stages? Can programs in high school remedy poor elementary programs? I believe we should think of these links between different stages in the evolution of opportunity as probabilistic rather than deterministic and about the overall process linking these stages as cumulative rather than stochastic.[16]

A dynamic view of educational opportunity is also important to understanding the relationship between social inequality and education, as is recognizing that people's circumstances change during their lifetime. Family income, relative to needs, varies over time. The needs of families change as the structure and composition of the family changes, or as they change location of residence. As a result, the influence of social circumstances on the learning chances of a child will vary during the lifespan of the child. If we think that the key resources that explain the influence of families on educational opportunities are education, money or material resources, time when adults interact with children, and other contacts with members of the family and community, we can see that these resources change during the life cycle of a family.[17] A single child may have relatively more opportunity early in life than later when there are siblings and perhaps other events—disease, death, changes in economic circumstances—that change the incentives for how the family is going to use its time and resources. Conversely, another child may have relatively more opportunities later in life, than earlier on, as a result of favorable changes in the family circumstances which allow them to spend more time together. An understanding of learning chances that takes either the learner or the characteristics of their education as "fixed" in time is inaccurate and fails

to capture what may be some of the most significant elements that could help to improve the conditions to foster the continued development of learners.[18]

A dynamic understanding of opportunity is important because it can help us focus
not just on the conditions that influence opportunity at any given stage, but on the relationship between different levels of opportunity and the transition from one to the
next. If we are to effectively counter the role of social inequalities in the learning
chances of children, we need to advance our understanding of opportunity as a dynamic
process—to garner evidence to understand how educational opportunity at different
stages in the lifespan of a person interacts with his or her cognitive, social, and emo-
tional development.

Returning to the model of educational opportunity levels, each level can be defined
in the following ways: The first stage of opportunity, the most basic level, is the
opportunity to enroll in the first grade of school. The second level is the opportunity
to have a sufficiently positive experience and to learn sufficiently in that first grade to
complete it with enough mastery of cognitive and social skills to continue learning in
school. The third level is the opportunity to complete each education cycle; that is, to
learn enough at each stage to continue to be promoted and to be able to afford attending school. The fourth level of opportunity relates to whether, having completed the
cycle, graduates have skills and knowledge comparable to those of other graduates
of the same cycle. Finally, the fifth level of opportunity relates to whether what was
learned in the cycle provides the graduate with other types of social and economic
opportunities that may expand his or her life chances.

What is required to have access to these five stages of opportunity? At each level
there are factors that stem from social opportunities, factors that result from what
teachers and schools do and factors that result from the interaction between the two.
A common way for economists to think about these factors involves supply- and
demand-side factors influencing educational opportunity, referring to conditions of
schools (supply) versus life circumstances (demand). While this classification may be
useful for some purposes, I find it inadequate to explain the presence of opportunity
at a given stage and particularly the transition from one stage to the next and the
interdependence of stages of opportunity.

Central to the educational opportunities of learners is how those learners spend their
time. If education (schooling) is to positively influence the development of students,
those children need to spend time engaged with others (teachers and peers) in ways that
are conducive to the achievement of curricular objectives (assuming the curriculum
fosters such development). How children spend their time is a family decision, and a
decision of the child, that reflects the incentives and circumstances faced by families.
These may include, but are not limited to, the children's experience in school. For example, poor parents may decide not to enroll their children in school if they believe that
what will be learned there will be of no use to the children. Of course, they may also
decide not to enroll the children because they cannot afford shoes or school uniforms
or because they need the children to stay home to fetch water or wood for cooking. The
same parents may choose not to send their children to a particular school if a teacher
shows up drunk frequently or abuses children, but instead send them to another school
or to another grade in the same school. Further, the decisions of a child about how
much time to spend on school-related activities outside school may be influenced by

the views and experience of older siblings. How children spend their time while in school reflects the skills and expectations of teachers for their students. Some teachers will succeed at engaging their students in challenging activities for more time than others. And some teachers will have students spend a large part of their time on activities that do not foster their development. The bottom line is that we need to understand the factors that play a role in the decisions students and their families make about how much time to spend on school-related activities. These decisions are the product not just of the preferences of the parents—though their cultural capital plays a significant role independent of other life circumstances—but of the objective conditions they face, including the level of material need (poverty) and the characteristics of the schools to which they can send their children.

The first level of opportunity, initial access to school, demands three conditions: a child who is sufficiently healthy to be enrolled in school, a school with space available within a reasonable distance of the home of the child, and a school in which the guardians of the child are willing to enroll her or him. This level of opportunity has been equally achieved in most of Latin America as will be demonstrated shortly.

The second level of educational opportunity, to learn during first grade, requires several conditions: enrollment in school; regular attendance; readiness to learn at the time of enrollment in school; adequately good health to learn; and teachers who have the skills, time, and resources to engage the child in activities that allow gradual mastery of the intended curriculum as well as the skills to accurately assess learning and provide feedback as children's understandings evolve. This second level of opportunity has not yet been universally achieved in Latin America. Children enroll in school in different conditions of health and nutrition. Only some children, typically not the children of the poor, have attended preschool. There are also quality differences between different first grades, stemming in part from different levels of resources going to each school. Some teachers cannot pitch the curriculum at a level or in a way that relates to understandings that are meaningful to their students. This is particularly problematic when the cultural and social backgrounds of teachers and students differ. These inequalities explain the different rates at which children learn in different schools. They are responsible for school failure and the high levels of repetition among first-graders. School failure, when children are just beginning school, is a process that begins to segment children by socioeconomic level at the very foundation of the education process. As we will see shortly, there is a high rate of failure in first grade in Latin America, primarily among the children of the poor.

The third level of educational opportunity, the possibility of completing the cycle, is a function of the preceding two levels and of regular enrollment and attendance by the child at each consecutive level. Early school failure increases the likelihood that children will drop out of school, in part because as they get older they can contribute more to the sustenance of their families and in part because families respond to signals they receive from schools regarding the academic potential of their children to complete the cycle. Several studies in Latin America show that early school failure leads to dropping out of school before completing the primary cycle (Munoz-Izquierdo et al. 1979; McGinn et al. 1991). Furthermore, poor families are more likely to decide that children should spend more time in work-related activities as they grow up and when family circumstances deteriorate.

The fourth level of educational opportunity, the possibility that having completed the cycle graduates have developed equal skills and knowledge, depends on the three prior levels and on whether the quality of schools are not just equal but can add value to the development of each child in equal proportion to the children's needs. The level of cognitive attainment of each basic education graduate, for example, is only in part a reflection of the work of schools. It also reflects the sociocultural environment in which children are raised. For graduates of different income groups to have the same level of command of the majority language, for instance, it is necessary that schools have provided them opportunities to compensate for the unequal sociocultural environments in which some of them live. The skills graduates master are the result of the sum of the contributions of schools and home environments and of how these two contexts interact. If schools did exactly the same for all children, skills of graduates would still be unequal, reflective of the differences between the sociocultural environments where children are raised. To achieve this fourth level of educational opportunity thus requires compensatory policies—policies of positive discrimination in favor of the lower income groups.[19] As we will see, low-income students have significantly lower levels of student achievement in all existing studies.[20]

The fifth level of educational opportunity, the possibility that having the same skills and competencies gives graduates the same life chances, depends on the existence of labor markets and societies that are meritocratic and democratic—markets in which access to any kind of occupation, to any social position, is not dependent upon the color of the skin, ethnicity, social origin, group of reference, political affiliation, or other characteristics unrelated to merit or ability. This level of educational opportunity can be influenced by schools in the long term, by their developing attitudes and values that foster inclusion; that value diversity, effort, and merit; and that recognize and counter all forms of discrimination, particularly those based on race, gender, or social class of origin.[21] Attention to this level of opportunity leads us in the direction of questioning the curricular objectives of schools. It may be that changes in the life circumstances of the poor require not just the development of cognitive skills in traditional school subjects but also the development of other forms of social and cultural capital such as the ability to associate and organize collectively, the ability to mobilize politically effectively, and an understanding of the political process and avenues to affect change.

To achieve equality of educational opportunity for children born into low-income families, Latin America needs to advance in the five levels of opportunity mentioned above. This requires generating systematic evidence on the role of different interventions to help low-income children learn in, progress in, and complete school. During the last several decades, much has been gained in the first level. The greatest challenges are in the remaining four levels. The simplification of reducing educational opportunity to just the first level is at the root of the paradox of having almost universal enrollment in first grade while significant differences in educational attainment for different income groups remain. Most children enroll in first grade and spend several years in primary education. Because of high rates of grade retention, which disproportionately affect children living in rural areas and the urban poor, only the children of the higher income groups complete primary education in a timely manner and proceed to secondary education.

Understanding why poor children repeat and eventually drop out of school at such high rates in Latin America is crucial to expanding equality of educational opportunity in the region. We know that most children do not drop out of school after completing just a year in school. Rather, most drop out after spending several years in school, especially if they repeat the same grade during those years (OAS 1997). Table 4.4 shows that there is almost universal access to first grade for all income groups in urban areas, while in some countries, rural areas are lagging behind.

In spite of the fact that most children enroll in school at the expected age, the disproportionately higher grade retention rates for poor children leads them to either drop out of primary school before completion or to enter secondary school at a much older age than their non-poor counterparts, when competing demands for their time will make success at this level less likely. Table 4.5 shows that rural and poor children in urban areas are significantly more likely to be "overage," that is, to exceed the expected age for the level they are studying by one or two years. In Brazil, for example, half of the children in rural areas and one in five in urban areas, most of them in the poorest 40 percent of homes, are repeating a grade. Half of the poorest 25 percent in urban areas are repeaters.[22]

As a result of the different rates at which children from different socioeconomic backgrounds progress up the education ladder, by the age of fourteen or fifteen, the basic contours of the education profiles that characterize different income groups are already dramatically different, as seen in Table 4.6. In Brazil a child in urban areas is twice as likely to have completed primary education at this age as a child in rural areas. A child living in one of the households with the highest income is two and a half times as likely to have completed sixth grade as a child in the poorer 25 percent. In all countries there are differences biased against the lower income children. These differences are greater in the urban areas of Brazil and Honduras and between the urban and rural areas of Mexico and Venezuela. Studying the factors that explain the variation observed between countries will facilitate formulating policy interventions that are more attuned to the mediating role of context in determining educational outcomes.

TABLE 4.4

Percentage of Children Enrolled in School at 8 or 9 in Urban and Rural Areas and by Quartile of Income in Urban Areas

| Country | Year | Urban | Rural | Quartile | | | |
				Q1	Q2	Q3	Q4
Argentina	1997	98.9		98.2	100.0	100.0	100.0
Brazil	1996	95.5	88.5	92.2	96.8	98.6	99.4
Chile	1996	99.7	99.5	99.6	99.7	99.8	100.0
Colombia	1997	95.1	91.1	91.6	97.3	97.6	97.8
Costa Rica	1997	97.8	96.8	96.9	97.8	100.0	100.0
Ecuador	1997	98.5		98.8	99.3	96.7	98.0
Honduras	1997	94.0	89.6	90.4	95.3	95.2	95.9
Mexico	1994	98.3	97.1	95.9	99.7	100.0	100.0
Panama	1997	99.3	98.8	99.3	98.5	100.0	100.0
Paraguay	1995	98.0		93.3	100.0	100.0	100.0
Uruguay	1997	98.8		98.8	98.3	100.0	100.0
Venezuela	1995	97.1	95.9	95.5	96.5	99.8	99.4

Source: CEPAL (1999, 174, 175).

TABLE 4.5

Estimates of Grade Repetition in Urban and Rural Areas and by Quartile of Income in Urban Areas (Children Enrolled in School at 9 or 10 Who Have Not Completed at Least Two Grades)

| Country | Year | Urban | Rural | Quartile | | | |
				Q1	Q2	Q3	Q4
Brazil	1996	25.6	52.9	43.5	20.5	9.4	4.7
Chile	1996	10.1	19.5	13.8	8.7	9.7	4.2
Colombia	1997	14.3	40.5	21.2	14.1	4.1	6.8
Costa Rica	1997	20.1	20.6	29.6	19.8	12.2	3.0
Ecuador	1997	7.2		12.7	4.9	4.1	0.3
Honduras	1997	10.9	24.8	19.0	8.3	6.9	3.4
Panama	1997	6.9	18.3	11.5	3.2	2.4	1.3
Paraguay	1995	10.2	16.9	17.1	7.5	7.4	3.1
Uruguay	1997	8.4		14.8	5.5	0.7	0.0
Venezuela	1995	11.0	20.9	15.9	8.3	9.1	2.2

Source: CEPAL (1999, 176, 177).

The differences in educational opportunities among income groups are greater the lower the overall level of enrollments at the particular grade or level. Enrollment rates are lower at the secondary and tertiary level. At the secondary level, 36 percent of those aged between twelve and seventeen are enrolled. Because of high repetition rates, however, an additional 27 percent of those in this age group are still enrolled in primary education (OAS 1997, 15). One in three children in this age group are not enrolled. Most of the children in the poorest 30 percent of the population do not have

TABLE 4.6

Percentage of Children Who Have Completed Six Grades of Primary Education at Age 14 or 15

| Country | Year | Urban | Rural | Quartile | | | |
				Q1	Q2	Q3	Q4
Argentina	1997	92.3		82.1	94.7	95.5	100.0
Brazil	1996	55.9	23.7	32.6	53.8	73.2	87.4
Chile	1996	92.1	78.8	85.6	95.1	97.1	98.0
Colombia	1997	75.8	41.0	65.3	75.8	85.5	87.8
Costa Rica	1997	85.9	70.8	76.9	86.0	95.4	95.7
Ecuador	1997	89.0		84.2	90.0	92.6	95.8
Honduras	1997	77.4	54.6	66.6	77.4	79.8	91.0
Mexico	1994	90.1	67.5	83.7	93.0	94.3	99.6
Panama	1997	92.0	82.6	87.8	94.0	95.0	97.7
Paraguay	1995	82.3		76.7	80.7	88.4	90.2
Uruguay	1997	92.3		87.3	94.5	95.7	100.0
Venezuela	1995	84.9	58.4	75.5	88.1	91.0	92.3

Source: CEPAL (1999, 180, 181).

access to secondary education. Table 4.7 summarizes differences in participation of the poor and the non-poor in preschool, primary, and secondary education in several countries in the region.

Educational attainment as a gateway to social opportunity is a moving bar. As access to education has expanded, the education divides between regions have moved to upper levels. In Argentina, while there are small differences in net enrollment ratios reflecting access to primary education between provinces, the differences are much larger for secondary education. Net enrollment ratios range from 70 percent in the Federal Capital to under 40 percent in Santiago del Estero, Chaco, and Misiones (Llach, Montoya, and Roldan 1999, 61).

The social inequalities in educational participation, and consequently attainment, are compounded at higher levels of the education system. At the age of twenty-one there is a significant difference in how many young people in different income groups are still in school. For the poorest 30 percent of the population, less than one in five is still studying. For the wealthiest 10 percent, more than one in two is still enrolled in school. At this age, the education gap between these two income groups is between four and five years in Mexico, Panama, Chile, and Costa Rica and more than six years in Brazil, Paraguay, and El Salvador. In Peru and Venezuela, the gap is the lowest in the region at about two years (IDB 1998). As explained earlier, it is the completion of secondary and tertiary education that offers the highest chances of social mobility, even though not completing primary education leads to the greatest social exclusion.

The social stratification of access to higher education is confirmed by the disproportionately small number of students from low-income households who go to college, and even more so where there is a greater attainment gap between rich and poor among young people. In El Salvador, for example, one of the countries with a larger gap in the educational attainment of the top decile versus the poorer 30 percent (six grades of difference), only 2 percent of university students come from the poorest 20 percent of families, and only 7 percent come from the poorest 40 percent of families. Conversely, 57 percent of the students in universities come from the wealthiest 20 percent of households (Reimers 1995, 72). In Venezuela, one of the countries with a smaller gap in educational

TABLE 4.7

Gross Enrollment Rates by Level and Income Group, circa 1995

Country	Preschool Quintile			Primary Quintile			Secondary Quintile		
	Q1	Q1, Q2	Q3, Q4, Q5	Q1	Q1, Q2	Q3, Q4, Q5	Q1	Q1, Q2	Q3, Q4, Q5
Brazil	51.6	57.2	77.8	83.3	86.8	96.7	53.9	57.2	77.9
Costa Rica	2.4	2.1	12.6	79.4	81.4	90.8	63.3	63.6	79.4
Chile	26.5	26.6	42.7	95.4	96.3	98.1	77.3	77.9	87.3
Ecuador	19.2	23.0	37.0	89.1	90.9	96.3	57.9	62.5	80.8
El Salvador	32.3	34.6	58.8	75.0	79.9	90.0	39.6	43.3	60.4
Honduras	31.7	30.5	34.1	86.9	87.6	93.5	50.5	45.9	64.7
Nicaragua	7.7	11.0	40.0	51.7	59.9	87.3	35.2	41.4	76.5
Peru	49.7	51.9	66.2	93.6	94.7	98.0	82.0	83.5	88.5

Source: Winkler (2000). Based on household surveys.

attainment, between these two groups (two years of schooling) only 7 percent of university students come from the poorest 20 percent of families, and only 16 percent come from the poorest 40 percent of families. Conversely, 43 percent of the students in college come from the wealthiest 20 percent of households (Republica de Venezuela 1995).

In Brazil and Mexico, eighteen- to twenty-four-year-olds from the lowest quintile account for less than 3 percent of all college enrollment, with enrollments from the poorest 40 percent accounting for less than 7 percent of all college enrollments. In Peru, one of the countries with a greater proportion of university students from low-income homes, those from the poorer 40 percent account for 10 percent of all enrollments in college (Winkler 1999).

To sum up, I have proposed a dynamic model to conceptualize educational opportunity and analyzed how the poor have significantly lower chances to move up to the higher stages of opportunity by completing primary education and proceeding to the secondary and tertiary levels. The next section reviews the influence of home circumstances and of school conditions on these lower opportunities.

HOW SCHOOLS PROVIDE UNEQUAL LEARNING CHANCES TO THE POOR

Education policies in the region have expanded existing education models by basically building more schools and hiring and training more teachers, rather than designing specific interventions responsive to the conditions of marginalized children. Many children have not been reached by this one-size-fits-all strategy. For instance, children who live in small rural communities that do not have the minimum number of children of primary school age required by Ministries of Education to open a school, as well as children of migrant farmers, go largely without schooling in parts of Mexico and Central America. This is especially the case for secondary education where children need to move to cities in order to access this level of schooling. In Brazil, for example, 95 percent of students enrolled in lower secondary (grades five to eight of basic schooling) and 99 percent of those in upper secondary (grades nine to eleven) are in urban areas. As a result, only 66 percent of all students who begin first grade will complete lower secondary and only one in three will eventually finish secondary education (World Bank 2000).

A more subtle, but equally important, form of inadequacy of expanding a one-size-fits-all model concerns how the curriculum is organized and delivered. For example, the school calendar and expected progression of the curriculum often reflects an urban bias that places children in rural areas at risk of failure.[23] Like the fox who invites the stork for dinner and serves the stork a delicious meal on a flat dish in the fable of LaFontaine, many teachers of low-income children in Latin America teach in ways that make it impossible for the students to partake of the educational banquet. They speak to children in languages they cannot understand, they use examples foreign to the life experiences of the children, and they convey to them and to their parents that their experiences have no value for the purposes of school. Teachers do not do this intentionally. It is not that they purposefully set out to disrespect or humiliate poor children. They just have other children in mind when they plan instruction. By not considering these specific students and their unique needs, teachers and policymakers invite poor and rural children to an educational meal they cannot digest.

Schools and teachers can teach only real children. While teachers may be educated to teach "average" children, children are situated in a specific social and cultural context. To the extent teachers are more adequately equipped and supported to address the children they face in the classroom, they can more successfully teach them. The failure of schools in Latin America to provide equal educational opportunity to the children of the poor is largely the result of failing to recognize these children as worthy co-constructors of a quality education. Beginning to redress this failure requires two steps: (1) recognizing these children, and identifying the social and cultural circumstances that define the context in which quality education can provide educational opportunity; and (2) equipping teachers and schools with skills, support, and resources to foster high levels of learning for these children. The current status quo is one of unequal learning chances due to social inequality outside the school (which schools fail to address) and unequal learning chances due to what happens (or does not happen) in schools.

Unequal Learning Chances Due to Social Inequality Outside the School

While these are factors that precede the schooling experience or appear to operate outside the school, I include them here because it is only by the failure of schools to recognize these factors, to compensate for them, that they lead to unequal educational outcomes. With responsive schools there is no reason why these factors, by themselves, should limit the educational opportunities of children (except in the extreme cases where malnutrition or poor health makes it impossible for children to show up in school, stay awake, or concentrate). Instruction can be organized in different ways to accommodate the circumstances of different groups of children.

Poor children have parents with less schooling and less education. They have less income and material commodities to support their health and well-being, and they may be stimulated to a lower extent to prepare them for school. Husen (1972) called these conditions "initial inequalities." Poor children lack physical capital that will get them ready to learn. Hungry, sick, and malnourished children do not learn well (Myers 2000). Because their families are poor, they may also be pressed to spend less time in school, to attend school irregularly, and to spend more time in various forms of work that contribute to family well-being. They also lack cultural capital that will make early success in school equally likely. In a nutshell, poor children have deficits to overcome that require greater efforts on the part of schools.

Some authors have questioned the concept of "deficit" implicit in the discussion of compensatory education, particularly as related to cultural dimensions (Bernstein 1971). I too argue that much can be gained by making teachers and schools responsive to the realities of poor children and by enabling teachers to teach them with respect. But the fact remains that by the time they enroll in first grade, many poor children have developed more restricted linguistic codes, which represent a delay in their developmental progression. The chances of success of low-income children in Latin America are limited because most of them enter school without sufficient prior cognitive stimulation, particularly with regard to language development. Of course this is compounded by the poor academic environments many face upon entering school.[24] A study of four-year-olds in Uruguay documents a significant relationship between language development and socioeconomic background of the children (ANEP 1999a). Much cognitive development occurs prior to enrolling in primary education. The expansion of Head Start in the United States as part of the War on Poverty was based on the realization that learning begins at birth.[25]

In Latin America, access to preschool education, at least to one or two years of pre-school prior to enrolling in primary school, has expanded significantly during the last thirty years. However, access has expanded primarily to serve the children of the non-poor. Forty-three percent of four-year-olds and 77 percent of five-year-olds are enrolled in preschool (OAS 1997). Even more so than with primary education, where access is greater, those excluded from access to preschool are the children of the poor. For example, in Chile, which has the highest rates of access to preschool in the region, the children from the wealthiest 60 percent of families are twice as likely to be enrolled in preschool in urban areas as the children in the 40 percent of families with less income (45 percent versus 24 percent, respectively). In rural areas, non-poor children are three times more likely to be enrolled than the poor (33 percent versus 11 percent) (Winkler 2000). In Nicaragua, the country with the second lowest enrollment rates in preschool in the region, the urban non-poor are twice as likely to participate in preschool as children from the poorer 40 percent (46 percent versus 20 percent). And in rural areas non-poor children are three times as likely to be enrolled in preschool as those from the poorer 40 percent (22 percent versus 7.6 percent) (World Bank 1993).

This disparity is compounded by the fact that students are typically tracked by skill level once they enter primary school. Much of this tracking results from school segregation. Some schools concentrate students with no preschool education into one group. Analyzing data from a nationally representative sample of primary schools and 50,000 students in Mexico, I found that among those who reached the sixth grade, the percentage with some form of preschool education was 59 percent in small rural schools, 59 percent in indigenous schools, 67 percent in rural schools, 73 percent in public urban schools, and 90 percent in private schools. These figures do not account for the likely differences in quality or for the differences in duration of the preschool experience between groups.

The influence of parental education on success in school extends beyond its impact in school readiness by the time children enroll in school.[26] Earlier I discussed the documented impact of parental education on school attainment. A similar impact is observed between parental education and student achievement in school. In Uruguay, for example, whether students are performing at grade level in language and math is related to the level of schooling of their mother. Whereas only 43.5 percent of the students met minimum language standards among those whose mothers had primary schooling or less, among those whose mothers had secondary education, 59 percent read at grade level; among those whose mothers had more than secondary schooling, 78 percent read at grade level. The corresponding figures for performance in math are 22 percent performing at grade level for those whose mothers had primary schooling or less, 35 percent for those whose mothers had secondary schooling, and 56 percent for those whose mothers had more than secondary schooling (ANEP 1999b, 16).

The pervasive influence of parental education on student achievement (an indicator of the intergenerational transmission of educational inequality) has been documented in most countries for which evidence is available. A recent comparative study of forty countries (TIMSS) confirms that parental education is one of the strongest predictors of student achievement in math and science. Children whose parents had a college education scored 32 points above the standardized international average in math (average of 513) and 30 points above the science average of 516. Students whose parents had secondary schooling were 15 and 13 points above the average, respectively. Students whose parents had completed only primary schooling, or less, were 26 and 24 points below the mean (TIMSS 1997). The same effects of parental education on student attainment and achievement are found in Argentina (Llach, Montoya, and Roldan 1999) and Brazil (World Bank 2000).

Initial inequality is also related to the frequently inadequate health and nutrition of poor children. Available evidence suggests that access to health services is lower for the poor in Nicaragua. For instance, only 15 percent among the poorest 20 percent report access to health services by ill children, compared to 20 percent among the poorest 40 percent and to 40 percent among the non-poor. In Peru, the respective figures are 30 percent, 38 percent, and 50 percent (Van der Gaag and Winkler 1996, 12). A good example that policy can affect children's futures, is found in statistics from Ecuador, Nicaragua, and Peru where poor children under five years have the same access to vaccination as their non-poor counterparts (Van der Gaag and Winkler 1996, 12). In Mexico, 13 percent of the sixth-graders in private schools wear glasses, compared to less than 5 percent in all other schools; assuming that the propensity to need glasses is the same across income groups, at least 8 percent of the children in public schools should wear glasses but do not. When these children were asked if they had had ear infections lately, only 10 percent in private schools, 13 percent in urban public schools, 16 percent in rural schools, 24 percent in indigenous schools, and 18 percent in small rural schools said yes. These differences reflect unequal access to sanitary conditions.

In addition to medical care, access to water and sewers is also important to sustaining health. Access is very different for children living in urban and rural areas and is biased against poor children in urban areas, as seen in Table 4.8. For example, in Bolivia, the likelihood of not having access to tap water is five times greater for children in the bottom 25 percent of the distribution of income than for children in the top 25 percent of the distribution of income. In Brazil, it is eight times greater; in Chile, eleven times greater; in Colombia, eight times greater; in Honduras, four times

TABLE 4.8

Percentage of Homes with Tap Water and Basic Sewers

Country	Year	Tap Water		Basic Sewers	
		Urban	Rural	Urban	Rural
Bolivia	1997	9.7	69.7	47.2	94.5
Brazil	1996	13.1	64.3	53.2	82.7
Chile	1996	1.6	49.9	12.3	79.5
Colombia	1997	1.7	32.4	8.7	43.7
Honduras	1997	12.7	61.6	41.6	90.7
Mexico	1994	7.2	35.4	20.3	60.1
Venezuela	1997	6.5		24.8	

Source: CEPAL (1999, 185).

greater; in Mexico, sixteen times greater; in Paraguay, four times greater; in Uruguay five times greater; and in Venezuela, six times greater (CEPAL 1999, 186).

In addition to poor health interfering with learning and progress in school, the children of the poor face greater direct and indirect costs of attending school, especially as they get older. As we saw earlier, they are more likely to be retained in grades in primary education and therefore less likely to have completed primary school, even after eight years of enrolling repeatedly at that level. Direct and indirect costs of schooling, starting at adolescence, will make it even more challenging for the children of the poor to stay in school. For women, the expectation that they will help significantly with household chores and have early pregnancies are additional barriers to educational progress as they enter adolescence.

Table 4.9 shows that already, at the age of thirteen to fourteen, children in rural areas are significantly more likely to be working than children in urban areas. To a much lesser extent, in urban areas, low-income children are more likely to be working than their non-poor peers in some countries. While children may attend school even as they work, the demands posed by work reduce the time available for school activities and may influence regular attendance.[27] In Brazil, for example, approximately 60 percent of the students enrolled in upper secondary education (ninth to eleventh grades) are enrolled in night schools because a majority of them must work full-time. Wealthier students spend more time in school, predominantly in daytime schools (World Bank 2000, 11).

For the region as a whole, children in rural areas are twice as likely to be working (30 percent) at the ages of thirteen to seventeen as children in urban areas (15 percent) (CEPAL 1990, 192). Twenty percent of young women aged fifteen to nineteen

TABLE 4.9

Percentage of Children Who Work at the Ages of 13–14 and 15–17 in Urban and Rural Areas and by Income Group in Urban Areas

Country	Year	Ages 13–14		Ages 15–17		Ages 13–17 in Urban Areas by Quartile			
		Urban	Rural	Urban	Rural	Q1	Q2	Q3	Q4
Argentina	1997	1		9		8	6	5	5
Bolivia	1997	10	58	22	76	14	20	19	17
Brazil	1996	17	52	38	67	30	32	30	21
Chile	1996	2	4	7	16	5	6	4	4
Colombia	1997	6	18	15	34	10	11	13	14
Costa Rica	1997	4	18	17	36	11	15	12	8
Ecuador	1997	9		20		15	17	15	17
Honduras	1997	14	30	34	51	25	26	29	25
Mexico	1994	7	22	22	41	19	19	12	7
Panama	1997	2	9	7	26	5	4	4	10
Paraguay	1996	22		34		31	29	27	27
Uruguay	1997	6		17		17	15	12	7
Venezuela	1997	6		19		12	15	16	11

Source: CEPAL (1999, 197–200).

are occupied only with household chores, another form of work. There are significant differences between urban and rural areas and between income groups. In urban areas, 10 percent of the women are occupied only with household chores, while in rural areas the figure is 30 percent. In urban areas, 17 percent of those in the first quartile are occupied only with household chores, compared to 4 percent in the fourth quartile (CEPAL 1990, 194).

Early pregnancies are another factor that constrains the educational opportunities of poor women. For the region as a whole, among women aged twenty to twenty-four, one in four (24 percent) gave birth in her teens. The rate of teenage mothers is 19 percent in urban areas and 30 percent in rural areas. In urban areas, one in three women in the poorer quartile becomes a mother in her teens, while in the upper quartile only 7 percent of women become mothers in their teens (CEPAL 1990, 196).

The opportunity cost of attending school is greater for youth than for children as they have higher earning potential. Data from six household surveys (for Venezuela, Paraguay, El Salvador, Costa Rica, Chile, and Bolivia), which asked reasons for not attending school, found that for six- to nine-year-olds, lack of family resources was the main reason offered. The need to work was cited as equally important for ten- to fourteen-year-olds and was the main reason offered among fifteen- to eighteen-year-olds (IDB 1998, 132). A study of secondary education in El Salvador found that the opportunity cost for attending secondary education is quite significant. Earnings of a seventeen-year-old with nine years of schooling and two years of work experience are equal to 34 percent of the monthly income of the homes of out-of-school youth. This is consistent with the average amount contributed by out-of-school youth to their families; one-third of the out-of-school youth surveyed brought in 40 percent of the family income. In addition, the direct costs of attending public secondary school equaled one month of family income for out-of-school youth, and the costs of attending private secondary schools were higher (World Bank 1999b, 16). The direct and indirect costs of attending schools are even higher for higher education. Therefore, one way in which poverty itself prevents educational opportunity is that many children of poor families do not attend school after they are fourteen or fifteen years old because they cannot afford to do so. There is, however, no evidence demonstrating that lowering the direct costs of secondary schooling increases enrollment or the probability of graduation.[28]

Poverty also influences the learning chances of children through the aggregate effects of living in disadvantaged areas. Concentrated poverty, in rural areas and marginalized urban communities, means fewer role models with high levels of education, fewer adults who can support students in their schoolwork, and lower aggregate capacity to effectively demand high-quality education. These aggregate effects of concentrated poverty relate to the regional and geographical education divides in each country. In Brazil, for example, people in the poorer Northeast have completed 4.4 years of schooling on average, while people in the richer Southeast have completed 6.6 years. Related to these differences in educational context, the percentage of students expected to complete eighth grade (basic education) is 35 percent in the Northeast, but 65 percent in the Southeast. Net enrollment in upper secondary education is 14 percent in the Northeast, but 43 percent in the Southeast (World Bank 2000, 23). The average years of education in the community was found to be a strong predictor of school attainment in Argentina and Brazil (Llach, Montoya, and Roldan 1999; World Bank 2000).

Table 4.10 demonstrates how children are segregated in schools in Mexico. On average, the percentage of fathers without schooling was 20 percent in small rural (Conafe) schools, compared to 13 percent in urban private schools. Equally interesting is the degree of inequality between schools of a given type, suggesting that there is segregation within school types. The last nine rows in the table show the percentile distribution of schools by the percentage of fathers without schooling. In 10 percent of the small rural schools, half of the fathers have never been to school, while in 60 percent of the urban private schools, less than 7 percent of the fathers have not been to school.

The segregation of children in schools where most parents have similar educational backgrounds was related to the resources and characteristics of teachers and schools. For example, the percentage of fathers without schooling was higher in schools where teachers described lighting as inadequate than in schools where they said they had adequate lighting. On average, where teachers said there were desks for all students, the percentage of fathers without schooling was 10 percent; where teachers said up to three desks were missing, the percentage of fathers without schooling was 15 percent; and where more than three desks were missing, the percentage of fathers without schooling was 20 percent. Similarly, where teachers said furniture was in good condition, the percentage of fathers without schooling was 10 percent, compared to 15 percent where teachers said more than 50 percent of the desks needed repairs. In schools without blackboards, 20 percent of the fathers had no schooling, compared to 10 percent in schools where there was a blackboard in good condition. Where teachers indicated that the number of textbooks received from the government was enough for all children, the

TABLE 4.10

Percentage of Fathers Who Have No Schooling in Different Types of Schools in Mexico

| | Types of Schools | | | | |
	Small Rural	Indigenous	Rural	Urban Public	Urban Private
Number of schools	357	433	1040	835	190
Mean percentage of fathers without schooling	20	14	16	16	13
Median (%)	11	7	8	8	4
Standard deviation (%)	25	19	21	23	20
Inequality (%)	126	142	133	141	156
Low 10%	0	0	0	0	0
20%	0	0	0	0	0
30%	2	0	2	2	0
40%	6	4	5	5	2
50%	11	7	8	8	4
60%	18	10	13	12	7
70%	25	15	18	17	14
80%	33	23	25	25	23
90%	53	38	44	47	33

Source: My estimates using data from the survey of Mexican primary schools described earlier.

percentage of fathers without schooling was 16 percent, compared to 11 percent where the number was sufficient or 10 percent where there were more textbooks than necessary. The percentage of fathers without schooling was much lower (7 percent) where teachers lived in the same community where the school was located than where teachers said they had no fixed residence (20 percent) or lived in another municipality or state (15 percent). Teachers had significantly lower levels of schooling in schools with a higher percentage of fathers without schooling. For example, for teachers with only a junior high school degree, 30 percent of the fathers had no schooling, compared to 9 percent for teachers who had a teaching degree from a tertiary institution. Where teachers had less experience, there was a greater percentage of fathers without schooling: 20 percent for teachers with less than five years of teaching experience, 14 percent for teachers with between five and ten years of experience, and under 10 percent for teachers with more than ten years of experience. A similar effect was observed for length of appointment in the school. Where teachers had been posted for less than a year, 18 percent of the fathers had no schooling, compared to 10 percent where teachers had been between four and six years in the school. The number of groups the teacher taught at the same time was also related to the level of education of the fathers. Where teachers taught only one group, 8 percent of the fathers were unschooled, compared to 17 percent where they taught two groups and 23 percent where they taught three or more groups. These effects were observed both within various Mexican states and within various types of school.

Unequal Chances in School

In addition to the unequal learning chances that stem from initial inequality, many of the constraints to equal educational opportunity are in the schools themselves. The kind of school children attend matters greatly for how much they learn. A significant portion of the variation in student learning outcomes is a result of differences between schools. Because students are grouped in schools in ways that reflect residential patterns of segregation, schools are socially segregated. The schools attended by low-income children are more likely to have substandard conditions, which make learning more challenging. The result of the differences between schools discussed in this section are unequal opportunities to learn for children from different income groups.

Assessment of student performance is a relatively recent undertaking in Latin America. Available evidence from these assessments, however, suggests that there are large inequalities between schools. For example, a recent study of student achievement in mathematics among fourth graders in Peru found that 54 percent of the differences were attributable to differences between schools (World Bank 1999a). Using fourth-grade student achievement data in language in the four poorer states in Mexico, I found that most of the variation between students could be accounted for by differences between schools (Table 4.11). As can be seen in Table 4.11, there are differences in the average levels of academic achievement among type of schools. Urban schools have the highest average level of achievement. However, the variation of achievement scores is equally large in the four types of schools. The percentage of that variation associated with differences between schools is higher for schools attended by proportionately more children from lower income families. The differences between schools explain 20 percent of the variation in achievement scores in urban areas, but 69 percent in

TABLE 4.11

Percentage of Variation of Student Achievement in a Spanish Test in Fourth Grade Explained by Differences Between Schools for Urban, Rural, Indigenous, and Remote Rural Schools in the South of Mexico

Type of School	Lowest Score	Highest Score	Average	Standard Deviation	% Explained by Differences Between Schools
Rural-remote	0	86.8	39.2	19.1	66
Indigenous	0	89.5	32.3	18.7	69
Rural	0	81.6	35.8	16.6	48
Urban	0	84.2	47.4	15.4	20

Source: My own estimates using data collected by the Centro de Estudios Educativos in Mexico, as described in Chapter 13 of this book.

indigenous areas and 66 percent in schools in remote rural areas. While these results are encouraging in that they suggest a great potential role for schools to equalize educational opportunity for all children, they also indicate the extent to which schools are currently reproducing social stratification in Latin America.[29]

Table 4.12 presents several indicators of educational inequality based on fourth-grade achievement data collected by Ministries of Education and UNESCO on student achievement in basic language and math skills in a sample of schools in several countries of the region. The second column is an index of socioeconomic segregation between schools.[30] There is a high degree of inequality in the social composition of schools in all countries included in the study. This suggests pervasive social segregation in schools. As would be expected, social segregation of schools is higher in the countries with the most educational inequality.[31] There are also significant inequalities in the levels of student achievement between these segregated schools as shown by columns 4 and 6, which represent the percentage of variance in student achievement due to differences between schools. There are also important differences between schools in the percentage of children who have repeated grades (column 8). The countries with the greatest degree of school segregation also show the greatest differences between schools in grade repetition.[32]

Because education authorities are more responsive to the social groups with greater social and political power, the resources necessary to support learning are also stratified in ways that reflect the social class of origin of the students. As a result, those who have more get more resources for learning. This stratification of resources begins with financial public resources for education, is aggravated by further stratification of private resources for education, and is finally reflected in the quality of schools attended by children from different income groups.

A study of educational expenditures in Brazil in the early 1990s found that per pupil expenditures in the poorest Northeast were only a third of the level of per pupil expenditures in the wealthiest Southeast, and only 44 percent of the national average. Per pupil costs are even lower in municipal schools. Some municipalities in the Northeast spend only 30 percent per pupil of what other municipalities spend in the rest of the country. State schools in São Paulo spend 100 times more per pupil than municipal schools in the Northeast. Throughout the country, municipal schools spend 63 percent of the amount state-funded schools spend (Brooke 1992, 40).

TABLE 4.12

Inequality in the Social Composition and Student Learning Outcomes Between Fourth-Grade Students in a Sample of Schools in Several Latin American Countries in 1997

Country	Percentage of Socioeconomic Segregation Between Schools	Ranking of Socioeconomic Segregation	School Differences in Language	Ranking of Differences in Language	School Differences in Mathematics	Ranking of Differences in Mathematics	School Differences in Repetition	Ranking of Differences in Repetition
Argentina	40	4	29	8	41	11		7
Bolivia	46	9	29	9	30	4	49	8
Brazil	47	10	25	6	31	6	58	5
Chile	39	2	17	1	31	5	48	4
Colombia	39	3	24	5	32	7	39	
Costa Rica								
Cuba	29	24	4	38	10	31	2	
Ecuador								
El Salvador								
Honduras	44	6	32	10	34	8	31	1
Mexico	46	8	27	7	25	2	65	10
Nicaragua								
Panama								
Paraguay	44	7	38	11	35	9	59	9
Peru	41	5	39	12	43	12	49	6
Dominican Republic	50	11	23	3	26	3	68	11
Uruguay								
Venezuela	33	1	20	2	21	1	38	3

Source: Derived from UNESCO-OREALC (2000).

Another study of educational expenditures in Mexico conducted in the mid-1990s found large differences in per pupil expenditures resulting from the financing formula used by the Mexican Federation to transfer resources to the states (Latapi and Ulloa 1997, 123). And a study of financing of secondary education in El Salvador found a significant urban bias, with nearly half of the resources alone being spent in the capital city, which accounts for less than a third of secondary school enrollments (World Bank 1999a, 10).

Inequality in the amount of resources going to children of different socioeconomic backgrounds results not just from differences in how public resources are allocated across schools, but also from the differences in the amount of the contributions made by parents to the education of their children, including private contributions to public schools. A recent study of education in Peru—which, as discussed earlier, has one of the lowest levels of income inequality and one of the lowest education gaps between rich and poor in the region—found that there were significant differences in private spending on education between income groups. Private spending on education in 1997 in Peru was equal to 2.4 percent of GDP, almost as much as total public spending on education, which was 3 percent of GDP. More than half of these private expenditures were for the education of children enrolled in public schools. There are very large differences between income groups in accounting for these private expenditures. Forty-five percent of them were incurred by the wealthiest 20 percent, while the poorest 20 percent incurred 5 percent of this total. For primary education, only 57 percent of all private expenditures are incurred by the wealthiest 20 percent. For public schools, only 68 percent of all private expenditures are incurred by the wealthiest group. These resources are used for teaching materials and to improve schools (World Bank 1999b, 20–21).

Another study in Brazil also found very large differences in the average family expenditures in education across income groups. Families in the top decile spent over twenty times more than the median value for all families. Up to the seventh decile, less than 2 percent of family income was spent on education versus 5 percent in the ninth decile and 16 percent in the tenth decile (World Bank 2000, 30).

Available data for a number of countries suggest that the amount privately contributed by parents to education is significant and higher than for OECD countries (see Table 4.13). Assuming that public expenditures are equally distributed across income groups, and assuming per pupil costs are the same across income groups, these differences in private expenditures lead to large differences in school resources for children in different income groups.

TABLE 4.13

Education Expenditures as a Percentage of GDP

	Public	Private
Colombia	4.2	3.6
Chile	3.1	2.6
Mexico	4.5	1.1
Peru	2.4	2.0
OECD	4.7	1.2

Source: OECD (1998).

In part, it is reasonable to expect that in a region with large income inequalities, private contributions to education would mirror these inequalities. Even if all families spent the same share of their resources for the education of their children, the net amount spent per child would be higher for the higher income groups which have significantly more income and fewer children. These differences in private expenditures will stratify public schools, and further stratify the system between public and private schools.

The percentage of children attending private schools varies significantly across countries in the region, as can be seen in Table 4.14. With the exception of some schools managed by religious orders that cater to disadvantaged children, such as the Fe y Alegria schools in thirteen countries in the region, most private schools serve the children of the wealthiest 20 percent of the population. In Colombia, for instance, among the children in the poorest quintile who attend primary school, 94 percent do so in public schools, compared to only 53 percent of children in the top quintile. The segmentation is more pronounced at the secondary level. Those in the poorest quintile who attend school do so in public schools, whereas only 39 percent of the wealthiest quintile who attend secondary school do so in public institutions (Sanchez and Nunez 1995, 77).

The fact that public and private schools, which on average have higher levels of student achievement (UNESCO 1998), have students of different social backgrounds makes it difficult to ascertain the extent to which these differences result from differences in school practices, from differences in the resources spent on the education of their children, or from differences in the educational background of the parents of children attending the various schools. A study examining the differences in levels of

TABLE 4.14

Percentage of Enrollment in Private Schools at Different Levels

Country	Pre-primary	Primary	Secondary
Argentina	31	21	30
Bolivia	11	8	
Brazil	23	12	
Chile	49	40	44
Colombia	56	18	39
Costa Rica	9	5	10
Dominican Republic	55	22	33
Ecuador	40	20	34
El Salvador	31	15	64
Guatemala	33	17	38
Haiti	63	58	84
Honduras	18	5	42
Mexico	8	6	12
Nicaragua	26	15	24
Panama	25	9	14
Paraguay	38	13	24
Peru	22	12	16
Uruguay	29	16	16
Venezuela	17	15	35

Source: UNESCO (1998).

student achievement among students attending public and private schools concluded that, controlling for the selectivity of private schools, there were no significant differences between the two kinds of schools (Carnoy 1998).

A World Bank study tried to separate the influence of public/private management from the contribution of the different level of resources in Brazilian secondary schools. The study concluded that most of the differences resulted from different facilities and instructional inputs and that "once equalized for these inputs, achievement differences among private, municipal, and state schools are eliminated. There appears to be nothing intrinsic to private education that cannot be attained in the public sector" (World Bank 2000, 45).

The differences in the financial resources between different public schools and between public and private schools lead to differences in the resources available to schools and classrooms and to differences in the quality of teachers. A survey of 400 primary schools in Peru demonstrated significant disparities in school resources between schools located in urban and rural areas. For example, while 81 percent of large schools in urban areas had a library, only 26 percent of small schools in rural areas had a library; 76 percent of large urban schools had latrines that worked, compared to 32 percent of small rural schools (World Bank 1998, 20).

A study of secondary schools in Brazil found that the vast majority of the schools attended by the rich feature more quality inputs. The most salient difference is access to computers; 60 percent of the schools catering to the rich have them, compared to only 20 percent of the schools catering to the poor. Despite state efforts to achieve standards comparable to private schools with regard to the availability of books, the wealthy still have greater access to books than do the poor. This finding supports the hypothesis that the wealthy attend the better public schools, while the less well off attend public schools of lower quality (World Bank 2000).

Similar differences in the facilities and resources of schools serving children from different socioeconomic backgrounds have been documented in Argentina (Llach, Montoya, and Roldan 1999) and Uruguay. In these countries, where 40 percent of the schools serve low socioeconomic status students, more than one-third are newly appointed teachers, compared to only 9 percent new teachers in the schools serving the students of highest socioeconomic background (ANEP 1999b). In a survey of 7,400 teachers in Mexico,[33] those teaching in disadvantaged areas reported very poor physical conditions. Table 4.15 summarizes the differences between schools with respect to physical characteristics.

In Mexico, all schools received free textbooks provided by the government, and all teachers reported that they had indeed received them. However, when asked if they had received enough textbooks for all students in the class, the responses indicated that those in the most disadvantaged areas were more likely to miss some textbooks. In indigenous and community rural schools, more than 35 percent of the teachers indicated that the textbooks were not sufficient. In rural schools, 18 percent; in urban public schools, 15 percent; and in urban private schools, 13 percent indicated that the textbooks received were not sufficient. While the Mexican Ministry of Education has demonstrated the capacity to reach all schools in distributing the officially sanctioned textbooks, it is more effective distributing enough textbooks to children in private schools and urban areas than to children in indigenous schools and small rural communities.

TABLE 4.15

Percentage of Classroom Characteristics by Type of School in Mexico

Characteristic	Urban Private	Urban Public	Rural	Indigenous	Community Rural
Poor lighting	9	27	21	34	38
Desks for all students	99	82	74	49	63
Some desks in disrepair	30	80	78	83	66
More than 25% of the desks in disrepair	2	27	29	36	16
Blackboard in good condition	74	34	33	25	44
No bookcase	26	76	70	83	61

Low-quality schools and teachers make it hard for many children to learn what is expected of them in the first grade. As we have seen, many children enter school at a disadvantage in that they have not been to preschool, while other children have. As a result, many children are retained in first grade—about one in three children repeat first grade in the region (OAS 1997, 18). High rates of repetition increase the level of difficulty for teachers facing classes where many children repeat because they increase the heterogeneity of the student population. Because these teachers have typically received less training and have the least resources, this greater challenge is faced by those least equipped to face it. The result is a perpetuation of the cycle of repetition that, as discussed earlier, leads many children to drop out of school before completing a primary education.

As discussed earlier, poor children are more likely to repeat grades. A study in Uruguay found that the percentage of students repeating a grade increased as the education level of the parents decreased and as income decreased. While 26 percent of children in the fourth grade whose parents had not completed primary education and who were in the bottom 50 percent of income in the sample had repeated a grade at least twice, only 1 percent of the children whose parents had at least upper secondary and who were in the top 50 percent of income had repeated (CEPAL 1991, 80). Grade retention is only an indirect proxy of student achievement. A study conducted in Northeast Brazil found no relationship between academic achievement and grade retention (Harbison and Hanushek 1992). Another study in Honduras found that, controlling for the level of reading ability of first- and third-graders, poorer children were more likely to be retained in the same grade and 20 percent of first-graders were retained even though they had met the official criteria to be promoted to the next grade (McGinn et al. 1991).

Another simple reason why many students do not complete six grades of primary education is that one-third of the primary schools in Latin America have less than six teachers to teach six grades (UNESCO 1996). These are called "incomplete schools"; some of them do not offer all six grades, and others offer the six grades asking some or all teachers to teach multiple grades. Because most teachers do not have adequate training to handle multigrade classes effectively or materials to support multigrade instruction, the children attending these schools, most of them living in rural areas, are at an educational disadvantage compared with their urban counterparts. For most of the children who reach the highest available grade in an "incomplete" primary school, the only feasible choice is to drop out of school with an equally incomplete primary education.

In Mexico, for example, 15 percent of the schools report that they have grades for which no teacher is assigned.[34] While this is a rare occurrence in urban schools, one in five indigenous and rural schools report having at least one group of children for whom no teacher is assigned. Only 57 percent of the schools in Mexico are "complete" (offering six grades with one teacher per grade); 21 percent are "incomplete," that is, they offer six grades but at least two of them are taught by the same teacher; and another 21 percent are "unitary," meaning one teacher teaches all grades offered. The percentage of unitary schools is highest among indigenous schools (26 percent) and rural schools (20 percent). The same is true for incomplete schools, which account for 35 percent of the indigenous schools and 39 percent of the rural schools. Communities that speak an indigenous language are clearly disadvantaged in the kind of school their children can attend. Nine percent of the principals reported that the parents of their children spoke primarily an indigenous language, and another 9 percent reported a combination of indigenous language and Spanish. The percentage of principals who report that they have a group of students without a teacher is 9 percent when the community speaks primarily Spanish, but 16 percent when the community speaks a mix of Spanish and an indigenous language and 22 percent when they speak primarily an indigenous language. In communities speaking primarily Spanish, the percentage of incomplete and unitary schools is 40 percent; in communities speaking a mix of Spanish and an indigenous language, 53 percent of the schools are incomplete or unitary; and in communities speaking primarily an indigenous language, 60 percent of the schools are incomplete or unitary. These differences in the educational opportunities of indigenous groups operate even within type of school. For example, in rural schools, only 12 percent of those in communities that speak primarily Spanish have a group without a teacher; in communities speaking Spanish and an indigenous language, 22 percent have a group without a teacher; and in communities speaking primarily an indigenous language, 35 percent have a group without a teacher. These differences are not a reflection of the size or type of organization of the school.

The quality of the education received by poor children is also weak, in part because those who teach them have limited abilities. Teaching well is hard. Helping low-income children reach standards of excellence should not be easier than practicing medicine or piloting airplanes. Arguably the education, work conditions, and incentives teachers encounter differ from those encountered by physicians and pilots and are worse than those faced by most professionals. This is partially due to the inadequate systems of teacher education (Tatto and Velez 1997; Villegas-Reimers 1998; Villegas-Reimers and Reimers 1996). Low teaching quality may also be a function of teacher salaries, careers, and work structure. Teaching is an occupation of last resort in most Latin American countries and those who teach poor children are often the least experienced. There is limited evidence to explain why the teaching profession fails to attract capable teachers. Arguably, unstable salaries and in some cases low salaries play a role in discouraging bright high school students from choosing to become teachers.

Teacher salaries declined significantly during the 1980s and increased during the 1990s. We do not know the long-term impact of these swings in salaries in attracting qualified students into the teaching profession, but we can assume that they signal that teaching is a career with an unstable reward structure. Teacher salaries in the region are lower, adjusted per working hours, than salaries of other professionals with comparable years of study, as shown in Table 4.16. The gap is between 25 percent and 30 percent in Brazil, Panama, Paraguay, and Uruguay and between 35 percent and 50 percent in Bolivia, Chile, and El Salvador. Only in Costa Rica are teacher salaries comparable to those of other professionals. Teachers in private schools receive on average 10–20 percent more per hour than do public school teachers (CEPAL 1999).

The lower salaries of teachers is confirmed by an independent study that looked at this issue in twelve Latin American countries (Liang 1999). This study found that teachers are paid, on average, less than other professionals with comparable levels of education. Adjusting for the longer summer vacation for the number of hours worked,[35] however, this differential disappears and in a few cases teachers are actually paid more. This study also found that teacher salaries are lower, controlling for other characteristics of teachers such as education and experience, in disadvantaged areas. Teachers working in rural or difficult areas receive between 10 percent and 30 percent less than those working in urban areas (Liang 1999, 27). The study also found that there is less variation in teacher's pay than in other professions and that teaching attracts candidates of lower socioeconomic background than other professions.

Given the low and unstable salaries, it should not be surprising that most of the applicants to teacher education colleges have the lowest academic scores among those who seek higher education and that in many countries teaching positions have to be filled by

TABLE 4.16

Average Teacher Salaries Standardized by Hours Worked for Teachers and for Other Professionals as a Multiple of the Poverty Line

Country	Year	Teachers	Other Professionals	
Bolivia	1997	2.4	7.1	(effective salary)
		4.8	8.1	(salary standardized for hours worked)
Brazil	1996	4.2	8.1	(effective salary)
		6.5	9.5	(salary standardized for hours worked)
Chile	1995	6.7	15.4	(effective salary)
		8.0	14.9	(salary standardized for hours worked)
Costa Rica	1997	7.9	9.2	(effective salary)
		10.1	9.5	(salary standardized for hours worked)
Ecuador	1997	3.3	5.6	(effective salary)
		3.7	5.6	(salary standardized for hours worked)
Panama	1997	6.6	9.8	(effective salary)
		8.1	10.1	(salary standardized for hours worked)
Paraguay	1996	3.9	6.2	(effective salary)
		5.0	6.6	(salary standardized for hours worked)
Uruguay	1997	4.5	8.4	(effective salary)
		6.8	8.9	(salary standardized for hours worked)

Source: CEPAL (1999) and Panorama Social de America Latina (1998, 124).

unqualified teachers (Schiefelbein and Tedesco 1995). The percentage of teachers without the officially required qualifications are 46 percent in Bolivia, 30 percent in Brazil, 10 percent in Colombia, 14 percent in Costa Rica, 26 percent in the Dominican Republic, 17 percent in Ecuador, 15 percent in Mexico, 25 percent in Nicaragua, 40 percent in Paraguay, and 26 percent in Peru. These unqualified teachers are assigned to rural schools and to schools in poor communities (UNESCO-OREALC 2000). As we have seen, the indices of grade repetition and of failure to complete primary school are significantly higher for these children.

In Mexico, teachers are more likely to live in the community when they teach in urban schools (in private schools 67 percent live in the community and in urban public schools 55 percent do) than in rural and indigenous schools where less than one in five teachers lives in the community where they teach. The level of teacher education is also lower in disadvantaged communities. In small rural schools, 97 percent of the teachers have a high school degree or less; in indigenous schools, 40 percent of the teachers have a high school degree or less; and in all other schools, less than 3 percent of the teachers have these low levels of education.

Teachers in urban schools tend to be more experienced. One in five teachers in indigenous and rural schools in Mexico has less than five years teaching experience, compared to 5 percent in urban schools and 14 percent in private schools. This suggests that most appointments are made to disadvantaged areas, frequently with teachers who do not live in these communities and often with unqualified teachers, and that as they gain experience and education, and therefore increase their salary, teachers transfer to urban schools.

With less experience and education, it should be expected that teachers in disadvantaged communities are less effective teachers. Ethnographic studies of pedagogical practices in schools attended by disadvantaged children in several countries in the region conclude that these teachers have limited instructional repertoires, have low expectations for the achievement of the children, spend limited time in instructional activities, and have to make do with a minimum of instructional resources. These conditions are opposite to what current research on school effectiveness suggests is necessary to foster student academic achievement (Avalos 1986; Carlson 2000; Ezpeleta and Weiss 1996; Portela and Santana 1998; Rockwell 1995).

One of the questions in the survey to 50,000 sixth-graders in Mexico asked students what their teacher does when students ask a question in class. The percentage of students who indicated that the teacher did not answer their question is clearly stratified along social contexts: 23 percent in small rural schools, 27 percent in indigenous schools, 19 percent in rural schools, 15 percent in public urban schools, and 13 percent in private schools. Responses to whether teachers' answers clarified the students' doubts reflect a similar gap between schools: 12 percent in small rural schools, 14 percent in indigenous schools, 9 percent in rural schools, 7 percent in urban public schools, and 6 percent in private schools.

These differences in the quality of teachers and instructional resources between schools account for the differences in learning outcomes for students who attend different schools discussed at the beginning of this section and for the differential rates of progress of the poor and the non-poor. Analyzing data for a nationally representative sample of sixth-graders in Mexico, I found important differences in the percentage of students who have the expected age in sixth grade (which as discussed earlier is a proxy for repetition) by socioeconomic background of the child. The differences between types of schools mirror the differences in quality discussed throughout this chapter. The percentage of students who are of an age appropriate to the grade is 43 percent in small rural schools, 39 percent in indigenous schools, 58 percent in rural schools, 71 percent in public urban schools, and 82 percent in private schools.

EDUCATION POLICY AND INEQUALITY

The sharp social inequalities in Latin America do matter for the chances children have to develop cognitive and social skills, hence reproducing inequality. The direct influences are the result of the gaps in cultural and financial capital between social groups which put the children of the poor at a disadvantage. These gaps were described earlier as "initial inequalities." Societies interested in equality of educational opportunity should seek to offer conditions in schools and other social policies that counterbalance those initial gaps resulting from social differences. But another channel of influence of social inequality in educational opportunity is even more problematic. Poor children attend schools where it is not possible to attain high levels of learning. Closing the gaps in quality between schools attended by the poor and the non-poor is crucial to moving forward toward more social justice in the region.

One way to close the gap in the educational opportunities faced by the most excluded and the rest of the children is to implement compensatory policies that give these children proportionately more resources to overcome the multifaceted forms of social disadvantage they face. This would mean, for example, providing opportunities for low-cost or free quality preschool education, which would foster children's school readiness. It would also require providing opportunities for health and nutrition in early childhood intervention programs, additional learning materials, specialized training to teachers, and support for the development of teaching approaches specifically tailored to their unique circumstances. An example of such support might include developing methodologies to teach effectively in multigrade settings or in classrooms with greater age heterogeneity because of high repetition rates.

A more basic way to address the gap in opportunities would be to ensure that the conditions faced by children in schools do not mirror the social gaps outside schools. At the very least, children of all backgrounds should have access to schools similarly endowed. As we have seen, this does not happen in Latin America, where poor children typically attend lousy schools in comparison to the schools attended by their wealthier peers.

While Latin America has espoused a long-standing rhetorical commitment to equality of educational opportunity, it is only recently that policy discourse has begun to address the initial inequality gap as well as the gap in the quality of schools between poor and non-poor. Equality of opportunity for most of the twentieth century has meant simply offering a space in school, though not always a chair and a desk or textbooks, to a growing number of children. Then and now, the gap between policy rhetoric and implementation of programs in schools has further limited the learning chances of poor children. While there are variations between countries in the region, it is possible to distinguish four periods with regard to how policy interpreted educational opportunity and to the priority policymakers assigned to this objective.

The Early Period of Establishment of Public Education Systems: Late 1800s to Mid-1900s

The emphasis of education policy during the late 1800s to mid-1900s was to contribute to the consolidation of nation-states and to serve the goal of providing citizens a common ground to share the values of the new republics. Domingo Faustino Sarmiento, a friend of Horace Mann, influenced the establishment of the public education system in Argentina, Chile, and Paraguay and, indirectly, in Uruguay. A few decades later, José de Vasconcelos promoted the public education system in Mexico. Equality of opportunity in this period meant the incorporation of a greater number of, but not all, students to primary education and the establishment of national public systems of education.

The Accelerated Expansion of Access in the 1950s

Following the approval of the Universal Declaration of Human Rights and the creation of UNESCO, a number of regional conferences were convened to foster the universalization of primary education and expansion of other levels of education. In addition to the global influences resulting from the role of the United Nations, UNESCO, and the popularization of human capital theory, which saw education as an investment, the economic development strategy adopted by Latin America (import substitution industrialization) called for the expansion of an internal market and for a more trained labor force that could work in industry. The rapid urbanization of the region made it possible for the education system to incorporate almost all children in primary school between 1950 and 1980. Access to secondary and tertiary education expanded rapidly, though the emphasis at these levels was not in incorporating all students, nor was it in achieving proportional representation of students from different social or ethnic backgrounds into the higher levels of education.

This period ended with the countries of the region subscribing to the Major Project in the Field of Education, an initiative spearheaded by UNESCO, which included as policy objectives for the 1980–2000 period achieving universal access to a basic education of eight years, overcoming illiteracy, and improving the quality and efficiency of education systems.

The Parenthesis of the Lost Decade, 1980–1990: The Obsession with Management and Financing Reforms

At the beginning of the 1980s, the region was hard hit with a debt and financial crisis that undermined the financial support necessary to achieve the goals of the Major Project in the Field of Education. As governments looked for ways to close the fiscal deficit, improving the administrative efficiency of educational spending became the central objective of education policy, while equality of educational opportunity took a back seat. Consistent with these educational priorities, governments in the region established systems to measure student achievement and to deepen experiments in educational decentralization, and some governments experimented with voucher systems. Policy rhetoric began to emphasize the relevance of education quality to support the integration of the countries of the region in the world economy.

The Late 1990s: The Discovery of Compensatory Policies

In 1990, a number of United Nations organizations convened a World Education Conference in Jomtien, Thailand, to recommit to the universalization of education. This conference emphasized the need to reach the excluded and the need to design innovative programs to address their basic learning needs. Some of these themes echoed the Major Project in the Field of Education, which had made little difference because of the financial crisis of the 1980s. In 1992, the United Nations Economic Commission for Latin America and the Regional Office of UNESCO prepared a policy framework (CEPAL-UNESCO 1992) emphasizing that the primary policy objectives for education should be fostering economic development and the promotion of equity. A number of countries in the region began reforms to improve quality and equity. However, it should be noted that equality of educational opportunity was not the central objective of these reforms, which spent great resources in fostering overall quality improvements and improvements in administrative efficiency (reflective of the policy emphases of the decade of the 1980s). The language of policy became more sharply focused on issues of equity toward the end of the decade. In 1998 a Summit of Presidents of the Americas in Santiago focused on education and specifically on links in education policy to the objective of alleviating poverty. The first item in the action plan called for the development of compensatory education policies. The report of UNESCO's regional office to the World Education Summit in Dakar[36] characterized the policy priorities of the region at the end of the 1990s in this way:

> Most of the countries assign a high priority to promoting equality of educational opportunity. The groups considered to be most important in this sense are children living in poverty, street children, working children, migrant children, children who are members of indigenous groups, as well as children with special learning needs. Among the efforts to promote equity are affirmative action programs which seek to target resources to at-risk populations and which encourage access to and permanence in basic education programs, especially for boys and girls who live in rural and in poor urban areas. Thus, compensatory programs are aimed at reducing educational gaps. These programs have gained in importance during the last half of the decade. (UNESCO-OREALC 2000, 18)

The concept of affirmative action, of positive discrimination, is relatively recent in education policy discourse in Latin America. It appears for the first time in education policy enacted by the newly democratic government of Chile in 1990 and in education policy documents in Mexico in 1993 (although the Mexican secretary of education established a unit of compensatory programs earlier in 1986). It extends to other countries in the region and was adopted in the Summit of the Americas in 1998.

Reflecting the new emphasis on equity, during the 1990s a number of education reforms in Latin America included improving equity as one of their objectives (Gajardo 1999). Gajardo identifies seven policy objectives driving the education reforms in Latin America in the 1990s, as summarized in Table 4.17. Given the multiplicity of these objectives, the priority of equity as a focus of these reforms is doubtful. The reforms aimed at improving equity have spanned the gamut from providing cash to students to allow them to attend schools, to trying to equalize per pupil expenditure, to trying to

TABLE 4.17

Policy Objectives of Current Education Reforms in Latin America

Policy Objective	Countries with Reforms Aimed at That Objective
Institutional reform and decentralization	Argentina, Colombia, Chile, Brazil, Mexico, Dominican Republic, El Salvador
Increased school autonomy	Bolivia, Paraguay, Chile, Brazil, Guatemala, El Salvador, Nicaragua
Improve quality and equity through targeted programs consisting of infrastructure improvement, teaching supplies	Argentina, Colombia, Chile, Brazil, Peru, Paraguay, Bolivia, Costa Rica, Guatemala, Uruguay, Dominican Republic
Curriculum reform	Argentina, Chile, Uruguay, Costa Rica, Bolivia, Dominican Republic, Brazil, Mexico
Extending school day	Colombia, Chile, Uruguay
Teacher education, improve teaching careers	Argentina, Colombia, Chile, Brazil, Uruguay, Costa Rica, Guatemala, Nicaragua, Dominican Republic
Increase spending on education	Argentina, Bolivia, Brazil, Chile, Colombia, Costa Rica, Guatemala, Mexico, Panama, Paraguay, Uruguay

Source: Gajardo (1999, 14).

improve the quality of education for all children, or particularly for schools attended by low-income children.

The largest programs to transfer cash to families in support of student attendance in school have been implemented in Mexico and Brazil. Mexico implemented a large program to provide cash to low-income families in marginalized communities if students attended school regularly and kept up with health checkups (Progresa). The Federal District of Brazil implemented a targeted cash transfer program to keep low-income children in school (Bolsa Escola). There appear to be positive results of this program in terms of focus and coverage. The dropout rate was lower for beneficiaries (0.2 percent) versus nonbeneficiaries (6.5 percent) (World Bank 2000). Preliminary evaluations of Progresa in Mexico suggest that it also had a positive impact on allowing students to remain in school (Schultz 2000).

The most significant policy to reduce disparities in per pupil expenditures was implemented in 1998 in Brazil, reforming the financing mechanism of primary education (the Fund for the Development of Fundamental Education and Valorization of Teachers [FUNDEF]). The new mechanism and formula guaranteed a minimum level of per student expenditure for basic education (first through eighth grade): $300. "The Fund promotes the redistribution of resources among state and municipal education systems within each state, in accordance with the number of students enrolled in each system. The Federal government provides supplemental resources for those states falling below the legislated minimum, thus reducing regional disparities in education spending" (World Bank 2000). Prior to the implementation of this reform, there were

wide disparities in per pupil spending. In 1995, per pupil expenditures in basic education in some northeastern states were just one-quarter the national average, compared
with three times the national average spent by some southern states. Within-state differences were also notable: in Rio de Janeiro, municipal systems spent less than one-third
that of state systems (World Bank 2000, 58). There are no evaluations documenting the
implementation or impact of this program.

Most compensatory policies during the 1990s supported the development of programs to improve the quality of schools attended by low-income children as well as
programs to expand early childhood care and preschool education targeted to disadvantaged children in Colombia, Mexico, Peru, and Venezuela. Targeted quality enhancing programs included those to improve the quality of rural multigrade schools in
Colombia and Chile, to reorganize the curriculum to facilitate automatic promotion
between grades in Brazil, to develop models to deliver education in small rural communities in Mexico; and to provide resources to improve schools attended by disadvantaged children in Chile and Mexico. Brazil also experimented with accelerated
summer instructional programs for students at risk to help students catch up with their
age cohort. Governments also made an effort to develop partnerships between the public sector and nongovernmental organizations to deliver quality education to disadvantaged children (Cardemil 1999; Filp 1993; Rodrigues and Campelo 1999; Schmelkes
1999; Swope and Latorre 1999).

Most of these programs were developed in a context of financial scarcity and with
greater sensitivity to their overall costs than to their cost-effectiveness. The aim was
to provide positive discrimination at low cost. There are few evaluations of these programs. Most of the evaluations focus on whether student achievement improves rather
than on the extent to which the programs close the educational achievement gap between low-income children and their more fortunate counterparts. There is some evidence that these programs indeed can increase student achievement, which should not
be surprising since the initial levels of achievement for the children of the excluded
are relatively low (Munoz-Izquierdo et al. 1997). Some of this evidence is examined
elsewhere in this book.

These programs, which characterize the most recent phase of education policies
in the region, effectively increased the level of resources to support the education of
low-income children and, as a result, are likely to have increased their educational
opportunities relative to previous eras. They are, however, unlikely to have equalized
educational opportunities between groups in terms of educational inputs or results. The
language of affirmative action or positive discrimination is more ambitious than the
actions to which it refers. In part, this reflects the limited ambitions of these programs,
focused on improving the education conditions of the poor, but not on closing the gap
and reducing inequality.[37] In part, this also reflects ambivalence regarding the priority
of equity vis-à-vis the objectives of improving quality and management efficiency. In
none of the reforms undertaken in the countries of the region was the achievement of
equality of educational opportunity the central policy priority during the 1990s. Rather,
the main priority was the overall improvement in education quality with some supple-
mentary programs to improve equity. During this period, the reforms to decentralize
education management, measure results, improve school autonomy, promote community participation in school management, and in some cases promote competition from

the private sector continue, although the rationale that links these reforms to the objectives of improving equity was never clearly articulated.

The policies of the 1990s reflect an improvement in the understanding of equality of educational opportunity as they focus on providing minimally adequate educational environments to the poor and in some cases on complementary income transfer and supportive social policies. But these policies are still insufficient from the point of view of reducing educational and social inequality.

What We Know about the Results of Implementing the Recent Wave of Compensatory Policies in Latin America

If the level of effort devoted to compensatory policies pales in comparison to the magnitude of the challenges to achieving equality of educational opportunity, the level of resources to assess these policies and programs is even more limited. In a context where policy formation is rarely influenced by public discussion of objectives, alternative strategies, or the results of past policies, and where there is limited accountability of education decision makers to the public or other constituencies for the content or implementation of policy, there are few incentives to spend much time reflecting on whether policies achieve their objectives and why. In addition, authoritarian traditions of public decision making limit access to information about program implementation and results to the academic communities. Much information about education programs is treated with levels of secrecy appropriate for matters of national security in times of war. Established scholars in countries of the region have difficulty obtaining data on levels of student achievement in standardized tests now collected in most countries of the region, on per pupil expenditures, or on the implementation records of education programs. The secrecy related to programs funded by international agencies is often even greater.

We know from studies of implementation of educational change in other contexts that implementing policies to change the learning chances of the poor is highly political (see Chapter 1)—that much policy is defined and recreated at the implementation stage. The unequal educational conditions discussed in this chapter reflect the unequal distribution of power between dominant and subdominant groups. The children of the poor do not go to lousy schools just because governments do not know better, but because governments have not been accountable to their parents and communities. Unless the political incentives faced by public officials change, we can expect that implementation, even of programs aimed to compensate for the harm caused to the poor by deficient education opportunities, will be flawed. In Brazil, for example, a program to distribute school lunches in schools was found to benefit primarily the non-poor. Half of the recipients belonged to the wealthier families (upper 30 percent of the income distribution), compared to 32 percent of the beneficiaries who came from the poorer 30 percent of households. Most of the recipients (51 percent) lived in the richer Southeast than in the poorer Northeast (28 percent). A similar program to benefit the poor, which provided free textbooks, still provided a fair amount of resources to children whose parents were able to buy these books. Twenty percent of the children receiving this benefit came from the richest 30 percent of the families, while 32 percent of the children receiving the books came from the poorest 30 percent. An equal percentage (29 percent) of children in the Northeast and the richer Southeast received books (World Bank 2000, 38).

In spite of constraints resulting from traditions of limited democratic dialogue about policy and its results, there are some evaluations and descriptive accounts of compensatory policies. Existing accounts tend to be descriptive, emphasizing mostly intended policy and short-term effects. When these reports are analytical they tend to focus on outcomes such as access or achievement on curriculum-based tests and they adopt a black-box approach to policy implementation, often assuming that policy output is implemented as intended. The designs employed rely on pre-post comparisons which are often inappropriately disaggregated, separating effects of the policies being evaluated from those of other policies or changes. Some are also disaggregated by comparisons between target populations and some quasi-control groups, often assuming learning from differences between groups and inappropriately accounting for the nonrandom selection of students to treatment schools. From the limited studies available, we know more about whether some desired outcome (more typically access, but also achievement levels) improves with the implementation of a compensatory policy than about whether the distance separating the beneficiaries of the policy shortens or widens as a result of the policy. Most studies concentrate on the effects of the policies, rather than on their costs. We also know little about the practical consequences of some of the effects (many of which are discussed as percentage increase in student achievement in a test or percentage change in access). In particular, we know almost nothing about the long-term effects of compensatory policies—whether they are sustained or interact with further interventions and what kinds of other long-term outcomes they have, such as access to higher levels of schooling, acquisition of skills, or life chances.

CONCLUSIONS

Countries in Latin America have very unequal structures of income distribution and, as a result, 90 million people, one in five persons in the region, do not have enough income to meet minimum caloric requirements necessary to stay alive and healthy. More than twice that number (204 million people, 44 percent of the population) are poor. Because of these high figures alone, it would make sense to elevate the elimination of poverty to a higher-level priority among the objectives of social policy. Even if the recent trends of decline in poverty incidence continue, they are so modest that it would take twenty to thirty years to halve current poverty rates. Because poverty and the social exclusion it generates are relative to the distribution of resources in a society, addressing inequality in social opportunity is central to efforts at providing the poor with access to the benefits of progress achieved by the region over the last decades.

Poverty, inequality, and education are related in multifaceted ways. For any given generation, the levels of education are related to levels of income. Low levels of education block access to the social and economic opportunities that would allow people to get out of poverty. Poverty, in turn, blocks opportunities for the children of the poor to attain levels of education sufficiently higher than their parents in order to move out of poverty. There are several processes that account for the low educational opportunity of children of the poor. Some stem directly from poverty—lower sanitation and living conditions—which lead to poor health and put children at a disadvantage to learn and progress in school. Greater economic needs put more pressure on the children of the poor to work at an early age. This is particularly true for children in rural areas. Greater pressure for the unpaid work of adolescent girls at home puts these girls at an additional disadvantage with regard to their pursuit of schooling. Greater rates of teenage pregnancies for the urban poor and for adolescent girls in rural areas create another obstacle on the path to completing secondary education.

Aside from the direct links between poverty of families and educational opportunity, there are major obstacles to opportunities to learn and succeed in school that stem from the poverty of the education system. Insufficient opportunities in preschool education and low-quality education account for the significantly high rates of grade retention for the poor. As students get older and lose pace with their cohorts of origin, factors directly related to poverty further reduce the chances that the children of the poor complete high school. These factors include the need for paid work; work in household chores; teenage pregnancies; and, related to the interaction between poverty and school factors, the higher direct costs of secondary and higher education. The result is an imperfect reproduction of the social structure through the education system. It is reproduction because the odds are that education gaps between the children of the poor and the non-poor will remain, even if schooling attainment increases on average for the population. It is imperfect because there are students who beat the odds, showing that the mechanisms discussed here are probabilistic but not deterministic.

There are five processes through which social inequality translates into unequal educational opportunities in Latin America:

1. *The differential access to different education levels for the poor and non-poor.* While most students enroll in first grade of primary school, the poor are less likely to complete it, and few of them have access to secondary and higher education.
2. *The differential treatment the poor and non-poor receive in school, where the poor receive an education of lower quality.* Students are socially segregated in schools. Those schools that serve low-income students have teachers with the least education and experience and who spend less time teaching. School organization is less focused on academic activities and there are fewer resources to support the work of teachers and students.
3. *The opportunity most students have to relate only with peers of a similar sociocultural background.* This is disadvantageous for all children, as it limits the development of social capital that would enable trust and collective action in diverse societies.
4. *The contributions parents make (or do not make) to the education of their children.* This includes the time parents spend with their children, the kind of language development and thinking their conversations stimulate, and the resources parents devote to developing communication and cognitive abilities. This is a direct transmission of cultural capital from parents to their children which occurs outside the school. Even if all parents devoted an equal proportion of their resources to stimulate the development of their children, those who have more are able to give more.
5. *The educational content and processes that are not specifically aimed at reducing inequality.* The absence of a project to foster social justice in schools explains, in good part, why they operate more as reproducers of the social structure than as transformers of that structure.

It is necessary to reform education policy in ways that will minimize social exclusion and foster significant educational mobility for the children of the poor. This task requires enabling all children to complete basic education, fostering social mobility, designing mechanisms to significantly increase the proportion of the children of the poor who complete secondary and higher education, and ensuring that all have access to an education of good quality. Completing primary education is already insufficient as a means to attain significantly higher incomes in the region.

While basic patterns of reproduction of the social structure through the education system are illustrated in all countries of the region, there are important differences between countries in their degrees of educational inequality. The countries with the greatest educational equality also have the greatest social equality. The systematic study of this variation, as well as the careful study of the impact of recent education reforms in many countries of the region, provides a potentially rich source of knowledge to inform policy and to answer basic questions about the two keys to understanding educational opportunity: How does opportunity differ among income and social groups, and what are the factors that explain the educational success of members of the most disadvantaged groups?

In recent years, education policy has focused more on improving equity. While actions trail policy, rhetoric is still insufficient to significantly alter the sharp inequalities discussed in this chapter. A number of experiments have sprung up stimulated by this new emphasis. They should be consolidated, carefully evaluated, and discussed to provide the foundation for more ambitious actions.

For education policy reform to contribute to protecting the basic human rights of all Latin American citizens and promote social inclusion, it must counter the current reproductive processes of schooling. This requires changing the odds currently working against poor children so that they may enjoy the same opportunities to learn, succeed, and attain social mobility. Countries of the region must invest in expanding knowledge regarding how the children who currently succeed are able to do so and how the various characteristics of the educational structures discussed here contribute to this process. Beyond this, it will require, above all, political will and policy entrepreneurship to articulate and give voice to the approximately 204 million people who currently comprise dispersed and fragile interest groups but who stand to benefit most directly from policy reforms aimed at making Latin American societies more inclusive.

NOTES

1. I am grateful to my colleagues Noel McGinn, Richard Murnane, and Gary Orfield who provided comments and suggestions to a draft of this chapter. While I cannot claim that I have consistently followed their advice, I appreciate their helping me think through these issues.

2. There are several dimensions of poverty. Insufficient access of income is only one of these dimensions (UNDP 1997). In this chapter poverty is understood as income poverty and three alternative definitions of poverty are used. One is poverty incidence, the number of people living below a comparable poverty line set at $2 per person per day at 1985 purchasing-equivalent prices. Whenever this measure is used, it will be indicated. Another measure of poverty incidence will use a country-specific poverty line, defined as the amount in local currency necessary to purchase a basic basket of goods to meet the minimum nutritional requirements to survive. Unless otherwise stated, this will be the principal definition of poverty

used in this chapter. Using this definition, the extreme poor will be defined as those with income below the poverty line, and the poor will be defined as those with income below two times the poverty line (CEPAL 1999). The unit of analysis will at times be households; at other times it will be individuals. Another definition of poverty used is a relative measure to the total income distribution in each country. It refers to the percentage of the population in the lower extreme of the income distribution. At times the emphasis will be on the poorest 10 percent (first decile); at other times on the poorest 20 percent (first quintile) or poorest 40 percent (second quintile). Inequality in this chapter is understood as disparities in access to income by different people or households in each country.

3. The number of people living below $2 a day declined from 60 percent in 1950 to 35 percent in 1980 (Londono 1996).

4. For a discussion of various dimensions of poverty, see Sen (2000).

5. I thank Richard Murnane for bringing this point to my attention.

6. For a discussion of how productivity growth is necessary, though not sufficient, to increase real incomes in the U.S. economy, see Levy (1999).

7. Note that this process will reduce poverty only in an absolute sense; because poverty is also a relative concept, growth does not necessarily lead to an improved distribution of income and therefore to a reduction in the social distance between the most excluded members of society and the rest.

8. The percentage of households living below the poverty line increased from 35 percent to 41 percent during this period. The percentage living in extreme poverty increased from 15 percent to 18 percent (CEPAL 1999).

9. Unless otherwise noted, the general statements on poverty for Latin America as a region are based on two sets of household surveys. One was conducted in fourteen countries in the region. The source for this analysis is IDB (1998). The countries included are Argentina, Bolivia, Brazil, Chile, Costa Rica, Ecuador, El Salvador, Honduras, Mexico, Panama, Paraguay, Peru, Uruguay, and Venezuela. All samples are national with the exceptions of Argentina, which covers only the Greater Buenos Aires, and Bolivia and Uruguay, which are urban. The other survey is more recent and includes twelve countries: Brazil, Colombia, Costa Rica, Chile, Dominican Republic, El Salvador, Honduras, Nicaragua, Panama, Paraguay, Uruguay, and Venezuela. This source is CEPAL (1999).

10. Participation of women in the labor force has grown continuously in Latin America. During the last decade, the poorer households have attempted to make ends meet by increasing the participation of women, and of younger members of households, in the labor force (CEPAL 1999).

11. These figures are averages of fourteen countries in the region (IDB 1998, 73) and are consistent with findings from Behrman (1997) and Behrman and Knowles (1997).

12. In this chapter, I cite data for Mexico at different times. Unless otherwise noted, these data are the results of my own analysis of a national survey of a representative sample of 4,000 primary schools and approximately 50,000 sixth-graders. These data were collected by the Federal Ministry of Education in 1997.

13. From data in the ENIGH-96 (Encuesta Nacional de Ingresos y Gastos de Hogares 1996). I thank Teresa Bracho for computing these averages and standard deviations.

14. This indicates that the variability of the distribution of educational attainments is still large. However, since the average level of schooling is higher for the younger groups, in relative terms, expressed as a fraction of the mean (this is the coefficient of variation), inequality has diminished. In Mexico, for example, the coefficient of variation of educational attainment for people over sixty is above 1 (with standard deviations of 4 years and an average level of schooling of 4), while it is 0.44 for twenty-five-year-olds (with standard deviations around 4 and an average level of schooling of 9).

15. This model is an elaboration of a concept of educational inequality, which suggested that equality can be distinguished on the basis of access, survival (completion), output (learning), and outcome (Schiefelbein and Farrell 1982; Farrell 1999). I have modified these levels and formulated the factors that account for equality at each level.

16. Because I have argued that we have no empirical evidence that would favor a stochastic model over a cumulative one, the basis for my preference is driven by the social implications of the choice, rather than by the truth value of each position which at this point cannot be determined. A cumulative view would lead to not give up on any child who has not received adequate opportunities early on; a stochastic view would lead to favor early intervention and then concentrate on the "survivors" of a very selective system. I think we need more and better research on the precise nature of the process of opportunity but, as mentioned in Chapter 1, many children's chances at present depend on choices that have to be made with incomplete knowledge.

17. This distinction among financial capital, human capital, and social capital results from the work of Coleman (1988).

18. Much of the research on educational effects, reviewed in Chapter 1, makes this assumption when it tries to explain differences in levels of achievement, or even learning gains, as a function of attributes or practices of teachers at a single point in the educational career of the student. The same assumption is implicit in evaluations that assess program effects assuming that the educational characteristics of children can be adequately captured in some indicator of social background, therefore assuming that their trajectories of opportunity are static.

19. Farrell argues that, from a perspective that values differences between individuals, different types of learning and ways of learning, as well as different uses of it throughout life, it is unclear what equality of results might mean (Farrell 1999, 158). While I agree with the view that equality of learning outputs is easier to define if we accept the desirability of equal learning outputs, I also think that a curriculum that explicitly defines varied learning outputs as objectives for different groups of children can be held to the same standards across groups. Equality of learning outputs is essentially a measure of success of the intended curriculum.

20. Assessing this stage of equality is complicated by the lack of evidence of equivalent outputs across students. Some might argue that there is something about the poor, their culture, or social background that prevents them from performing at comparable levels to the non-poor. Others might argue that the tests are irrelevant to measure meaningful learning outcomes for the poor. It is important to study the variability in learning outputs among the poor and not just the average differences between poor and non-poor, because it clearly demonstrates that poor children are capable, under the right circumstances, of performing at levels comparable or superior to their non-poor counterparts.

21. As I explain later, schools in Latin America segregate students by socioeconomic background. It is unlikely that students can learn to value diversity in segregated schools.

22. These figures are consistent with those reported in an independent assessment which reported 40 percent of repetition in first grade, 20 percent in second grade, peaking to 25 percent in fifth grade and ninth grade (World Bank 2000, 11).

23. Many of these children take leave from school during the harvest period. Some countries have introduced alternate schedules either to make school holidays overlap with the harvest in the particular region or to allow for individualized progression of students in the curriculum.

24. A stochastic model of opportunity would see the lack of early intervention as critical and unsolvable at higher levels; a cumulative model would emphasize the lack of adequate environments to stimulate such development of poorly stimulated children in school.

25. Head Start and most compensatory policies in the United States reflect an implicit bias toward a stochastic model of opportunity.

26. After children enroll in school it becomes more difficult to establish the causal linkages involved. Presumably, some direct influence of the cultural capital of the parents continues even

as children progress in school. Where the characteristics of schools are lower for children who have parents with lower levels of education, such as in Latin America, the pervasiveness of this influence may over time reflect the impact of poorer school conditions.

27. Post (2000) has demonstrated that education policy can accommodate the need for children to work and that, consequently, different education systems exhibit different forms of trade-offs between education and work.

28. This illustrates the point made in Chapter 1: Examining factors that are associated with educational conditions of low-income children does not tell us what to do, even if it is suggestive of hypotheses. An evaluation of a program that systematically examined the impact of lowering the cost of secondary schooling on participation rates would provide this kind of evidence. Because such systematic evaluations are rare, we need to take stock of germane research to inform our understanding of the constraints to educational opportunity, even if we are aware of the limits of such research.

29. The lower percentage of variance in student learning outcomes in urban areas can also reflect that there are more alternative sources of learning in this setting than in rural areas.

30. It is the percentage of variance between schools in a multilevel Hierarchical Linear Modelling (HLM) analysis of variance of a composite index of social background including parental education, occupation, and home characteristics.

31. The Pearson correlation coefficient between the education Gini and the percentage of socioeconomic status variance between schools is 0.637; the statistical significance of this coefficient is 0.035.

32. The Pearson correlation coefficient between the percentage of socioeconomic variance between schools and the percentage of variance in repetition rates between schools is 0.75; the statistical significance of this coefficient is 0.008.

33. My estimates are based on the survey in Mexico described earlier.

34. I have calculated these figures from data obtained on the survey of 4,000 primary schools and 50,000 students described earlier.

35. The adjustment for hours worked is problematic because it assumes that teachers' work is done only in the workplace, in schools. As most teachers know, however, teacher preparation and response to students' work, as well as further professional development and some administrative duties, often take place at home.

36. This summit was convened by the United Nations to assess the progress made in the accomplishment of the goals set in Jomtien in 1990.

37. This reflects a larger philosophical debate between those who see poverty alleviation strategies as consisting of improving the conditions and opportunities of the poor and those who see poverty as a relative concept and therefore consider the reduction of inequality essential to reduce poverty.

REFERENCES

Administracion Nacional de Educacion Publica. 1999a. Estudio del lenguaje en los ninos de cuatro anos del Uruguay. Montevideo: MECAEP-ANEP/BIRF.

Administracion Nacional de Educacion Publica. 1999b. Estudio de los factores institucionales y pedagogicos que inciden en los aprendizajes en escuelas primarias de contextos sociales desfavorecidos en el Uruguay. Montevideo: MECAEP-ANEP/BIRF.

Avalos, Beatrice, ed. 1986. *Teaching Children of the Poor.* Ottawa: International Development Research Center.

Behrman, Jere. 1997. Women's schooling and child education: A survey. Mimeograph. Philadelphia: University of Pennsylvania.

Behrman, Jere, and Jeremy Knowles. 1997. How strong is child schooling associated with household income? Mimeograph. Philadelphia: University of Pennsylvania.

Bernstein, Basil. 1971. A critique of the concept of compensatory education. In *Class, Codes and Control. Volume 1. Theoretical Studies Towards a Sociology of Language,* Chapter 10. London: Routledge and Kegan.

Brooke, Nancy. 1992. The equalization of resources for primary education in Brazil. *International Journal for Educational Development* 12(1): 37–49.

Cardemil, Cecilia. 1999. Prevention of repetition and dropout: Quality and equity in the first years of primary education in chile—Two programs to achieve them. In *Schooling for Success,* ed. Laura Randall and Joan Anderson, 152–162. New York: Sharpe.

Carlson, Beverly. 2000. Achieving educational quality: What schools teach us. Santiago, Chile: CEPAL, United Nations.

Carnoy, Martin. 1998. National voucher plans in Chile and Sweden: Did privatization reforms make for better education? *Comparative Education Review* 42(3): 309–337.

CEPAL (Comision Economica para America Latina). 1991. *Que Aprenden y Quienes Aprenden en las Escuelas Uruguayas.* Montevideo: CEPAL.

CEPAL. 1999. *Panorama Social.* Santiago, Chile: United Nations.

Coleman, James. 1988. Social capital in the creation of human capital. *American Journal of Sociology* 94(Supplement): 95–120.

Coleman, James, et al. 1966. *Equality of Educational Opportunity.* Washington, D.C.: U.S. Government Printing Office.

Conway, Jill, and Susan Bourque, eds. 1995. *The Politics of Women's Education.* Ann Arbor: The University of Michigan Press.

Duryea, Suzanne, and Miguel Szekely. 1999. The determinants of the distribution of schooling in Latin America. Mimeograph. Washington, D.C.: IDB.

ECLAC/UNESCO. 1992. *Education and Knowledge.* Santiago, Chile: United Nations.

Ezpeleta, Justa, and Eduardo Weiss. 1996. Las escuelas rurales en zonas de pobreza y sus maestros. *Revista Mexicana de Investigacion Educativa* I(1).

Farrell, Joseph. 1999. Changing conceptions of equality of education. In *Comparative Education: The Dialectic of the Global and the Local,* ed. Robert Arnove and Carlos Alberto Torres, 149–177. Lanham, Md.: Roman and Littlefield.

Filp, Joanna. 1993. *The 900 Schools Program: Improving the Quality of Primary Schools in Impoverished Areas of Chile.* Paris: UNESCO, International Institute for Educational Planning.

Gajardo, Marcela. 1999. *Reformas Educativas en America Latina: Balance de una Decada.* Santiago, Chile: PREAL.

Harbison, Ralph, and Eric Hanushek. 1992. *Educational Performance of the Poor: Lessons from Rural Northeast Brazil.* Washington, D.C.: World Bank.

Husen, Torsten. 1972. *Social Background and Educational Career.* Paris: OECD.

InterAmerican Development Bank. 1998. *Facing up to Inequality in Latin America.* Washington, D.C.: IDB.

Latapi, Pablo, and Manuel Ulloa. 1997. *El Financiamiento de la Educacion Basica en el Marco del Federalismo.* Mexico City: UNAM, Centro de Estudios Sobre la Universidad.

Latorre, Marcela, and John Swope. 1999. Fe y Alegria: An alternative proposal for primary education in Latin America. In *Schooling for Success,* ed. Laura Randall and Joan Anderson, 33–42. New York: Sharpe.

Llach, Juan Jose, Silvia Montoya, and Flavia Roldan. 1999. *Education para Todos.* Buenos Aires: IERAL.

Levy, Frank. 1999. *The New Dollars and Dreams.* New York: Russell Sage.

Liang, Xiaoyan. 1999. Teacher pay in 12 Latin American countries: How does teacher pay compare to other professions, what determines teacher pay, and who are the teachers? Presented at the Conference on Teachers in Latin America: New Perspectives on Their Development and Performance. San Jose, Costa Rica, June 28–30.

Lindquist-Wong, Pia. 1995. Constructing a public popular education in São Paulo, Brazil. *Comparative Education Review* 39(1): 120–141.

Lockheed, Marlaine, and Emmanuel Jimenz. 1994. *Public and Private Secondary Schools in Developing Countries.* Washington, D.C.: World Bank.

Londono, Juan Luis. 1996. *Poverty, Inequality, and Human Capital Development in Latin America, 1950–2025.* Washington, D.C.: World Bank.

Macisaac, Donna. 1994. Peru. In *Indigenous People and Poverty in Latin America,* ed. George Psacharopoulos and Harry Patrinos, 165–204. Washington, D.C.: World Bank.

McGinn, Noel, Fernando Reimers, Armando Loera, Maria del Carmen Soto, and Sagrario Lopez. 1991. *Why Do Children Repeat Grades? A Study of Rural Primary Schools in Honduras.* Cambridge, Mass.: Harvard University.

Mision Social. 1997. Los planteles, la calidad de la educacion y el residuo. Mimeograph. Colombia: Mision Social.

Molina, Carlos Gerardo. 1999. Las reformas educativas en America Latina. Hacia mas equidad? Mimeograph. Washington, D.C.: IDB.

Munoz-Izquierdo, Carlos, Pedro Rodriguez, Patricia Restrepo, and Claudia Borrani. 1979. El sindrome del atraso escolar y el abandono del sistema educativo. *Revista Latinoamericana de Estudios Educativos* IX(3).

Munoz-Izquierdo, Carlos, Raquel Ahuja, Carmen Noriega, Patricia Schurmann, and Magda Campillo. 1997. Valoracion del impacto educativo de un programa compensatorio, orientado a abatir el rezago escolar en la educacion primaria. *Revista Latinoamericana de Estudios Educativos* XXV(4): 11–58.

Myers, Robert. 2000. Primary school repetition and drop-out in two rural Mexian communities: A follow-up study. Mimeograph. Mexico City: World Bank.

Organization of American States. 1997. Educacion en las Americas: Calidad, equidad y ciudadania. Mimeograph. Washington, D.C.: OAS.

Organization of American States. 1998. Declaracion de la Cumbre de las Americas, Santiago. OAS Web page. <www.oas.org/udse/summit.htm>.

Organization of Economic Cooperation and Development. 1998. *Basic Education Indicators.* Paris: OECD.

Panagides, Alexis. 1994. Mexico. In *Indigenous People and Poverty in Latin America,* ed. George Psacharopoulos and Harry Patrinos, 127–164. Washington, D.C.: World Bank.

Plank, David. 1996. *The Means of Our Salvation. Public Education in Brazil 1930–1995.* Boulder, Colo.: Westview Press.

Portela, Adelia, and Eni Santana Barretto Bastos. 1998. *O (Des) Conhecido Universo da Sala de Aula.* Brasilia, Brazil: Ministerio da Educacao e do Desporto. Projecto Nordeste.

Post, David. 2000. Left behind? Child labor and schooling in Latin America. Paper presented at the Annual Conference of the Comparative and International Education Society. San Antonio, Texas, March 11.

Post, David. Expected 2001. *Children's Work, Education, and Family Welfare in Latin America.* Boulder, Colo.: Westview Press.

Psacharopoulos, George, and Harry Patrinos, eds. 1994. *Indigenous People and Poverty in Latin America.* Washington, D.C.: World Bank.

Reimers, Fernando, ed. 1995. *La Educacion en El Salvador de Cara al Siglo XXI. Desafios y Oportunidades.* San Salvador: Universidad Centro Americana.

Reimers, Fernando. 1999a. Educational chances of the poor at the end of the twentieth century. *Prospects* XXIX(4): 481–491.

Reimers, Fernando. 1999b. Educational opportunities for low income families in Latin America. *Prospects* XXIX(4): 535–549.

Reimers, Fernando. 1999c. El estudio de las oportunidades educativas de los pobres en America Latina. *Revista Latinoamericana de Estudios Educativos* XXIX(1): 17–68.

Reimers, Fernando. 1999d. Politicas compensatorias en America latina. Insuficientes, subfinanciadas y fragiles. *La Educacion* XLIII(132–134): 15–59.

Reimers, Fernando. 2000a. Educacion, desigualdad y opciones de politica en America latina en el siglo XXI. *Revista Iberoamericana de Educacion* 23(mayo agosto): 21–50.

Reimers, Fernando. Expected 2000b. Educacion, inclusion y justicia social en America Latina. In *Educacion y Desarrollo en America Latina. Ensayos en Honor a Pablo Latapi,* ed. C. Ornelas, forthcoming. Mexico City: Fondo de Cultura Economica.

Reimers, Fernando. 2000c. La igualdad de oportunidades educativas como prioridad de politicas en America Latina. In *Perspectivas sobre la Reforma Educativa,* ed. Juan Carlos Navarro, Katherine Taylor, Andres Bernasconi, and Lewis Tyler, 47–80. Washington, D.C.: InterAmerican Development Bank.

Reimers, Fernando. Expected 2000d. Oportunidad educativa en Mexico. Logros y desafios de las politicas educativas. In *La Educacion en Mexico: Historia, Realidad y Desafios,* ed. Sergio Chazaro, forthcoming. Mexico City: Editorial Mexico Desconocido.

Reimers, Fernando. 2000e. Pueden aprender los hijos de los pobres en las escuelas de America Latina? *Revista Mexicana de Investigacion Educativa* V(9): 11–69.

Republica de Colombia. 1997. *Tercer Estudio Internacional de Matematicas y Ciencias.* Santafe de Bogota: Ministerio de Educacion Nacional.

Republica de Venezuela. 1995. *Encuesta de Hogares por Muestreo.* Caracas, Venezuela: Oficina Central de Estadistica e Informatica.

Rockwell, Elsie, ed. 1995. *La Escuela Cotidiana.* Mexico City: Fondo de Cultura Economica.

Rodrigues Pino, Ivany, and Mariane Campelo Koslinsky. 1999. Government programs to eliminate repetition, school dropout, and exclusion in Brazil. In *Schooling for Success,* ed. Laura Randall and Joan Anderson, 142–151. New York: Sharpe.

Sanchez, Fausto, and Javier Nunez. 1995. Porque los ninos pobres no van a la escuela? *Planeacion y Desarrollo* XXIV(4): 73–110.

Schiefelbein, Ernesto, and Joseph Farrell. 1982. *Eight Years of Their Lives.* Ottawa: IDRC.

Schiefelbein, Ernesto, and Juan Carlos Tedesco. 1995. *El Desafio Educativo.* Madrid: Santillana.

Schiefelbein, Ernesto, and Lawrence Wolff. 1992. *Repetition and Inadequate Achievement in Latin America's Primary Schools.* Washington, D.C.: World Bank.

Schmelkes, Sylvia. 1999. Policies against school failure in Mexico—An overview. In *Schooling for Success,* ed. Laura Randall and Joan Anderson, 163–175. New York: Sharpe.

Schultz, Paul. 2000. Final report on the impact of Progresa on school enrollment. Mimeograph. New Haven: Yale University.

Sen, Amartya. 2000. *Development as Freedom.* New York: Knopf.

Steele, Diane. 1994. Guatemala. In *Indigenous People and Poverty in Latin America,* ed. George Psacharopoulos and Harry Patrinos, 97–126. Washington, D.C.: World Bank.

Stromquist, Nelly, ed. 1996. *Gender Dimensions in Education in Latin America.* Washington, D.C.: OAS.

Swope, John, and Marcela Latorre. 1998. *Comunidades Educativas Donde Termina el Asfalto.* Santiago, Chile: Centro de Investigacion y Desarrollo de la Educacion.

Tatto, Maria Teresa, and Eduardo Velez. 1997. Teacher education reform initiatives. The case of Mexico. In *Latin American Education: Comparative Perspectives,* ed. Carlos Alberto Torres and Adriana Puiggros, 165–218. Boulder, Colo.: Westview Press.

Third International Mathematics and Science Study. 1997. *Mathematics Achievement in the Primary School Years and Science Achievement in the Primary School Years.* Chestnut Hill, Mass.: Boston College.

UNDP (United Nations Development Program). 1997. *Human Development Report.* New York: Oxford University Press.

UNDP. 1998. *Human Development Report.* New York: Oxford University Press.

UNESCO. 1996. *Situation Educativa de America Latina y El Caribe, 1980–1994.* Santiago, Chile: UNESCO.

UNESCO. 1998. *World Education Report.* Paris: UNESCO.

UNESCO-OREALC. 2000. *Regional Report of the Americas. An Assessment of the Education for All Program in the Year 2000.* Santiago, Chile: UNESCO-OREALC.

Van der Gaag, Jacques, and Donald Winkler. 1996. *Children of the Poor in Latin America and the Caribbean.* Washington, D.C.: World Bank.

Villegas-Reimers, Eleanora. 1998. *The Preparation of Teachers in Latin America.* Washington, D.C.: World Bank.

Villegas-Reimers, Eleanora, and Fernando Reimers. 1996. Where are 60 million teachers? The missing voice in educational reforms around the world. *Prospects* XXVI(3): 469–492.

Winkler, Donald. 1999. Reforma educativa en America Latina. El rol del sector privado. Presentation in Foro Internacional. Educacion Economia y Sociedad. Mexico City, March 11–12.

Winkler, Donald. 2000. Educating the poor in Latin America and the Caribbean: Examples of compensatory education. Chapter 5 in this book.

Wood, Bill, and Harry Patrinos. 1994. Urban Bolivia. In *Indigenous People and Poverty in Latin America,* ed. George Psacharopoulos and Harry Patrinos, 55–96. Washington, D.C.: World Bank.

World Bank. 1999a. *Secondary Education in El Salvador: Education Reform in Progress.* Washington, D.C.: World Bank.

World Bank. 1999b. *Sector Study on Education Finance and Rural Education in Peru.* Washington, D.C.: World Bank.

World Bank. 2000. *Brazil. Secondary Education in Brazil.* Washington, D.C.: World Bank.

Commentary

**Teresa Bracho, Centro de Investigación y
Docencia Económicas, Mexico**

Chapter 4 presents a comprehensive view of the links among education, poverty, and inequality in Latin America. This is an important task because it provides a clear review of the problems and achievements that can characterize the region. At the same time, in this global view, the author points to differences between countries in the region.

Even though specific national case studies are provided in other chapters of this book, we should highlight not only differences between countries, but also the fact that within most of them the internal inequalities are significant (for example, the Mexican and Brazilian cases). The analysis of the regional set of countries also allows us to identify the possibilities of groupings at the supranational level. Though this is clearly not the objective of this study, we know that for some purposes, the country is not the best unit of analysis to reflect differentiation. National averages can hide internal differences. In addition, the similarities may have a geographical and cultural character, which makes the political frontiers fade away and different units emerge (for instance, between the South of Mexico and Guatemala).

Chapter 4 is critical of the approaches to "development" that emphasize economic development to reduce poverty and social inequality. Along these lines, it highlights the importance of the type of growth, which in the Latin American case is primarily oriented toward the links between external economies and sectors of the economy of high productivity which also require a high quality of human resources. I believe it is important to make explicit, among the proposals aimed at fostering equality, the importance of growth that includes job creation and increases in salaries. That is, it is necessary to specify what constitutes *quality* growth.

The main theme of the chapter is increasingly central in the academic discussions about education and its contributions to national and regional development, as well as in several agencies charged with educational planning and investment. For this reason, I think it is necessary to specify some relationships among inequality, poverty, and education in ways that allow us to distinguish the different notions implied in this chapter. Just as economic growth can have different characteristics and these can have different consequences for social distribution, educational growth can also exhibit different levels of quality in its distribution, as well as different levels of quality in the education addressed to different social sectors. The links between education—even in its broadest definition as used in the chapter—and poverty allow one to distinguish analytically between educational expansion and educational inequality, on the one hand, and social inequality and income distribution on the other. In other words, just as the concepts of poverty and inequality refer to different processes, those of education and educational distribution are also different processes. One of the terms refers to "stocks" or "capabilities," while the other alludes to its distribution in a given society.

While from a point of view of political philosophy or of social ethics, poverty can hardly be compatible with equity, there may be redistribution that leads to greater social equality but that has little impact on poverty incidence or intensity. Such would be the case with redistribution between the middle and upper sectors of the distribution. On the other hand, it is possible to think of redistributions that, while having modest impacts over the global distribution, from the point of view of social ethics could have great importance. An example of this would be the reduction of the intensity of poverty in small segments, even if poverty incidence did not change, and even if the general distribution of income was relatively unchanged.

This distinction is important not just in this particular chapter but in other chapters in this book. The proposal to eliminate poverty has a clear foundation in the order of substantive social ethics, expressed in the Universal Declaration of Human Rights: to allow the development of the potentialities of all people. It also has a political base. This development can stimulate social, political, and economic development of the countries of the region. Hence, guaranteeing universal basic education and the expansion of quality educational opportunities for all, even if they refer to smaller proportions of the population, is a condition sine qua non for the development of the region.

Along the same lines, as can be read in several parts throughout the chapter, the author recognizes that educational expansion has been associated with an increase in income inequality, at least over time. The result would appear paradoxical when we expect to increase equity in the region through an increase in the education level of the population, given the role education can play in the reduction of poverty. Fernando Reimers offers several hypotheses about these links, which lead to several implicit policy options, among them different levels of educational attainment and insufficient equality of educational opportunities, which lead to the increase in the education level of social differentiation.

The chapter emphasizes five levels of educational opportunity and highlights that equity should be achieved in all of them. The distinction is important in that it highlights that it is not enough to guarantee equality in access to the education system, but that the objective should be that all complete at least basic education with the appropriate skills. While we may agree with this premise, we concur with the author in pointing out that the last level is not an area that can be influenced directly by the education system. That is, education may contribute to the last level of equality through the formation of values and attitudes, but the life chances and the opportunities in the labor market and in the social and political spheres do not depend on actions in the education system.

Based on the figures and arguments of the chapter, it could be stated that the level of basic education is no longer sufficient to contribute to the reduction of gaps between the upper and lower extremes of the social distribution, which leads to the recognition that social differentiation has increased and now reaches secondary and higher education. This poses greater difficulties, in a context of resource constraints, in determining how to guarantee basic education to the poor who do not yet have the first levels of educational opportunities and, at the same time, expanding the opportunities to access quality secondary and higher education. To leave the poorer and middle-income groups to compete on their own with the upper-income groups in the search of post-basic educational opportunities would lead to widening the education gaps and the advantages associated with higher education. When we think about strategies to overcome poverty, it is important to recognize the gaps between the poor and the non-poor. However, when we address the problem of distribution and inequality in all of society, to these gaps we should add those that exist between all social groups.

The importance of these remarks follows from the fact that the education system has become a quasi-monopoly as a differentiating agency, as was supposed by the classical theory of social stratification. The problem, however, is that facing conditions of deficiencies in educational expansion—that is, in conditions of educational exclusion—and facing a persistent and growing educational inequality in the distribution of income, the education system also has a centrality in the definition of entry to other agencies that stratify and define social participation and, therefore, social exclusion.

Four girls read in the courtyard of the "Foyer Maurice Sixto," a UNICEF-assisted center for five-to-eighteen-year-old live-in child domestic servants, in Carrefour, Haiti.
[UNICEF/95-0642/Nicole Toutounji (Haiti)]

5

Educating the Poor in Latin America and the Caribbean: Examples of Compensatory Education

Donald Winkler
The World Bank, Latin America and the Caribbean Region

Though Latin American and Caribbean countries made important social gains over the last generation, they remain unable to provide adequate education services to large segments of their populations. Disadvantaged groups—particularly rural inhabitants—continue to suffer from limited access to schools. And even when schools are accessible, poor children often represent too valuable a source of labor to their families to attend school full-time.

Meanwhile, those disadvantaged children who do attend school often do so in substandard environments. In these cases, the quality of teaching, educational materials, and physical facilities are typically so poor as to undermine the value of their time investment. In addition to these sources of inequality, factors outside of the physical school environment hinder the educational development of poor children. These include factors such as a hostile or nonsupportive family environment and substandard living conditions which can affect the child's health and psychological well-being. The incidence of these are disproportionately high among disadvantaged children because of poor access to health services and sanitation facilities as well as the low levels of education often held by their parents. These factors have a direct influence on their performance at school.

To address these problems, countries develop compensatory education programs. The hope is that by accommodating the varied needs laid out above, countries can provide disadvantaged students with the educational opportunities they have traditionally gone without. However, just as the needs of disadvantaged children are far from homogeneous, neither are the programs designed to alleviate them. Consequently, we find tremendous variety among compensatory education programs, both in planning and practice.

After an explicit diagnosis of needs, therefore, this chapter attempts to classify the wide range of compensatory programs. The exercise should provide insight into how ·

the needs of disadvantaged children are being met and, ultimately, a prism through which to assess our ability to meet those needs.

The compensatory programs highlighted are classified according to their focus on either supply- or demand-driven interventions and the means employed to target the beneficiaries. This chapter addresses the structure of the program, how potential beneficiaries are identified, how the program is implemented, and what aspects of the problem it attempts to solve. The chapter concludes by identifying patterns of success and failure at meeting needs through compensatory education.

DIAGNOSIS OF THE PROBLEM

The Rural versus Urban Divide

Many of the problems compensatory programs address are most acute among rural children. No doubt this arises from the systematically higher incidence of child poverty in rural areas. The relative measure of poverty used here is based on per capita household income and consumption distribution in the countries selected. "Very poor children" are those living in the bottom 20 percent of households (first quintile). "Poor children" are those living in the bottom 40 percent of households (first and second quintiles). "Non-poor children" are those living in the remaining 60 percent of households (Waiser 1995, 9).

Over 80 percent of households with children in rural Brazil are considered either "poor" or "very poor," as compared to only 44.7 percent of such households in urban areas. Indeed, this pattern holds across much of Latin America and the Caribbean (hereafter LAC). Chile, Ecuador, El Salvador, Nicaragua, and Peru all report that more than two-thirds of rural households with children live in poverty, as compared to less than one-third of similar households in these countries' urban areas (with the exception of Chile, in which 46.4 percent of households with children live in poverty).

Table 5.1 reflects poverty levels among children below age fifteen and reveals a similar pattern. Nearly 90 percent of Brazil's rural children live in poverty, while Chile, Ecuador, El Salvador, Nicaragua, and Peru all suffer from rates at or above 75 percent.

Access to schools also tends to be lower in rural areas and the quality of these schools is very poor. Rural dropout and repetition rates are typically higher than those of urban schools, a likely result of the frequently inadequate teaching methods employed in rural, multigrade schools. (These methods frequently emphasize mechanical rules and memorization.) Beyond this, many rural schools are simply incomplete—that is, they do not offer all six grades of primary school—and rarely do rural students have exposure to pre-primary programs. Many rural schools also lack safe water, adequate sanitation facilities, and electricity.

Low levels of formal education are commonly found among heads of households of the "very poor" and "poor" in this region. These circumstances are concentrated particularly in rural areas, as illustrated in Table 5.2. A child raised in a household where formal education is not a priority will not step into the classroom with the same system of support as other children where this is not the case.

Not surprisingly, problems relating to health and malnutrition—problems that tend to dramatically limit educational opportunities by lowering attendance and impeding

TABLE 5.1

Distribution of Children Below Fifteen Years of Age by Poverty Level and Area
(percentage by poverty level)

	Total (Rural and Urban)		
Country	Very Poor	Poor	Non-Poor
Brazil	38.6	61.9	38.1
Colombia	n/a	n/a	n/a
Costa Rica	33.8	60.0	40.0
Chile	32.2	57.5	42.5
Ecuador	30.9	56.4	43.6
El Salvador	32.3	57.2	42.8
Honduras	27.5	53.4	46.6
Jamaica	32.3	58.4	41.6
Nicaragua	31.1	53.1	46.9
Peru	33.6	58.9	41.1

	Rural			Urban		
Country	Very Poor	Poor	Non-Poor	Very Poor	Poor	Non-Poor
Brazil	68.7	88.4	11.6	29.1	53.4	46.6
Colombia	n/a	n/a	n/a	31.9	56.5	43.5
Costa Rica	46.0	73.0	27.0	20.7	46.0	54.0
Chile	49.9	78.5	21.5	27.8	52.3	47.7
Ecuador	44.4	74.6	25.4	18.1	39.2	60.8
El Salvador	49.3	76.0	24.0	14.5	37.6	62.4
Honduras	36.1	64.6	35.4	14.1	36.1	63.9
Jamaica	43.4	69.2	30.8	18.4	45.0	55.0
Nicaragua	50.2	76.7	23.3	12.4	30.0	70.0
Peru	57.9	83.5	16.5	19.5	44.6	55.4

concentration and cognitive development—are also most acute in rural areas. In particular, diarrhea and respiratory infections are the leading causes of mortality among young children in rural locales, where issues of access typically explain why they get sick, and why, once sick, they frequently go without treatment (Winkler and van der Gaag 1996).

To illustrate, consider Tables 5.3, 5.4, and 5.5. Less than 21 percent of rural households with children in Brazil, Chile, Honduras, and Peru have access to sewerage facilities, a number that falls to just 3.6 percent in Nicaragua (Table 5.3). Similarly, less than 30 percent of households with children have access to piped water in Brazil, El Salvador, Nicaragua, and Peru (Table 5.4). And though the data for health services are less complete, we see that less than 45 percent of the rural inhabitants of Jamaica, Nicaragua, and Peru have access to health services (Table 5.5).

Regardless of the access to and quality of the school facilities, if the child does not have a healthy and supportive home environment, his or her educational development and success will be significantly hindered.

TABLE 5.2

Years of Schooling of Household Head, in Households with Children, by Poverty Level and Area (average years)

| Country | Total (Rural and Urban) | | | |
	Very Poor	Poor	Non-Poor	Total
Brazil	2.7	3.3	7.5	5.4
Colombia	n/a	n/a	n/a	n/a
Costa Rica	4.9	5.5	8.7	7.1
Chile	6.9	7.2	10.3	8.7
Ecuador	3.9	4.5	8.0	6.4
El Salvador	2.1	2.4	5.6	4.1
Honduras	2.3	2.7	5.7	4.3
Jamaica	6.8	7.0	8.0	7.5
Nicaragua	1.2	1.8	5.6	3.9
Peru	5.5	6.3	10.0	8.3

| Country | Rural | | | | Urban | | | |
	Very Poor	Poor	Non-Poor	Total	Very Poor	Poor	Non-Poor	Total
Brazil	1.8	2.3	5.0	2.7	3.2	3.7	7.7	6.1
Colombia	n/a	n/a	n/a	n/a	6.0	6.4	10.3	8.4
Costa Rica	4.5	4.9	7.1	5.7	5.7	6.5	9.5	8.4
Chile	5.2	5.2	7.2	5.7	7.7	8.0	10.7	9.4
Ecuador	3.5	3.9	5.4	4.4	4.7	5.4	8.9	7.9
El Salvador	1.8	1.9	3.0	2.2	3.1	3.5	6.5	5.7
Honduras	1.9	2.2	3.6	2.8	3.9	3.9	7.3	6.3
Jamaica	6.7	6.7	7.3	6.9	6.8	7.5	8.3	8.1
Nicaragua	0.9	1.2	3.3	1.8	2.4	3.2	6.4	5.6
Peru	5.2	5.4	6.7	5.7	6.1	7.2	10.5	9.4

Finally, differences in language ability of students is a problem common, but not exclusive, to rural areas. Regardless of the locale, native speakers of the indigenous language are far more likely to repeat, dropout, and work as children and have much lower achievement than native Spanish speakers.

Coverage, Quality, Enrollment, and Efficiency by Level of Schooling

Preschool enrollment is low among poor children across the board, but, as mentioned above, it is virtually nonexistent in rural areas. As reported in Table 5.6, *overall* gross enrollment rates at the pre-primary level are less then 40 percent in Chile, Ecuador, Honduras, and Nicaragua, and the number descends to as low as 5.9 percent in Costa Rica. The lack of pre-primary coverage is concentrated in the rural areas of these countries.

Coverage is generally not as urgent an issue at the primary level. Table 5.7 reveals overall gross enrollment rates exceeding 84 percent in all of the countries but Nicaragua, and, with the exception of El Salvador and Nicaragua, these rates remain above 80 percent in rural areas.

TABLE 5.3

Access to Sewerage for Households with Children

Country	Urban	Rural	Total
Brazil	67.1	13.5	56.1
Colombia	93.8	n/a	n/a
Costa Rica	92.0	68.5	80.9
Chile	86.0	20.7	73.6
Ecuador	82.9	42.6	65.2
El Salvador	88.3	76.2	83.0
Honduras	62.8	19.7	38.2
Jamaica	n/a	n/a	n/a
Nicaragua	54.8	3.6	32.3
Peru	77.8	15.3	58.0

The more salient problem at the primary level is poor quality and inefficiency, as reflected in high dropout and repetition rates and, ultimately, low transition rates to the secondary level. These problems typically result from teacher incompetence and excessively low expenditures on textbooks and school-related equipment.

In Colombia, for example, 50 percent of teachers lack postsecondary degrees. And in Honduras, where politics is often the sole criterion for hiring new teachers, the candidate with the better credentials frequently gets left behind. For that matter, teachers throughout the region face weak incentives because promotion policies rarely reward high performance. Moreover, this only exacerbates problems of quality given the obvious link between poor teachers and underprovision of basic teaching materials: inflated spending on the former crowds out investment in the latter.

Finally, on the secondary level, the combination of poor primary school quality (which leads to high dropout rates as discussed above) and a shortage of classroom space seem to underlie low coverage. As Table 5.8 reveals, Brazil, El Salvador, Honduras, and Nicaragua all have secondary gross enrollment rates of less than 70 percent, while these rates exceed 80 percent only in Chile and Peru. Once again, however, the

TABLE 5.4

Access to Piped Water for Households with Children

Country	Urban	Rural	Total
Brazil	83.6	12.2	69.0
Colombia	97.1	n/a	n/a
Costa Rica	97.3	72.9	85.9
Chile	98.7	43.0	88.0
Ecuador	74.0	41.4	59.7
El Salvador	67.5	28.2	50.1
Honduras	83.8	73.7	78.0
Jamaica	90.0	62.3	76.5
Nicaragua	88.4	28.8	62.2
Peru	83.9	27.9	66.2

TABLE 5.5

Access to Health Services for Households with Children

Country	Urban	Rural	Total
Brazil	n/a	n/a	n/a
Colombia	84.5	n/a	n/a
Costa Rica	75.7	81.2	78.3
Chile	98.5	97.6	98.4
Ecuador	79.8	69.2	74.7
Jamaica	46.0	44.2	45.2
Nicaragua	51.7	35.4	43.5
Peru	34.2	40.7	36.5

problem is more concentrated among rural inhabitants. The rural areas of Brazil, El Salvador, Honduras, and Nicaragua all suffer from secondary enrollment rates of less than 50 percent, while only rural Peru has a rate above 70 percent.

Other obstacles to secondary enrollment appear on the demand side. In particular, secondary-age children may leave school because the opportunity cost of attending becomes prohibitive. This is most prevalent among poor families, which typically rely on older children to earn outside income or to make full-time contributions around the house (perhaps on a family farm or by supervising other children). Moreover, depending on the area, this phenomenon may disproportionately affect one or the other gender.

TYPOLOGY OF SOLUTIONS

For the purpose of the classification and evaluation of compensatory programs in LAC, the programs will be viewed according to the type of intervention that they are structured around, demand-side or supply-side, as well as the methods of targeting that were adopted to select the beneficiaries.

TABLE 5.6

Preschool Gross Enrollment Rates by Poverty Level and Area

Country	Total (Rural and Urban)			
	Very Poor	Poor	Non-Poor	Total
Brazil	51.6	57.2	77.8	63.8
Colombia	n/a	n/a	n/a	n/a
Costa Rica	2.4	2.1	12.6	5.9
Chile	26.5	26.6	42.7	33.5
Ecuador	19.2	23.0	37.0	29.1
El Salvador	32.3	34.6	58.8	44.4
Honduras	31.7	30.5	34.1	32.2
Jamaica	75.3	79.1	91.4	84.2
Nicaragua	7.7	11.0	40.0	24.2
Peru	49.7	51.9	66.2	57.4

TABLE 5.7

Primary School Gross Enrollment Rates by Poverty Level and Area

| Country | Total (Rural and Urban) | | | |
	Very Poor	Poor	Non-Poor	Total
Brazil	83.3	86.8	96.7	90.3
Colombia	n/a	n/a	n/a	n/a
Costa Rica	79.4	81.4	90.8	85.1
Chile	95.4	96.3	98.1	97.1
Ecuador	89.1	90.9	96.3	93.3
El Salvador	75.0	79.9	90.0	84.4
Honduras	86.9	87.6	93.5	90.2
Jamaica	98.5	98.3	99.0	98.6
Nicaragua	51.7	59.9	87.3	72.8
Peru	93.6	94.7	98.0	96.1

Two variables determine a given program's structure, each occupying one axis of our plane. On the vertical axis, we answer the question of what type of intervention is being attempted. Supply-driven interventions are those programs whose emphasis is on improving the quality of and access to education by increasing the number of schools, the number of student places, and the inputs required for learning. Demand-driven interventions target specific groups or individuals who have a need for increased access to education by providing them with the means to obtain it. These interventions include vouchers, stipends, loans, and scholarships.

To varied degrees, both of these types of interventions attempt to either increase coverage or improve the quality of education. Though two nonmutually exclusive goals, they do tend to prescribe different measures, which, in a resource-constrained environment, may force a tradeoff. It is therefore useful to distinguish whether the program focuses primarily on improving school quality, on increasing access to schools, or on some combination of the two.

TABLE 5.8

Secondary School Gross Enrollment Rates by Poverty Level and Area

| Country | Total (Rural and Urban) | | | |
	Very Poor	Poor	Non-Poor	Total
Brazil	53.9	57.2	77.9	66.7
Colombia	n/a	n/a	n/a	n/a
Costa Rica	63.3	63.6	79.4	71.2
Chile	77.3	77.9	87.3	82.4
Ecuador	57.9	62.5	80.8	71.5
El Salvador	39.6	43.3	60.4	52.8
Honduras	50.5	45.9	64.7	55.5
Jamaica	67.6	68.2	76.9	72.2
Nicaragua	35.2	41.4	76.5	59.2
Peru	82.0	83.5	88.5	85.9

Programs concerned with quality tend to conceive of education as an explicit production process. More important, the efficiency of this process can be enhanced and its output can be improved through the manipulation of relevant inputs. The idea is that a greater volume of some inputs and higher quality of others will improve academic performance and ultimately reduce inefficiently high dropout and repetition rates. In practical terms, this may mean upgrading dilapidated classrooms, strengthening curriculum and pedagogical techniques, procuring new textbooks and instructional materials, hiring better-trained teachers, investing in educational equipment like computers and calculators, even providing meals, nutritional supplements, and health screenings.

An alternative approach to quality improvement comes by way of incentives. That is, rather than directly finance an input like teacher training, a program can provide teachers with a monetary inducement to improve their skills, reduce absenteeism, or otherwise effect an improvement in student performance. Of course, as with the division between quality and access, it is certainly possible to make use of both inputs and incentives. A program may, for example, provide periodic teacher in-service training while at the same time rewarding more committed teachers with additional compensation.

The rationale behind access, on the other hand, is to provide educational opportunities for children who would not otherwise enjoy them. As described previously, there remain large populations of children, particularly rural children, who have no prospect of obtaining an education. This can occur for one of two reasons. The first derives from the conventional notion of access: there is simply no school close enough to the child's home to make attendance feasible, or, if there is an accessible school, it is too crowded to accommodate additional students. For obvious reasons, this is said to be a problem of supply. The child would be willing to attend if a school existed and could accommodate him or her, but cannot attend for shortage of supply. The supply-side solution, then, is to build more schools and classrooms.

Yet this is hardly the end of the story. The data reveal a considerable number of students who have access to schools—in the conventional sense—but who, for whatever reason, still elect not to attend. For these students, we must therefore conclude that the problem is one of demand. Though these children may wish to attend school, the precarious socioeconomic status of their family renders the opportunity cost prohibitive. The solution, then, is to increase the child's demand for education by decreasing its cost. This can take the form of a voucher that lowers the direct cost of attending school or a subsidy that offsets the opportunity cost of attending school rather than working.

Needless to say, there are situations that blur the somewhat artificial distinction between quality and access. We might ask, for example, if providing textbooks to a school that previously did without them is a quality or access improvement. For the sake of our classification, however, we take quality improvements to imply strengthening performance and efficiency among existing consumers of education, and access improvements to imply delivering this service to those not currently consuming. By this criteria, the textbook scenario is clearly a quality improvement. Though it technically "expands access" to textbooks, it does so to improve the performance of those who are already consumers of education services.

That said, there are clearly situations in which the problems of quality and access cannot be disentangled. Consider, as alluded to above, that many students drop out of school because the opportunity cost of attending is prohibitive. This would appear to be a problem of access. Give them a scholarship and the cost of attending school will no longer prevent them from doing so. But it may be no less an issue of quality. That is, because quality is low, students expect that the return from their education will also be low. The result is that they have little incentive to continue their education. One might therefore be able to further increase attendance by simultaneously improving quality.

Because compensatory programs, by their very nature, serve only a segment of the population, the method of selecting this segment forms a crucial component of the program. The second determinant of program structure is therefore the *targeting mechanism,* the method of identifying eligible candidates.

Three basic targeting mechanisms are commonly used in compensatory education programs. The *geographic targeting mechanism* targets benefits at specific regions with the qualifying characteristic usually being average welfare (Grosh 1994, 96). No member is excluded (according to this characteristic) once the geographic area is established, so the accuracy of the target depends on the group's relative homogeneity. Therefore, the more homogeneous the region, the smaller the number of unintended beneficiaries.

Further, because smaller geographical groups are more likely to be homogeneous, the accuracy of the target generally decreases with the size of the region. For example, while targeting poor communities is fairly efficient—to say that poor people almost exclusively inhabit poor communities is essentially tautological—their larger income variation means targeting states creates beneficiaries who would not be eligible as individuals (Grosh 1994, 96–97).

The second form of targeting mechanism is the *group characteristic mechanism.* Rather than scrutinize individuals, this mechanism identifies groups whose members tend to exhibit a certain qualifying characteristic. Gender and ethnic groups commonly serve as a basis for group targeting. For example, because there are areas in which girls enjoy far fewer educational opportunities than boys, it sometimes makes sense to target them specifically. Likewise for ethnicity. Indigenous students are frequently much worse off than even the poorest native Spanish speakers, so a rationale exists for targeting benefits to them. A group of schools that are performing below national standards may also be targeted using this mechanism. Group targeting can also refer to targeting by age and/or grade level.

The final mechanism, *self-targeting,* is the most subtle of the three. It leaves the participation decision entirely to the individual, relying instead on program design to discourage more well-off consumers (Grosh 1994, 33). For example, some programs require participants to wait in long lines. Because the opportunity cost of waiting rises with the size of one's wage—while the marginal benefit often falls—it is assumed that higher wage earners will forgo the compensatory service (Grosh 1994, 111–112). Other opportunities for self-targeting derive from the stigma surrounding these services or from their poorer quality (Grosh 1994, 113–115). That is, wealthier people will elect to consume more expensive services when they either perceive or genuinely experience a difference in quality. These last two elements typically underlie self-targeting in education.

Although these are the three targeting mechanisms most relevant to our discussion, it is important to be aware that there is another form of targeting called the *individual assessment mechanism.* This requires individual selection on the basis of a specified set of criteria, such as means tests, the gender of the household head, or the nutritional status of the applicant (Grosh 1994, 33). This can be used in conjunction with other mechanisms and is typically the most administratively difficult and costly to implement. For the purpose of our discussion, this mechanism will only be mentioned when it appears in a program in collaboration with another mechanism.

A few final words on targeting. In many cases programs employ more than one targeting mechanism. Some programs explicitly combine two mechanisms—for example, it is possible to target both a given municipality and, within it, only students whose families fall below a certain income level. Other programs implicitly combine a second mechanism with the more explicit one. Consider, for example, a program that targets a specific municipality, but within which the snob appeal of private schools ciphons off children of more privileged families. To keep the classification as simple as possible, then, the scheme below identifies programs according to which mechanism is intended as the primary means of targeting.

Finally, it is important to recognize that the existence of intrafamily inequality means targeted compensatory services may fail to increase the family's investment in a given child. The family may instead reduce its own investment so that the overall level of investment in the child remains the same before and after the provision of benefits.

EXAMPLES OF COMPENSATORY EDUCATION PROGRAMS IN LAC

Figure 5.1 lists programs in Latin America and the Caribbean that illustrate the different targeting mechanisms and types of intervention.

Supply-Side Intervention: Geographic Targeting

Mexico's *Telesecundaria* program affords one of the best examples of supply-side intervention using a geographic targeting mechanism. The program provides lower secondary instruction (grades 7–9) to students in rural communities through a series of daily satellite broadcasts. Each lesson consists of a fifteen-minute television program,

FIGURE 5.1

Compensatory Education Programs in LAC by Targeting Mechanisms and Types of Intervention

	Geographic Targeting	Group Targeting	Self-Targeting
Supply-Side	Telesecundaria (Mexico) MECE-RURAL (Chile) PARE (Mexico)	P-900 (Chile) ROSE (Jamaica)	Fe y Alegría (Bolivia) Hogares de Bienestar Infantil (Colombia)
Demand-Side	Bolsa Escola (Brazil) Progresa (Mexico)	Eduque a la Niña (Guatemala) Voucher Program (Colombia)	

followed by a thirty-five-minute teacher-student discussion, and then a ten-minute break before the next lesson. The school day consists of six of these periods, and students attend 200 days per year, just as they would in a conventional school setting.

Communities can enter the program by furnishing at least fifteen primary school graduates with an instructional facility. At this point, the ministry of education provides a college-trained and nationally certified teacher, a television, digital signal decoder, satellite dish, wiring, instructional program, and textbooks. The ministry also sponsors teacher training. This includes periodic afternoon and weekend in-services, as well as more elaborate seminars and workshops.

Telesecundaria geographically targets its resources to expand coverage to rural areas in Mexico. At its inception in 1968, programming reached rural villages in the seven states surrounding Mexico City. Today, Telesecundaria reaches over 800,000 students in 13,785 rural communities.

Chile's Program for the Improvement of Rural Schools (*MECE-RURAL*) provides a second example of a compensatory program that features both supply-driven and geographic targeting components. MECE-RURAL targets those primary schools in rural areas in need of improvement. It designs new teaching methods for rural settings, supplies schools with first- and sixth-grade textbooks that incorporate these methods, sponsors additional new rural-oriented methods by way of a curriculum development manual, and trains teachers to implement educational reforms. The program relies on a strong supervision component to monitor the progress of these reforms.

One of the more novel elements of MECE-RURAL is a network of "rural education microcenters," each intended to bring together teachers within a given rural area. The idea is to facilitate the exchange of ideas and experiences among rural teachers. Beyond this, the centers also assist in the provision of technical support.

On the level of access, meanwhile, MECE-RURAL supports classroom construction and the hiring of teachers in schools that cannot accommodate students through the eighth-grade level (the final year of compulsory education in Chile).

A third example of this type of program, *PARE,* falls under the group of compensatory programs under the aegis of Mexico's National Council for Educational Development (CONAFE). The CONAFE programs are run on the national level and are designed to improve the delivery of education services to remote areas.

The PARE program operates in Mexico's four poorest states—most of whose inhabitants are indigenous. Its curriculum corresponds to the national curriculum through the first six grades, but is delivered in two three-year cycles. A parallel program, *PRODEI,* was designed to expand access to early childhood education and included home visits to upgrade parenting skills. The two programs have recently been combined under the heading *PAREB,* which now includes ten additional low-income states.

On the input side, PARE provided books for school libraries and developed textbooks in the eight main indigenous languages through the fourth-grade level. To improve the quality of teaching, it provided a series of training sessions on Saturdays and during summers. The training addressed subject matter knowledge; pedagogic techniques, including multigrade teaching; and approaches to student evaluation and monitoring. As a complement to the training, PARE provided monetary incentives equal to the teacher's base salary. Parent associations meted out the incentives according to a specific set of criteria for teacher performance.

Regarding physical structures, PARE supported the upgrading and replacement of schools in disrepair. At the same time, it earmarked a small annual sum to the parent associations for school improvement and maintenance.

PARE also increased funding for supervisory functions, making it possible for 1,230 supervisors to visit remote schools in both monitoring and technical support capacities. It sought to further strengthen management and administration by instructing mid- and high-level administrators in organizational and pedagogic reform, decentralization, and information systems.

In the realm of access, PARE supported the construction of modest rural schools and annexes in the most remote locations. The program realized large cost savings when responsibility for construction was transferred from large national contractors to municipalities employing local labor.

PARE was targeted by way of a geographic mechanism, as alluded to above. Nearly two-thirds of the four targeted states' populations fell below the poverty line. The states also include almost 40 percent of the country's indigenous population.

Supply-Side Intervention: Group Targeting

Chile's *P-900* program supplies a concrete example of a supply-driven and group-targeted compensatory scheme. The program, which came into being at the behest of Chile's new democratic government in 1990, seeks to improve the quality of the country's worst-performing primary schools. It trains teachers to encourage creativity and innovation through a series of in-services and workshops, and it trains young "extension workers" to provide remedial reading instruction to third- and fourth-grade students outside of school hours. P-900 also provides classrooms with a set of educational materials, including libraries, teacher guides, games, and calculators. It funds the repair and upgrading of the physical facilities teachers deem most relevant to learning and regularly dispatches teams of technical and educational supervisors to participating schools. All of these efforts are coordinated and funded by the national education ministry.

P-900 employs a group-targeting mechanism, focusing on schools as the basic targeting unit. Using data from Chile's National Education Quality Assessment System (SIMCE), the program originally directed its resources at the lowest-achieving 10 percent of Chilean primary schools, all of which served indigent student populations. The criteria has since been altered to include all schools falling well below the regional SIMCE average for student achievement, which increased the number of eligible schools from the original 900 in 1990 to 1,300 by 1991 (the number had fallen to 1,000 by 1996). Schools "graduate" from the program once they have caught up to the regional average, while others become eligible as they fall farther below it. As a consequence, the number of participating schools fluctuates regularly.

Jamaica's Reform of Secondary Education project (*ROSE*) is a characteristic attempt to incorporate a combination of quality and access objectives into compensatory programming by means of supply-driven interventions and group targeting. The project, in some respects like Chile's P-900 program, directs curriculum reform, teacher guides, teacher training, and textbooks to underperforming schools. ROSE's seventy-two participating schools were selected according to the incidence of poverty in their student populations, a targeting arrangement based on Jamaica's Survey of Living Conditions. The survey reveals that ROSE schools serve 79 percent of the poorest quintile of students.

The curriculum consists of a core of math, science, social studies, language arts, technology training, and career education. In terms of pedagogy, the emphasis is on both basic skills and problem-solving activities, and the project provides local consultants to develop daily assignments and conduct curriculum research. The central Ministry of Education and Culture coordinates teacher training designed to complement these changes. It entails overseas training in daily teaching methods, periodic in-service training, summer workshops, distance education, and school visits. The ministry also trains regional education officers, school administrators, and school board members.

Textbooks and instructional materials also reflect an emphasis on basic skills and are developed to accommodate four different levels of advancement. To support other educational inputs, meanwhile, the ministry identifies a minimum set of materials necessary to meet the core educational goals and requires each school to conduct an "inventory" of these materials. The ministry then supplements the schools' inputs—typically chairs, desks, blackboards, and laboratory equipment—according to the disparity between the actual inventories and minimum requirements.

The final component of ROSE's quality improvement efforts is a rigorous evaluation process. The new student evaluation attempts to consolidate earlier tests into a new ninth-grade Junior High School Certification Exam. The exam was to become a requirement for employment and promotion to upper secondary school.

Supply-Side Intervention: Self-Targeting

Fe y Alegría (FYA), a private, nongovernmental organization (NGO), supports formal and nonformal education for the poor in twelve Latin American countries through supply-driven interventions and self-targeting mechanisms. Jesuit priests manage the NGO, and though it makes frequent use of public sector delivery systems, it insists on strong functional autonomy in all countries of operation.

FYA schools serve students of all grade levels and in all regions—whether urban, peri-urban, or rural. When FYA opens a school, it quickly engages local organizations and community members, involving them as much as possible in construction, management, and administration. In return for these contributions, community members are given considerable say in how to spend school resources.

The defining feature of FYA's philosophy is its focus on community development and local culture. Teachers are encouraged to live on school grounds to better integrate themselves into the community. In this capacity, they are expected to promote FYA's vision of democratic participation, supervising rather than dictating wherever possible.

FYA activity in Bolivia is fairly representative of its work internationally. A national FYA office handles matters of accounting, budgeting, personnel, finance, and project development, while seven regional offices—with staffs of two to five each—manage nearly 200 schools nationally. From these centers, field coordinators visit schools to conduct in-service training, help schools prepare curricular plans, and acquaint schools with FYA's basic guidelines. The Bolivian government pays teacher and principal salaries, while the community bears the remaining costs. This gives the Bolivian government some control over personnel decisions, but it respects FYA's autonomy in most other areas.

FYA's participants are identified through a self-targeting mechanism requiring parents to apply if they want to enroll their children in the program. As a result of this personal choice, affluent households choose to enroll their children in the more prestigious schools.

Colombia's early childhood development program, *Hogares de Bienestar Infantil,* provides access to pre-primary education for young disadvantaged children. Hogares consists of two components, a supplemental feeding program and a day care program. Volunteer mothers organize the program, which places groups of fifteen children in a neighborhood home. For its part, the Institute for Family Well-Being (ICBF), a government agency, trains the volunteers, pays them nominal stipends, and even helps them procure home improvement loans. The ICBF also supplies all necessary food and nutritional material.

This program makes use of a self-targeting mechanism because more affluent households will generally elect not to have their children participate in this program because of the perceived better quality of other pre-primary institutions. It also utilizes the geographic targeting mechanism as it targets specific neighborhoods.

Demand-Side Intervention: Geographic Targeting

Brazil's *Bolsa Escola* program serves as an example of a demand-side intervention using a geographic targeting mechanism. The program consists of two components. The first is a scholarship to needy children aged seven to fourteen. Families of these students receive a monthly payment equivalent to the minimum wage. As poor families typically rely on the wages of older children, the aim is to reduce dropouts by offsetting the opportunity cost of attending school. The scholarships are redeemable at public primary schools within the Federal District of Brazil (Brasilia)—all of which are administered on the state (Federal District) level. Payment is conditional upon the child attending at least 90 percent of all school days.

Bolsa Escola's second component, the School Savings Program, focuses on the students whose families receive the stipend. Following the eligible child's promotion to each new grade, the program deposits one annual minimum wage into a savings account managed by the Federal District's Solidarity Fund. The student is then permitted to withdraw half the money upon completing fourth or eighth grade and receives the remainder of the balance after graduating from high school. Students that fail a grade for two years in a row are dropped from the program, and their accrued savings reinvested in the general savings fund.

Bolsa Escola makes primary use of the geographic targeting mechanism. This program operates solely within the Federal District of Brasilia; however, within this specified region, individual assessment mechanisms identify the participants. To qualify for the program, the per capita income of the child's family must not exceed half the minimum wage. If any adult family members are unemployed, they must provide periodic verification that they are actively searching for a job (this is accomplished through enrollment in the National Employment System). Finally, the family must provide proof of residence within the Federal District for the previous five years.

Like Bolsa Escola, Mexico's *Progresa* scholarships take a demand-side approach to the problem of access. Progresa provides educational grants for children under the age of eighteen and between the third year of primary and the third year of secondary school. The value of the scholarship is between 5 and 9 percent of the annual income of a family living in extreme poverty—roughly 15 percent of the average potential income for children—but is slightly higher for girls over the age of twelve because of their higher dropout rates. Stipends are generally larger for secondary school students, who must typically pay for their own textbooks.

Progresa allocates funds by way of both geographic targeting and an individual assessment mechanism. It first identifies eligible localities on the basis of poverty and access to basic services, then screens individual families according to family structure, literacy, and other household characteristics.

Demand-Side Intervention: Group Targeting

Guatemala's *Eduque a la Niña* program is designed to address the low school attendance of primary-age girls (aged seven to fourteen) in rural Guatemala. It is funded by several donor organizations—USAID being the most prominent—though it receives a small contribution from the Ministry of Education. These funds are coordinated by Fundazucar, a local NGO that supports community development, housing, and education projects generally within the sugar plantation areas along the southern coast. In the case of Eduque, however, Fundazucar works with twelve rural communities in the country's highlands region.

Fundazucar presides over Eduque's four components, which include the following: First, Eduque provides a monthly scholarship worth about $4, equivalent to about one-quarter of the monthly income for women with less than one year of schooling. Second, it organizes the parent committees whose job is to select recipients of the scholarship and monitor program activities. Third, Eduque provides community outreach workers to offer tutoring and support to scholarship recipients. Finally, the program distributes educational materials for students and teachers in Spanish and four Mayan languages. The materials are oriented to the educational needs of girls.

Eduque targets the participants based on gender; however, it implicitly utilizes the geographic and self-assessment targeting mechanisms as well. It targets those rural communities with the largest disparities in primary enrollment between boys and girls and it requires parent committees to conduct a socioeconomic survey of each candidate's parents before awarding the scholarship entirely on the basis of need.

In response to severe overcrowding in public secondary schools and excess capacity in private schools, the Colombian government initiated a private school voucher program in 1991. This program makes use of a demand-side intervention and a group targeting mechanism to increase secondary school coverage by providing vouchers that cover the cost of private school tuition for children under sixteen in grades six through eleven. Its value is set according to the average tuition of lower- to middle-income-level private schools in the country's three largest cities. Students who fail a grade lose their voucher automatically. The Colombian Institute of Educational Credit

(ICETEX), a national education agency, administers the vouchers, while the ministry of education finances 80 percent of the program (and municipalities cover the rest).

The decision about whether to participate in the program occurs first at the municipal level, after which individual private schools make their own participation decision. Schools that elect to participate must submit a three-year curriculum plan to the ministry of education before receiving funding, and this funding has been limited to not-for-profit private schools since 1996.

The program provides vouchers to all graduates of public primary schools who have been admitted to a participating private school and meet an income eligibility requirement. Students must demonstrate their status in the bottom third of the socioeconomic spectrum, typically through a utility bill which indicates the income stratum of the child's neighborhood. It should be pointed out that in accepting only public school graduates, the program benefits from a fairly strong self-targeting mechanism as well.

DO COMPENSATORY EDUCATION PROGRAMS HELP POOR STUDENTS?

To the extent that we can generalize about the successes of compensatory programs, most seem to come in the areas of expanding access, increasing the volume of inputs, and strengthening community involvement. Difficulties arise in improving quality, at least in ways that affect student achievement. Though students generally perform no worse than their counterparts in conventional programs, neither do they exhibit marked improvements.

Of course, for those programs whose primary goal is access, the fact that students score as well as more traditional students is no small achievement. Such is the case for Mexico's distance learning program, Telesecundaria, whose students are actually more likely to pass the state-administered ninth-grade final exam than their more conventional counterparts (though it is important to note that the two groups take different exams).

On the local level, community involvement and the use of monetary incentives can be effective in reducing teacher absenteeism and the number of school days lost due to absenteeism, as well as positively affecting students' achievement. El Salvador's *EDUCO* program is typical of this phenomenon. The program has succeeded in expanding access to primary school among rural children, at involving parents in the management and direction of their children's schools, and at reducing the number of days missed by students (by 10 percent as compared to students in traditional schools)—probably the result of a reduction in teacher absenteeism (Jimenez and Sawada 1998). Despite the lower socioeconomic status of EDUCO students, their achievement was comparable to that of the students in traditional schools. In some cases, such as in first- and second-grade mathematics, they scored significantly higher (World Bank 1994).

Early childhood interventions have typically proved successful at increasing the quality of education for its participants. Like the other levels of compensatory programming, these programs provided services to previously uncovered children. These programs also led to a marked improvement in cognitive development and achievement with the child's subsequent entry to primary school. A 1992 evaluation of Colombia's

Hogares de Bienestar Infantil program revealed that the "psychosocial development" of participants improved relative to nonparticipants (Waiser 1995), even though nutritional status showed little sign of improvement. Compensatory preschool programs in Chile and Brazil reported that participants were socially and intellectually better prepared for primary school than nonparticipants (Waiser 1995).

Of course, whether these programs genuinely contribute to child development or merely reflect a self-selective process—suppose, for example, that better parents are more likely to take advantage of compensatory early childhood programs when they become available, but would raise higher achieving kids independent of these programs—is difficult to determine. Still, if for no other reason than the fact that they provide a steady source of nourishment and therefore allow cognitive development to run its natural course, it is likely that these programs have some causal effect on subsequent academic performance.

The cost-effectiveness of compensatory education programs in LAC, the relationship between the cost of the inputs and the success of the outputs, is an important aspect to consider when evaluating the impact a given program has had on improving the education of poor children. However, it has been an area where little study and evaluation has taken place, and existing data have not been gathered in a consistent format that would allow effective comparison.

Figure 5.2 illustrates examples of compensatory education in relation to what they achieve in terms of increasing the access of education to disadvantaged children and improving the quality of their educational experience, in addition to what these programs cost.

CONCLUSION

The experiences of the varied compensatory education programs in Latin America reveal three basic patterns:

- Indirect interventions like school health and nutrition programs—particularly at the early childhood level—seem to yield positive improvements in the academic performance of disadvantaged children.
- The implementation of programs designed to expand access and improve the quality of educational inputs tends to be fairly successful, though quality may suffer when resources are spread too thinly.
- Compensatory education programs are generally successful at expanding access to the poor—from both the supply- and demand-sides. The success of programs that target quality tends to be more elusive, however, if success is defined as improved academic achievement. Of course, part of this ambiguity is attributable to poor systems of evaluation and information management.

The key, therefore, is to neither rejoice unduly in the successes nor to despair excessively in the failures. While the experience of compensatory education in LAC teaches that the needs of children remain great—and that much progress remains to be made—it also demonstrates the power of a well-targeted intervention.

FIGURE 5.2

Lessons Learned Regarding the Effects and Costs of Several Compensatory Policies

	IMPACT ON ACCESS	IMPACT ON QUALITY	COST
Telesecundaria	Available in 12,700 rural communities, almost 800,000 students in grades 7–9 are enrolled in this program.	Almost 75 percent of students who enter Telesecundaria at grade 7 successfully complete grade 9. These students are substantially more likely than other groups to pass a grade 9 state-administered test.	Per-child cost in Telesecundaria is approximately equal to that of traditional students.
P-900		After one year of implementation, scores in Spanish and math increased. However, some schools did not show much improvement as seen by their extended stay in the program or returning soon after they "graduated" from it.	Per-child cost in a P-900 school is 25 percent greater (approximately $60 more per child) than the per-child cost in a nonparticipating school.
MECE-Rural	Supported classroom construction and the hiring of teachers.	Students scored 50 percent better in math and reading/writing exams than those in nontargeted schools.	Not available.
Hogares de Bienestar Infantil	Of the 877,710 enrolled in 1992, only 305,659 were actually attending. Less than 20 percent of households in extreme poverty use these services.	Nearly a third of participants had not received the complete nutritional benefits offered under the program. However, psychosocial development improved relative to nonparticipants.	Annual per-child cost is $340.
EDUCO	Increased coverage of preschool and basic education.	Despite being poorer, EDUCO students do as well as non-EDUCO students in achievement tests and had higher scores in first- and second-grade mathematics.	Overall cost of EDUCO program is about equal to the costs of the traditional school program.
ROSE	Civil works, the refurbishing and construction of schools, is progressing.	1996–1997 grade 7 and 8 test scores show that achievement was significantly higher in comprehensive (ROSE) and secondary high (ROSE) schools in comparison to non-ROSE schools. Primary and junior high (ROSE) schools did not show improvement.	Not available.
PARE		Increase in performance for the average student in the range of 45–90 percent for indigenous students and from 19 to 38 percent among rural students.	Program increased the per-pupil cost of education by 38 percent in indigenous schools and by 24 percent in rural schools.
Eduque a la Niña	Higher attendance of girls than in nonproject schools.	Lower dropout rates, higher completion rates, greater amount of active participation, and increased teacher participation in comparison to nonproject schools.	Program costs approximately $370 more than traditional schools to produce a sixth-grade graduate; however, costs should decrease over time as efficiency of program increases.

REFERENCES

Amaral, A. L., A. Guedes, T. Lobo, and R. Walker. 1995. Decentralized management of education in Minas Gerais, Brazil. Human Development Department, Education Group. Washington, D.C.: World Bank.

Baker, Judy L. 1998. *Poverty, Education, and Compensatory Programs in Mexico.* Washington, D.C.: World Bank.

Behrman, Jere. 1996. *Human Resources in Latin America and the Caribbean.* Washington, D.C.: InterAmerican Development Bank.

Birdsall, Nancy. 1996. Public spending on higher education in developing countries: Too much or too little. *Economics of Education Review* 15(4): 407–419.

Calderoni, José. 1998. Telesecundaria: Using TV to bring education to rural Mexico. *Education and Technology Technical Notes Series* 3(2). Human Development Network. Washington, D.C.: World Bank.

Carlson, Beverly A. 1999. Achieving educational quality: What schools teach us. División de Desarollo Productivo y Empresarial. Santiago, Chile: Comisión Económica para América Latina y el Caribe de las Naciones Unidas.

Chesterfield, Ray, and Fernando E. Rubio. 1995. Incentives for the participation of Guatemalan indigenous girls in primary education: The first year of implementation of the *Eduque a la Niña* project. Washington, D.C.: Academy for Educational Development.

Consultative Group on Early Childhood Care and Development. Program strategies in early childhood care and development. <http://www.ecdgroup.com/prstrat.html>.

Estudio de evaluación de la linea de educación rural del programa MECE. 1998. Valdivia–Valparaíso, Chile: Universidad Austral de Chile and Universidad de Playa Ancha de Ciencias de la Educación.

Filp, Johana. 1994. Todos los niños aprenden. Evaluaciones del P-900. *Cooperación Internacional y Desarollo de la Educación,* 179–249.

Gaynor, Cathy. 1998. *Decentralization of Education: Teacher Management.* Washington, D.C.: World Bank.

Grosh, Margaret. 1994. *Administering Targeted Social Programs in Latin America: From Platitudes to Practice.* Washington, D.C.: World Bank.

Hanushek, Eric A. 1995. Interpreting recent research on schooling in developing countries. *The World Bank Research Observer* 10(2): 227–246.

Jimenez, Emmanuel, and Yasuyuki Sawada. 1998. Do community-managed schools work? An evaluation of El Salvador's EDUCO program. Paper No. 8, Development Research Group. Washington, D.C.: World Bank.

Levinger, Beryl. 1994. *Nutrition, Health and Education for All.* Newton, Mass.: Education Development Center.

Liang, Xiaoyan, and Kari Marble. 1996. Guatemala—*Eduque a la Niña:* Girls' scholarship pilot. Human Development Department. Washington, D.C.: World Bank.

Mexico—Advancing educational equity and productivity in the context of decentralization. 1998. Phase I Report, Education Sector, LCSHD. Washington, D.C.: World Bank.

Peirano, Claudia, and Robert W. McMeekin. 1994. Gastos y costos del P-900. *Cooperación Internacional y Desarollo de la Educación,* 73–97.

Pollitt, Ernesto. 1990. *Malnutrition and Infection in the Classroom.* Paris: UNESCO.

Psacharopoulos, George. 1994. Returns to investment in education: A global update. *World Development* 22(9): 1325–1343.

Psacharopoulos, George, Carlos Rojas, and Eduardo Velez. 1993. Achievement evaluation of Colombia's *Escuela Nueva:* Is multi-grade the answer. *Comparative Education Review* 37 (August): 263–276.

Schiefelbein, Ernesto, Jorge Valenzuela, and Eduardo Velez. 1993. Factors affecting achievement in primary education: A review of the literature for Latin America and the Caribbean. Paper No. 2, Human Resources Development and Operations Policy. Washington, D.C.: World Bank.

Tilak, Jandhyala, B. G. 1989. Education and its relationship to economic growth, poverty, and income distribution: Past evidence and further analysis. Discussion Paper No. 46. Washington, D.C.: World Bank.

Waiser, Myriam. 1995. Early childhood care and development programs in Latin America: How much do they cost? Technical Advisory Group, LAC. Washington, D.C.: World Bank.

Winkler, Donald, and Jacques van der Gaag. 1996. Children of the poor in Latin America and the Caribbean. Paper No. 1, LASHC. Washington, D.C.: World Bank.

World Bank. 1994. El Salvador—Community education strategy: Decentralized school management. Sector Report No. 13502, Education Sector, LCSHD. Washington, D.C.: World Bank.

Wu, Kin Bing. 1998. Aide-memoire of the World Bank supervision mission: Reform of secondary education project and social policy analysis component. LCSHD. Washington, D.C.: World Bank.

Young, Mary Eming. 1995. Early child development: Investing in the future. Human Development Department. Washington, D.C.: World Bank.

Commentary

Jorge Padua, Colegio de Mexico

Donald Winkler's chapter examines one of the most problematic issues when examining the educational distribution among different social groups in Latin America: the limited access of schooling for disadvantaged populations. These populations are considered disadvantaged in relation to the distribution of other social dimensions in the population, such as status, occupation, income, level of well-being, and power. From the perspective of equality, they are the groups historically marginalized.

Winkler establishes this idea from the beginning of his discussion as a problem of compensatory education. He uses as an example of this phenomenon, compensatory programs evident in other countries, and he analyzes how those programs have accentuated issues of supply and demand with their targeting mechanisms and intent to identify program participants in poverty.

Compensatory education for special segments of the population is an issue with old roots in Latin America, associated with colonial times in which traditional populations of indigenous, mestizo, and blacks were initially marginalized, particularly in urban areas. This tradition continued at different rates in different countries during the nineteenth century, with some variation that depended on the size of those groups and on the importance that the government gave to the formidable task of formulating a "community." This work was inspired by the ideology of the liberation movements of the French and North American revolutions. Simon Rodriguez, Domingo F. Sarmiento, Andres Bello, Jose M. L. Mora, and many more considered public school as the principal instrument for the creation of a national culture.

The diagnosis of Winkler, almost fifty years later, not only signifies the disparities between rural and urban areas, between different ethnic groups, or between different generations, but also their common link: an endemic poverty in some countries that appears through new means and unusual intensity. Although the above list is incomplete, at the end of the century, the number of poor living in misery in Latin America is astonishing. Even in countries like Chile and Costa Rica that at the middle of the century demonstrated advances relatively important in the distribution of resources in the social structure, poverty continues to plague vast numbers of their population.

Although Winkler's analysis does not directly elaborate on the consequences of inequality, the content of the problem has to do with issues of economic and social developments, in light of economic and political organizations and social structures that favor cooperation and minimum conflict in society. In these dimensions, "compensation" can be thought of as a strategy that implies a counterbalance to society's structure, not simply a remedy. In other words, give more of one thing to make up for a scarcity of another social resource. For example, offer more or better schooling to compensate for lower incomes.

But in actuality, that is not the situation described in Winkler's analysis on the distribution of incomes, health, and nutrition, according to the characteristics of coverage, quality, and enrollment by school level in rural areas. In sociological terms, the social structure is one of two polarized classes, with some intermediary strata that in the last decades have diminished in volume. Winkler also makes reference to relevant issues on the diversity of necessities given the heterogeneity and volume of the population that needs special assistance.

The typology that Winkler uses to analyze the structure of programs and the means of identifying beneficiaries has virtue in that it emphasizes the importance of giving attention to special groups in the population. This is done in reference to education, health, and nutrition; the provision of special support for materials and finances to schools and families; and the impulses of creativity and innovation across the interchanges of ideas and experiences among teachers. Even though in political discourse there has always been a reference to participation in these respects, current programs now appear to foster implementation in practice. The typology also allows us to see that in most recent times increases in supply have been followed by concrete results in the number of children and young people who have opportunities to access and stay in the school system. However, some programs are not made effective due to fiscal dependence.

But to establish issues of education in terms of compensatory education and in terms of supply, demand, clients, evaluations, and monetary incentives could distract debate from the nature of the problem and from defining the purpose of education. Using market metaphors to justify interventions not only offers the temptation to think of the distribution of society's resources like a service for purely instrumental resources, but may lead us to forget that basic education is a right and not an item of consumption. Educational distribution has as much symbolic value as instrumental usage, just like other dimensions of the state that refer to the principles of equality, citizenship, justice, and in general, the rights borne by social contracts.

Simply posed as a problem of poverty, compensatory programs thought of in their specific connotation and taken to sociological extremes may in actuality generate undesired effects due to problems in their instrumentation. In the face of heterogeneity, the idea of alternative strategies for a common goal seems more appropriate than having different social systems for citizens of the "first" or "second" class. For example, some forms of schooling like distance education could accommodate the needs of diverse populations rather than forcing them to fit into a certain mold.

In general, urban and rural families value education positively. To what extent they conform to (or resign themselves to) the quantity and quality of education they receive is a more complex problem. Standards of satisfaction tend to be low in rural areas in comparison to urban ones, particularly when problems of supply continue. School coverage problems exist at the preschool and secondary levels, and much of the coverage provided by primary schools is substandard. The problem of the quantity and quality of schools for the poorest sectors is intense. To put it in the author's words, there are problems of supply in terms of access, as there are in permanence, terminal efficiency, and quality.

The author's conclusions signal important issues: compensatory programs have expanded access and have improved the quality of educational achievements. Compensatory programs in some countries have allowed for the unraveling of important dynamics, but they have not been implemented in the public sector due to bureaucratic problems.

The effects of the health and nutrition programs on academic achievement have been most pronounced in improving intellectual capacity during the prenatal period and during the first months of infancy. Obviously, there is a need to give special attention to expectant and postnatal mothers. But not all children suffer from these problems. Nonetheless, many children suffer from nutritional deficiencies; therefore, having schools provide meals may be effective and even necessary to attend to other aspects of growth, especially with extended school days. Abundant data exist on the need to utilize nutritional plans and more investigation is necessary to diagnose the specific needs of children in certain localities. As Winkler finalizes his discussion, the needs of children are great and much is left to be accomplished.

The active learning principles of the Escuela Nueva (New School) model have been incorporated into education reform in a number of countries in Latin America, as demonstrated at Calle Larga Escuela Nueva in Barcelona, Colombia.
[UNICEF/90-0020/Ellen Tolmie (Colombia)]

6

Can Education Measure up to Poverty in Argentina?

Inés Aguerrondo
Ministerio de Educación, Argentina and Facultad
Latinoamericana de Ciencias Sociales, Argentina

Despite numerous and long-term efforts to eradicate the structural phenomenon of poverty, it continues to permeate Latin America. Even among the most modern societies in the region such as Argentina, poverty can enter and leave a permanent mark, as was the case in the 1970s. Minujin and Kessler (1995) report that "the depth and persistence of the crisis which began in the mid-1970s saw hundreds of middle class families who had escaped misery in the past suffer such losses of income that they fell below the 'poverty line,' defined as the income necessary to acquire the basic basket of goods and services." For a brief discussion of alternative ways to measure poverty, see the Appendix to this chapter. As a result, "the lost decade" had a previously unknown effect on that sector of society: an increase in poverty and, as a consequence, a rise in the number of what is now known as "the new poor" (Minujin 1992).

Argentina, a nation of immigrants, developed a strategy to integrate the late nineteenth and early twentieth century contingent: an education system based on high-quality public schools. As a result of this strategy, Argentina positioned itself early as one of the most advanced countries in Latin America in terms of economic growth and educational development. National Population Census figures reveal high enrollment rates and constantly falling illiteracy rates. In 1914, an illiteracy rate of 35.9 percent fell to 13.6 percent in 1947, 8.5 percent in 1960, 7.4 percent in 1970, 6.1 percent in 1980, and finally dropped to 3.9 percent in 1991. The development of university education paralleled the development of primary education. Argentina gave birth to the university reform in Latin America,[1] positioning itself at the forefront of the "democratic university," a free institution for all without any admission requirements.

As economic and social changes following World War II caused large numbers of people to move from rural to urban areas, public schools once again became the mechanism for integrating these new groups into urban society. But the supply of education would experience important fundamental changes in loss of quality—in other words, in its ability to transmit knowledge. Although the expansion of education services played an important role in integrating these new groups, the education system was as much affected by the difficulty it had in adapting to the cultural characteristics of these new groups as its own inability to meet society's new demands.

General population censuses and other research on this topic indicate that many more children, including those from varying sectors of society, attend school today than thirty or forty years ago.[2] All available data point to enrollment rates of nearly 100 percent of children between the ages of five and twelve (IPA 1989). But how will the persistent presence of poverty afflicting the population affect education? This chapter begins by answering this question and then dips into the visible effects of poverty in the educational system, labeled as marginalization through inclusion and exclusion. We then examine how Argentina has responded to marginalization in light of the differences present in its citizenry. This is followed by a look at the new forms of marginalization evident in the school system today and the efforts made by the country, especially through the Social Education Plan to bring forth equality in education. We will close with an optimistic sense that education can indeed narrow the opportunity gap between different sectors of society and offer other points and avenues to consider in the search for social equity.

POVERTY AND EDUCATION

The state-of-the-art definition of *poverty* defines it as a syndrome made up of a series of characteristics of which two in particular stand out: *employment,* because it determines the income level which in turn permits access to goods and materials; and *education,* which provides access to cultural goods and in great measure determines the type of employment a person can obtain. For this reason, when we speak of the link between poverty and education, the central question behind all discussions of poverty has to be, Can education help in the face of poverty?

Empirical research has found that education has a decisive influence in that the majority of a population's characteristics vary with education. In other words, education is directly related to poverty. What is still not clear is the nature of this relationship. Is it the cause? That is to say, are the poor poor because they have little education? Or if not that, is it an effect? Why do the poor have less education?

As with many social phenomena, it seems that the relationship is not a strictly linear one. At a given moment, one variable may cause the other, and at other times, it becomes the effect. In one way we may consider poverty as the reason that children receive less education and education of poorer quality. In general, a middle-class child is more likely to have access to better quality and an increased quantity of education than a poor child. This tells us that the education system's (society's) structure leads to the least amount of education to the poorest, in terms of quantity and quality.

For adults the relationship is reversed. Limited education causes people to remain poor. A poorly educated adult has fewer opportunities to access the benefits of society than a better educated one. These benefits may be intangible (cultural, recreational, attitudinal) as well as material (type of employment, access to health services, etc.).

As a result, a vicious cycle exists between these two phenomena where, on the one hand, poverty results in less education and, on the other, having less education prevents getting out of poverty. How to break this cycle is the question that remains unanswered.

The structural factors that reinforce poverty through the education system have been constructed as the true mechanisms of social marginalization, above all in societies where economic determinants made it necessary to make choices in the face of successive social groups' demands to enter the education system. Three types of marginalization in education continue to make their relative presence known (Braslavsky 1985):

- Marginalization through total exclusion: no entry into the education system and no access at all to formal learning, in particular learning to read and write and perform basic math functions
- Marginalization through early exclusion: expulsion or rejection from the formal education system before having had the opportunity to solidify basic skills[3]
- Marginalization through inclusion: education is provided through "tracks" of differing quality for some sectors of society where students remain in the school system but without guaranteed access to some skills

These social marginalization processes are of major significance in a "knowledge society" where the skills and competencies acquired as a consequence of receiving an education are increasingly critical. Each of these processes is manifested differently in the diverse strata of society.

The relationship between education and poverty can be examined from two perspectives. The first, the *retrospective,* explains the answers provided in the last century: equity is to give the same to all; this means, in the case of education, "equal opportunity" in terms of access to school. A second perspective, the *prospective,* implies that equity is to give to each according to his or her needs; this means giving more to those who have less. Facing problems by compensating for differences is the foundation upon which modern political science decisions are based and opens up interesting possibilities.

THE RETROSPECTIVE OUTLOOK: EQUITY AS "EQUAL OPPORTUNITY" OF ACCESS TO SCHOOL (*EVERYONE ATTENDS SCHOOL TODAY.*)[4]

Education systems arose in response to the needs of a new industrial society to, at a minimum, homogenize the collective knowledge of society. In order to achieve this objective, a new institution, the school, was organized to provide access for all children to the education system. This marked the growth, and later the expansion of education systems, where the main idea was "equal opportunity."

The expansion of education to provide access for all groups of society marked the first positive outcome of the retrospective movement. This process occurred in Argentina at the end of the nineteenth century through the first half of the twentieth century. Today, children from all strata of society between the ages of seven and twelve go to school. As presented in Table 6.1, few differences exist in enrollment rates[5] between the structural, "new," and non-poor.

The method and the circumstances under which education expansion was implemented had positive aspects and negative consequences. On the one hand, expansion of the education system aided social integration, but on the other, its characteristics brought with them the social differentiation that underlies the process of stratification in school systems today.

TABLE 6.1

Enrollment Rates for Ages 4–24 by Poverty Level[6] (Argentina, 1988)

Age (in years)	Structural Poor	"New Poor"	Non-Poor	Total
4	30.8	41.8	80.7	55.2
5	64.2	76.8	91.0	78.4
6	79.3	99.3	100.0	93.5
7	97.4	100.0	100.0	99.3
8	91.9	100.0	100.0	97.9
9	93.0	100.0	100.0	98.2
10	92.1	100.0	100.0	98.0
11	92.3	100.0	100.0	97.9
12	86.7	100.0	100.0	97.0
13	86.4	94.5	92.3	91.4
14	73.2	81.0	94.4	87.3
15	58.3	64.4	80.9	71.6
16	32.5	64.0	65.6	60.2
17	40.1	48.1	56.0	50.6
18	12.4	31.6	50.6	38.1
19	7.3	18.2	40.2	28.2
20	15.1	18.3	49.1	26.0
21	2.7	34.4	34.3	30.5
22	6.0	4.8	35.6	26.1
23	2.6	8.6	14.6	11.1
24	1.2	6.8	18.7	14.2

Source: Inés Aguerrondo, *Schooling, Failure and Poverty: How to Break the Vicious Cycle* (Washington, D.C.: DAE/OEA, 1994).

The Negative Effect: Differentiated Expansion

As a consequence of the fact that access and permanence in the education system were originally not the same for all sectors of society, expansion of the system did not have the same effect either. In the first place, the system absorbed groups without previous access and, as a result, net enrollment rates increased.[7] In addition, those groups already incorporated into the education system remained for longer periods of time because schooling acquired a "credentialing effect."

In this way, two phenomena occurred simultaneously: the *expansion* of the education system and *differentiation*. This means we are dealing with a differentiated expansion where the process of "education for all" translated into "different education for all." The following data present objective differences in terms of the level of education attained in relation to the degree of poverty for different groups.

To analyze this differentiated expansion, we examined the education levels of the population of young adults (those between twenty and twenty-nine years of age) because this age group reflects the most recent performance of the education system. In Table 6.2, we can see once again not only the education expansion process, but also clear evidence of differentiation.

TABLE 6.2

Education Level of Young Adults Grouped by Poverty Level (Argentina, 1988)

Education Level*	Age (in years)	Structural Poor	"New Poor"	Non-Poor
No schooling	20–29	1.6	0.6	1.4
Up to third grade	20–29	12.7	2.5	0.7
Completed primary (grade 7)	20–29	71.6	90.5	96.3
Primary and beyond	20–29	8.7	19.4	44.6

*In all categories the difference to make 100 percent corresponds to the population that leaves between fourth and sixth grades.

Source: Inés Aguerrondo, *Schooling, Failure and Poverty: How to Break the Vicious Cycle* (Washington, D.C.: DAE/OEA, 1994).

These data seem to indicate that the Argentine education system has overcome the first mechanism of marginalization: total exclusion. Clearly, there is inclusion given that only 1.6 percent of poor young adults have not attended school. But these data also indicate that marginalization exists, in this case marginalization through exclusion (drop outs? expulsion?) because a greater percentage of structural children left school during the first cycle of education (up to the third grade) than the non-poor.

The third mechanism, marginalization by inclusion, the existence of different pathways that correspond to different socioeconomic sectors, is described in the next two sections. Different studies have shown that marginalization by inclusion exists in primary school as evidenced in the differences in the stratum of primary school leavers, with a range that runs from 71.6 percent of structurally poor graduates to 96.3 percent of the non-poor. Its effect can also be seen in the different distributions of the poor and non-poor in the last category (primary and beyond). The structural poor, even when they complete primary school, are much less likely to complete the noncompulsory levels of the education system than the non-poor (8.7 percent versus 44.6 percent).

The Positive Effect: Inclusion to Put All on the Same Level

First Effect: Increase in the Supply of Education   After the more than 100 years[8] since the creation of the education system, it is clear that if indeed the total population increased its participation in education, so, too, did the most disadvantaged groups and in very relevant proportions. As noted in Table 6.3, comparisons among the levels of education attained by different age groups of different sectors illustrate the continuous progress of educational attainment within groups.

An analysis of the different age groups that never completed a single grade reveals that there has undoubtedly been a progressive reduction in marginalization due to early exclusion. The first expansion occurred only through the first few decades of the twentieth century so that fifty years ago about 15 percent of the structural poor did not enter primary school versus 5.7 percent of the non-poor. At the present time, these figures are about even: approximately 1.5 percent of either group is excluded. In addition, the expansion of the education system (in urban areas) may have reached its

TABLE 6.3

Level of Education for the Adult Population (20–60 and older)
by Poverty and Age Group (Argentina, 1988)

Education Level Attained	Age	Structural Poor	"New Poor"	Non-poor
Never completed a single grade	20–29	1.5	0.6	1.4
	30–39	3.6	1.6	0.5
	40–49	10.5	5.9	1.4
	50–59	12.6	4.9	2.4
	60 and older	15.9	7.4	5.7
Left school between first and third grades	20–29	12.7	2.5	0.7
	30–39	19.9	6.4	2.0
	40–49	37.8	16.8	6.1
	50–59	40.8	22.0	15.8
	60 and older	45.4	26.7	19.9
Completed primary school (seventh grade)	20–29	71.6	90.5	96.3
	30–39	59.7	80.6	93.3
	40–49	37.0	63.1	83.5
	50–59	32.2	51.7	65.5
	60 and older	18.0	48.7	56.7
Completed secondary or tertiary studies	20–29	8.7	19.4	44.6
	30–39	4.2	9.5	27.7
	40–49	3.4	7.4	31.3
	50–59	4.7	9.9	14.9
	60 and older	1.3	3.1	7.3

Source: Inés Aguerrondo, *Schooling, Failure and Poverty: How to Break the Vicious Cycle* (Washington, D.C.: DAE/OEA, 1994).

limit. In the youngest age group (20–29) the percentages of total marginalization from school are negligible. Today, at least in urban areas, everyone in Argentina enters school. The figures show that for this first aspect of marginalization, the differences between the poor and the non-poor have been tangibly reduced.

We observe similar trends among the second group, the population that leaves school between the first and third grades. Schools have increased in general efficiency because, as much among the poor as the non-poor, the younger the students, the lower the leaving rate. This process benefits the poorest, whose rate has been reduced from 45.4 percent to 12.7 percent over the past fifty years.

Perhaps the greatest impact of the expansion of the education system in Argentina can be seen in the group that completes primary education. The structural poor have made important gains in completing compulsory education through seventh grade, rising from 18 percent among those older than sixty to 71.6 percent among young people between twenty and twenty-nine. Even though significant differences remain between the completion rates of the poor and non-poor, these figures also tell us that the quota of education offered to the poor as a result of the expansion of the education system has increased noticeably. This process, indeed sustained across time, has accelerated in the last two age groups where the differences between the structural poor and the non-poor have shrunk considerably.

Second Effect: Greater Access to Social Benefits   A notable loss in the quality of education accompanies the expansion of education, which has permitted the poor to attend and finish school in proportions never before seen in Argentina (Bertoni 1984; Braslavsky and Filmus 1987; SNECE Scores 1994, 1995, 1996, 1997, 1998). This has raised serious questions about the role of school and its usefulness, especially in relation to public schools and the public sector. Nevertheless, even when the transformation of education in some respects is one of the most urgent challenges to be faced today,[9] we cannot ignore the positive effects that schooling continues to have on greater social equity.

The first direct benefit can be seen in terms of acquiring and strengthening useful basic skills (reading, writing, and math). As a literate society, schooling for the poorest sectors provides access to information and facilities that otherwise would be inaccessible. In this sense, the IPA study has shown that the poor gain a real benefit from attending school. Even when the quality of teaching is in crisis and even when the pedagogy is inadequate to attend to their needs, those who pass through school (including those who do not finish) improve their chances of acquiring basic literacy skills.

The data in Table 6.4 demonstrate the great difference between having gone to school, even if for only a few years, and not having gone to school. Notice the astonishing disparities between mothers who never went to school (only 5 percent read) and those who went to school and left before the end of third grade (73.9 percent read).

Schooling has a positive impact: the greater the amount of education received, the greater the proportion of mothers capable of reading. These differences are also clear in relation to the different social sectors. Some 60 percent of structurally poor mothers read without difficulty and only 15 percent cannot read. According to Table 6.5, regardless of poverty level, those who have completed primary school or further have similar high percentages of fundamental reading skills. This finding suggests that completion of primary education guarantees, as a minimum, adequate reading skills.[10]

Going to school has a positive impact in terms of acquiring useful and essential knowledge for participation in a literate society; but completing primary school, even

TABLE 6.4

Percentage of Mothers Between the Ages of 35 and 59
Who Acquired/Did Not Acquire Literacy Skills Grouped by Level
of Education (Argentina, 1988)

Last Grade Completed	Did Not Learn to Read	Learned to Read
Never attended school	94.8	5.2
From first to third grade	26.1	73.9
From fourth to sixth grade	11.1	88.8
Completed primary (seventh grade)	7.4	92.6
Attended past seventh grade	3.5	96.5

Source: Inés Aguerrondo, *Schooling, Failure and Poverty: How to Break the Vicious Cycle* (Washington, D.C.: DAE/OEA, 1994).

TABLE 6.5

Percentage of Mothers Between the Ages of 35 and 59 Grouped by
Reading Achievement and Poverty Level (Argentina, 1988)

	Structural Poor	"New Poor"	Non-Poor	Total
Reads without difficulty	60.2	81.0	88.4	76.7
Reads with difficulty	18.9	12.4	5.3	11.1
Reads without understanding	1.5	5.7	5.3	2.5
Non-reader	15.0	4.5	0.4	8.9

Source: Inés Aguerrondo, *Schooling, Failure and Poverty: How to Break the Vicious Cycle* (Washington, D.C.: DAE/OEA, 1994).

though for the poor it means overcoming a series of difficulties to do so, has other concrete results. Thanks to the role education plays in facilitating access to other social benefits and its power to modify and disseminate modern cultural practices, the poor who have completed primary school are more likely to have access to these other economic and cultural benefits.

Access to benefits and opportunities by the poor varies significantly by education level attained. The poor who complete primary school have increased access to credit to buy their own homes; they are more likely to have health coverage (probably through their place of employment); and women are more likely to use birth control and receive improved prenatal care as well as regular, well-child care. This study confirms that these relationships are clear in all cases and, in addition, strengthen with age. It is precisely among the young who are structurally poor (20–29) where education appears to have the clearest influence (Aguerrondo 1993).

Consequently, education appears to facilitate the redistribution of the probability of acquiring the scarce benefits available to society among social sectors. This means that schooling still impacts access to greater benefits for the most overlooked sectors. The inclusion of the poorer sectors of society in the education system continues to have the same effect that it had a half-century ago for the middle class: integration into society and facilitated access to improved quality of life.

Education as a Battleground: New Forms of Marginalization

The benefits obtained by the most overlooked sectors of society as a result of acquiring more education were not obtained because the social system (or the education system) kept its promise of equal opportunity. The elements of the process of marginalization, intrinsic in the logic of the classic education system, are recycled in new forms and once again act as powerful and selective forces against the neediest sectors of society.

The education system was transformed into a battleground where, on the one hand, there is evidence of structural mechanisms of marginalization and, on the other, different social sectors demand to enter and remain in school. In this way, we can understand the interplay between inclusion-exclusion/sorting-leveling and the inner processes of the system. Two of these processes stand out: repetition and "shifting forward," or what can be called the new mechanisms of exclusion.

Originally, a school's organized structure attracted the middle class. The first consequence of social groups with different cultural foundations gaining access to education was what was usually known as "school leaving" or "dropping out." Under a perspective of equity, it might better be called "rejection." A school formally created for the middle class conditionally *rejects* children from other sectors.

As the education system incorporates different sectors into its realm, these "sectors" develop resistance mechanisms to fight the rejection they confront in the system. The phenomenon of repetition represents the conflict between an education system that rejects and discriminates against the poorest sectors who want to remain. It is customarily understood to be the precursor and the primary cause of dropping out, perhaps because the majority of statistical analyses can detect both events in the same social sectors. This interpretation may be the result of a methodological strategy that routinely compares both phenomena collectively (countries, provinces, schools), where universal results indicate that the groups with the highest repetition rates also have the highest dropout rates. This procedure can lead to a logical fallacy if the argument proposes explanations for *individual* behavior, but proof can be found in certain data for *group* behavior.

It is interesting to take into account certain findings that place these facts in doubt:[11]

- Not all students who drop out have repeated a grade. Furthermore, among those that drop out, approximately half repeated a grade and the other half did not.
- Among those who repeat, not all drop out. A third of those who are in school have repeated a grade, some up to three times.
- Students who have repeated a grade and drop out have completed higher levels of education than those who drop out and did not repeat (Aguerrondo 1988).[12]

Recognizing the phenomenon of "shifting forward" is another way in which we can see education as a battleground. The expansion of education has done nothing more than to bring to the forefront the mechanisms of marginalization built into the education system.

If at the present time all of the poor attend school and three-quarters of them finish primary school, it has not been because of this participation that barriers have been lifted. Differences have not been erased, only shifted, showing up before primary school or in subsequent years of schooling. Every traditional mechanism of marginalization has a modern substitute.

New Marginalization by Total Exclusion　In the case of total exclusion (never entering school), the door to education has shifted. It is no longer the first grade but kindergarten where we notice the differences. Returning to Table 6.1, we can see that children of six or seven years of age from all sectors are in school, but there is a big difference between the poor and others when we examine enrollment rates for four and five year olds.

Other findings from the same study permit us to consider a new form of exclusion: the active role played by kindergarten attendance. Even though the supply of kindergarten slots has been increased to meet a strong demand from the poorest sectors, this does not imply support of equal opportunity. Since kindergarten instruction, like that of primary school, is predicated on the characteristics of middle-class children, and evaluations are based on these criteria, children from the poorer sectors who attend kindergarten enter first grade already at a disadvantage.[13]

New Marginalization by Early Exclusion   The same thing occurs with the second mechanism, marginalization by early exclusion (rejection or dropping out). In spite of the fact that many more children today complete primary school and go on to secondary education, the vast majority of those from the poorest sectors do not complete this level.

As evidenced in the highlighted boxes in Table 6.6, there are apparent differences between the poor and the non-poor in primary school completion rates, but the differences widen for completion rates at either the secondary or tertiary levels.

New Marginalization by Inclusion   Marginalization by inclusion, or "tracking," has deepened differences at the primary and successive school levels (Braslavsky and Filmus 1987). With the entry of the neediest children into the education system, this mechanism permits the education system to shift its main concern away from transmitting knowledge to incorporating services to aid the poor.[14] The decision to convert schools into assistance centers has diminished their function as distributors of knowledge. This causes schools to turn their attention to meeting prerequisites for learning demands, not a problem in and of itself, but the fact that schools provide this assistance means that they are not proposing strategies to improve current levels of learning. Therefore, differences in learning achievement, or the causes of school failure, are found to be the student's "fault" because he or she has socioeconomic problems or "learning disabilities."

The previous explanation for school failure generates different responses: the establishment of psychological services inside or outside the school (where children "with problems" are referred), the hiring of remedial education teachers, and other responses

TABLE 6.6

Adults (20–60 and Older) Who Completed Primary or Other Education Levels by Poverty and Age Groups (Argentina, 1988)

Education Level Attained	Age	Structural Poor	"New Poor"	Non-Poor
Completed primary school	20–29	71.6	90.5	96.3
	30–39	59.7	80.6	93.3
	40–49	37.0	63.1	83.5
	50–59	32.2	51.7	65.5
	60 and older	18.0	48.7	56.7
Completed secondary or tertiary studies	20–29	8.7	19.4	44.6
	30–39	4.2	9.5	27.7
	40–49	3.4	7.4	31.3
	50–59	4.7	9.9	14.9
	60 and older	1.3	3.1	7.3

Source: Inés Aguerrondo, *Schooling, Failure and Poverty: How to Break the Vicious Cycle* (Washington, D.C.: DAE/OEA, 1994).

that have in common placing responsibility for learning failure squarely on the individual child and that do not assume any institutional responsibility for poor results.[15]

The education system has employed special strategies to avoid taking any blame for discrimination, thereby placing the blame for school failure on the socioeconomic conditions of the family or on the child's "learning problems." This does not lead to the creation of pedagogical solutions. The end result is a perverse cycle that reinforces poverty instead of attenuating it.

THE PROSPECTIVE OUTLOOK: IS IT POSSIBLE TO CLOSE THE ACHIEVEMENT GAP?

Transforming Education: A Real Possibility

The prospective outlook on equity appropriates resources to each child according to his or her needs and consequently provides more to those who have less. Increasing the supply of education to the poorest sectors of society is not enough because of the "tiptoe effect"—in essence, when everyone has a certain level of education, just attaining that level is not enough. In order to compete in a global society, a student today must have more education than a student at the end of the past century.

What is needed to close the gap? Basically, education must counteract the structural mechanisms of exclusion, as much as in their original version as in the more modern one, something possible only through an integral transformation of education.

Ambitiously, Argentina attempted to transform education during a period of profound economic and institutional reform with the passage of the 1993 Federal Education Act (No. 24.195). It proposes an educational transformation that not only seeks to establish the basis for education in the future, but also to repay the debts of the past—that is, to compensate for the pockets of inequity that are the result of the classic education system.

Among the most evident debts of the past is the need to overcome marginalization in education in its three forms. One strategy is to design a new education and educational policies that take into account the characteristics of different social groups in school.

Currently, educational policies take aim at correcting the mechanism of exclusion by modifying the levels and cycles of the system's structure. In effect, Act 24.195 replaces the old structure of seven years of compulsory primary education and five years of secondary education with twelve years divided into nine compulsory years of general basic education (EGB)[16] (divided into three cycles of three years each) and three of polymodal education. The last three years of EGB, called the third cycle of EGB, and the polymodal make up the new secondary level.

By including compulsory instruction for five year olds, the government clearly indicates its commitment to take on the responsibility of offering education to the entire population, beginning with the youngest children. In order to take on disparities and increase equity, the government has enacted two major approaches: a focus on the first two cycles of EGB to confront the learning problems that arise in the lower grades and different treatment for the third cycle by focusing on retaining all adolescents in school.

As we have seen in previous sections of this chapter, large differences of educational attainment and achievement proliferate between different socioeconomic sectors. The Federal Education Act obligates the national government[17] to reduce these differences. In light of this obligation, the government has put into effect a program of compensatory policies called the Social Education Plan. It includes numerous elements from material compensation for schools and students to the provision of instructional materials, in-service courses for teachers, programs to support institutional initiatives, and so on. After some five years, the plan's results are auspicious.

The Social Education Plan and Its Effects

The plan includes a set of actions organized into programs and projects to tackle the fundamental components of the education system that give rise to a quality education. It is designed to provide compensation for financial and material resources as well as technical assistance in the form of guidance for institutional management and training. All of its combined actions have a pedagogical end and are sustained over time as a way to influence school practice.

In 1998, the Social Education Plan impacted 21,542 schools and nearly 3 million students,[18] primarily at the preschool and basic primary levels, although some of its activities included secondary schools.[19] These schools were selected on the basis of achievement indicators such as dropout and repetition rates and number of overage students; the condition of school buildings; and the lack of furniture, other equipment, or instructional materials. The plan consists of three programs: (1) Better Education for All Program, (2) School Infrastructure Improvement Program, and (3) National Student Scholarship Program.

The Better Education for All Program is directed at the poorest children and proposes implementation of pedagogy designed to meet their specific needs. At a minimum, it ensures that the same instructional materials are made available to them as to the most advantaged students. Additionally, teachers use special teaching techniques that require specific preparation. To meet this need, instructional materials designed for individual and group work are delivered to the schools. The program is designed to motivate teachers—through incentives—to take the initiative, support innovative proposals, and facilitate the exchange of successful experiences. It is complemented by training and in-service components for teachers in these schools.

The School Infrastructure Improvement Program designates funds to construct buildings and classrooms or to make repairs. Construction has taken place in rural and marginal urban areas to replace, enlarge, or reconfigure schools deemed inadequate workplaces for students and teachers.

The National Student Scholarship Program is designed to create the conditions to make it possible for students from the most socioeconomically vulnerable families to remain in both the third cycle of EGB and the polymodal cycle, to improve student achievement by supporting attendance and promotion, to reduce the number of young people who do not attend the compulsory cycles, and to improve their prospects for future employment. Toward this end, a scholarship system provides money to help families keep students in school. This program is also supposed to develop specific instructional strategies to improve student retention.

Management of the Social Education Plan has been decentralized so that the Ministry of Education delivers benefits directly to the participating schools:

For classrooms: textbooks, teachers' guides, dictionaries, notebooks, student equipment, children's literature libraries, encyclopedias, atlases, science books, and history books

For teachers by school: computers, printers, and professional libraries

Under the plan, financial resources are transferred to each school's Special Savings Account. Local school authorities and the community administer the accounts. This is both efficient and transparent, both of which are indispensable for meeting a high efficiency level of state management.

Overcoming the "aid mentality," together with decentralizing management functions, promotes the education community's participation in the plan's activities, delegating to it some of the decision making for the acquisition and utilization of resources to improve instructional quality. Achieving participation through decentralized management models is also an indispensable requirement for the success of the plan's activities and sustaining them over time. This compensatory task takes leave of traditional public administration in Argentina. Surmounting the traditional model created favorable conditions for successful management of the Social Education Plan: budgets by program, work by project, and decentralization of resource distribution. This management model reduces management costs to 3 percent, thus making it possible to take maximum advantage of the designated resources.

One of the conditions for an effective fight for equity is represented in the total amount of resources assigned to compensation. In order for the effects to be visible, the investment needs to be sustained. Between 1993 and 1998, Argentina designated $703,546,514 to the Social Education Plan.[20] Table 6.7 presents a detailed account of the plan's investments.

The results obtained over these five years can be represented by a series of indicators. Investment in infrastructure was important and was made at practically the same level as instructional materials. Of the many important outcomes of the plan's activities, one is of special significance: the ability to settle an old debt to marginalized and rural groups by completely eliminating "country schools" in three years.[21] It also bears mention that prioritizing the construction of preschool and third cycle EGB classrooms facilitated the inclusion of children younger than six and students in the eighth and ninth grades in compulsory education. Between 1991 and 1998, the enrollment rates for both preschool and middle school rose dramatically. In the first instance, enrollment rates jumped from 72.7 percent in 1991 to 97.5 percent in 1998; for middle school, enrollment rates went from 59.3 percent in 1991 to 69.2 percent in 1998 (Ministry of Education 1998).

Two pieces of information are particularly relevant in relation to increasing equity. The first has to do with a decline in the repetition rate in primary school and the second with an increase in students' academic achievement. Both results clearly demonstrate that the most positive results have been found in those provinces with the largest number of homes where Basic Needs are Unmet (NBI); these most disadvantaged areas are also the provinces where the Social Education Plan covers all the primary schools as well as a fairly high percentage of the middle schools.

TABLE 6.7

Social Education Plan Investments in Schools (1993–1998)

	1993	1994	1995	1996	1997	1998*	Totals
Number of students	412,539	1,051,235	2,167,331	2,684,523	3,303,212	3,625,894	3,625,894
Number of schools	1,000	4,277	10,119	14,174	16,530	17,763	17,763
Number of textbooks delivered	1,000,000	2,000,000	2,500,000	2,432,461	3,373,032	1,938,746	13,244,239
Investment in textbooks	$5,058,000	$17,217,000	$16,362,854	$16,048,661	$26,011,189	$19,728,104	$100,425,808
Financing for equipment and other material	$3,183,040	$28,610,800	$15,949,272	$12,210,703	$22,440,159	$17,385,149	$99,779,123
Financing for institutional projects		$6,507,000	$4,185,000	$12,735,000	$11,486,453	$10,403,794	$45,317,247
Number of computers delivered	2,000	3,600					5,600
Investment in computers	$2,750,000	$4,950,000			$2,718,950	$3,498,390	$13,917,340
Investment in school supplies (including funds and notebooks)	$1,196,960	$2,000,000	$15,171,317	$17,856,102	$17,787,573	$12,044,479	$66,056,431
Total investment in the Education for All Program	**$12,188,000**	**$59,284,800**	**$51,668,443**	**$58,850,466**	**$80,444,324**	**$63,059,916**	**$325,495,949**
Replacement buildings for the "country schools"	785	1,057	97				1,939
Kindergarten classroom construction (in square meters)	45,270	42,300	20,269	32,398	9,320	3,497	149,557
Classroom construction (in square meters)	1,170	37,980	16,407	25,721	24,159	9,724	105,437
Retrofiting and renovations (number of schools impacted)	1,140	878	805	1,044	911	412	4,778
Services (in square meters)				50,735	39,443	13,060	90,178
Total investment in the School Improvement Program	**$49,641,696**	**$66,415,271**	**$47,482,271**	**$70,916,937**	**$82,740,256**	**$35,403,373**	**$317,196,290**
Number of scholarship students					37,986	106,045	106,045
Total investment in the Scholarship Program					**$10,482,900**	**$50,371,375**	**$60,854,275**
Total investment 1993–1998, Social Education Plan	**$61,829,696**	**$125,700,071**	**$99,150,714**	**$129,767,403**	**$173,667,480**	**$148,834,664**	**$703,546,514**

*Investments made by September 1998.

Source: Ministry of Education and Culture, "Better Education for All Program," Social Education Plan, Compensatory Programs in Argentina, 1993–1998, Buenos Aires, 1998.

In 1994, as part of widespread education reform, the National Evaluation System of the Quality of Education (SNECE) initiated its first activities for accountability. The annual testing program administered through SNECE consists of self-administered objective tests completed by a sample of third, sixth, ninth, and twelfth grade general education students. The test scores for the 1993–1998 period reveal some important results.

Figure 6.1 shows that repetition rates are falling more rapidly in the provinces with the highest percentage of NBI homes—in other words, the poorest areas. Figure 6.2 shows that SNECE test scores improve most notably in those provinces with the highest percentage of NBI homes.

FIGURE 6.1

Variation in Repetition Rates by Province Classified by the Percentage of NBI Homes

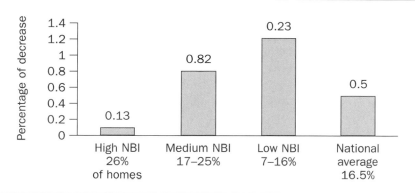

Source: Ministry of Education and Culture, "Better Education for All Program," Social Education Plan, Compensatory Programs in Argentina, 1993–1998, Buenos Aires, 1998.

FIGURE 6.2

Variation in SNECE Test Scores by Province Classified by the Percentage of NBI Homes

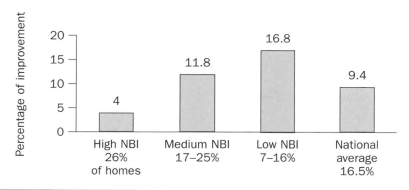

Source: Ministry of Education and Culture, "Better Education for All Program," Social Education Plan, Compensatory Programs in Argentina, 1993–1998, Buenos Aires, 1998.

CONCLUSION: THE FIGHT FOR EQUITY

Argentina continues to serve the most disadvantaged sectors of society even though the mechanisms of exclusion are alive and well. Nevertheless, this does not mean that urgent, deep changes are unnecessary. They are, in fact, quite necessary, not only for the poor, but also to meet society's demands. In spite of this, real change will only occur if, in addition to working out the technical-pedagogical problems of change, alternatives to the image of schools and education can be found.

In agreement with the literature critical of education development, such as the classic work of Bourdieu and Passeron (1977), the development of education that we have categorized as "expansion-differentiation" brought as a consequence the appearance of a fragmented network of education quality. This is contrary to the initial role of education at the beginning of this process. Instead of facilitating social mobility, it had the opposite effect: it reinforced the social origins of diverse groups.

"Poverty is not the problem of the chronically poor, rather it is the problem of societies which create poverty as an integral component of their success and failures" (Blanco 1993); consequently, we have to suppose that education really can be society's antidote to counteract this evil. But, again according to Blanco, "it is not about finding a way to peacefully coexist with poverty, it's about eradicating it . . . it's about changing the way poverty is perceived in order to fight it. It isn't only about aid, although aid is certainly a part of it, but about fundamentally altering the sources that give rise to poverty."

In fact, it is not only about a fight against poverty but even more about creating the conditions so that society can respond to the demands and necessities of all of its members. If education effectively contributes to society's growth in what we understand by this challenge in today's terms, it helps increase competitiveness in society. In this sense,

> [T]here is increasing agreement to point to the greatest challenge faced by nations trying to increase their competitiveness[—]to transform the quality of education. . . . Paradoxically, speaking in general terms, there is equal consensus that points to a strong disconnect between education systems and the hopes placed upon them and reality. They appear to be the children of a rapidly eroding industrial society, with structures and orientation more closely linked to the nineteenth rather than the twenty-first century. The effectiveness of education systems began to fade as society's paradigm changed and it began to have new expectations of them. (Ottone 1998)

As a result, education can somewhat realistically and validly fight against poverty only if it structurally modifies its model (its purpose). The classic model worked in Argentina to provide equity to the immigrant classes. In other words, it permitted equity through a model of increased democracy. The expansion of education after World War II was accompanied by an interesting phenomenon, the incorporation of vast populations of rural migrants into the urban education system. But repetition increased, a phenomenon that, on the one hand, is of concern but, on the other, somewhat interesting in the sense that it guarantees that the student, whatever the age, stays in school.

Finally, recreating the education system such that inequity is reduced is not merely a social justice response. The sustainability over time of the processes of growth and development are more and more determined by the capacity of countries to adapt to international demands and by the progressive addition of technical progress being exported. Increasingly, the capacity to compete in international markets depends on human capital.

It is important not to base these processes on a spurious competitiveness where the advantages produced by international commerce depend on low wages and the destructive use of natural resources. Rather, they should be based on authentic competitiveness which includes incorporating technical progress and increasing productivity and wages (Fajnzylber 1992). This would require a fundamental change in the purpose of education.

APPENDIX

MEASUREMENT OF POVERTY

The two methods traditionally used to measure poverty are the so-called poverty line (PL) and unmet basic needs (UBN). The first presupposes that a basket of basic goods and services can be established that takes into account a society's consumer habits at a particular point in time. This normative basket, once established, determines the poverty line. The basket is adjusted to take into consideration the protein and calorie requirements defined by the Food Administration Organization and World Health Organization (FAO-WHO) for each age group, sex, level of activity, and biological needs. The value of the food basket constitutes the indigence line (IL). Based on the proportion that food expenses represent as a percentage of the total expenses for the average level of consumption, the poverty line is defined as 2.07 times the indigence line. This calculation allows other necessities such as transportation, clothing, housing, education, and health to be taken into consideration.

The second form of poverty measurement, "unmet basic needs," defines poverty as a lack of access to certain goods. This method requires the definition of minimum levels of satisfaction of basic needs. If a home falls in at least one of the following categories, it is considered poor:

Stacking: dwellings with more than three people per room
Precarious structures: dwellings constructed from scraps, trash, or disposable materials
No basic plumbing: dwellings that do not have a bathroom with running water
Dropouts: homes where there is at least one child between the ages of six and twelve who does not attend school
Lack of subsistence capacity: homes with four or more persons where the head of the household has only completed second grade or less

By combining these two methods of measuring poverty, the following poverty groups can be constructed:

Structural poor: those who do not meet one or more of the basic needs and are either above or below the poverty line
Impoverished or the "new poor": those whose per capita incomes are lower than the per capita poverty line

Non-poor: those whose per capita incomes are higher than the poverty line and have their basic needs met

The "new poor" category allows us to measure the impact of the downward transition because it takes into consideration those groups that have their basic needs met, but whose incomes are lower than the poverty line.

NOTES

1. University reform began in 1918 in Córdoba, a city in the center of Argentina under the banner of democratizing the university course system by incorporating a system of competitive exams.
2. Net enrollment rates for primary education (grades 1–7) according to the last four National Censuses have been 83.5 percent in 1960, 87.7 percent in 1970, 90.5 percent in 1980, and 95.7 percent in 1991.
3. This form of marginalization is usually referred to as "school leaving." It is interesting that this term has not been questioned as of now. It should have been a given that it supposes that the blame for not receiving an education falls on the student (who leaves) or on the family (which makes the student leave), thus hiding the structural causes of the problem.
4. The information analyzed comes from the Quality of Life Survey that was completed as part of the Argentine Poverty Study (IPA) in INDEC between April and July 1988. The sample included data from Greater Buenos Aires, Posadas, Santiago del Estero, Neuquén, and General Roca. The data were analyzed on two occasions. The first time was as part of the report for the Argentine Poverty Study (IPA) and the second as part of the work completed by CIPPA (Center for Public Policy Research) where only the data from the nineteen Greater Buenos Aires Districts were included.
5. Rather than presenting figures that correspond to the 1991 National Census, which are not available for all levels of poverty, I present information from the Argentina Poverty Study (IPA). I will refer to the number of people and homes with unsatisfied basic needs as poor. Please see the Appendix to this chapter for a discussion of alternative poverty measures.
6. Data from three groups were used:

   Structural poor: They do not have one or more of the basic necessities and are either above or below the poverty line (PL).
   "New poor": They have per capita income lower than the poverty line (prorated per capita).
   Non-poor: They have per capita income higher than the poverty line and can meet their basic needs.

7. The 1980 Census shows something more than 90 percent of primary enrollment. In the two studies we analyzed (IPA) and Survey and Evaluation of the National Social Promotion and Nutrition Program-School Lunch Programs (PPSN), we found a schooling rate between 96 percent and 100 percent for ages 6–14, which is nearly the same rate of schooling as under the old education system structure (Law 1.420, 1884) which was in effect at the time.
8. In 1884, when Law 1.420 went into effect, a compulsory primary education system was established; it is usually the date used in Argentina as to when the education system was created. It has been estimated that at that time 85 percent of the population between six and fourteen years of age were excluded from basic education.
9. Since 1993, the Federal Education Act (No. 24.195) has been in effect to establish substantive reform in the structure, content, and functioning of the education system.
10. We are not referring here to reading quality in the strictest sense, simply the possibility of reading short pieces fluidly, as was required by the test.

11. The unit of analysis for both studies was at the individual level (IPA and CIPPA).
12. These results are from a study of the nutritional and educational impact of school food programs (see Ministerio de Educación y Justicia 1985–1986). The unit of analysis for this study was also at the individual level.
13. Here a perverse control comes into play where the child is diagnosed as "too immature" to enter first grade and is obligated to repeat kindergarten.
14. Major approaches to providing assistance are the school food program, medical or dental service, and the distribution of clothes and shoes.
15. A result of this same phenomenon is the ridiculous number of children found to be "slightly mentally disabled" and who are placed in our special education schools (making up some 80 percent of the entire special education population). This is another structural expulsion mechanism incorporated into the education system.
16. In reality, compulsory education has been extended to ten years since it now includes preschool classrooms for five year olds.
17. The Republic of Argentina is a federal state in which each of the twenty-four provinces administers its own education system (within the framework of national agreements). According to federal law, the national ministry has three objectives: defend the unity of the education system, defend its quality, and protect equity.
18. There are 45,269 schools and 8,411,232 students in Argentina (Ministry of Education, National Information Network, 1997). The Social Education Plan covers 47.6 percent of schools and 34.5 percent of students.
19. In 1998, coverage by level was as follows:

Social Education Plan Coverage (1998)

Level	Schools	Students
Preschool	6,249	265,892
EGB	12,858	2,015,795
Middle	1,705	550,021
Special education	730	70,634
Total	21,542	2,902,342

20. One Argentine peso is approximately equal to one U.S. dollar.
21. These "country schools" were precarious constructions (adobe walls with straw roofs) that generally did not have electricity or bathrooms with running water, making them unsuitable for instruction and dangerous in terms of public health.

REFERENCES

Aguerrondo, Inés. 1998. La marginación educativa en los diferentes grupos socioeconómicos: Exclusión, abandono y repitencia en la escuela primaria. Paper presented at the XXI Latin American Congress of Sociology, Montevideo, December.

Aguerrondo, Inés. 1993. Escuela, fracaso y pobreza: Cómo salir del círculo vicioso. Department of Educational Affairs. Washington, D.C.: Organization of American States.

Blanco, Carlos. 1993. Prólogo. In Pobreza, un Tema Impostergable: Nuevas Respuestas a Nivel Mundial, ed. B. Kliksberg, 7–8. Mexico City: Fondo de Cultura Económica.

Bertoni, Alicia, et al. 1984. Los perfiles de aprendizaje de los alumnos de las escuelas primarias de la MCBA según el nivel de logro de los objetivos curriculares—Areas lengua, matemática, estudios sociales y ciencias naturales. Secretaría de Educación, Proyecto 3 (Ministry of Education, Project 3). Buenos Aires: MCBA.

Bourdieu, Pierre, and Jean Claude Passeron. 1977. La reproducción. Barcelona: Editorial Laia.

Braslavsky, Cecilia. 1985. *La Discriminación Educativa en la Argentina.* Buenos Aires: Facultad Latinoamericana de Ciencias Sociales/Grupo Editor Latinoamericano.

Braslavsky, Cecilia, and Daniel Filmus. 1987. Ultimo año de colegio secundario y discriminación educativa. Serie Documentos e informes de investigación No. 50. Buenos Aires: Facultad Latinoamericana de Ciencias Sociales.

Estudio de Costos del Sistema Educativo. 1998. *Pobreza, Repetición, y Resultados de Calidad (1993–1997).* Buenos Aires: Ministerio de Cultura y Educación de la Nación, Secretaría de Programación y Evaluación Educativa.

Fajnzylber, Fernando. 1992. Industrialización y desarrollo tecnológico, Informe No. 12, División Conjunta. Santiago, Chile: CEPAL/ONUDI.

Finkel, Sara. 1978. El sistema de educación y la alianza de clases. La clase medfia como beneficiaria de la expansión del sistema educacional argentino. In *La Educación Burguesa,* ed. G. Labarca, T. Vasconi, S. Finkel, and I. Recca, 93–136. Mexico City: Editorial Nueva Imagen.

Investigación sobre Pobreza en Argentina (IPA). 1989. Buenos Aires: Instituto Nacional de Estadísticas y Censos (INDEC).

Jauregui, Silvia, María Luisa Lemos, and Norma Paviglianiti. 1983. El sistema educativo argentino: características y problemas. *Cuadernos Fundación Eugenio A. Blanco* I(3): 35–49.

Kliksberg, Bernardo. 1993. La escalada de la pobreza en América Latina. In *Pobreza, un Tema Impostergable. Nuevas Respuestas a Nivel Mundial,* ed. B. Kliksberg. Mexico City: Fondo de Cultura Económica.

Ministerio de Cultura y Educación. 1998. Mejor educación para todos: Plan social educativo, programas compensatorios en Argentina. 1993–1998. Buenos Aires: MCE.

Ministerio de Cultura y Educación. 1998. Pobreza, repetición y resultados de calidad: 1993–1997. Programa Estudio de Costos del Sistema Educativo, Secretaría de Programación y Evaluación Educativa. Buenos Aires: MCE.

Ministerio de Cultura y Educación, Sistema Nacional de Evaluación de la Calidad de la Educación (SNECE). 1994, 1995, 1996, 1997, 1998. Operativos nacionales de evaluación 1994, 1995, 1996, 1997, 1998. Buenos Aires: Informes anuales (annual reports). MCE, Subsecretaría de Evaluación de la Calidad de la Educación.

Ministerio de Educación y Justicia. 1985–1986. Evaluación del programa nacional de promoción social y nutricional (PPSN) (Comedores escolares). Buenos Aires: Convenio Ministerio de Educación y Justicia/Ministerio de Salud y Acción Social/FAO-OPS.

Minujin, Alberto, ed. 1992. *Cuesta Abajo. Los Nuevos Pobres: Efectos de la Crisis en la Sociedad Argentina.* Buenos Aires: UNICEF/Editorial Losada.

Minujin, Alberto, and Germán Kessler. 1995. *La Nueva Pobreza en la Argentina.* Buenos Aires: Editorial Planeta.

Ottone, Ernesto. 1998. Educación y competitividad. Paper presented at the first forum "La formación de Recursos Humanos para la gestión educativa en América Latina" at the Instituto Internacional de Planificación de la Educación (International Institute for Educational Planning), Buenos Aires, November 22.

Tedesco, Juan Carlos. 1970. *Educación y Sociedad en la Argentina (1880–1900).* Buenos Aires: Ediciones Pannedille.

Commentary

Terrence Tivnan, Harvard Graduate School of Education

This chapter raises and discusses a number of important issues, and it provides a description of a program that is designed to address some of the problems and challenges raised. So this chapter does a lot: it combines a set of theoretical and practical issues, issues that will be familiar to educators in all kinds of settings and in all parts of the world.

Can education help address economic and social conditions? As educators, we like to think that the answer to this question will be yes. We certainly hope that education, or improvements in educational programs, will lead to increased learning on the part of students, to better jobs and better lives for them later on, and to better conditions for society in general. But how will these changes occur? And why are our efforts often less successful than we would like? Why are we not even more successful in reducing poverty and improving lives through educational changes? These are the types of questions that are addressed in this chapter.

Inés Aguerrondo raises a series of important questions. Some of these make us confront some fundamental assumptions about the role of education in society. Data from Argentina show how the expansion of the education system has resulted in very high participation rates in some types of schooling. Even among the most poverty-stricken sectors there have been major increases in participation in public schooling. Along with participation in schooling have come higher levels of literacy. Even among those who attend school for only a few years, basic literacy levels have improved remarkably over the levels of the past: the greater the amount of education received, the greater the proportion of literate mothers. Literacy appears to be a concrete result of greater participation in education. But despite these changes in the system, major problems remain. Indeed, despite the trends toward greater participation in schooling, data from Argentina actually show that there are now more people below the poverty line than was the case twenty-five years ago. These would appear to be contradictory trends if we believe that education can have a positive role in reducing poverty.

Are there new forms of marginalization at work? Aguerrondo suggests that perhaps we can still see the education system perpetuating its older role. Her chapter summarizes some influential ideas about the interrelationship of education and poverty. She suggests that education systems have actually helped to exclude, or at least socially marginalize, certain groups from full participation in the society. There might be marginalization by excluding some groups from education entirely. Or perhaps there could be marginalization through early exclusion—expulsion or rejection from the formal education system before having had the opportunity to solidify basic skills. Or a third form of marginalization could occur through inclusion that includes a form of tracking that restricts certain groups to a kind of "second-class" education that will limit their opportunities.

Is there evidence that these forms of marginalization are still working today? In Argentina—and undoubtedly in other countries—evidence suggests that the answer is yes. While there is greater participation in lower levels of education, we still see major differences in participation in secondary and certainly postsecondary schooling. The poor and non-poor still differ dramatically in their completion rates at secondary levels and beyond. Another form of possible marginalization comes through the establishment of different learning tracks or the availability of special services that serve to separate and isolate a disproportionate share of students from poor backgrounds. In fact, Aguerrondo argues, every traditional mechanism of marginalization has a modern equivalent. If education systems excluded some students totally in the past, they now do something similar by making higher levels of education a requirement for better jobs, but then limiting access to these higher levels. Different tracks of the educational program can serve to exclude certain students instead of giving them access to the quality of education that would lead to better outcomes.

But here is a point that deserves serious discussion. Even if this is the case, policymakers should be asking *why* these conditions occur. Why does the expansion of education—expansion designed to include more children in the system and improve their opportunities for better lives—lead to a reduction in the quality of education? Does it always happen? Does expansion actually diminish or dilute the quality of existing schools? Does the availability of a new school have to lead to a decrease in the quality of an existing school? It would seem as though this would not have to be the case, but if we see this relationship holding, we should work hard to understand why.

Similarly, we wonder about why the "modern mechanisms of marginalization" should appear when education has expanded to become more democratic. Why would this be so? Is the expansion of education seen as a threat to the existing social order? Is there some active set of political forces that oppose the more democratic or egalitarian approaches? Or is there a more benign explanation? Are these questionable effects a result of well-intentioned policies leading to unintended and sometimes harmful consequences? Is it possible that we might be trying to design programs that will be better suited to certain students, but then we end up marginalizing them out of the mainstream program?

Many papers raise these issues without attempting any serious resolution or providing any suggestions for future work. We often are presented with the history of a system and an analysis of historical records, but we are not provided with specific ideas for new programs. One of the features of this chapter that I enjoyed most was that it presented the historically based critique, but then it also presented a report of a promising program that is intended to address the shortcomings (at least some of them) that were identified. We hear about the Social Education Plan, begun in 1993 and involving over 21,000 schools and 3 million students.

The three major components of the plan attempt to address the major challenges facing Argentina. First, the plan is aimed at providing better education for all, and so it addresses the issue of differential access to quality education. It is directed at the poorest children, and the pedagogical approach is intended to meet the specific needs of these children. Second, the program addresses differences in school resources by providing funds for buildings and repairs. This is an attempt to make the physical facilities more suitable for learning. A third important component addresses incentives for continuing schooling. Families are given scholarships to help keep their children in school.

These features sound promising. They will look familiar to educators in other countries and in other settings, as they capture features of other initiatives that have been developed to meet the needs of school systems confronted with increasingly diverse populations of students. But at the same time, in keeping with the themes raised earlier in the chapter, we might ask about some of the possible unintended consequences that might arise. What would we say by way of critique here? I think several questions might be raised.

First, is the development of pedagogy specifically designed to meet the needs of poor children just another form of exclusionary practice? Will this really lead to similar levels of learning and similar outcomes for these children? Or will the different approaches be regarded as "inferior" or "lower" or "the poor children's way" of education? In attempting to tailor something to meet special needs, are we likely to develop a separate track that will marginalize those who take it?

Second, will the resources and materials for teacher training that are provided as part of the new program produce or lead to a dilution of resources for regular education programs? Are we not leading ourselves toward the very problem we criticized earlier? As we expand education, are we almost inevitably lowering the average quality of what we provide? How can we determine if this is happening? How can we guard against these possibilities?

A similar concern can be raised about the provision of funds for buildings and repairs. Will there be no drawing away of resources from other schools?

The results available thus far from the first several years of the new plan are encouraging. There have been reports of large increases in enrollment and reductions in repetitions of grades, and these are especially noted in areas that are poorer. Achievement test scores are increasing. So these indications are encouraging. But we certainly need to keep monitoring the results. In fact, as the chapter points out, it will be increasingly important to monitor possible changes in other areas of the system to see if the new plan is having unexpected or unintended effects on other features of the existing system. Are repairs for some schools being delayed because of the emphasis on the new plan schools, for example? What might be the long-term consequences of this?

The chapter is an ambitious attempt to raise some of the important issues, to explain some of the important critiques that can be raised about the limitations of education in helping to deal with reducing poverty, and to present some ideas about new programs and approaches that are being tried out on a grand scale. I hope that the results of the evaluation studies on the new plan will be shared widely and internationally. The issues being addressed in Argentina are similar to those being addressed in the United States and other countries, and evaluators and policymakers can benefit greatly by having an increased pool of studies and findings.

The chapter starts out on a somewhat cautionary note by reminding us of the many challenges facing educators and pointing out the many shortcomings of earlier attempts at education reform. But the chapter ends on a more optimistic note, sharing ideas about new approaches that will help us learn more about the relationships between educational change and economic changes. It reminds us that education can help to reduce poverty, not just by helping people do better in the existing system, but by educating people so that the system can be transformed into one that is more helpful and truly educational.

Students read texts from a school library in Chile.
[Arnaldo Guevara/Ministerio de Educación, Chile]

7

Educational Policies and Equity in Chile

Juan Eduardo García-Huidobro
Ministerio de Educación, Chile

This chapter analyzes some measures taken under the Chilean Education Reform (1990–1998) that have been geared toward achieving equity in education. The chapter begins with a general reflection about the growing importance of education in the quest for equity. It then examines educational policy through the lens of equity, highlighting two programs as examples of positive discrimination. Finally, the last section discusses how much success these policies have had in reaching their goals.

THE IMPORTANCE OF EDUCATION FOR EQUITY

From 1990 to the present, the role of education in fostering equitable and sustainable human development has been stressed more than in previous decades, as evidenced by the various debates and forums held throughout the decade.

Although a perennial theme, the role of education in achieving equity merits special consideration given the current context of globalization. Chile's ex-minister of education and newly elected president, Ricardo Lagos, expressed its timeliness when he said, "Did you know the difference between the inheritors and the disinherited of the seventeenth century? . . . land ownership. Marx arrived at the beginning of the nineteenth century and said the difference was rooted in ownership of the means of production, factories. The differences between inheritors and the disinherited of the next century will be access to education. That is why education is so important" (BID 1998).

The 1990 World Conference for Education for All in Jomtien, Thailand, ushered in the decade.[1] It underscored the universality that the learning process must have, advocating "education for all." It also established education as a special type of human necessity, as basic as food and shelter. Learning is a fundamental need of people, be it children, youth, or adults, that is inextricably linked to equity because it provides people with the capacity to develop themselves and to achieve autonomy or independence in different spheres of knowledge.[2]

In Latin America, the importance of education for equity has also dawned during the last few years. Education has become more of a focus in light of the need to evaluate the present and future of the region in terms of its economic incorporation into the international context. The model for this "economic insertion" that has had the most success is presented by the Comisión Económica Para America Latina (CEPAL), a UN economic commission for Latin America, and the United Nations Educational, Cultural, and Scientific Organization (UNESCO) in their publication *Education and Growth: The Axis of Productive Transformation with Equity*.[3] The publication proposes that productive transformation is compatible with political democratization and growing social equity given that it is accompanied by an equitable expansion and improvement of education. The expansion of education also would require the incorporation and deliberate and systematic distribution of technical progress (CEPAL-UNESCO 1992, 15).[4]

The arguments to justify a strong relationship between access to education and social justice are long running, but they acquire new force in the current context. Neoliberal strategies intend to reduce equity by overcoming poverty while simultaneously negating the problematic character of the lack of social mobility and equality of opportunities. These policies also fail to acknowledge that the appeal of democracy is that it not only represents a form of governance but also forwards an ideal of justice and community life. Given this perspective, by expanding the range of democracy, the theme of equity in education is seen as one of enhancing equality of opportunities in education which in turn is closely tied with the legitimacy of social order and specifically with the market as the provider of goods.

Another way to propose equality of opportunities is to relate it to certain basic rights that society must guarantee—in other words, to the "basic rights of citizenship" (Rivas 1996). This equality forms the foundation of social order. The legitimacy of a democratic order is upheld in the sustained effectiveness that this principle of equality of opportunity holds or does not hold. Furthermore, there is no other area that makes this more evident than educational equity. If all children truly had the same opportunities to access the "dominant cultural scripts" that allow them to move freely throughout society, social mobility would be an everyday occurrence and the legitimacy of the social order would be unshakable. However, when inequality is transmitted intergenerationally, the social order that preserves inequalities becomes more illegitimate based on those very privileges. The former becomes even clearer when the society has chosen the market to assign resources so basic to well-being, such as work. An answer to this concern would be an educational system that provides greater equality to enter this market.

Education is also offered as a palliative against the piercing inequalities created by economic growth. Today it is widely known that economic development does not necessarily increase the quality and quantity of human development (PNUD 1996). Growth, polarized and concentrated, is experienced by some without increased employment for others. There are 358 people worldwide whose assets surpass the combined annual wages of countries inhabited by 45 percent of the world population. Chile is beginning to dangerously resemble the countries that possess the greatest differences between the rich and the poor. At the present time there are differences of forty times per capita between the highest and lowest tenth of the population. The presence and persistence of educational inequality reinforce economic disparities perpetuated over time and in turn are reflected in disparities in the quality of citizenship experienced by people. As an alternative to this schema, one of the most effective means to align human development to economic growth is to invest in education and training.

In summary, educational opportunities in contemporary society are assuming growing importance. The advance of democratic ideas, the modern idea of equality between people and the existence of a meritocracy, is inextricably tied to the condition of equality of opportunity in education for all. Today we see with greater clarity that the realization of this condition entails the elimination of barriers to academic success based on social origin along with the provision of substantial support and the opening of avenues toward educational success to the poorest members of society.

For education to contribute to societal justice, it first must be fair to all. However, it is known that the poor have fewer opportunities to access educational services. This inequality feeds and creates another vehicle by which inequality is transmitted and multiplied. Primary school becomes a means of reproducing social inequalities that are inevitably tied to the different levels of skills acquired by the children of the poor and the non-poor. It also generates great differences as well as potential exclusion that are overcome only with great difficulty by those who start off marginalized (Zúñiga 1989).

So how do you achieve equality in education? The world consensus with respect to equality of opportunities in education has led to insisting that everyone receive a similar education (United Nations 1949). This parity in education has not yet been achieved, and if achieved, it still would be an insufficient mechanism. In order to guarantee similar outcomes between diverse members of society, education must be different in that it "discriminates" positively in favor of children, youth, and adults who have fewer opportunities to learn. In other words, education must be in favor of the poorest and those with the least cultural capital. Furthermore, this redistributive and compensatory property is economically rational, given that it avoids wastage of scarce resources that results from policies that favor access without regard for learning achievement.

EQUITY IN THE CHILEAN SYSTEM OF EDUCATION

In 1990, at the beginning of President Patricio Aylwin's term, the Chilean education system demonstrated important gains in coverage, an increase in the average number of school years of Chileans, and a reduction of illiteracy. In 1990 close to 100 percent of Chilean children went to school, more than 75 percent of fourteen to seventeen year olds attended institutions of secondary education, illiteracy declined to 5.3 percent, and the average number of school years per citizen was 8.6.[5]

Despite these gains, indicators of educational quality showed low levels of quality and especially equity. For that reason, since 1988 a standardized test, the System of Measurement of Quality of Education (SIMCE) has been administered to measure student performance.[6] The results have brought deficiencies in the performance of primary education to public attention. For example, fourth graders countrywide scored only 60.1 percent in math and 61.2 percent in Spanish on the 1990 SIMCE test. The SIMCE test has only recently been given to secondary school students. The results of these tests confirm what can only be expected, that the poor quality of primary education leads to continued and amplified poor quality of secondary school performance levels.[7]

Nevertheless, these averages cloak the gross disparities in the quality of education received and the results obtained by children of different social sectors. Preparation for school is not equal for each of the groups. While half of the children in the top twentieth percentile of the highest income families attend more than one year of preschool, only two out of ten children coming from the lowest income families do. To highlight the disparities even further, the gap between students who attend the "best" and the "worst" schools is more than forty points on the SIMCE test.[8] This disparity is also evident when comparing private and public schools. Students in private schools (which account for 8 percent of all students) scored 80 percent on the SIMCE test, students in schools privately subsidized by the state scored 63.9 percent, and public school students scored 56.7 percent.[9]

To overcome this reality, educational policies from 1990 onward have been geared toward increasing quality and reducing inequalities in education. These two strategies are intimately intertwined, constituting a unified and directed strategy to attack the poor quality of education that affects the majority of the Chilean population. Policies aimed at bettering the whole of subsidized education (those that are administered by local governments as well as those administered privately) promote the goal of equity.

In the rest of this chapter, I will summarize the principal policies that affect subsidized education, underscore some relevant strategies of positive discrimination within those policies, and explain focused programs that support the most vulnerable primary schools. In the last section, I will discuss the reach and limitations of these policies.

Educational Policies, 1990–1998

The first thing to keep in mind with respect to the expanding policies aimed at achieving equity is that they occur in a context of extensive effort to improve subsidized education. This effort has substantially improved the conditions of primary and secondary schools in the country. One way to assess the magnitude of this change is to look at the shift in public funds directed to education. From 1990 to 1997 there was an increase of $2.641 billion (all dollar amounts are in U.S. dollars unless otherwise specified) invested in education by the government. This shift in monies has produced the following changes: an increase of teachers' salaries by 99.3 percent, free distribution of textbooks from the first grade in primary school through the second year of secondary school, books for all primary school classes, and the creation of school libraries. In addition, a computer network that connects approximately 3,000 primary and secondary schools has been created and within a year will connect up to 5,000 schools. Funds have also been siphoned to improve school infrastructure increasing from $262 million in 1990 to $872 million in 1997. Since 1997, all schools in the country have begun to transition from half school days to full school days, allowing for an eight-hour school day. So far 4,200 schools have fully incorporated the changes affecting 500,000 students, which comprise 18 percent of the total student population in Chile.

Based on this new foundation, pedagogy and curricular reforms have been forged that seek to make the content of education and the method of teaching and learning current. From a strategic point of view, the crux of these changes has been in the transformation of primary and secondary schools, generating conditions so schools have the possibility to become dynamic and fine-tuned to the necessities of their students with growing independence and creativity. Along this line, improvement programs geared toward achieving quality and equity in both primary and secondary education[10] have been housed under the Fund for Educational Improvement Projects. This umbrella agency receives proposals from schools that want to improve the learning and teaching process according to their local context and reality. So far more than 7,000 schools have accessed funds. More recently, with the full school day, two hours per week have been allotted for collective technical work of teachers. These two hours make up part of the hours remunerated for all teachers of educational institutions that have phased in the full school day.

Diverse Methods of Positive Discrimination

Based on the general improvement experienced in the educational system previously discussed, some policies are designed to lend more support to primary and secondary schools that serve children from the lowest-income families and with the least cultural capital. The following is a summary of some significant examples of this shift in policy:

- In July 1991, the Statute of Professionals in Education established a supplement in the salary of teachers working in high-need areas. These high-need areas were educational institutions with one or more of the following characteristics: difficult to access, in an area of high urban conflict, serving families of extreme poverty, or serving indigenous populations.
- Different programs have favored various methods of positively discriminating in favor of the most vulnerable schools. For example, in the Educational Improvement Projects more opportunities are given to projects in schools at the highest academic risk. The secondary schools most at risk entered into the MECE Program (Program for the Improvement of the Quality of Education). Currently, primary and secondary schools that serve the most needy populations have been given access to funding to improve school infrastructure in order to accommodate the full school day.[11]
- Various compensatory programs have been created such as the School Health Program. This program enables children from first grade to be checked and provided with the necessary medical treatments each year. The Summer Camp Program, created in 1991, makes it possible for 41,000 "high-risk" children to attend camps for one week during the summer. Preexisting programs have also been amplified, such as the distribution of free textbooks and school lunches. These programs were expanded to include all students classified as vulnerable, approximately 900,000 students, which makes up one-third of the student population in Chile.
- In an effort to prevent repetition in educational institutions that serve poor populations, a special grant provides funding for teachers to provide academic reinforcement during the second half of the year and after-school hours to children who have demonstrated that they are slow to master the learning process in some subjects.[12]
- Since 1996, grants to rural primary and secondary schools that were small in size and isolated increased to compensate for difficulties incurred in running the schools. The result is that 4,290 educational institutions that serve 12 percent of the student population have the right to access this additional funding proportionately based on the size of the school.

Targeted Programs

This section refers to educational interventions that give special support, or positive discrimination, to schools that present conditions of high academic risk.

The 900 Schools Program[13]   In March 1990, the first education reform undertaken by President Patricio Aylwin's administration was the implementation of the 900 Schools Program. It aimed at supporting 10 percent of the worst performing primary schools so that children attending these schools could achieve the basic culturally accepted skills.

The program focused its efforts on educational institutions that demonstrated the greatest deficits in quality as determined by the SIMCE test. The 900 Schools Program seeks to make up for the differences that children come with to school, giving opportunities to the most needy to guarantee acceptable levels of learning.[14] The objective is to improve the learning gains of children from first to fourth grade in reading, writing, and mathematics, considered the fundamental base of further learning.[15]

During its first two years, the 900 Schools Program concentrated on actions to improve conditions in schools. These included the improvement of school infrastructure; the provision of textbooks for all children in the first cycle of primary education (first to fourth grade); and the supply of school libraries, didactic materials, and other materials such as ditto and mimeograph machines. Since 1992, these actions extended to subsidized schools, which have received support of a more pedagogical nature

Teacher workshops have also been offered to improve the practices of teachers in the first cycle of primary education in each of the schools. The workshops have focused on analyzing the learning process with respect to the teaching of language arts and mathematics as well as identifying the adequate tools to tackle these subjects. The goal is to increase teaching capacity to promote effective learning of the culturally relevant basic skills (reading, writing, and mathematics) of the students. These workshops also work to identify strategies that favor expression, creativity, and self-esteem of students. Particular importance is given to teachers' understanding of their students' cultural environment, as well as relations among the school, families, and the community. These activities take place during the teachers' work time in weekly or biweekly sessions supported by the technical-pedagogical supervisors from the Ministry of Education.

The workshops open up spaces in schools for participatory technical work as well as give teachers autonomy. These spaces give teachers the opportunity to take hold of their practice and see it as a place of innovation and of professional responsibility.

The program also directly supports children through learning workshops (referred to as TAP). These workshops serve children from third to fourth grades who are not performing at grade level. Community monitors work with fifteen to twenty children after school twice a week. The activities of the workshops seek to reinforce what is taught at school and simultaneously increase the self-esteem of children who have had challenging experiences at school. The methodology used is active-participatory, incorporating games as educational tools. The children also receive special notebooks, so they practice with their families at home what they have learned in school.

The community monitors are adolescents (eighteen or older) who have gone to secondary school in the community. They are selected by the principal and teachers of the school and then trained and supported in workshops by technical supervisors from the Ministry of Education.

Additionally, didactic materials were created that permit the principals of schools to work with teams of teachers in the conception and implementation of school improvement plans that integrate the various emphases of the program while inviting the participation of teachers, parents, and students. From 1993, through a partnership with the Pontificia Universidad Católica de Chile and the Center for Educational Research and Development (CIDE), this work was expanded and further geared toward the promotion of education by bringing community officials into the process. Thirty-nine neighborhoods have worked within this framework.

Between 1990 and 1997, 2,260 schools have participated in the 900 Schools Program. With their entry into the program, the performance of their students has significantly improved. Table 7.1 shows the number of participating schools and students in the program from 1990 to 1997.

The decision to maintain coverage at approximately 10 percent of the schools is relatively arbitrary. It has been a priority to serve schools according to necessity so that the available personnel and tasks that the supervisors must handle can be given due attention. In any case, two things must be taken into account: 10 percent of the schools in Chile represent 15 percent of the total student population and schools leaving the program, upon attaining satisfactory levels of quality and independence, allows the Ministry to begin to serve other schools.[16]

The Rural Primary Education Program   Rural education is an extreme example of the low quality and the lack of equity that is seen in primary education. All of the qualitative indicators show that there is a gross disparity between rural education and urban education. A phenomenon of rural schools is that here are many schools that serve few students; the average number of students per school is ninety. Forty-five percent of Chilean schools are rural, amounting to more than 400 schools, but only 15.8 percent of the total student population is rural. Despite the small size of the majority of these schools, close to 80 percent are multigrade and 75 percent have only one, two, or three teachers. Because of the low number of teaching staff, they are often "incomplete," not offering seventh or eighth grades. Student performance is low. These schools have the

TABLE 7.1

Coverage of the 900 Schools Program (1990–1997)

Participants	1990	1991	1992	1993	1994	1995	1996	1997
Schools	969	1,278	1,123	1,097	1,060	988	900	862
Teachers	5,237	7,129	6,494	5,406	5,626	5,135	4,806	4,414
Students								
(grades 1–4)	160,182	219,594	191,451	170,214	165,758	152,326	141,316	137,689
Monitors	2,086	2,800	2,500	2,350	2,300	2,186	1,802	1,745
Children in								
learning								
workshops	34,000	50,000	40,000	38,000	35,000	32,900	28,000	26,000

lowest scores in performance tests, and most rural regions also have the lowest level of learning (see Table 7.2).

These conditions justified the creation of a special program targeting multigraded rural schools. This program was an offshoot of the 900 Schools Program in 1991, serving 106 schools with one to two teachers in seven neighborhoods pertaining to the IX and X regions. The program was then based in the Ministry of Education in 1992 and included all schools with three or fewer teachers. In 1996 the program was expanded to include all rural schools. Table 7.3 provides information on the expansion of the program.

The Rural Primary Education Program aimed to improve the quality and equity of these rural schools, defining the central problems and outlining strategies to face them. Teachers at these schools felt severe professional isolation. They lacked professional groups that would allow them to examine their pedagogical practice, a serious concern because these teachers confront extremely complicated tasks, where they must teach combined grades without proper training or materials to do so. At the same time, the overwhelming and imposing influence of urban culture on the system has deeply influenced the curriculum and textbooks. This urban bias constitutes an obstacle to teaching rural children.

To face these challenges, the Rural Primary Education Program delineated three lines of action:

- Teacher training that seeks to overcome the isolation of the rural teacher by establishing micro-centers. These micro-centers are sites for monthly meetings for teachers from an average of seven to eight schools. The first stage of training, during the first year of the project, consists of three days of workshops. Between workshops during the first year and monthly in the following years, teachers meet for one entire day at the micro-center. It is a day of team planning, exchange of experiences, and evaluation. There are 507 micro-centers serving the 3,338 rural schools.
- The design of a pedagogy that accommodates the local cultures and elaborates a strategy of multigrade schooling. These designs have been incorporated into the *Handbook for Curriculum Development* for multigrade schools, which makes up the core of the teacher training.

TABLE 7.2

Number of Students Attending Urban and Rural Schools in 1993 and Their Efficiency Indicators

Data	Urban	Rural	Total
Enrollment	1,733,833	326,866	2,060,699
Schools*	4,613	4,000	8,613
Passed	91.95%	87.48%	91.24%
Failed	6.26%	10.31%	6.90%
Left school	1.80%	2.21%	1.86%

*Estimate.

TABLE 7.3

Expansion of the Coverage of Rural MECE (1992–1996)[a]

Year	Schools	%	Teachers	%	Students	%
1992	629	18.8	944	18.4	20,993	21.7
1993	701	21.0	1,078	21.0	20,438	21.2
1994	711	21.3	1,038	20.3	21,527	22.3
1995	969	29.0	1,555	30.3	24,127	25.0
1996	328	9.8	506	9.9	9,514	9.8
Total	3,338[b]	100.0	5,121	100.0	96,540[c]	100.0

[a]The figures are cumulative; they indicate schools that enter each year into the program with the understanding that once in the program, they will remain incorporated.
[b]Of these schools, the majority (65 percent) have only one teacher, 23 percent have two teachers, and the remaining 12 percent have three teachers.
[c]By adding to this figure the number of students participating in the 900 Schools Program, 21 percent of all students in basic education are reached by targeted programs.

- The design and production of auxiliary texts, specially created to aid teachers in rural multigrade schools. They allow for both individual and group strategies while taking into account the context of the rural environment as a starting point for further learning. All children in these schools have received auxiliary texts each year of the program.

THE REACH AND LIMITATIONS OF EQUITY POLICIES

Overall Analysis

The educational policies discussed can be viewed as successful. For example, if the results of the SIMCE test are examined, they show a sustained improvement in the learning of primary school students since 1990. The national results in math and language in fourth and eighth grade have increased by eleven points in six years (see Figure 7.1). To evaluate this information, it is important to keep in mind that they are tests that cut across all sectors of society and that the improvement of eleven points is equivalent to an overall improvement of 18 percent in fourth-grade scores and 20.2 percent in eighth-grade scores. Furthermore, it is important to observe in the case of the fourth-grade tests that the SIMCE aims to measure basic cultural skills that are difficult to quantify. The exams can downplay the complexity of the skills being tested. Furthermore, the tests can become easier with time as the children become used to taking them.

The results in Figure 7.1 indicate that the majority of Chilean children today know more than students six years ago.[17] Also, despite the persistence of strong inequalities in the country, there is a reduction in the gap in performance between low-performing and high-performing schools based on the SIMCE results for the fourth grade. There is no evidence for this in the eighth grade (see Tables 7.4 and 7.5). These results are in accordance with the program's emphasis on the first cycle of primary education.[18]

Judging from this evidence, the policy demonstrates a successful and promising beginning. However, the direction and emphases must be sustained and deepened in order to reach the goals of the reform, making quality education a reality for all.

FIGURE 7.1

National Results of Primary Education (1990–1997)

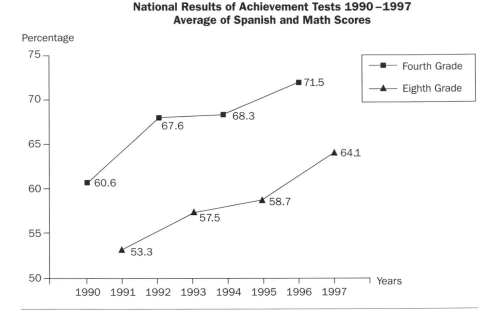

National Results of Achievement Tests 1990–1997
Average of Spanish and Math Scores

Evaluation of the 900 Schools Program

To evaluate the achievement of the program's goals of increasing the learning of primary school students attending poorly performing schools, the SIMCE test that measures the level of academic performance in fourth grade is used. Schools that entered the program in 1990 scored an average of 43.1 points in 1988. By the end of 1990, the average score had increased to 52.1 points. Scores continued to increase; in 1992 the average was 60.9 points, in 1994 it increased to 61.6, and in 1996 the average score was at 64.3 points. Because this improvement in scores was accompanied by a general increase in scores across the country, the only way to attribute them to the 900 Schools

TABLE 7.4

Comparison of the SIMCE Results in the Fourth Grade Between
the Performance of the Highest and Lowest Tenth Percentiles

	Average for Math and Spanish				Changes Between Selected Periods			
	1990	1992	1994	1996	90–96	90–92	92–94	94–96
Type A schools (Highest 10%)	78.2	85.5	84.8	86.7				
Type B schools (Lowest 10%)	40.2	46.3	48.8	53.6				
Gap	38.0	39.2	36.0	33.1	−4.9	+1.1	−3.2	−2.9

TABLE 7.5

Comparison of the SIMCE Results in the Eighth Grade Between
the Performance of the Highest and Lowest Tenth Percentiles

	Average for Math and Spanish				Changes Between Selected Periods			
	1991	1993	1995	1997	91–97	93–95	95–97	93–97
Type A schools								
(Highest 10%)	73.1	78.0	78.1	82.6				
Type B schools								
(Lowest 10%)	34.3	38.5	40.9	44.6				
Gap	38.8	39.5	37.2	38.0	−0.8	−2.3	+0.8	−1.5

Program is to compare the achievement of these schools with the rest of the schools not involved in the program. Table 7.6 and Figure 7.2 show that schools in the program have increased by an average of 5.8 points more than the rest of subsidized schools,[19] which implies that the gap between the performance of the worst-performing and the best-performing schools has decreased.

Given this average increase, it is interesting to note the different courses of action taken by schools in the program. In the first place, it is important to show that 60.4 percent of the schools that are part of the program have shown an improvement in performance results of 24.1 percent, a sizable improvement given that the results have begun to surpass the average of public schools of their region (from being 10 percent of the worst performing to 50 percent). A number (34.6 percent) of schools in the program have not been able to improve, and among them, 194 schools have not been able to improve despite their participation in the program for four years.

An external evaluation has been conducted by the Center of Educational Research and Development (CIDE) since the inception of the 900 Schools Program. UNESCO and the Swedish Cooperation Agency (which funded the program in 1990 and 1991) have also conducted evaluations. In 1991, the evaluation conducted by CIDE researchers aimed to test basic and higher skills pertaining to math and language arts.

TABLE 7.6

Comparison of SIMCE Scores Between Subsidized Schools and Schools
in the 900 Schools Program (Test of Achievement in Spanish/Mathematics
in Fourth Grade)*

	1988	1990	1992	1994	1996	Gap Between 1988 and 1996
Free (subsidized) schools	52.5	59.0	66.4	67.7	67.9	15.4
900 Schools Program schools	43.1	52.1	60.9	61.6	64.3	21.2
Gap	−9.4	−6.9	−5.5	−6.1	−3.6	5.8

*Subsidized schools correspond to the average of the total municipal schools as well as municipal schools that receive subsidies measured by the SIMCE test. The schools that make up the 900 Schools Program have been disaggregated. Schools in the 900 Schools Program are those that entered into the program between 1990 and 1996. Therefore, the results reflect the performance of the 2,099 schools that had participated one or more years in the program.

FIGURE 7.2

Changes in SIMCE Scores in Free Schools and in Schools Participating
in the 900 Schools Program (1988–1996)

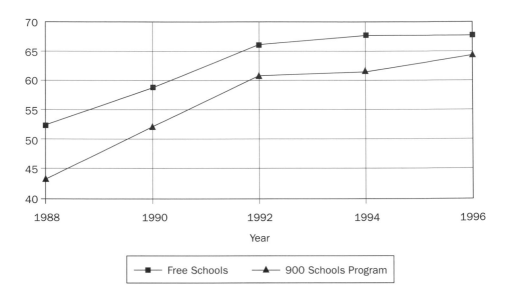

Year

- ■ - Free Schools   - ▲ - 900 Schools Program

The tests were administered to a group of schools participating in the 900 Schools Program and another group that, although similar, did not receive the benefits offered by the program. In language, the greatest improvement was in the fourth grade (3.3 percent). Smaller improvements were seen in first and second grades as well. In math, the results ranged from 9.7 percent in second grade to 3.7 percent in first grade. This same evaluation observed teachers in Spanish and math classes at the beginning of the implementation of the program and in the second half of the school year. These observations confirmed that for schools involved in the program, an interactive style became more pervasive later in the year, there was less repetition, and there was greater opportunity for students to take initiative and engage in individual and group work. Furthermore, class libraries were used more frequently, although silent reading suggested by the program was seldom conducted. In math, it was observed that students and teachers engaged in oral work and the resolution of problems. In the opinion of the supervisors that were interviewed, professors were reexamining their practice critically, they had reevaluated the expectations they had for their students, and they showed more respect for the cultural context of the children they taught.

UNESCO's evaluation of the program in 1992 provides some perspective about the impact of the program. Its study emphasizes the most efficient use of resources upon implementing the wide range of actions geared to improving the quality of education. It integrated inputs from the Ministry of Education, experts from universities and independent academic centers, as well as information about successful experiments in nonformal education (TAP). The participants from various institutions, despite having a positive regard of the program, stated that they did not have enough evidence on which to base a judgment and delineate explicit concrete achievements of the teachers. Furthermore, the information was not sufficient to make decisions with respect to the learning needs of the students and their families.

An evaluation of the TAP program (Cardemil 1993; Cardemil et al. 1994) concluded that it improves the learning outcomes of children who have been identified as having the greatest difficulties in the educational system. It also concludes that the community monitors are an important contribution to the success of the students in the program. Furthermore, the experience of working with children and in sharing space with other adolescents has had a great impact on the community monitors' lives.

In summary, the evidence shows that the 900 Schools Program has been successful in the majority of cases. With only a few resources, significant gains have been attained. Furthermore, the concept and practice of positive discrimination has been incorporated into Chilean educational policies. The problem that remains is the work to do in a third of schools that were not reached by this program.

Evaluation of the Rural Primary Education Program

The Rural Primary Education Program has been in place for nearly seven years. During the last three years of the program, all schools have transitioned into multigrade teaching. Multigrade classrooms are now an integral piece of the Chilean rural landscape and make up an important part of the life and work of the teachers of these schools. A notable aspect of the program is the enthusiasm with which a majority of rural teachers talk about it, attributing the alleviation of professional isolation and anonymity to the program.

Based on the available test results, the increases in student achievement are extraordinary (see Table 7.7). To evaluate the importance of these results, we can compare them with national performance levels. The gap between these schools and others decreased by two-thirds. It is not an exaggeration to say that because of the program, rural schools with three teachers or less entered into the world of national education (see Table 7.8).[20] Furthermore, other measures of efficiency confirm the improvement. Students who were left back decreased from 12.7 percent in 1990 to 7.5 percent in 1996. In addition, dropouts decreased from 2.4 percent to 1.8 percent.

These promising figures are supported by the difference in enthusiasm expressed by the teachers and the students in these schools. One testimony of a teacher from Ninhue expressed it like this: "As rural professors we have always been alone; no one listened to us. Now we have the possibility to analyze how the children behave. We have learned to know ourselves with each other" (MINEDUC 1998, 36). Another teacher from Los Lagos adds, "The micro-center is very positive because we have been able to exchange ideas and have conversations. It's an experience you wait for. The other positive aspect is that we have learned to organize ourselves and to work independently" (Universidad Austral and Universidad de Playa Ancha 1998).

TABLE 7.7

SIMCE Fourth-Grade Test Results of the Rural Primary Education Program*

	1992	1996	Variation
Mathematics	34.3	60.8	26.5
Spanish	34.1	59.4	25.3

*This information is based on data from the Departamento de Estudios del Ministerio de Educación. All schools in the Rural Primary Education Program that had been part of the program since 1992 and for which SIMCE measurements existed in 1992 and 1996 are included. Total: 196 schools, which is equivalent to 6.1 percent of the schools in the program and 31.1 percent of the schools in 1992.

Final Considerations

The overall results of the policies are positive. There is a considerable and well-distributed improvement in the quality of education of the majority of schools involved, which signals a powerful advance in achieving equality of opportunities in the country. Furthermore, the slow but continual decrease in the gap between the highest- and lowest-performing extremes provides us with evidence that we must continue in the direction of positive discrimination started in 1990. It continues to be reasonable to think that children with less family cultural capital can begin to enjoy the results of growing quality if they attend schools that have well-trained and motivated teachers and that have resources (books, appropriate and adequate didactic materials, access to computer technology, and appropriate infrastructure).

However, several critiques of the current policies have been made from the point of view of equity. These critiques offer suggestions for improvement and increased commitment to the actions taken so far.[21]

One group of critiques centers around the delays in implementing the reforms and the low level of financial investment rather than the policies themselves. "In Chile there has been a slowness to respond to the needs of the poorest groups and as a result, to achieve greater equity in the distribution of the educational service" (Espínola 1996). To increase the pace of reform, there must be a greater commitment to increasing investment in positive discrimination; "the poor quality of learning of the neediest children and the lack of educational opportunities of youth of these same sectors demands more radical targeted policies." This is demonstrated through the case of the 900 Schools Program. This program's total cost from 1990 to 1992 was $16.8 million,

TABLE 7.8

Comparison Between Results of the Schools in the Rural Primary Education Program and National Averages*

	1992	1996	Variation
National average	67.7	71.5	+3.8
Rural schools	34.2	60.5	+26.3
Gap	33.8	11.0	−22.8

*The results are the average of Spanish and mathematics scores.

which did not "make up 1 percent of the expenses used for primary education in 1992" (Espínola 1996).

It is difficult to estimate a reasonable proportion of resources for compensatory programs. One possible response is to tie the contribution of the state to the lowest-income sectors with the expenses that the highest-income families spend on their children. Two possibilities may be promising to study. One proposal is that if Chile's private education comprises about 8 percent of total enrollments, the state is saving this amount of money and can therefore siphon this proportion of funding to the poorest members of society.[22] The second alternative is to direct funds, in the name of positive discrimination, to poor public schools in the amount that parents contribute to schools cofinanced by the public and private sectors, $44 billion in 1997. These resources can be used to improve the subsidies of poor urban schools and provide nonexisting services to poor sectors such as preprimary education from four years of age onward.

Two other viewpoints expose other limitations of the policy. One critiques the policy for being too intra-school and the other asserts that resorting to the market will not benefit the poor.

In relation to the unilateral character of educational policies, it is important to note that the policies do not consider factors external to schools, such as families. This is a serious exclusion, given that 60 percent of the difference in school performance is explained by factors external to school, one of the most important being the educational climate of the home. Forty to 50 percent of the impact of this environment can be attributed to characteristics of the socioeconomic and familial contexts (Cohen 1996; Gerstenfeld 1995). The suggestion that comes from this critique is the necessity to attune educational and social policies with actions underway in communities, assuring the participation of parents in the education of the poorest groups (Cohen 1996; Hopenhayn 1996).

On the other hand, it should be noted that the introduction of decentralization and market mechanisms worsen equity as proposed by Espínola (1996). Those who possess the greatest economic and cultural capital quickly access the available resources, while the poor remain cautious of taking advantage of offers that progressively deteriorate and vanish. "In Chile, a market system, apparently neutral, operates.[23] However, the weak intervention of the state to counteract the disadvantages of the resource poor social strata transforms the system into one that is highly inequitable" (Espínola 1996). In contrast to municipal schools, private schools are not obligated to accept all children who seek admission. The result is stratification and segregation of schools. Forty-two percent of the students attending municipal schools are from the poorest 20 percent of homes, while only 28.8 percent of private school students are from that social sector. Private schools tend to avoid having a high number of low-income children because they cost more to teach. To compound inequities, there is a tendency for private schools to accept families that are more willing and able to fund school activities.

These critiques suggest that what has been done remains insufficient and that positive discrimination should be pursued further. Furthermore, two concrete proposals can be drawn from this study. One is the possibility of exploring and studying the effect of sliding subsidies, allotting more to those who need the most.[24] The other is to improve and strengthen regulations governing institutions that work with public funds so as not to ignore the needs of the poorest in society.

NOTES

1. See *Satisfaction of the Basic Necessities of Learning: A Vision for the Decade of the 90s,* Reference Document, World Conference on Education for All (New York: UNICEF, 1990).
2. This term refers to basic abilities required for autonomous learning: reading, writing, oral expression, arithmetic, resolution of math problems, and given the social context, other abilities such as computer skills, library skills, as well as the ability to interpret messages transmitted by mass media.
3. Analysis of education is undertaken in CEPAL's proposal of "productive transformation with equity."
4. In other places, "authentic or structural competition" versus "spurious competition" is discussed. Latin America, during the period between 1980 and 1990, is a case of spurious competition: the region opened to the rest of the world, and competition existed, but the minimum salary decreased by 40 percent.
5. The positive aspect of these figures is clear when compared to figures from thirty years earlier. In 1960 only 80 percent of children attended primary school, 14 percent of the population attended secondary school, and illiteracy was at 16.4 percent.
6. The SIMCE are standardized tests to measure the objectives of the program of study through testing of fourth and eighth graders every other two years.
7. For the math test in the second year of secondary school, the national average score was 47.2 percent in the general track and 38.6 percent in the vocational track.
8. For the fourth grade SIMCE test, 5 percent of students from the best schools scored 80.9 percent correct answers and 5 percent of students from the worst schools scored 40.5 percent.
9. These scores are average figures for Spanish language and math from 1990. It is important to keep in mind that these are schools that serve populations with different cultural capital. The mothers of children from private schools attended school for an average of 14.7 years, subsidized schools for an average of 10.4 years, and public schools for an average of 8.6 years (Ministerio de Educación 1998).
10. The programs contained under the Primary Education Quality and Equity Improvement Plan (1992–1997) have been a series of unified systematic interventions first targeting preschool and primary education and followed by secondary education. Both programs have been developed from loans offered by the World Bank.
11. The transition from double-shift schools to full-day schools requires schools to amplify the school infrastructure so that all children can go to class at the same time. This requires investments projected at $700 million. It also implies an increase in state subsidies of 34 percent to cover the greatest costs of the project.
12. This program was started in 1996 and serves each year close to 450,000 children, who make up approximately 18 percent of the students who attend subsidized schools.
13. For a complete discussion of this program, see *International Cooperation and Educational Development,* ed. M. Gajardo (Santiago: AGCI and CIDE, 1994), and particularly the articles by Filp, Undurraga, García-Huidobro, and Jara within this title.
14. See García-Huidobro (1994) for related information.
15. The 900 Schools Program has three foci: (1) to identify the schools at the lowest 10 percent of academic performance; (2) at these schools, to lend support to strengthen instruction from first to fourth grade; and (3) to include extra supports and innovation to assure learning in the fundamental culturally required competencies (language and mathematics).
16. This process of entry and exit occurred until 1997. Since 1998, schools are allowed to enter for a period of three years.
17. It is possible to argue that real improvement may be less than what is shown because students can become accustomed to these types of tests. But it is very difficult to isolate the

real learning when testing basic competencies. One may think that these tests are becoming easier each year. This is easily proven empirically by giving children one of the older tests. So far this has not been done.

18. The 900 Schools Program, until 1998, focused its programs only on the first cycle of education in rural primary schools. Given that the former do not have seventh and eighth grades, effects are most strongly felt in the primary cycle.

19. In Chile, 92 percent of basic education receives state subsidies. Sixty percent of the subsidies are administered by local governments and 32 percent come through private administration, though they are state funds.

20. The idea of "entry" into national education means that the schools began to have learning outcomes comparable with the rest of the nation with the enormous leap in points that these schools achieved.

21. The same centrality awarded to education in the quest for equity has multiplied the number of conversations about the theme. For example, two seminars were organized by CEPAL: Seminar-Workshop, "Secondary School Reform in Chile: Approaching Greater Equity?" which occurred April 11–15, 1995, and Seminar-Workshop, "Resource Provision for the Improvement of Quality and Education Equality," which took place January 10, 1996.

22. If we estimate, 8 percent of that which is spent on subsidies in 1996 is equivalent to $43,440,000,000 Chilean pesos, which is approximately $104 million.

23. Subsidies are the central mechanism of this system. The state offers an equal contribution to the municipal public schools and to not-for profit private schools per each student. The logic is that subsidies are dictated by demand. Theoretically, the mechanism allows for the family to freely choose the education for their children. In reality, there is unequal opportunity to utilize this choice and public service.

24. As of yet these measures have only been carried out in rural settings to allow the functioning of very small schools; they have not been related to the socioeconomic vulnerability of students.

REFERENCES

Banco Interamericano de Desarrollo. 1998. *America Latina Frente a la Desigualdad.* Washington, D.C.: Banco Interamericano de Desarrollo.

Cardemil, Cecilia. 1993. *Evaluación de los Talleres de Aprendizaje: Programa de las 900 Escuelas.* Santiago, Chile: Ministerio de Educación.

Cardemil, Cecilia, et al. 1994. Los talleres de aprendizaje: Evaluación de lo no-formal en el programa de las 900 escuelas. In *Cooperación Internacional y Desarrollo de la Educación,* ed. Marcela Gajardo, 251–296. Santiago, Chile: Centro de Investigación y Desarrollo de la Educación.

Comision Economica para America Latina. 1990. *Transformación Productiva con Equidad.* Santiago, Chile: United Nations.

CEPAL-UNESCO. 1992. *Educación y Conocimiento: Eje de la Transformación Productiva con Equidad.* Santiago, Chile: CEPAL-UNESCO.

Cohen, Ernesto. 1996. Educación y equidad: Una difícil convivencia. In Seminario-Taller, Asignación de recursos para el mejoramiento de la calidad y la equidad educativa. Santiago, Chile: CEPAL, January 10.

Espínola, Viola. 1996. Revisión de 15 años de política educativa en Chile: Ajustes en función de la equidad. In Seminario-Taller, Asignación de recursos para el mejoramiento de la calidad y la equidad educativa. Santiago, Chile: CEPAL, January 10.

Gajardo, Marcela, ed. 1994. *Cooperación Internacional y Desarrollo de la Educación.* Santiago, Chile: Centro de Investigación y Desarrollo de la Educación.

García-Huidobro, Juan Eduardo. 1994. Positive discrimination in education: Its justification and a Chilean example. *International Review of Education* 40(3–5): 209–221.

Gerstenfeld, Pascual. 1995. *Variables Extrapedagógicas y Equidad en la Educación Media.* Serie Políticas Sociales 9. Santiago, Chile: Comision Economica para America Latina.

Hopenhayn, Martín. 1996. El desafío educativo: En busca de la equidad perdida. In Seminario-Taller, Asignación de recursos para el mejoramiento de la calidad y la equidad educativa. Santiago, Chile: CEPAL, January 10.

Ministerio de Educación. 1998. *Prueba SIMCE 1997: Octavos Básicos.* Santiago, Chile: Ministerio de Educación.

Ministerio de Educación. 1998. *Reforma en Marcha: Buena Educación para Todos.* Santiago, Chile: Ministerio de Educación.

PNUD (United Nations Development Program). 1996. *Informe Sobre Desarrollo Humano 1996.* New York: Oxford University Press.

Rivas, Gonzalo. 1996. Rol del desarrollo productivo en el logro de la equidad. In *Los Caminos de la Equidad,* ed. Partido por la Democracia. Santiago, Chile: Partido Popular Democratico, Secretaria de Programas y Estudios.

UNICEF. 1990. Satisfacción de las necesidades básicas de aprendizaje: Una visión para el decenio de 1990. Reference Document for World Conference of Education for All, New York.

United Nations General Assembly. 1949. *Universal Declaration of Human Rights.* Lake Success, N.Y.: United Nations.

Universidad Austral y Universidad de Playa Ancha. 1998. *Estudio de Evaluación de la Línea de Educación Rural del Programa MECE.* Tercer Informe. Valdivia–Valparaíso, Chile: Universidad Austral and Universidad de Playa Ancha.

Zuñiga, Luis. 1989. La educación y la política social: El lugar de la educación de los niños en las estrategias de superación de la pobreza. In *¿Qué Pueden Esperar los Pobres de la Educación?* eds. Juan Eduardo García-Huidobro and Luis Zuñiga, 107–124. Santiago, Chile: Centro de Investigación y Desarrollo de la Educación.

Commentary

Noel F. McGinn, Harvard Graduate School of Education

This chapter contains an exciting message. It is possible to improve education dramatically! We now know how to generate large improvements in student achievement. Through these improvements we can reduce the difference in learning outcomes of poor and rural students, as compared to those who are urban and more wealthy.

García-Huidobro reports the latest results of education reforms carried out by the democratic governments that took power in Chile in 1990. Their motivation and impact should be understood in the context of a long history of education reforms. In the early 1960s, a conservative government in Chile attempted a major revision of curriculum aimed primarily at improvements in quality. Between 1965 and 1970 the Christian Democrats expanded access to primary schools and restructured secondary education. The Popular Unity government elected in 1970 attempted to provide equal opportunity and equal access to quality through a "unified school."

Strong reaction against this proposal to improve equity was one of the factors contributing to the military coup in 1973. The military government had its own set of reforms, designed principally to achieve higher efficiency (and eventually higher quality). Their main effect was to expand enrollments in publicly subsidized, privately owned schools that do not charge fees. As there are few private schools in rural areas, the policy increased disparities in access and retention between urban and rural areas.

The democratic government that took power in 1990 was committed to addressing the urban-rural imbalance and to improving the performance of schools that serve primarily poor children, urban or rural. In the government's view, these inequities were primarily a result of imbalances in the resources allocated to schools in the different areas. The reforms carried out under previous governments were left in place, but spending on education was increased dramatically.

Over the past nine years the democratic government has doubled spending on education, for both public and subsidized, non-fee-charging or "free" private schools. The central policy has been designed as "positive discrimination." García-Huidobro describes the various programs funded under the Projects of Educational Improvement (MECE). The list is impressive: the Chileans obviously had a well-developed understanding of how schooling works and where resources are required.

The impact of these programs (and growing public concern for education) on the quality of education is shown by reference to gains in scores on the national achievement test. Between 1990 and 1996, scores in Spanish and mathematics went from 60.5 to 71.5 for fourth grade, and from 53.3 to 64.1 for eighth grade. These improvements benefited all schools in Chile.

The most innovative program identified the 900 schools with average student achievement scores in the lowest decile on the national achievement test. The program provides learning workshops for students, training for teachers and principals, and materials and supplies. Parental participation is strongly encouraged. More than 2,000 schools have passed through the program.

García-Huidobro shows how the gap between scores of students in the 900 Schools Program and the "free" private schools has narrowed significantly between 1988 and 1996. Average scores in both kinds of schools have improved, but the gain in private schools was only 15 points, while it was 21 points for the schools that received positive discrimination. Other positive discrimination programs have produced equally encouraging results.

These results are taken as proof that it is possible to achieve equity and that one highly effective way to do so is to spend more in favor of those currently disfavored. García-Huidobro points out that other reforms, such as the decentralization and privatization of the military government, can have no positive effect unless they attack directly the root causes of poor student performance. Positive discrimination is the way to overcome the inequitable access to resources that plagues students and their families. What has been achieved is promising, he argues, but it is not enough. More resources are required to achieve equity.

The significance of García-Huidobro's work is so great it merits very careful scrutiny. Positive discrimination as a policy involves both a political decision to increase equity and a choice among means to do so. The stated assumption in García-Huidobro's presentation is that reducing inequity in terms of allocation of resources to education will reduce differences in learning outcomes, which will result in greater equity in terms of life outcomes, such as employment and income. This latter assumption is part of the "myth of progress" in which equality of education is assumed to ensure equality in all other aspects of life (Ramirez 1997).

It is called a myth as there is little convincing evidence to show that in fact equalization of educational opportunity results in social or economic equity. For example, in the United States white men continue to earn one-third more than women or minorities in equivalent occupations and with equivalent education. This inequity has persisted for thirty years despite rapid increases in the amount of education for all three groups. The distribution of income in industrialized societies is becoming more unequal despite increases in average level of educational attainment. More than equity in education is required to produce equity in society, and it is possible that a society can achieve high levels of social and political equity even though equity in education is relatively low.

The second part of the justification of positive discrimination is that it will reduce differences in learning outcomes. The evidence appears clear: students in schools receiving the additional resources and assistance improved their test scores more than students in schools not receiving resources and assistance. The gains are clear, and statistically significant. There is no doubt that positive discrimination had some impact.

There are, however, two points of concern. The first is about the current content of the positive discrimination program. All schools in Chile showed improved scores between 1988 and 1996, and those gains are much greater than the reduction in differences between schools receiving and not receiving additional resources and assistance. In other words, there are other factors improving education in Chile that are more effective than the positive discrimination undertaken by the government. We do not know what those factors are. Would it not be better to identify those factors, and to spend more on them for disadvantaged schools, than to continue the current program of positive discrimination?

The second concern is more fundamental. Although scores have improved in every time period measured, the rate of improvement has slowed with time. In fact, according to the data that García-Huidobro reports, scores appear to be leveling off. In other words, although positive discrimination had a big impact at the beginning, its impact is declining and may disappear. This is to be expected. As the program moves schools out of the bottom decile on average test scores, it takes in schools that initially were not as bad off as the first group. Each successive group, although it is at the bottom, is better than the bottom group before it. Probably (the data are not sufficient to tell) the difference between schools in resource availability is also declining, as a result of positive discrimination.

School resources are not the only determinant of student achievement. In fact, García-Huidobro tells us they account for only half of student learning. In other words, positive discrimination cannot be expected to achieve full equality in educational outcomes (test scores). More important, it may have achieved all that is possible in terms of reduction of differences in achievement test scores. Increased spending on this form of positive discrimination would therefore be a waste of valuable resources.

What then might be done to further reduce equity? We should admire what has been achieved in Chile, but recognize that it is an incomplete solution to the problem of inequity. The answer probably lies in focusing on the educational process itself. That is, rather than just spend more on schooling, we should explore whether other forms of education can overcome the disadvantages that children bring with them to the classroom. The schooling form of education that dominates in Chile and elsewhere in the world was designed more than 200 years ago. That design, which makes the teacher the prime source of knowledge and emphasizes transmission from teacher to student, favors children from middle- and upper-class urban families. Alternative designs focus on student production of personal knowledge and minimize the importance of "cultural capital" in learning. These new forms of education could, perhaps, reduce the heavy hand of social class that limits all efforts to achieve equity in schools.

The Chileans have shown that it is possible to achieve significant improvements in educational outcomes but that it requires spending more. Once countries are persuaded that equity is an achievable goal, we can work on creating an education more likely (than schooling) to overcome social and economic inequities in the larger society.

REFERENCE

Ramirez, F. O. 1997. The nation-state, citizenship, and educational change: Institutionalization and globalization. In *International Handbook of Education and Development: Preparing Schools, Students and Nations for the Twenty-First Century,* eds. W. K. Cummings and N. F. McGinn, 47–62. Oxford, England: Elsevier Science.

Students work on a school project in an elementary school in Santiago, Chile.
[Arnaldo Guevara/Ministerio de Educación, Chile]

8

Education and Poverty in Chile: Affirmative Action in the 1990s

Ernesto Schiefelbein and Paulina Schiefelbein
Universidad Santo Tomás and Centro de Investigación y
Desarrollo de la Educación, Santiago, Chile

Over the past decade, several diagnoses of the Chilean education system identified serious quality and equity issues which led the government to implement diverse strategies, none of which have managed to offer more individualized education where students construct their own knowledge. Problems with quality persist and teachers continue to use traditional methods of instruction suggesting that the many initiatives pushed by the government and various private organizations have not been able to change educational practice in the classroom. We believe that the limited impact of these efforts is due to the contaminating effect of traditional pedagogical approaches which conceive of people as biological universalities instead of as unique psychological beings and perpetuate the use of teaching methods centered on the average student, ignoring students' basic needs (Schiefelbein 1994).

Implementation of traditional pedagogy renders the national education system incapable of achieving objectives that pay greater attention to particular types of intelligences, incapable of accepting that learning is a personal construction of understanding, and incapable of respecting minorities' cultures (whatever they might be). Traditional pedagogy assumes that students' knowledge, values, and aptitudes are acquired in a cumulative, uniform fashion and that individual differences depend only upon the speed with which each student memorizes certain concepts and their applications. Nevertheless, it is acceptable today to pay attention to the differences among people and, given that there are different types of intelligence (Gardner 1991), to facilitate the progress of each according to individual characteristics. In short, whenever twentieth-century solutions have been applied to twenty-first-century problems, it has been impossible to meet the challenges faced by Chilean education today.

In the first section of this chapter, we describe changes in enrollment rates in the education system. In the second section, we comment on education policies implemented in the 1990s at all levels of education and then describe the degree to which the quality of basic public education in Chile has changed. We follow with a discussion of the reasons why the education policies that were implemented have not substantially changed the quality of education, and finally we draw some conclusions.

CHANGES IN PUBLIC EDUCATION ENROLLMENT RATES

Public education enrollment rates rose considerably between 1960 and 1996 (see Table 8.1), but differences in access were associated with the socioeconomic level of families (see Table 8.2). All children now enroll in the education system at some point and stay in school an average of ten years. It is remarkable that 82 percent of the corresponding age group now attends secondary school. Nevertheless, only one in four attends preschool.

The major difficulty that the poorest children have in terms of access to education can be seen in the distribution of enrollment by quintile of family income at different education levels (Table 8.2). Now that the country has near universal primary enrollment, and the differences among quintiles are indeed small and tend to decrease at the primary level, there are considerable differences at the other levels. In secondary school, there is a difference of 21.9 points between the most extreme quintiles and that difference is even greater for postsecondary education (51.2 points).

Provided there are no serious space limitations restricting access to the secondary level, these inequities in enrollment (the last column in Table 8.2) also imply differences in the opportunity to enroll, number of years in the system, and repetition rates (always associated with academic achievement). All of this information suggests that, up until now, even though there have been considerable increases in enrollment, incentives or conditions to permit timely access and adequate quality do not exist.

POLICIES OF THE 1990S TO PROMOTE EQUITY AND QUALITY

Diverse education reform efforts in Chile during the 1990s have sought to ensure equity in terms of access to education, as much at the primary level as the secondary and post-secondary levels, and in terms of quality of education, particularly among the urban and rural areas where half of the children whose parents have the lowest incomes can be found. Since 1990, affirmative action[1] programs targeted to improve equity and quality have been implemented to support improvements and innovations in pedagogy at all levels (preschool, primary, secondary, postsecondary) according to the needs of each level. It should also be noted that the government increased education spending between

TABLE 8.1

Net Enrollment Rates for All Levels of Education in Chile

Level	1960	1996
Preschool	2%	25%
Primary	80%	96%
Secondary	14%	82%
Postsecondary	8%	26%

Sources: MINEDUC (1998); Schiefelbein (1969); León (1998).

TABLE 8.2

Enrollment by Family Income Quintiles

Level	I	II	III	IV	V	Difference Between Extremes
Preschool	22.3	26.8	30.0	36.8	48.4	26.1
Primary	96.5	98.4	98.0	99.4	99.7	3.2
Secondary	75.3	81.0	89.3	95.3	97.2	21.9
Postsecondary	8.5	15.1	21.5	34.7	59.7	51.2

Source: MINEDUC (1998).

1990 and 1998 by $50 million a year (beginning with an initial budget of $600 million) and regulated and increased teachers' salaries in accordance with the Teacher Act.

Preschool Education

Assuming that it is beneficial for children of all socioeconomic levels to attend preschool, preschool enrollment rates reflect inequities in access to this level of education (Zona Pública 25, 1998). While half of the children from the highest income quintile attend preschool, only one in five from the lowest quintile attends (Table 8.2). In order to respond to these children's needs, the government has developed a set of programs designed to increase enrollment and improve the quality of education offered. These programs seek to:

- Increase government offerings through some decentralized alternatives.
- Maximize the coverage of existing programs by filling unused slots and extending geographic boundaries.
- Incorporate nonformal preschool programs, primarily for children in extreme poverty and isolated areas.
- Integrate diverse actors in the education process: mothers, fathers, family, and community.

The following is a summary of the major programs that seek to improve the preschool sector.

Enrollment

- Create new spaces and adapt existing facilities (MINEDUC 1998).
- Create preschool classes in public schools[2] for five and six year olds, to be taught by early childhood teachers, using existing space or newly constructed classrooms, providing furniture where necessary. Nutrition programs and instructional materials are also provided, thus benefiting 2,000 children (0.2 percent of the preschool population[3]).
- Use unfilled slots in the INTEGRA Open Centers (community centers) in order to provide a full-day program for children ages four and five; hire early childhood

teaching assistants. Nutrition programs and instructional materials are included, thus benefiting 12,000 children (1 percent of the age cohort).
- Use unfilled slots at the National Kindergarten Board's kindergartens (JUNJI) and create Family Centers to provide four and five year olds either full- or half-day programs; hire early childhood teaching assistants. Include nutrition programs and instructional materials, thus benefiting 4,000 children (0.3 percent of the preschool population).
- Provide full-time programs at the INTEGRA Rural Centers utilizing community members trained and supervised by early childhood educators. Include nutrition programs and instructional materials, thus benefiting 2,000 children (0.2 percent of the population).

Learning Conditions (MINEDUC 1998; Zona 2, 1995)

- Provide instructional materials and classroom libraries for 100 percent of the second transition levels (children ages four and five) in the subsidized schools.[4]
- Improve the adult-child ratios in JUNJI, INTEGRA, and MINEDUC kindergartens and family centers by hiring personnel to reduce existing deficits.
- Provide in-service training for personnel at higher levels so that they can replicate the process at the next lowest level. This program is coordinated by the Center for Pedagogical Research and Improvement (CPEIP) and reaches 100 percent of JUNJI, INTEGRA, and MINEDUC personnel. It benefits 3,450 professionals.

Nonformal Education: Parents' Participation and Quality of Life

- The Know Your Child Program was developed and tested by CPEIP for rural children who have not attended preschool. It operates under the local education authority and is composed of mothers and fathers who act as advisers to train the parents in their region. It provides printed material for children's use at home. The program serves 4,200 children (0.3 percent of the population) and functions in 245 rural communities in 13 regions of the country (Zona 25, 1998).
- The Infancy Improvement Program (PMI) is a nonformal education program that works with poor children under the age of six who are not served by any institution. It functions through key community members with the support of their community organizations. There are 105 local projects and between 1995 and 1997 approximately 20,000 children (1.7 percent of the population) benefited from its services (Zona 25, 1998).
- Through the National Local Integration Workshop (TILNA), the MINEDUC, together with the Educational Research and Interdisciplinary Program (PIIE), implemented workshops for teachers and parents at preschool centers to (1) exchange experiences among centers, (2) develop Education Improvement Programs, and (3) train education agents (Zona 2, 1995). This program benefits 5,882 formal and nonformal education agents, 800 teachers, and 4,000 parents (MINEDUC 1998).
- The Family Participation with Early Childhood–Primary Education Integration Program is an interdisciplinary team model made up of teachers, parents, and advisers who implement education activities in conjunction with the family at the education sites. It seeks to support development and learning in the social, affective,

logical, mathematical thinking, and language areas. Since 1994, 6,500 people have been trained; approximately 920 educational centers are implementing the program and 100,400 have benefited directly from it (Zona 25, 1998).

- Children and parents learn together in the Manolo and Margarita Program. Teaching guides and educators provide training for parents of children in the second transition level. Up until 1994, 60,000 parents in the Metropolitan Region and in Regions V, XI, and XII (Zona 2, 1995) received training. The program was extended to first grade in order to support articulation efforts between the preschool and primary sectors. It benefits 26,845 families and 1,586 education centers (Zona 25, 1998).
- Distance education, through communication media, is used to develop a mass parental education campaign. It is intended to make parents aware of the importance of the preschool years and promotes positive skills and practices in child rearing and education.

Primary Education

Programs at this level seek to improve the learning process by targeting high-risk groups. If indeed universal primary enrollment has been reached, there is still inequity in the academic achievement of children in the poorest sectors. The government's education policies seek to:

- Achieve equity in the quality of education by implementing programs in the neediest sectors.
- Decentralize resources and decision making, delegate management functions, but maintain salary negotiations as a centralized function.
- Support community participation in education.
- Design a basic curriculum that permits some local adaptation.
- Acquire and distribute books and equipment in a centralized fashion.

The following is a summary of the major programs that seek to improve primary education.

Conditions for Learning

- Provide textbooks for students in grades one to eight in four subject areas (Spanish, mathematics, history and geography, and natural sciences) together with teachers' guides and training in the use of these materials, and provide classroom libraries of some eighty volumes for all primary school grades (MINEDUC 1998).
- Provide resources to repair infrastructure, including playground equipment and landscaping, and to improve rural schools so that they can offer instruction for all primary grades (MINEDUC 1998).
- Prevent risks and provide health services to students through a program run by the National School Assistance and Scholarships Board (JUNAEB). This program benefits school children in first grade at subsidized primary schools (Zona 2, 1995).
- Generate an education information network among schools ("Enlace"). Since it began in 1992, 25 percent of primary schools have been incorporated in the network (Zona 13, 1996).

- Promote individualized instruction by CPEIP at 200 schools.
- Extend the school day by two hours for a total of seven hours.
- Improve teachers' salaries. Purchasing power was doubled during this period.

Programs Targeted at High-Risk Sectors

- Since 1990, the 900 Schools Program (P-900) has been implemented in 10 percent of the public schools with the lowest levels of learning and the highest levels of poverty in order to raise the quality of education in sectors-at-risk and incorporate the community into the school. The 900 Schools Program includes (1) implementation of Learning Workshops (TAP) where specially trained young people from the community work after school with third and fourth graders who have learning difficulties; (2) teacher training workshops in language arts and mathematics; (3) provision of textbooks and classroom libraries; (4) interdisciplinary and/or multisector teams made up of principals, pedagogical specialists, classroom teachers, heads of public education departments, and technical-pedagogical supervisors; and (5) cooperation with the Ministry of Justice to prevent problems such as dropouts and falling behind in school (MINEDUC 1998).
- The Improvement in Education Quality in Multigrade Rural Schools Program (MECE-Rural) assumes that pedagogical practices utilized in urban schools are not applicable to the improvement of student learning in the 3,338 multigrade, rural schools. This program's activities include (1) provision of textbooks and instructional materials for students in grades one to six that are suitable for rural areas and include local, concrete examples; (2) creation and operation of pedagogical coordination microcenters where local classroom teachers analyze and follow up on educational innovations and promote the development and implementation of Education Improvement Projects (PMEs); (3) teacher training to empower teachers to assume a leading role in overcoming their isolation; and (4) development of a new curriculum that relates local cultural information with global knowledge (MINEDUC 1998).

Out-of-School Programs   Family and student risk prevention assistance programs provide nutrition programs for primary and secondary students, room and board, scholarships for indigenous students at all levels, and school supplies (MINEDUC 1998).

Secondary Education

Secondary education enrollment rates rose quickly over the past thirty years, from 14 percent in 1960 to 82 percent in 1996. This increase in participation in public education represents a significant accomplishment for Chilean education, but it brought with it new problems and challenges. In 1991 the government was faced with a crisis in secondary education. Over the next two years, it developed an education improvement program along three lines of attack: (1) research efforts to describe and evaluate education quality, including curriculum, school administration, finance, and teacher preparation; (2) public opinion surveys; and (3) preparation of an education budget. In 1994 a pilot project, Secondary School Quality and Equity Improvement Program

(MECE-Media), was initiated in 124 secondary schools and by 1997, all education communities were involved, from the scientific-humanist to the technical-professional. There were two interventions at this level.

Investment in Resources and Conditions for Educational Development

- Create or modernize each institution's library.
- Deliver maps, videos, CDs, and other instructional materials for teachers and students.
- Deliver texts for use with a variety of teaching techniques.
- Expand facilities and improve equipment.
- Connect each institution to the education information network. This network consists of a two-year technical assistance program led by a national coordinator and seven regional centers, coordinated by the MECE program in Santiago and the University in Temuco (Zona 13, 1996).
- Implement the Youth Workforce Training Program ("Chile Joven"). Started in 1991, this program provides scholarships to assist students who drop out or leave the education system with entry into society and the workforce. In 1996 this program, inspired by the German dual training system, trained 7,500 low-income young people (Zona 14, 1996).

Improvement in Educational Processes and Learning Outcomes

- Strengthen the school administration team's work (human resources, human relations, and decision making), make changes in administration practices, and develop proposals to improve school management (Zona 2, 1995).
- Provide systematic support for teachers and instructional leaders through reflection and evaluation techniques, motivating them to work in teams and focus their efforts more on pedagogy than administration (Zona 2, 1995).
- Lend technical, education assistance to professional labor groups (GPT), organizing teachers in interdisciplinary groups to improve pedagogical practice (Zona 2, 1995).
- Train teachers to design new methodological and curricular strategies to incorporate the students' reality (Zona 2, 1995).
- Stimulate the production of Education Improvement Projects (PME).
- Create opportunities to incorporate the community by disseminating student work (Zona 2, 1995).
- Provide for flexibility in the curriculum within the national framework of objectives and content areas so that each institution can develop its own plans and programs (Zona 9, 1996; Zona 20, 1997).
- Give students various choices in curriculum activities (ACLE) as a means to foster social development.
- Promote youth workshops in art, the environment, and communication (Zona 2, 1995).
- Provide student leadership training at each school (Zona 2, 1995).
- Offer career and guidance counseling to assist students in planning their futures (Zona 2, 1995).

• Develop and support at the school level a new curriculum framework (Montegrande Project) for secondary education that complements the MECE-Media Program. In 1997, fifty-one high-risk schools were selected to develop proposals for curriculum innovations. During the final years of the project, the most successful experiences will be systematized and disseminated (Zona 23, 1997).

Postsecondary Education

Postsecondary education at all levels in Chile offers preparation for a number of different careers (academic, professional, technical). Enrollment in postsecondary education rose considerably between 1960 and 1996 (the actual enrollment rate, 26 percent, was three times greater than it was in 1960), but this increase was concentrated in the highest income quintile (Léon 1998). In addition, students in the lowest income quintile have the highest leaving and dropout rates. The government considered two dimensions of equity at this level, access and completion rates, in order to develop programs to address this situation.

It is difficult for students with low academic achievement (usually from the poorest public schools) to enter postsecondary education. Financial aid, be it scholarships or university loans provided by the central government, is given primarily to graduates of private secondary institutions who enter publicly subsidized, traditional universities with better facilities and usually more selective admissions policies.

High dropout and leaving rates represent a breakdown between the entrance requirements (preference is given to the PAA[5] score over the grades received during the last four years of secondary education) and program of study requirements. The government has awarded a significant number of scholarships and will develop the Postsecondary Equity and Quality Improvement Project (MECESUP) to establish a national accreditation system for all postsecondary institutions (Léon 1998). The different forms of student aid are as follows:

• The University Common Credit Fund, started in 1980, is a loan system initially administered by the Public Treasury, but now run by the universities. The loan system was jeopardized by reduced state funds for universities, administrative problems, and late payments. In 1991, the system was reformed and in 1994 the University Common Credit Fund was established. The Council of University Presidents (from traditional universities) provides loans through the Common Credit Fund, with an annual interest rate of 2 percent, which partially or completely finance the costs of a university education. Conditions for repayment of the loans depend on the salary earned as a result of obtaining a university education. At the end of twelve years, any remaining debt is forgiven. Debtors who repay their loans provide the system with the funds to make new loans. One hundred percent of the students from the two lowest income quintiles and some 48 percent of all students enrolled in traditional universities benefit from this loan system (with loans paying on average more than 60 percent of the costs of a university education).
• The Postsecondary Scholarship Program benefits those students with the highest academic achievement and the lowest economic resources. Unlike a loan, these scholarships do not have to be repaid. This program includes the Juan Gomez

Millas Scholarships (1,142 scholarships for high school graduates) and Scholarships for Outstanding Future Teachers (121 scholarships for students who plan teaching careers).
• The Savings Plan for Private Postsecondary Education enables families to finance future university expenses. Students with such accounts receive preference when applying for university loans.

CHANGES IN THE QUALITY OF PUBLIC PRIMARY EDUCATION

Huge government expenditures on public education programs to improve the quality of primary education have not achieved the desired results. While only some 70 percent of the objectives for fourth grade in private schools have been achieved, there is a considerable gap with respect to the public schools. Repetition and school leaving rates in traditional schools have not changed significantly. School system success can be measured in three ways: high levels of student achievement, low repetition rates, and few dropouts. Problems with any one of these can cause a chain reaction that affects the others (McGinn et al. 1992). The analysis of the change in education quality that follows is focused on primary education because it is still too early to evaluate the impact of the programs to improve secondary education that were started in 1995. We think it is worthwhile to examine the evolution of these three processes in primary education.

Student Achievement

Raw scores on the SIMCE[6] achievement tests given to students in the fourth and eighth grades at various institutions around the country have improved in subsidized schools over the past eight years (MINEDUC 1996). Raw scores at public schools, for example, have risen 18 percentage points. Nevertheless, since these test results are not designed to be compared directly, careful analysis of these data is necessary. This means that adjusted scores[7] must be calculated to control for test quality, given that the fourth-grade scores for students in private schools have not changed (the same is true for the eighth grade). With adjusted scores, it is possible to see the true increase in student achievement, thereby reducing considerably what seem to be initial improvements. See the adjusted scores column in Table 8.3.

The 20 percent increase in public school fourth-grade scores from 1988 to 1996 is not large enough to allow primary school graduates to acquire the skills needed to meet the demands of today's labor market. A fair number of them are unable to understand what they read (Schiefelbein et al. 1998). Teaching methods currently in use are essentially designed to transfer and accumulate mostly obsolete knowledge and do not meet rapidly increasing technological and scientific demands such as (1) lifelong learning, (2) adaptation to change, (3) application of knowledge to unexpected situations, (4) adoption of new methods, (5) organization of new tasks and functions, (6) openness to learning new ideas and information, (7) taking the initiative, (8) accepting responsibility, and (9) continuous training in how to use critical thinking skills (Schiefelbein et al. 1998). It is also worth mentioning that, according to both the "Chile Reads Its Future" study (Bravo 1998) and the CASEN survey (MIDEPLAN 1996), the other reason why children decide to leave school is because they are disinterested, bored, and find

TABLE 8.3

Raw and Adjusted Scores on the SIMCE Achievement Test (1988–1996)

School Category	Grade 4					Grade 8		
	1988 Raw	1992 Raw	1992 Adjusted	1996 Raw	1996 Adjusted	1989 Raw	1993 Raw	1995 Raw
Public	49.3	63.9	56.6	68.0	60.3	52.3	54.0	55.0
Private subsidized	56.4	70.2	62.1	73.7	65.4	57.6	59.4	60.6
Private	76.2	86.1	76.2	85.9	76.2	76.3	75.8	76.1

Note: The adjusted scores are calculated by holding constant private schools' scores (assuming there has been no change in teaching methods or teachers' quality).

Source: Mizala and Romaguera (1998).

little relevance in what they are studying.[8] (Note: Forty years ago the rate was 9 percent, but today it fluctuates between 25 and 28 percent for the two surveys, respectively.)

Controlling for a family's socioeconomic status and the size of the city, there are no statistically significant differences between the quality of public schools and the subsidized private schools in terms of SIMCE achievement scores for fourth grade. Furthermore, in rural areas, achievement scores for the subsidized schools are lower than the public schools.

If indeed there have been gains in student achievement at each socioeconomic level and according to population center size—metropolitan areas, provincial cities, and rural area (Schiefelbein and Schiefelbein 1998a)—achievement gains for students in the lowest income quintile are equal to about half of those for students in the highest income quintile (Wolff, Schiefelbein, and Valenzuela 1993). In every case, achievement gains for students in private schools are significantly higher even when the schools have not received any financial support through government education projects, the World Bank, or other sources. They also have the best teachers in the country, adequate facilities, and internationally prepared instructional materials.

Repetition

In 1997, the average repetition rate for Chilean first graders was under 10 percent (UNESCO 1996). The number of students in each of the first three grades of primary school beyond the population of the corresponding age cohort for that grade is an approximation of the number of repeaters in that grade.[9] It is interesting, however, that as the repetition rate declined, the number of students enrolled in first grade also declined from 436,100 in 1971 to 322,880 in 1981.

While repetition affects students from all socioeconomic groups, it primarily affects the most needy. Children from the most impoverished families are disadvantaged by a lack of early stimulation (particularly in the first three years of life), poor nutrition, limited family support, few resources in the home, and their parents' cultural level. All of these factors affect their ability to learn (Gajardo and de Andraca 1988; Fausto and Cervini 1992; UNESCO 1996). Children in depressed areas (rural and urban) are affected by different combinations of these elements resulting in schools made up of very heterogeneous groups. It is difficult to teach these groups using the traditional instructional methods favored by most teachers (Edwards 1996; Schiefelbein and Schiefelbein 1998b). In these poor, isolated subgroups, repetition rates are higher among indigenous children whose home language is not Spanish.

Repetition leads to more heterogeneous classes and lower academic achievement for students who are repeating the grade. The majority of students eight years of age and older who are repeating first grade have an impact on both pedagogy and the quality of education. Increased heterogeneity makes it difficult for teachers to rely on traditional pedagogy. This form of pedagogy, which is the most commonly used in Chile, is usually more efficient for homogeneous groups (see the discussion on program limitations of traditional teaching methods). Teachers in rural, multigrade classrooms utilizing these traditional techniques end up "teaching to the average." This has a negative impact on learning because these methods do not meet individual students' needs. Repeaters suffer from poor self-esteem and feel inferior to their peers who go on to the next grade. This poor self-esteem is reflected in their achievement scores, which are lower than their classmates' scores (Schiefelbein and Clavel 1983). In the United States, reading performance of children who repeat is 18 percent lower than those who have not repeated (Wolff, Schiefelbein, and Valenzuela 1993). Repetition also reduces the possibility of completing primary school because, once a student is fourteen years old, economic pressures force the most disadvantaged to leave the system to enter the workforce.

Dropouts

In general, students remain enrolled in school (even if they attend school only infrequently) until they are fourteen years old. The dropout rate in Chile starts with 3 percent of fifteen year olds and rises to 12 percent of sixteen year olds.

Dropout rates increase directly in proportion to children's failure rates (McGinn 1988). A followup study revealed that 25 percent of dropouts said they left school because of poor performance or because of irrelevant curriculum, even though what they stated as reasons for dropping out might be very different from the true reasons (Schiefelbein and Farrell 1982). Permanent dropouts who have repeated several primary school grades entered the workforce because they found it more stimulating— personally, socially, and economically—than continuing to perform poorly in school. A higher quality education would probably result in higher promotion rates and probably encourage students to finish primary school before dropping out, which would substantially improve the total return from education.

It is worth mentioning that students' families must meet numerous educational expenses while at the same time foregoing the income that children might generate. Even though education in Chile is "free" by law, there are a number of additional costs that parents must bear in order to educate their children: transportation, uniforms, bookbags, books, notebooks, pencils, and other school supplies. These additional costs can be as much as 2 percent of families' salaries (Schiefelbein 1997). In addition to the lost income from children's labor, many parents feel that educating their children is a great economic expense which leads them to consider other options (Anker and Melkas 1995). In sum, an education that results in insufficient learning and additional costs to the family causes many parents to consider it more beneficial to take them out of school and send them to work (Schiefelbein et al. 1998; Schiefelbein 1997).

IMPACT OF THESE PROGRAMS

Even as primary education resources have resulted in a 5.7 percent increase in the cost per pupil between 1990 and 1998, there has been only a 20 percent increase in the national SIMCE scores in fourth grade. Using both figures, we estimate cost-effectiveness at 0.7 percent (Schiefelbein, Swope, and Schiefelbein 1999), which is considerably lower than the cost-effectiveness of some forty improvement alternatives estimated by a group of experts (Schiefelbein, Wolff, and Schiefelbein 1998). The 20 percent increase in scores is similar to that achieved by the 900 Schools Program in the 1,000 lowest achieving schools of 1990 (Latorre 1993). Nevertheless, experiences in rural and marginalized urban schools indicate that there is greater potential for improvement (Schiefelbein et al. 1992).

We examined characteristics of these programs to determine the degree to which they provide the conditions necessary to respond to the problems identified and to estimate their possible impact. According to our estimates, nine of the programs had low or less than average impact on student achievement, one was about average, and only one had a high impact (but only for about 200 of the more than 10,000 schools in the country). Table 8.4 presents the scope and expected impact on student achievement for each program.

Assessment of the Programs We Analyzed

In general, the programs we analyzed seek to improve certain factors that influence student learning: (1) minimize the impact of the socioeconomic characteristics of students and their environment by subsidizing nutrition and health services, providing room and board, awarding scholarships, and providing school supplies; (2) increase access to preschool education in order to improve achievement in primary school, increase enrollment, and create nonformal education systems; (3) respond to the needs of multigrade classrooms by delivering textbooks to rural schools; (4) increase opportunity for primary education by improving rural schools so that all the primary grades are offered; (5) increase access to instructional material by providing public schools with textbooks, classroom libraries, and hookups to the education information network (Enlace); (6) increase instructional time by extending the school day by two hours to be more like developed countries; and (7) raise salaries and increase social prestige for the teaching profession.

These programs have not met the fundamental needs of the students. Programs are still needed to change aspects of the instructional process that do not permit adequate learning: (1) traditional instructional methods that rely primarily on memorization and do not allow teachers to work effectively with heterogeneous groups; (2) instructional materials of very poor quality—whose design requires that teachers spend too much time adapting them to students' needs—and a lack of teachers' guides to help teachers

TABLE 8.4

Analysis of Chilean Education Improvement Programs

Comments on the Program's Scope	Expected Impact on Student Achievement

Learning Conditions

(a) Traditional texts adapted by the teacher to meet students' learning needs.	(a) Low; teachers have little time and few resources.
(b) Better school facilities improve the learning environment and increase capacity.	(b) Low; this only improves the physical plant.
(c) Health services raise attendance for students with problems.	(c) Increases in proportion to increased time in class.
(d) Information networks provide access to databases and allow contact between students and teachers.	(d) Low; not much time on this and it does not lead to significant learning experiences.
(e) Individualized instruction more effectively meets students' needs.	(e) High in 200 schools, but low in the 10,000 schools in the national system.
(f) More time in school increases the opportunity to learn.	(f) Average; more of the same.
(g) Appropriate salaries contribute to good teaching.	(g) Low; this has not been the case for either short- or medium-term levels of achievement.

Programs Targeting At-Risk Students

(a) 900 Schools Program: an integrated program that offers good opportunities for learning for students with problems.	(a) Average; learning workshops solve problems in the classroom, but do not change traditional instruction.
(b) MECE-Rural: provides textbooks, training, and curriculum revision for rural schools.	(b) Low; locally based curriculums are presented in traditional texts; teacher training is also done using traditional methods.
(c) PME: schools and teachers develop education improvement plans.	(c) Low; teachers only know traditional methods and do not come up with viable alternatives.

Support Programs

(a) Nutrition programs, scholarships, and other initiatives to improve attendance among the neediest students.	(a) Low; increases proportionately to the time students are in class.

Source: Schiefelbein, Wolff, and Schiefelbein (1998); Schiefelbein and Schiefelbein (1998a; 1998b).

develop interactive teaching techniques; and (3) teacher training that promotes traditional teaching methods.

Traditional Teaching Methods   Education improvement programs have not been able to change the teaching methods most frequently used throughout the country. These methods do not address students' learning problems and tend to lead to excessive repetition. Teacher-centered learning or "chalk and talk" emphasizes verbal transmission of information and passive memorization by the entire class. These methods minimize (1) students' use of previously acquired knowledge; (2) the effective use of instructional time because the teacher has to maintain order in the classroom, some-times using upwards of 30 percent of the time on disciplinary matters; (3) considera-tion of alternative interpretations; (4) making connections to the context in which students live; and (5) written communication—either in class or as homework.

Teacher-centered learning seems to be effective with homogeneous groups—where the majority of students are like the imaginary "average" student—but it is not effec-tive with heterogeneous groups, particularly those found in the poorest areas of the country, where many students are not capable of keeping up with the pace in the class-room. If we add to this other huge differences in factors such as time to study at home, individual intellectual ability, health, and parental support, it is very difficult to deter-mine what is meant by the average student (Schiefelbein 1994). If these students do not receive individualized instruction, their reading comprehension levels decline and their repetition rates increase, which leads to increases in the heterogeneity of age groups in the classroom, making it just that much more difficult for traditional teaching methods to be effective (Thomas and Shaw 1992). It is not easy to break the vicious cycle created by heterogeneity of age and intellect (Ezpeleta 1989). Nonetheless, research suggests that it is possible to improve the quality of learning, to personalize learning—that is, to minimize the use of pedagogy focused on explanation and repetition of infor-mation; to increase the use of instructional materials that promote individual, interactive, and cooperative learning; and to train teachers to use active teaching methods to deal with heterogeneous and/or multigrade groups (Purves 1973; Schiefelbein and Clavel 1977; Costa 1977; Husen et al. 1978; Jamison et al. 1981; Farrell and Heyneman 1989; Munoz Izquierdo 1996; Pogrow 1996).

Poor Textbook Quality and Lack of Interactive Teacher Guides   Studies have shown that the textbooks and teacher guides used in Chile are of poor quality (Schiefelbein 1994; Eyzaguirre and Fontaine 1997). Because investment in effective instructional materials is one of the best short-term investments in terms of cost-effectiveness, gov-ernment programs should not only provide these materials, but also make sure that their use leads to interactive learning appropriate for each educational environment. The use of interactive teacher guides makes it easier for teachers to make the transi-tion from traditional instructional methods to individualized and group instruction (Schiefelbein and Tedesco 1995) and to build on students' previous knowledge and their family's culture as part of the active process of learning (Tenti 1997).

Teacher Training   Proposals to modernize education and the curriculum of teacher preparation programs are not aligned. Existing teacher preparation and training pro-grams do not meet the demands of individualized and interactive methodologies and programs. In workshops throughout the country, teachers have been found to be predisposed to traditional teaching methods, but at the same time they are open to change if they have the experience, techniques, and instructional materials to foster it. This suggests that teachers need appropriate training to change their pedagogy. For teachers to internalize a more individualized, interactive approach to teaching, they themselves must be trained through such an approach and not through traditional methods which not only reinforce what they already know, but end up being the very methods they will use.

Finally, it is essential to consider the importance of a national consensus on education policy, given that long-term policies are politically viable only to the degree that they are supported by political groups as well as civil society. This process will require establishing information systems in the field of education. The fulfillment of any government policy will depend on society adopting it as its own, a step that can take place only when society understands its nature and its purpose. For this reason, the Ministry of Education should provide information to inform public opinion at three levels: the general public, through mass publicity campaigns; those who manage the education process; and teachers in schools.

CONCLUSIONS

Given the considerable inequity in terms of access as well as quality of education, the Chilean education system is not responding to the socioeconomic needs of the country. Enrollments, although generally quite high, vary according to geographic regions. The low academic achievement of poor children is a reflection of the poor quality of the teaching-learning process in public schools. Finally, the government's education improvement programs are not designed to make substantive changes and are, therefore, not effective. Without some evaluation of their weaknesses, it will not be possible to strengthen and improve these programs.

There have been considerable increases in enrollment in Chile's education system during recent years, especially in secondary education (68 percentage points in the past thirty years). Practically all children in a given age cohort enroll in primary school (see Table 8.1). Nevertheless, as enrollments have increased in three of the four levels of education—preschool, secondary, and postsecondary—equity has not been achieved. There are large differences among the family income quintiles (see Table 8.2). Enrollment rates in preschool programs have risen more slowly for children from the most disadvantaged homes, but more concrete efforts to increase these enrollment rates are needed. Preschool programs prepare children for primary school, improve their achievement, and permit their mothers to find work and, therefore, improve the quality of family life. It is not yet known if the nonformal programs will provide such expected benefits for preschoolers as transforming and improving primary schools' efficiency by building on preschool learning. This is due, in part, to the abrupt change in methodology faced by children as they go from child-centered instruction, group activities, and learning through play in preschool to the traditional pedagogical methods of the primary school where education is teacher-centered.

Government programs that seek equity in terms of quality are targeting the neediest sectors, providing schools with supplies (textbooks, libraries, computers), training teachers, and approving education improvement projects (PMEs) at the poorest schools. At the same time, there are no strategies in place to introduce a new pedagogical focus, one centered on the individual needs of students, and so these government programs have not yet met their objectives. This is clear from national achievement test scores on the SIMCE, which reveal that there is inequity in the distribution of knowledge. With a difference of 16 points, academic achievement at public schools, and particularly at subsidized schools, is clearly inferior to that of the private schools. In addition, repetition and dropout rates increase in public and subsidized schools because children from the most disadvantaged sectors attend them. It will be necessary to gradually introduce innovations, including the delivery of suitable teaching materials (together with interactive guides) supported by in-service training to introduce teachers to their use. At the secondary level, government programs have not yet borne fruit (they have been in effect only since 1997), but if they do not also change teaching methods used in classrooms, they will not improve students' academic achievement. For teachers to implement interactive, cooperative, and individualized instructional methods that are presented in the teachers' guides, they will have to experience these methods and see them in practice.

The fact that national education improvement programs are mandated by the Ministry of Education prevents local actors—teachers, principals, parents, and students—from taking ownership of them. For these actors to fully participate in proposed changes, the Ministry of Education must allow for information gathering, participation, and decision making at local levels. Finally, all of these government-generated innovations require evaluation, where possible by third parties. If evaluation of these innovations can demonstrate their impact on academic achievement, then they should be replicated and modified where necessary for use in other areas.

NOTES

1. Affirmative action refers to the programs designed to target equity and quality.
2. Public or municipal schools are administered by each municipality and subsidized by the government.
3. Percentages are based on preschool-age children (three to six years old).
4. These are schools run by individuals that receive a state subsidy based on average monthly attendance.
5. The Academic Aptitude Test (PAA) is a national test required for admittance to postsecondary education.
6. SIMCE (Education Quality Measurement System) is a two-part test of mathematics and Spanish language. It is taken by fourth-grade students during even-numbered years and eighth-grade students during odd-numbered years. The results are made available nationally so that parents can choose the schools with the best results.
7. Adjusted scores allow comparisons of changes over time because they are calculated by holding constant private schools' scores.
8. Students leave school primarily because of economic problems and the need to work.
9. For example, in 1995 there were 312,996 students in first grade, which is 20,000 more than the corresponding age group (close to 290,000 children). This means that if 100 percent of the age group enrolls, close to 7 percent of the first-grade students are repeating that grade. Since nearly all students currently enroll on time for first grade, the calculations are simpler and have a very small margin of error (1–2 percent). Traditional pedagogy in this case refers to the teacher standing at the front of the classroom facing the students with the students seated in rows facing the teacher. It may also be called "chalk and talk" or "teacher-centered instruction."

REFERENCES

Anker, Richard, and Helina Melkas. 1995. *Economic Incentives for Children and Families Intended to Eliminate or Reduce Child Labour.* Geneva: International Labor Organization.

Bravo, David. 1998. *Chile Lee su Futuro.* Santiago: Universidad de Chile, Facultad de Ciencias Económicas.

Costa, Mesias. 1977. School outputs and the determinants of scholastic achievement. Unpublished Ph.D. dissertation. Palo Alto, Calif.: Stanford University.

Edwards, Verónica. 1996. *Estado del Arte sobre Trabajo Infantil y Educación*. Santiago: Programa Interdisciplinario de Investigaciones en Educación-UNESCO.

Eyzaguirre, Barbara, and Loreto Fontaine, eds. 1997. *El Futuro en Riesgo: Nuestros Textos Escolares*. Santiago: Centro de Estudios Públicos.

Ezpeleta, Justa. 1989. *Escuelas y Maestros: Condiciones del Trabajo Docente en Argentina*. Santiago: UNESCO/OREALC.

Farrell, Joseph, and Steve Heynemann. 1989. *Textbooks in the Developing World: Economic and Educational Choices*. Washington, D.C.: World Bank.

Fausto, Ayrton, and Ruben Cervini, eds. 1992. *O Trabalho e a Rua. Criancas e Adolescentes no Brasil Urbano dos Anos 80*. São Paulo: Cortez Editora.

Gajardo, Marcela, and Ana María de Andraca. 1988. *Trabajo Infantil y Escuela. Las Zonas Rurales*. Santiago: Facultad Latinoamericana de Ciencias Sociales.

Gardner, Howard. 1991. *The Unschooled Mind*. New York: Basic Books.

Husen, Torsten, Lawrence Saha, and Richard Noonan. 1978. *Teacher Training and Student Achievement in Less Developed Countries*. Washington, D.C.: World Bank.

Jamison, Dean, Barbara Searle, Steve Heynemann, and K. Galda. 1981. *Improving Elementary Mathematics Education in Nicaragua: An Experimental Study of the Impact of Textbooks and Radio on Achievement*. Washington, D.C.: World Bank, Population and Human Resources Division.

Latorre, Marcela. 1993. *Evaluación de Rendimiento Escolar de los Alumnos de las Escuelas del P-900*. Santiago: Ministerio de Educación.

León, José. 1998. *Equidad y Educación Superior*. Santiago: Ministerio de Educación, División de Educación Superior.

McGinn, Noel. 1988. Foreword. In Mary Anderson, *Access to Schooling in the Third World: An Overview*. Cambridge, Mass.: Harvard University.

McGinn, Noel, Fernando Reimers, Armando Loera, Maria del Carmen Soto, and Sagrario López. 1992. Why do children repeat grades? A study of rural primary schools in Honduras. Cambridge, Mass.: Harvard University.

MIDEPLAN (Ministerio de Planeación). 1996. *Encuesta Caracterización Socioeconómica-CASEN*. Santiago: MIDEPLAN, Departamento de Información.

MINEDUC (Ministerio de Educación). 1996. *Compendio de Información Estadística*. Santiago: Ministerio de Educación.

MINEDUC. 1998. *Reforma en Marcha: Buena Educación para Todos*. Santiago: Ministerio de Educación.

Mizala, Alejandra, and Pilar Romaguera. 1998. Desempeño escolar y elección de colegios: La experiencia Chilena. Serie Economía No. 36. Centro de Economía Aplicada, Departamento de Ingeniería Industrial, Facultad de Ciencias Físicas y Matemáticas, Universidad de Chile.

Muñoz Izquierdo, Carlos. 1996. La tranformación de los sistemas educativos Latinoamericanos ante los nuevos requerimientos de las economías de la región. *La Educacion* 106: 25–44.

Pogrow, Stanley. 1996. Reforming the wannabe reformers. Why education reforms almost always end up making things worse. *Kappan* 77(10): 656–663.

Purves, Alan C. 1973. *Literature Education in Ten Countries: An Empirical Study*. Washington, D.C.: Almquist and Wiksell.

Schiefelbein, Ernesto. 1969. Las universidades. Santiago: Centro Perfeccionamiento Universitario CPU.

Schiefelbein, Ernesto. 1994. Estrategias para elevar la calidad de la educación. *Revista Interamericana de Desarrollo Educativo de OEA* 117: 10–24.

Schiefelbein, Ernesto. 1995. Education reform in Latin America and the Caribbean. *UNESCO-OREALC* 37: 15–23.

Schiefelbein, Ernesto. 1997. School-related economic incentives in Latin America: Reducing drop-out and repetition and combating child labour. Florence, Italy: Innocenti Occasional Pares, Child Rights Series, No. 12, UNICEF International Child Development Centre.

Schiefelbein, Ernesto, and Carlos Clavel. 1977. Stability over time of educational input-output relationships. Santiago: Programa ECIEL del PIIE-Departamento de Economía de la Universidad de Chile.

Schiefelbein, Ernesto, and Carlos Clavel. 1983. Variables exógenas que inciden en el rendimiento escolar en 4o y 6o años de la escuela básica y que convendría usar en futuros análisis del PER. Santiago: Centro de Perfeccionamiento Educativo y de Instrucción de Profesores y Organización de Estados Americanos.

Schiefelbein, Ernesto, and Joseph Farrell. 1982. *Eight Years of Their Lives*. Ottawa: International Development Research Centre.

Schiefelbein, Ernesto, Benno Sander, Leonel Zuñiga, Getulio Carvalho, Beatrice Edwards, Lawrence Wolff, and Michael Alleyne. 1998. *Education in the Americas: Quality, Equity and Citizenship*. Washington, D.C.: Organization of American States.

Schiefelbein, Ernesto, and Paulina Schiefelbein. 1998a. Evolución de la repetición, deserción y calidad de la educación en Chile, 1999–1997. Document prepared for the workshop organized by the JUNAEB, Santiago, Chile.

Schiefelbein, Ernesto, and Paulina Schiefelbein. 1998b. Expectativas y cambios metodológicos: Una visión desde el mundo de los profesores. Santiago: Centro de Investigación y Desarrollo de la Educación.

Schiefelbein, Ernesto, and Juan Carlos Tedesco. 1995. *Una Nueva Oportunidad: El Rol de la Educación en el Desarrollo de América Latina*. Buenos Aires: Editorial Santillana, Aula XXI.

Schiefelbein, Ernesto, Eduardo Velez, and José Valenzuela. 1992. Factors affecting achievement in primary education: A review of the literature for Latin America and the Caribbean. Washington, D.C.: World Bank.

Schiefelbein, Ernesto, Laurence Wolff, and Paulina Schiefelbein. 1998. Cost effectiveness of education policies in Latin America: A survey of expert opinion. Washington, D.C.: InterAmerican Development Bank.

Tenti Fanfani, Emilio. 1997. Escuela y Cotidianeidad. Paper presented at the Seminar on Education and Daily Life, 1997 Book Fair, Argentina.

Thomas, Christopher, and Christopher Shaw. 1992. Issues in the development of multigrade schools. Washington, D.C.: World Bank.

UNESCO. 1996. *State of Education in Latin America and the Caribbean, 1980–1994*. Santiago: UNESCO-OREALC.

Wolff, Laurence, Ernesto Schiefelbein, and Jorge Valenzuela. 1993. Improving the quality of primary education in Latin America and the Caribbean. Washington, D.C.: World Bank.

Zona Pública 2. 1995. Programa MECE: Educación, calidad y equidad. Santiago: Secretaría de Comunicación y Cultura (SECC), pp. 18–25.

Zona Pública 9. 1996. Modernización y educación: Descentralización curricular. Santiago: SECC, pp. 10–15.

Zona Pública 13. 1996. Programa enlaces. El computador llega a la escuela. Santiago: SECC, pp. 38–47.

Zona Pública 14. 1996. Mece—Rural. Mañana será otro día. Santiago: SECC, pp. 10–18.

Zona Pública 20. 1997. Cambio curricular para la educación media. Un marco flexible para contener el futuro. Santiago: SECC, pp. 2–12.

Zona Pública 23. 1997. Proyecto montegrande. El hábito de innovar en la educación. Santiago: SECC, pp. 2–17.

Zona Pública 25. 1998. Educación parvularia. Programación sólo para menores. Santiago: SECC, pp. 2–14.

Commentary

Lewis A. Tyler, Harvard Graduate School of Education

Overall, this chapter is a useful inventory and criticism of Chilean education programs and policies of the 1990s. My comments focus on two or three areas of the chapter that influenced my appreciation of the authors' work.

I found it necessary to overcome the authors' highly pessimistic tone. Even given the intention of the authors to be critical, they cite statistics that are still remote dreams for policymakers in other countries and would, in other contexts, be cause for celebration: Coverage is virtually universal in basic education, 80 percent in secondary and 26 percent in higher education, and there has been a 20 percent improvement in the SIMCE over the past eight or nine years with only a modest increase in per-pupil expenditures.

In some respects the chapter was weakened by the recurring criticism of traditional "chalk and talk" instructional methods. Such pervasive criticism elevates this subject to the principal theme of the chapter.

The teacher training section buried the important commentary regarding the importance of generating national consensus in education policy.

Finally, in the section of the chapter dealing with the impact of programs upon educational improvement, neither the programs analyzed nor the measures of analysis were evident to me.

This fourteen-year-old student, a national peace movement leader, interviews classmates during an internal public-address broadcast at the Colegio Yermo y Parres in Bogota, Colombia.
[UNICEF/99-0231/Jeremy Horner (Colombia)]

9

Equity and Education in Colombia

Alfredo Sarmiento Gómez
Misión Social, Dirección de Planeación Nacional, Colombia

EDUCATION, EQUITY, AND POVERTY

Equity as the foundation of society is the great challenge of the late twentieth century and will continue to challenge societal foundations to be built in the twenty-first century. John Rawls, in his book *Theory of Justice* (Rawls 1971)—which Amartya Sen considers the "most important theory of justice presented in this century" (Sen 1995, 75)—has defined the two basic principles of justice: "1) Every person has the same right to a fully valid scheme of equal basic freedoms which are compatible with a similar scheme of freedoms for all. 2) Social and economic inequalities should satisfy two conditions. In the first place, they should be associated with jobs and positions open to all in equality of opportunities; in the second place, they should assume the greatest benefit for the least advantaged members of the society" (Rawls 1971, 13).

This chapter will examine the conditions of social equality in terms of education in Colombia. Additionally, it will examine those external factors that are inextricably connected to an individual's education, income, and labor. Then the chapter will look at current expenditures on education and how they differ for children of varying socioeconomic backgrounds. Finally, it will investigate and describe current programs in Colombia that attempt to mitigate differences between schools and the poor with a special emphasis on positive discrimination in funding and in educational programs.

According to Rawls, collaboration—the foundation of a just society—implies the ideas of reciprocity and mutuality and can be summed up as the fact that one citizen, fully within his or her rights, is willing to collaborate with all members of society for his or her lifetime on the basis of mutual respect, on the condition that all others also do so. This is reasonable behavior. This behavior is perfectly compatible with the search for multiple finalities or rationalities. The existence of reciprocity and mutuality among the members of the community as the fundamental idea in the organization of society is what demands that preferential treatment be given to the weak as a way of guaranteeing the equality of all (Rawls 1988, 20–24).

Sen has also contributed to the development of a methodology for addressing the understanding and measurement of inequality as well as to the development of substantive ideas about this topic. Individual advantage is judged by the freedom to achieve, incorporating but going beyond actually realized achievement, within a space of specified values (Sen 1992, 129–132). With respect to Rawls, Sen emphasizes that differences in the capability to convert resources into freedoms and functionings make the consideration of capabilities more appropriate than the consideration of freedoms for judging individual advantages (Sen 1997, 121).

Differences related to personal characteristics such as sex, age, and genetic endowment, allow Sen to insist on the point that equality in the freedom to pursue diverse ends is not generated only by equality in the distribution of primary goods. It requires, in addition, consideration of personal differences for transforming resources into capabilities for achieving objectives. This variability among people for converting means into "capabilities" and capabilities into achievements, which is more difficult for the poor, is what justifies a special treatment for them and for other traditionally excluded groups such as women, the elderly, and ethnic minorities (Sen 1995, 85–87).

Thus, seen from the theory of justice, or from economic welfare theory, preferential treatment for the weakest—or, in economic terms, for the poorest—is a basic condition of the social order. It is not a value judgment tacked on to economic analysis, but rather a condition more basic than economics for establishing the existence of a just society (see Sarmiento and Arteaga 1998).

Analyzing the relationship between education and income, it has been found that both variables are highly correlated. For any age, more educated workers obtain better incomes on average than less educated workers, an ever-increasing trend. It has similarly been found that the educational status of the person in charge of child rearing influences the level of education of his or her children. This phenomenon demonstrates an intergenerational educational relationship. Moreover, education not only influences the individual and families, but also impacts the well-being of the greater society.

The economic effect of education is not solely felt in the economic productivity of firms and the incomes of educated workers. Education produces a large impact on the conditions of life of the entire population in basic areas such as health, nutrition, civic behavior, and community participation in development. For example, the best way to prevent child malnutrition and infectious diseases is through education. We find a myriad of implications for education, and thus it has developed into a policy tool with the potential to reproduce inequity or to correct it.

Human capital theory posits that increases in the productivity of individuals, firms, and nations result from the education levels of the labor force. This theory was developed in the 1960s with the work of T. W. Schultz. The reemergence of interest in neoclassical economics to explain economic growth provided further evidence of the role of investments in human capital in explaining unlimited sustained growth (Romer 1996). Later, activities involving technological development and government action were incorporated (Romer 1987; Barro and Sala-I-Martin 1995). A model of this last type, applied by Barro to 87 countries, showed that one extra year in the average number of years of education at the secondary and university level, for men over twenty-five years of age, produces an increase of 1.2 percent per year in the rate of growth (Barro 1997, 19–28).

Thus education has been shown to be critical for long-term economic growth, both for what it means to have more educated people with increased productivity and because education increases the development and use of innovations and new technologies. For example, the same study by Barro (1997) showed that the completion of primary education had numerous benefits for women and their families, including the reduction in fertility rates with a consequential greater share of resources for all members of the smaller families.

Amartya Sen (1998), while recognizing the contribution that human capital theory has made to "soften and humanize the conception of development," warns at the same time against the traditional interpretation which considers man as a means and not the end of development. His proposal to value growth according to the broadening of human capabilities emphasizes two features that are often forgotten. He argues that increasing capabilities for the present generation is important, not only as a better means for future production but also so that the person can enjoy today the possibilities achieved by the society.

DISTRIBUTION AND EDUCATION IN COLOMBIA

Poverty and Education in Colombia: Magnitude, Profile, and Tendencies

The Evolution of Poverty: 1993–1997   The incidence of poverty varies according to the concept used for measuring it. The instruments most often used to measure the incidence of poverty are the Unsatisfied Basic Needs Index (UBN) and the poverty line. The UBN defines five needs as basic (see Table 9.1). According to the index, in 1997 there were 10.5 million poor Colombians, those who could not satisfy at least one of the five needs defined as basic, or 26.5 percent of the total population. Compared with 1993, this represents a decrease of 663,000 persons, or 4 percentage points (from 30 to 26 percent). The number of indigents—people with two or more UBN—was 3.5 million in 1997, 850,000 less than in 1993.

Although these numbers indicate a decreasing poverty trend as measured by the UBN, concentrated poverty continues to plague rural zones more so than urban zones. According to the UBN, 50 percent of the rural population is considered poor, a figure three times greater than that in urban areas. This urban-rural difference widened in the 1993–1997 period, as the decrease was more pronounced in cities than in the countryside. Additionally, 22 percent of the rural population are indigent, contrasted to 3.5 percent in urban zones.

Misery measured by the indigence line. As seen in Table 9.2, in 1997, out of a population of close to 40 million, 7.3 million had an income level so low that even if they invested it all in food, it would not be enough to satisfy their minimum food needs. In the country as a whole, that was 1 million more than in 1993, but with different performance in the rural sector, whose population in misery decreased by 1 million, and the urban zone where it increased by 2 million.

These figures allow us to state that a good part of the increase in urban misery is explained by the increase in urban unemployment (nearly 50 percent growth in the rate of unemployment) and the massive displacement from the countryside to the cities due to the combined effect of economic recession and growing factors of armed confrontation between insurgent and paramilitary groups. The poverty line in Colombia is

TABLE 9.1

Extent of Poverty by Type of Deficiency According to UBN Indicators

		Housing	Services	Crowding	School Non-Attendance	Economic Dependency	Total
1993							
Urban	Number Poor	1,355,281	1,250,719	2,861,050	746,960	1,468,384	7,682,394
	Incidence (%)	5.2	4.8	11.1	2.9	5.7	21.4
Rural	Number Poor	2,430,011	1,752,220	2,368,754	1,170,839	1,988,656	5,704,033
	Incidence (%)	22.2	16	21.7	10.7	18.2	52.1
Total	Number Poor	3,785,292	3,002,939	5,229,804	1,917,799	3,457,040	11,225,719
	Incidence (%)	10.3	8.2	14.2	5.2	9.4	30.5
1997							
Urban	Number Poor	778,701	641,793	2,401,650	552,732	1,788,951	4,947,623
	Incidence (%)	2.7	2.2	8.4	1.9	6.2	17.2
Rural	Number Poor	2,251,063	1,732,692	1,975,425	1,016,258	2,374,143	5,614,792
	Incidence (%)	20.3	15.6	17.8	9.1	21.4	50.5
Total	Number Poor	3,029,764	2,374,485	4,377,075	1,568,990	4,163,094	10,562,415
	Incidence (%)	7.6	6	11	3.9	10.4	26.5

Note: Incidence is defined as the proportion of the affected population with respect to the total population.

Source: Calculations by Duarte Guterman and Company from the Socioeconomic Characterization Survey (1993) and the Quality of Life Survey (1997).

TABLE 9.2
The Evolution of Poverty (1993–1997)

	1993			1997		
	Urban	Rural	Total	Urban	Rural	Total
Indigent population by income	2,817,267	3,502,606	6,317,873	4,876,382	2,431,651	7,308,033
Incidence (%)	10.9	32.0	17.2	17.0	21.9	18.3
Poor population by UBN	5,521,686	5,704,033	11,225,719	4,951,951	5,610,464	10,562,415
Incidence (%)	21.4	52.1	30.5	17.2	50.5	26.5
Indigent population by UBN	1,629,512	2,663,869	4,293,381	1,007,357	2,440,686	3,448,043
Incidence (%)	6.3	24.4	11.7	3.5	22.0	8.7
Poor population by poverty line	10,414,839	7,561,708	17,976,547	11,868,372	6,909,064	18,777,436
Incidence (%)	40.3	69.1	48.9	41.3	62.2	47.1
Poor population by UBN or poverty line	11,882,114	8,538,683	20,420,797	12,865,947	8,254,228	21,120,175
Incidence (%)	4.6	76.1	55.5	44.8	74.3	53.0
Poor population by UBN and poverty line	4,054,400	4,727,057	8,781,457	3,946,096	4,273,580	8,219,676
Incidence (percent)	15.7	43.2	23.9	13.7	38.5	20.6
Poverty deficit	36.9	49.6	43.4	44.8	46.2	45.3
Intensity of poverty (%)	15.7	34.3	21.2	18.5	28.8	21.3
Severity of poverty (%)	8.4	2.1	12.1	11.2	17.1	12.9
SEN Index	0.209	0.433	0.261	0.248	0.375	0.288

Note: Incidence is defined as the proportion of the affected population with respect to the total population.

Source: Calculations by Duarte Guterman and Company from the Socioeconomic Characterization Survey (1993) and the Quality of Life Survey (1997).

fixed at 2.1 times the misery line. The population that had income below this poverty line[1] was 47 percent in 1997, almost 2 percentage points less than in 1993, but 800,000 people more in absolute numbers. In this case too the increase is different by zone: an increase of 1.5 million people in the urban zone and a decrease of 0.5 million in the rural zone.

Distribution of Income   The behavior of the Gini coefficient shows that in the concentration of total income there was also a deterioration in the urban sector and an improvement in the rural sector. Table 9.3 shows that the variation by income quintiles displays a general impoverishment of all other income groups in favor of the richest 20 percent. The biggest losers are the second and third quintiles comprised of the poorest 20 percent to 60 percent, which lose 1.3 and 1.5 percentage points of income participation. On the other hand, the richest 20 percent increase their part of income by 5 percentage points.

Disaggregation, using the Theil index,[2] lets us see that differences between urban groups are more important for total inequality than urban/rural differences. There is, however, a change between the situation of 1993 and that of 1999; the difference between urban and rural zones grows in importance, while the heterogeneity of groups in the rural area decreases.

TABLE 9.3

Distribution of Income (1993–1997)

	1993			1997		
	Urban	Rural	Total	Urban	Rural	Total
Total population						
20%	4.38	4.41	3.71	3.01	4.41	2.77
40%	12.93	13.04	11.54	10.06	13.84	9.28
60%	25.92	26.05	24.08	21.57	27.96	20.25
80%	45.78	46.42	44.14	41.47	49.21	39.30
100%	100.00	100.00	100.00	100.00	100.00	100.00
Gini coefficient						
Total population	0.488	0.482	0.512	0.541	0.456	0.562
Poor by income	0.211	0.259	0.250	0.275	0.260	0.290
According to QLI						
(Quality of Life Index)	0.106	0.240	0.183	0.088	0.223	0.163
Theil index						
Total population	0.489	0.490	0.546	0.563	0.401	0.610
Contribution (%)[1]	75.28	14.42	100.00	80.28	7.63	100.00
Decomposition[2]	0.411	0.079	0.546	0.489	0.047	0.610

[1]Contribution between zones (urban/rural): 1993: 10.30; 1997: 12.09.
[2]Decomposition between zones (urban/rural): 1993: 0.056; 1997: 0.074.

Source: Calculations by Duarte Guterman and Company from the Socioeconomic Characterization Survey (1993) and the Quality of Life Survey (1997).

Education and Poverty   How much education are poor children exposed to prior to their inception in the school system? This section attempts to understand what the levels of education are in poor households and how they differ between regions, the rural and urban. In terms of average education, the heads of the poor households have a fourth-grade education, 80 percent less than the rest. This difference is 25 percent higher in the rural sector than in the urban sector. An interesting fact is that the education of the spouse is 0.2 grades higher for the poorest in 1997, while in 1993 it was practically the same for both. The urban sector has witnessed the widening of this difference. In both zones it is clear that the difference in the number of years of education is less in 1997, both for the head of the household and for his or her spouse. Between 1993 and 1997 an increase of 0.7 grades was achieved for non-poor urban heads of households, while there was almost no change for the poor. There was a very small (0.05) growth in the rural sector for the non-poor, and 0.2 for the poor. A very similar pattern is seen in the education of spouses.

As far as school attendance, poor homes have quadrupled the number of children who do not attend, and the difference is 5 times in the urban zone and only 2.4 in the rural. Notable changes have taken place in the four years under consideration. The decrease in this period in school nonattendance per 10,000 was greater, in absolute terms, for the poor, and within this category for the rural poor. However, in relative terms, the biggest improvement is found among the urban non-poor.

To evaluate the effects of a number of attributes on the possibility of being poor, the effect of a change in each one on the incidence of poverty was measured, holding all other factors constant (scc Table 9.4).

The probability of being poor increases with household size. When the household reaches five children, the average for rural homes, the probability of being poor is 61 percent. At the other extreme, for 3.79 children, the average for the urban non-poor, the probability is 36.1 percent. In all cases, the probability of being poor due to an increase in the number of household members is less in the urban sector.

The risk of poverty for having one child under 12 years old begins, in rural households, at 51 percent, a figure 16 percentage points above that for the urban sector. The increase in the risk is lower in the rural zone until four children, at which point the two probabilities differ by only 4 percentage points. In any case, the increased risk due to having another child is larger than that produced due to another person in the household.

The number of employed members of the household decreases the risk of being poor. It begins with a higher probability in the rural sector with one employed person, and decreases more slowly as that number increases. This demonstrates that employment as a generator of income is more important in the urban sector.

A fourth of households have a female head. The incidence of poverty is higher in these homes than in those headed by men. This situation is especially notable in the urban sector, where the differential in the incidence of poverty is 13 percentage points, compared to only 4 points in the rural area.

The education of the head of household is the main factor in decreasing the probability of being poor. Illiteracy is one of the best predictors of poverty. Being absolutely or functionally (incomplete primary school) illiterate produces practically the same probability of poverty. Reaching nine years of education practically equalizes the probabilities of poverty in the urban and rural zones and diminishes the risk of poverty to

TABLE 9.4

Incidence of Poverty (%) (1997)

Variable	Urban	Rural	Total	Variable	Urban	Rural	Total
Number of persons in household				Children under 12 years old			
1	27.85	29.20	28.17	0	27.10	46.52	31.25
2	28.26	41.88	31.58	1	35.10	50.89	38.72
3	32.49	45.17	35.32	2	48.82	61.17	52.12
4	37.30	54.30	41.18	3	66.88	74.086	9.63
5	38.58	61.13	44.07	4	77.90	81.79	79.86
6	46.17	70.84	53.19	5 or more	72.50	93.62	84.75
7	51.39	73.05	60.28				
8	49.21	71.78	57.11				
9 or more	70.74	75.24	72.64				
Number of employed in household				Sex of head of household			
0	68.94	84.46	72.09	Male	38.10	61.60	45.33
1	52.32	71.62	58.31	Female	50.53	65.85	53.29
2	34.87	59.84	41.11				
3	28.13	50.87	34.19				
4	25.26	41.87	30.13				
5 or more	18.37	37.49	25.30				
				Years of education of spouse of head of household			
Years of education of head of household				None	50.95	70.43	60.99
None	54.51	69.22	62.10	1–3	62.48	67.77	65.43
1–3	59.68	66.95	63.07	4–5	49.97	59.30	53.00
4–5	51.53	57.90	53.31	6–8	38.71	47.01	39.80
6–8	44.63	42.79	44.41	9–11	24.23	17.76	23.82
9–11	28.67	28.35	28.64	12 or more	6.26	22.46	6.91
12 or more	6.42	14.81	6.66				
Age of head of household				Age of spouse of head of household			
Less than 20 years	55.69	40.51	52.68	Less than 20 years			
21–30 years	47.42	57.89	50.07	21–30 years	45.06	65.53	51.48
31–40 years	43.35	65.32	49.63	31–40 years	39.16	65.07	46.52
41–50 years	37.66	62.81	44.30	41–50 years	32.01	60.41	40.39
More than 50 years	39.87	61.35	46.21	More than 50 years	35.21	60.58	42.98

Source: Calculations by Duarte Guterman and Company from the Socioeconomic Characterization Survey (1993) and the Quality of Life Survey (1997).

28 percent. But reaching 12 or more years reduces the risk by half in the rural zone and to one-fourth as much in the urban zone. A similar pattern is found for the education of the spouse.

The effect of the age of both the head of household and the spouse shows a different pattern for the rural and urban zones. For the urban sector, the age of the head or the spouse decreases the probability from twenty years of age to fifty. For the rural sector, the risk of poverty increases with the age of the head or the spouse up to forty years of age and decreases slowly from there on.

Inequality in Access

This section reviews the differences in how different income groups participate in different levels of schooling and examines which factors are associated with those differences. The section is prefaced by a description of the policies of educational decentralization that have characterized the educational context over the last decades.

The Institutional Framework: Decentralization   Within the general context of state reorganization in the period since 1991, sectorial motivations were multiple and contradictory. The national technical stratum sought the municipalization of education, the weakening of the teachers' union, and the greatest possible neutrality of spending in the face of party politics. The teachers sought guarantees of payment of the benefits they had won and the least possible decentralization. The private sector, and in particular the Catholic schools, wanted to maintain their freedom to provide education and to reduce state intervention to the greatest extent possible.

One-fifth of the current income of the nation is distributed to the municipalities as Participation in Current Income (PICN), of which 30 percent must be dedicated to education, 20 percent to health, and 50 percent to different ends from a list set by law. This money must be spent on financing the investment needed to support improvements in the quality of education, but during a period of transition it may be spent on functioning expenses.

The most interesting part of this financing scheme is the definition of criteria for territorial distribution. The first criterion is the population, the second is the relative poverty of the territorial entity, and the third is administrative and fiscal efficiency.

Of the organizational changes in the sector, what should be stressed are the regulatory changes that lead the Ministry of Education to reorient its role toward leadership, technical design, evaluation of management, evaluation of quality, impact measurement, and the disappearance of the vestiges of central administration and operation.

Educational Achievements: Slow, Insufficient, and Inequitable   Education is a long-term process. Finishing basic education takes ten years or more depending on the number of years spent in preparation and preschool. Finishing a university education can take from seven to twelve additional years. Thus short-term achievements should be analyzed in light of long-term tendencies, since part of their effect is the result of a cumulative effort.

In Colombia, education as measured in average number of years completed for people over five years of age has increased from 2.4 years in the mid-1960s to nearly six grades in 1997. At this pace the country took more than twenty years to double its educational accumulation—a worthwhile but slow effort. The speed at which this accumulation has taken place has differed in time and has favored the urban sector. The first push for rapid growth was formally initiated in 1958, based on the creation of a fixed percentage of state resources directed to education. This measure produced stability and allowed a level of planning that undoubtedly provided results and is currently substantiated by the Constitution of 1991.

Figure 9.1 clearly highlights these two acceleration points. The first, initiated by law in 1958, but actually put into practice some four years later for the urban sector and somewhat more than ten years later for the rural sector, runs out in the mid-1980s.

Average Years of Schooling of the Population over Five Years
of Age by Type of Locality for the Years 1964, 1973, 1985,
1993, and 1997

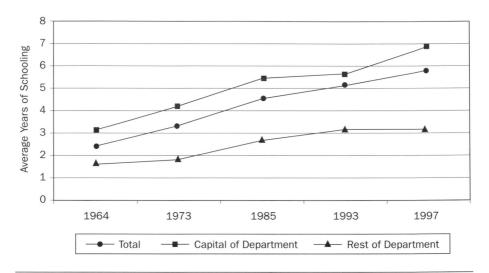

The second impulse, formally initiated in 1991, takes effect two years later in the urban sector and remains unfelt in the rural sector.[3] The pace of growth in the first twenty years was an average of one grade of education for ten calendar years, and the speed of growth has increased to one grade for six calendar years in the urban sector, but with little probability of sustainability given the difficult fiscal conjuncture. In consideration of these trends, we can expect the rural sector to be more than thirty years behind the urban. Even if the rural sector is brought up to the pace of the urban in the last four years, it will still lag by fifteen years. Faced with the needs for growth, these achievements are not sufficient. Growth has been considerably less than in the Eastern emerging nations and even some of the Latin American countries. Thus its development in the long term has been insufficient.

To compare achievements in equity we look at the evolution over the last ten years of average grades of education by income deciles for persons over five years old and for the economically active population (EAP).[4] The difference in educational achievement between the first and last income deciles is seven years. The richest 10 percent of the population has more than double the education of the poorest. The relative difference is decreasing until the fourth decile and increases from there on, both for the population as a whole and for the EAP, which shows us how education has been distributed—more and more equitably in basic education and increasingly inequitably above this level. This difference widens between 1985 and 1997, in absolute and relative terms, up to the fifth decile.

One way to compare the impact of education on distribution in the short term is to look at how its benefits are distributed given the existing distribution of income. This was done using a simplified partial equilibrium model which approximates the measure of the impact of services with respect to the value of the subsidies given to households.[5] The measure that sums up this effect is the progressivity coefficient, deduced from the concentration coefficient, originally used by Kakwani (1976) to measure the impact of subsidies. The concentration coefficient is calculated with a methodology similar to the Gini and varies between −1 and +1. It relates the percentage of subsidies received for each service with the percent of the population ordered by per capita income. To calculate the progressivity coefficient (P), the difference between the concentration coefficient (C) of the variable in question and the Gini coefficient (G) of income distribution is measured. This P coefficient will be less than zero when the variable is distributed progressively (relatively favoring the poorest) and positive in the opposite case. Thus the progressivity coefficient comes from subtracting the concentration coefficient of subsidies, school attendance, or in general the variable whose progressivity is being investigated, from the concentration coefficient that exists in the same population group before being affected by that variable.

The population of working age (PWA) numbers 28.9 million people, of which 22.8 million are not in school. The average level of education attained by the people who are and are not studying is measured for the population, ranked by income deciles. The analysis on the education of this population demonstrates that between 1993 and 1997 there is a growing trend of unequal distribution (see Table 9.5). The table provides frequencies of individuals enrolled in school as well as the mean, or average, level of education each group within the PWA has attained.

The progressivity coefficient between 1993 and 1997 is positive and growing. Thus the distribution of education as a whole is regressive and is associated with growing inequality. Eighty-five percent of the population between 7 and 17 years of age are in the education system. Variation by income quintiles is, however, very large. In the 7–11-year-old group, the target population for primary education, while practically all children of school age in the richest 20 percent attend school, of the poorest 20 percent, 12 percent of children do not attend school. Among 12–17 year olds, 12 percent of the richest group do not attend, compared to 30 percent of the poorest. At the university level, only 18 percent of the poorest go to universities compared to 50 percent of the richest.

Is the opportunity to stay within the system the same for all social groups, or do differences exist? To respond to this question, the gross and net rates are analyzed by income quintiles. At the primary level the net rates by quintile are quite similar. This is not so at the other levels, where coverage rises with income quintile, especially for university education, where the gross coverage rate is 3 percent for the poorest quintile and 74 percent for the richest. The difference is less marked at the preschool and secondary levels—somewhat less than 40 percentage points for the former and close to 20 for the latter. This difference indicates that, in spite of having achieved relative equity for access to primary education, there are still clear barriers associated with income level which make it harder for people with lower incomes to progress through secondary and higher education.

To understand why universal coverage has not been attained, the reasons given for not attending are analyzed for both 1993 and 1997. For the first three quintiles, the main cause given was "high costs," which is also the cause that has grown the most compared

TABLE 9.5

The Stock of Education and Its Distribution in the Population of Working Age (PWA) (1997)

Decile	1	2	3	4	5	6	7	8	9	10	Total	C	P
PWA													
Individual													
Total (millions)	2.9	3	3	3	3	2.8	3	2.8	2.7	2.7	28.9	−0.02	0
%	9.9	10.5	10.4	10.4	10.5	9.9	10.3	9.6	9.2	9.3	100		
Education													
Mean	3.6	4.4	5	5.5	5.8	6.7	7.5	8.6	9.8	11.6	6.8	0.17	0.193
Standard deviation	3.1	3.2	3.3	3.6	3.4	3.8	3.7	4	4.2	4.3	4.4		
Total (millions)	10.3	13.2	15	16.6	17.7	19.2	22.2	23.8	26.1	31.1	195		
%	5.3	6.8	7.7	8.5	9.1	9.8	11.4	12.2	13.4	15.9	100		
PWA not in school													
Individuals													
Total (millions)	2.3	2.4	2.4	2.4	2.4	2.3	2.3	2.2	2.1	2	22.8	−0.03	0
%	10.2	10.5	10.4	10.6	10.7	9.9	10.3	9.5	9.1	8.8	100		
Education													
Mean	3.2	4	4.6	5.1	5.5	6.4	7.2	8.3	9.7	11.7	6.4	0.18	0.213
Standard deviation	33.2	3.3	3.7	3.5	3.9	3.9	4.2	4.4	4.6	4.5			
Total (millions)	7.4	9.6	10.9	12.4	13.5	14.5	16.9	18.1	20	23.6	147		
%	5	6.5	7.4	8.4	9.2	9.9	11.5	12.3	13.6	16.1	100		

Source: Calculations by the CDH, based on the Quality of Life Survey (1997) and CASEN (1993).

with 1993. On the other hand, for the 40 percent with the highest incomes, the main cause is that they "don't like it."

In spite of its magnitude, a majority of the people that report nonattendance due to high costs are young people of 12–17 years old who have not finished secondary school and children (5–6 years old) who have not entered the school system. In any case, it is the most important cause, so that it can be stated that to achieve universal coverage in basic education, the targeting of actions toward the poorest must receive special emphasis. There is a concentration among the poorest 40 percent (78.5). The greatest increase is found in the second quintile, especially for children under 11 years old, and in the third quintile, mainly in those over 12. This result is consistent with what was found in the analysis of poverty as the impoverishment of the second and third quintiles in the urban sector.

It is interesting to note that all the other causes decrease between 1993 and 1997, especially "not being the right age" (–52 percent) and "needs to work" (–40 percent), which is consistent with what was found in the income and expenses survey with respect to families' financial demands, which shows that expenses for transportation and uniforms represent as high a cost as tuition for the poorest groups. This reason is given in the lower quintiles. The reason "not being the right age" is concentrated in the 5–6-year-old group and reflects a cultural fact about families who prefer to keep their children at home. The decreased weight of "lack of vacancies" and of "schools too far away" reflects efforts to increase educational supply during this period.

The reason "don't like it" is notably concentrated in the 12–17-year-old group among those who have not finished their basic education. Although the information does not allow a definitive judgment, it appears to reflect a perception of lack of relevance of education for urban youth of marginal means. This magnitude, which decreases as the level of income increases, affects 68 percent of the poorest 40 percent.

Looking at income quintiles, the reasons that are mainly affected by supply, such as "lack of vacancies" and "schools too far away," are concentrated (74 percent) among the two poorest quintiles. The latter practically disappears in the highest quintiles. From 1993 to 1997, "lack of vacancies" increases in the fourth and second quintiles and decreases in the first and third. The "needs to work" is claimed mainly by the middle income groups.

The next question to approach is the effect that government intervention has had on enrollments. To analyze this, the state of the target population is studied at each level with the following indicators:

• Percentage of private and official participation, to measure the relative effort of the two sectors, for the total population and for each of the income deciles
• The net rate of private and public coverage, to see this effort in relation to the target population
• The percentage of the population that does not attend school, to measure the effort that remains to be made
• The percentage of the population that has not finished its level
• The percentage of the population that has passed on to the next level

The indicators are examined comparatively from 1993 to 1997.

Preschool   Preschool is still a level with low coverage: only 40 percent of preschool-age children go to preschool. This rate varies between 26 out of each 100 for the poorest and 63 out of 100 in the case of the richest 20 percent. There has been an increase in public sector coverage, which went from 19 to 24 percent, with a slight decrease in private coverage, which means that part of the official growth substituted public attendance for private efforts. Supply is official for 64 out of 100 children. By income level, four out of five children in the poorest 20 percent who attend school go to an official establishment, which is true for only one out of three among the richest 20 percent.

Primary Education[6]   Of the population between 7 and 11 years of age, 83 percent were enrolled in primary school in 1993 and 1997. Official attendance is clearly concentrated among the poorest by income, and in the rural sector. In the rural sector, public education is predominant—more than 97 percent of children in the poorest 40 percent of households, and 82 percent in the richest 40 percent, attend an official establishment. In the urban sector, in contrast, the proportion is 92 percent among the poorest and 45 percent in the 20 percent highest income group. In the four years being examined, the private sector increased its attendance by 2.5 points and official sector attendance decreased by 2 points.

Secondary Education   At the secondary level, the net rate of coverage is 59.7 percent. Of the people who attend school between sixth and eleventh grade, two out of three go to public institutions. Attendance differs by income groups: 85 percent in the lowest income quintile and 45 percent in the highest. This situation is reflected in the *P* coefficient, which is regressive for private and progressive for official attendance. The growth of coverage over the four years being analyzed has been 4.8 percentage points for public supply and 1.3 for private.

Higher Education   Net coverage at this educational level among the 18–25-year-old population is 15 percent. In contrast to the primary and secondary levels, enrollment is primarily private. At this age, only 3 percent of the lowest income quintile goes to a university, and of these more than 50 percent pay for their education in private universities. In contrast, more than 40 percent of people of this age group in the highest quintile attend universities, and 75 percent of these attend private institutions. This is the only educational level in which the increase in coverage is larger in the private sector (5 percentage points) than in the public sector (1.7 percentage points).

The Labor Market and Education

In the labor market, education provides advantages not only for income but for the opportunity to participate and find work.

Educational Level of the Economically Active Population (EAP)[7]   Analysis of household surveys administered periodically by the government demonstrates an increase in the educational levels of the labor force. In general, the less educated groups, including the secondary school unfinished group, have reduced their participation as part of the total number of active members, in both the urban and rural zones and in the seven cities. In contrast, the middle and higher levels increase participation, in particular for the "finished secondary school" group in the urban sector and in the seven cities, where the increase of almost 4 percentage points from 1991 to 1997 for people who have finished university level education is notable.

One aspect that should be pointed out is the difference in the educational levels of the urban EAP and the rural EAP. The proportion of people without education in the rural sector is four times greater than in the urban sector (and eight times greater than in the seven major cities). In the rural zone, 70 percent of the EAP has a level of primary or less, while in the urban zone this percentage is slightly higher than 30 percent. The proportion of the active population with secondary school unfinished oscillates between 27 and 25 percent in the urban zone and accounts for only a bit more than 10 percent in the rural zone. The levels of secondary school finished and above, which reach more than 30 percent, are almost exclusively from the urban sector, as in the rural zone they reach only 5 percent.

The biggest change in educational levels is found in women. Presently, the women who comprise part of the EAP are more educated than the men, and this tendency is growing stronger. The opening of greater educational oppportunities for women has made possible their growing links to the labor market and an increase in general educational levels of the EAP. This statement is true for all levels of education, but especially for people with secondary education finished and above. At these levels, both sexes increase their participation, but women do so more rapidly: in 1997, 24 percent of women have finished secondary studies (17 percent for men) and 16 percent have finished university studies (11 percent for men) (see Table 9.6).

The Income of the Employed by Educational Level   To observe the change in income by educational level of the workforce, relative income is defined as the quotient of the natural logarithm of the average income of the most educated and the corresponding logarithm of the average income of five other groups: no education, primary education, secondary unfinished, secondary finished, and university unfinished. Figure 9.2 provides a comparison of the incomes of university graduates employed relative to other groups.

The first observation is that the differentials in income are higher in the urban zone than in the rural zone, independent of educational level. In the urban zone, the seven cities have lower differentials than the urban sector as a whole. But the behavior of income is not the same throughout the period. Between 1991 and 1993, people with more education show increments in their incomes relative to the other groups. From 1993 onward the incomes of the most educated group begin to fall relatively. The increase in the rates of unemployment beginning in that year could explain this situation, and it is to be expected that the returns of education would have diminished since then.

Unemployment and Education   By income level, it can be observed at the national level as well as both the urban and rural levels that the people found in the lower income groups have lower educational levels and suffer in a greater degree from unemployment. Unemployment rates diminish as income rises, such that for the country as a whole the unemployment rates for the poorest 60 percent are greater than the national average.

In the urban zone, the unemployment rate for the poorest 10 percent was four times higher than that of the richest in 1991. This relationship increases to more than nine

TABLE 9.6

Distribution of the Economically Active Population (EAP) by Educational Level and Sex, National Total (1991, 1997)

Year	1991			1997		
Sex	Women	Men	All	Women	Men	All
Without education (%)	7.0	8.8	8.1	4.5	8.7	7.2
Some primary (%)	39.2	48.2	45.0	31.6	42.7	38.5
Secondary unfinished (%)	23.2	21.9	22.3	22.7	20.2	21.2
Secondary finished (%)	18.4	12.5	14.6	24.4	16.9	19.7
University unfinished (%)	6.1	3.5	4.4	7.4	4.5	5.6
University finished (%)	6.1	5.2	5.5	9.3	7.0	7.9
Total (%)	100	100	100	100	100	100
Total number	5,040,983	8,896,766	13,937,749	6,378,270	10,553,135	16,931,405

Source: Author's calculations based on DANE, National Household Surveys.

FIGURE 9.2

Relative Incomes of Employed University Graduates Compared to Other Educational Groups[1] (1978–1997)

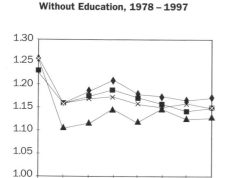

Without Education, 1978 – 1997

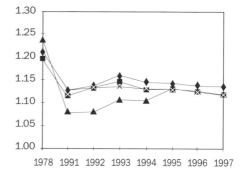

Some Primary, 1978 – 1997

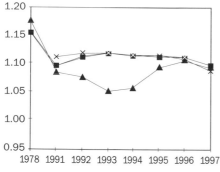

Secondary Unfinished, 1978 – 1997

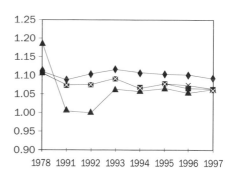

Secondary Finished, 1978 – 1997

—◆— Total   —■— Municipal capital   —▲— Rest   —✕— 7 Cities[2]

[1]The graphs in each figure represent the ratios in the earnings of university graduates to the earnings of the groups described in each case.

[2]"7 Cities" refers to the seven principal cities of Colombia, namely Bogotá, Medellín, Cali, Barranquilla, Bucaramanga, Pasto, and Manizales.

times in 1997. While the growth of unemployment has affected all income groups except the wealthiest, it has done so in an especially strong way among the poorest. The increase in the educational levels of the EAP has not been sufficient to counteract this tendency, because it has not been equitable. The average educational level rose over the period from 6.1 to 6.7 years for the nation as a whole, an increase explained by the evolution of the urban sector (from 7.2 to 7.8 years), while in the rural sector the increase is very low. People who belong to the highest income deciles (9 and 10) increased their education in the urban sector by almost one year, while the other deciles increased by only a half year. The difference in years between the poorest and the richest decile is five years, and the distances do not get shorter over the course of the decade. In the rural sector the increases are important only in the highest decile, while the differentials are small between groups (two years between the poorest and the richest), and the averages are half of those in the urban sector.

Returns of Education   Does education benefit the different groups in Colombian society in terms of labor and wage-earning potential? The following section examines how education and the labor market interact. The data were gathered from National Household Surveys administered between 1991 and 1997 and for 1978. The term *rate of return* signifies the percent change in income with increasing levels of education, net of the costs of acquiring that additional level of education. Therefore, if the analysis refers to a 10 percent increase in rate of return, that can be interpreted as, with an additional unit of education, the individual's income increased by 10 percent. Estimates of income functions were made using data from the National Household Survey between 1991 and 1997 and for 1978. The model used corresponds to the basic formulation developed by Mincer (1974), to which was added the components of the Spline transformation, which lets us estimate rates of return for different educational levels. Table 9.7 presents the regression coefficients for the Mincerian equations corresponding to various years since 1978.

Urban zone. The economic opening that the country experienced from the beginning of the 1990s and developments within the educational system generated changes in the requirements for skilled labor that affect the relationship between education and labor income, or variations in the productivity of labor expressed in the rates of return to education. We begin with two basic assumptions: first, that the most educated workers are better qualified to critically evaluate new information and to use new technologies more efficiently; and second, that employers, upon seeing productivity increased, reward the workers who made that possible with higher salaries. Training is an intermediate variable in the causal relationship between technology and productivity, and the differential income levels capture a large part of their effect.

After the significant reduction in the internal rate of return to education experienced through the end of the 1980s, its behavior in the 1990s tended, if not to revert, at least to stabilize the returns of education, which had a significant contribution, together with experience, in explaining labor incomes. The rate of return to education stabilized over the course of the 1990s at levels close to 10 percent, lower than the levels it had in the 1980s, when it oscillated between 15 and 13 percent.

Our analysis of the household surveys revealed that, in fact, different rates of return on education exist between educational levels. In other words, we found discrepancies

TABLE 9.7

Main Results of the Regression Models, Urban Zone (1978–1997)

Variables	1978	1991	1993	1994	1995	1997
Schooling	0.10572	0.101734	0.104290	0.108218	0.106362	0.112258
Experience	0.04153	0.039850	0.036340	0.034523	0.033423	0.034316
Hours worked	nd*	0.006486	0.008095	0.007492	0.008800	0.007398
Sex	0.28410	0.364632	0.285167	0.286593	0.303319	0.314559
Secondary (6–11)	0.01511	−0.031133	−0.067506	−0.089050	−0.090964	−0.114452
Experience^2	−0.00041	−0.000473	−0.000418	−0.000376	−0.000379	−0.000307
Permanent/ temporary	nd	0.198735	0.159759	0.183096	0.186479	0.179497
Migration condition	nd	0.042385	0.057111	0.063203	0.077301	−0.050000
School/work	−0.22233	−0.074197	−0.063849	−0.082620	−0.080653	−0.108716
University (>11)	0.01511	0.244863	0.241429	0.239138	0.252838	0.195320
Constant	7.26208	9.329145	9.752877	9.985202	10.109527	10.594002
R^2	0.35164	0.407600	0.354900	0.369680	0.380930	0.415240

*nd = No data are available for this year.
Note: For the coefficients sex, migration condition, permanent/temporary $y^\wedge = (e \exp(\beta^\wedge - \frac{1}{2} \text{Var}(\beta)) - 1)$, see Robert Halvorsen and Raymond Palmquist, "The Interpretation of Dummy Variables Is Semilogarithmic," *American Economic Review* (June 1980), 70. Peter Kennedy, "Estimation with Correctly Interpreted Dummy Variables in Semilogarithmic Equations," *American Economic Review* (1981), 71.
Source: Author's calculations based on DANE, National Household Surveys.

between individuals who attained a primary education compared to those with a university education. Primary education has a return slightly lower than the rate we estimated, while surprisingly, secondary education has a lower rate of return than primary education, especially at the end of the period under consideration, 1997. The explanation for this phenomenon could be provided by the generalization of secondary education, given that in the urban zone the proportion of the economically active population with full or unfinished secondary education went from 46 percent in 1991 to 49 percent in 1997. With higher education, the opposite occurred. While increasing, the proportion of people with some postsecondary education was still small—close to 13 percent in 1991 and 17 percent in 1997. Higher education had higher returns, although decreasing over the course of the decade.

The differential by sex. Table 9.8 provides regression coefficients computed separately for men and women. These results lead to the question of whether stabilization in the internal rate of return can be attributed to the increase in women's education and, likewise, can explain why men and women with similar characteristics of education and experience obtain different incomes. Previous studies that differentiated the income functions by gender demonstrated lower effects of education and experience in women. This pattern, in the case of schooling, has changed. The returns of education for women have grown during this period and are slightly higher than for men. On the other hand, experience continues to count much less for women than for men. For men, the net impact of experience, while decreasing over the years being considered, compensates for the loss in education.

TABLE 9.8

Income Functions by Sex (1991–1997)

Men	1978	1991	1993	1995	1997
Schooling	0.10860	0.09448	0.10536	0.10298	0.10555
School/work	−0.24307	−0.09551	−0.12160	−0.13503	−0.15770
Experience	0.05560	0.04785	0.04234	0.04030	0.04071
Experience^2	−0.00060	−0.00057	−0.00048	−0.00046	−0.00040
Hours worked	nd*	0.00394	0.00526	0.00573	0.00643
Migration condition	nd	0.04484	0.07834	0.08272	−0.07408
Secondary (6–11)	0.04832	−0.00768	−0.05301	−0.07709	−0.09384
Permanent/temporary	nd	0.17891	0.13017	0.16199	0.18782
University (>11)	0.3411	0.35196	0.28117	0.31457	0.28375
R^2	0.36782	0.39804	0.35799	0.36871	0.40194

Women	1978	1991	1993	1995	1997
Schooling	0.09381	0.10823	0.09999	0.10678	0.11717
School/work	−0.19008	−0.05450	−0.00545	−0.03386	−0.08356
Experience	0.01459	0.03182	0.03050	0.02658	0.02941
Experience^2	−0.00004	−0.00040	−0.00038	−0.00032	−0.00029
Hours worked	nd	0.00893	0.01097	0.01194	0.00944
Migration condition	nd	0.03123	0.01799	0.06442	−0.08293
Secondary (6–11)	−0.00347	−0.04403	−0.07710	−0.08923	−0.12056
Permanent/temporary	nd	0.20835	0.18272	0.20546	0.15954
University (>11)	0.24816	0.13467	0.19906	0.20664	0.10801
Constant		9.29658	9.76409	10.06225	10.57233
R^2	0.24942	0.37410	0.31889	0.36975	0.40502

*nd = No data are available for this year.

Source: Author's calculations based on DANE, National Household Surveys.

The variables that seek to measure the differentials in the rates of return of education by educational level show the same sign for men and women. Secondary education shows the negative aforementioned pattern, while for university education it is positive, but much higher for men than for women. The returns of secondary education, which in all cases is lower than primary education returns for men, is similar to primary education for women, except in 1993. University education, on the contrary, seems to have greater returns for men than for women. This is probably associated with two simultaneous phenomena: on the one hand, women work in different and lower-paid professions than men, and on the other hand, even when they work in the same professions as men, they are paid less. Thus achieving higher education levels has not been sufficient for women to be rewarded by the market in the same way as men.

FINANCING

This section examines the methods by which education is financed in Colombia, both through the contributions made privately and those administered publicly, and the incidence of the distribution of expenditures on equity.

Private Spending by Decile

An important factor in the equity of educational service is to analyze the way that the different elements of education are financed.[8] Various types of payments that families make to schools (tuition, entrance fees, graduation fees, and monthly fees) are grouped together under the category of "supply expenses." These expenses represent between 43 and 67 percent of spending on education. This means that between 40 and 60 percent of families' expenses for education are for items other than supply expenses. In aggregated terms for the country, families' spending represents 4.3 percent of GDP, which means that families dedicate to education a percentage very similar to the state's expenditure.

The Total Public Expenditure

Current national revenues finance a majority of educational services, which by constitutional mandate comes to the sector in two forms: the "situado fiscal," a transfer from the federal government to the departments, and "municipal participations," a transfer to the municipalities. Beginning in 1995, during the transition toward decentralization, there was a compensation fund, also of national origin. Part of the tributary incomes and contributions are of municipal origin and constitute their own resources, which are also dedicated to education.

Total social spending[9] multiplied fivefold from 1973 to 1997, growing continuously in real terms, while the population grew by only 60 percent. The speed of growth of the 1970s declined in the next decade as a result of the difficult economic conjuncture and of the fiscal adjustment in the middle of the decade. In the 1990s, public spending recuperated its dynamism, and since 1991 has been growing continuously, passing 40 percent in 1997. However, the country is going through a difficult economic situation which naturally has repercussions on fiscal behavior. Public spending grew very little in 1998 and it is even possible that it decreased in 1999. The state, which in the early 1970s spent 259,000 pesos per inhabitant, in 1980 spent close to double that amount, and in 1995 spent 739,000 pesos per inhabitant (all figures are based on constant pesos of 1996).[10]

With respect to GDP, the growth of the last 25 years has represented a doubling of the state's imput, as public spending went from representing 16 percent of GDP in 1973 to 33 percent in 1995. The largest growth of state spending, close to 25 percent in real terms, occurred between 1990 and 1994. Of this growth, the largest part was made in general administration, in defense and public order, and in social spending, as an effect of the reform of the state and of the new obligations established in the Constitution of 1991. From the point of view of public spending, the contribution of the new constitution is the obligation to transfer resources to the departments and municipalities, leaving the initiative for spending to them. The transition to this form of transfers was made in a very short period of time, which has generated problems of rigidity in macroeconomic management and of increased levels of regional indebtedness, which has meant serious fiscal difficulties for a large portion of the departmental and municipal entities.

Another characteristic of public spending in the 1990s was the declining participation of economic services in government spending, as a consequence of the privatization of some goods and services previously produced or lent by the state.

Expenditures on Education

Even during times of recession, Colombia maintains its financing for social spending. While it is not anticyclical, because it does not increase in a recession, it falls by less than what is customary in other countries because of its financing from revenues with specific destinations. Before the Constitution of 1991, growth of the GDP or of state spending did not necessarily produce growth of social spending.[11] Neither of the two peaks of growth, from 1977 to 1978 and from 1985 to 1986, were accompanied by a similar growth in social spending. Moreover, from 1984 to 1986 spending on education fell. The economic adjustment of 1985 increased the state's participation in the economy, but in favor of sectors other than the social sector, while decreasing spending on education and increasing debt participation.

In the 1990s the situation was different. Both public and social spending were growing, but the latter did so at a greater speed. While in real terms total public expenditures grew by 50 percent from 1990 to 1995, social spending doubled. In this way it compensated for the relative backwardness it had since 1973, with some exceptions such as education and other services, whose accumulated indices were still lower than those of social spending and total state expenditures. Only since the Constitution of 1991, with its framework of decentralization, was there a clear turnaround in favor of social spending which reversed and compensated for this eighteen-year trend.

During the 1980s, per capita social spending oscillated between 135,000 and 160,000 pesos. The steadiness of expenditures can be attributed in large part to the revenues with specific destinations for social spending which exist since the plebiscite of 1958. These specific allocations to social spending were kept in the rules of value-added-tax transfers in the 1970s, and were later reaffirmed in the Constitution of 1991. Even though it is necessary to seek ways to periodically evaluate the size of those revenues in order to adjust it to the economic conjuncture, revenues with specific destinations have turned out to be one of the few instruments of long-term programming.

Figure 9.3 shows that public per capita spending on education increased fivefold in real terms from 1973 to 1997, while the population of school age (five to twenty-five years) grew by only 30 percent. Growth was most rapid in the 1990s, from 62,000 pesos at the beginning of the decade to 128,000 pesos, approximately $127, in 1996.

With respect to GDP as shown in Figure 9.4, spending on education reached 3.7 percent in 1984, but started to decrease beginning with the economic adjustment of 1985 until reaching 3.13 percent in 1991, the lowest participation since 1979. Starting in 1991, as an effect of the impulse toward social spending provided by the new Constitution, it grew until reaching 5.71 percent in 1996. If we add to this percentage 4.2 percent in private spending, the resulting percentage is above the average for Latin America. Thus it could be said that education took on a growing importance in Colombian society judging by its GDP participation.

Looking at participation in government expenditures, however, education has passed the 11.1 percent it represented in 1989 but reached only 13.6 percent in 1996, far from the 21 percent it had in the first half of the 1970s. This is because government spending increased considerably in recent years and targeted health and social security.

FIGURE 9.3

Total Government Expenditure by Destination (1973–1996)

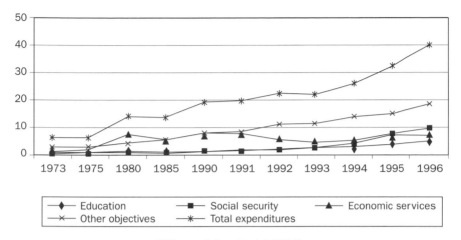

Billions of Constant 1996 Pesos

Source: 1973–1995: DANE, Registro F-400. Calculations by Misión Social DNP-PNUD.
          1996–1997: Calculations by Misión Social based on Contraloría General de la República.

FIGURE 9.4

Public Spending on Education by Levels as a Percentage of GDP

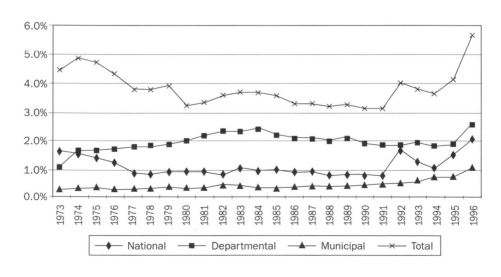

Source: 1980–1996: Calculations by Misión Social based on Registro F-400, National Accounts, DANE.

Analyzing the structure of expenditures in education by levels (primary, secondary, and higher education), administrative expenditures grew the most in the whole period, from 0.2 percent of GDP in 1981 to 0.83 percent in 1996, as can be seen in Table 9.9. However, there was a large growth in this expenditure from 1991 to 1993 when decentralization was initiated, which in 1992 reached close to 30 percent of the expenditure on education. From then on, it decreased its relative weight to close to 15 percent for 1996, the last year for which there are comparable spending data.

Primary education expenditures grew the most (602 percent) from 1973 to 1996. However, through 1995 university education exemplified the largest growth—447 percent, compared to an average growth of 352 percent for the entire sector. Looking at the behavior of expenditures in primary education, it is found that this area lost the most with the adjustment of 1984. Its financing in real terms diminished from 1983 to 1986 but then recovered. In the last five years it was doubled in constant terms and in its participation in GDP. Expenditures on secondary education were the ones that grew the least of the three levels, but since 1992 they have doubled.

In the twenty-three years under consideration, higher education has more than doubled its participation in GDP, going from 0.52 to 1.18 percent. This index is more than the average for the sector but less than for administration and primary education. In the last period, its growth accelerated such that its participation in the sector grew from 14 percent in 1992 to 21 percent in 1996.

Impact of Social Spending by Income Levels

Analysis of the enrollment differential by income quintiles for public and private institutions offers a first approximation of equity in public spending. However, spending per student is different for the rural and urban sectors and for the primary and secondary levels. Statistics for national fiscal accounts inform us on the direct expenditures for primary and secondary education, but not on the division between the rural and urban sectors. The direct expenditure was used as the allocation criterion for administrative expenditures, and the average cost of teachers was used to differentiate between urban and rural costs.[12] Taking the difference in costs on the teachers' pay scale and the difference in the proportion of students per teacher, the cost relationship obtained was 40 percent higher for the urban sector at the primary level and 12 percent at the secondary level.

The cost of primary education has increased relatively more than secondary education. Between 1985 and 1997, the cost per student in primary school rose by 145 percent, while at the secondary level it rose by only 39 percent. This higher cost is due to the unification of primary and secondary teacher pay scales and to the facilities for the formation of educators. However, an increase in cost has not been accompanied by an enormous improvement in efficiency, the time needed to complete a level of schooling as measured by the average cost of each sector. Over these sixteen years, the time needed to graduate primary school has been reduced by about 1.6 percent. The system is more expensive and only a little more efficient.[13]

Distribution of Spending Between Urban and Rural Areas   For 1997 spending at the primary level clearly favored the poorest 50 percent of the population in both the urban and rural sectors. The growth of the expenditure on secondary education in the

TABLE 9.9

Public Spending on Education by Subdestination (Millions of Current Pesos)

Year	Administration	Primary	Secondary	Higher	Other	Auxiliary	Total
1973	762.72	1,924.48	2,061.31	1,271.34	904.41	32.49	6,956.74
1975	795.90	4,239.37	4,587.28	2,130.73	1,671.34	66.32	13,490.94
1977	1,364.56	7,636.20	5,054.81	4,075.00	2,553.46	107.93	20,791.96
1979	2,098.71	11,309.90	9,784.39	7,991.76	4,738.15	349.14	36,272.05
1981	4,732.81	22,975.83	13,891.81	14,181.49	9,017.51	959.74	65,759.20
1983	9,307.11	36,237.88	26,978.11	24,929.39	13,694.02	321.73	111,468.24
1985	15,837.82	53,146.01	43,735.57	36,239.07	26,352.50	161.15	175,472.11
1987	32,336.00	95,144.00	70,080.00	56,525.00	35,960.00	432.00	290,477.00
1989	57,685.00	163,353.00	120,136.00	95,225.00	61,117.00	492.00	498,008.00
1990	73,321.00	206,541.00	166,651.00	124,834.00	66,053.00	482.00	637,882.00
1991	67,817.00	283,235.00	216,069.00	160,907.00	89,245.00	514.00	817,787.00
1992	389,390.00	375,096.00	265,806.00	191,962.00	115,013.00	958.00	1,338,225.00
1993	340,357.00	507,316.00	370,235.00	289,342.00	144,684.00	3,302.00	1,655,236.00
1994	319,167.00	640,223.00	479,095.00	459,098.00	181,574.00	6,896.00	2,086,053.00
1995	429,590.00	924,953.00	652,058.00	699,547.00	300,186.00	8,075.00	3,014,409.00
1996	736,483.00	1,690,558.00	1,185,948.00	1,048,024.00	387,607.00	19,488.00	5,068,108.00

Source: 1980–1996: Calculations by Misión Social based on Registro F-400, National Accounts, DANE.

1993–1997 period was clearly redistributive, especially in the rural sector. In terms of impact, the rural primary and secondary expenditure represents 40 percent of the real incomes of the poorest 10 percent of families, both rural and urban. For the second decile, it represents 18 percent in the urban zone and somewhat more than 50 percent in the rural zone, while this proportion is less than 4 percent for families above the fifth income decile.

Public spending on education is distributed in a progressive manner, as shown in Table 9.10; that is, the lower income groups receive the largest part of public expenditures, especially at the primary level. In the case of higher education, the distribution is regressive, as expenditures are concentrated in the higher income quintiles. Only 12 percent of the poorest 40 percent attend a university, and 60 percent of those attend private universities where they pay for their education. In addition, more than 40 percent of those who belong to the highest quintiles go to public institutions even though they could pay private tuitions.

INTERVENTIONS FOR POSITIVE DISCRIMINATION

As we have shown, the 1990s marked a period of generalized policy intervention that favored the poorest sectors. Most important, this era realized the urgent need for the redistribution of current expenditures, which timely interventions can support. This characterized the change in the management of services. For the management of production of goods, change has come mainly in the orientation of investment, in accumulating greater productive capacity and directing that capacity toward new destinations. In the case of services in general and social services in particular, assuring change in current expenditures is most important. This is the case in the management of the education sector; the creation of people's human capabilities so that they can lead their individual and collective lives is done mainly with what has traditionally been called current expenditures.

From the perspective of the economic supply of public services, the issue is one of a merit good which society decides to put within the reach of all people without excluding any groups. Public leadership considers universal access as a clear and essential collective achievement of development.

The effect, from the point of view of resource management, is that the results of universal provision and subsidy of education should be evaluated in terms of the reorientation and rationalization of current expenditures. From 1985 through 1997, the following instruments of positive discrimination have had significant positive impacts on current expenditures for the poor: stability in official financing for basic education; reorientation toward the poor of national transfers in a decentralized framework; the New School, a high-quality intervention aimed at the poorest strata; and a set of instruments and programs still in the process of evaluation which try to involve the whole society in the management of public education, such as private administration of public institutions, peer accompaniment in daily management, and official financing of services provided by private organizations (PACES grants). Another program in progress, which is only just beginning its activity with the formulation of the latest development plan, is the establishment of the complementary schoolday.

TABLE 9.10

The Distribution of the Primary and Secondary Education Subsidy by Income Decile (Constant 1996 Pesos)

Decile	1	2	3	4	5	6	7	8	9	10	Total
Income per household		Gini 0.526									
Urban	810,934	2,137,218	3,012,173	3,669,176	4,596,278	5,900,323	7,105,438	9,237,504	13,639,950	40,787,575	10,762,564
Rural	1,066,833	2,188,486	2,919,745	3,689,655	4,406,199	5,369,664	6,042,394	7,708,140	10,421,203	21,742,511	3,701,984
Subsidy—Primary		Concentration Coefficient −0.336			Progressivity Coefficient −0.862						
Urban %	12.4%	14.7%	13.8%	14.2%	15.1%	10.1%	8.6%	5.3%	3.9%	1.9%	100.0%
Impact (%)	26.8%	12.1%	6.4%	5.0%	3.8%	1.8%	1.2%	0.6%	0.3%	0.0%	1.1%
Rural %	25.5%	26.7%	17.8%	12.3%	8.3%	5.2%	2.0%	1.2%	0.8%	0.1%	100.0%
Impact (%)	21.39%	10.86%	7.18%	4.45%	3.45%	2.21%	0.99%	0.65%	0.46%	0.05%	4.78%
Total %	17.0%	18.9%	15.2%	13.5%	12.8%	8.4%	6.3%	3.9%	2.8%	1.3%	100.0%
Impact (%)	23.68%	11.46%	6.73%	4.84%	3.70%	1.89%	1.21%	0.56%	0.28%	0.04%	1.47%
Subsidy—Secondary											
Urban %	9.9%	10.8%	12.2%	13.2%	12.0%	14.6%	11.3%	7.3%	6.6%	2.2%	100.0%
Impact (%)	14.10%	5.89%	3.73%	3.09%	1.97%	1.73%	1.07%	0.50%	0.29%	0.03%	0.71%
Rural %	16.2%	24.7%	17.2%	15.5%	7.5%	8.5%	5.7%	3.1%	1.4%	0.3%	100.0%
Impact (%)	4.33%	3.19%	2.21%	1.78%	0.99%	1.15%	0.87%	0.54%	0.25%	0.06%	1.52%
Total %	11.2%	13.7%	13.2%	13.6%	11.1%	13.3%	10.1%	6.5%	5.5%	1.8%	100.0%
Impact (%)	8.44%	4.49%	3.15%	2.63%	1.73%	1.62%	1.04%	0.50%	0.29%	0.03%	0.79%
Total		Concentration Coefficient −0.336			Progressivity Coefficient −0.862	Gini 0.504				

Source: Calculations by the Misión Social based on the Quality of Life Survey (1997).

The Distribution of Transfers

The reorientation of national transfers toward the poorest departments and municipalities is the most important instrument of positive discrimination to come out of the
latest stage of the decentralization process. National transfers have notably affected
current expenditures on education. The most eminent positive characteristics of this
intervention are:

- The stability of the sector's financing
- The clear objective of favoring the poorest
- Decentralization of its management and operations

The main limitations in its development have been the following:

- The attempt to achieve more than one objective with a single policy instrument
  has been problematic. While this attempt has affected distribution, it has not succeeded in completely correcting it, particularly in terms of distribution between
  municipalities within the departments.
- It has been difficult to change the Ministry of Education from an executive and controlling institution to one of orientation and evaluation of quality and management.
- The design and use of management instruments have been precarious and have
  only very partially achieved social control over the sector.

The Stability of Financing   Stable financing has critically influenced the development of the sector. In practice, it has allowed Colombian society to confront the short-
term political profitability of physical public works with long-term social returns in
the form of human capabilities. The fundamental achievement of this stability is that
it increased spending on basic education.

Preferential Spending on the Poorest   A clear direction toward the basic levels has
been achieved, which between 1994 and 1997 has been mainly toward the secondary
level. The impact on family income has notably favored the lowest deciles and has had
a significant effect on the general concentration and distribution coefficients. Its redistributive effect has been twofold. First, it maintained a preference for the poorest
sectors in social spending, and second, it maintained subsidies mainly for basic schooling levels, despite the indubitable preference of society for university education.

Decentralization of Management and Operation   This has been a clear achievement
since the Constitution of 1991. As we showed earlier, it has most clearly affected the
role of the municipality. However, evidence on the way that this spending takes place
raises doubts about the quality of the fiscal management of several of these departments and municipalities.

The Mix of Objectives   The attempt to achieve more than one policy objective with
the same instrument can be seen in what has occurred in the distribution of transfers
in recent years. Even though the constitutional reform was made in 1991, the inertial
effect is very large in the allocation of transfers since 1994 because the formulas for
distribution are applied gradually to a growing part of expenditures.

The formula is problematic in that it attempts to distribute a great majority of its resources via the poverty indicator but at the same time attempts to rectify this issue through administrative and fiscal efficiency. The intent is laudable, because it tries to avoid fiscal laziness and reward the most efficient. What experience has shown, however, is that these objectives can be contradictory in a given year.

When educational departments, as specified by region, are placed in order by the Quality of Life Index (QLI), where those with the highest indices are the richest, it is evident that the effect of the formula clearly favors eleven departments, compared to nine in the initial situation. However, it maintains the discrimination against eight of them, compared to ten in 1994. The situation has improved, but the mix of the three criteria impedes the redistributive effect from increasing. Even among the richest departments, though corrected for in Bogotá, the formula favors the Atlantic department inequitably as seen in Table 9.11. The situation repeats itself when the distribution made by the departments between municipalities is analyzed. Thus the formula has improved distribution but not with the expected speed.

Changes in the Ministry of Education   Although expected, it has been very difficult to change the role of the Ministry of Education. The problem is reflected in the growing expenditures at the national level; even if they have grown less than municipal expenditures, the desired effect was a substantial reduction. This difficulty is due not only to the will of the central level, but also to the age-old reliance upon it to resolve the financial troubles of municipalities and departments and the slow rate of social control over these institutions. The Ministry is not prepared for its new functions. Ministers remain in their positions for an average of nine months, which makes the development of the technical capacity to advise and evaluate territorial entities difficult. The result is that the functionaries prefer to continue doing their traditional jobs.

The Instruments   Clearly one of the major limitations is the design, the application, and most important, the use of the decision-making instruments. The traditional annual census, similar to those used in the majority of Latin American countries, is inadequate, less for its variables than for its antiquated conception of central processing, lack of foresight about the quality control of information, and the banking conception of information as a way of documenting history. Systems for the evaluation of management and for the precise continuous measurement of costs must be decidedly encouraged. In this area the traditional mistrust of the sector toward quantitative measurement must be overcome, as well as the erroneous attempt to replace it with a set of unsystematic opinions which are defended with the argument that qualitative observation conflicts with the quantitative. Evaluation is an activity that combines scientific measurement with political and cultural evaluations.

The tendency to neither ask for nor provide accountability, to make the opinions of the authorities predominate over demonstrable knowledge, is clearly reflected in the resistance of the teachers' organizations to the sorts of evaluations that they routinely practice on their students. The most undesirable effect of this lack of accountability is the difficulty in getting the base communities (parents, students, and nonschool institutions) to have a way of exercising social control over the results of school management.

TABLE 9.11

Comparative Chart of the Per Capita Transfer for Education by Department (1994–1998)

1994			1998 with CEF[1]			Variation from 1994 to 1998		
Department	QLI[2]	Per Capita Transfer	Department	QLI	Per Capita Transfer	Department	QLI	Per Capita Transfer
Departments with QLI below the national average and per capita transfers below average								
Córdoba	52.7	(61,043)	Córdoba	52.7	(47,822)	Chocó	47.9	(1,456)
Sucre	54.7	(84,671)	Sucre	54.7	(80,561)	Nariño	55.0	(19,262)
Nariño	55.0	(26,585)	Nariño	55.0	(45,848)	Magdalena	61.3	(9,824)
Cauca	58.3	(17,644)	Cauca	58.3	(1,065)	Bolívar	62.7	(9,610)
Cesar	60.0	(6,757)	Magdalena	61.3	(81,005)	Huila	64.5	(17,354)
Magdalena	61.3	(71,182)	Bolívar	62.7	(55,445)	Guajira	66.1	(530)
Bolívar	62.7	(45,835)	Huila	64.5	(50,584)	Meta	66.8	(10,259)
Huila	64.5	(33,230)	Guajira	66.1	(41,622)	Tolima	66.9	(15,827)
Guajira	66.1	(41,091)	Meta	66.8	(24,394)			
Meta	66.8	(14,135)	Tolima	66.9	(4,047)			
Departments with QLI below the national average and per capita transfers above average								
Chocó	47.9	28,163	Chocó	47.9	26,707	Córdoba	52.7	13,222
Caquetá	55.6	52,226	Caquetá	55.6	79,889	Sucre	54.7	4,110
Boyacá	60.0	45,545	Boyacá	60.0	58,494	Caquetá	55.6	27,663
ATTNN	63.6	128,762	Cesar	60.0	18,937	Cauca	58.3	16,578
Norte Santander	66.3	14,361	ATTNN	63.6	185,358	Boyacá	60.0	12,948
Tolima	66.9	11,780	Norte Santander	66.3	41,980	Cesar	60.0	25,693
Cundinamarca	67.5	78,002	Cundinamarca	67.5	82,585	ATTNN	63.6	56,596
Santander	69.4	22,174	Santander	69.4	38,769	Norte Santander	66.3	27,619
Caldas	71.8	46,804	Caldas	71.8	65,356	Cundinamarca	67.5	4,583
						Santander	69.4	16,595
						Caldas	71.8	18,553
Departments with QLI above the national average and per capita transfers below average								
Antioquia	73.3	(36,933)	Antioquia	73.3	(53,274)	Antioquia	73.3	(16,341)
Risaralda	74.3	(2,573)	Risaralda	74.3	(24,473)	Risaralda	74.3	(21,900)
Atlántico	77.0	(116,307)	Valle	77.8	(27,078)	Bogotá	84.4	(49,522)
Valle	77.8	(27,626)						
Departments with QLI above the national average and per capita transfers above average								
Quindio	76.2	80,982	Quindio	76.2	133,239	Quindio	76.2	52,257
Bogotá	84.4	76,815	Atlántico	77.0	15,312	Atlántico	77.0	131,619
			Bogotá	84.4	27,293	Valle	77.8	548

[1] CEF = Compensation Educational Fund
[2] QLI = Quality of Life Index

Source: Calculations by the Misión Social based on DNP-UDT (transfers); DNP-UDS (FEC); Misión Social, "La educación en cifras" (enrollments); Misión Social, ICV 1993.

The New School

In the area of instruments of positive discrimination with generalized effects, the New School should be mentioned. From the indicators presented in the first sections of this chapter, it is clearly deduced that poverty is concentrated in the rural sector and that educational achievement, as measured by average years, is a clear measure of its relative backwardness. Thus educational efforts that favor basic education in the rural sector imply efforts in favor of the poor.

The causes of the relative backwardness of the countryside are widely known:

- Difficulties in achieving complete basic education due to the dispersion of the population which has few children for each grade, making it uneconomical to have one professor per course
- Difficulties in keeping children in school all year because of the tendency of parents to use them in seasonal production and harvesting work
- Deficient training of teachers, who are not familiar with the curricula or with adequate teaching methods, especially for multigrade teaching
- Frequent absence of teachers who must travel long distances from the school to receive their salaries, get certified, or attend to family emergencies
- Difficulty in introducing modern pedagogical methods and bringing the teachers up to date
- Lack of relevant knowledge and absence of updating parental involvement

The New School was consolidated as a framework for resolving these problems in an economically sustainable and pedagogically skilled manner. It has the advantage of the multigrade school for all grades, but it does so with modern, semi-individualized, and cooperative learning methods. These instructional mechanisms permit the teacher to guide the learning process through heterogeneous grouping, breaking the rigidity of fixed grades and allowing students to move according to their own pace. Consequently, there is a lower incidence of dropout. Both teachers and students profit from the learning that takes place in the New School. The school pedagogically orients teachers and becomes an interactive textbook between the teacher and the student. Curricular materials indicate the time for teacher intervention, individual/group study, and the use of support materials.

In addition, the school has developed forms of social interaction that promote children's responsibility and their participation in the organization and management of authority in the school. It has obtained the participation of parents, both in the way it organizes school government and in the way it guides children and teachers in the production of their support materials, thus increasing the relevance of education, incorporating the needs of the community into school activities, and promoting the use of materials from the region. The educational microcenters, or teacher's learning groups, allow interchanges of experiences and solutions among teachers.

More than each particular element, what is important about the New School (Escuela Nueva) is the combination of all of them in a feasible model, which since 1986 has become the desirable new learning paradigm for the entire rural sector and which in 1997 was recognized as the study system for 40 percent of the children who attend rural primary school.

The design of the New School has demonstrated effectiveness in terms of discrimination in favor of the poor because it is located in rural areas. In terms of quality, quality evaluations (Psacharopoulos et al. 1992; McEwan 1995), various examinations by Saber (National System of Student Assessment) (Misión Social 1997), efficiency studies (Uribe 1998), and the analysis by the Latin American Quality in Education Laboratory (UNESCO 1998) have produced flattering results for the model. It has been found that students have attained better results in learning, self-esteem, creativity, and solidarity, and that there have been significant effects on diverse activities in the rural sector such as agricultural extension and sanitation campaigns (Rojas and Castillo 1998). In terms of standardized tests, the 1997 study found the top achievements in language and very similar ones in mathematics. What is interesting is that these results, which were from only a few rural schools in the 1992 study, are taken from a larger population and have now included 30 percent of rural schools in a process of expansion which, in spite of management errors in its massive implementation, was able to preserve the desirable characteristics of the New School. What is most important about the New School model is not so much its individual components as their balanced, integrated, and continuous use in daily routines. The new forms of school organization foreseen by the 1994 General Law on Education learned from the experience with the New School. The formal participation of parents in school government encouraged teachers to adopt student-centered approaches and to make adjustments in the curriculum to be more responsive to the characteristics and demands of the community.

The study of efficiency in the use of resources carried out by Uribe showed that the New School is more efficient than the traditional schools. New evidence from comparative studies contributed by the Latin American Quality in Education Laboratory (UNESCO 1998) shows that, while rural schools in Latin America present low achievements compared with their urban counterparts, in Colombia they obtain higher third-grade language scores than urban schools. In third-grade mathematics, they do not exceed all of the urban schools, but they are placed after the megacities.

The third-grade results show that different levels of achievement exist within countries, depending on whether students belong to schools located in megacities, urban centers, or rural zones. These generally follow a pattern of diminishing returns in the order megacity, urban, rural. In the cases of Chile and Cuba, this pattern changes, since schools located in the urban centers have higher scores. On the other hand, for fourth-grade mathematics, rural schools in Colombia (263), Brazil (257), and Argentina (253) have median scores above the regional average, though lower than those of Cuba. On the intra-country level, in Colombia rural schools show performance that, compared to those located in other zones, not only exceeds expectations but also exceeds that of the urban centers.

From the point of view of increasing schooling in terms of grades approved, the expansion of the New School in the rural zones broke the stagnation of the early 1980s in the education sector. McEwan (1995) proposes two hypotheses to explain why the significant difference in the third grade diminishes in the fifth grade:

- The New School receives students who would be repeating grades in the traditional schools. Instead of forcing them to repeat, they stimulate them. Their incorporation is successful because, in spite of their limitations, the fifth-grade students as a whole show better results than in the traditional schools.

• In the fifth grade of the New School there are a larger number of students coming from the traditional schools than in the third grade. Their lower quality puts downward pressure on the average.

Support to Demand: Grants, Aid in Money, and Aid in Kind

In Colombia educational aid and support traditionally have been given by the government to families for the education of their children. In private schools of the middle strata and in the official universities, honor grants are awarded for the best academic performance. Even during the last years in which there were tuition controls (they were eliminated in 1994), to have an increase in funding approved by the government, schools had to provide some percentage of grants to their students. In addition, as part of their welfare policies, firms provide educational aid to employees and their children.

In 1992 the Ministry of Education, as part of its credit program with the World Bank, initiated a grant program called the Program for Aid to Poor Students, to allow poor students to pursue their studies in sixth through eleventh grade. This program, called PACES, in 1997 reached a total of 216 municipalities (out of about 1,200 in the country); about 90,000 students and more than 1,800 private schools participated in the program. The majority of the participating schools are in urban areas where the private schools are concentrated. The ten largest municipalities have 55 percent of the students with grants and 62 percent of the participating schools (King et al. 1997).[14]

In late 1997 the Quality of Life Survey measured these factors, which can be grouped into grants, aid in money, and aid in kind, in disaggregated form. Of the people of school age who attend any level of education, 14 percent (1,644,998 people) received some type of aid in 1977. Table 9.12 disagregates grant beneficiaries by income quintile and Table 9.13 by level of education. Among grant recipients, close to half a million received grants and a similar amount received aid in money. Aid in kind reached slightly more than 900,000.[15] The highest percentage of aid by educational level went to the secondary level, and the lowest to graduate studies. The number of benefits offered by private agencies is higher than for public agencies. Recipients of private aid are concentrated in undergraduate and graduate higher education, while public aid goes mostly to the basic educational levels. However, more than 80 percent of total aid is for basic education.

By income quintiles there is a more progressive distribution for public than for private aid. Some 50 percent of aid from public agencies go to the poorest 40 percent of the population, while this group receives only 30 percent of private aid. The richest 40 percent still receive 23 percent of public aid, indicating that there is still room for better targeting of state subsidies.

The PACES Grants   While grants represent a small percentage of total aid to demand, they are 30 percent of the aid offered for secondary schooling. Students must have finished fifth grade, be less than sixteen years old, belong to the first or second stratum,[16] come from a public school, and have been accepted by a school already registered with

TABLE 9.12

Distribution of Educational Aid: Grants, Money, and Aid in Kind by Per Capita Income Quintiles, Sector, and Number of Beneficiaries (1997)

Level	Sector	Quintile					Total
		One	Two	Three	Four	Five	
Primary	Public agency	156,683	107,448	93,893	49,377	4,275	411,676
	Private agency	68,099	79,857	77,072	63,928	61,979	350,935
	All	224,782	187,305	170,965	113,305	66,254	762,611
Secondary	Public agency	66,412	63,893	108,576	72,725	25,871	337,477
	Private agency	29,374	53,099	101,613	99,394	59,772	343,252
	All	95,786	116,992	210,189	172,119	85,643	680,729
University	Public agency	282	3,554	5,732	12,755	17,787	40,110
	Private agency	938	7,098	3,981	42,772	94,152	148,941
	All	1,220	10,652	9,713	55,527	111,939	189,051
Graduate	Public agency				2,131		2,131
	Private agency				10,476		10,476
	All	0	0	0	12,607	0	12,607
Total	Public agency	223,377	174,895	208,201	136,988	47,933	791,394
	Private agency	98,411	140,054	182,666	216,570	215,903	853,604
	All	321,788	314,949	390,867	353,558	263,836	1,644,998

Source: Calculations by the Misión Social based on the Quality of Life Survey (1997).

the Ministry of Education. The grant is renewed until graduation as long as the student does not fail any grade. Grants are authorized at random if the demand exceeds supply, and only not-for-profit schools participate. Financing is shared between the central and local governments (80 percent and 20 percent, respectively). The stratum and having gone to primary school in a public institution are two instruments for identifying a child as poor.

The program had its widest coverage in 1995 as seen in Table 9.14. The decline from then onward is explained by the declining political support for the program as a consequence of the change of mayors in 1996. In the measurements of King and her team (1997), the most important factors explaining the participation of municipalities are excess demand for secondary education and greater participation of private enrollment in the total. Larger schools, vocational schools, and schools with less than average tuition (40 percent less) participate most. In the measurement of the causes of quality in mathematics and language, no significant differences were found between participating students from private and public schools—that is, quality is at least preserved.

However, differences were found between the private schools that participate in the program and those that do not, but since socioeconomic background was not controlled for, it cannot be stated that the public schools are worse. According to the results of a Misión Social study over the universe of private and public schools, the largest part of quality differences is explained by the socioeconomic origin of the students.

A study in progress coordinated by Joshua Angrist of MIT, Erick Bloom of the Misión Social, Elizabeth King of the World Bank, and Michael Kremer of MIT/Harvard[17] is analyzing the effects of the program. Preliminary results on the effects of the program

TABLE 9.13

Persons Receiving Grants, Money Subsidies, or Subsidies in Kind, by Educational Level

	Primary		Secondary		Level University		Graduate		Total	
	Persons	%	Persons	%	Persons	%	Persons	%	Persons	%
Grant	76,399	1.50%	249,691	6.02%	87,703	6.69%	2,648	2.60%	416,441	3.91%
Money subsidy	170,454	3.36%	222,402	5.36%	83,084	6.33%	8,972	8.81%	484,912	4.56%
Subsidy in kind	515,758	10.16%	208,638	5.03%	18,264	1.39%	987	0.97%	743,647	6.99%
Grant or subsidy	729,834	14.37%	615,828	14.85%	158,806	12.11%	12,607	12.38%	1,517,075	14.26%

Source: Calculations by the Misión Social based on the Quality of Life Survey (1997).

TABLE 9.14

Number of Municipalities, Schools, and Students in the Program

	1992	1993	1994	1995	1996
Number of municipalities	78	173	215	216	211
Number of schools	1,529	1,688	1,786	1,795	1,744
Number of students	49,573	67,149	90,809	88,634	81,009

Source: King et al. (1997).

on permanence in school, taking into account the ages of students and parents, the mother's work condition, and parents' education and salaries, find that the grant has positively affected permanence in the system and has done so in direct relation with the highest educational grade reached. Higher age of the student, working, or living as a couple reduces the probability of staying in school. Finally, this probability is different for men and women.

New Programs of Positive Discrimination

Here we describe a set of programs of positive discrimination, which have not yet been evaluated but which indicate the level of consciousness that exists in the state about the need to give preferential attention to the poorest and which demonstrate how research results influence the formulation of policies and programs. Of these, of special importance is the establishment of the additional day, which is beginning to be applied with the new development plan that the current government presented to the legislative houses in late 1998. This additional day aims at facilitating access for students of the poorest public and private schools to complementary activities of a cultural and recreational nature (theater, sports, music) and to informational and interactive media and systems (libraries, Internet, lectures, etc.). These activities are supervised and directed by adults who are not necessarily teachers, but who are oriented toward supporting classroom study.

The design of the program responds to the discovery that activities and factors found in the family explain 70 percent of quality achievements, while only 30 percent is explained by factors related to the educational institution. It therefore seeks to publicly provide to middle-class and poor children the facilities and elements of support that the rich have in their families. An additional result sought by the program is to multiply the possibilities for polyclass interaction in a school atmosphere, which is increasingly difficult given the great social segmentation that exists in Colombia.

Another activity is delegated administration or peer assistance. In several cities a program is being implemented that seeks to give schools with administrative problems continuous support for a period of time for the purpose of improving its management. This support can be provided by schools of accepted excellence or by nongovernmental organizations of recognized experience, such as Fe y Alegría[18] and the Carvajal Foundation, or entrepreneurs interested in education. In some cases the municipality contracts these advisers, while in other cases an individual firm "adopts" a school, and in others an organization makes a commitment to managing one or several public schools. The program responds to two diagnosed needs: first, the lack of systematization of management practices proven in the sphere of the public sector, and therefore the importance of identifying them empirically; and second, the lack of skilled personnel in the departmental and municipal education departments who can adequately and continuously support the numerous existing educational establishments, and the need to create consciousness that the quality of official education should be a concern and an objective of everyone.

CONCLUSIONS, CHALLENGES, AND RECOMMENDATIONS

The great challenge at the start of the twenty-first century in Colombian society is equity. The main unresolved subject from the political point of view is democracy; from the economic point of view it is equity. Preference for the weakest has become the meeting point for analyses of economic and social development. It is the indispensable foundation for society, as Rawls emphasizes, and it is the foundation for development as analysts of endogenous growth have demonstrated. Equity is not a value judgment but rather a condition for growth.

For achieving social equity, access to education holds a privileged position as the indispensable basis for the creation, appropriation, diffusion, and application of innovation, which has been shown to be the driving force for secularly sustained development.

In Colombia access to education is a sign of social and economic inequality. Education has great potential as a distributor of opportunities, but when its access is restricted, it becomes a factor in reproducing inequity across generations. The noneducational variable that, in standardized tests of achievement, best explains quality variations is children's socioeconomic background.

The challenge for achieving the universalization of basic education is, while sustaining the stability of financing, to improve social efficiency by means of positive discrimination more decidedly in favor of the poor. This increase in the social efficiency of allocation implies better knowledge and more careful use of resources. But it also implies social mobilization in favor of the poor and social control of quality. If the results expected of the educational institutions are not expressed in an understandable and measurable form, social control will only be a utopian desire.

The behavior of the labor market shows that, even though there has been a decline in the returns of education with the rise of unemployment, this has stabilized, and education continues to be one of the best long-term investments in individual terms. In social terms it is a condition for increasing social capital and has proven its positive effect in reducing violence. Women's education, which has grown more than men's, has reduced gender discrimination and has favored growing women's participation in economic activity, although it still has not been able to completely overcome inequality in remuneration. University education seems to have greater returns for men than for women, which is probably associated with two simultaneous phenomena: on the one hand, women exercise different professions than men and these are valued lower by the market, and on the other hand, even when they practice the same professions as men, women are paid less.

As we have shown, the most important fact in terms of equity in the 1990s is that intervention in favor of the poorest groups has been a generalized policy in the sector. What has been important is the rising consciousness that the most urgent change is the redistribution of current expenditures, for which timely interventions are one of the support instruments.

The way that decentralization has been carried out has had an influence in creating a more equitable allocation between departments, but the challenge still remains of taking this more decidedly to the municipalities. More aggressiveness is required to support the poorest groups and to do so where their expenses weigh the most in their family incomes: textbooks, school supplies, and uniforms. A great effort remains to be made in terms of the information needed to achieve effective accountability.

The results of the New School with respect to educational achievement must be highlighted, not only because it has enabled rural children, the poorest in the country, to compete advantageously with their counterparts in the cities, but also because it has been sustained over time. Since the time it went from an experimental project to a national program, many serious administrative mistakes were made. Nevertheless, it was a good experiment that grew to a massive scale, absorbed educational innovations well, and was able to influence the development of education in the whole country.

Social spending on education in Colombia has been redistributive with the exception of the university level. In real terms the educational subsidy has an important effect on the average incomes of the poorest families. The rural primary and secondary expenditure represents 40 percent of the real incomes of the poorest 10 percent of families, both rural and urban. For the second decile, it represents 18 percent in the urban zone and somewhat more than 50 percent in the rural zone, while this proportion is less than 4 percent for families above the fifth income decile.

While the figures calculated here are not definitive, they illustrate how bringing basic education to the entire population could be done economically as long as there exists determination; the participation of the poor in their own solutions; and above all an effective, efficient, and transparent management.

The level of inequality in Colombian society is one of the highest in Latin America and must be a principal target of public action. Given the incidence of inequality, actions with the greatest coverage should receive the top priority. Education is one of the most efficient ways to improve equity, but it is not an inherent characteristic of public education. This must be explicitly proposed as a goal. Given that the current situation is the accumulation of past inequities, new policies must affect the existing distribution with explicit preference for the poor.

Can poverty be affected through education? Yes, because higher levels of education lead to more welfare. Education is a desirable good and, in economic terms, a superior good whose consumption increases with income. It is better to be educated than not to be.

This affirmation leads to three corollaries: (1) To increase the effect of the programs with positive discrimination toward the poor, it is necessary to have the participation of the affected population. (2) The evaluation of educational programs should identify the winning group and the effect that the program has had on the incidence of poverty, the intensity of this effect, and the effect on income distribution. (3) The educational system also affects equity, depending on who pays and who takes advantage of it. To benefit the poor, there must be an explicit positive discrimination.

In the implementation of public policies in education, particularly those operated by the government, there are significant weaknesses in two critical aspects: (1) management among the different levels of government and (2) regulatory bodies, which are necessary to help strengthen civil society.

Equity that favors basic education does not imply abandoning the university. The creation of a solid base in science and technology is important for competitiveness and development. Public subsidies must give preference to basic education but also support strategic disciplines for scientific and technological development. It is not acceptable to subsidize the future income of professionals before guaranteeing basic education and the creation of a scientific base.

NOTES

1. According to the National Statistics Department (DANE), the poverty line is 2 times the indigence line for the countryside and 2.3 times for the urban sector.
2. The Theil coefficient of inequality is an index that identifies the factors associated with the differences in the share of income held by different groups, thus permitting the "decomposition" of inequality. It does not vary with the scale used to measure income, but it is sensitive to income transfers between individuals at different income levels.

$$T = \Sigma_i \, X_i \, ln \, (x_i n)/ln$$

where n is the number of people receiving income and X_i are their participations in total income, or the share of each group in the total income available in the country.
3. It should be noted, however, that the information from 1991 does not include the new departments, formerly referred to as national territories, where about 10 percent of the population live and which have had an accelerated development in the last four years.
4. National Planning Department (DANE) household surveys from September of each year are used in this analysis.
5. This is the method used by the Misión Social of Colombia to measure the impact of public social spending programs on equity. For a discussion of their foundations, see Vélez (1996).
6. Official participation is undervalued because neither of the two surveys (CASEN 1993 and Quality of Life 1997) are representative of the new departments or old national territories, whose enrollment is in large part official.
7. Six educational groups were considered within the EAP: without education (0 years of schooling); primary studies (between 1 and 5 years of schooling); secondary unfinished (between 6 and 10 years of schooling); secondary finished (11 years of schooling); university unfinished (between 12 and 15 years of schooling); and university finished (16 or more years of schooling).
8. The data are based on the survey of income and expenditures carried out by DANE between 1994 and 1995 as the basis for the price index. One is done every ten years.
9. For a broader analysis of social spending in Colombia, see Sarmiento, Delgado, and Reyes (1999).
10. In 1996 the exchange rate was $1,036 pesos per dollar.
11. *Social spending* means spending by the state on education, health, welfare, housing, social security, potable water, and "other" expenditures such as culture and recreation. The information covers the period 1980–1997 and was derived from the National Accounts series of

DANE, which makes possible the aggregation of national, departmental, and municipal expenditures net of transfers.

12. The difference between levels on the pay scale for 1997 was 5.89 rural primary, 8.36 urban primary, 10.57 urban secondary, and 9.25 rural secondary.

13. For a broader analysis of internal efficiency, see Sarmiento and Caro (1998, Tables 13 and 26).

14. The World Bank carried out an initial evaluation coordinated by Elizabeth King, whose results are summarized here, and has another group of researchers working on an evaluation now in progress.

15. The difference between the sum of these three categories and the total is due to the fact that the forms of aid are not mutually exclusive.

16. Households in Colombia are classified into six strata according to physical conditions of their housing, for purposes of assigning rates for public services. Stratum 1 has the worst conditions and Stratum 6 has the best.

17. This study is from a combined sample from their surveys in Bogotá (1995 and 1997) and Jamundí (1993).

18. Fe y Alegría, literally *faith and joy,* is a nongovernmental organization that runs schools in marginalized communities in thirteen countries in Latin America. Managed by Jesuits with most of the staff being lay personnel, the organization typically works in partnership with governments that subsidize teachers' salaries.

REFERENCES

Aristóteles de Estagira. 1989. *Book III, 6. Politeia.* Direct translation from Greek into Spanish by Manuel Briceño Jáuregui. Bogotá, Colombia: Publicaciones del Instituto Caro y Cuervo.

Baldión, Edgar. 1995. Estrategias de capacitación y productividad en la empresa. Report to the World Bank. Mimeograph. Bogotá, Colombia: World Bank.

Barro, Robert. 1997. *Determinants of Economic Growth: A Cross-Country Empirical Study.* Cambridge, Mass.: MIT Press.

Barro, Robert, and Xavier Sala-i-Martin. 1995. *Economic Growth.* New York: McGraw-Hill.

Corporación para el Desarrollo Humano. 1998. Analisis del servicio educativo 1993–1997. Mimeograph. Bogotá, Colombia: Misión Social.

Departamento Nacional de Estadísticas (DANE) (National Department of Statistics). Encuestas de hogares, septiembre de cada año. Bogotá, Colombia: DANE.

Departamento Nacional de Estadísticas (DANE). 1997. Encuesta de calidad de vida. Bogotá, Colombia: DANE.

Departamento Nacional de Planeación. 1983. *Cambio con Equidad: Plan Nacional de Desarrollo 1983–1986.* Bogotá, Colombia: DNP.

Departamento Nacional de Planeación. 1985. El programa macroeconómico: Autodisciplina para el desarrollo, 1985–1986. Bogotá, Colombia: DNP.

Duarte, Guterman, and Cia, Ltd. 1998. Análisis de pobreza y equidad 1993–1997. Misión Social. Mimeograph. Bogotá, Colombia.

Duarte, Guterman, and Cia. 1997. Report on Quality of Life survey. Mimeograph. Bogotá, Colombia.

Duarte, Guterman, and Cia. 1993. Report on socioeconomic household survey. Mimeograph. Bogotá, Colombia.

Kakwani, Nanak. 1976. Measurement of tax progressivity: An international comparison. *Economic Journal* 87(345): 71–80.

King, Elizabeth, et al. 1997. Colombia's targeted education voucher program: Features, coverage, and participation. Working paper series on impact evaluation of education reform, paper no. 3. Mimeograph. Washington, D.C.: World Bank.

Laboratorio Latinoamericano de Calidad de la Educación. 1998. *Primer Estudio Comparativo sobre Lenguaje y Matemáticas y Factores Asociados en Tercero y Cuarto Grado*. Santiago, Chile: UNESCO.

McEwan, Patrick. 1995. Primary school reform for rural development: An evaluation of Colombian new schools. Washington, D.C.: InterAmerican Development Bank.

Mincer, Jacob. 1974. Schooling experience and earnings. New York: National Bureau of Economic Research, Columbia University Press, pp. 80–82.

Misión Social, Departamento Nacional de Planeación (DNP). 1997. La calidad de la educación y el logro de los planteles educativos. *Planeación y Desarrollo* XXVIII(1): 25–62.

Nuñez, Jairo, and Fabio Sánchez. 1998. Educación y salarios relativos—1976–1995: Implicaciones para la distribución del ingreso. In *La Distribución del Ingreso en Colombia*, ed. Fabio Sanchez, 129–171. Bogotá, Colombia: Tercer Mundo Editores-Departamento Nacional de Planeacion.

Oficina de Planificacion y Estadistica, Ministerio de Educacion Nacional. 1985. Eficiencia interna del sistema educativo Colombiano en el nivel primario: 1961–1983. Bogotá, Colombia.

Oficina de Planificacion y Estadistica, Ministerio de Educación Nacional. 1987. Eficiencia interna de básica secundaria y media vocacional: 1978–1984. Bogotá, Colombia.

Psacharopoulos, George, Carlos Rojas, and Eduardo Vélez. 1992. Achievement evaluation of Colombia's escuela nueva. Washington, D.C.: World Bank.

Rawls, John. 1971. *Teoria de la Justica*. Mexico City: Fondo de Cultura Económica.

Rawls, John, Charles Fried, Amartya Sen, and Thomas C. Schelling. 1988. *Libertad Igualdad y Derecho*. Barcelona: Editorial Ariel.

Rojas, Carlos, and Zoraida Castillo. 1998. Evaluación del programa de escuela nueva en Colombia. Bogotá, Colombia: Instituto SER.

Romer, David. 1996. *Advanced Macroeconomics*. New York: McGraw-Hill.

Romer, David. 1987. Growth based on increasing returns due to specialization. *American Economic Review* 27(2): 56–62.

Sarmiento Gomez, Alfredo, and Leticia Arteaga. 1998. Focalizar para universalizar. *Cuadernos de Economía* XVII(29): 197–210.

Sarmiento Gomez, Alfredo, and Blanca Lilia Caro. 1999. La educación en cifras. Boletin Sistema de Indicadores Sociodemograficos para Planeacion. Bogotá, Colombia: DNP.

Sarmiento Gomez, Alfredo, Liliana Delgado, and Carlos Reyes. 1999. El gasto público en los servicios sociales básicos en Colombia: Iniciativa 20/20. In *Gasto en Servicios Sociales Básicos en America Latina y el Caribe: Análisis de la Perspectiva de la Iniciativa 20/20*, eds. Enrique Ganuza, Artura Leon, and Pablo Sauma, 289–333. Bogotá, Colombia: PNUD, CEPAL, UNICEF.

Sen, Amartya. 1992. *Inequality Reexamined*. Cambridge, Mass.: Harvard University Press.

Sen, Amartya. 1997. *On Economic Inequality*. Oxford, England: Clarendon Press.

Sen, Amartya. 1998. Teorías del desarrollo a principios del siglo XXI. In *El Desarrollo Económico y Social en los Umbrales del Siglo XXI*, eds. Louis Emmerij and José Nuñez, 589–614. Washington, D.C.: InterAmerican Development Bank.

Sen, Amartya. 1995. The political economy of targeting. In *Public Spending and the Poor*, eds. Dominique Van de Walle and Kimberly Nead. Baltimore, Md.: Johns Hopkins University Press.

Tenjo, Jaime. 1993. Evolución de los retornos a la inversión en educación, 1976–1989. In *Planeación y Desarrollo* XXIV (special edition):85–102.

UNESCO/OREALC. 1998. *Laboratorio Latinoamericano de Calidad de la Educación: Primer Estudio Comparativo Sobre Lenguaje, Matemáticas y Factores Asociados en Tercero y Cuarto Grado.* Santiago, Chile: UNESCO.

Uribe, Maria Camila. 1998. Eficiencia del gasto publico en educacion. Bogotá, Colombia: Departamento Nacional de Planeción.

Van de Walle, Dominique, and Nead Kimberly, eds. 1995. *Public Spending and the Poor.* Washington, D.C.: Johns Hopkins University Press.

Vélez, Carlos Eduardo. 1996. *Gasto Social y Desigualdad: Logros y Extravíos.* Departamento Nacional de Planeación/Misión Social. Bogotá, Colombia: Tercer Mundo Editores.

Commentary

Jorge Padua, Colegio de Mexico

Sarmiento Gomez's description of Colombian schooling is intense in quantity and detail. The information provided to diagnose educational problems and the descriptive analyses of different educational participants allow one to gain a better picture of schooling in Colombia. However, his intentions are weak in explicitly defining the content and the intentions of certain political public sectors toward the marginalized populations in poverty seen with greater intensity among many Latin American countries.

Unsurprisingly, Colombia is increasingly a country less and less unique in its unstable and unsafe social network. Aggravated by open group conflict—with particularly violent ethical norms, like those of "drug lords," guerillas, paramilitary groups, and common delinquents—with authorities and forces of security, Colombian society is maintained by a state of permanent warfare. The crisis induced by public politics, together with the dispositions of reform in the country, are included in this political, economic, and cultural scene.

Sarmiento Gomez's initial investigation only brushes over issues of migratory trends from rural populations to urban. On the other hand, his brief incorporation of theories on social justice from Rawls in conjunction with his discussion of public school expenditures and of programs to assist the poor in search of equity bring to light more explicit arguments. In search of equity, schooling would have a positive privilege as the distributor of opportunities, a worthy investment for individuals, institutions, and society in general. Sarmiento Gomez describes education as the most important predictor variable in general life opportunities and in labor markets. At the same time, he diagnoses the actual schooling situation as one that perpetuates social and economic inequalities and that is unable to increase equity. To resolve the problem, Sarmiento Gomez justifies the use of positive discrimination to universalize basic education in favor of the poor. This is in addition to the following: an increase in privatization efficiency, decentralization, education innovation, participation of the population to control quality, the improvement of public school administrative systems, and a diminishing subsidy for superior education.

In addition, Sarmiento Gomez's analysis of the characteristics and evolution of poverty during the period of 1993–1997, although it covers only a brief period of time, is important to understand the real concentration of poverty in Colombia. Although the country attempts to offer the impression of making significant strides in increasing the standard of living among its populous, poverty indicators show otherwise. As Sarmiento Gomez points out, indigents comprise 18.3 percent of the population and those in extreme poverty, 47.1 percent (1997).

The most important data and that most indicative of the situation in Latin America refer to the decreased distribution of income in rural areas and the redistribution of income in rural areas. In general, during the period discussed, the analysis examining varying quintiles of the population shows that income distribution favors those groups in the highest quintiles.

I will now address Sarmiento Gomez's discussion on educational distribution across different sectors of society. The analysis clearly shows that in the last years in relation to other countries, educational accomplishments have been insufficient, unequal, and slow. Why slow? Slow because average years of schooling for the population accelerated at a high speed beginning in the 1960s and then stagnated forcefully in the 1980s, only to slightly recuperate their growth in the 1990s. Sarmiento Gomez's analysis on the evolution of public school clearly shows that in the case of Colombia, there has been a decrease in funding since 1974 sustained until 1991, and recently surpassed in 1996. This phenomenon has unveiled significant financial problems for the public sector in 1998.

In sum, Colombia has heightened a trend of segmentation in the last years with respect to schooling and labor, as evidenced by the fact that groups with low levels of education have reduced their participation in the economic active population (EAP), equally in rural and urban areas. The groups in the lowest income deciles have unemployment rates four times that of those in the highest deciles. At the same time, the average number of school years completed for the poorest sectors is not sufficient to counteract these tendencies. It is probable that a certain "credentialing" effect has taken place in superior levels of schooling, although the author prefers to offer relative explanations to differences in economic productivity.

Furthermore, the description and analysis of programs oriented toward the poor are indicative of positive results in learning, self-esteem, creativity, and independence. This is not evident in secondary school programs or in the incorporation of vouchers to increase the privatization of schooling. Program descriptions at the primary public level clearly indicate a different type of organization that fosters the participation of parents, teachers, students, agencies, and actors that facilitate innovation.

Overall, the mechanisms employed to institutionally restructure the school system have focused on the following: decentralization; the weakening of teacher unions, a reduction in state intervention and the opening of the provision of private services, and decreasing public subsidies at the basic public level and in poor rural populations.

Finally, social injustice and the general upward trend of poverty and increased segmentation in the population are not a direct consequence of the public school system. On the contrary, the unequal distribution of schooling stems from social structures and systems of institutionalized injustice. Although there isn't sufficient space to elaborate on this topic, it is important to remember that the problems that emerge during Sarmiento Gomez's analysis of constructing a just society are large and complex. Even though education in general, and particularly basic education, is important in the present and future, it cannot solely resolve problems evident in social and economic structures. It is not sufficient to ask for modernization in which the current objectives favor self-interest and inequality. The triumph of liberalism-capitalism-utilitarianism is the triumph of social classes in society that together move toward equality. The opposite, or compensatory society, runs against the notion of liberty.

The proposition of viewing education as the individual and social intervention for democracy is sensational, reasonable, and desired. However, under the perspective of assuming that formal education could possibly influence the development of psycho-social well-being and in lieu of the type of appropriate regulated development, much remains for debate.

Elementary-school students during a school ceremony in Veracruz, Mexico.
[Enrique Barradas/Diario AZ/Veracruz]

10

Poverty and Education in Mexico, 1984–1996

Teresa Bracho, Centro de Investigación y Docencia Económicas, Mexico

It is part of the international consensus that the development of human capital is a crucial element in obtaining economic growth, and education has been highlighted in practically all recent discussions about inequality and poverty. Nevertheless, the relationship between education and poverty has not been explored in depth from the perspective of education theory.

In the case of Mexico, there is widespread recognition of the intensity and incidence of poverty, as well as of the impact of the reform policies of the 1980s and the most recent economic crisis of 1995 on households in more vulnerable conditions. Because most recent social policies were oriented toward the eradication of poverty, or at least attempted to diminish its effects, the variety of measures implemented during the 1980s and 1990s is important. Recent approaches in the literature as well as policy planning include at least one of the following components:

- Policies for stable economic growth
- Policies that facilitate the access of jobs to poor people and assure that they are better remunerated
- Programs that offer direct support to poor families in order to break the vicious cycle of extreme poverty
- Sustained investment in social infrastructure—in particular, in the regions and microregions with the largest concentration of the poor

Within this general context of development, educational policies can be identified at least in the last two components mentioned above. One factor deemed fundamental in breaking the cycle of poverty is the improvement of educational conditions among the "lagged" social segments of society.[1]

The purpose of this chapter is to present a general overview of Mexico's income distribution, poverty, educational distribution, and their relationships, based on household data. The information is based on household surveys taken between 1984 and 1996.[2]

The chapter is divided in two parts. The first, of a general character, refers to the definitions of poverty and the main approaches used in its analysis. The second part focuses on the empirical analysis of the Mexican case. It describes some of the poverty and educational conditions within an important segment of the households and compares it with the national situation. It focuses on the analysis of household heads and their chances of being poor according to their educational backgrounds. In addition, it describes the educational status of younger household members and school enrollment. The intention is to allow a better understanding of the relationship between poverty conditions and access to education. Because this is an ambitious goal, I will present my arguments in a simplified, descriptive manner, in order to identify the dimensions of the problem and prompt us to ask new questions.

POVERTY AND THE ROLE OF EDUCATION IN ITS DEFINITIONS

The definitions of *poverty* are abundant. Among them, there is not a clear agreement on what should be understood as the "poor," "minimal levels of well-being," or "quality of life," to mention just some of the concepts associated with poverty. However, the concept always suggests a notion of scarcity of the necessary means to survival.

The different approaches to poverty analysis may be classified in a few categories.[3] The first two approaches have dominated the economic analysis on poverty. First, the most common approach in the literature establishes minimum requirements for survival. A poverty line is defined from either a basic nutritional basket and the income required to purchase it, or living conditions and access to public services.[4] The second approach emphasizes inequality, defining the differences between the segments of society with larger and smaller incomes.[5] The emphasis on relative deprivation, defining the level of poverty in relation to another group or person, has been most common in the sociological literature.[6] The notion of relativity had been expanded to conform to a fourth approach, defining poverty as a value judgment and, as such, as an exercise in social philosophy and as an exercise in political measures oriented toward a redistribution of social goods based on the idea of "basic rights," similar to the idea of "basic needs."

Amartya Sen expands the ideas behind these approaches. He points out that the notion of basic needs can be better expressed in terms of basic capabilities in order to distinguish "the capability to satisfy certain crucial needs and to achieve a certain basic level" (Sen 1996, 67). As a consequence, the poverty line, rather than being defined in terms of a basic nutritional basket or fulfillment of basic needs, should be a measure of a failure to achieve a certain level of functioning. He does not reject the minimum income approaches but interprets the cause of poverty based on income.

Education Within Poverty Analysis

The notions of poverty described above imply different possible interpretations of the relations between education and poverty and between the educational system and its role in society. We must recognize, however, that the most recent developments in the area have taken place in the fields of philosophy and economy, rather than in the educational field.[7] I suggest here that, in accordance with Sen's approach, education should be considered a basic capability, and as such its relative dimension based on its societal and cultural context must play a role in its analysis.

Access to literacy is considered a basic need in most of the literature on poverty, with some authors extending the definition to basic schooling. Education also may be associated with the notion of basic need and basic right, when enrollment rates or average schooling is contrasted with minimum educational standards such as those established by the Universal Declaration of Human Rights.

However, schooling is far more than a basic need. It is part of a group of goods available to the individual (or household) for exchange as part of his or her social and cultural capital. It also has a particular value, with at least part of it determined by its exchange power or its capacity to achieve other social goods, such as access to employment, level of income, and other personal and social benefits.[8] The following empirical analysis relates education to poverty, based on the concept of education as a basic human right, with the value of education relative to the standards and subcultures of each society.

EMPIRICAL ANALYSIS

The purpose of this part of the chapter is to describe the educational characteristics of the poorest sector of the population and its position relative to national income and educational levels. The estimates presented are based on microdata from the Mexican National Household Income and Expenditure Surveys (ENIGH) produced by the National Institute of Statistics, Geography, and Informatics (INEGI 1984; 1989; 1992; 1994; and 1996). In the Appendix, I briefly describe the contents of these national surveys, their comparability, and the variables used in this analysis.

The first section describes the distribution and concentration of income. The estimates of income distribution and poverty are based on income per capita. A brief description of poverty distribution, exclusion, and educational averages by state is included to highlight the regional disparities embedded in the study of poverty.

The second section analyzes the educational distribution among household heads by income quintiles and the differences between urban and rural areas. It explores the possibilities of educational expansion among the poorest sectors to promote social mobility.

The third section analyzes the educational levels of school-age populations. Emphasis is put on those who do not attend school, as well as households with educational exclusion in relation to income distribution. Young members of the household who are part of the labor force are not described at length, although the general tendencies of the population between six and fifteen years old, corresponding to the mandatory level of basic education, are described. The expansion of compulsory education at the political level—since 1992—to secondary education often poses a conflict between the household decision to send children to school and the need for the household's participation in raising its income.[9] The levels at which these decisions are made for Mexican households are identified.

Distribution of Income and Poverty

Before discussing income distribution, it should be noted that there is no agreement among different researchers on where to establish the poverty threshold in Mexico. The poverty line is usually established between the second and fourth deciles. Some authors assert that about 20 percent of the households are in poverty (the most commonly used definition of poverty), while others extend this estimate to 30 percent to 40 percent of the population. Here I choose to define poverty by income quintiles, identifying the bottom 20 percent of the distribution as extreme poverty. The second quintile constitutes the income strata with moderate levels of poverty. I compare both groups with the remaining strata of income distribution.[10]

There is an increasing concentration of income in the top quintile, particularly among the top 10 percent of the distribution. In contrast, there is an income deterioration in the remaining quintiles (except for the fourth and fifth, since 1989). The deterioration is constant and noticeable in the poorest bottom 40 percent of the population. The redistribution of income found in 1996 is concurrent to a general impoverishment of the entire population (see the Appendix, Table A.1).

Table 10.1 summarizes the income distribution by quintiles. In 1984, the top income segments of society made twelve times more than the bottom 20 percent of households under extreme forms of poverty. The disparity in income between the top and bottom segments increased in 1989 (fifteen times higher), in 1994 (fifteen times higher), and in 1996 (fourteen times higher). According to these data, income inequality is a key issue along with poverty; while the poorest 40 percent of the distribution received only 12 percent of total income, the top decile received 40.3 percent of the wealth.

Table 10.2 shows that poverty is identified mainly in rural areas. In 1996, 10.8 million people within the bottom quintile lived in rural areas, representing 60 percent of the quintile. In contrast, 93 percent of the population in the top quintile lived in an urban area. The information presented in the table illustrates that poverty is mainly a rural problem, although 7.3 million poor (from the bottom quintile) live in the urban areas. This poses a problem to the policies oriented mainly to alleviate poverty among the rural population, particularly to educational programs within them.

In the Appendix, I also show some information about the structure and composition of households according to income decile (see the Appendix, Table A.3). In Table A.3, I emphasize the most relevant information for educational analysis: urban/rural distinctions, household size, and labor. One important factor to consider is a decrease in birth rates, translating into a decrease in household size in all income strata (from an average of 5.1 members in 1984 to 4.4 members in 1996), a parallel decrease in the average number of young members (from 2.8 in 1984 to 2.3 in 1996),[11] and a larger concentration of children at the bottom of the income distribution. Finally, in relation to participation in the labor market, there was an increase in the number of individuals above twelve years old who worked, as well as an increase in the average number of income earners per household.[12] This increase is constant and reached its peak in 1996, with an average of 1.7 income earners per household. These data add a vital dimension in understanding school distribution.

Although this chapter does not seek to analyze regional differences in income distribution and poverty in Mexico, it should be noted that poverty is a phenomenon with

TABLE 10.1

Distribution of Income per Capita (1994 = 100)

Year	Percentile	Individuals (thousands)	Total PCI* (millions)	% PCI
1984	I-II	14,361.02	3,713.43	4.48
	III-IV	14,349.66	6,967.43	8.42
	V-VI	14,369.80	11,076.54	13.37
	VII-VIII	14,364.44	17,886.70	21.60
	IX-X	14,360.95	43,165.43	52.13
1989	I-II	15,831.00	4,396.10	3.88
	III-IV	15,822.96	8,769.88	7.74
	V-VI	15,829.98	13,765.77	12.15
	VII-VIII	15,831.80	21,890.13	19.33
	IX-X	15,825.26	64,426.27	56.89
1992	I-II	16,841.85	5,180.25	3.69
	III-IV	16,873.81	10,477.27	7.47
	V-VI	16,863.00	16,516.29	11.77
	VII-VIII	16,864.45	27,302.39	19.45
	IX-X	16,897.51	80,879.12	57.63
1994	I-II	17,971.10	6,036.71	3.77
	III-IV	17,966.25	11,754.11	7.35
	V-VI	17,962.86	18,843.15	11.79
	VII-VIII	17,962.31	30,718.50	19.21
	IX-X	17,952.49	92,542.92	57.88
1996	I-II	18,608.06	4,935.84	4.13
	III-IV	18,599.01	9,431.96	7.88
	V-VI	18,592.32	14,709.44	12.29
	VII-VIII	18,597.61	23,452.96	19.60
	IX-X	18,585.71	67,153.89	56.11

*Quarterly current income.

Source: Calculated by the author based on ENIGH and INEGI (1984–1996).

TABLE 10.2

Population by PCI Quintile, 1996 (thousands)

	Rural	Urban	Total	% by Income Strata		% by Rural/Urban	
				Rural	Urban	Rural	Urban
I-II	10,823.6	7,330.9	18,154	59.6	40.4	43.8	11.1
III-IV	6,742.0	11,483.1	18,225	37.0	63.0	27.3	17.4
V-VI	3,926.7	14,304.0	18,231	21.5	78.5	15.9	21.7
VII-VIII	1,935.7	16,209.4	18,145	10.7	89.3	7.8	24.6
IX-X	1,269.6	16,563.6	17,833	7.1	92.9	5.1	25.1
Total	24,697.7	65,890.9	90,589	27.3	72.7	100	100

Source: Calculated by the author based on ENIGH and INEGI (1996).

a clear regional delimitation in the national context, in which indigenous population is mainly affected. Here I display some information that allows us to identify this problem, even though it will not be analyzed in depth.

Table 10.3 represents the indicators of exclusion at the state level estimated by CONAPO, the proportion of the population below the moderate levels of poverty (H index), and the average level of education among the adult and indigenous populations. The regional division presented in the table is based on the distribution of education (compare Bracho 1999).[13] This information allows us to show that both the phenomena of exclusion and poverty as well as educational distribution vary according to region. We can observe higher levels of development in the capital and in the north of the country, a deterioration or slower progress in states in the peripheral central region, and a clear delay in the south. In terms of education, the differences between the regions shown in the 1990 Census correspond to those that can be identified at the beginning of the twentieth century (Padua 1998). These historical legacies of underdevelopment persist despite the advances in the average educational levels of the population. On the other hand, the problem of educational distribution among indigenous populations has been identified throughout the century. However, as shown by their average level of schooling, this is still a problem.

Finally, although I cannot address the issue extensively, it should be acknowledged that the states with greater educational lag within the adult population also present high proportions of children who do not attend schools. They have the highest dropout and repetition rates, as well as the lowest rates of transition from primary to secondary education.[14]

Educational Profile of Income Groups

I describe and compare the educational profile of income groups based on the educational level of the household heads.[15] Table 10.4 identifies an important change in the educational profile of household heads between 1984 and 1996 and a parallel increase in the overall education distribution in the country. This shift is shown on the line corresponding to the total rows for each year. While in 1984 more than half of the household heads (57 percent) did not complete primary education, in 1996 this percentage fell to less than half (40 percent), and one-fifth had reached the primary level of education. Beyond the elementary level, important increases are evident: an increase from 10 percent in 1984 to 15 percent in 1996 of household heads who completed secondary education; an increase from 6 percent to 12 percent in the upper-middle level of education; and an increase from 7 percent to 12 percent in higher education.

Taking into account the educational composition of each income level, the change in levels of schooling has been matched by a larger concentration of household heads with post-basic education in the top of the distribution. While in 1984, 32 percent of the household heads from the top quintile had some post-basic education (upper-secondary plus higher level), in 1996 that number increased to 55 percent. At the same time, educational levels for those with basic education deteriorated; in 1984, only 8 percent of household heads had primary education in the bottom quintile. In 1996 this percentage increased to 19 percent. In the second quintile, the change was from 15 percent to 25 percent. Household heads with secondary education, who in 1984 were only 2 percent

TABLE 10.3

Margination and Average Schooling by State and Region, 1990

Region	State	Margination Index[1]	Margination Intensity[1]	Poverty Incidence (H)[2]	Average of Adult Schooling[3]	Average of Indigenous Schooling[3]
North	Baja California	−1.34464	Very low	0.4589	7.53	5.80
Pacific	Baja California Sur	−0.96851	Low	0.5890	7.69	5.01
	Sonora	−0.85979	Low	0.5783	7.40	3.41
North	Coahuila	−1.05344	Very low	0.6560	7.34	9.55
	Chihuahua	−0.87224	Low	0.5920	6.87	2.30
	Nuevo Leon	−1.37660	Very low	0.6328	8.17	4.21
	Tamaulipas	−0.60855	Low	0.6669	7.11	5.97
Capital	Distrito Federal	−1.68846	Very low	0.5362	9.08	5.97
West	Aguascalientes	−0.88969	Low	0.6645	6.68	8.00
	Colima	−0.75783	Low	0.5461	6.54	7.43
	Durango	0.01175	High	0.7245	6.18	1.90
	Jalisco	−0.76764	Low	0.6044	6.65	4.05
	Nayarit	−0.13366	Medium	0.6023	6.22	2.02
	Sinaloa	−0.14100	Medium	0.6173	6.64	3.29
Central	Mexico	−0.60422	Low	0.6723	7.05	3.39
Mexico	Morelos	−0.45714	Low	0.6383	6.81	3.49
	Queretaro	0.16086	High	0.6520	6.01	3.91
	Tlaxcala	−0.03620	Medium	0.7645	6.25	3.60
Peripheral	Guanajuato	0.21157	High	0.6806	5.08	4.19
Center	Hidalgo	1.16952	Very high	0.7903	5.20	2.62
	Michoacan	0.36274	High	0.7012	5.19	3.22
	Puebla	0.83108	Very high	0.7680	5.60	2.33
	San Luis Potosi	0.74878	High	0.7703	5.62	3.09
	Veracruz	1.13030	Very high	0.7602	5.43	2.64
	Zacatecas	0.56805	High	0.7876	5.32	5.00
South	Chiapas	2.36046	Very high	0.8466	3.93	1.94
	Guerrero	1.74666	Very high	0.7520	4.85	1.70
	Oaxaca	2.05526	Very high	0.8338	4.32	2.87
Southeast	Campeche	0.47741	High	0.7403	5.90	3.43
	Quintana Roo	−0.19119	Medium	0.5703	6.17	3.87
	Tabasco	0.51677	High	0.7184	5.78	4.18
	Yucatan	0.39959	High	0.7678	5.76	3.36

[1] Population National Council (CONAPO) (1990).
[2] De la Torre (1997).
[3] Bracho (1999b).

of the extremely poor, in 1996 reached 8 percent. In the dynamics of income and educational distribution, the latter is better distributed, but this improvement seems to parallel a worsening in income distribution.

When educational profiles are broken down by urban/rural areas, I identify important and systematic differences. Table 10.5 summarizes the results for 1996. In rural areas, 70 percent of the household heads did not finish primary education, 18 percent

TABLE 10.4

Level of Education of the Household Head (percentages)

| | | | Level of Education | | | | |
| | | | Basic | | Post-Basic | | |
Year	Percentile	Less Than Primary	Primary	Secondary	Upper-Secondary	Higher Education	Total
1984	I-II	89.4	8.1	2.1	0.2	0.1	100
	III-IV	77.7	14.8	5.9	1.4	0.2	100
	V-VI	65.6	21.8	9.0	2.1	1.5	100
	VII-VIII	46.0	24.7	14.3	7.7	7.4	100
	IX-X	30.5	24.9	12.7	12.6	19.2	100
	Total	56.9	20.2	9.7	5.9	7.4	100
1989	I-II	79.3	13.8	5.3	1.3	0.3	100
	III-IV	62.2	23.2	9.0	2.9	2.6	100
	V-VI	50.8	22.8	15.8	7.0	3.7	100
	VII-VIII	41.8	22.7	13.8	12.4	9.3	100
	IX-X	22.2	18.9	13.2	15.1	30.7	100
	Total	47.3	20.5	11.9	8.8	11.5	100
1992	I-II	77.2	18.2	3.8	0.6	0.1	100
	III-IV	64.2	21.8	10.9	2.5	0.6	100
	V-VI	48.4	26.1	15.7	7.4	2.3	100
	VII-VIII	37.6	24.0	17.1	13.2	8.1	100
	IX-X	19.3	15.4	13.4	19.6	32.4	100
	Total	44.9	20.8	12.8	10.2	11.2	100
1994	I-II	77.3	16.3	4.4	1.2	0.7	100
	III-IV	63.5	22.0	11.3	2.7	0.6	100
	V-VI	48.0	23.5	18.1	7.4	3.0	100
	VII-VIII	34.7	23.7	19.8	13.1	8.7	100
	IX-X	19.3	16.5	12.6	19.1	32.4	100
	Total	44.0	20.3	13.8	10.2	11.7	100
1996	I-II	70.8	19.4	7.6	1.7	0.5	100
	III-IV	54.7	25.2	13.1	5.5	1.4	100
	V-VI	45.2	22.8	18.2	10.5	3.4	100
	VII-VIII	33.0	24.7	20.1	14.1	8.1	100
	IX-X	18.2	14.6	12.6	20.5	34.0	100
	Total	40.1	20.9	14.8	12.0	12.3	100

Source: Calculated by the author based on ENIGH and INEGI (1984–1996).

had completed primary education, 8 percent had graduated from secondary school, and only 5 percent had some post-basic education. In urban areas, the percentage of household heads with less than primary education was reduced to 31 percent and the percentage that completed primary education increased to 22 percent and to 17 percent with secondary education. Among the 31 percent with post-basic education, 16 percent had higher education.

TABLE 10.5
Household-Head Educational Attainment by PCI, 1996

		Level of Educational Attainment					
Region	*Income Deciles*	*Less Than Primary*	*Primary*	*Secondary*	*Upper-Secondary*	*Higher Education*	*Total*
Rural	I-II	77.5	16.7	5.4	0.4	0.0	100
	III-IV	68.6	21.4	6.8	2.5	0.8	100
	V-VI	68.5	17.2	9.8	3.6	0.8	100
	VII-VIII	64.7	15.8	12.1	5.0	2.5	100
	IX-X	51.0	16.0	14.5	9.6	8.9	100
	Total	69.5	17.9	8.2	2.9	1.5	100
Urban	I-II	61.6	23.0	10.6	3.5	1.3	100
	III-IV	46.4	27.5	16.9	7.4	1.8	100
	V-VI	38.3	24.4	20.7	12.5	4.1	100
	VII-VIII	28.6	25.9	21.2	15.4	8.9	100
	IX-X	15.5	14.5	12.4	21.4	36.1	100
	Total	31.1	21.8	16.8	14.8	15.6	100

Source: Calculated by the author based on ENIGH and INEGI (1996).

The differences between income strata are important. In households with extreme poverty (strata I-II), more than 77 percent of household heads in rural areas had less than primary education. In the urban areas, that percentage was reduced to 62 percent. Within the same income level, the percentage of household heads with complete primary education in the rural zones was 17 percent and 23 percent in the urban zones. For post-basic education, this percentage went from 1 percent to 5 percent. When I compare the profile above with the educational background in the top quintile, in the rural areas, half of them had less than primary education even though one-fifth had some post-basic education. Household heads from the top quintile in urban areas showed a large concentration of post-basic (58 percent) and, in particular, higher education (36 percent). The percentages of those with basic education at this income level were 12 percent with secondary education, 15 percent with primary education, and 16 percent with less than primary.

From these data, we can identify the impact of schooling on income. It is evident that without improving the educational distribution, we should expect a worsening of the relative conditions of income inequality, even with a process of increased education.

The data also show some results that might appear difficult to explain. For example, among households at the bottom of the income distribution, particularly those under extreme forms of poverty, there are household heads with post-basic education.[16] Although no one would expect a perfect correlation between education and income, we must try to explore some hypothesis that would allow us to understand those particular cases of educational success. These cases might contribute to our understanding of the possibilities of decreasing poverty conditions through educational expansion. The remaining part of this section will address this issue.

As suggested before, education may be considered part of the individual capabilities or opportunities to potentially select "better" living conditions. In this section, I analyze changes in relative social position as a function of schooling. The analysis enables us to view education as part of a system of individual opportunities, within the context of income distribution, rather than a system of social mobility. It will also provide the plausibility and the importance of considering the different household life cycles in further educational analysis, in particular the relevance of their relationship with income distribution and poverty.

The data presented in Figures 10.1, 10.2, and 10.3 refer to five-year quasi-cohorts. I identified the percentages of household heads with different educational levels within each income strata. I took five-year age groups of household heads (for example, those born between 1964 and 1968, who in 1984 were twenty to twenty-four years old), identifying their educational level and, within it, their income strata. I compared them with their educational household head equivalents in 1989 (in the example, the ones who in 1989 were between twenty-five and twenty-nine years old) and in 1994 (the ones who were between thirty and thirty-four years old). I recognize the limitations of these quasi-cohorts. First, the period covered by the national surveys, as has been pointed out before, represents changes in the distribution of education, which here I controlled only upon analyzing the educational distribution at each level (without taking into account the role of any particular level in the overall educational distribution). Second, these five-year groups cover a relatively short period of time (ten years). Finally, the period represents important shifts in the national economy, as mentioned above.

For each cohort, in particular the youngest, those who begin with less than primary education are highly represented at the bottom of the income distribution. In the case of the younger cohort, the ones who in 1984 were between twenty and twenty-four years old, 28 percent of the heads who did not complete primary education were in the I-II quintile. Ten years later, 42 percent of them were identified among the extremely poor. Starting with the thirty- to thirty-four-year-old cohort, there is a stabilization and slight variation, with about one-fourth to one-third of household heads with less than primary education and in the lowest income strata. So far, it is impossible to know if their conditions are due to the distribution of education or if without education their opportunities might have changed.

In contrast, household heads with complete primary education represent a smaller percentage at the lower income strata than those with less than primary school: between 10 percent and 15 percent of household heads with primary education are extremely poor. Added to the second quintile, they represent no more than one-third (except for the first cohort in 1994). This result contrasts with the household heads with less than primary education and who find a higher representation in the two bottom quintiles (reaching two-thirds). The results could express that even some access to education is not enough to protect one from poverty and that the culmination of the first cycle of the educational system might be interpreted as some kind of "safety net" in relation to poverty.

Those with secondary education have a lower representation in the first and second quintiles and increase their representation at the third and fourth quintiles (including the top quintile for the thirty- to thirty-four-year-old cohort), representing around one-third of those households.

For household heads with post-basic education the situation is quite different. Not only do they have a very low representation in the first quintile, but their participation in the top of the income distribution increases over time, especially for the thirty-year-old

FIGURE 10.1

Household Heads Born in 1964–1968: Distribution by Income Quintile and Educational Level

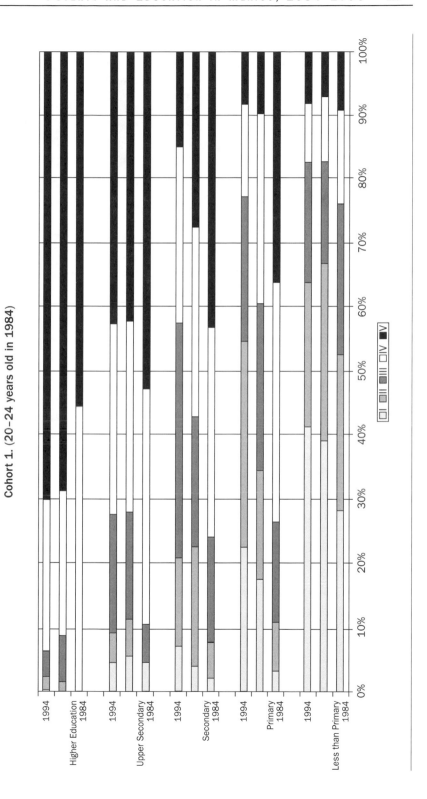

Cohort 1. (20–24 years old in 1984)

FIGURE 10.2

Household Heads Born in 1954–1958: Distribution by Income Quintile and Educational Level

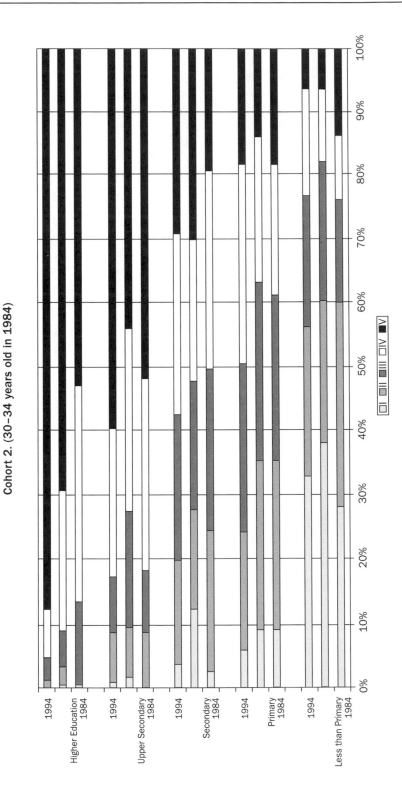

Cohort 2. (30–34 years old in 1984)

FIGURE 10.3

Household Heads Born in 1944–1948: Distribution by Income Quintile and Educational Level

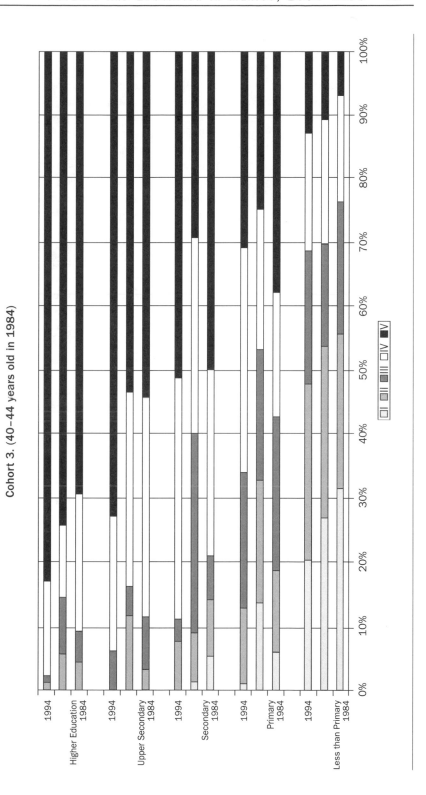

Cohort 3. (40–44 years old in 1984)

and older cohorts. We must note that the changes in representation become evident when the other levels have "stabilized" their participation in the lower- and middle-income strata. Between 50 percent and 80 percent with higher education from all cohorts show an increase in participation in the top quintile, representing a clear decrease in their participation among the bottom 60 percent of the income distribution.

Research devoted to the relationship between education and poverty does not take into account the family life cycle implicit in this brief description, even though there is an increasing number of studies oriented to the analysis of poverty among aging populations, the presence of minors in household (as dependents), and so forth.[17] This first descriptive exercise suggests that it must be included, since it might represent a critical variable for understanding the relationships among educational distribution, poverty conditions, and income distribution. For example, in 1984 household heads between twenty and twenty-four years old with post-basic education and with income levels I-IV prompted us to raise some questions: Could those individuals be studying or initiating a work path different from their counterparts? Can the family life cycle as well as the different household structures explain that phenomenon? Could it represent a social differentiation of the moment in the individual's life cycle to establish their own household? In any case, what is interesting to point out is that in addressing these questions we do not face a problem of absolute poverty, but relative poverty. Simultaneously, the issues involved might not be about poverty in terms of income, but might be better stated in terms of a differentiation of opportunities.

The last problem that can be identified from this analysis is the changes over time in the representation in the income distribution of the different educational levels. The different income levels among and within cohorts at different points in time might be attributable to changes in the distribution of education or to a change in the returns of education. The change in the returns may come from the expansion of basic education that is not matched with an expansion of post-basic educational opportunities. That is, educational expansion and its concentration might be part of the problem as well as of the solution for the improvement of the distribution of resources in society. Looking at the problem in a more dynamic dimension can contribute to better explanations of the relations among education, inequality, and poverty.

Educational Lag and Exclusion

This section describes the school attainment of young household members, defined as those between six and twenty-four years old, not household heads (or their spouses), and who are related to the head. In order to identify the educational lag, first I distinguished the individuals who attend school from those not studying in each age group and analyzed them both in relation to income levels and urban/rural areas. Second, I analyzed the educational exclusion at the household level, defined as a household in which at least one minor was not studying. Finally, I presented the information relevant to identify the relationship between schooling and working decisions within the households.

Educational Delay at the Individual Level   It is common to address the problems of school attendance and school delay at the individual level, and based on these, to estimate the levels of school participation. In this section[18] we describe educational delay or lag as the percentage of school-age children who are not in the appropriate grade for their age group, either because they do not study or because they are enrolled at grade levels below those appropriate for their age. We must emphasize that due to the nature of this chapter, we think it is relevant to include post-basic education in that it shows a possible extension of the educational gap between the different income strata.

Table 10.6 summarizes the evolution of educational lag at the individual level—the young members in each age group who should be studying at their appropriate school levels.[19] The lag in primary education (see "Total" rows) for rural areas in 1992 was 11 percent for children between six and twelve years old. These figures decreased by half (5 percent) in 1996. In the urban areas, the percentages were 4 percent and 3 percent, respectively. These data reflect the efforts that took place since the 1990 Census that identified a large number of children who were out of primary school, despite ten years of public discourse that affirmed complete coverage for the demand for primary education.[20] Beginning in 1992, important reforms were implemented to promote total coverage for primary education in the whole country.[21]

Table 10.6 shows the gap between the first and second quintile and between them and the top quintile. In the rural areas, in 1992, 14 percent of children between six and twelve years old in the first quintile were not enrolled in primary education. In 1996, this percentage decreased to 7 percent. In the second quintile, the percentages are closer to the rest of the distribution, ranging from 3 percent to 5 percent in 1996. For the urban zones, the proportion of children in this age group who were not studying decreased in a constant manner from the bottom to the top quintile, with 8 percent in the first quintile and less than 1 percent in the top quintile in 1996. In the second quintile in urban areas, we noticed a very similar percentage to the rural area in general, with the exception of the extremely poor in rural areas. Finally, it should be noted that the first quintile in the urban area showed little improvement in this indicator, probably reflecting the particular attention of policies toward poverty alleviation among the rural population, with little questioning of the presence of urban poverty and its particularities.

For the age group between thirteen and fifteen, which corresponds to secondary education, the lag found in 1996 was 47 percent among the rural population and 20 percent among the urban. This educational lag is significant considering that secondary education is compulsory according to the 1992 amendment to Article 3 of the Constitution. The table also shows that the lag for this age group decreased between 1992 and 1994 and increased in 1996 both in urban and rural areas, which may be attributed to the economic crisis of 1995, its impact over educational programs, and on the household strategies to face it. Taking into account the differences by income strata, increases in the secondary education lag is significant mostly in the groups under extreme and moderate levels of poverty in the rural areas and the extremely poor in the urban areas. So far, it is impossible to determine how much of this phenomenon can be attributed to problems in educational supply or attributed to household decisions not to matriculate their children in secondary school.

For the age group between sixteen and nineteen, corresponding to the upper-middle level of education, an increasing percentage of youth who are not studying, both in rural and urban areas, can be identified. Only in the top 40 percent of the distribution in urban areas do we find a decrease in this educational lag during the period. Within

TABLE 10.6

Age-Group Population Not Attending School by Educational Level by PCI (percentage) (Data: individuals)

	1992				1994				1996			
	6–12	13–15	16–19	20–24	6–12	13–15	16–19	20–24	6–12	13–15	16–19	20–24
Rural	10.9	42.3	79.3	96.7	6.8	40.5	82.0	95.2	5.4	47.0	86.9	98.3
I-II	14.0	48.2	86.6	98.0	7.7	43.8	85.7	97.9	6.9	56.4	92.1	100.0
III-IV	7.9	39.1	74.6	95.3	6.5	37.7	81.9	95.1	3.3	43.9	89.7	99.5
V-VI	5.1	34.6	76.3	97.9	4.3	38.9	79.6	94.3	4.9	32.3	79.1	96.8
VII-VIII	4.7	28.9	71.6	96.2	6.8	33.7	73.1	95.1	2.9	32.2	77.8	96.4
IX-X	2.9	33.3	62.5	91.4	0.0	21.1	69.2	78.2	2.7	33.3	69.1	92.0
Urban	4.1	17.4	49.2	77.0	3.4	16.6	48.4	78.0	2.9	19.7	52.2	80.6
I-II	9.0	30.3	66.4	91.3	10.8	36.2	70.5	94.7	8.0	43.8	78.9	98.0
III-IV	5.0	27.0	63.4	91.7	4.5	28.2	65.2	94.0	3.1	26.3	66.1	92.3
V-VI	2.6	17.8	54.0	87.1	1.4	13.2	54.5	85.5	1.9	18.2	56.0	88.8
VII-VIII	3.2	10.7	51.0	79.2	1.0	9.4	47.9	78.6	1.3	10.1	46.2	85.1
IX-X	1.6	5.4	26.1	58.7	1.0	3.2	19.9	55.9	0.3	3.1	22.8	55.5

Source: Calculated by the author based on ENIGH and INEGI (1992–1996).

this age group, the lag ranges from about 90 percent among the rural population in the first two quintiles to nearly 70 percent in the quintile IX-X. In the urban areas those percentages are smaller, although almost 80 percent of the age group lagged within the poorest quintile and 23 percent within the upper one. The data show a decrease in the population not studying only for the top of the distribution. This allows us to distinguish a growing educational gap between the affluent segments of the society and the rest of the population within post-basic education.

Finally, within the age group between twenty and twenty-four, corresponding to higher education, the total educational lag reaches more than 80 percent in the urban areas and 98 percent in the rural areas. Like the preceding age group, there is a growing gap between the top quintile urban (with 56 percent delayed) compared to the rest of the distribution (with more than 85 percent delayed).

To conclude this section, it is informative to notice the enormous percentage of young individuals without basic education who possibly join the workforce or start a family of their own. Even though in 1996 there was a decrease in the percentage of youth between sixteen and twenty-four years old who were under those conditions, the numbers are still not very encouraging when we compare them to the results observed in the previous section regarding household head's educational level. The second problem that should be emphasized is the increase in the distance at the post-basic level of education between the top income quintile in urban areas and the rest of the distribution, both urban and rural.

Household Educational Exclusion by Income Level   Educational exclusion or households with at least one child excluded from school is summarized for basic and post-basic levels of education. Table 10.7 in the first part shows a global decrease in the number of households with basic education exclusion for all income levels, urban and rural. However, the differences in the profiles among income levels are maintained, with a much higher proportion of households with basic education exclusion in the poorest sectors (one-third in quintile I-II and one-fourth in quintile III-IV in 1996).

Taking into account the distribution of educational exclusion (second part of Table 10.7), we can point out where these households with exclusion rates are according to their income strata. In 1996, more than half of the households with exclusion in basic education (55 percent) are identified in the first quintile, in the rural areas, and one fifth (23 percent) of the urban households with exclusion are in this bottom strata. What stands out is that these proportions represent an improvement for the rural zone and a worsening of the urban condition of educational exclusion. In quintile V-VI there is an increase in exclusion both in urban and rural areas. The contrast between the first and second parts of the table allows us to conclude that despite the decrease in exclusion at the basic level of education in households, the social profile of exclusion remains almost the same.

Table 10.8 shows a global decrease in post-basic educational exclusion, both in rural and urban areas, mainly attributable to changes in the top 40 percent of the income distribution, particularly in the urban areas. Changes in the distribution of households with post-basic educational exclusion (second part in Table 10.8) can be identified, with a smaller representation of households with exclusion in urban areas at the top 20 percent of the income distribution. In contrast, the bottom quintile shows

TABLE 10.7

Educational Exclusion: Basic Education (Data: households)

Profile of Educational Exclusion

	1992				1994				1996			
	With Exclusions	No Exclusions	Total	Cases	With Exclusions	No Exclusions	Total	Cases	With Exclusions	No Exclusions	Total	Cases
Total	24.8	75.2	100	5,930	74.3	25.7	100	7,019	18.6	81.4	100	7,281
I-II	40.9	59.1	100	1,248	91.8	8.2	100	1,493	31.1	68.9	100	1,555
III-IV	30.7	69.3	100	1,294	90.0	10.0	100	1,510	20.6	79.4	100	1,635
V-VI	19.4	80.6	100	1,269	82.1	17.9	100	1,473	16.7	83.3	100	1,603
VII-VIII	18.4	81.6	100	1,114	74.0	26.0	100	1,381	11.6	88.4	100	1,416
IX-X	11.0	89.0	100	1,005	41.8	58.2	100	1,162	9.6	90.4	100	1,072
Rural	39.1	60.9	100	1,596	30.0	70.0	100	1,955	26.9	73.1	100	2,009
I-II	44.9	55.1	100	817	34.0	66.0	100	947	32.7	67.3	100	915
III-IV	37.1	62.9	100	420	29.1	70.9	100	554	24.6	75.4	100	585
V-VI	27.8	72.2	100	216	23.7	76.3	100	278	21.0	79.0	100	315
VII-VIII	30.3	69.7	100	109	25.8	74.2	100	128	16.5	83.5	100	127
IX-X	23.5	76.5	100	34	8.3	91.7	100	48	14.9	85.1	100	67
Urban	19.5	80.5	100	4,336	16.0	84.0	100	5,064	15.4	84.6	100	5,272
I-II	33.3	66.7	100	432	29.1	70.9	100	547	28.9	71.1	100	640
III-IV	27.6	72.4	100	874	24.4	75.6	100	956	18.3	81.7	100	1,050
V-VI	17.7	82.3	100	1,054	13.0	87.0	100	1,195	15.6	84.4	100	1,288
VII-VIII	17.1	82.9	100	1,005	12.1	87.9	100	1,253	11.1	88.9	100	1,289
IX-X	10.6	89.4	100	971	10.2	89.8	100	1,113	9.3	90.7	100	1,005

Social Distribution of Educational Exclusion

	1992				1994				1996			
	With Exclusions	No Exclusions	Total	Cases	With Exclusions	No Exclusions	Total	Cases	With Exclusions	No Exclusions	Total	Cases
Total	100	100	100	5,930	100	100	100	7,019	100	100	100	7,281
I-II	34.7	16.5	21.0	1,248	34.3	18.0	21.3	1,493	35.7	18.1	21.4	1,555
III-IV	27.0	20.1	21.8	1,294	28.2	19.9	21.5	1,510	24.8	21.9	22.5	1,635
V-VI	16.7	22.9	21.4	1,269	15.8	22.3	21.0	1,473	19.7	22.5	22.0	1,603
VII-VIII	14.0	20.4	18.8	1,114	13.2	21.3	19.7	1,381	12.1	21.1	19.4	1,416
IX-X	7.6	20.0	16.9	1,005	8.4	18.6	16.6	1,162	7.6	16.3	14.7	1,072
Rural	100	100	100	1,596	100	100	100	1,955	100	100	100	2,009
I-II	58.8	46.3	51.2	817	54.9	45.7	48.4	947	55.4	41.9	45.5	915
III-IV	25.0	27.2	26.3	420	27.5	28.7	28.3	554	26.7	30.0	29.1	585
V-VI	9.6	16.0	13.5	216	11.3	15.5	14.2	278	12.2	17.0	15.7	315
VII-VIII	5.3	7.8	6.8	109	5.6	6.9	6.5	128	3.9	7.2	6.3	127
IX-X	1.3	2.7	2.1	34	0.7	3.2	2.5	48	1.9	3.9	3.3	67
Urban	100	100	100	4,336	100	100	100	5,064	100	100	100	5,272
I-II	17.0	8.3	10.0	432	19.6	9.1	10.8	547	22.7	10.2	12.1	640
III-IV	28.5	18.1	20.2	874	28.7	17.0	18.9	956	23.6	19.2	19.9	1,050
V-VI	22.1	24.8	24.3	1,054	19.1	24.5	23.6	1,195	24.7	24.4	24.4	1,288
VII-VIII	20.3	23.9	23.2	1,005	18.7	25.9	24.7	1,253	17.6	25.7	24.4	1,289
IX-X	12.2	24.9	22.4	971	13.9	23.5	22.0	1,113	11.4	20.5	19.1	1,005

Source: Calculated by the author based on ENIGH and INEGI (1992–1996).

TABLE 10.8

Educational Exclusion: Post-Basic Education (Data: households)

Profile of Educational Exclusion

	1992				1994				1996			
	With Exclusions	No Exclusions	Total	Cases	With Exclusions	No Exclusions	Total	Cases	With Exclusions	No Exclusions	Total	Cases
Total	74.6	25.4	100	3,869	74.3	25.7	100	4,755	71.4	28.6	100	4,709
I-II	96.3	3.7	100	540	91.8	8.2	100	682	93.0	7.0	100	719
III-IV	83.8	16.2	100	709	90.0	10.0	100	869	87.1	12.9	100	866
V-VI	80.6	19.4	100	777	82.1	17.9	100	1,038	78.0	22.0	100	1,017
VII-VIII	72.6	27.4	100	925	74.0	26.0	100	1,134	67.0	33.0	100	1,113
IX-X	51.9	48.1	100	918	41.8	58.2	100	1,032	40.4	59.6	100	994
Rural	93.1	6.9	100	885	93.9	6.1	100	1,116	91.3	8.7	100	1,144
I-II	98.9	1.1	100	358	96.5	3.5	100	429	96.2	3.8	100	425
III-IV	88.9	11.1	100	261	93.5	6.5	100	322	91.5	8.5	100	342
V-VI	88.3	11.7	100	145	93.7	6.3	100	205	90.5	9.5	100	222
VII-VIII	92.4	7.6	100	92	93.5	6.5	100	123	85.1	14.9	100	87
IX-X	86.2	13.8	100	29	70.3	29.7	100	37	70.6	29.4	100	68
Urban	69.2	30.8	100	2,983	68.2	31.8	100	3,640	65.0	35.0	100	3,564
I-II	91.7	8.3	100	181	83.8	16.2	100	253	88.4	11.6	100	294
III-IV	80.8	19.2	100	448	87.9	12.1	100	547	84.1	15.9	100	523
V-VI	78.6	21.4	100	632	79.2	20.8	100	833	74.5	25.5	100	795
VII-VIII	70.5	29.5	100	833	71.5	28.5	100	1,012	65.5	34.5	100	1,026
IX-X	50.7	49.3	100	889	40.8	59.2	100	995	38.2	61.8	100	926

Social Distribution of Educational Exclusion

	1992				1994				1996			
	With Exclusions	No Exclusions	Total	Cases	With Exclusions	No Exclusions	Total	Cases	With Exclusions	No Exclusions	Total	Cases
Total	100	100	100	3,869	100	100	100	4,755	100	100	100	4,709
I-II	18.0	2.0	14.0	540	17.7	4.6	14.3	682	19.9	3.7	15.3	719
III-IV	20.6	11.7	18.3	709	22.2	7.1	18.3	869	22.4	8.3	18.4	866
V-VI	21.7	15.4	20.1	777	24.1	15.2	21.8	1,038	23.6	16.7	21.6	1,017
VII-VIII	23.3	25.8	23.9	925	23.8	24.1	23.9	1,134	22.2	27.3	23.6	1,113
IX-X	16.5	45.1	23.7	918	12.2	49.0	21.7	1,032	12.0	44.0	21.1	994
Rural	100	100	100	885	100	100	100	1,116	100	100	100	1,144
I-II	43.0	6.6	40.5	358	39.5	22.1	38.4	429	39.1	16.2	37.2	425
III-IV	28.2	47.5	29.5	261	28.7	30.9	28.9	322	30.0	29.3	29.9	342
V-VI	15.5	27.9	16.4	145	18.3	19.1	18.4	205	19.2	21.2	19.4	222
VII-VIII	10.3	11.5	10.4	92	11.0	11.8	11.0	123	7.1	13.1	7.6	87
IX-X	3.0	6.6	3.3	29	2.5	16.2	3.3	37	4.6	20.2	5.9	68
Urban	100	100	100	2,983	100	100	100	3,640	100	100	100	3,564
I-II	8.0	1.6	6.1	181	8.5	3.5	7.0	253	11.2	2.7	8.2	294
III-IV	17.5	9.3	15.0	448	19.4	5.7	15.0	547	19.0	6.7	14.7	523
V-VI	24.1	14.7	21.2	632	26.6	15.0	22.9	833	25.5	16.3	22.3	795
VII-VIII	28.5	26.7	27.9	833	29.2	24.9	27.8	1,012	29.0	28.4	28.8	1,026
IX-X	21.9	47.6	29.8	889	16.4	50.9	27.3	995	15.3	45.9	26.0	926

Source: Calculated by the author based on ENIGH and INEGI (1992–1996).

an increase in the representation of households with this educational exclusion. The remaining income strata keep a relatively constant rate of exclusion during the period.

In summary, the high proportions of households that register exclusion of at least one of its young members from education, facing the overall increase in the school participation rate, continues to be problematic. The exclusion concentration in the bottom income strata may represent the difficulty faced by the poor of maintaining their children in the educational system. In contrast, we observe important efforts at the intermediate and upper levels of society to expand the educational level of household members to post-basic education. The main issue that should be highlighted with this scenario is the probable increase in the educational gap among social groups, even without taking into account the differences in the quality of education available to the different groups.

Young Income Earners In order to identify the possible relationships between the educational lags explained earlier in the chapter and working minors, I display the distribution of income earners[22] by age group and income quintile. Here I concentrate on the relevant age group for the analysis of basic education, that is, children between the ages of six and fifteen. With this preliminary description I intend to question if the possibility of choosing between work and education can generate a decision conflict.[23] Income earners at the ages to attend primary and secondary schools might be crucial in explaining, at least in part, the decrease in school participation—and the corresponding increase in educational exclusion—in the bottom income levels shown in the former section.

Table 10.9 summarizes the results for the 1996 survey,[24] considering the percentages of earners among the six to twelve and thirteen to fifteen age groups and school attendance of these earners. Of the total children in the six to twelve age group, 4.4 percent were registered as earners in the first quintile, in contrast to 1.6 percent of the children in the IX-X quintile. Among the earners in the first quintile, only 8 percent did not attend school. All of the earners within the top quintile attended school.

For the thirteen to fifteen age group, 16 percent of children in the I-II quintile were declared as earners, compared to 5 percent in the top quintile. But, as opposed to their younger counterparts described earlier, the earner condition had a strong correlation with school attendance, particularly in the quintile I-II, where 73 percent of the earners did not study. In the top quintile, this percentage decreased to 11 percent.

When we compare by rural/urban, the table indicates that about one-fifth of rural children and 10 percent of the urban received some income. Finally, of the total earners in the thirteen to fifteen age group, 73 percent of the rural and 52 percent of the urban did not attend school. Further research should address these problems. There is a possibility that scarce resources are only part of the explanation of the incorporation of the young into the labor market; the "necessity of work" may also be part of the socialization process. If this is the case, educational policies not only should address the problem of the expansion of opportunities, but also should be able to convey the idea that school is a better learning and socialization resource for children (including teenagers) than work.

These results show the relevance of the participation of all household members in raising income for its survival. It is possible to assume that the choice between work

TABLE 10.9

Earners by Age Group (6–15) and School Attendance, 1996 (percentages)

By Income Quintile

| | Age Group | | | | | |
| | 6–12 Years Old | | | 13–15 Years Old | | |
	Earners in Group	Not Attending School	Attending School	Earners in Group	Not Attending School	Attending School
I-II	4.4	8.2	91.8	16.1	73.1	26.9
III-IV	4.7	3.6	96.4	18.2	65.8	34.2
V-VI	2.8	1.9	98.1	12.9	59.6	40.4
VII-VIII	2.2	0.0	100.0	11.6	42.2	57.8
IX-X	1.6	0.0	100.0	4.7	11.1	88.9
Total	3.5	4.6	3.5	13.9	30.0	7.5

By Rural/Urban

| | Age Group | |
	6–12	13–15
Rural	5.4	17.6
Urban	2.8	9.9
Total	3.6	12.2

Age Group: 13–15
Earners by School Attendance

	Not Attending	Attending
Rural	73.1	26.9
Urban	51.8	48.2

Source: Calculated by the author based on ENIGH and INEGI (1996).

and school is a paradox, probably faced as a "Solomonic judgment" in the case of secondary education (but not for primary education). Further analysis is fundamental to find better explanations concerning family decisions on schooling, and their relationship to income, work, and social perceptions of "learning." In addition to its analytical importance, the consequences in terms of recent programs directed to address educational lags, based on monetary incentives to minors (such as Progresa), would allow us to evaluate their achievements and limitations.

CONCLUSIONS

This chapter questioned the issue of education in studies of poverty and rested on the idea that schooling is a product of political and individual decisions that take place within a particular social distribution of economic and educational resources. It emphasized that the phenomenon of poverty may be distinct for each household life cycle and that there might be a distinct relationship between education and the ideas of absolute and relative poverty in relation to those life cycles.

Based on the analysis of school participation among younger household members, similar results to traditional works were found: children who are not in school are highly represented in the poorest social sectors. I identified to what extent this phenomenon is related to children's participation in the labor market by considering their condition as income earners. The results enabled us to establish that the institutional distinction between the primary and secondary basic levels of education may well be associated with distinct social images of their necessity. The comparison between low and decreasing rates in primary educational exclusion and the high and growing exclusion rates for secondary education, especially in the bottom 40 percent of the income distribution, could be expressing a very clear commitment to fulfill the constitutional mandate of compulsory primary education. The lack of secondary school participation among the poor could also express a deficient coverage of secondary education or a difficulty among households to break with traditions for survival, beginning with the early insertion of their children in the labor market.

In addition, I identified efforts from middle- and upper-income strata to advance their children up to post-basic education. In the context of poverty analysis and the distribution of social resources, the finding is important. It is known that post-basic educational levels are by now a minimum requirement for participating in the most dynamic sectors of the economy, allowing a privileged position in relation to employment and income. The results remind us to understand the educational problems within a context of social distribution and the increase in educational standards for social participation as school expansion goes further. If these trends continue, we will find a concentrated number of highly educated individuals among a small, privileged proportion of the population.

Despite the fact that both primary and secondary levels of education are now constitutionally mandated, national surveys report educational lags at these levels. It seems that equality has not been part of the sociopolitical agenda, beyond the discourse level, even given that education is better distributed than other social resources. This is part of a vicious cycle that reproduces a coexistence of a culture of poverty and a culture of privilege, in which the persistence of inequality and the concentration of social resources among a few becomes justified as "normal" and even "natural."

We need to broaden the images we have about the relationship between education and poverty by incorporating into the discussion issues of human capabilities and the context in which household (or family) decisions take place. This should not be a way to transfer the state educational responsibility to families. Instead, we should attempt to find within households the mechanisms conducive to their educational decisions, given an unequal distribution of resources. This decision-making process can be socially determined and part of a process that allows a household to establish alternatives that favor its survival and expansion of opportunities as a whole; among these decisions are included the possibility for selecting the members who will (and will not) attend school.

APPENDIX: METHOD, DATA, AND VARIABLES

I briefly explain here the information used in this chapter and some of the methodological decisions that took place in order to allow me to interpret the data for the purposes of this research.

For the estimates presented in this analysis, I used the data from the *Encuestas Nacionales de Ingresos y Gastos de los Hogares* (National Surveys of Household Income and Expenditures) (1984, 1989, 1992, 1994, and 1996—both at the individual and household levels), identified in the text as ENIGH. Based on nationwide stratified samples, they are compiled by the Instituto Nacional de Estadística, Geografía e Informática (INEGI), the National Institute of Statistics, Geography, and Information Technology. They are comparable samples, using the same sampling procedures, the same questions, and covering the same time of the year (third trimester), between September and November. All the results presented here are my own calculations based on the original data.

Income and Income per Capita Deciles

There are differences between the results for income and consumption variables released by ENIGH and the ones presented by the system of *Cuentas Nacionales;* for examples, see INEGI, CONAPO (1992), and Lustig and Székely (1997). The first explains the differences in the type of information collected in both systems and attributes the difference to the possibility of overestimating income in the 1989 survey. In the latter, the possibility of underreporting income for the 1984 survey is suggested. Other authors take into account the variations in "nonmonetary expenditures" and suggest its elimination for income estimates (for instance, see Cortés [1998]).

I recognize there are differences that are difficult to explain. However, I decided to calculate total income according to the procedure suggested by INEGI, including all current income,[25] and without making any corrections to those variables. This allows an interested reader to make a more general comparison with the results published by INEGI. By maintaining the parameter established by INEGI, I recognize the possibility of overestimating income, particularly among the bottom deciles, through the consideration of nonmonetary income. However, I preferred that to its underestimation. By not doing any adjustments to income, it is possible that I underestimate it, as Lustig and Székely point out.

One important difference between this analysis and those published by INEGI is the procedure for estimation of income deciles. INEGI presents estimates of income distribution by deciles based on total household income. That is, the distribution compiles the incomes of all members taking the household as a unit, regardless of the number of earners and the number of residents in the household. Cortés's works (1995, 1998) show that the above approach represents a problem in establishing inequality, by overestimating households with a larger number of income earners among the top deciles and with larger numbers of members. On the other hand, there is common recognition in the literature on inequality that the effect of the number of members on estimates of income distribution is significant and should be taken into account as "disposable income per individual"[26] (see Burniaux et al. [1998] and Cortés [1998]).

Equivalent household income, or per capita income (PCI), was used to estimate the distribution. Household income is divided by the total number of members. In so doing, I assume there is no scale economy in the household or other factors affecting income distribution within it (such as age, family position, or being an earner).

Finally, the deciles estimate based on PCI that uses the household as the unit of analysis produces an overrepresentation of the largest households in the bottom deciles and, as a consequence, of one-person households in the top deciles. In order to avoid this effect and obtain a distribution of households in income deciles that takes into account the number of its members, we used individual per capita income as the unit of analysis. The distribution that results does not break the household unit and maintains the order and analytical starting point in individuals and their PCI.[27]

Table A.1 shows the PCI distribution and the Gini coefficient for the five years of the surveys. The table includes the percentage of individuals and of households in each decile. There is a smaller percentage of households in the bottom deciles in comparison with individuals (who correspond to 10 percent). This is a product of the combined estimation of individuals-households referred to above.

As I point out in the chapter, there is no consensus on the definition of poverty for the case of Mexico. However, it is not difficult to support that the first quintile, the bottom 20 percent of the distribution, includes households under "extreme forms of poverty" and that the line for "moderate poverty" would be in the second quintile, the bottom 40 percent. Table A.2 summarizes the average monetary income per capita, distinguishing by rural/urban area and income distribution. Based on the definition of a "basic basket" from INEGI for 1994, the extreme poverty line in rural settings is $147.28 per person per month. For urban settings, the amount is $198.29. For moderate levels of poverty in the rural setting, that amount is $257.74, and in urban areas, $396.77. If we compare these poverty lines with the per capita income per trimester, we find, in fact, the plausibility of the threshold proposed in this work.

Table A.3 outlines some of the information about household size, composition, and structure. The difference between the columns "Residents" and "Size" is that the former includes all individuals living in the household (original data from ENIGH), and the latter excludes co-residents, guests, servants, and absent household heads. The last sample is the one taken in consideration for the analysis, as it intends to reflect the notion of family—nuclear or extended—within the restrictive context imposed by the information offered by these surveys.

Table A.4 shows the distribution of the younger population (six to twenty-four years old) by income strata. Its value rests in the fact that the greater concentrations of the younger children (six to fifteen years old) are among the lower strata, while the population relevant to the analysis of post-basic education is distributed across the whole spectrum. Finally, Table A.5 identifies the earner conditions within each age group. I maintain sample values in the table to call attention to the low numbers found in the ENIGH and the fragility of the indicator for more complete analysis (however, these values are weighted). Within the lower strata, there is an increase in working minors between the ages of six and fifteen. At the bottom 40 percent of the income distribution, earner minors constitute a huge representation, mainly in the rural areas.

All the tables included in the text compile income quintiles, as it is usual in the international literature, in order to allow for further comparisons.

Education

The analysis takes into account only the main structural differentiation of the Mexican educational system by levels of schooling. It begins with elementary or primary education (*primaria*), lasting six years, which corresponds to the age group between six and twelve years old. The next level is secondary (*secundaria*), lasting three years and corresponding to thirteen to fifteen years old. These two levels make up the basic compulsory education since 1992 (primary was compulsory before this last amendment to

TABLE A.1

Per Capita Income Distribution*

Year	Percentile	Individuals (thousands)	Total PCI (millions)	% PCI	% PCI Cumulative	% Cases	% House- holds	Gini Coefficient[†]
1984	I	7,174.51	1,369.16	1.7	1.7	10.0	7.0	0.4705
	II	7,186.51	2,344.27	2.8	4.5	10.0	7.8	
	III	7,174.09	3,094.00	3.7	8.2	10.0	7.9	
	IV	7,175.57	3,873.43	4.7	12.9	10.0	8.6	
	V	7,192.95	4,921.89	5.9	18.8	10.0	9.4	
	VI	7,176.85	6,154.65	7.4	26.3	10.0	10.0	
	VII	7,188.16	7,793.03	9.4	35.7	10.0	10.5	
	VIII	7,176.29	10,093.67	12.2	47.9	10.0	11.1	
	IX	7,186.18	13,970.51	16.9	64.7	10.0	12.7	
	X	7,174.77	29,194.92	35.3	100.0	10.0	15.1	
1989	I	7,917.36	1,563.72	1.4	1.4	10.0	7.0	0.5189
	II	7,913.64	2,832.38	2.5	3.9	10.0	7.8	
	III	7,909.58	3,855.41	3.4	7.3	10.0	8.4	
	IV	7,913.38	4,914.48	4.3	11.6	10.0	8.8	
	V	7,914.49	6,131.43	5.4	17.0	10.0	9.4	
	VI	7,915.50	7,634.34	6.7	23.8	10.0	9.9	
	VII	7,915.38	9,585.14	8.5	32.3	10.0	10.3	
	VIII	7,916.42	12,304.99	10.9	43.1	10.0	11.2	
	IX	7,913.87	17,693.91	15.6	58.7	10.0	12.5	
	X	7,911.39	46,732.36	41.3	100.0	10.0	14.5	
1992	I	8,435.64	1,855.83	1.3	1.3	10.0	6.9	0.5262
	II	8,406.20	3,324.42	2.4	3.7	10.0	7.9	
	III	8,438.98	4,589.01	3.3	7.0	10.0	8.0	
	IV	8,434.83	5,888.26	4.2	11.2	10.0	8.8	
	V	8,439.65	7,320.46	5.2	16.4	10.0	9.2	
	VI	8,423.34	9,195.83	6.6	22.9	10.0	9.9	
	VII	8,429.66	11,748.07	8.4	31.3	10.0	10.5	
	VIII	8,434.78	15,554.32	11.1	42.4	10.0	11.6	
	IX	8,383.76	22,481.06	16.0	58.4	9.9	12.9	
	X	8,513.75	58,398.06	41.6	100.0	10.1	14.3	
1994	I	8,994.12	2,228.59	1.4	1.4	10.0	6.8	0.5282
	II	8,976.98	3,808.12	2.4	3.8	10.0	7.6	
	III	8,984.07	5,174.64	3.2	7.0	10.0	8.4	
	IV	8,982.18	6,579.47	4.1	11.1	10.0	8.8	
	V	8,981.87	8,355.30	5.2	16.4	10.0	9.5	
	VI	8,980.99	10,487.85	6.6	22.9	10.0	9.9	
	VII	8,981.60	13,300.11	8.3	31.2	10.0	10.4	
	VIII	8,980.71	17,418.38	10.9	42.1	10.0	11.2	
	IX	8,979.15	25,344.35	15.9	58.0	10.0	12.8	
	X	8,973.34	67,198.57	42.0	100.0	10.0	14.5	
1996	I	9,308.42	1,817.35	1.5	1.5	10.0	6.3	0.5085
	II	9,299.63	3,118.49	2.6	4.1	10.0	7.4	
	III	9,298.85	4,170.50	3.5	7.6	10.0	8.2	
	IV	9,300.16	5,261.46	4.4	12.0	10.0	8.8	
	V	9,297.02	6,572.43	5.5	17.5	10.0	9.4	
	VI	9,295.30	8,137.01	6.8	24.3	10.0	10.0	
	VII	9,297.99	10,207.61	8.5	32.8	10.0	10.7	
	VIII	9,299.62	13,245.35	11.1	43.9	10.0	11.3	
	IX	9,298.86	18,961.01	15.8	59.7	10.0	12.9	
	X	9,286.85	48,192.88	40.3	100.0	10.0	14.8	

*Based on current income for every three months (1994 = 100).

[†]Calculated by the formula (Cortes et al. [1998]): $1 - (p1(Q1 + Q0) + p2(Q2 + Q1) + \ldots + pn(Qn + Qn - 1))$.

Source: Calculated by the author based on ENIGH and INEGI (1984–1996).

TABLE A.2

Per Capita Monetary Current Income* (1994 = 100)

| Decile | Area | Monetary per Capita Current Income Average | | | | |
		1984	1989	1992	1994	1996
I	Rural	134.88	131.69	123.82	151.71	119.63
	Urban	138.39	146.12	173.42	183.24	154.26
	Total	135.76	134.75	132.93	159.36	127.04
II	Rural	229.17	254.77	256.28	280.80	223.38
	Urban	268.45	305.47	304.05	320.48	255.85
	Total	241.93	269.07	276.81	300.36	243.50
III	Rural	322.44	360.03	377.88	390.70	317.60
	Urban	360.81	393.18	420.21	430.53	350.12
	Total	342.28	376.11	414.46	413.18	337.45
IV	Rural	392.60	469.61	496.09	505.45	402.30
	Urban	443.04	514.52	546.56	558.94	439.35
	Total	418.85	493.94	528.68	539.32	424.35
V	Rural	502.28	572.86	605.43	632.16	514.12
	Urban	566.72	636.29	686.28	687.01	547.34
	Total	542.77	611.88	672.70	672.08	539.93
VI	Rural	659.31	707.04	744.98	771.48	640.28
	Urban	682.12	760.31	840.55	863.31	643.52
	Total	673.82	742.26	829.84	847.57	643.15
VII	Rural	805.71	934.28	1,004.56	1,000.41	786.59
	Urban	881.67	952.71	1,029.10	1,079.20	820.47
	Total	858.70	948.33	1,027.74	1,069.25	813.86
VIII	Rural	1,106.47	1,185.55	1,309.21	1,358.70	1,027.76
	Urban	1,105.19	1,197.30	1,330.95	1,358.73	1,073.70
	Total	1,105.40	1,194.55	1,320.78	1,358.73	1,068.73
IX	Rural	1,367.61	1,639.31	1,745.08	1,804.84	1,509.62
	Urban	1,454.92	1,710.13	1,960.81	2,015.39	1,499.75
	Total	1,439.69	1,696.80	1,938.77	1,999.01	1,499.79
X	Rural	3,380.14	3,316.41	3,378.75	4,416.09	2,728.12
	Urban	3,433.79	4,674.80	3,813.33	5,882.67	3,026.05
	Total	3,425.77	4,525.46	3,807.80	5,830.46	3,007.60
Total	Rural	688.59	693.42	364.55	616.72	342.03
	Urban	1,354.87	1,695.69	1,038.07	1,954.71	820.47
	Total	1,121.35	1,339.63	830.46	1,629.95	675.43

*Current income for every three months.

Source: Calculated by the author based on ENIGH and INEGI (1984–1996).

TABLE A.3

Household Composition: Residents, Earners, and Age Structure (means)

	Household Structure			Earners		Age Structure							
	Size	Children	Residents	Workers	Earners	<5	6–12	13–15	16–19	20–24	25–44	45–64	65+
1984													
I	7.24	4.61	7.24	1.65	1.45	1.62	1.94	0.59	0.54	0.38	1.38	0.56	0.24
II	6.54	4.10	6.54	1.49	1.49	1.45	1.87	0.55	0.45	0.38	1.17	0.51	0.16
III	6.43	3.90	6.44	1.54	1.47	1.45	1.72	0.48	0.45	0.38	1.27	0.52	0.16
IV	5.91	3.43	5.92	1.64	1.56	0.96	1.54	0.55	0.44	0.44	1.19	0.57	0.22
V	5.42	3.15	5.42	1.51	1.58	0.84	1.12	0.52	0.60	0.50	1.04	0.64	0.16
VI	5.09	2.74	5.09	1.45	1.52	0.83	1.02	0.44	0.47	0.40	1.12	0.59	0.24
VII	4.81	2.51	4.83	1.48	1.63	0.70	0.81	0.37	0.49	0.58	1.11	0.56	0.20
VIII	4.58	2.30	4.60	1.60	1.67	0.62	0.74	0.37	0.45	0.54	1.12	0.54	0.20
IX	3.99	1.87	4.02	1.52	1.73	0.46	0.59	0.27	0.31	0.48	1.10	0.48	0.30
X	3.29	1.42	3.37	1.39	1.53	0.30	0.42	0.20	0.27	0.34	0.99	0.56	0.21
Total	5.07	2.78	5.09	1.51	1.57	0.83	1.06	0.41	0.43	0.44	1.13	0.55	0.21
1989													
I	7.08	4.34	7.08	1.61	1.44	1.46	2.00	0.61	0.52	0.36	1.31	0.57	0.26
II	6.32	3.73	6.32	1.69	1.51	1.19	1.57	0.56	0.51	0.44	1.24	0.59	0.22
III	5.92	3.46	5.92	1.54	1.54	1.01	1.39	0.54	0.52	0.48	1.24	0.53	0.20
IV	5.62	3.17	5.63	1.61	1.66	0.87	1.11	0.52	0.67	0.44	1.15	0.67	0.19
V	5.26	2.84	5.27	1.60	1.70	0.76	1.08	0.41	0.48	0.46	1.27	0.53	0.26
VI	4.98	2.60	4.99	1.61	1.72	0.66	0.87	0.38	0.55	0.49	1.14	0.62	0.28
VII	4.78	2.50	4.80	1.71	1.81	0.62	0.76	0.34	0.56	0.46	1.18	0.62	0.24
VIII	4.40	2.19	4.42	1.67	1.86	0.56	0.57	0.32	0.45	0.47	1.22	0.58	0.23
IX	3.94	1.88	3.97	1.59	1.80	0.48	0.52	0.24	0.35	0.44	1.15	0.55	0.22
X	3.28	1.39	3.41	1.49	1.70	0.35	0.36	0.16	0.24	0.36	1.09	0.52	0.20
Total	4.93	2.63	4.96	1.61	1.69	0.73	0.93	0.38	0.47	0.44	1.19	0.57	0.23
1992													
I	6.83	4.12	6.83	1.68	1.39	1.46	1.87	0.57	0.48	0.38	1.41	0.46	0.20
II	5.95	3.44	5.95	1.65	1.51	1.10	1.50	0.50	0.44	0.39	1.33	0.48	0.21
III	5.92	3.34	5.92	1.67	1.57	0.96	1.37	0.52	0.44	0.49	1.38	0.53	0.23
IV	5.41	2.96	5.41	1.74	1.71	0.83	1.13	0.47	0.60	0.41	1.29	0.47	0.21
V	5.14	2.81	5.14	1.63	1.69	0.77	1.05	0.43	0.50	0.49	1.23	0.48	0.19

(continued)

TABLE A.3 (continued)

	Household Structure			Earners		Age Structure							
	Size	Children	Residents	Workers	Earners	<5	6–12	13–15	16–19	20–24	25–44	45–64	65+
1992 (continued)													
VI	4.79	2.40	4.79	1.68	1.80	0.64	0.80	0.37	0.48	0.51	1.18	0.55	0.25
VII	4.47	2.23	4.49	1.68	1.86	0.59	0.62	0.29	0.53	0.51	1.19	0.56	0.18
VIII	4.08	1.97	4.10	1.59	1.75	0.48	0.59	0.27	0.40	0.45	1.16	0.50	0.23
IX	3.62	1.58	3.65	1.53	1.73	0.40	0.45	0.20	0.31	0.47	1.10	0.49	0.21
X	3.27	1.35	3.33	1.49	1.65	0.31	0.35	0.14	0.25	0.35	1.05	0.62	0.20
Total	4.71	2.44	4.73	1.62	1.68	0.69	0.87	0.34	0.43	0.44	1.21	0.52	0.21
1994													
I	6.78	4.06	6.78	1.86	1.67	1.44	1.81	0.56	0.46	0.37	1.39	0.51	0.24
II	6.06	3.53	6.06	1.70	1.60	1.19	1.41	0.54	0.50	0.41	1.23	0.54	0.25
III	5.53	3.07	5.53	1.78	1.74	0.95	1.18	0.49	0.47	0.45	1.18	0.59	0.22
IV	5.23	2.73	5.23	1.76	1.74	0.82	1.01	0.42	0.45	0.50	1.21	0.61	0.21
V	4.86	2.47	4.86	1.68	1.75	0.68	0.88	0.35	0.51	0.52	1.19	0.53	0.20
VI	4.65	2.26	4.65	1.75	1.77	0.64	0.73	0.34	0.44	0.56	1.17	0.56	0.22
VII	4.40	2.19	4.43	1.70	1.81	0.56	0.69	0.29	0.44	0.51	1.17	0.54	0.20
VIII	4.11	1.98	4.13	1.73	1.82	0.42	0.57	0.25	0.40	0.59	1.07	0.59	0.23
IX	3.57	1.56	3.60	1.58	1.73	0.38	0.43	0.19	0.29	0.39	1.12	0.53	0.24
X	3.08	1.20	3.18	1.49	1.65	0.25	0.31	0.13	0.20	0.29	1.08	0.60	0.22
Total	4.59	2.33	4.62	1.68	1.73	0.66	0.81	0.32	0.40	0.45	1.16	0.56	0.22
1996													
I	6.99	4.16	7.16	2.11	1.71	1.49	1.94	0.60	0.45	0.32	1.42	0.57	0.18
II	5.98	3.47	6.13	1.97	1.80	1.17	1.40	0.49	0.48	0.42	1.32	0.51	0.20
III	5.40	3.06	5.51	1.84	1.81	0.87	1.13	0.48	0.47	0.43	1.27	0.53	0.21
IV	5.05	2.72	5.15	1.79	1.79	0.86	0.98	0.40	0.43	0.39	1.29	0.47	0.23
V	4.74	2.51	4.82	1.72	1.75	0.68	0.85	0.36	0.46	0.42	1.22	0.52	0.22
VI	4.46	2.25	4.56	1.78	1.80	0.59	0.71	0.31	0.40	0.42	1.24	0.59	0.19
VII	4.15	1.99	4.24	1.66	1.75	0.54	0.59	0.28	0.36	0.47	1.13	0.57	0.21
VIII	3.90	1.83	4.00	1.74	1.79	0.50	0.48	0.21	0.34	0.44	1.18	0.57	0.19
IX	3.41	1.48	3.51	1.55	1.66	0.38	0.40	0.17	0.22	0.33	1.09	0.59	0.24
X	2.91	1.12	3.07	1.48	1.60	0.26	0.28	0.12	0.20	0.25	1.07	0.53	0.20
Total	4.43	2.25	4.54	1.72	1.73	0.65	0.77	0.31	0.36	0.38	1.20	0.55	0.21

Source: Calculated by the author based on ENIGH and INEGI (1984–1996).

TABLE A.4

Population Distribution: Age Group by Quintile (Data: individuals)

	Age Group			
	6–12	*13–15*	*16–19*	*20–24*
1992				
I-II	28.4	22.9	16.0	13.0
III-IV	23.8	23.9	20.6	16.9
V-VI	20.1	22.3	21.8	21.5
VII-VIII	15.3	17.8	23.8	24.0
IX-X	12.3	13.1	17.9	24.7
Total	100.0	100.0	100.0	100.0
1994				
I-II	28.5	24.2	17.4	12.4
III-IV	23.2	24.1	20.0	17.9
V-VI	19.2	20.5	23.0	23.2
VII-VIII	16.7	17.9	22.9	26.3
IX-X	12.3	13.3	16.6	20.2
Total	100.0	100.0	100.0	100.0
1996				
I-II	29.6	24.1	17.9	13.4
III-IV	23.4	24.2	21.3	18.3
V-VI	19.7	21.3	23.4	21.2
VII-VIII	15.3	17.5	21.4	26.3
IX-X	12.0	12.9	16.1	20.7
Total	100.0	100.0	100.0	100.0

Source: Calculated by the author based on ENIGH (1992–1996).

the Constitution). The upper-middle educational level includes preparatory, vocational, and technical education, an additional three years of schooling covering the sixteen- to nineteen-year-old population. It corresponds to high school. Finally, higher education offered by universities and technical higher education institutions covers the population of twenty- to twenty-four-year-olds. Post-basic education includes the last two levels of schooling. INEGI's original variables for education were processed in order to reconstruct this educational structure and to estimate participation rates on education.

TABLE A.5

Younger Earners by Age Group

Zone		1992		1994		1996	
		N	%	N	%	N	%
Earners 6–12 (primary)							
Rural	I-II	25	35.2	69	48.9	81	43.1
	III-IV	21	29.6	42	29.8	71	37.8
	V-VI	19	26.8	25	17.7	21	11.2
	VII-VIII	6	8.5	4	2.8	13	6.9
	IX-X	0	0.0	1	0.7	2	1.1
	Total	71	100.0	141	100.0	188	100.0
Urban	I-II	3	5.3	19	14.5	59	28.6
	III-IV	17	29.8	29	22.1	49	23.8
	V-VI	16	28.1	29	22.1	40	19.4
	VII-VIII	9	15.8	39	29.8	33	16.0
	IX-X	12	21.1	15	11.5	25	12.1
	Total	57	100.0	131	100.0	206	100.0
Earners 13–15 (secondary)							
Rural	I-II	41	33.3	67	48.9	106	45.9
	III-IV	46	37.4	49	29.8	72	31.2
	V-VI	21	17.1	22	17.7	36	15.6
	VII-VIII	13	10.6	6	2.8	15	6.5
	IX-X	2	1.6	2	0.7	2	0.9
	Total	123	100.0	146	100.0	231	100.0
Urban	I-II	26	10.5	26	14.5	46	15.4
	III-IV	68	27.5	66	22.1	106	35.5
	V-VI	68	27.5	46	22.1	68	22.7
	VII-VIII	52	21.1	49	29.8	58	19.4
	IX-X	33	13.4	18	11.5	21	7.0
	Total	247	100.0	205	100.0	299	100.0
Young Earners (16–24)							
Rural	I-II	253	30.4	321	32.9	355	28.8
	III-IV	236	28.4	287	29.4	429	34.8
	V-VI	178	21.4	204	20.9	249	20.2
	VII-VIII	124	14.9	125	12.8	123	10.0
	IX-X	40	4.8	38	3.9	75	6.1
	Total	831	100.0	975	100.0	1231	100.0
Urban	I-II	133	4.1	247	6.1	275	7.8
	III-IV	390	12.1	610	15.1	555	15.7
	V-VI	750	23.2	1006	24.8	841	23.8
	VII-VIII	1018	31.5	1326	32.7	1129	32.0
	IX-X	943	29.2	862	21.3	732	20.7
	Total	3234	100.0	4051	100.0	3532	100.0

Source: Calculated by the author based on ENIGH and INEGI (1996).

NOTES

1. *Lagged*, within the analysis of schooling of household heads, refers to those who have not completed mandatory basic education which is constitutionally guaranteed to every Mexican citizen; within the analysis of the young, to those not attending school, to the delayed entrance to the system, to repetition, and to dropout, as well as to educational exclusion within households. See the Appendix for a brief description of the Mexican educational system.

2. One should recognize that the time period represents significant fluctuations in the national economy—from crisis, to recovery, and even to euphoria—with important effects in employment conditions as well as in individual choices about schooling and participation in the labor market.

3. This classification is based on Sen (1992).

4. For the national case, the former is developed in INEGI (1993). For a description of the latter, see Boltvinik (1994, 1995a, 1995b).

5. For example, see Székely (1994; 1995). For an analysis on educational inequality, see Bracho (1995) and COMIE (1998).

6. In Townsend's words, "Society and specially the State, is creating or 'manufacturing' as well as reconstituting needs at the same time as it is determining the allocation of resources in the first place—and not just the redistribution of income—with which those needs can or will be met" (1985, 663).

7. Even more, the most recent state programs oriented toward the relief of poverty by the distribution of education, such as Progresa, are based on economic theory, rather than on educational theories. In addition, Progresa has its administrative center outside the educational system.

8. This value of education as a "good" derives from its value as "capability," not restricted to a utilitarian or consequential notion, but representing in itself a value for the individual and overall social development.

9. This particular problem refers to the limits of rationality as the basis of decision making or, following Elster (1995), as a "Solomonic judgment."

10. The Appendix presents a general synopsis of the main indicators of the distribution of per capita household income distribution and the method used to obtain this estimate. Here I show indicators only by income quintiles relevant to the purpose of this analysis.

11. For the purposes of this analysis, the young members are those who are not household heads, or their spouses, and who are relevant to an educational analysis, up until the age of twenty-four. I restricted the analysis to those that have some kindred relation with the household head.

12. The term *earner* refers to individuals at any age that received any form of income during the last six months.

13. The first is generated by CONAPO, Consejo Nacional de Poblacion (National Population Council), based on municipal level information, and is the indicator used by Progresa, Programa de Educacion, Salud y Alimentacion (Program of Education, Health, and Nutrition), in the first place in its targeting selection method. The H index, estimated by PEA, Poblacion Economicamente Activa (Economically Active Population), with income below two minimum wages, is due to de la Torre (1997). The educational indicators are estimations from the author (Bracho 1999b) and refer to the "adult population" between twenty and sixty-four years old.

14. See Bracho (1999a), based on *Informe de Labores*, Secretaría de Educación Pública.

15. The analysis is limited to the educational level of household heads over twenty years old. We compiled our data by educational levels, omitting the estimates based on average years of

schooling in order to identify general educational standards rather than a specific number of years of schooling. We recognize that a more in-depth analysis of the household educational profile must be done including information about the spouses, as it is relevant for an analysis of school participation. However, this goal exceeds the objective of this chapter.

16. There are also some household heads at the bottom of the income distribution who have completed higher education, even though the percentage is low.

17. See, in particular, the works developed at OECD.

18. In this section the information is restricted to the ENIGH from 1992, 1994, and 1996 which included the variable "school attendance." For surveys conducted in 1984 and 1989, it is possible to take into account only individuals twelve years old or older from the labor indicators. I prefer to omit that information.

19. The estimation corresponds to net rates; the population who studies at an older and younger age appropriate for their level are excluded. Those who concluded a school level at the appropriate age were incorporated in the "without lag" category.

20. The argument used at that time to explain the distance between public discourse and Census information was that government provided for 100 percent of the population "who demanded" education, and not the total potential demand. In our view, if that argument was prevalent, the attention to educational demand would be a problem of procedural justice instead of substantial justice, following Elster's characterization (1995), ignoring the notion of human rights involved in public responsibility of educational distribution.

21. Public efforts were oriented to decrease the lag in the age beginning primary school. From 1990 to 1996, SEP reported increases in enrollment for the six-year-old population, from 90 percent to 93 percent. See Bracho (1998).

22. Cortés (1998) emphasized its relevance for income distribution analysis. As pointed out earlier, an "earner" does not necessarily refer to individuals who work or who make income contributions to the household.

23. In order to provide a deeper analysis of the problem, we would have to consider other factors related to the structure and composition of households and the differential roles its members have in assuring household survival. The problem is beyond the scope of this chapter.

24. The Appendix compiles general information on minors for 1992–1996 (see Tables A.4 and A.5), in relation to the changes during the period and the problems with sample representations. Here we selected the data for 1996, mainly for its sample size.

25. Total income includes all current income, monetary and nonmonetary, but excludes capital income.

26. One procedure to weight by household size is an estimation (or attribution) of equivalence elasticity scales, that is, how much household needs increase based on the number of its members. See the recent works produced by OECD, in particular, Forster (1994) and Burniaux et al. (1998). Others suggest adjusting the estimate to the household structure and not only the number of family members (Atkinson [1991], Haddad and Kanbur [1990], and others).

27. For this estimate I used the statistical program developed by Cortés, Rubalcava, and Ramírez (1998).

REFERENCES

Atkinson, A. B. (1991) Measuring poverty and differences in family composition. *Economica* 59: 1–16.

Boltvinik, Julio. (1992). Pobreza, naturaleza humana y necesidades. In *América Latina: El Reto de la Pobreza—Características, Evolución y Perspectivas,* eds. Luis Beccaria, Julio Boltvinik, Juan Carlos Feres, Oscar Fresnada, Arturo León, and Amartya Sen, 63–80. Santa Fe de Bogotá, Colombia: PNUD.

Boltvinik, Julio. 1994, La evolución de la pobreza según INEGI. Mimeograph. México City: El Colegio de México.

Boltvinik, Julio 1995a. La pobreza en México: Metodología y evolución. *Salud Pública de México* 37(4): 288–297.

Boltvinik, Julio. 1995b. *Pobreza y Estratificación Social en México.* México City: INEGI, IISUNAM, El Colegio de México.

Bracho, Teresa. 1995. Distribución y desigualdad educativa: México, 1990. *Estudios Sociológicos* 13(37): 23–56

Bracho, Teresa. 1999a. Basic education in Mexico: An overview. In *Schooling for Success: Preventing Repetition and Dropout in Latin American Primary Schools,* eds. Laura Randall and Joan Anderson, 103–118. New York: Sharpe.

Bracho, Teresa. 1999b. Perfil educativo regional en México. *Estudios Sociológicos* XVII(51): 703–742.

Burniaux, Jean-Marc, Thai-Thanh Dang, Douglas Fore, Michael Förster, Marco Mira d'Ercole, and Howard Oxley. 1998. Income distribution and poverty in selected OECD countries. Economic Department Working Paper No. 189. Paris: Organization for Economic Cooperation and Development.

COMIE. 1998. Educación y desigualdad social. *Revista Mexicana de Investigación Educativa* III(6): 317–345.

CONAPO. 1990. *Indicadores Socioeconómicos e Índice de Marginación Municipal.* México City: Consejo Nacional de Población.

Cortés, Fernando. 1998. *La Distribución del Ingreso en México en Épocas de Estabilización y Reforma.* México City: El Colegio de México.

Cortés, Fernando. 1995. Procesos sociales y demográficos en auxilio de la economía neoliberal: Un análisis de la distribución del ingreso en México durante los ochenta. *Revista Mexicana de Sociología* LVII(2): 73–90.

Cortés, Fernando, Rosa María Rubalcava, and Mario Ramírez. 1998. Programa Desigualimetro. Version 3.0.

de la Torre, Rodolfo. 1997. Indicadores de desarrollo regional con información limitada. In *Pobreza y Política Social en México,* ed. Gabriel Martínez, 273–295. México City: Instituto Tecnológico Autónomo de Méxcio, El Trimestre Económico, F.C.E.

Elster, Jon. 1995. *Juicios Salomónicos: Las Limitaciones de la Racionalidad Como Principio de Decisión.* Barcelona: Gedisa.

Förster, Michael F. 1994. Measurement of low incomes and poverty in a perspective of international comparisons. Labour Market and Social Policy Occasional Papers, no. 14. Paris: Organization for Economic Cooperation and Development.

Haddad, Lawrence, and Ravi Kanbur. 1990. How serious is the neglect of intra-household inequality? *Economic Journal* 100(September): 866–888.

INEGI. 1984, 1989, 1992, 1994, 1996. *Encuesta Nacional de Ingresos y Gastos de los Hogares.* México City: Instituto Nacional de Estadística, Geografía e Informática.

INEGI. 1993. *Magnitud y Evolución de la Pobreza en México: 1984–1992. Informe Metodológico.* México City: Instituto Nacional de Estadística, Geografía e Informática.

Jencks, Christopher. 1972. *Inequality. A Reassessment of the Effect of Family and Schooling in America.* New York: Harper Colophon.

Lustig, Nora, and Miguel Székely. 1997. *México: Evolución Económica, Pobreza y Desigualdad.* Technical Study, Sustainable Development Department. Washington, D.C.: InterAmerican Development Bank.

Padua, Jorge. 1990. Algunos efectos de la crisis en la educación superior y la reforma en las universidades. In *La Modernización Educativa en Perspectiva,* ed. Teresa Bracho, 350–390. México City: Flacso-SEP.

Padua, Jorge. 1998. La educación en las transformaciones sociales. In *Un Siglo de Educación en México,* ed. Pablo Latapí, vol. I, 84–149. México City: Fondo de Cultura Económica/ CONACULTA.

Secretaría de Desarrollo Social. 1997. *Programa de Educación, Salud y Alimentación (Progresa).* México City: SEDESOL.

Secretaría de Educación Pública. Various years. *Informe de Labores.* México City: SEP.

Sen, Amartya. 1992. Conceptos de pobreza. In *América Latina: El Reto de la Pobreza: Características, Evolución y Perspectivas,* eds. Luis Beccaria, Julio Boltvinik, Juan Carlos Feres, Oscar Fresnada, Arturo León, and Amartya Sen, 27–40. Santa Fe de Bogotá, Colombia: PNUD.

Sen, Amartya. 1995. *Nuevo Examen de la Desigualdad.* Madrid: Alianza.

Sen, Amartya. 1996. Capacidad y bienestar. In *La Calidad de Vida,* eds. Martha C. Nussbaum and Amartya Sen, 54–100. México City: FCE.

Sen, Amartya. 1997a. *Bienestar, Justicia y Mercado.* Barcelona: Paidós.

Sen, Amartya. 1997b. Editorial: Human capital and human capability. *World Development* 25(12): 1959–1961.

Székely, Miguel. 1994. Estabilización y ajuste con desigualdad y pobreza: El caso de México. *El Trimestre Económico* LXI(1): 135–175.

Székely, Miguel. 1995. Aspectos de la desigualdad en México. *El Trimestre Económico* LXII(2): 201–243.

Townsend, Peter. 1985. A sociological approach to the measurement of poverty—A rejoinder to Professor Amartya Sen. *Oxford Economic Papers* 37: 659–668.

Commentary

Emily Hannum, Harvard Graduate School of Education

In reading Chapter 10, I was struck by three themes: the ambiguous nature of the relationship between education and social inequality, the importance of considering the demographic context of schooling, and the usefulness of the life-course perspective in examining educational exclusion. These themes are significant not only in the case of Mexico, but also as emerging topics for debate among scholars and policymakers in many nations around the world. My comments focus on these themes.

EDUCATION, POVERTY, AND INEQUALITY: AMBIGUOUS RELATIONSHIPS

In a critical discussion, the author makes explicit the problems inherent in an overly simplistic view of the implications of rising levels of education for poverty and inequality. We know that in many nations around the world a long-term trend of increasing education has emerged. Improved access to some basic level of schooling for the poor is certainly a favorable development. However, changes in inequality implied by rising levels of education are less clear. A recent cross-national empirical study of school-to-work transitions in thirteen nations illustrated very clearly the problem of credential inflation: as ever-larger proportions of the population obtain a given educational credential, the labor market value of that credential declines (Muller and Shavit 1998).

The author notes that despite a global decrease in exclusion from education in Mexico, inequalities in exclusion remain. She cites the striking example that regional differences in educational attainment evident in the 1990 Census mirror those in existence in the early part of the twentieth century. This example illustrates the broad point that historical social hierarchies are often mirrored in the quantity and quality of educational facilities, and thus the distribution of educational credentials tends to reinforce existing patterns of inequality. A recent comparative study of educational stratification trends in thirteen countries showed stable levels of class inequality at higher-level, valuable educational transitions (Blossfeld and Shavit 1993). The case of Brazil clearly illustrates the ambiguous relationship between economic development and associated educational expansion and various dimensions of social inequality. One study (Bills and Haller 1984) showed that the effects of parental socioeconomic status on sons' educational levels were not weakening over time and were stronger in more developed regions than in less developed regions. Another (Telles 1994) indicated that development and educational expansion in Brazil had reinforced, and even increased, racial inequality in white-collar occupational attainment.

In short, while increasing participation in education is obviously desirable for many reasons, rising absolute levels of education will not necessarily affect the relative position of children from different social backgrounds in the distribution of educational credentials. As the author notes, the quality and quantity of credentials needed for social participation differ depending on context and tend to rise over time. This statement implies that rising levels of education will not detract from income inequality without a fundamental shift in the distribution of education across social groups.

THE DEMOGRAPHIC CONTEXT OF SCHOOLING

The implications of demographic change for education described by the author also illustrate issues significant in the global context. It is important for educational planners to understand the implications of demographic shifts for the size and composition of the school-aged populations that they will be serving in the near future. Fertility transition in Mexico, as in much of the rest of the world, means that the ever-increasing cohorts of school-aged children that characterize pre-transition and transitioning societies will soon be a characteristic of the past. This change is favorable from the perspective of reducing strain on the school system and in the sense of providing a stable context for planning. Smaller family sizes may also be favorable from the perspective that smaller numbers of siblings are associated in many societies with the devotion of greater resources to educating children. However, the fact that fertility decline tends to occur more quickly among higher socioeconomic status (SES) groups implies two important facts: first, children of higher SES groups are likely to disproportionately reap any educational benefits of smaller numbers of children in families, and second, children as a group will increasingly be concentrated in low SES, large families at greatest educational risk. These are important issues for education planners to bear in mind.

Dealing effectively with the changing demographic context of education is critical for societies undergoing transition. The declining ratio of school-aged cohorts to the working-age population will eventually become a declining ratio of workers to elderly dependents. The coming population aging highlights the economic imperative of providing an education to children that prepares them for a productive working life.

It is worth noting, however, that recent population projections for Mexico indicate that the transition to smaller families has not yet accompanied a transition to smaller school-aged cohorts. This phenomenon typically occurs as a result of "population momentum": as large cohorts of women (reflecting high levels of fertility among previous generations) pass through the reproductive ages, it is common to find continued growth in the overall size of cohorts of children for some time despite smaller numbers of children per woman. In Mexico, cohorts entering school will continue to increase at a slow pace for the next few years (see Figure C10.1).

The Life-Course Perspective

The author advocates a life-course perspective in this chapter, noting that income inequalities associated with schooling become heightened among older cohorts. The life-course perspective highlights longitudinal studies of changes across the lives of individuals, rather than cross-sectional studies that draw inferences from comparisons

FIGURE C10.1

Population Pyramids for Mexico, Selected Years

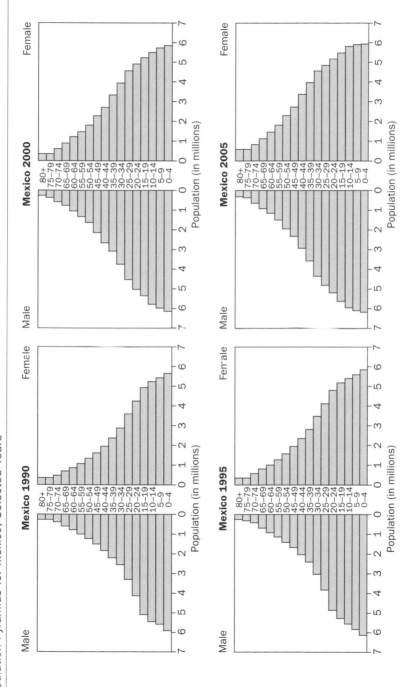

Note: Data updated 12/28/98 (http://www.census.gov/ipc/www/, accessed 6/26/99)
Source: U.S. Census Bureau, international database.

of different individuals. This perspective is particularly important in the context of studies of the economic outcomes of education, where inferences about the effects of more education for poorly educated individuals may be quite misleading if they are drawn from comparisons with the experiences of those whose circumstances permitted them to obtain more education. Further, measurement of poverty itself can be greatly improved if data collection occurs at more than one time point. The importance of longitudinal approaches as tools for examining the impact of poverty on children has been prioritized by poverty researchers and data collection agencies in the United States (Brooks-Gunn et al. 1995, 27–97); this chapter illustrates strongly the case for a similar approach in the context of Mexico.

In closing, I would like to thank the author for a thoughtful investigation of issues of poverty and educational inequality. Detailed empirical investigation guided by a well-thought-out theoretical framework makes this work an important contribution to the knowledge base on equity issues.

REFERENCES

Bills, D. B., and A. O. Haller. 1984. Socio-economic development and social stratification: Reassessing the Brazilian case. *Journal of Developing Areas* 19: 59–70.

Blossfeld, Hans-Peter, and Yossi Shavit. 1993. Persisting barriers: Changes in educational opportunities in thirteen countries. In *Persistent Inequality: Changing Educational Attainment in Thirteen Countries,* ed. Yossi Shavit and Hans-Peter Blossfeld, 1–24. Boulder, Colo.: Westview Press.

Brooks-Gunn, Jeanne, Brett Brown, Greg J. Duncan, and Kristin Anderson Moore. 1995. Child development in the context of family and community resources. In *Integrating Federal Statistics on Children: Report on a Workshop,* 27–97. Board on Children and Families, Committee on National Statistics, Commission on Behavioral and Social Sciences and Education, National Research Council, Institute of Medicine. Washington, D.C.: National Academy Press.

Muller, Walter, and Yossi Shavit. 1998. The institutional embeddedness of the stratification process: A comparative study of qualifications and occupations in 13 countries. In *From School to Work: A Comparative Study of Educational Qualifications and Occupational Destinations,* ed. Yossi Shavit and Walter Muller, 1–48. Oxford: Clarendon Press.

Telles, Edward. 1994. Industrialization and racial inequality in employment: The Brazilian example. *American Sociological Review* 59: 46–63.

Elementary-school students in the Escuela Nezahualcoyotl in Chalco, Mexico.
[Jose C. Gonzalez]

11

The Schooling Situation of Children in Highly Underprivileged Rural Localities in Mexico

Patricia E. Muñiz
Education, Health, and Nutrition Program (*Progresa*), Mexico

Continuous efforts by the state to broaden the coverage of the educational system have characterized recent decades in Mexican education. At least since 1990, official statistics reveal that the proportion of children (six to sixteen years old) who never attended school has decreased systematically, estimating 2.5 percent by 1995. According to experts, it is practically impossible to go beyond these levels, because they mainly reflect part of the rural population located in very small and hard to reach sites, where schools are nonexistent and their settlement would be hardly feasible.

Despite some breakthroughs, the problem still exists regarding the high proportion of children who do not attend school and who have fallen behind in their education, or who dropped out before the end of their basic education years (Muñoz and Suárez 1996). In this regard, a strong decline in school attendance has been observed from one school cycle to the other, as well as a continuous shrinkage in the number of students as the educational ladder ascends (Guevara Niebla 1992).

Particular attention has been drawn to the high proportion of children who drop out of school after four or five years of attendance, as well as to the gradual increase in the average school age throughout the population. Likewise, gender-based differences have been observed, especially in the shift from primary to secondary education onward, which implies fewer opportunities in the labor market for girls.

The economic crisis of the 1980s, the deterioration of the population's life style, advances in social research, and the growing perception of the role played by gender drivers, in particular in poorer areas, have led to the development of special programs aimed at addressing poverty from various fronts. Based on the assumption that access to minimum education is critical for enhancing future opportunities for poorer children, these programs seek to increase schooling for children of both genders, but particularly for girls. The programs have enabled educators to obtain detailed information on school access problems, educational lagging, and dropout trends in localities representative of the situations that limit the coverage of the educational system and that are supposedly the ones less benefited by development processes.

This chapter addresses these concerns and analyzes the schooling situation of children ranging from six to sixteen years old in highly marginalized localities throughout Mexico in spite of previous and current efforts to improve their access to schooling. After describing the sources of information used, I will focus on school attendance, dropout, and lagging trends, comparing national data with the data for children in marginalized localities. The last section deals with a preliminary analysis of the factors associated with nonattendance, addressing children aged six to ten and eleven to sixteen, highlighting variables related to the characteristics of the children and their households. We hope that this analysis will serve as an informational tool for continued research and development of programs that will increase student access to both primary and secondary levels of schooling with special consideration to marginalized rural communities.

INFORMATION SOURCES AND SCOPE OF ANALYSIS

The information used in this study has two sources: the 1995 National Census on Population and Households (Conteo-95) of the National Institute of Statistics, Geography, and Information Technology (INEGI) and the Survey on Social and Economic Characteristics of Households (ENCASEH) of the Education, Health, and Nutrition Program.[1]

The Conteo-95 census combined a comprehensive count of all the population and dwellings in the country with a survey that delved into the characteristics gathered by the count. The field work lasted from November 6 to December 2, 1995. The units for census analysis were private dwellings and their customary occupants. The survey also gathered information about households as units of analysis (a questionnaire was carried through for each household inside a dwelling). The Conteo-95 questionnaire gathered information on dwelling utilities and some characteristics of their customary occupants, such as gender, age, literacy, and language. The survey included the same subjects in more detail and dealt with additional issues.

The second primary source for analysis was the ENCASEH. The ENCASEH is the instrument used by Progresa, a program for increasing school access to highly marginalized localities, to carry out the census on the localities selected for the program. Progresa targets marginalized localities on the basis of nationwide homogeneous elements and abides by a standardized procedure emerging from the generation of a Marginalization Index for each of the localities in the country for which social and demographic census information is available.[2]

The first section of the ENCASEH questionnaire collects sociodemographics about household members (gender, age, illiteracy, schooling, attendance, occupation, income, allowances from government programs, etc.), and the second section inquires about building materials, availability and building infrastructure, existence of dwelling, goods, animals, and ground, as well as family relations, size, and migration of household members. A census schedule is also issued bearing information on existing utilities.

For this chapter I used information from a random sample of 100,000 households out of the 1,950,000 surveyed by Progresa between December 1996 and May 1998 in 36,948 highly and very highly maginalized rural localities in thirty states of the

Mexican Republic. These represent 35.4 percent of the localities of less than 5,000 inhabitants and 47.5 percent of the total number of more highly marginalized localities. The 15.3 million people residing in these localities account for 76.5 percent of the total population living in rural areas of less than 5,000 inhabitants. The first approach to the families living in extreme poverty conditions is based on family income and the extreme poverty line,[3] sorting households into two groups: (1) extremely poor and (2) non-extremely poor. From this preliminary identification, a second household classification is made considering a set of social and economic indicators obtained from the information provided by survey respondents in each household. The aim is to achieve a multidimensional approach to a household's poverty conditions; for this purpose, a discriminant analysis is carried out, which enables categorizing a household in either of the relevant sets—that is, extreme poverty or non-extreme poverty.

It is worth noticing that, given the support characteristics delivered by Progresa, it was necessary to ensure that basic education services were available at the locality itself, or no farther than five kilometers away from it. Therefore, in these analyses, the problem of educational supply—which would impact child and teenage school attendance, dropout ratios, and low schooling levels—has already been considered in the selection of localities where schools exist. No generalizations can be made about localities without schools. However, the localities spanned by the program could evince problems such as differences in distance and transportation costs. In conclusion, the data from both sources came from similar questions; those pertaining to Conteo-95 present the expanded data of the national sample, whereas the Progresa observations reflect the total number of boys and girls in the sample which refers only to rural marginalized communities.

THE SCHOOLING SITUATION OF CHILDREN

Attendance

The first approach for studying access to the school system is in reviewing the proportion of children between six and sixteen years old who never attended school. Table 11.1 provides information for 1995. In 1995, 2.5 percent of all children between six and sixteen years old had never attended school. Considering the information by single age, the percentage of children in this situation reaches its peak at the age of six (6.4 percent) and declines from age seven until eleven, where it reaches the minimum value (1.1 percent). At age twelve, the percentage rises again and reaches 2.3 percent at age sixteen. These numbers indicate that indeed a majority of the school-aged population does have access to schools. However, we must investigate who lacks access specifically, looking at age, gender, and place of residence.

Differences in school access initially appear when considering the children's place of residence.[4] In urban areas, 1.4 percent of all the children never attended school compared with 4.2 percent for rural areas. The highest percentages are observed in children between six and seven—11.6 percent and 5.7 percent for rural children, and 4.1 percent and 1.6 percent for urban children. These percentages follow the same downward trend observed in the nationwide total until the age of eleven, but the proportion of children never attending school after this age is much higher in the rural population,

TABLE 11.1

Proportion of Children and Teenagers Who Have Never Attended School,
by Age and Gender According to Their Place of Residence

Age	Nationwide	Urban	Rural	Boys	Girls	Rural Boys	Rural Girls
6	6.35	4.08	11.35	6.27	6.45	11.78	10.91
7	2.78	1.60	5.65	2.70	2.87	5.98	5.30
8	1.75	0.98	3.37	1.76	1.73	3.22	3.52
9	1.41	0.77	2.81	1.42	1.41	2.42	3.20
10	1.61	1.15	2.63	1.69	1.53	2.76	2.50
11	1.19	0.88	1.87	1.18	1.20	1.53	2.23
12	1.48	0.85	2.85	1.27	1.70	2.38	3.37
13	1.66	0.99	3.21	1.55	1.77	2.86	3.54
14	1.49	0.91	2.82	1.43	1.55	2.87	2.76
15	2.04	1.07	4.28	2.23	1.86	4.48	4.07
16	2.33	1.61	4.11	2.12	2.54	3.89	4.36

Source: Own calculations from Conteo-1995.

amounting to three or four times the percentages of urban children in senior years. Thus we find causes to further investigate why children in the rural areas do not attend schools at the same rates as those in urban areas and whether these trends are more pronounced when taking gender into account.

With respect to gender, boys and girls do not differ in either aggregate form (nationwide proportions are 2.2 percent and 2.3 percent, respectively) or in age differences. In other words, regardless of age, boys and girls exemplify similar trends in school attendance nationally. The table also illustrates a similar phenomenon when solely observing rural localities (around 4 percent).

Additional information on nonattendance is presented in Table 11.2. The data provided by Table 11.2 refer to school-aged children from marginalized rural localities for the years 1996–1998. Of the total school-aged population, 7.17 percent have never attended school, a figure much higher than that reported by the census some years earlier in rural areas. An all-encompassing view of the table shows how the proportion of extremely poor children with absolute nonattendance more than doubles the percentage of non-poor children of all ages and both genders.[5]

More specifically, when we review the information by single age, we notice very high percentages of children not attending at an early age, particularly for six-year-old poor children. Both poor boys and poor girls of this age group amount to one-fifth of the total who have never attended school (21.2 percent for boys and 21.2 percent for girls). In non-poor children, the percentage of nonattendance is lower starting at eight years of age and shows nonsystematic gender-based differences; in some ages, the proportion of boys is higher, whereas in other ages the opposite trend is true. With regard to poverty conditions, the proportion of nonattending children is still high at age eight and remains at similar levels for all ages, with slight variations. For extremely poor children, there are more systematic gender-based differences: in almost all ages the proportion of girls who have never attended is higher than boys. The lowest proportion of nonattending poor children takes place at age nine—that is, one year earlier than

TABLE 11.2

Proportion of Children and Teenagers Who Have Never Attended School,
by Age and Gender in Marginalized Rural Localities

	Non-Poor		Poor	
Age	Boys	Girls	Boys	Girls
6	9.04	10.78	21.18	21.23
7	4.10	4.97	9.91	10.21
8	1.68	1.79	6.01	6.14
9	2.34	1.02	4.66	4.73
10	1.01	2.16	4.65	4.85
11	1.73	1.58	4.28	4.23
12	2.24	1.41	4.40	5.53
13	1.42	1.94	4.53	5.05
14	2.49	3.11	5.47	6.18
15	1.88	2.08	5.75	7.31
16	2.92	3.91	6.89	7.94
Total	2.64	2.94	7.22	7.75

Source: Own calculations from Progresa database.

non-poor children in marginalized rural localities and two years earlier than rural children as noted in the Conteo-95.

Even though these data provide a broad approximation to the analysis of the coverage of the schooling system and might be complemented with additional information, they point out another matter of concern: how far the rule-based assumption that defines the regular educational trajectory, as relating to the child's age when entering school, is true. What we have noticed thus far is that children from various backgrounds access schooling at different ages and, therefore, we need to understand with more depth how the Mexican school system is structured and how that structure expects children to progress through elementary and secondary levels.

The state undertakes the delivery of basic education (that is, primary and secondary) to all school-aged children. From the standpoint of the minimum acceptable school age in Mexico, this means that schools only accept children of at least six full years of age, and that for at least nine years, the child will be a student, according to the time required for education. A rule or criterion is thus set forth, which assumes regularity in the child's basic educational record and which enables assessing certain aspects of the coverage of the schooling system and the child's performance. If this assumption is true and there are no factors undermining it, it would be expected that a child enrolled at age six would advance one school term every year of age. Should this be the case, the child's primary education trajectory should last six years, whereas his or her secondary education would take another three years. A child enrolled in school at age six and attending regularly would be twelve years old when finishing primary school and fifteen at the end of secondary school. However, since the dates of the beginning of the school terms are not always consistent with the time a child turns six, a certain age fluctuation is to be expected in the age of beginning studies and, therefore, in the age of the child at the end of each school term. If the absence of an educational trajectory points to the lack of school access, a regular trajectory then defines two other situations: the child has either lagged behind or dropped out. The first case has to do with the fact that the child accessing the school system does not keep the expected relationship between age and grade attended, whereas the latter means that the child has dropped school completely at a given moment.

In marginalized rural areas—and particularly in conditions of extreme poverty—the high percentages of children ranging from six to eight who have never attended school may signify that these children may be subjected to an ex-ante delayed education. Perhaps external factors influence whether or not these children begin school at the expected age but will not necessarily impair their ability to complete their education "normally." On the other hand, it has been proved that the delay in a child's educational record may be a critical element in explaining dropout trends (for Mexico, see Muñoz Izquierdo [1994]). Therefore, large proportions of children in marginalized localities begin school in a disadvantageous situation due to late entry, which may lead them to drop out. This brings us to our next subject for examination, dropout trends.

Dropout Trends

Another important issue of examining the situation of children attending school is the dropout trend at an early age. Between the ages of seven and eleven, over 96 percent of children attend school. However, after eleven years of age, this proportion starts to decrease remarkably, reducing attendance to half for sixteen-year-olds. If a distinction is made based on places of residence, clearly rural children have a disadvantaged situation compared to urban children, with the dropout proportions being much higher as age increases. Thus, among rural fifteen-year-olds, the proportion of children still attending school is 40.7 percent, whereas among urban children the percentage is 69.3 percent. Likewise, the rural sixteen-year-olds who attend school amount to 28.5 percent, whereas for urban children the proportion is 60.6 percent (see Table 11.3).

With regard to gender information, the data show similar trends as the ones described above, and there is no gender difference, except for eleven years of age, where

TABLE 11.3

Percentage of Children Attending School by Age, Gender, and Place of Residence

Age	Total	Rural	Urban	Boys	Girls	Rural Boys	Rural Girls
6	92.36	87.10	94.75	92.31	92.41	86.73	87.48
7	96.67	93.76	97.87	96.88	96.45	93.62	93.91
8	97.24	95.04	98.27	96.94	97.53	94.81	95.28
9	97.65	95.76	98.51	97.62	97.67	95.83	95.69
10	97.00	94.90	97.95	96.88	97.12	94.80	94.99
11	96.12	93.84	97.14	96.32	95.91	93.98	93.68
12	91.11	84.14	94.28	92.93	89.11	87.05	80.88
13	84.20	72.32	89.40	86.57	81.98	76.35	68.48
14	76.96	60.15	84.24	79.07	74.83	64.03	56.14
15	60.59	40.66	69.29	63.03	58.23	47.36	34.08
16	51.38	28.52	60.58	53.51	49.42	32.42	24.28

Source: Own calculations from Conteo-1995.

the proportion of girls attending school becomes lower than that for boys. This situation becomes more dramatic when looking at rural girls, because only close to one-third of fifteen-year-old girls and less than one-fourth of sixteen-year-old girls attend school. The latter fraction represents less than half of the women on a nationwide basis.

In marginalized rural areas, six-year-olds attend school in a similar fashion as the ones already discussed, with consideration of the delayed entry that has already been pointed out (see Table 11.4). For non-poor children between seven and ten years of age, the proportion of attending children is equal to or higher than 95 percent. At ten, the percentage of regular school-goers decreases, until attendance becomes reduced to just one-third of the sixteen-year-olds, with a steeper reduction in girls twelve years old and onward.

Among poor children, younger children have lower attendance rates than middle-school-aged children. While three-fourths of both six-year-old boys and girls attend school, the proportion of seven-year-old poor children enrolled in school is very similar to the proportion of six-year-old non-poor children enrolled, indicating that indeed children in poor households begin school at a later age. Between eight and eleven years old, attendees average 91 percent. Although the attendance of extremely poor children at all ages is approximately 5 percent less than the non-poor, from eleven years old onward, the gap widens. Whereas 64 percent of fifteen-year-old non-poor boys and 54 percent of girls of the same age and social conditions attend school, in poor children the percentages are 44.7 percent and 36.1 percent, respectively—a difference of 19 percent in boys and 17 percent in girls. Therefore, just as we noted differences in young children attending school, we see a similar phenomenon in older children, those expected to be in secondary schooling. Thus, within marginalized rural areas, it is precisely the children of extremely poor households who report the lowest attendance percentages, and this is especially true with girls, whose attendance starts

TABLE 11.4

Attendance Percentages by Age, Gender, and State of Poverty
in Marginalized Rural Areas

| Age | Non-Extremely Poor | | Extremely Poor | |
	Boys	Girls	Boys	Girls
6	90.11	87.97	76.77	77.04
7	94.71	93.37	88.23	87.50
8	97.59	97.07	91.47	91.35
9	95.83	96.93	92.41	92.13
10	96.85	96.04	91.50	91.30
11	94.20	95.50	90.05	90.02
12	91.47	88.35	84.88	79.65
13	87.03	78.32	74.62	65.52
14	77.62	67.88	59.73	51.66
15	63.94	53.39	44.75	36.14
16	37.13	33.98	33.76	25.12
Total	81.17	77.24	76.96	73.67

Source: Own calculations from Progresa database.

to decline earlier than boys. The systematic nature of nonattendance from ten or eleven years old onward leads us to verify the existence of a dropout trend.

If the information reviewed so far is considered as a whole, the outlook of schooling trajectories from populations of differing backgrounds turns out to be quite different from the one assumed by the regulatory criteria of educational policies. A significant percentage of children, especially in marginalized rural areas, start school late and drop out early. These children's school trajectories are, in fact, reduced to a small number of years and, to make matters worse, seem to lag from the very start. This turns our focus to examine the relationship between age and accomplished school years. If the regulatory school record assumption is accepted, lagging exists whenever the child's age is higher than that required if he or she had started school at age six and had passed all the school terms. This relationship should then be analyzed.

Age at Start of Basic Education

With the aim of reviewing the lagging of children in marginalized rural areas in terms of the regulatory age set forth by the school system, two indicators will be used: (1) the average age of girls and boys and (2) the median age on passing each school year. Because the information has been sourced from household surveys and the school-related questions refer to aspects such as last school grade attained, the tables point to the age of the child at the moment of the survey and the last year passed by him or her. Thus it is expected that the children within the scope of the survey would be attending the class following the above-mentioned average grade. As with the previous sections, we will first review nationwide observations in 1995, and the information on children in the selected marginalized areas later, controlling in both cases between attendees and nonattendees. For contextual analysis, comparisons are made only on the basis of gender and place of residence.

The left-hand side of Table 11.5 refers to urban and rural children who attend school and reveals that the average age of urban boys in each of the school years is slightly higher than that of urban girls—a difference worth noting, but not of essential significance. On the other hand, the average age of urban children passing each school year is lower than that of rural children, indicating that rural children tend to be older for the appropriate grade level. Additionally, we notice a situation similar to the one delineated for boys and girls in urban areas. In rural areas, boys and girls tend to be of similar age across grade levels.

With regard to nonattendees (right-hand side of Table 11.5), the situation is entirely different and may imply significant lagging or dropout trends. Keep in mind that the percentage of nonattendees increases as the children grow up. However, what is remarkable is the similarity between boys and girls independent of their place of residence. Remember that these data reflect the age of the children at the time of the survey with respect to their last completed school term. Therefore, the average age of nonattendees in first grade primary reflects the average age of individuals who reported only completing preschool, never attending school, or dropping out. Will these findings be replicated in marginalized rural areas? Table 11.6 illustrates the average age of boys and girls in marginalized rural areas by school year and thus leads us to make comparisons between boys and girls who attended school at the moment of the interview and

TABLE 11.5

Average Attendance Age in Each School Term by Gender and Place of Residence

Urban Children

| | Attendees | | | | Nonattendees | | | |
| | Boys | | Girls | | Boys | | Girls | |
	Average	Median	Average	Median	Average	Median	Average	Median
Primary Grade								
1	7.50	7	7.43	7	12.07	12	12.58	13
2	8.61	8	8.49	8	13.37	14	13.19	13
3	9.58	9	9.36	9	13.68	14	13.76	14
4	10.61	10	10.39	10	14.38	14	14.03	14
5	11.60	11	11.45	11	14.52	15	14.67	15
6	12.56	12	12.40	12	14.77	15	14.51	15
Secondary Grade								
1	13.46	13	13.31	13	15.11	15	14.77	15
2	14.43	14	14.22	14	15.31	15	15.25	16
3	15.22	15	15.17	15	15.55	16	15.48	16

Rural Children

| | Attendees | | | | Nonattendees | | | |
| | Boys | | Girls | | Boys | | Girls | |
	Average	Median	Average	Median	Average	Median	Average	Median
Primary Grade								
1	8 13	8	7.95	8	12.76	13	12.62	13
2	9.21	9	9.01	9	13.59	14	13.58	14
3	10.26	10	9.99	10	14.19	15	14.00	14
4	11.16	11	10.89	11	14.34	15	14.23	15
5	12.02	12	11.90	12	14.62	15	14.46	15
6	12.87	13	12.76	12	14.54	15	14.45	15
Secondary Grade								
1	13.77	14	13.49	13	14.91	15	14.68	15
2	14.63	15	14.36	14	15.17	15	14.94	15
3	15.20	15	15.16	15	15.56	16	15.46	16

Source: Own calculations from Conteo-1995.

those who had ceased to attend. On reviewing the information in the first left-hand side column, notice that children begin to fall behind when starting primary school. Both non-poor and poor boys and girls are 6.6 years old on average when they complete preschool and 7.8 years if they complete first grade of primary education, suggesting that on average, it has taken them over one year to be in first grade. For the second year, the children's average ages are similar, although median ages indicate that girls are in a more favorable position; whereas half of the boys in second grade are nine years old, the same proportion among girls are eight years of age. From the third to the sixth grade of primary school, children advance one year of age for each school term without any gender differences in median ages, with average ages remaining at a slightly lower level in the case of girls. Starting the first year of high school, the similarity between the average ages of boys and girls is preserved, and girls are again in a good position. However, it should be noted that from the moment children turn twelve, the proportion of girls that go on attending classes dramatically decreases.

Lagging

After this discussion of the average age of individuals by school year I now turn our attention to lagging (years of delay relative to appropriate age for grade), which is derived from the average number of school years completed by the observed population

TABLE 11.6

Average Age of Children in Marginalized Rural Areas per School Term, by Gender, Poverty, and Attendance

| | Non-Poor Attendees | | | | Non-Poor Nonattendees | | | |
| | Boys | | Girls | | Boys | | Girls | |
	Average	Median	Average	Median	Average	Median	Average	Median
Primary Grade								
1	7.84	7	7.85	7	9.36	8.5	7.78	7
2	8.86	9	8.81	8	12.79	14	11.75	12
3	9.99	10	9.81	10	14.05	14	13.50	15
4	11.04	11	10.83	11	14.12	15	14.20	15
5	12.10	12	11.87	12	14.27	15	14.44	15
6	12.99	13	12.78	13	14.44	15	14.16	14
Secondary Grade								
1	13.78	14	13.60	13	14.86	15	14.66	15
2	14.53	15	14.43	14	15.07	15	14.70	15
3	15.07	15	15.13	15	15.17	16	15.04	15

| | Poor Attendees | | | | Poor Nonattendees | | | |
| | Boys | | Girls | | Boys | | Girls | |
	Average	Median	Average	Median	Average	Median	Average	Median
Primary Grade								
1	7.85	7	7.75	7	8.26	7	8.65	7
2	9.06	9	8.86	9	11.57	12	11.08	11
3	10.12	10	9.94	10	12.75	13	12.74	13
4	11.12	11	10.92	11	13.45	14	13.45	14
5	12.12	12	11.95	12	13.81	14	13.92	14
6	13.06	13	12.89	13	14.12	15	14.13	14
Secondary Grade								
1	13.80	14	13.63	14	14.54	15	14.42	15
2	14.62	15	14.44	14	14.62	15	14.53	15
3	15.16	15	15.10	15	15.08	15	14.97	15

Source: Own calculations from Progresa database.

separated by age group (Tables 11.7 and 11.8). This information should help explain why differences in age were noted previously because it is sensible to perceive that an individual will be older at any given grade if it has taken him or her longer to complete a certain number of school years.

Let us begin by concentrating on the median ages stated in Table 11.7. In urban attendees, practically no differences are observed between boys and girls. Children advance one school term per year of age (no lagging), pursuant to the official norms, and half of the fifteen- and sixteen-year-old boys and girls accomplish nine years of schooling.

TABLE 11.7

Average Schooling Years by Age, Gender, and Place of Residence, Based on Attendance

	Urban Children							
	Attendees				Nonattendees			
	Boys		Girls		Boys		Girls	
Age	Average	Median	Average	Median	Average	Median	Average	Median
6	2.38	0	2.41	0	1.02	0	0.69	0
7	1.52	1	1.35	1	0.33	0	1.09	0
8	1.86	2	1.95	2	0.83	0	0.51	0
9	2.67	3	2.82	3	0.88	0	1.22	0
10	3.52	4	3.67	4	0.95	0	0.74	0
11	4.43	5	4.63	5	2.03	1	2.87	3
12	5.37	6	5.48	6	3.41	3	3.85	4
13	6.20	7	6.47	7	4.41	6	4.58	6
14	7.15	8	7.38	8	5.12	6	5.31	6
15	8.09	9	8.40	9	6.06	6	6.59	6
16	8.87	9	9.09	9	6.57	6	6.58	6

	Rural Children							
	Attendees				Nonattendees			
	Boys		Girls		Boys		Girls	
Age	Average	Median	Average	Median	Average	Median	Average	Median
6	2.01	0	2.23	0	0.31	0	0.53	0
7	1.46	1	1.36	1	0.06	0	0.17	0
8	1.67	2	1.66	2	1.11	0	0.37	0
9	2.39	2	2.42	3	0.90	0	0.38	0
10	2.95	3	3.23	3	0.99	0	1.12	0
11	3.93	4	3.94	4	2.42	2	2.07	2
12	4.47	5	4.64	5	3.24	3	3.88	5
13	5.30	6	5.64	6	4.07	6	4.25	6
14	6.21	7	6.26	7	4.45	6	4.72	6
15	7.04	8	7.18	8	5.13	6	5.46	6
16	7.87	8	8.12	9	5.62	6	5.57	6

Source: Own calculations from Conteo-1995.

With regard to the rural population, at age nine, half of the boys have accomplished only two years of schooling, whereas half of the girls have already covered three years. Additionally, at age sixteen, half of the boys passed eight years of their school record, whereas girls accomplished nine years.

For nonattendees, the situation is akin to the one described for children's average age in each school year. Half of the thirteen-year-olds and older teenagers have attended classes for a total of only six years, a statistic not associated with place of residence.

Table 11.8 includes the data for children in marginalized localities. The official norm stipulates one grade should be passed with each year of age. Therefore, it would be expected that at age eight, the child should have covered two years of schooling and would already be attending the third school term. After reviewing the information

TABLE 11.8

Average Schooling Years by Single Age in Marginalized Rural Areas, by Poverty Conditions and Gender

| | Non-Poor Attendees | | | | Non-Poor Nonattendees | | | |
| | Boys | | Girls | | Boys | | Girls | |
Age	Average	Median	Average	Median	Average	Median	Average	Median
6	0.27	0	0.25	0	0.00	0	0.03	0
7	0.90	1	0.90	1	0.20	0	0.20	0
8	1.74	2	1.71	2	0.35	0	0.57	0
9	2.60	3	2.64	3	0.91	0	1.68	2
10	3.34	3	3.41	4	1.92	2	1.00	0
11	4.04	4	4.20	4	2.18	2	2.09	2
12	4.54	5	4.73	5	2.17	2	2.94	4
13	5.74	5	5.94	7	3.08	3	3.67	4
14	6.84	7	6.97	8	3.75	4	3.86	4
15	7.47	8	7.56	8	5.73	5	5.83	7
16	7.66	8	7.76	8	6.44	9	6.08	8

| | Poor Attendees | | | | Poor Nonattendees | | | |
| | Boys | | Girls | | Boys | | Girls | |
Age	Average	Median	Average	Median	Average	Median	Average	Median
6	0.28	0	0.28	0	0.02	0	0.03	0
7	0.89	1	0.95	1	0.13	0	0.18	0
8	1.62	2	1.64	2	0.46	0	0.46	0
9	2.37	2	2.42	2	0.83	0	0.83	0
10	3.07	3	3.18	3	1.28	0	1.14	0
11	3.76	4	3.87	4	1.66	1	1.59	1
12	4.16	4	4.33	5	1.88	2	2.05	2
13	5.02	5	5.27	5	2.43	2	2.59	3
14	6.09	7	6.30	7	3.12	3	3.16	3
15	6.91	8	7.06	8	4.19	4	4.00	4
16	7.17	8	7.28	8	4.75	4	4.55	4

Source: Own calculations from Progresa database.

in Table 11.8, we notice that among attendees, non-poor ten-year-old boys average 3.3 years of schooling, with half of them accomplishing three years. This situation differs with non-poor girls of the same age; half of them already have four years of schooling. Both fifteen- and sixteen-year-old boys and girls are more likely to lag behind in the average accumulated years of study, and half of them have only eight years of schooling.

On the other hand, extremely poor children start to lag behind at earlier ages than the non-poor. Because poor children are more likely to repeat a grade they are also more likely to be delayed relative to age-appropriateness than their non-poor counterparts. Both nine-year-old boys and girls have completed only two years of schooling, and when they turn twelve, they average 4.16 and 4.33 grades of study, respectively. Significant gender differences only appear in examining median school years completed (grades) by twelve-year-olds. Half of the twelve-year-old boys completed four years of education in comparison to five years for girls. However, from the reported data we know that the proportion of girls who attend school at that age is slightly lower than that of the boys. Regardless, of those enrolled in school, the numbers suggest that girls complete more grades of schooling with age than boys.

The information on nonattendees presents a much more dramatic situation and could well suggest that the level of schooling reached by them may never progress, this being particularly true with older children. Half of non-poor eight-year-old boys and girls have not accrued any schooling years; twelve-year-old boys have accomplished barely two years, whereas the girls of the same age have accomplished four years. With extremely poor children, the situation is similar with eight- and twelve-year-olds, except that in this case half of the poor girls have only two years of schooling. Finally, the average number of years of study among sixteen-year-olds does not go beyond 4.5 years—a stunning and problematic statistic when evaluating opportunities for children in marginalized areas.

We continue to support our discussion of lagging by employing a different method of analysis. Using the regulatory criteria as a basis for comparison, and considering that the available age-related information refers to full years rather than to the exact age, a "broad-based" criterion was established, which considers that a child at a certain full age could have passed any of three school terms close to the ones established by the regulations. Thus an eight-year-old might have passed the first, second, or third grade of primary school. Therefore, our analysis will refer to lagging in terms of number of years that they lag behind following our established criterion.

Broadly speaking, it may be said that as children grow up, lagging tends to be higher, both in the proportion of laggers and in the number of lagging years accumulated. This situation holds true with both boys and girls. However, the proportion of lagging children in extremely poor households is higher than the proportion of non-poor children (Table 11.9).

As evidenced in Table 11.9, approximately 18.4 percent of non-poor-ten-year-old boys and 23.3 percent of eleven-year-olds are considered laggers in school. A greater majority of the lagging boys of this age, without considering poverty (14.4 percent in ten-year-olds and 13.7 percent in eleven-year-olds) lag for one year. With eleven-year-old boys, those that have been lagging for two, three, or more years reveal very similar percentages (13.7 percent and 6.8 percent, respectively). For non-poor girls, we find

TABLE 11.9

Proportion of Children Lagging Behind the Expected Grade for Their Age Among School-Going Children, by Age, Gender, and State of Poverty

	Non-Poor Boys				Non-Poor Girls			
Age	Total	1 Year	2 Years	3 and More Years	Total	1 Year	2 Years	3 and More Years
8	5.67	5.67	0	0	4.86	4.86	0	0
9	9.10	7.61	1.49	0	8.17	6.72	1.45	0
10	18.35	14.40	3.02	0.93	15.63	11.13	4.13	0.38
11	23.30	13.74	6.81	7.75	17.07	10.96	4.71	1.40
12	30.43	18.84	7.07	4.53	20.85	11.81	5.32	3.72
13	35.47	19.59	8.81	7.07	31.21	18.14	7.07	6.01
14	36.46	16.57	11.05	8.84	30.93	14.42	8.39	8.13
15	39.33	17.73	10.00	11.60	33.39	14.41	8.31	10.68
16	49.61	24.80	9.25	15.55	45.52	22.53	10.11	12.87

	Poor Boys				Poor Girls			
Age	Total	1 Year	2 Years	3 and More Years	Total	1 Year	2 Years	3 and More Years
8	7.02	7.02	0	0	6.56	6.56	0	0
9	18.16	15.91	2.24	0	16.31	14.23	2.08	0
10	28.29	19.21	7.83	1.26	24.11	16.39	6.86	0.85
11	33.26	19.36	9.25	4.66	29.56	18.04	7.60	3.92
12	43.15	20.35	12.67	10.12	36.76	18.58	11.01	7.17
13	52.83	24.72	14.46	13.65	47.12	25.01	11.32	10.79
14	53.12	18.79	16.96	17.38	48.57	17.67	15.87	15.03
15	54.15	18.15	15.38	20.63	49.15	16.53	14.46	18.17
16	67.15	26.62	13.72	26.81	58.72	22.54	11.23	24.96

Source: Own calculations from Conteo-1995.

smaller proportions of lagging than that of boys with varying differences at each age but reaching a high variance of 10 percentage points at age twelve.

For children in extremely poor households, the lagging ratio is much higher than with their non-poor peers. Between nine and twelve years old, the proportion of poor lagging boys is 10 percent higher than with non-poor laggers. With twelve-year-olds, whereas poor boys with two and three years of lagging are in proportions higher than 10 percent (12.7 percent and 10.1 percent, respectively), non-poor boys reveal percentages no higher than 7 percent and 4.5 percent. Poor girls reveal similar lags as poor boys, the lengths of which are alike in both genders, except that the percentages for girls in each age are inferior by 5 or 7 percentage points.

As a way of supplementing the information reviewed so far, Figure 11.1 displays a set of charts that show the proportion of children of different ages in each of the school years, with each slot representing one school year.

Remember that these school years refer to the last term accomplished by the child. A first look at the data reveals the differences between poor and non-poor children, as well as between boys and girls in all the school years. It is clear that the most significant lag

FIGURE 11.1

Proportion of Children Attending School by School Grade, Age, Gender, and
Poverty Conditions in Highly Marginalized Localities

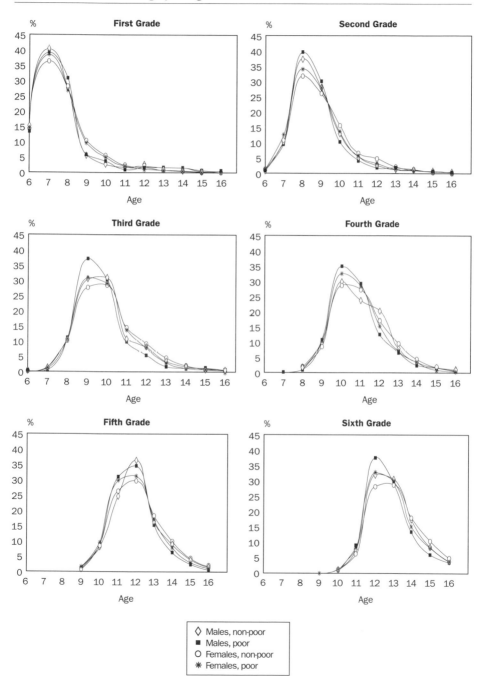

◇ Males, non-poor
■ Males, poor
O Females, non-poor
✱ Females, poor

at the beginning of school takes place with poor children. As children move to higher grades in school, it becomes evident that girls are better off than boys in the same state of poverty, that is those who stay attain higher grades, even though it should not be overlooked that in the senior school years, only a third of the girls continue attending.

We have already reviewed the schooling situation of children, particularly those who live in highly marginalized rural areas. We have noticed that a large percentage of children, especially in extremely poor households, start school at a late age. We also observed that a large proportion of children drop out from age eleven onward. Because it was not possible to establish a direct relationship between these two phenomena, we looked for another proxy of analyzing the average age of children in each school grade attained and the average number of school grades attained at each age. The analysis revealed significant results for lagging attendees in marginalized areas. This lagging becomes even bigger with children who have never attended school, particularly after they turn eleven. In many cases the difference between the child's age and the last accomplished school year is so great that it might be supposed that the child will never resume his or her studies. In other words, with marginalized rural localities, there is a causal relationship among age on school entry, lagging, and dropout trends.

When we first described the information sources used for this analysis, we pointed out that Progresa operates in marginalized localities where school services are available in the locality or in a nearby one, although there may be differences in distance and transportation costs. Because we can consider educational supply a constant between the populations in question, our analysis suggests that other household characteristics (that is, poverty) influence a child's progression and initial access to the school system. The problem may be posed as follows: In a context where educational services are available and the quality of education is supposedly similar for all schools, what other factors may help in explaining the children's educational situation? The following section examines the role of household characteristics in school attendance of marginalized rural children.

ATTENDANCE-RELATED FACTORS

Since the end of the 1970s and beginning of the 1980s, Mexican research has focused on life strategies, insertion of household members in labor markets, women's participation in the labor market, migrations, and so on, and how they influence children's educational opportunities. This research trend has emphasized household characteristics, in particular, the composition of the household members, the role of the household head, and the consumer-worker relationship and has proved useful in the various fields where it has been applied. Moreover, recent nationwide studies of educational exclusion have attempted to include these factors in analysis (Bracho 1997).

Along similar lines, the following analysis includes interesting aspects of this perspective, sourced from studies on heads of households and educational trajectories of university students (Hernández and Muñiz 1996; Muñiz 1997; and Muñiz and Hernández 1999). The variables related with individual characteristics of children in highly marginalized areas are also included here. This information should provide illuminating insight in understanding the observed disparities between the educational trajectories of marginalized rural primary and secondary school children and their counterparts.

Characteristics of the Marginalized Rural Population

Out of the 155,691 children included in the sample, a majority (134,019, 86.1 percent) live in extremely poor households. Gender distribution is practically equal (51.3 percent of boys and 48.7 percent of girls) and gender percentages in each poverty category are similar (see Table 11.10).

With regard to age (see Table 11.11) whereas the proportion of children ranging from six to ten years old in non-poor households is around 7 percent, the figure for poor households is 10 percent. The opposite is true in the groups ranging from eleven to sixteen. The gender distribution is similar, whatever the age.

We will now describe specific household characteristics, and afterward we will supply additional information on the children, differentiating it by poverty condition. The data indicate that a higher proportion of poor children live in nuclear households that include more than one family member. Additionally, the average number of workers in these households is higher than in non-poor ones, and there are practically no gender-based differences. Little more than nine out of ten poor families have a male household head who is three years younger than the non-poor heads.

As the main producer of family income, it is necessary to further investigate the characteristics of household heads. State of poverty tends to be associated with schooling and occupation, with the poor at a disadvantage, as noted in Table 11.12. Whereas 17 percent of non-poor heads received no schooling, and 45 percent and 36 percent of them received primary and secondary education, respectively, 29 percent of poor household heads have received no schooling, 50 percent completed only their primary education, and only 21 percent accomplished one or more high school years. With regard to occupational differences between household heads, 29 percent of the non-poor are unskilled laborers and a similar proportion are manual and self-employed workers (21 percent). In extremely poor households, unskilled workers account for 45 percent of the heads, craftsmen represent 12 percent, and self-employed workers account for 18 percent. Finally, the extremely poor households with children between zero and five years old exceed by 30 percent the number of non-extremely poor households with children the same age.

With regard to the characteristics of children between the ages of six and sixteen, we observe that while in non-extremely poor households indigenous language speakers

TABLE 11.10

Household Poverty Condition by Gender in Marginalized Rural Localities

	Gender		
	Boys	Girls	Total
Non-poor	11,126	10,546	21,672
	(14.1)	(13.8)	(13.9)
Poor	67,935	66,081	134,019
	(85.9)	(86.2)	(86.1)
Total	79,061	76,627	155,691
	100	100	100

Source: Own calculations from Progresa database.

TABLE 11.11

Age, Gender, and Household Poverty Condition Distribution
in Marginalized Rural Areas

Age	Non-Extremely Poor			Poor		
	Boys	Girls	Total	Boys	Girls	Total
6	6.54	6.17	6.36	9.98	10.26	10.12
7	7.06	6.46	6.76	9.82	10.17	9.99
8	7.70	7.72	7.71	10.06	10.01	10.04
9	7.05	7.62	7.33	9.17	9.35	9.26
10	8.24	8.25	8.25	10.19	9.83	10.01
11	7.54	8.03	7.78	8.99	8.88	8.93
12	11.20	10.58	10.90	9.41	9.42	9.42
13	9.95	10.68	10.30	8.55	8.64	8.60
14	10.87	11.01	10.94	8.50	8.33	8.42
15	10.97	10.90	10.94	8.24	7.91	8.08
16	12.89	12.57	12.74	7.09	7.19	7.14
Total	100	100	100	100	100	100

Source: Own calculations from Progresa database.

account for 14 percent of the children, in extremely poor homes this proportion is slightly over 25 percent, with no gender-based differences. In a context where the large majority of children are unmarried, it is worth highlighting the small proportion of girls who are by now married or living with a partner (2 percent of non-poor girls and 1.7 percent of poor girls).

Children's participation in work markets reveals gender differences, regardless of poverty conditions; the boys' share more than doubles the girls'.[6] School attendance evinces a similar situation as the one described for the study: poor girls are the ones with the lowest attendance and account for the largest proportion of children who have never attended classes. By combining work and attendance, we notice that around 5 percent of both poor and non-poor children perform both activities, but in this case the percentage of girls is lower than the percentage of boys. The largest gender-based differences appear in nonworking and nonattending children: here the highest percentages lie with girls (17.30 percent for non-poor girls and 21.40 percent for poor girls), whereas boys account for 7.5 percent and 12.2 percent, respectively.

In essence, the data direct our attention to drastic differences in household characteristics of poor and non-poor children in marginalized rural areas. Are these differences significant enough for us to conclude that they will influence a child's attendance in school? In order to answer this question, more elaborate statistical analysis is warranted. Regression analysis enables us to make predictions on the likelihood of any one of the aforementioned to influence school attendance. I believe that this is the most important problem reviewed so far, because as long as children continue attending school, schooling levels will increase and lagging will decrease—an important issue in equalizing the educational opportunities for children of varying backgrounds.

TABLE 11.12

Characteristics of Households and Children in Marginalized Rural Areas by Gender and Poverty Condition

	Non-Extremely Poor		Poor	
	Boys	Girls	Boys	Girls
Household membership				
Nuclear	70.2	69.7	74.6	73.7
Composite	28.8	29.3	24.9	25.7
Other	1.0	1.0	0.5	0.6
Average household size	6.19	6.23	7.24	7.27
Household head gender				
Male	90.6	90.4	92.3	92.1
Female	9.4	9.6	7.7	7.9
Average number of workers	3.44	3.44	3.79	3.80
Average head age	46.52	46.62	43.46	43.31
Head schooling				
No schooling	17.8	17.4	29.2	28.7
Primary	45.5	45.8	49.7	49.7
Secondary and beyond	36.6	36.8	21.1	21.5
Head's occupation				
Unemployed	10.5	10.5	9.8	9.7
Unskilled laborer	29.2	28.7	45.1	44.6
Manual worker	20.6	20.6	12.2	12.9
Self-employed	22.0	22.4	18.1	17.8
Other	17.7	17.9	14.8	15.0
Children ranging 0 to 5 years old				
None	67.7	66.9	36.4	35.2
In existence	32.3	33.1	63.6	64.8
Speaker of indigenous language				
Yes	14.1	14.4	27.9	28.0
No	85.9	85.6	72.1	72.0
Marital status				
Married	0.2	2.0	0.2	1.7
Single	99.7	97.9	99.7	98.2
Other	0.1	0.1	0.1	0.2
Works?				
Yes	16.9	7.7	16.2	7.4
No	83.1	92.3	83.8	92.6
School attendee				
Yes	80.6	77.2	77.0	73.7
No	16.8	19.9	15.9	18.6
Never	2.6	2.9	7.1	7.6
School attendee and working				
Works-attends	5.0	2.1	5.3	2.5
Works only	11.9	5.5	10.9	4.9
Attends only	75.6	75.0	71.6	71.2
Does not work–does not attend	7.5	17.3	12.2	21.4
Child's position in terms of the other children				
Eldest	52.0	51.1	38.8	38.4
Other	28.6	30.3	50.5	51.6
Youngest	19.4	18.5	10.7	10.0

Source: Own calculations from Progresa database.

Attendance-Related Factors in Children

A logistic regression model was used to review the impact of these factors, enabling an analysis of all the elements jointly on the dependent variable which was school attendance.[7] Table 11.13 presents the estimated adjusted odds ratios, which are the result of the models. These odds ratios may be interpreted as an "increased risk" measure of the likelihood of the event—that is, that children should attend school—when the child has a specific characteristic that differentiates him or her from the other children (who are defined as a reference). If the risk of the event taking place does not increase or becomes reduced, the odds ratio will be close to one.

For this model, we used thirteen variables, four of which are related to the characteristics of the households where the children live: poverty condition, household head gender, schooling level and occupation, and existence of children below five years old. Two child-related variables were included: the child's relation with the household members, such as family relation with the head and position of the child with regard to the siblings or other minors integrating the home. Some of the more relevant characteristics of the child are also incorporated: gender, age, marital status, use of indigenous language, work market participation, income, and accomplished school years.

Table 11.13 shows the results of three different models, including the set of variables used and the estimated and adjusted odds ratio for the significant variables ($p < 0.05$). We start by observing the information of children from six to sixteen that appears in the first column.

School attendance relates to three factors associated with the traits of the children's households. First, children in non-poor households, where household heads have higher schooling levels and work at a paid job, have a stronger likelihood of being able to go to school. Second, in contrast, children who live in extremely poor households, the head of which has a lower schooling level and a more disadvantageous position in the work market, are less likely to attend school. Third, out of the two variables that relate the children with the other home members, if the child is under five years old, it is less likely that he or she will be sent to school; being of an intermediate age within the group of children in the household slightly increases the child's schooling opportunities. The relationship of the child to the household head is independent from his or her attendance.

On the other side of the spectrum, younger children, single boys who speak an indigenous language, and those who do not have a share in the work market are more likely to attend school than their counterparts. In other words, as children grow up, their likelihood of attending school diminishes, boys have more opportunities than girls do, and unmarried children substantially multiply their likelihood, as well as non-working children.

Given the significance of age as an attendance driver, and considering the lag with which children are incorporated into the schooling system, as well as the age when attendance starts to decline, we believe that we should explore the factors for two different groups of children: from six to ten and from eleven to sixteen. The results are illustrated in Table 11.13. It should be noted how the number of significant variables is reduced in the model for children from six to ten. If the child's household is in extreme poverty condition, his or her likelihood of attendance will be reduced to around

TABLE 11.13

Attendance-Related Factors in Children Between 6 and 16
in Marginalized Rural Areas

	Odds Ratio at Different Ages		
Attendance-Related Factors	6–16 Years	6–10 Years	11–16 Years
Poverty condition			
Poor	0.6123	0.6058	0.6444
Non-extremely poor	1.00	1.00	1.00
Schooling of the household head			
No schooling	0.3752	0.4362	0.4095
Up to primary education	0.5502	0.6538	0.5768
Secondary education or more	1.00	1.00	1.00
Child's years of schooling	0.7114	0.6501	0.9461
Child's positions related to the other children			
Eldest			
Middle	1.2442		
Youngest	1.00	1.00	1.00
Total child's income	0.9952		0.9963
Child's marital status			
Single	31.47		15.5758
Other	34.56		8.5347
Married	1.00	1.00	1.00
Speaker of indigenous language			
Yes	1.1727		1.2546
No	1.00	1.00	1.00
Gender			
Boy	1.6301		2.0948
Girl	1.00	1.00	1.00
Child's age	0.8531	0.8731	0.6086
Child's share in the work market			
Yes	0.1653	1.0735	0.1694
No	1.00	1.00	1.00
Head's occupation			
Unemployed	0.8561	0.8598	0.8294
Unskilled laborer	0.8397	0.8066	0.8320
Manual worker		0.8487	
Self-employed		0.8761	
Other	1.00	1.00	1.00
Children below five years old			
No	1.3017	1.1547	1.2402
Yes	1.00	1.00	1.00
Family relation with the head			
Son or daughter			
Other	1.00	1.00	1.00

Source: Own calculations from Progresa database.

40 percent. Something similar happens if the head of the household has received little schooling and engages in a low-level occupation. Age and accrued schooling years also play a relevant role in the attendance-related factors. The higher the number of schooling years, the lower the likelihood that the child will attend school when controlling the remaining factors. In this group, the child's age presents a slightly lower dropout probability, especially if it is compared with the eleven to sixteen age group.

On the other hand, by reviewing the eleven to sixteen age group, the same predictors which are significant for the six to sixteen age group are statistically significant, except for the child's place in relation with the other minors in the household. The first model reflects family and personal attendance-related factors in the eleven to sixteen age group more clearly. A remarkable point is the reduced impact on the model of the state of poverty of the children's households and the number of accrued schooling years, as well as the increase in the risk caused by the child's age.

CLOSING COMMENTS

This chapter has attempted to review attendance in children between six and sixteen years old, focusing on those who live in highly marginalized localities. This review addressed late entry problems, as well as lagging in terms of the regulatory record and the dropout trend. The analysis makes it clear that the proportion of children who have never attended school is differential in terms of places of residence, and the disadvantage lies with children who live in rural areas, and especially in marginalized localities within these areas. We also identified an age problem on school entry, which points to an ex-ante delay in poor children in general and in poor girls in particular. The data on attendance also reveal irregularities in the schooling trajectories for these groups of children. All this leads us to believe that the actual school record is very different from the regulatory one, and it seems to be related with variations in the lives of poor children that mark their opportunities for education. This situation thus requires cautionary reaction to the uncritical acceptance of the regulatory trajectory assumptions usually applied in research. Most studies in Mexico are apparently influenced by the idea that the problem of access has been taken care of. They have considered that the high dropout ratios, still in existence, result from school deficiencies and factors related to the school environment, which may not directly be the case. Obviously, schools have been unable to respond to the different needs of children in marginalized areas. Research has shown time and again that school lagging plays a critical role in the dropout trend. These considerations have led researchers to ignore the role played by social and demographic contexts in children's school records.

This analysis has tried to revive social and demographic considerations by assuming a relation among the various aspects of the problem. Problems such as lagging are not necessarily associated with the child's abilities or with flaws in the school environment, but rather with preexisting living conditions in different sectors of the population. In marginalized rural localities, these living conditions impact the child at an early age; thus the child enters the schooling system already behind. These living conditions also hamper regular attendance and lead to early dropout trends. The child's life course defines the age ranges at which he or she ought to study rather than the one imposed by the school system. That is why school-aged children within these ranges will attend classes with only late entry or the need to work obstructing their passage. However, when children exceed these age ranges, attendance is hindered by factors such as the number of accomplished school terms, the number of household members, the child's marital status and participation in the work market, and the child's income. All this is set within a clear role distribution and gender differentiation that bring about major disadvantages for girls, especially if they are poor.

NOTES

1. By mid-1997, a new program was implemented to fight extreme poverty in Mexico. This program tries to help extremely poor households in accessing genuine opportunities for meeting the basic needs of education, health, and feeding. Progresa's main objectives are (1) supporting extremely poor households and broadening their opportunities and ability of achieving a higher welfare level; (2) enhancing the conditions of education, health, and nourishment in poor families, focusing on children and their mothers, by providing school and health care services, as well as food support; and (3) integrating these measures so that school development may not be damaged by children's or teenager's poor health or malnutrition, or by labor tasks that might impair their school record. Toward the end of 1998, the program was already supporting nearly 1.95 million households.

2. The Marginalization Index is generated with marginalized indicators, and a principal components analysis is performed on these indicators to obtain a summary variable concentrating the largest variation of information among localities. Index values are constructed by means of a comparative analysis among localities. The indicators used for the Marginalization Index are the following: percentage of illiterate population of fifteen or more years of age, percentage of dwellings without water supply, percentage of dwellings without drainage, percentage of dwellings without power supply, average number of occupants per room, percentage of dwellings with a soil floor, and percentage of the population in the primary sector.

3. The extreme poverty line is obtained by assessing the monthly per capita income of the households and comparing it with the cost of the basic food basket required for minimum needs and thus preventing malnutrition, disease, and anthropometric deficiencies.

4. The definition of place of residence follows a criterion based on population size. Thus, rural localities are defined as those with less than 2,500 inhabitants, whereas urban localities are those with 2,501 or more inhabitants.

5. Notice that when we are talking about non-poor children, we are always making reference to the non-extremely poor.

6. Data on the work market share of children were gathered for children over eight. This means that the analysis considered that six- and seven-year-olds do not work.

7. The selection of models of this kind is due to the fact that the variable here is dichotomous and regression enables deriving an estimator of the likelihood of the event taking place. The event at stake here is that of a child going to school. The estimator obtained through logistic regression allows calculating *odds* ratios, which are indicators of the relative risk of an event taking place (Hosmer and Lemeshow 1989).

REFERENCES

Bracho González, Teresa. 1997. La exclusión de la educación básica: Desiciones familiares sobre escolarización. Documentos de trabajo, número 58, División de Administración Pública, Centro de Investigacion y Docencia Economicas, México.

Guevara Niebla, Gilberto, ed. 1992. *La Catástrofe Silenciosa.* México City: Fondo de Cultura Económica.

Hernández Franco, Daniel, and Patricia E. Muñiz Martelon. 1996. ¿Qué es un jefe de Hogar? *Sociológica* 11(32): 23–49.

Hosmer, David, and Stanley Lemeshow. 1989. *Applied Logistic Regression.* New York: Wiley.

Muñiz Martelon, Patricia Emma. 1997. *Trayectorias Educativas y Deserción Universitaria en los Ochenta.* Colección temas de hoy en la educación superior, número 19. México City: Asociacion Nacional de Universidades e Instituciones de Educacion Superior.

Muñiz Martelon, Patricia Emma, and Daniel Hernández Franco. 1999. Los atributos de la jefatura del hogar. *Estudios Demográficos y Urbanos,* 14(2): 383–409.

Muñoz García, Humberto, and María Herlinda Suárez Zozaya. 1996. *Perfil Educativo de la Población Mexicana.* Aguascalientes, México: Instituto Nacional de Estadística, Geografía e Informática, CRIM-UNAM e ISSUNAM.

Muñoz Izquierdo, Carlos, et al. 1994. El síndrome del atraso escolar y el abandono del sistema educativo. In *La Contribución de la Educación al Cambio Social,* ed. Carlos Muñoz Izquierdo, 27–105. México City: Guernica.

Muñoz Izquierdo, Carlos, and Sonia Lavín de Arrivé. 1988. Estrategias para mejorar el acceso y la permanencia en educación primaria. In *Calidad, Equidad y Eficiencia de la Educación Primaria: Estado Actual de las Investigaciones Realizadas en América Latina,* ed. Carlos Muñoz Izquierdo, 121–187. México City: Centro de Estudios Educativos.

Commentary

Suzanne Grant Lewis, Harvard Graduate School of Education

This chapter serves as a valuable introduction to subsequent chapters exploring the relationship between education and poverty in Mexico. In this chapter, Patricia Muñiz addresses two questions. The first is "What is the schooling situation of children, age six to sixteen, in extreme poverty in Mexico and how does it compare to others (a) in the same locations and (b) in urban and rural populations throughout the country?" The second research question is "In a context where educational services are available and the quality is similar for all schools, what factors help explain children's schooling situation?" The first question is analyzed more completely than the latter. Let me focus first on the descriptive analysis that forms the main body of the chapter.

In choosing her sample from the Progresa database, Muñiz controlled for the supply of schools. This allows her analysis to identify the factors specific to disadvantaged rural areas where the availability of schooling through secondary level is not a constraint. This is an important variable to control, but this strategy then begs the question of "What quality of schooling?"

By structuring the analysis at two levels—comparing urban/rural differences and, within the underprivileged rural areas, the most highly impoverished with the less impoverished—the analysis is deepened. The chapter provides useful descriptions of the children least likely to ever attend school, the school-leaving trends, and the contribution of age to school attendance patterns. The repetition analysis is based on proxy indicators, mainly based on age, and is not very persuasive. Age of entry data are unfortunately not available from the data sets used and without them and an indication of the extent of temporary "stopping out," the discussion of "lagging" remains inconclusive. It remains a puzzle in the chapter why urban children start school younger than rural children but that by the third year of secondary education there is no age difference and children are progressing at the same pace: one year of age per grade. A more complex analysis is required to take into account the ages of the school leavers and repeaters.

One of the most important contributions of the chapter is in showing the heterogeneity within the rural population. Starting first with the urban-rural dicotomy, Muñiz moves on to look within the rural setting to the disadvantaged areas of Mexico. She then breaks down that category to focus on children in the most impoverished households and identifies how much more dire these children's schooling situation is compared to others in the same locations.

Another important finding is the compounding effect of different forms of discrimination, specifically the double burden of poverty and gender faced by the most impoverished, rural girls. Rural children are less likely to ever attend school, and rural girls are more likely to leave school before rural boys. Girls in the most impoverished homes are even more likely to leave school before either their national rural counterparts or their poor male counterparts in the same households. At times, however, poverty is a stronger factor than sex, as in the case of "ever attending" school and "average age of schooling per age." This interaction of poverty and gender deserves greater discussion in the chapter.

Moving on to the second research question, I see that the chapter's major limitation is on focusing solely on family factors, providing only a partial picture of factors explaining children's educational situation. A more comprehensive analysis requires attention to school factors. This should include distance to school, transport availability, and transport costs—all identified as missing from the supply of schools condition—as well as data capturing educational quality and curriculum relevance as they would likely affect student and parental motivation for educational persistence. There are many reasons why children do not attend school. The work on the second research question explains who is more likely to attend or not attend but stops short of exploring why.

Generally, the analysis would benefit from more probing of explanations for the patterns identified in the data. Perhaps other educational research in Mexico would be suggestive. Faced with some powerful statistics, the reader is left desirous of the author's views—even if just suppositions—on the phenomena behind the numbers as well as on the most pressing questions coming out of the analysis.

Related to this need for greater discussion of possible explanations for the findings is a need for greater explication of the sociopolitical context. For example, does the explanation of why school leavers' average ages at lower grades are so high lie in the policy initiatives of two to five years earlier? When were compensatory programs introduced? Here again, reference to any other research or data sets to "fill in" the picture, such as time series data, would be valuable.

More generally, the chapter would benefit from a clearer definition of terms such as "dropout"—which is a misnomer in any event—and "nonattendees." How are they calculated?

The data could be made more digestible by calculating summary indicators such as completion rates or cycle times (through a cohort analysis) and by providing more summary statements along the lines of "Nationally, rural girls are twice as likely to be out of school than urban girls of sixteen years."

The author suggests that there is a causal link between age of entry, repeating ("lagging"), and school leaving trends but has not demonstrated this. There is a need to treat two issues analytically separately, looking separately at (1) the children who never attended, and how as age increases, likelihood of enrolling decreases, and (2) the relationship between children's age of entry, repetition, and school leaving. Much is made of the discussion of late entry and early school leaving, without discussing why these might be problematic.

Elementary students listen attentively to their teacher in an indigenous school in Mexico.
[Carlos Blanco/CONAFE]

12

Education and Indian Peoples in Mexico: An Example of Policy Failure

Sylvia Schmelkes
Departamento de Investigaciones Educativas,
Centro de Investigación y de Estudios Avanzados
del Instituto Politécnico Nacional, Mexico City

This chapter[1] describes the current state of Indian[2] educational policy in Mexico, identifying numerous challenges and problems in the education system that contribute to the position of extreme disadvantage faced by the Indian population in Mexico. To understand the present failure of schools to effectively serve the Indian population, the chapter provides general background on the Indian population and briefly traces the history of educational policies specifically geared toward the Indians.

THE INDIAN POPULATION

Indian culture and Indian blood explain a very important part of Mexican identity. Unlike what occurred in other countries in Latin America, the Indian and the Spanish population mingled during the three centuries in which Mexico was a Spanish colony. The enormous majority of the Mexican population is *mestizo*, a mixture of Indian and Spanish ancestors.

Mexico, however, is a multicultural country. Many Indian communities refused to become integrated into the Spanish society and what it implied, and avoided contact or fled to the highlands in order to continue living according to their culture. Only missionaries reached many of these groups, and mingling was rare. According to 1995 census data, 7.4 percent of the Mexican population is culturally Indian—that is, speaks an Indian language. This represents almost 6,700,000 people. There are fifty-six distinct linguistic Indian groups in Mexico living across the country. Nine out of thirty-two states (Mexico is a Federation), however, concentrate 84.2 percent of the Indian population (Oaxaca, Veracruz, Chiapas, Puebla, Yucatán, Hidalgo, the State of Mexico, Guerrero, and San Luis Potosí). These states are home to the numerically most important Indian groups: Náhuatl, Maya, Mixteco, Zapoteco, Hñahñú, Tseltal, Tsotsil, Totonaco, Mazateco, Chol, and Mazahua. Thirty-eight percent of the Indian population (2,600,000) are children under fifteen years of age.

It is grievous to note that the Indian population of Mexico is among the poorest in the country. There are many reasons for this. A very important one is historical: These Indian groups fled to the highlands that no Spaniard was interested in—poor, unsowable, rain-fed land that barely yields what the small communities need to survive. Another reason is that Indians have been marginalized for centuries, and this century is no exception. Mexican history is full of Indian revolts that have been easily put down. Indian organizations are recent and still weak, and for too many years they have had neither voice nor means to put pressure on local and national governments to receive adequate and sufficient basic services. In Mexico, discrimination and racism exist, especially in those areas where Indians and *ladinos* (culturally white people) have coexisted without mingling—in Chiapas, for example. The condition of poverty of the great majority of the Indian population, together with other factors which we will also analyze, seriously affect the efficiency and the quality of the education they receive.

EDUCATION FOR THE INDIAN POPULATION: A BRIEF HISTORY OF RECENT DEVELOPMENTS

Primary schools were the first to reach Indian communities which, needless to say, were also among the last to be reached by primary education. Primary schools started to spread over the countryside very slowly, from 1920 to 1960, and much faster after that. However, primary schools for the Indian population were (and many of them still are) poor imitations of the traditional urban schools.[3] Instruction was in Spanish. Generally, schools were multigrade (one teacher for more than one grade, very often in one-room schoolhouses). Many schools were incomplete, offering only the first three grades of primary schooling. Complete schools (six grades) were established next to Indian hostels, where children ate and slept five days of the week and went home over the weekend. Repetition and dropout rates were the highest in the country among the Indian population.

It was not until 1979 that bilingual-bicultural education was formally established and operated through the newly created General Directorate for Indian Education within the Ministry of Education. In part, this was a result of pressure put on the system by the Association of Indian Teachers and Professionals. Despite very important experiences with bilingual education in the past—Indian lay teachers have been active for the past fifty-five years—emphasis was placed on teaching Spanish (*castellanización*).

Bilingual-bicultural education, once officially defined, means that instruction is in the Indian language during the first two years of primary school (the years for attaining literacy skills). After third grade, Spanish is gradually introduced, and by the sixth grade (the last grade of primary education), instruction is predominantly in Spanish. What "bicultural" education there is involves teaching the culture of those who speak the mother tongue.

An important consequence of the bilingual policy was the need to hire lay teachers (with nine grades of education) for teaching primary education, especially in the first grades, because there were practically no certified Indian teachers who spoke the different Indian languages. This is still the case in most Indian schools, though many Indian teachers have studied during the summers or through open learning systems and have already obtained their degrees. At present, and only since 1990, in order to be a teacher in an Indian school, twelve years of schooling are required.

Primary schools were generalized across the country in 1980. Efforts were made to complete incomplete schools and to have at least two teachers in the very small communities. Enrollment of Indian population grew rapidly during the late 1970s and early 1980s, though repetition and dropout rates remained (and still remain) high.

Once the primary schools were more or less universal in Indian communities, other educational services started reaching them. Early childhood, preschool, and secondary schools (grades seven to nine), as well as special education, have been established in many communities and have increased during the past few years.

CURRENT POLICY

Bilingual-bicultural basic education is offered to forty-five Indian groups in twenty-three states of the country. Two institutions specifically offer Indian education: Intercultural Bilingual Schools (DGEI; decentralized but regulated by the General Directorate for Indian Education within the Ministry of Education) and the Program for the Educational Attention of Indian Population at the Preschool and Primary Levels (regulated by CONAFE, a deconcentrated but federal institution set up to address Indian children living in very small communities). Table 12.1 indicates the number of students and schools covered by these programs.

Mexico is now in a process of redefining Indian education. The Indian revolt in Chiapas has posed very clear demands regarding education for the Indian population. The present program for basic education (Poder Ejecutivo Federal 1995) has defined two complementary global policies for Indian education:

- The supply of educational services specifically destined to Indian groups and adapted to their needs, demands, linguistic and cultural conditions, type of settlements, social organization, and type of production and work.
- An active struggle against overt and covert forms of racism and discrimination by means of the national primary school curriculum. Indian peoples' historic contribution to the building of the nation, as well as the understanding of their situation and problems and the recognition of their contribution to Mexican life in general, will be accentuated.

TABLE 12.1

Number of Students and Schools Supported by Indigenous Education Programs

	DGEI		CONAFE	
Educational Level	Students	Schools	Students	Schools
Early childhood	29,000*			
Preschool	270,000	7,519	8,462	868
Primary	700,000	7,948[†]	16,779	1,462

*Nonformal early childhood education consists of educating parents for adequate care of their newborns to four-year-olds.

[†]About 60,000 children receive primary education in schools attached to hostels where the children eat and sleep during the weekdays and are free to go home for the weekends.

The present regime has abandoned the notion of "bicultural" education and has substituted it for the concept of "intercultural" education. This concept emphasizes the relationships among different cultures. The accent is now placed on learning to value differences and to live together in a multicultural society.[4]

Among the specific policies that the DGEI has defined in order to achieve these aims, the following are worth noting:

- Social participation of Indian communities in initial and basic intercultural and bilingual education is encouraged.
- Adding flexiblity to the curriculum, methodology, and educational material is designed to allow for the cultural relevance of each school. The main objectives of the national curriculum that have to do with the development of basic skills must be equally pursued in all schools, but the knowledge and values of each Indian group should form an important part of the specific curriculum. Teaching and assessment methods also should be adapted to the characteristics and needs of Indian children.
- School organization and academic norms should be flexible and adaptable to the different needs and conditions of Indian groups.
- New and better ways of training in-service teachers for the development of more respectful modes of working with children, parents, and communities are being developed.
- Greater autonomy is given to the schools in order to allow them to improve conditions for access, retention, and learning. This implies emphasizing collective decision making on the part of school communities.
- Special attention is given to the education of girls and teenage women.[5] This implies working with parents and the larger community.
- Compensatory programs operate in all Indian schools within the selected areas. There is a strong compensatory policy that strengthens investment in schools and teachers in the poorest states and in the poorest municipalities in the rest of the states. Indian schools in these states and municipalities are automatically included in the programs, which differ among the states, but which in general include an incentive for the teacher, training courses for headmasters and teachers, school libraries and educational material for the schools, and school supplies for the students. It is worthwhile noting that it was one of these compensatory programs that began the development of textbooks in eight Indian languages for children from first to fourth grades. There are now such textbooks in thirty-three different Indian languages and nineteen linguistic variations.

There is an ongoing process toward the definition of an intercultural bilingual model of basic education for Indian children. This process is explicitly and necessarily slow and gradual because it involves a strong ingredient of social participation. The construction of the model is seen as a permanent process, and it is conceived as the dynamic articulation of the following components: educational aims and objectives, pre-service and in-service teacher training, teaching-learning processes, and school management.

Basic and teacher education for Indian groups was decentralized in 1992, as was basic and teacher education in general. Even though the General Directorate for Indian Education is still the normative organ for Indian education in the country, it is now the twenty-three states with Indian populations that administer this mode of education with resources transferred from the federal government. This gives more autonomy to the states for the development of special programs in Indian education, as well as the theoretical possibility of specific policies that are more adapted to the characteristics of the Indian groups in each state. It also implies decision making regarding the use of resources in more limited areas where political factors, and, perhaps, more in-grained racism may play a more important role than they did at the national level. It is too early to evaluate the consequences of this important structural transformation of the Mexican educational system for Indian education, but close monitoring is obviously necessary.

PREVALENT PROBLEMS

In spite of these renovated ideas regarding Indian education in the country, many of which are very sound and logical, the situation with Indian education is so critical that it begs the question of whether what is required is a totally new approach to the problem. In this section, some of these problems are analyzed using available information. It is important to note that information about Indian education is very difficult to obtain and that which is available is often not comparable with information regarding the regular system. Nevertheless, the data to which we had access do in fact reinforce the critical situation of education for Indian populations.

Not all Indian children have access to bilingual-intercultural schools. The percentage of enrollment in primary school represented by children enrolled in bilingual-bicultural schools is less than their percentage in the population as a whole. As can be seen in Figure 12.1, enrollment in these schools represents 5 percent of the primary school population.[6] Because of higher dropout rates among the Indian population, the percentage decreases noticeably in the higher grades. But the percentage of the Indian population with respect to the total population is, as we mentioned, 7.4 percent, and due to lower life expectancy rates, even higher for the school-aged population. We do not know what happens to these other Indian children. Some of them simply do not attend school—the percentage of school-aged children who do not attend school is certainly greater among the Indian population than among the population as a whole. Many of these Indian children live in communities that are so small that neither conventional nor unconventional schools are provided. Another important group are migrant agricultural workers who travel with their parents to the highly mechanized agricultural fields in the northern part of the country for the harvest, but who are never in one place for enough time to be enrolled in school. There is no certain information about the dimension of this phenomenon, but it is known that between 400,000 and 700,000 school-aged children live in this situation. A high percentage of them are Indian. Thus it is likely that Indian children are overrepresented in the 1,300,000 school-aged children who do not go to school. Perhaps it would not be too implausible to presume that most of these children are Indian.

FIGURE 12.1

Indigenous and Rural Students as a Percentage of Total Enrollment, 1997–1998

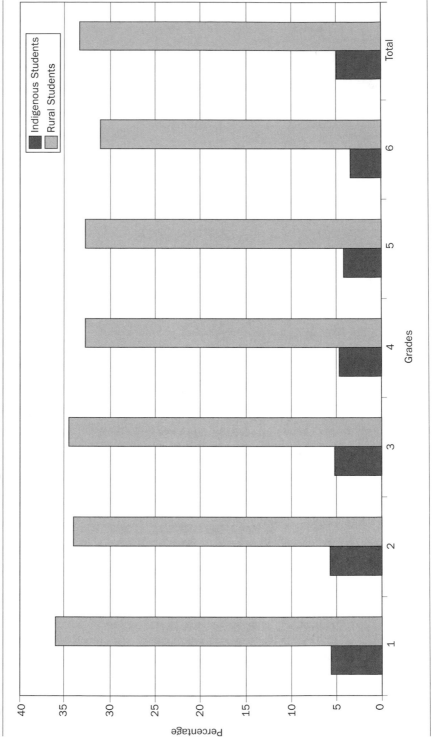

Many other Indian children, surely, attend regular schools. This is especially true in the cities where large groups of Indians live but where no bilingual-intercultural schools operate.

It is also a well-known fact, though no quantification is available, that many Indian teachers work in communities that speak a different language from their own. Bilingual education, in these circumstances, is impossible.

Dropout rates, but especially repetition rates, are much higher in Indian schools than in regular schools. Dropout rates within the same school year are not much different, and even lower, in Indian schools than in regular schools (4.75 percent at the national level; 4.10 percent in Indian schools). This is due to a well-defined phenomenon that occurs in rural and remote areas: Teachers do not report their children as dropouts when they stop attending school. Instead, they wait until the end of the year, when they report them as "failed." This is why there is, in fact, a large difference in failure rates among different types of schools, as can be seen in Figure 12.2 (expressed as "passing"—the inverse expression of failing). This figure shows the different rates for the national population; the rural population (which includes the Indian schools); the Indian schools; and the states of Oaxaca and Chiapas, which are the two states with the highest amount of Indians. Differences are much greater in the early grades, due perhaps to a process of "natural selection" of those who remain in school. In the first grade, for example, the difference between the national average and the Indian schools amounts to 7.8 percentage points. With Chiapas, the difference is more than 12 percentage points.

Enrollment in Indian schools is still pyramidal at the primary level. A universalized school structure should have the form, more or less, of a rectangle. However, as can be seen in Figure 12.3, this is much more the case at the national level than in the Indian schools. There are relatively more Indian children in the first three grades than in the last three. The difference with respect to the rural population (which includes the Indian population) is not as great, but still noticeable.

Terminal efficiency rates are, therefore, much lower in Indian schools than in regular schools. Terminal efficiency is an indicator of how many children complete primary school in the expected time. It is estimated as the percentage of children completing primary school in a given year relative to the total enrollment in first grade six years earlier. Terminal efficiency is significantly lower in indigenous schools, where only 48 percent of the students complete primary school on time. The average percentage of on-time primary completion is 30 percentage points greater. While terminal efficiency in indigenous schools has increased consistently over the last five years, indigenous schools are still far from providing universal completion of a sixth-grade primary education at the same time that secondary education has already been declared compulsory.

Educational supply is poor, coinciding with the poverty of educational demand. In Mexico, in general, the poorer the population receiving the educational service, the poorer the educational supply. We were not able to obtain information regarding comparative per student costs of primary education. However, in spite of the fact that Indian communities are mostly small (and thus the teacher-student ratio is high), the cost per student in Indian schools is clearly lower than that of regular schools. The study carried out in the state of Puebla, already mentioned, illustrates this fact. Table 12.2 compares data of school infrastructure in schools belonging to different contexts

FIGURE 12.2

Passing Rates among Different Types of Schools, 1997–1998

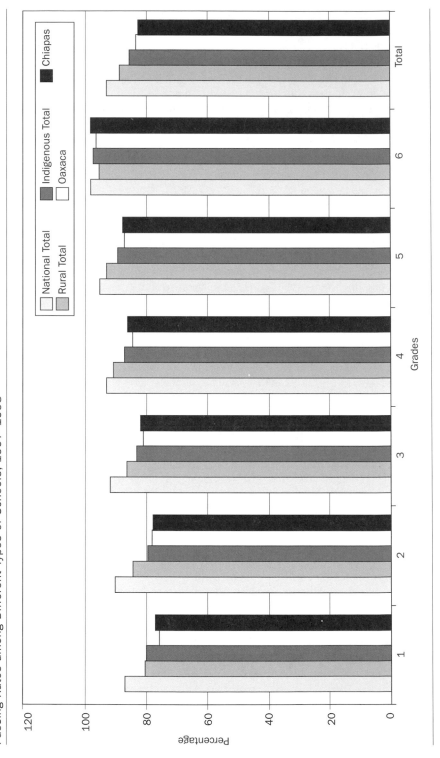

FIGURE 12.3

Percentage of Students by Grade among Different Types of Schools, 1997–1998

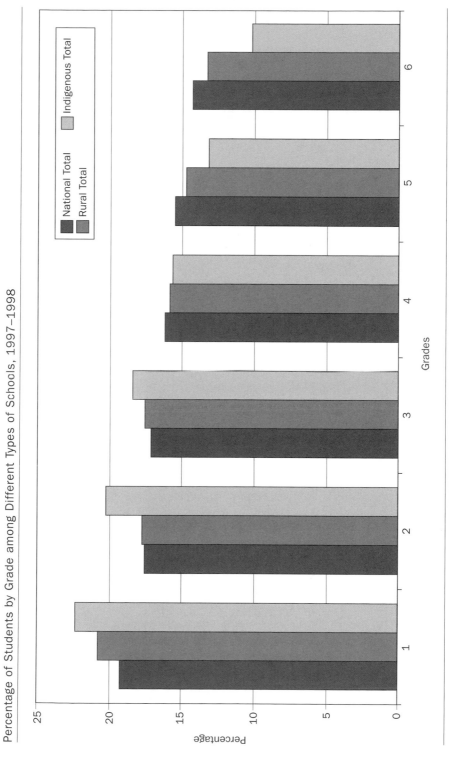

TABLE 12.2

Infrastructure in Schools

Zone	Urban Middle Class (%)	Urban Marginal (%)	Rural Developed (%)	Rural Marginal (%)	Indian (%)
Drinking water	81.3	50.0	60.0	7.1	37.5
Electricity	87.5	87.5	86.7	57.1	37.5
Bathrooms or latrines	87.5	87.5	93.3	78.6	31.3
Sports court	75.0	37.5	40.0	42.9	50.0
Office	37.5	43.8	46.7	14.3	12.5
Patio	87.5	75.0	86.7	71.4	25.0
Auditorium	37.5	12.5	26.7	0.0	12.5
Teacher's house	43.8	37.5	26.7	78.6	6.3

Percentage of classrooms in good infrastructural condition, according to classroom observation

Walls	74.2	46.7	53.6	76.5	33.3
Door	73.3	16.7	53.6	41.2	21.7
Floor	77.4	50.0	60.7	47.1	29.2
Ceiling	80.6	53.3	64.3	41.0	33.3
Light	8639	43.3	57.0	52.9	58.3
Ventilation	80.6	50.0	64.3	47.1	70.8

Percentage of schools with books other than textbooks

Books in classroom	77.0	38.5	37.1	20.8	37.8
Books in office	68.8	31.3	73.3	14.3	37.5
"Rincón de Lectura"*	43.8	18.8	33.3	14.3	25.0

Availability of textbooks

Arrive on time	81.6	35.5	50.0	14.3	75.0
Arrive complete	81.3	56.3	66.7	71.4	68.8

*The Federal Ministry distributed children's literature for all grades, beginning with rural schools. The program is presently in all public primary schools, at least in theory. This was not yet the case when this study was carried out.

(sixteen schools per context). The poverty of Indian schools is evident in all indicators with the exception of textbooks and books, where the situation is comparable, or even better, than schools in other contexts.

Table 12.3 shows the difference between the staff of Indian schools and the staff of schools in other contexts. Head teachers are also classroom teachers in 80 percent of the schools (versus 6 percent in urban middle-class schools). Most teachers are male (66 percent versus 15 percent in urban middle-class schools) and, what is most evident, teacher's schooling is much lower in the Indian regions.

The coincidence of both poverties—of the supply and of the demand—has to do, of course, with the lack of pressure on the part of the population who, due to little or no information as to what type of service they should expect, as well as no reference

TABLE 12.3

Data on School Staff

Zone	Urban Middle Class	Urban Marginal	Rural Developed	Rural Marginal	Indian
Schools with full-time head teachers (%)	94	50	30	5	20
Male teachers (%)	15	30	45	38	66
Teacher's schooling					
9 years or less	1.1	0.0	0.0	0.0	20.9
10–11 years	4.3	3.3	1.4	0.0	9.3
12–13 years	33.9	35.9	45.1	64.0	58.1
14–15 years	6.3	22.9	18.3	12.0	9.3
16 years or more	54.0	38.0	35.2	24.0	2.3

points for the quality of the service elsewhere, are in general satisfied with what they receive. An important proportion of the adult population in these communities have had little experience in school (the majority of the students' fathers in these schools in Puebla did not complete their primary education; the majority of the mothers did not attend school). Given what we know about the importance of cultural capital (that is, schooling) of the parents, and especially of the mothers, for the educational success of their children, it certainly is a question of social injustice that where quality educational services are most needed is precisely where they are lacking.

Children who attend Indian schools learn much less than children who attend regular schools (and even nonconventional schools). Given the facts above, and especially the coincidence of poverties between supply and demand, it is certainly no surprise that educational quality, as measured by learning outcomes of the students, is alarmingly low in Indian schools.

Table 12.4 shows the results of the Puebla study. A test of basic skills was given to the fourth and sixth grades of schools in all five contexts. There is a significant difference with respect to urban middle-class schools (not, however, with respect to schools in the other three contexts). The difference is enormous: the mean in the urban middle-class schools is 20 and 25 points higher than in the Indian schools in the communication skills test, and 11 and 14 points higher in the mathematics skills test. Nevertheless, there is no difference between Indian schools and schools in other rural or marginal contexts, so that one can say that Indian schools are just as bad as these others.

However, in a national assessment exercise recently carried out in Mexico, with a national sample of different types of schools, we found a significant difference in the learning outcomes of Indian schools with respect to all other types of schools: private urban schools, public urban schools, public rural schools, and *cursos comunitarios*.[7] Again two tests, based on national standards in reading comprehension skills and mathematics skills, were given to children who had finished third and fifth grades.[8] The results are shown in Table 12.5. The numbers show the percentage of students who meet the national standards in these two subject areas. The disadvantage of the Indian schools is alarming. Students are far from reaching the national standards in primary schools.

TABLE 12.4

Results of the Puebla Study

Correct Answers (%)	Total Sample	Urban Middle Class	Urban Marginal	Rural Developed	Rural Marginal	Indian
Communication (Reading and Writing)						
Fourth grade						
50% or less	75.0	46.7	84.2	88.7	96.5	86.2
51–70%	18.7	37.5	11.9	10.5	3.5	11.5
More than 70%	6.3	15.8	3.9	0.8	0.0	2.3
Mean	34.0	49.9	27.2	26.8	25.9	28.6
Sixth grade						
50% or less	49.1	13.0	63.2	68.5	74.7	76.3
51–70%	35.3	49.1	32.7	28.2	23.1	18.3
More than 70%	15.6	37.9	4.1	3.3	2.2	5.4
Mean	50.0	65.1	41.4	41.8	41.8	39.7
Mathematics (Solution of Real-Life Problems)						
Fourth grade						
50% or less	90.1	77.7	95.5	96.6	98.2	91.5
51–70%	9.0	20.4	4.5	3.0	1.8	6.2
More than 70%	0.9	1.9	0.0	0.4	0.0	2.3
Mean	27.0	36.7	22.5	21.6	20.0	25.7
Sixth grade						
50% or less	97.2	92.1	99.6	100.0	100.0	100.0
51–70%	2.6	7.4	0.4	0.0	0.0	0.0
More than 70%	0.2	0.6	0.0	0.0	0.0	0.0
Mean	23.0	30.0	18.9	19.7	18.1	15.8

The problems mentioned so far are evidence of an educational policy that has failed. The problems that follow have to do with the obstacles that must be overcome in order to improve the quality of Indian education.

Indian teachers are not adequately trained. The teachers are not adequately trained as teachers, and many of them do not have the necessary mastery of their native language to teach the children to read and write. Teachers are hard to reach for in-service training because they work in far-away and inaccessible villages.

Bilingual education has been rigidly defined and/or understood. Current policy assumes that all Indian children are monolingual. However, the linguistic situation of Indian children is much more complex. There are very different degrees of bilingualism of the population. Bilingual education should operate differently in monolingual (Indian or Spanish) situations and in bilingual situations, and should make space for differences in degrees of bilingualism among communities and among children within the same community.

In many Indian communities, parents are opposed to bilingual education. Parents understand bilingual education as monolingual education in the mother tongue,

TABLE 12.5

Percentage of Students Meeting National Standards
on Reading and Math Tests

Test and Grade	Type of School					
	Urban Private	Urban Public	Rural Public	Cursos Comunitarios	Indian	National
Reading, Third	38	20	15	11	8	20
Reading, Fifth	50	21	12	8	6	19
Math, Third	30	17	15	17	9	17
Math, Fifth	11	5	4	2	5	5

and they are against that, because one of the main reasons for sending their children to school is for them to learn Spanish to be able to get along in the outside world. The parents are right. What the system has not done correctly is to explain to parents that bilingual education is the best way of reaching a mastery of oral and written Spanish.

Many Indian teachers do not value their own culture and do not believe in teaching children their own language. This is in part the result of the education that they experienced when studying in their primary and secondary school courses, which tended to "de-culturate" and transmitted the idea of Mexico as a monocultural Western country. Unfortunately, when the culture of the Indian group is not very strong, these de-culturating trends persist.

A relatively recent phenomenon is the large concentrations of Indian population in big cities. This is clearly the case in Tijuana, where there are many Indians, especially from Oaxaca, who are unable to enter the United States and therefore stay along the border. These Indians are being serviced by bilingual education. But something similar occurs in Mexico City, Guadalajara, and middle-sized cities in the country. Although one or two linguistic groups predominate, there is in fact a mixture of several different Indian peoples in the cities. Most of the children are attending conventional schools that are unprepared for adequately receiving Indian children. Urban Indian education is new and clearly multicultural, something with which Mexico has almost no experience.

CONCLUDING REMARKS

The problems mentioned in this chapter are severe and continue to pose enormous challenges to those preoccupied with the improvement of Indian education. The situation is very complex. Important historical factors are not easily reversed. Poverty is of course a limitation for access, perseverance, and learning outcomes. The system can only gradually undo the trend of giving less to the poorest, and that requires sustained political will.

From a different perspective, Indian groups are very heterogeneous. Perhaps the most important difference from the educational perspective among these groups is their own cultural strength and their consequent interest in maintaining and developing their culture and their language.

The most coherent Indian proposal for an education that takes the Indian population into account is without doubt the one in Chiapas, as crystallized in the San Andrés Agreements (Comisión de Concordia y Pacificación 1996). Among the important points in these agreements are the following:

- The recognition of the right of all Mexicans to receive a multicultural education. National education must foster the knowledge and understanding of Mexican Indian cultures.
- The recognition of the right to cultural difference.
- The promotion of all types of cultural manifestations of Indian groups by institutions where Indian groups are represented.
- The recognition of the right of Indian groups to carrying out their own forms of education in their own cultural spaces and the adequate distribution of resources to make this possible.
- The recognition of the need for Indian education to foster the development of Indian culture and at the same time to make universal knowledge, science, and technology accessible to the Indian population.
- The promotion of equity in opportunities of access and learning at all levels of education.

As we have seen, many of these demands have already been incorporated as part of the discourse sustaining the educational policy for the 1995–2000 period. Some of these—though very few—have begun to acquire operational form. Others are being gradually developed with the participation of Indian groups and Indian teachers.

The San Andrés Agreements, however, have not been respected entirely by the government. Political will is weak, and the challenge is enormous. We must adequately face the need to develop educational spaces and institutions that will strengthen Indian cultures and languages while at the same time ensuring access to universal knowledge. We must meet the challenge of educating for a multicultural society. We must do this with the active participation of the different Indian groups. At the same time, we have to demonstrate effective learning of all Indian children in a situation characterized by poverty, and often extreme poverty, of both supply and demand.

The improvement of the quality of education destined to Indian populations necessarily has to take the Indian communities into account. Education must be relevant for the Indian communities, and relevance has to be jointly defined. The need to be able to get along in the outside world is real and must be satisfied by schools. The importance of strengthening Indian culture and language is clear to many educators as well as to some, but not all, Indian groups.

Mexico is now in a process of redefining Indian education. The Indian revolt in Chiapas has posed very concrete demands regarding education for Indian populations. The need for rethinking Indian education is clear—it is not a question of supplying more of the same, because "the same" is always a poor imitation of what works in urban Western societies. In this process, one thing is certain: The future of Indian education cannot continue without an active and increasing participation of the Indian groups themselves.

NOTES

1. An important part of this chapter is based on a presentation prepared for the OECD-CEA Conference on Combating Failure at School, held in Toronto, Ontario, Canada, in September 1997. I am indebted to Alexis López, then general director of Indian education, who contributed much of the information as well as appreciative remarks regarding Indian schools, as well as to María Elena Guerra, from CONAFE, who contributed all the information on the PAEPI-CONAFE program for very small Indian communities.
2. We use the term *Indian* because we consider it the best translation of *indio,* which is the way Indian organizations have decided they wish to be called. *Indígena* is considered to be a term used by the government when dealing with Indian affairs. In Mexico, *native population, aboriginal population,* and *First Nations* are terms that are not used either to refer to Indians or by the Indians themselves.
3. The Program for the Development of Education (1995–2000) states: "The deficiencies of education in Indian regions are a consequence not only of the irregularity and limitations in the services offered, but also of an inadequate pedagogical and cultural approach, originated in the attempt to reproduce, with marginal adaptations and under precarious conditions, the generic model of the urban school" (Poder Ejecutivo Federal 1995).
4. Mexico defines itself as a pluriethnic and multicultural society since 1992, when Article 4 of the Constitution was amended to that effect.
5. In Mexico, the participation of girls and women in basic education is almost proportional to their representation in the population at large. This, however, is not the case for the Indian population, especially among teenagers and where educational services are concentrated and imply living in a hostel.
6. These and most of the national statistical data included in this chapter are taken from Secretaría de Educación Pública (1998).
7. *Cursos comunitarios* are nonconventional one-room schools where lower or higher secondary school graduates teach students in very small communities where no other school exists. They operate in disperse rural areas (with more than five and less than thirty school-aged children) and are administrated by CONAFE.
8. Because the test was administered in October, at the beginnning of the school year, sixth-grade graduates were tested in the first grade of secondary school. There is no way of knowing which children in secondary schools are Indian.

REFERENCES

Comisión de Concordia y Pacificación. 1996. Acuerdos de San Andrés. México City: Comisión de Concordia y Pacificación.

Poder Ejecutivo Federal. 1995. Programa de desarrollo educativo 1995–2000. México City: Poder Ejecutivo Federal.

Secretaría de Educación Pública. 1998. *Estadística Básica del Sistema Educativo Nacional: Preescolar y Primaria, Fin de Cursos 1996–1997, Medios Urbano y Rural.* México City: Secretaría de Educación Pública.

Schmelkes, Sylvia, Sonia Lavin, Francisco Martinez, and Carmen Noriega. 1996. *The Quality of Primary Education in Mexico: The Case of Puebla.* Paris: International Institute for Educational Planning.

Commentary

John H. Coatsworth, Harvard University

The title of Sylvia Schmelkes' chapter well summarizes the history and current condition of indigenous education in Mexico. It is an alarming example of "policy failure." This failure has historical roots as well as contemporary consequences that demand the urgent attention of citizens and policymakers alike.

Mexico's failure began more than five hundred years ago. The Europeans who conquered and colonized New Spain came from one of the least literate societies of Western Europe. Spaniards did not devote much attention to educating their own sons, and still less their daughters, until the late nineteenth century (Nuñez 1990). In 1860, only 27 percent of Spaniards could read and write; England had reached this level at the time of the Civil War two centuries earlier. In the European colonial empires, literacy and schooling were generally neglected except in settlement colonies with homogeneous populations of European origin. New England and Argentina did better than New Spain, Brazil, and British India. Slave populations remained largely illiterate nearly everywhere. At comparable levels of ethnic subordination, however, the colonies of Great Britain generally did better than those of Spain and Portugal.

This pattern could be related to differences in economic performance. From at least the late seventeenth century, British GDP per capita exceeded that of Spain and Portugal. Differences in educational attainment may have been due to differences in productivity; richer countries and their colonies can afford more schools. There are three reasons for rejecting this suggestion. First, at comparable levels of GDP per capita, Spain consistently lagged behind Great Britain in literacy and schooling well into the twentieth century.[1] Second, literacy rates were higher in British North America by the eighteenth century than in Spanish colonies with comparable or higher levels of GDP per capita.[2] And third, as Nuñez (1992) points out for Spain, literacy is statistically correlated with income per capita, but only when literacy lags; this means that literacy has tended to increase *before* the onset of economic growth and not initially as a result of growth.[3]

Independence in Latin America came as a consequence of what might be called "settler" revolts, like the Rhodesian rebellion against Britain in 1970. Cultural, political, and social changes after independence took decades to consummate. When change did occur, it tended to celebrate and promote mobility for urban mestizo or mulatto groups to the neglect of rural areas of predominantly indigenous or African ancestry. Literacy and education varied across regions within countries in ways consistent with the international comparisons. The Afro-Brazilian northeast of Brazil, for example, has lagged educationally in contrast to São Paulo and the south. In Mexico, the southern states have suffered in contrast to the center and north, though predominantly indige-nous areas in such northern states as Sonora and Chihuahua have also lagged behind.

Mexico's failure stands out most sharply when compared to its northern neighbor. As early as 1800, more than 80 percent of the U.S. free population (and over 60 percent of the total population) could read and write (Niemi 1980). Mexico did not reach the U.S. 1800 level of literacy until the 1950s to 1980s, a lag of more than a century and a half.[4] Mexico's high illiteracy rate persisted well into the twentieth century. At the time of the Mexican Revolution of 1910, barely a quarter of the school-aged population went to pri-mary school and less than 5 percent reached secondary school (Instituto Nacional de Estadística Geografía e Informatica 1985, 85).

Schmelkes' chapter suggests that these patterns of relative neglect and discrimina-tion against the indigenous population may have persisted in Mexico until today, despite policies nominally committed to equality of educational opportunity. This hypothesis makes sense, but it is difficult to test. The data pose a serious identification problem. To put the issue succinctly, it is not clear whether Mexico still has a specifically "in-digenous" problem or a broader problem of educating the poor whether indigenous or not. This issue has both an historical and a contemporary dimension.

Historically, poverty and ethnicity are linked in two contradictory ways. On the one hand, poor Mexicans today are more likely to be indigenous than the population as a whole. On the other hand, social mobility has tended to go hand in hand with assimi-lation. As indigenous peasants have migrated to cities, they or their children have been transformed in language and culture into mestizos. That is, in the wealthier center and north of the country, economic advance provided incentives to assimilate and the heavy-handed assimilationism of Mexico's public schools abetted the process. His-torically, indigenous people of higher income are those who speak Spanish and adapt to the dominant mestizo culture. In effect, when indigenous people cease to be poor and rural, they cease to be counted as indigenous and disappear from the data. For this reason, a successful policy of assimilationist education would produce exactly what the data show.

What proportion of Mexico's population consists of people whose DNA markers are exclusively indigenous no one knows. What we do know is that those whose speech and culture mark them as indigenous, whatever their DNA says, are always predominantly poor and rural, by definition. Only in the past decade or so have the as-similationist practices of the Mexican state begun to allow for a self-respecting diver-sity. Hence the analytical question: Does Mexico have a specific problem educating its indigenous population or rather a more general problem of delivering educational services to the poor, especially the rural poor, regardless of race or ethnicity?

Schmelkes cites indicators of educational failure that show striking parallels be-tween the indigenous population and nonindigenous urban marginals and rural poor. The nonindigenous rural population appears to have even less access to full-time teachers as well as fewer textbooks and sports facilities on average than the indigenous population. The data also suggest that the ethnically isolated schools operated for in-digenous, mostly male, students may be working better than other public schools that serve the poor and marginal populations of the country. Is it possible that the policy failure in indigenous education has now become more class-based and region-specific than racial or ethnic in nature? Perhaps race or ethnicity has become less significant in Mexican higher education than class and place of residence in determining access to education, as William Julius Wilson (1978) argued with respect to poverty among African Americans in the United States a decade ago. Or, to put it differently, Mexico is now discriminating against indigenous people even after they have assimilated.

Curiously, just as race and ethnicity are declining in significance, Mexican policy and politics have moved to embrace multiculturalism for the first time in the nation's history, as Schmelkes reports. Though this process began with the adoption of bilingual education in 1979, it received an important boost with the restructuring of the Instituto Nacional Indigenista (INI) and the constitutional amendments adopted during the presidency of Carlos Salinas de Gortari. These changes were championed by Arturo Warman, one of Mexico's most distinguished anthropologists, who served both as director of INI and in the newly created post of "procurador" or ombudsman for the indigenous population in the federal government. During the Zedillo administration, bilingual education has been renamed "intercultural" education, while administrative and fiscal responsibility for public education has been further decentralized.

It is not yet clear what the long-term implications of these changes will be, either in promoting respect for indigenous rights and cultures or for promoting improved access to education. Assigning greater value to indigenous cultures and languages in the curriculum could help to improve attendance and performance. Giving more power to state and local school authorities could reduce waste and rigidity while empowering parents and communities to make improvements. On the other hand, creating more "separate but equal" schools for indigenous children could backfire; decentralization already has, in many cases, turned power over to local bosses and bureaucrats who have more important things to do than improving education for the children of indigenous villagers.

In the twentieth century, but not earlier, Mexico achieved major advances in literacy and education. According to the National Census of 1900, only 22.3 percent of the Mexican population could read and write. Today, nearly 90 percent are counted as literate. The literacy transition, which education historians define as passing from a threshold of less than 30 percent to over 70 percent literacy, occurred between the 1920s and the 1960s. These national averages disguise regional, social, and racial differences. In rural, poor, and largely indigenous Chiapas, only 9.1 percent were literate in 1900; 30 percent literacy was not achieved until the late 1940s and 70 percent in the 1990s. Education at all levels has also improved, but schooling in all its dimensions remains far behind the rest of the country, as it does in Guerrero, Oaxaca, and other states where rural poverty, not all of it indigenous, is endemic.

Mexico's policymakers have yet to design and implement policies to eliminate or substantially reduce the illiteracy and lack of quality schooling for the still large proportion of its population that is poor, marginal, rural, and indigenous. This failure persists despite the many examples of success in this field in other countries with no more resources than Mexico. To correct it, Mexico will need to clear away institutional bottlenecks, reformulate national priorities, and divert resources from other worthy uses. If the Mexican government continues to fail to provide a modern education for so many of its people, the price the country pays for its neglect in slower growth, political turmoil, and socioethnic conflict will get even higher.

NOTES

1. For the English data, see Nicholas (1990).
2. For rough estimates of GDP per capita in 1700 and 1800, see Coatsworth (1998).
3. A twenty-year lag fits the Spanish data best (Coatsworth 1998, 130–133). For a fuller discussion of the methodology employed, see Nuñez's excellent book (1992, Chapter 5).
4. Literacy in Mexico reached 56.8 percent in 1950, 66.5 percent in 1960, 76.3 percent in 1970, and 83 percent in 1980 (Instituto Nacional de Estadística, Geografía e Informática 1985, 91).

REFERENCES

Coatsworth, John H. 1998. Economic and Institutional Trajectories in Nineteenth-Century Latin America. In *Latin America and the World Economy Since 1800,* ed. John Coatsworth and Alan Taylor, 23–54. Cambridge, Mass.: Harvard University Press.

Instituto Nacional de Estadística, Geografía e Informática. 1985. *Estadísticas Históricas de México,* vol. 1. Aguascalientes, Mexico: INEGI, 91.

Nicholas, Stephen. 1990. Literacy and the Industrial Revolution. In *Education and Economic Development Since the Industrial Revolution,* ed. Gabriel Tortella, 47–68. Valencia: Generalitat Valenciana.

Niemi, Albert W., Jr. 1980. *U.S. Economic History,* 2nd ed. Chicago: Rand McNally.

Nuñez, Clara Eugenia. 1990. Literacy and economic growth in Spain. In *Education and Economic Development Since the Industrial Revolution,* ed. Gabriel Tortella, 136. Valencia: Generalitat Valenciana.

Nuñez, Clara Eugenia. 1992. *La Fuente de la Riqueza: Educación y Desarrollo Económico en la España Contemporánea.* Madrid: Alianza Universidad.

Wilson, William Julius. 1978. *The Declining Significance of Race: Blacks and Changing American Institutions.* Chicago: University of Chicago Press.

A student listens to her teacher at the Escuela 18 de Marzo in Guadalupe Victoria, Mexico.
[Robert Myers/Mexico]

13

Function and Evaluation of a Compensatory Program Directed at the Poorest Mexican States: Chiapas, Guerrero, Hidalgo, and Oaxaca

Carlos Muñoz Izquierdo
Raquel Ahuja Sánchez
Universidad Iberoamericana, Campus Santa Fe, Mexico City

One of the Mexican government's proposed solutions to an inequitable, inefficient education system is the Program to Overcome the Educational Gap, or PARE (from the initials in *Programa para Abatir el Rezago Educativo*). This program is considered compensatory in that it targets the poorest states for additional education services and resources. This chapter analyzes the implementation and effects of PARE in the different types of communities that received assistance. The results of this detailed study highlight the shortcomings of PARE in its current form. The authors provide valuable suggestions for improving the program to better address the needs of Mexico's most disadvantaged students.

BACKGROUND

As a result of diverse public policies that began in 1960 to satisfy the demand for primary education, since 1982 Mexico has been able to enroll practically all children in the first grade. This improvement, however, was insufficient, resulting in an expanded but inefficient and inequitable education system. Despite 100 percent enrollment in the first grade, many students do not finish school on time. The coefficient of terminal efficiency of primary education (obtained by dividing the number of students who complete sixth grade by those that began the cycle six years earlier) is 70.1 percent. Consequently, the coefficient of satisfaction of demand that is close to 100 percent for children six years old falls to 60 percent for children twelve years old. This indicator varies, however, between 85.6 percent in the Federal District and 28.5 percent in the state of Chiapas.

The level of efficiency of primary education corresponds to the socioeconomic level of the states. Between 1970 and 1990, the efficiency of primary education was maintained above the national average in the states that enjoyed the highest living standards in 1970. In contrast, school efficiency decreased in the states that had the lowest levels of economic development in 1970.[1] This is significant because it indicates that the educational development experienced within these two decades was pushed primarily by factors external to the education system, and not by policies expressly designed to improve education in the poorest states.

The achievement of primary school children is related directly to the level of socioeconomic development of the regions in which their respective schools are found.[2] Much like the observation in the preceding paragraph, this means that the expansion of the school system has not contributed to reducing the gaps that have traditionally existed between the levels of socioeconomic and cultural development of the different regions of the country.

The average schooling of the population fifteen years old and older is 6.6 grades. However, in the Federal District, it is 9 grades and in Chiapas it reaches only 4.3 grades. In addition, the indicator of functional illiteracy among the population 15 years old and older is 28.9 percent for the entire country. It does, however, vary significantly by region: 12.5 percent in the Federal District, 46.2 percent in Oaxaca, and 52.2 percent in Chiapas.

Finally, the index that measures inequality of the distribution of schooling among the inhabitants of the different states of the Republic (estimated in agreement with the Gini coefficient) is 0.39 at the national level. However, this indicator varies between 0.29 in the Federal District and 0.54 in the state of Chiapas.[3]

PUBLIC POLICIES DIRECTED AT OVERCOMING THE GAP

The problems described above have accumulated in spite of the fact that, since the 1970s, the federal government has designed different educational reforms directed at overcoming them. However, the fact that the advances that have been successful have been situated in the geographic zones with the highest levels of socioeconomic development—such that the educational gaps persist in the poorest regions of the country— clearly indicates that none of these reforms was capable of producing the hoped-for effects.

Since 1992, the federal government has carried out new actions directed at combating the factors that have contributed to the development and persistence of the problems described above. These actions began when the National Agreement for the Modernization of Basic Education (ANMEB) was created in 1992, an agreement underwritten by the president of the Republic, the governors of all the states, and the National Teachers' Union. Subsequently, the measures contained in this agreement were incorporated into the General Law of Education (drawn up in 1993). They referred, fundamentally, to the following:

- Reorganization of the school system
- Participation of the community in the educational process
- Reformation of didactic contents and materials

• Social upgrading of the teaching profession
• Equal distribution of educational opportunities

The measures that were designed to counteract, in the short term, the effects of the problems that have impeded the provision of quality and equitable educational opportunities are known conventionally as preventative, compensatory, or corrective (remedial). They are typified in Chapter III of the General Law of Education which, in turn, was based on ANMEB. These strategies can be condensed into five points:

• To assign resources with compensatory objectives
• To diversify the provision of education
• To satisfy the demand for initial and preschool education
• To improve the educational process
• To combat the effects of different external obstacles that interfere with learning

One of the most important arrangements of Chapter III is that schools that are attended primarily by students from socially marginalized strata will receive special attention. For this, the law requires "the assignment, to said schools, of resources and investments of greater quality" (Article 33, Section I). This arrangement is complemented by that of the federal executive "that it should carry out compensatory programs by virtue of those that it would support with specific resources for the governments of those federal entities with the greatest educational gaps" (Article 34).

The Program to Overcome the Educational Gap (PARE)

The Program to Overcome the Educational Gap (PARE), started in 1991, was the first program implemented in accordance with ANMEB. Its budget climbed to $352 million, distributed over four years; $250 million of the budget was covered with loans from the World Bank (Ornelas, 1995, 237).[4] It was invested in two areas, improvement of educational services and institutional strengthening.

The general objective of the program was to improve the quality and efficiency of primary education of rural schools in the states lagging behind most of the country. The specific objectives were to increase levels of learning in primary education, to improve the preparation and motivation of teachers, and to strengthen the organization and educational administration.

The four states selected as beneficiaries, Chiapas, Guerrero, Oaxaca, and Hidalgo, were chosen because they were considered the most disadvantaged at a national level, as much in terms of poverty as scholastic failure. Some indicators of the socioeconomic and educational situation of the states selected to participate in PARE, and their comparison with other parameters, are shown in Table 13.1. Within these states, the program is oriented primarily toward public primary schools in communities with the greatest poverty and school failure—that is, toward rural, indigenous, and community courses of CONAFE.[5]

The means of achieving the objectives of the program included a series of educational investments and support for institutional fortification. The initial budget of PARE was structured as shown in Table 13.2. The component "mechanisms of social

TABLE 13.1

Indicators of Poverty and Education of the Participating States

State	Poverty Index	Educational Attainment	Gini Index (Related to Educational Attainment)	Functional Illiteracy (%)	Terminal Efficiency of Primary Education (%)
Hidalgo	83.23	5.64	0.44	37.6	53.2
Guerrero	86.12	5.24	0.50	42.6	40.4
Oaxaca	89.73	4.62	0.50	46.2	40.2
Chiapas	88.85	4.33	0.54	52.2	28.5
Federal District	41.48	8.95	0.29	12.5	85.6
National average	70.47	6.65	0.39	28.9	54.7

Sources: Martinez Rizo (1992); Muñoz Izquierdo and Ulloa (1992); SEP (1985–1991).

participation in the finance and educational tasks" was directed at participation with the school community; however, it was cancelled before the initiation of the program. The component "distance education and training" was dedicated to producing audio and video materials, but until 1995 it had not been integrated in the schools. The component "improvement of information systems" was implemented in coordination between state and central offices in the Ministry of Education to homogenize the management of data and reports, following information distributed by the central coordinators of PARE.

TABLE 13.2

Distribution of Budget of the PARE Project by Component

Component	Budget (1991–1994) Millions of U.S. Dollars	%
Provision of didactic material	54.0	15.3
Provision of textbooks for indigenous education	3.1	0.9
Endowment of school libraries	4.4	1.3
Construction of regional warehouses	3.1	0.9
Training and modernization of the teaching profession	43.0	12.2
Distance education and training	8.6	2.4
School infrastructure and equipment	131.0	37.2
Improvement of school supervision	27.5	7.8
Incentives for good teacher performance	52.0	14.8
Improvement of information systems	2.1	0.6
Evaluation of scholastic achievement	4.1	1.2
Mechanisms of social participation in the finance and educational tasks	0.3	0.1
Impact of the program	1.2	0.3
Unforeseen expenditures	17.5	5.0
Total	352.0	100.0
National funds	102.0	
International financing	250.0	

Until the end of the school cycle 1994–1995 eight components had been offered to the beneficiaries (schools and educational agents). The community courses received only the component of didactic material and libraries; the urban schools initially received only training courses for teachers, but they all received the investments minus infrastructure and teacher incentives; the rural and indigenous schools received all of the components.

EVALUATION OF THE IMPACT OF PARE

In this section we describe the methods followed in this study, describe the conditions in which the program operated during the first three years of implementation, and characterize the communities in which it operated.

Methodology

The general objectives of this investigation were to examine whether student academic achievement would increase with the provision of the diverse components of the program, to determine the cost-effectiveness of the components of the program, and, finally, to provide some explanation for the variability in success across schools.

The study has a quasi-experimental, longitudinal design with three measurements: at the beginning of the school cycle 1992–1993, at the beginning of the school cycle 1993–1994, and near the end of the school cycle 1994–1995. The state of Michoacan was included as a control group because of its similarity to the rest of the states in terms of socioeconomic and educational characteristics.[6]

The design of the sample followed a random and systematic selection method. Four sample strata were used to select the schools: urban schools, rural schools, indigenous schools, and community courses. A sample of 206 schools was chosen, with the following distribution between strata: 27 were urban, 71 were rural, 64 were Indian schools, and 44 were community courses.

The subjects of the study were students who began the fourth grade of primary school in the 1992–1993 cycle and continued on to fifth and sixth grades. The initial size of this cohort was 3,546 children.

Ninety-three percent of the schools in the initial sample remained in the study until the last wave of data collection. The losses were due to difficulties in access, final or temporary closures of some scholastic centers, and conflicts in the communities that impeded collecting the data (this was particularly the case in the state of Chiapas).

The following independent variables were included in the study:

Variables referring to conditions of children and their families

• Distance of the locality in relation to the capital of the state
• Level of urbanization of the localities
• Standard of living of the families
• Cultural capital of the family
• Learning environment provided by the family
• Conditions that dispose the student to study
• School history of the child

• Health of the child
• Nutritional intake of the student
• Self-esteem of the student

Variables relating to school provision

• Conditions of the classrooms
• Performance of the group teacher
• Performance of the director of the school
• Participation of the parents and the community in the educational process
• Quality of school supervision

Variables about the program

• Exposition of each component of the program
• Quality of the implementation process of each component of the program

The data were analyzed through multivariate statistical models. To analyze the impact of PARE, two regression models were constructed. The first investigated whether schools that received a determined component of the program exhibited different levels of achievement than the rest. The second consisted of determining if some relationship existed between school achievement and the form in which PARE investments were distributed and utilized by the schools.

Conditions of the Schools in Which PARE Operated

Based on the information collected by the longitudinal survey of teachers and parents, we characterize the conditions of the schools targeted by the program, as well as the teachers and students in those schools.

Schools   The majority of schools were complete; that is, they offered all grades. Previously, however, in rural areas multigrade schools predominated (in the rural strata, there was an average of four teachers per school, five in indigenous schools, and eleven in urban schools). Fourteen percent of rural schools and 25 percent of bilingual schools were functioning in buildings not designed specifically to provide educational services.

Teachers   On average, less than 20 percent of the teachers and directors of rural schools were living in the same communities in which they worked, which is necessarily related to teacher absenteeism. According to information provided by teachers themselves, they were absent from work, on average, eleven days of the year in rural and indigenous strata, twenty-three days in community courses, and seven days in urban strata.[7]

In all of the sampled strata, there was more than one teacher who solicited a change of assignment during the three school cycles (1992–1993, 1993–1994, and 1994–1995). In addition, 90 percent of rural schools, 80 percent of bilingual schools, and 61 percent of the urban schools reported having had some change of faculty during the same period.[8]

One indicator confirms a recognized problem. The faculty with the most schooling and experience are assigned to urban schools and not to schools that, because of their low socioeducational status, require the best-prepared teachers.

Students   On average, more than a third of the children in each stratum were over-age for the grade they were studying. In indigenous schools, 50 percent of the children were overage. According to school principals, it is more common that children abandon school during the same school year than between one cycle and another. The fact that there are not more children dropping out of school between years means, upon first analysis, that it is not fundamentally caused by a scarcity of places in the schools. Upon second analysis, it means that children of lesser academic achievement make the decision to leave school even before taking final exams—probably because they anticipate that they will not be able to pass them. These data are also compatible with the hypothesis that school drop out is in part generated by extra-academic phenomena (related, presumably, to family dynamics and to the precarious conditions of the lives of the children).

Of the indigenous schools, 57.6 percent in the sample include monolingual students. The averages for federal schools fluctuate between 11.8 percent in Michoacan and 29.4 percent in Oaxaca. In turn, children who do not speak Spanish represent, on average, 50.9 percent of those enrolled in these public schools.[9]

The proportions of monolingual students are larger in first grade (in which monolingual children represent 59 percent), as would be expected. However, those children represent only a little more than a fourth (26.5 percent) of those enrolled in sixth grade, suggesting that the schools are not succeeding in *castilianizing* (teaching students Spanish, which replaces their native languages) all their students during primary school.

Eleven percent of teachers (ranging between 0 percent in Guerrero to 24 percent in Chiapas) do not speak the language of the communities in which they work. It is very likely that this problem influenced the observations cited above.

The Communities, Families, and Children

The urban schools are situated in locations that rely on public services (piped water, drainage, pavement, etc.). The others are found in populations that lack these services. Almost none of the students in schools located outside of cities utilize some vehicle to transport themselves to school.

In the nonurban strata, the proportions of heads of family whose economic activities correspond to the primary sector fluctuates between 76 percent and 98 percent. In the cities, 62 percent of the heads of families work in the service sector. The indicator that measures the occupational position of the heads of family assumes its lesser value in the communities in which community courses are found. In comparison with this parameter, the corresponding value for heads of family of bilingual schools is higher at 22.2 percent; the value corresponding to rural schools is 83.3 percent higher. The value corresponding to heads of family of urban schools is 7.6 times higher than that.

Family revenue (indirectly estimated) is less in the localities in which bilingual schools are found. Family revenue in community courses is greater, at 40 percent;

family revenue in rural schools is 3.4 times higher; and family revenue in urban schools is 10.4 times greater.

The indicator that measures the cultural capital of the family is lowest in bilingual schools. This is followed by the rural schools (33.3 percent greater), community courses (41 percent greater), and urban schools (64 percent greater).

A succinct summary of the principal characteristics of educational demand is as follows:

- The localities where community courses and indigenous schools function are, on average, the farthest from the state capitals (in relation to travel time). Likewise, these communities also have the lowest indicators of urbanization.
- In all strata, there were insufficiencies in the provision of educational services. Some community members had to travel up to eight hours to receive the services they needed.
- A high indicator of illiteracy of the parents, accentuated in rural zones, reflects family conditions that do not favor an adequate school performance by the children. Books and written materials are lacking, limiting support to the children and the development of basic abilities such as reading and writing that are not stimulated in the home.
- In the urban stratum, more than 80 percent of the children had access to preschool education. In contrast, in the rural and indigenous strata, only 60 percent had access. In the community courses, the proportion of children with access to preschool drops to 20 percent.
- Delayed admission into primary school is higher in the indigenous stratum, where 35 percent of the children pertaining to this stratum entered school after the age of six. This phenomenon, in general, is present more frequently in rural zones than in urban zones.
- In all the strata, there are schools in which the teachers of second and sixth grade report that 100 percent of their students exceed the age corresponding to the grade.
- In agreement with information provided by parents, half of the children in community courses have failed some grade. In the urban stratum, one of every five children has failed; in the indigenous stratum, one of every four has failed; and in the rural stratum, one in every three has failed.
- The proportions of children who have left school for at least a year or who have had to interrupt their studies in a school cycle fluctuate between 6 percent and 13 percent among the different strata. Temporary desertion is most evident in rural zones, particularly in community courses and indigenous schools.

PRINCIPAL RESULTS

In this section we present the results as changes in the levels of student achievement over time in the schools targeted by the program, and we examine the extent to which these changes, measured in a wide range of indices, relate to program characteristics and interventions.

School Achievement

The evaluation of academic achievement was carried out through multiple-choice tests, in the areas of Spanish and mathematics, produced by the General Office of Evaluation (SEP). It is important to clarify that the tests of the different grades, although not pedagogically comparable, permit the observation of changes experienced by the children.

Though various subsamples of PARE students increased their achievement levels, the data do not signify an educationally significant improvement because students still do not reach minimum passing levels. In all grades and areas (with the exception of mathematics in fourth grade), the results show higher scores for students in urban schools than those in rural schools. Among the students of the last three grades of primary education, those in the bilingual programs attain the lowest scores in Spanish. In general, students had higher levels of achievement in Spanish than in math.

About the Operation of the Program

To research the operation of the program, data were obtained from three sources of information:

- Interviews with the central coordinators of the eight components
- Interviews with 728 users from the PARE groups, including participating teachers from the rural strata, school directors (148), supervisors (128), and representatives from the associations of parents (145)
- The receipts from didactic material, libraries, and bilingual texts from the schools in the study, distributed by the state coordinators of the program, to confirm data on the investments in each school

Two basic aspects concerning the operation of the program's components are explored in this section: timely delivery and sufficiency.

Timely Delivery   The timely delivery of the components was considered to be one of the conditions necessary for the program to achieve the intended goals. Timeliness of delivery was measured in different ways depending on the objectives of each component.

An important indicator of timeliness is the arrival of textbooks to the schools in the first month of classes. Not all schools received textbooks on time during the last three school cycles. In the indigenous stratum, only 18 percent of schools were able to rely on textbooks in the first month of classes. In the rural stratum and community courses, more materials arrived on time, though they still arrived late to half of the schools.

With regard to didactic materials, a comparison was made between months of use in accordance with the date on which the school received the materials. Results show that in the 1993–1994 school cycle, the materials could be used for only four of the ten months the school cycle covers. In the 1994–1995 school cycle, however, the reported average for months of use was 8.7 in urban schools; elsewhere, delivery opportunity worsened: from 3.8 months to 2.9 months of use in community schools, from 4.1 to 3.8 months in bilingual schools, and from 4.3 to 3.9 in rural schools.

The distribution of bilingual texts was not timely either. Only 12 percent received texts at the beginning of classes, and 46 percent of the schools received texts after the first three months of classes, while the rest of the schools received their texts within the first three months but not at the beginning of classes.

Sufficiency of Components   The sufficiency of the components granted by the program is understood as the correspondence between the requirements of the school and the quantity of investments received.

Books/didactic materials. Thirty-five percent of the indigenous schools declared that they had received an insufficient number of bilingual texts. It is notable that almost half of the teachers said they found little correspondence between the bilingual texts and the local language. Conversely, 27 percent felt that there was a lot of correspondence between the texts and the language. Still, 60 percent of teachers said that they had not been able to integrate these texts into their teaching.

The community course teachers reported the lowest average of books per student delivered by the program. In the community courses and in the urban stratum, one book for every two students was received from PARE, while in the rural stratum, two books for every student were received. Another important shortage was in the support materials for libraries: 69 percent of schools did not receive instruction manuals and more than 95 percent did not receive bookshelves or file cabinets.

Problems that impeded the transfer of didactic materials, libraries, and bilingual texts to the schools were detected. Materials did not arrive directly to the schools, except in the urban stratum. The didactic materials were usually distributed to the stores of PARE, not to the communities directly. The textbooks were generally delivered to the supervisors or zone headquarters. The community or the teachers had to go collect the materials (and cover the cost of transportation as well) on a workday, implying the loss of workdays or classes.

The time needed to travel between the school and the PARE center to pick up materials reached an average of five hours in the community courses and indigenous stratum. Supervisors in the rural and indigenous stratum had to travel an average of three hours to reach the distribution centers. In urban areas, the average travel time was only one hour.

Teachers/teacher training. Between 1992 and 1995, the teaching personnel of the indigenous schools benefited most from the training component, with an average of 2.5 courses per teacher out of three available courses. The lowest average of coverage was found in the urban stratum, with less than two courses per teacher. All of the schools getting incentives received training.

There were great shortages in training teachers to incorporate didactic materials from PARE into their pedagogy. In the indigenous and rural strata, only 20 percent of the teachers declared having received some type of formal orientation for the utilization of didactic material. Only 40 percent of the community instructors received training.

With respect to the use of library books, the proportions of teachers who received some training were also small: 40 percent of the instructors, 30 percent of the teachers from the rural stratum, and 10 percent of the teachers from the indigenous stratum. However, 80 percent of teachers from indigenous schools said they had received training to use the bilingual texts, although only 20 percent had received follow-up orientations.

Many of the teachers receiving incentives did not fully understand the objectives of providing the extra funds. Eighty-four percent of the teachers receiving incentives felt that their school had been selected because of its location in an extremely marginalized zone. Sixteen percent indicated that it was chosen because of a shortage of access roads. Only 5 percent said it was due to the high rotation of teachers, which is one of the most important objectives of the component.

There was also some confusion about the requirements for receiving the incentive: 68 percent of the teachers thought they needed to carry out community development activities to receive the incentive, 53 percent understood that they were obligated to remain in the community; and 47 percent thought they had to teach literacy to the adults. No teacher made reference to their work with the students. The requirements actually included the four items mentioned.

Supervisors. Seventy-six percent of the supervisors of indigenous schools said they did not utilize the trucks from PARE to carry out their work. The supervisors who made the most use of the trucks were from the rural stratum; however, only 40 percent of those able to use them did so. A third of the supervisors from the urban stratum used the trucks, calling attention to the fact that they had greater access to the trucks than did supervisors of bilingual schools.

The economic support for supervisors was insufficient and did not mitigate the difficulties that supervisors had in arriving at communities. In the indigenous stratum, nearly 50 percent of the supervisors did not visit at least half of their schools.

Supervisory support also had limitations. The supervisors reported that the dimensions and the design of the offices were not adequate in space, temperature, and safety. Regarding office equipment, a third of the supervisors reported that the sector headquarters received mimeographs, but close to 40 percent did not know of their existence; only three supervisors of the sample had used them.

The greatest benefits to supervisors were the investments that were delivered to the supervisors directly (office, equipment, economic support) as opposed to the sector headquarters (trucks, mimeographs).

Infrastructure. The assignment of classrooms was sufficient for the majority of the schools, as much for the rural stratum as the indigenous stratum. Data shows twenty-five students per classroom in rural schools and twenty-seven in indigenous schools.

PARE covers all the infrastructure costs. However, high percentages of contribution from the communities are found. The support solicited from parents consisted of materials, free labor, and infrequently money, generally from contractors.

Impact of the Program

In this section we fit several multiple regression models to examine the impact of the program on changes in student achievement. We first describe the rationale for the analysis that we conducted and then present the results of the regressions.

Rationale of the Analysis   One of the principal purposes of this study was to determine the impact produced through time on school achievement in those schools that received different PARE supports. The investigation was designed to identify the contribution of different PARE components to the achievement of the objectives of improving children's learning and ensuring the permanence of children in the school system. The ample literature available on this theme permitted the anticipation of the need to carry out our analysis based on multivariate statistical methods.

Different multiple linear regression models were fitted to the data with the objective of determining which measurement, as much PARE as the other variables considered in the study, contributes to school achievement and retention. The equations that were devised followed a "production function approach," developed by economists to analyze the contribution that different factors utilized to obtain goods and services make on the product of a given enterprise. In this case the multiple regression equations establish the contribution that multiple factors (independent variables) make to several learning outcomes of children who participated in the program.

To reduce the probability that the results of the equations would attribute to some variables the effects that in reality had been generated by others, two measures were taken. One measure created independent equations for a collection of relatively homogeneous subsamples. The purpose was to maintain intrasample variances constant in relation to the variables representative of educational demand and the variances of the variables related to the investments distributed to the school system and with school provision. To construct these equations, a method of stratification based on "clusters" was utilized.[10] That is, we examined the effect of independent variables in subgroups of children of similar socioeconomic backgrounds.

We conducted analyses within five strata, whose denominations and respective sizes indicate the following:

- *Lower Rural stratum* ($n = 650$): integrated by students enrolled in rural schools, pertaining to families who in comparative terms are found at the lowest socioeconomic levels (in this stratum, the majority of students pertain to indigenous populations)
- *Middle Rural stratum* ($n = 294$): integrated by students enrolled in rural schools, pertaining to families who in comparative terms are found at intermediate socioeconomic levels
- *Upper Rural stratum* ($n = 59$): integrated by students enrolled in rural schools, pertaining to families who in comparative terms are found at the highest socioeconomic levels
- *Lower Urban stratum* ($n = 263$): integrated by students enrolled in urban schools, pertaining to families who in comparative terms are found at the lowest socioeconomic levels
- *Upper Urban stratum* ($n = 628$): integrated by students enrolled in urban schools, pertaining to families who in comparative terms are found at the highest socioeconomic levels

The second measure taken to reduce the risk mentioned above was to use a stepwise approach to multiple regression method. The method permits the determination of whether the introduction of an independent variable (or of a combination of independent variables) in the regression equation generates a statistically significant effect in addition ،o the effects generated by the variables that have already been introduced in the same equation.

In various models generated with this step-wise approach, distinct dependent variables were utilized, through which other such regression equations were estimated for each cluster. These variables were constructed as follows:

1. Difference between the grade obtained by each sixth-grade student in a Spanish course and the same student's grade in Spanish at the end of fourth grade, expressed by the following formula:

   DV1 (Dependent or Outcome Variable) = (6th Spanish − 4th Spanish)

2. Difference between the sum of the scores obtained by each student in the Spanish course upon completing fifth and sixth grades and the same student's grade in Spanish at the end of fourth grade, expressed by the following formula:

   DV2 = (5th Spanish + 6th Spanish) − 4th Spanish

3. Difference between the sixth-grade student's test score in mathematics and the same student's score in mathematics at the end of fourth grade, expressed by the following formula:

   DV3 = (6th Mathematics − 4th Mathematics)

4. Difference between the sum of the grades obtained by each student in mathematics upon completing fifth and sixth grades and the same student's grade in mathematics at the end of fourth grade, expressed by the following formula:

   DV4 = (5th Mathematics + 6th Mathematics) − 4th Mathematics

In agreement with the methodology chosen, the independent variables were introduced into the equations in three successive stages. The order in which this was carried out was based on the theory of the program. Therefore, in the first stage, representative variables of educational demand were considered; in the second, representative variables of school provision were included; and in the last, representative variables of the investments of PARE were included. Whether the introduction of the combination of variables being considered increased the R^2 in a statistically significant form (or the multiple regression coefficient elevated to square) was considered at each stage. (The R^2 expresses the percentage of variation of the outcome variable which is explained by the independent or predictor variables.)

Finally, the impact of the program was analyzed through two regression models. The objective of the first consisted of investigating whether the fact that schools had received a determined component of PARE had some impact on the achievement of the children. This necessitates including in the equation, in addition to the schools that received investments in the program, others that did not participate in it (the control group from Michoacan). In doing this, a natural dummy variable was included in the corresponding regression model for each of the program's investments.

The objective of the second model was to determine whether some relationship existed between school achievement and the way in which the investments of PARE were utilized in the schools. Therefore, this model was constructed with variables that not only reflect whether schools received determined investments from PARE but that also measure, through different scales, the intensity with which each investment was utilized; the degree to which the schools had access to the investments (measured by the time during which the schools had access to them); and whether the investments received were sufficient in terms of the size of each school.

Behavior of the Variables Included in the Models

Dependent variables. The scores obtained on the different achievement tests (and the dependent variables that were constructed from them) in each sample stratum were submitted to an analysis of variance. Table 13.3 shows the averages of students' scores—classified in each of the previously described stratum—on the achievement tests corresponding to the courses mentioned above when those students completed the fourth, fifth, and sixth grades. The averages also appear in the constructs related to each of the dependent variables, defined in the previous paragraphs.

In Table 13.3, the strata are numbered from 1 to 5 corresponding to socioeconomic levels of the families of the students. Number 1 corresponds to the stratum composed of the students that have, in the total sample, the highest socioeconomic backgrounds (Upper Urban stratum). Number 5 corresponds to those children in the Lower Rural stratum.

Table 13.3 shows the low levels of achievement obtained by the children on all the tests that were given to them. Given that a score below 60 percent is considered failing, all averages that appear in the table are failing scores. This problem is most acute in mathematics. The second item for each dependent variable corresponds to the strata whose averages are significantly less than those noted in the respective stratum.

The students in the Upper Urban stratum obtained the highest averages in five of the six measurements taken. In the remaining measurements (which correspond to the grades obtained on the tests of fourth-grade mathematics), the highest average corresponded to the students of the Lower Urban stratum. Generally, the average scores tend to be positively related to their socioeconomic strata.

Upon examining the behavior of the averages of the four dependent variables, it is evident that the urban strata surpass the rural in three measurements. However, in the remaining measurement (the difference between the sixth-grade and fourth-grade marks in Spanish), the Lower Rural stratum shows the greatest advances. Although this occurred with only one of the four variables used, this discovery is encouraging, especially because most of the indigenous population pertains to the Lower Rural stratum. However, the achievement in Spanish of students in the other strata tended to diminish or, at least, to remain constant. It should concern the educational authorities that in four strata the achievement in Spanish, on average, remained at failing levels in fourth grade.

Independent variables. To analyze the patterns of distribution of the different independent variables among each of the sample strata, an analysis of variance was carried out. The results appear in Tables 13.4, 13.5, and 13.6. These tables show the averages obtained for the independent variables in the different strata. The numbers that appear below some averages identify the sample strata whose averages are lower than the average in question.

Table 13.4 shows the analysis of the variables that represent conditions of educational demand. They refer, therefore, to the children, their families, and the communities in which the schools are found. The averages corresponding to the urban strata are greater

TABLE 13.3

Distribution of the Averages of School Achievement Between the Different Strata

		Upper Urban (1)	Lower Urban (2)	Upper Rural (3)	Middle Rural (4)	Lower Rural (5)
Global evaluation in Spanish in fourth grade	$\bar{X}$* $\neq$[†]	**50.26** > 5, 4, 3	46.87 > 5, 4	43.35 > 5	41.41 > 5	31.98
Global evaluation in Spanish in fifth grade	$\bar{X}$ $\neq$	**68.61** > 5, 4, 3, 2	57.52 > 5, 4, 3	48.61 > 5	45.34 > 5	39.66
Global evaluation in Spanish in sixth grade	$\bar{X}$ $\neq$	**42.88** > 5, 4, 3, 2	39.60 > 5, 4, 3	33.88	33.20 > 5	30.40
Differences among the evaluations of Spanish in fourth and sixth grades (with evaluations standardized and configured to 100)	$\bar{X}$ $\neq$	−0.64	−0.90	−4.37	−3.34	**3.59** > 3, 4, 2, 1
Differences among the evaluations of Spanish in fourth, fifth, and sixth grades (with evaluations standardized and configured to 100)	$\bar{X}$ $\neq$	**68.19** > 4, 5, 3, 2	55.98 > 4, 5, 3	44.27	42.62	43.30
Global evaluation in mathematics in fourth grade	$\bar{X}$ $\neq$	28.07	**29.26** > 5	28.79	28.46	27.00
Global evaluation in mathematics in fifth grade	$\bar{X}$ $\neq$	**34.52** > 5, 3, 4	32.08 > 5, 4	28.08	28.39	26.24
Global evaluation in mathematics in sixth grade	$\bar{X}$ $\neq$	**38.49** > 5, 4, 3, 2	34.58 > 5	32.86	32.50 > 5	29.57
Differences among the evaluations of mathematics in fourth and sixth grades (with evaluations standardized and configured to 100)	$\bar{X}$ $\neq$	**4.26** > 5, 3, 4, 2	−2.85	−4.41	−4.40	−6.08
Difference among the evaluations of mathematics in fourth, fifth, and sixth grades (with evaluations standardized and configured to 100)	$\bar{X}$ $\neq$	**51.19** 5, 4, 3, 2	38.55 > 5	34.33	34.20	29.58

*$\bar{X}$ indicates mean.

[†]$\neq$ indicates which strata [Upper Urban (1), Lower Urban (2), etc.] have average levels of achievement significantly different from the strata noted in each column. For instance, the first cell notes that the achievement levels in Spanish in fourth grade for the Upper Urban stratum are higher than for 5 (Lower Rural), 4 (Middle Rural), and 3 (Upper Rural).

TABLE 13.4

Distribution of the Averages of the Variables of Demand
among the Different Strata

		Upper Urban (1)	Lower Urban (2)	Upper Rural (3)	Middle Rural (4)	Lower Rural (5)
Participation of the association of parents (sixth grade)	$\overline{X}^*$ $\neq^\dagger$	37.02 > 5, 4	**39.41** > 5, 4	34.86	33.41	33.11
Total self-esteem of the student measured in fifth and sixth grades	$\overline{X}$ $\neq$	**155.55** > 5, 4, 2	147.73	149.41	145.71	143.27
Cultural capital of the family of the student	$\overline{X}$ $\neq$	**69.38** > 5, 2, 4	50.61 > 5	64.70 > 5, 2, 4	55.69 > 5, 2	43.44
Conditions for studying for the student	$\overline{X}$ $\neq$	**79.54** > 5, 3, 4, 2	73.82 > 5	71.67	72.54 > 5	69.35
Educational background of the student's family	$\overline{X}$ $\neq$	**48.75** > 5, 2, 3	42.12	46.87 > 5, 2	44.91 > 5, 2	40.88
School history of the student	$\overline{X}$ $\neq$	**84.15** > 5, 2, 4, 3	66.42	73.87 > 5	68.51 > 5	62.81
Nutrition index of the student	$\overline{X}$ $\neq$	**91.70** > 5, 3, 2, 4	79.83 > 5	79.06 > 5	87.00 > 5, 3, 2	68.20
Standard of living of the student's family	$\overline{X}$ $\neq$	**61.44** > 5, 4, 2, 3	36.54 > 5, 4	39.74 > 5, 4	32.74 > 5	18.09

*$\overline{X}$ indicates mean.
†$\neq$ indicates which strata [Upper Urban (1), Lower Urban (2), etc.] have average levels of achievement significantly different from the strata noted in each column.

than those obtained for the rural strata. This confirms that the method of stratification adopted produced the expected results.

Variables related to school provision. Table 13.5 presents the distribution among the different strata of the independent variables that refer to the conditions of school centers and to the operation of educational investments. As was evident in the preceding section, this analysis shows that the urban strata are in conditions clearly superior to those that correspond to the rural strata. This difference reflects a strong inequity in the distribution of the quality of the resources of schools that, in time, contribute to perpetuating the existing inequalities among school achievement of the diverse strata. The data confirm, again, that the variables representative of school provision are positively related to those that represent the characteristics of educational demand.

Variables representative of access to the investments of PARE (model 1). The results of the analysis of variance carried out to examine the form in which the different investments of PARE were distributed among the different sample strata appear in Table 13.6. The distribution of these investments among the schools was measured through dichotomous variables, which indicated whether each establishment received some component of the program or whether it remained on the periphery.

TABLE 13.5

Distribution of the Averages of the Variables of Provision
among the Different Strata

		Upper Urban (1)	Lower Urban (2)	Upper Rural (3)	Middle Rural (4)	Lower Rural (5)
Total matriculation (average of the three cycles) among total faculty	$\overline{X}$* $\neq^{\dagger}$	**36.09** > 3, 5, 4, 2	31.41 > 3, 5, 4	24.43	25.74	25.06
Performance of the teacher of fourth grade	$\overline{X}$ $\neq$	**55.90** > 5, 3, 4	54.76 > 5	53.53	53.87 > 5	51.96
Performance of the teacher of sixth grade	$\overline{X}$ $\neq$	**44.11** > 3, 4, 5	43.35 > 3	39.99	41.69	42.65 > 3
Academic performance of the director of the school	$\overline{X}$ $\neq$	**57.11** > 3, 4, 5, 2	52.87 > 3, 4, 5	49.64	49.67	51.05 > 4
Quality of the supervision of the school	$\overline{X}$ $\neq$	**66.48** >2, 4	61.03	60.69	62.16	64.30

*$\overline{X}$ indicates mean.
$^{\dagger}\neq$ indicates which strata [Upper Urban (1), Lower Urban (2), etc.] have average levels of achievement significantly
different from the strata noted in each column.

In general terms, it can be affirmed that program resources were distributed according to expectations. Unlike the observation in the preceding section, a tendency toward compensation for educational inequalities is noticeable. In almost all the investments analyzed, greater proportions of investments were assigned to the schools in which students pertaining to the Lower Rural stratum were enrolled. However, upon analyzing the distribution of the investments from the program destined to strengthen the process of school supervision, it was found that the schools attended by children pertaining to the Upper Urban stratum were favored, contrary to expectations, to a greater degree than the others.

Variables representative of the operation of PARE (model 2). Finally, Table 13.7 shows the results of the analysis of variance carried out to compare the way in which different investments from the program operated in the different strata. In eight of the eleven comparisons that showed statistically significant differences, it was found that the investments of PARE functioned in the most adequate form in those schools attended by children corresponding to the Lower Rural stratum. In all these cases, PARE managed to correct educational inequalities.

In the three remaining comparisons, however, the investments of the program functioned most adequately in those schools in which students are part of the Upper Urban stratum. These comparisons refer to the quality of the distribution of textbooks and guides for teachers and to the quantity of training courses that zone supervisors and technical trainers received.

TABLE 13.6

Distribution of the Averages of the Variables of PARE (Model 1)
among the Different Strata

		Upper Urban (1)	Lower Urban (2)	Upper Rural (3)	Middle Rural (4)	Lower Rural (5)
Dichotomy of the reception of the component of didactic materials in the three cycles	$\bar{X}^*$ $\neq^\dagger$	0.32	0.35	0.65 > 1, 2	0.60 > 1, 2	**0.85** >1, 2, 4, 3
Dichotomy of the reception of the component of textbooks in the three cycles	$\bar{X}$ $\neq$	0.71 > 2, 4	0.55	0.56	0.62	**0.79** > 2, 3, 4, 1
Dichotomy of the reception of the component of training in the three cycles	$\bar{X}$ $\neq$	0.82 > 2, 3, 4	0.58	0.63	0.63	**0.83** > 2, 3, 4
Dichotomy of the reception of the component of construction in the three cycles	$\bar{X}$ $\neq$	0.00	0.00	0.03	0.04	**0.22** > 2, 1, 3, 4
Dichotomy of the reception of the component of supervisory support in the three cycles	$\bar{X}$ $\neq$	**0.85** > 2, 3, 4	0.59	0.62	0.62	0.82 > 2, 3, 4
Dichotomy of the reception of the component of teacher incentives in the three cycles	$\bar{X}$ $\neq$	0.00	0.00	0.00	0.04 > 2, 1	**0.05** > 2, 1

*$\bar{X}$ indicates mean.
†$\neq$ indicates which strata [Upper Urban (1), Lower Urban (2), etc.] have average levels of achievement significantly different from the strata noted in each column.

Results of the Educational Impact of the Program   Table 13.8 reports the values assumed by the R^2 in the equations corresponding to the five clusters, to the two regression models described above, and to the four dependent variables that were constructed to carry out this study. In addition to the statistics mentioned above, the number of cases analyzed in each equation and the values obtained by performing the Durbin-Watson test[11] appear in Table 13.8.

The statistically significant values of the R^2 fluctuate between 0.025 and 0.515. It is interesting to note that in practically all the equations, the coefficients corresponding to model 2 are greater than those corresponding to model 1. All the coefficients of model 2 are statistically significant, and the highest has a value of 0.515. On the other hand,

TABLE 13.7

Distribution of the Averages of the Variables of PARE (Model 2) among the Different Strata

		Upper Urban (1)	Lower Urban (2)	Upper Rural (3)	Middle Rural (4)	Lower Rural (5)
Pedagogical operation of the didactic material for the students in the three cycles (quantity of material received per student balanced with the months the material was present in the school)	$\bar{X}^*$ $\neq^\dagger$	0.04	0.00	15.98 > 2, 1, 4	6.70 > 2, 1	**32.33** > 2, 1, 4, 3
Pedagogical operation of the didactic material for the teacher in the three cycles (quantity of each material received by months of exposure)	$\bar{X}$ $\neq$	3.32	23.79	139.19 > 1, 2, 4	87.00 > 1, 2	**182.41** > 1, 2, 4, 3
Pedagogical operation of office material in the three cycles (quantity of each material received by months of exposure)	$\bar{X}$ $\neq$	44.46	26.82	600.23 > 2, 1	579.86 > 2, 1	**872.19** > 2, 1, 4, 3
Pedagogical operation of the libraries in the three cycles (quantity of books granted per student)	$\bar{X}$ $\neq$	0.57	0.58	1.43	1.85 > 1, 2	**2.54** > 1, 2, 3, 4
Pedagogical operation of the quality of distribution (delivery opportunity, sufficiency) of the teacher guides in the three cycles	$\bar{X}$ $\neq$	**34.77** > 2, 3, 4	14.45	19.07	23.17 > 2	32.15 > 2, 3, 4
Pedagogical operation of the quality of distribution (delivery opportunity, sufficiency) of the textbooks in the three cycles	$\bar{X}$ $\neq$	**45.95** > 4, 2, 3, 5	30.94	32.14	30.40	37.33 > 4, 2
Pedagogical operation of the number of courses taken in the school among the total teachers (including the director) in the three cycles	$\bar{X}$ $\neq$	1.27	1.18	1.53	1.53 > 2, 1	**2.04** > 2, 1, 4, 3

(continued)

*$\bar{X}$ indicates mean.

$\dagger\neq$ indicates which strata [Upper Urban (1), Lower Urban (2), etc.] have average levels of achievement significantly different from the strata noted in each column.

TABLE 13.7*(continued)*

		Upper Urban (1)	Lower Urban (2)	Upper Rural (3)	Middle Rural (4)	Lower Rural (5)
Pedagogical operation of the office equipment[1] distributed to the supervisor (typewriter and mimeograph) in the three cycles	$\overline{X}$ ≠	0.49	0.58	0.58	0.62 > 1	**0.76** > 1, 2, 4
Pedagogical operation of the use of the truck[2] on the part of the supervisor in the three cycles	$\overline{X}$ ≠	—	—	—	—	—
Pedagogical operation of the training[3] received by the supervisor and by the technical assistant in the three cycles	$\overline{X}$ ≠	**5.40** > 3, 2, 4	4.26	4.04	4.62	5.15 > 2
Pedagogical operation of the office of supervision[4] constructed by PARE in the three cycles	$\overline{X}$ ≠	13.54 > 2	4.33	15.04 > 2	14.03 > 2	**16.43** > 2, 1
Pedagogical operation of the trimestrial economic incentive[5] received by the supervisor in the three cycles (months that they were received)	$\overline{X}$ ≠	—	—	—	—	—
Pedagogical operation of the economic incentive received by the teachers in the three cycles (months that it was received by number of teachers balanced by the cycles in which it was received)	$\overline{X}$ ≠	0.00	0.00	0.00	0.32	**0.49** > 2, 1

[1]The construct referring to office equipment adds up whether the supervisor has used the mimeograph assigned to the sector headquarters and whether he or she relies on the typewriter from PARE in the three cycles.

[2]The construct refers to the access and distribution of materials to schools which evaluates whether the supervisor made use of the truck distributed through PARE.

[3]The construct refers to the training component that adds up the courses taken by the supervisor and the technical assistant.

[4]The construct refers to the infrastructure component that quantifies months of office use on the part of the supervisor in the three cycles.

[5]The construct refers to economic incentives that quantifies the months that the supervisor received the incentive in the three cycles.

TABLE 13.8

Proportion of the Variances Explained by Each Model in the Different Equations

Equation		Lower Rural		Middle Rural		Upper Rural		Lower Urban		Upper Urban	
		Model 1	Model 2	Model 1	Model 2	Model 1	Model 2	Model 1	Model 2	Model 1	Model 2
I[1]	Total	0.097	0.144	0.237	0.246	NS*	0.355	0.131	0.145	0.117	0.127
	Cases	650	630	284	284	59	59	261	261	626	626
	D-W†	1.17	1.28	1.86	1.93	1.79	2.12	2.13	2.21	2.05	2.09
II[2]	Total	0.096	0.122	NS	0.180	NS	NS	0.125	0.193	0.152	0.154
	Cases	613	593	273	273	57	57	226	226	608	608
	D-W	1.22	1.24	1.45	1.51	2.14	2.50	2.00	2.15	2.07	2.09
III[3]	Total	NS	0.025	0.065	0.135	NS	NS	NS	0.224	0.087	0.109
	Cases	650	630	294	294	59	59	263	263	628	628
	D-W	1.75	1.82	1.73	1.87	2.52	2.67	1.66	1.95	2.02	2.09
IV[4]	Total	NS	0.052	0.049	0.089	0.438	0.515	0.164	0.178	0.109	0.142
	Cases	612	593	282	282	57	57	226	226	604	604
	D-W	1.81	1.88	1.85	2.00	2.45	2.68	2.14	2.18	2.01	2.08

I[1]   Vd (Dependent variable) = (6th Spanish – 4th Spanish)
II[2]   Vd (Dependent variable) = (5th Spanish + 6th Spanish) – 4th Span:sh
III[3]   Vd (Dependent variable) = (6th Mathematics – 4th Mathematics)
IV[4]   Vd (Dependent variable) = (5th Mathematics + 6th Mathematics) – 4th Mathematics

*NS = Not statistically significant
†D-W = Durbin Watson coefficient

some of the coefficients of model 1 are not statistically significant and the highest assumes a value of 0.438. In the rural clusters, the models have a greater capacity to explain the variance of the increases in achievement in the Spanish course. In the urban clusters, the opposite occurs.

In effect, in two clusters (Lower Rural and Middle Rural), the equations explained greater proportions of the dependent variable expressing learning gains—that is, the equation of the variable: (6th Spanish – 4th Spanish).[12]

In the other two groups (Upper Rural and Upper Urban), the models could explain a greater proportion of the variance of the dependent variable to which the number 4 was assigned, which was obtained through the formula (5th Mathematics + 6th Mathematics) – 4th Mathematics.[13]

Finally, in the Lower Urban stratum, the models had a greater capacity to explain the variance of the dependent variable to which the number 3 was assigned, which was constructed through the following expression: (6th Mathematics – 4th Mathematics).[14] This observation could be attributed to the fact that, as was already pointed out, the children pertaining to the Lower Rural stratum increased their achievement more rapidly than the students corresponding to the urban strata.

On the other hand, the greatest increases in achievement in mathematics corresponded to the students pertaining to the urban strata, which probably contributed to generating a greater correspondence between the behavior of the independent variables and the dependent variables that reflect achievement in this course. Remember that the regression equations that are being commented upon were designed from the concept of "educational production of operation," in which the independent variables (characteristic of the investments of the school system) are positively related to the dependent variables (resulting from the same system).

Contribution of the variables representative of educational demand. Table 13.9 shows the standard regression coefficients corresponding to the representative variables related to children's and families' conditions. These coefficients were obtained in the first stage of regression analysis (it is important to point out that in this table, and in subsequent tables, only regression coefficients are reported that, through the tests carried out, came out to be statistically significant).

As noted in the table, these variables have a greater explanatory capacity in the Upper Urban stratum (in which the R^2 assumes a value of 0.105, in relation to the dependent variable number 2: (6th Mathematics – 4th Mathematics). The opposite occurs in the Lower Rural and Middle Rural strata (in which the values of the R^2 fluctuate between 0 and 0.02). This may be attributable to the fact that, contrary to what happens in the rural strata, children integral to the Upper Urban stratum have relatively heterogeneous economic backgrounds. This is confirmed upon observing that the representative variable of the family's standard of living only intervenes with statistically significant regression coefficients in the equations corresponding to this stratum.

Attention is called to the importance of variables like cultural capital of the family, the school history of the student, and self-esteem in explaining student achievement. It is important to note that in only one of the equations (corresponding to the Upper Urban stratum), the variable that measures participation of the parents of families in school activities intervened with a statistically significant coefficient.

TABLE 13.9

Regression Coefficients: Variables Representative of Demand

	Equation 2 β	Equation 3 β	Equation 4 β
Lower Rural Stratum			
Cultural capital of the family			0.146
School history	0.107		
Contribution to the R^2 (model 1)	**0.017**		**0.014**
Contribution to the R^2 (model 2)	**0.020**		**0.013**
Middle Rural Stratum			
Self-esteem	0.194		
School history			0.132
Contribution to the R^2 (model 1)	**NS***		**NS**
Contribution to the R^2 (model 2)	**NS**		**NS**
Lower Urban Stratum			
Self-esteem	0.136		
Contribution to the R^2 (model 1)	**NS**		
Contribution to the R^2 (model 2)	**NS**		
Upper Urban Stratum			
Participation by parents of the family (sixth grade)			0.409
Standard of living of the family	0.155	0.099	0.101
Self-esteem	0.139		0.105
Contribution to the R^2 (model 1)	**0.105**	**0.030**	**0.040**
Contribution to the R^2 (model 2)	**0.105**	**0.030**	**0.040**

*NS = Not statistically significant

Contribution of the variables representative of school provision. As previously indicated, the variables representative of school provision were introduced into the regression equations in the second stage of analysis, after considering the contribution of the dependent variables that could be attributed to the variables representative of educational demand.

In the first place (see Table 13.10), it is evident that these variables explain more for the Middle Rural stratum (reflected in the two equations with the dependent variables referring to achievement in Spanish). The opposite occurs in the Upper Urban stratum.

As explained earlier, in the Upper Urban stratum the variable representing educational demand had greater weight. It is probable, therefore, that the variables corresponding to provision of education have less influence because of the existing interrelationship—above all, in this stratum—between the quality of the school investments and the characteristics of educational demand.

Upon analyzing the regression coefficients obtained in the equations referring to the rural strata, it is evident that the coefficients that correspond to the quality of teacher performance in sixth grade, the quality of the academic performance of the director, and the quality of school supervision are important.

TABLE 13.10

Regression Coefficients: Variables Representative of Provision

	Equation 1 β	Equation 2 β	Equation 3 β	Equation 4 β
Lower Rural Stratum				
Teacher performance (sixth grade)	0.154	0.132		0.115
Quality of supervision	0.142			
Contribution to the R^2 (model 1)	**0.047**	**0.035**		**NS**
Contribution to the R^2 (model 2)	**0.044**	**0.030**		**0.012**
Middle Rural Stratum				
Teacher performance (sixth grade)		0.229		0.142
Academic performance of the director	0.294	0.240		
Quality of supervision	0.283	0.237		
Student-teacher ratio		−0.174	−0.190	−0.217
Contribution to the R^2 (model 1)	**0.200**	**0.121**	**NS**	**NS**
Contribution to the R^2 (model 2)	**0.200**	**0.121**	**NS**	**NS**
Upper Rural Stratum				
Academic performance of the director			0.466	0.640
Quality of supervision	0.523			
Student-teacher ratio		−0.539		
Contribution to the R^2 (model 1)	**NS***	**NS**	**NS**	**0.309**
Contribution to the R^2 (model 2)	**NS**	**NS**	**NS**	**0.309**
Lower Urban Stratum				
Quality of supervision	0.217			
Contribution to the R^2 (model 1)	**NS**			
Contribution to the R^2 (model 2)	**0.043**			
Upper Urban Stratum				
Academic performance of the director	0.270	0.279	0.295	0.236
Quality of supervision	0.240	0.231		
Student-teacher ratio	−0.153			
Contribution to the R^2 (model 1)	**NS**	**0.025**	**NS**	**0.016**
Contribution to the R^2 (model 2)	**NS**	**0.025**	**NS**	**0.016**

*NS = Not statistically significant

The variable that reflects the quantity of students who are taught by each teacher intervenes in the regression coefficients with a negative sign indicating that the greatest variable is the size of the group, not school achievement. This finding is contrary to that reported in the international literature, in which it has been affirmed that school achievement is not significantly related to the size of the group.[15] Therefore, other studies should be taken into account. It is probable that the coefficients obtained in this case could be attributed to the fact the students who attend schools that rely on few teachers (for example, multigrade schools in which some teachers have to perform, in addition to their functions as teachers, managerial tasks) have lower academic achievement.

Contribution of the variables representative of access to the investments of PARE (model 1). As previously indicated, access to investments from PARE was measured through dichotomous variables, which were introduced in the regression equations in the third stage of analysis after having taken into account the effects generated by the variables representative of school provision and educational demand. Table 13.11 shows the coefficients of the variables in this group, which intervened in the equations with statistically significant values.

Having had access to the investments of the program—or even having remained on the periphery—has a greater explanatory power in the achievement of children who attend urban schools than for those enrolled in rural schools. However, it is important to note that almost all the coefficients that form part of the equations corresponding to the urban strata have negative signs (only the coefficients corresponding to the variable that reflects access to the component of PARE related to supervision have positive signs). This does not mean that having access to definite investments reduces school achievement. In reality, it is much more probable that the negative signs of these coefficients indicate that the children of greatest academic capacity are enrolled in schools that, because of their socioeconomic characteristics, were not assisted by PARE.

TABLE 13.11

Regression Coefficients: Variables Representative of Access
to the Components of PARE (Model 1)

	Equation 1 β	Equation 2 β	Equation 3 β	Equation 4 β
Lower Rural Stratum				
Didactic material	−0.121			
School libraries	0.229	0.326		
Supervisory support	−0.169	−0.153		
Teacher incentives			0.109	
Contribution to the R^2	**0.035**	**0.044**	**NS**	**NS**
Middle Rural Stratum				
Didactic material	0.455	0.364	0.375	
Teacher incentives			0.165	0.215
Contribution to the R^2	**0.037**	**NS***	**0.065**	**0.049**
Lower Urban Stratum				
Didactic material		0.361		
School libraries	−0.489	−0.489		
Teacher training	-0.632	−0.888		
Supervisory support	0.705	1.051		0.517
Contribution to the R^2	**0.088**	**0.125**		**0.049**
Upper Urban Stratum				
Didactic material			-0.251	-0.145
School libraries	-0.337	-0.147		0.262
Teacher incentives	-0.732	-0.314		0.209
Supervisory support	0.990	0.485		
Contribution to the R^2	**0.117**	**0.022**	**0.057**	**0.053**

*NS = Not statistically significant

Following the same rationale, upon analyzing the coefficients corresponding to the different components of PARE separately, it is possible to construct some explanatory hypotheses such as the following:

- *Didactic materials.* The students enrolled in schools that correspond to the Middle Rural and the Upper Urban strata that had access to these materials were able to improve their achievement. In addition, children who attend schools that correspond to the Upper Urban stratum that obtained high levels of achievement did not receive this particular PARE investment. Likewise, the children who attend schools that correspond to the Lower Rural stratum who improved their achievement most significantly achieved it without having had access to this investment. This last observation should be analyzed in greater detail in further studies because of doubts about the relevance of the materials offered in schools integral to this stratum.
- *School libraries.* The children enrolled in schools that correspond to the urban strata improved their returns without having had access to this component of PARE. On the contrary, those who attend schools in the Lower Rural stratum that had access to this investment improved their achievement in the Spanish course.
- *Teacher training.* The students integral to the Lower Urban stratum improved their returns in the Spanish course without having had access to this investment of the program.
- *Supervisory support.* The students of the urban schools who most significantly improved their achievements had access to this component of the program. Students in the Lower Rural stratum did not have access to this component of the program.
- *Teacher incentives.* Contrary to what was previously observed, the distribution of this investment seems to have been based on policies designed by the administrators of the program. In effect, the regression coefficients indicate that the students in schools in the Lower Rural and Middle Rural strata who had access to these incentives were able to improve their returns in the Spanish course. In contrast, the students pertaining to the Upper Urban stratum who achieved higher returns attend schools that, because of their socioeconomic characteristics, did not receive incentives.

Contribution of the variables representative of the operation of PARE (model 2). As stated earlier, these variables were designed to measure with greater precision the way in which the different investments of PARE functioned in the schools that received them. Those that obtained statistically significant regression coefficients appear in Table 13.12 with the values of the coefficients. It is important to note, however, that the contributions of these variables to the explanation of the dependent variables fluctuates: in the Lower Rural stratum, between 0.025 and 0.077; in the Middle Rural stratum, between 0.045 and 0.135; in the Upper Rural, between 0.207 and 0.355; and in the urban strata, between 0.038 and 0.193.

The behavior of the regression coefficients corresponding to the different components of PARE had the following characteristics:

- *Didactic materials for the students.* The variable that reflects the investment of didactic materials for students has coefficients with a negative sign in the equations related to achievement in Spanish in the Lower Rural stratum.
- *Didactic materials for the teachers.* In contrast to the previous observation, the variable that reports the operation of didactic materials for teachers has positive

Table 13.12

Regression Coefficients: Variables Representative of the Operation of the Components of PARE (Model 2)

	Equation 1 β	Equation 2 β	Equation 3 β	Equation 4 β
Lower Rural Stratum				
Teacher training		0.157		
Distribution of guides to the teachers	0.236	0.199		
Didactic material (students)		−0.128		
Didactic material (teachers)		0.137	0.114	0.133
Didactic material (office)		−0.125	−0.260	−0.161
Use of the truck by the supervisor	0.101		−0.096	
Supervisor training		−0.130		
Construction of the office for the supervisor		−0.121		
Incentive for the supervisors	−0.131		0.125	0.175
Incentive for the teachers	−0.097	−0.155		
Contribution to the R^2	**0.077**	**0.072**	**0.025**	**0.028**
Middle Rural Stratum				
Teacher training	−0.326	−0.505	−0.542	−0.408
Distribution of guides to the teachers			−0.430	−0.391
Distribution of textbooks				0.298
Use of the truck by the supervisor		−0.385		
Supervisor training			0.821	
Incentive for the teachers	−0.207	−0.188		
Contribution to the R^2	**0.045**	**0.059**	**0.135**	**0.089**
Upper Rural Stratum				
Teacher training				−0.825
Distribution of guides to the teachers	0.831			−0.597
Distribution of textbooks	−0.870			
Didactic material (office)	−0.647			
Incentive for the supervisors	1.389			
Contribution to the R^2	**0.355**			**0.207**
Lower Urban Stratum				
School libraries			−0.659	
Teacher training				−0.415
Distribution of guides to the teachers		−0.415		
Distribution of textbooks			−0.826	
Use of the truck by the supervisor		0.590	0.552	
Supervisor training		1.227	1.524	
Construction of the office for the supervisor				0.501
Incentive for the supervisors	−0.384			
Contribution to the R^2	**0.102**	**0.193**	**0.123**	**0.038**
Upper Urban Stratum				
School libraries	−0.685			
Distribution of guides to the teachers		0.531		
Distribution of textbooks	−0.699			
Didactic material (teachers)				0.508
Use of the truck by the supervisor	0.380			
Supervisor training	0.978			
Contribution to the R^2	**0.127**	**0.025**	**0.078**	**0.086**

coefficients in equations referring to the returns in Spanish and mathematics in the Lower Rural stratum. This may indicate that the didactic materials for teachers were designed and administered in an adequate manner.

- *Materials and equipment for school offices.* The variables for these materials and equipment have negative coefficients in the Lower Rural stratum. One can deduce that the children enrolled in schools pertaining to this stratum who obtained higher returns raised their achievement without these investments.

- *School libraries.* Upon measuring with greater precision the administration of this component, the regression coefficients indicate that only students in schools in the urban strata who improved their achievement in mathematics did not have access to school libraries. This may be attributed to the fact that, because of their high socioeconomic characteristics, these schools were not included in the universe targeted by the PARE program.

- *Distribution of teacher guides and textbooks.* The coefficients corresponding to these variables show that, in general, the administration of these investments had the expected corrective effects in the Lower Rural stratum for achievement in Spanish. At the same time, it can be inferred from the coefficients that the children enrolled in the schools pertaining to the other strata improved their achievement (especially in mathematics) without these investments operating adequately.

- *Teacher training.* The coefficients of the variable that reflects teacher training have positive signs in the models that refer to the achievement in Spanish for the Lower Rural and Middle Rural strata. In other functions, these coefficients have negative signs, principally in the functions relating to achievement in mathematics corresponding to the Middle Rural, Upper Rural, Lower Urban, and Upper Urban strata. These results could indicate—above all, in the case of the urban strata—that some schools with high levels of student achievement did not have access to this component of the program.

- *School supervisory support.* The operation of this component was analyzed through four variables: the training of supervisors, the construction of offices for functionaries, the use of trucks, and the distribution of incentives. The majority of the coefficients are negative in various equations corresponding to the Lower Rural stratum and positive in the equations corresponding to the urban strata. Therefore, it can be affirmed that the administration of supervisory support was generally not implemented in accordance with the design of the program.

- *Incentives for teachers.* In agreement with the analysis carried out, the distribution of this component had corrective effects only in those strata where incentives were allotted. The negative regression coefficients could indicate that the students of the schools in the Lower Rural stratum who improved their achievement in Spanish attended schools in which this component did not function adequately. However, it is necessary to clarify that this observation is based on a sample of schools that is too small for the results to be conclusive.

CONCLUSIONS AND RECOMMENDATIONS

In this section we summarize the main findings of this study and highlight the implications of these findings for policy reform and implementation.

Conclusions

PARE was based on a theoretical model that stemmed from the supposition that school achievement would improve if the inequalities that historically existed in school investments in different sociogeographic environments were reduced. To reduce these inequalities, PARE proposed providing schools with diverse investments directed at improving academic achievement through a strategy of positive discrimination. The results from the evaluation show that PARE did not sufficiently achieve its goals.

Despite some improvements in PARE schools, the scores on the achievement tests were not satisfactory. The scores were not high enough for students to pass their courses. Mathematics scores were generally lower than Spanish scores. Even the scores of students who had obtained higher scores at the beginning of the investigation remained stable or decreased over time.

The need for some type of compensatory program is highlighted by the fact that the achievement levels tended to be positively related to the family's socioeconomic level. Related to this, poor nutrition of the children also seems to be related to low achievement levels. Children in bilingual schools had especially low nutrition indicators, though children with low nutrition were also in the urban strata. Possibly related to their low nutritional levels, a high proportion of fourth-grade students in bilingual schools failed some course. The illiteracy rates of the parents—and to a greater degree that of the mothers—of the students in rural and bilingual schools is a variable that clearly intervenes in the achievement of the investigated schools. The indicators corresponding to the parents and to the mothers of the students are 9 percent and 11 percent, respectively, in urban schools; 15 percent and 14 percent, respectively, in rural schools; 11 percent and 26 percent, respectively, in bilingual schools; and 15 percent and 27 percent, respectively, in the community courses.

Many flaws in the implementation of PARE can be improved upon. The implementation of the program did not reflect many of the characteristics implicit in the model from which it originated. The selection of the program components were not based on an investigation of the needs that were unsatisfied. In general, the components were administered in a disjointed form, and some were not provided in a timely fashion. These problems are exemplified in the gap between the pedagogical theories on which the training courses were based (constructivism) and those that directed the design of some didactic materials. These teacher training courses were not always given by qualified personnel. Often supervisors did not help with training teachers as they should have.

Recommendations

The achievement results indicate the importance of planning the distribution of educational resources according to the principle of positive discrimination. The study confirmed a positive relationship between educational demands and available investments for schools. The strategy of positive discrimination should be expanded to include the placement of teachers and support for supervisors. Currently, the most educated and experienced teachers are sent to urban schools. Instead, they should be sent to the poorer rural schools where the most skilled teachers are needed due to the additional challenges related to poverty. Additionally, supervisory support should be greater for rural schools. Though this component was included in the plans for PARE, it was not implemented according to the strategy of positive discrimination.

The previous sections illustrate that the model on which PARE was based was not implemented. Therefore, the unsatisfactory results cannot all be attributed to the conception of the program. The data from this study only permit affirming that the results were generated through inadequate implementation of the program. To see what could be achieved through a program of this nature, implementation of the current PARE must be improved. The following recommendations are based on the problems highlighted in this study.

PARE attempted to simultaneously reduce educational inequalities and radically transform the learning and teaching processes of the poorest sectors. Unfortunately, the new educational models aimed at improving the quality of the educational processes were not tested in the context of Mexico's poorest communities. It therefore is impossible to guarantee the effectiveness of the new pedagogical models transplanted to a context for which they were not designed. Nonetheless, the teacher trainings for PARE were geared toward introducing the innovative techniques designed by SEP.

New compensatory programs should propose at least two objectives. The first consists of improving the quality of the school investments and school conditions, a prerequisite for effective teaching and learning. Logically, there must be adequate planning of the distribution of the corrective resources, based on a knowledge of the needs that should be satisfied.

The second objective is to develop experimental educational models that could produce satisfactory effects in precarious sociogeographic conditions.[16]

To achieve the first objective, the compensation of inequalities, three distinct actions are necessary. First, identify the central needs of students in different types of schools. Second, identify strategies that can reddress, in the short-term, the needs identified within each type of school. These could include strategies aimed at enhancing student achievement, retaining school leavers, and fostering parental participation in instructional activities. Third, identify the curriculum of training programs that would enable teachers to design the strategies mentioned above, as well as to produce the learning materials to support teachers in this process.

To achieve the second objective, the development of alternative educational approaches, it would be necessary to develop an instructional system that allows for more individualized learning.

To carry out these recommendations, there must be coordination between an interdisciplinary team of specialists and SEP. Many of the problems with PARE may be solved with better-coordinated implementation. With its fundamental strategy based on positive discrimination, PARE has great potential for significantly improving the achievement of Mexico's poorest students if it is fully implemented with the above recommendations. Programs such as PARE that address the dire educational situation should be the priority for Mexico's government.

NOTES

1. Compare Muñoz Izquierdo and Ulloa (1992).
2. Compare Schmelkes (1994).

3. As the Gini coefficient, this index ranges from 0 to 1, the closer to 0 the greater equality and the closer to 1 the greater the inequality.
4. The budget of the program in relation to public education's expenses during the period 1991–1994 represented 0.7 percent (this figure is based on calculations with data provided by Prawda [1999]).
5. In Mexico, primary education for the school-aged population is provided through three types of services: general, bilingual-bicultural, and community courses. The primary modality is provided through the state or private organizations in urban and rural mediums (they are distinguished by the quantity of inhabitants: a location with more than 2,500 inhabitants is considered urban). In this type of school, the standardization and evaluation of instruction are national and depend on the SEP. The bilingual-bicultural schools are provided in indigenous communities. They adapt the primary school programs to the regional necessities. They are under the jurisdiction of the General Direction of Indigenous Education. The community courses function in communities that, because of their poverty and isolation, have not received the benefits of education. All the schools are unitary—that is, they have one teacher for all grades—and depend on CONAFE (the decentralized organ of SEP).
6. Available data showed that in 1990 Michoacan scored below the national average on the following statistics: school retention, promotion rates, functional illiteracy, and terminal efficiency.
7. Annual teacher absences can reach seventy days in community courses and rural schools, forty-five days in bilingual schools, and thirty days in urban schools.
8. The directors and supervisors decide on the rotation of teachers who live in localities different from those in which they work and who prefer to work in different geographic zones.
9. A deep analysis of Indian educational conditions is found in Sylvia Schmelkes' chapter in this book.
10. We arrived at the conclusion to proceed in this manner once different efforts to control the variables of demand and provision were exhausted. We had tried to control the variables through the segmentation at the interior of each stratum in agreement with terciles of representative variables.
11. In general, specialists agree that a statistically significant multicollinearity exists when the values resulting from the application of this procedure fluctuate between 1.8 and 2.2.
12. The values assumed by the R^2 are 0.144 and 0.246, respectively.
13. The values assumed by the R^2 are 0.515 and 0.142, respectively.
14. The value assumed by the R^2 is 0.244.
15. From a review of the different studies carried out about this theme, the following conclusion was drawn: "It cannot be concluded that an increase in the size of the class necessarily brings about a decrease in the level of academic achievement of the students" (cf. Haddad Wadi in Latapí 1991).
16. See the References to this chapter.

REFERENCES

Bacchus, Kazim. 1990. Curriculum reform: Quality in basic education. Background policy paper. *Improving the Quality of Basic Education,* vol I. London: Commonwealth Secretariat.
Berman, Paul, and Milbrey W. McLaughlin. 1977. *Federal Programs Supporting Educational Change. Volume IV: The Findings in Review.* Santa Monica, Calif.: Rand Corporation.
Calvo, Gloria. 1997. *Nuevas Formas de Enseñar y de Aprender.* Santiago: Programa Regional de Educación en América Latina (PREAL).
Carnoy, Martin, and Claudio Mora Castro. 1996. ¿Qué rumbo debe tomar el mejoramiento de la educación en América Latina? Buenos Aires: Seminario sobre Reforma Educativa, Banco Interamericano de Desarrollo.

Colbert, Vicky, Clemencia Chiappe, and Jairo Arboleda. 1993. The New School Program: More and better primary education for children in rural areas in Colombia. In *Effective Schools in Developing Countries,* eds. Henry M. Levin and Marlaine E. Lockheed, 52–68. Stanford, Calif.: Stanford University Press.

Consejo Nacional de Fomento Educativo. 1993. Programa para abatir el rezago educativo en educación básica. Mexico City: UPC-PAREB, CONAFE (July).

Crandall, David, et al. 1982. *People, Policies and Practice: Examining the Chain of School Improvement,* vols. 1–10. Andover, Mass.: The Network.

Dalin, Per. 1973. *Case Studies of Educational Innovation. Volume IV: Strategies for Educational Innovation.* Paris: Center for Educational Research and Improvement/OECD.

Dalin, Per, Tekle Ayono, A. Biazen, B. Dibaba, M. Jahan, Mathew B. Miles, and Carlos Rojas. 1994. *How Schools Improve: An International Report.* London: Cassell.

Dalin, Per, and Hans G. Rolff. 1993. *Changing the School Culture.* London: Cassell.

Fullan, Michael G., and Suzanne Stiegelbauer. 1991. *The New Meaning of Educational Change.* New York: Teachers College Press.

Haddad, Wadi. 1991. Efectos educacionales del tamaño de la clase. In *Educación y Escuela: Lecturas Básicas para Investigadores de la Educación,* Vol. 1, ed. Pablo Latapí, 95–110. Mexico City: Nueva Imagen.

Huberman, Michael A., and Matthew B. Miles. 1984. *Innovation up Close; How School Improvements Work.* New York: Plenum Press.

McEwan, Patrick. 1995. Primary school reform for rural development: An evaluation of Colombian new schools. Mimeograph. Washington, D.C.: InterAmerican Development Bank.

Martinez Rizo, Felipe. 1994. La desigualdad educativa en Mexico. *Revista Latinoamericana de Estudios Educativos* XXII(2): 59–120.

Muñoz Izquierdo, Carlos, and Manuel Ulloa. 1994. Cuatro tesis sobre el origen de las desigualdades educativas: Una reflexión. *Revista Latinoamericana de Estudios Educativos* XXII (2): 11–58.

Noriega Ramírez, Carmen. 1996. Estudio sobre el programa para abatir el rezago educativo 1991–1995. Mexico City: Universidad Autónoma Metropolitana.

OECD. 1996. *Combating Failure at School: Report on the Activity.* Paris: OECD.

Ornelas, Carlos. 1995. *El Sistema Educativo Mexicano: La Transición de Fin de Siglo.* Mexico City: Fondo de Cultura Económica.

Prawda, Juan. 1999. Reflexiones en torno al sistema educativo mexicano. Mimeograph. Mexico City (May).

Psacharopoulos, George, Carlos Rojas, and Eduardo Velez. 1993. Achievement evaluation of Colombia's Escuela Nueva: Is multigrade the answer? *Comparative Education Review* 37(3): 263–276.

Reimers, Fernando. 1996. The role of nongovernmental organizations in promoting educational innovation: A case study in Latin America. In *Education and Development: Tradition and Innovation,* eds. James Lynch, Celia Modgil, and Sohan Modgil, 33–44. London: Cassell.

Rojas, Carlos, and Zoraida Castillo. 1988. Evaluación del programa Escuela Nueva en Colombia. Bogotá: Instituto SER de Investigación.

Schiefelbein, Ernesto. 1991. *In Search of the School of the XXI Century: Is the Escuela Nueva the Right Pathfinder?* Santiago: UNESCO-UNICEF.

Schmelkes del Valle, Sylvia I. 1993. Mejoramiento de la calidad de la educación primaria: Estudio comparativo de cinco zonas del estado de Puebla. Mexico City: Universidad Iberoamericana.

Secretaría de Educación Pública. 1992. *Acuerdo Nacional para la Modernización de la Educación Básica.* Mexico City: SEP.

Secretaría de Educación Pública. 1993. *Articulo 3°. Constitucional y Ley General de Educación.* Mexico City: SEP.

Secretaría de Educación Pública. 1985–1991. *Estadísticas Básicas del Sistema Educativo Nacional. Inicio y Fin de Cursos Ciclos Escolares 1985–1986, 1987–1988 y 1990–1991*. Mexico City: SEP.

Slavin, Robert E., et al. 1984. Combining cooperative learning and individualized instruction: Effects on student mathematics achievement, attitudes and behaviors. *Elementary School Journal* 84(4): 409–422.

Thomas, Christopher, and Christopher Shaw. 1992. *Issues in the Development of Multigrade Schools*. Washington, D.C.: World Bank, Technical Paper No. 172.

Verspoor, Adriaan M. 1989. *Pathways to Change: Improving the Quality of Education in Developing Countries*. Washington, D.C.: World Bank, Discussion Paper No. 53.

Weeler, Christopher W., Stephen Raudenbush, and Aida Pasigna. 1989. Policy initiatives to improve school quality in Thailand: An essay on implementation, constraints and opportunities for educational improvement. Cambridge, Mass: Harvard Institute for International Development, Bridges Research Report Series, No. 5.

Williams, Phillip. 1996. Changing schools. In *Our Children at Risk*, ed. Centre for Educational Research and Innovation, 79–111. Paris: Organization for Economic Cooperation and Development.

Commentary

Emily Hannum, Harvard Graduate School of Education

Social reproduction emerges as a key concern in this chapter. The authors thoroughly examine the policy and social context of schooling in Mexico, then discuss the implications of PARE for educational equity. The chapter is a useful resource for those interested in education policy or educational inequality in Mexico, as it devotes much space to discussions of policy and inequality and to presentation of relevant data.

I found interesting the point that children are more likely to abandon school during the same school year than between school years. School leaving comes about when children with lower levels of academic achievement withdraw *in anticipation* of failing exams. The authors conclude that school leaving in this case stems more from family pull-outs than from institutional push-outs. The authors highlight family-related barriers to schooling, including illiteracy and lack of support in the household for schooling.

A boy sells ice cream in the central market in Lima, Peru.
[UNICEF/96-0469/Alejandro Balaguer (Peru)]

14

Education and Poverty in Peru

Kin Bing Wu, The World Bank
Patricia Arregui, Grupo de Analisis para el Desarrollo (GRADE), Peru
Pete Goldschmidt, University of California, Los Angeles
Arturo Miranda, Universidad de San Marcos, Peru
Suhas Parandekar, The World Bank
Jaime Saavedra, GRADE, Peru
Juan Pablo Silva, Universidad Catolica, Peru

In the late 1980s and early 1990s, Peru experienced enormous economic and political upheavals. Hyperinflation reached 7,000 percent by 1990, and the country was torn by civil unrest. Structural reforms and the ending of the Shining Path insurgency brought stability to the country by 1994. Within three years, inflation was reduced to 7 percent and GDP growth reached 7 percent in real terms, among the highest in the region second only to that of Chile (World Bank 1999a). In 1997, Peru enjoyed a gross domestic product (GDP) per capita of $2,460 (World Bank 1998). Despite impressive growth, however, disparity in income distribution remains among the highest in the region. In 1997, about 49 percent of the population of 24 million people in Peru lived in poverty and 15 percent in extreme poverty, with a concentration in the highland and the jungle (World Bank 1999b).

Viewed against this larger political and economic background, Peru has achieved rates of participation in education that are particularly impressive. In 1997, the education system enrolled practically all of the six- to eleven-year-olds, nearly 80 percent of the twelve- to sixteen-year-olds, and over 30 percent of the seventeen- to twenty-five-year-olds. This progress was made from a very low base only half a century ago. Between 1950 and 1997, enrollment expanded 6.6 times, more than double the threefold increase of the population (Diaz et al. 1995). Total enrollment grew from a mere 14 percent of the population in 1950 to 36 percent in 1997. As a consequence, over the period, the average education level of the population of age fifteen and over increased from 1.9 years to 8.6 years, and the illiteracy rate was reduced from 58 percent to 11 percent. Female illiteracy was reduced from 70 to 18 percent, and rural illiteracy from over 60 to 29 percent. Other countries, by contrast, have achieved far less: Figure 14.1 shows Peruvian gross enrollment ratios in a remarkably favorable light in international comparison.

FIGURE 14.1

International Comparison of Enrollment of Students Between the Ages of 3 and 23

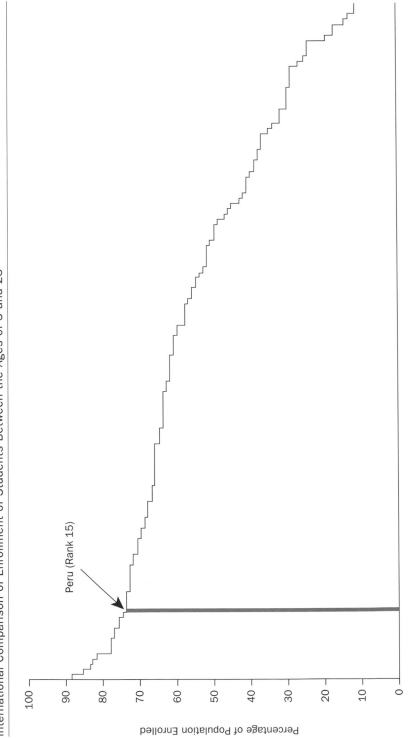

Peru (Rank 15)

Percentage of Population Enrolled

Source: Edstats Database of the World Bank.

These accomplishments in education are all the more remarkable when taking into account Peru's historically low level of public spending on education, which stood at only 3 percent of GDP in 1997. When its level of public spending on education as a percentage of GDP is compared with other countries', as in Figure 14.2, Peru's position changes markedly from the enrollment position that Figure 14.1 portrayed. In comparison with a group of nonsocialist, lower-middle-income countries, Peru's level of public expenditure on education is lower than what should be expected of countries with its income level (Figure 14.3).

Furthermore, because pensions of retired teachers and administrators in Peru were paid out of the recurrent expenditure on education, actual government expenditures that went to operate the public education system were only about 2.4 percent of GDP in 1997. This was far below the Latin American and Caribbean regional average of about 4.5 percent (which were net of pensions) (UNESCO 1998). The Organization for Economic Cooperation and Development (OECD) average was around 4.6 percent (OECD 1998). Even if the level of public spending on education as a percentage of GDP had been similar, Peru's need for educational services is much greater because the proportion of its school-aged population is much higher (36 percent) than those in, for example, France and the United Kingdom (16 percent), Mexico (28 percent), Colombia (26 percent), and Chile (23 percent).

What can explain the puzzle that Peru has been able to achieve an unusually high participation rate with such a low level of public spending on education? Is it because public resources have been better used and targeted than those in other countries? Is it because Peruvian households have invested heavily in education? Has expansion of basic education come at the expense of qualitative improvement? This chapter[1] aims to answer these questions by examining public and private finance on education and their impact on quality, internal efficiency, and labor market outcomes. It will address these issues particularly from the perspective of the poor—of what the outcomes of policy for the poor have been and of how future education policies might best serve the task of poverty reduction.

This chapter argues that both the government's ability to contain personnel costs and limit spending on tertiary education and households' willingness to bear the direct and indirect costs of education have contributed to the attainment of high enrollment at a relatively low level of public spending on education. However, this achievement has come at the expense of quality and opportunities for the poor. The very low level of public spending, despite being distributed relatively evenly across consumption quintiles overall, has resulted in unequal outcomes because of the need for complementary financial inputs from households, which can impose a heavy burden on the poor. Increasing public expenditures on education and targeting specific assistance to the disadvantaged groups, particularly to indigenous people, is necessary to provide the educational opportunities for the poor that are essential to a long-term reduction in poverty.

PUBLIC EXPENDITURES ON EDUCATION

Government allocation constitutes the most important source of funding for education, accounting for 17 percent of central government spending in 1997. Between 1970 and 1997, public expenditures on education fluctuated widely, peaking in 1972 at 3.7 percent

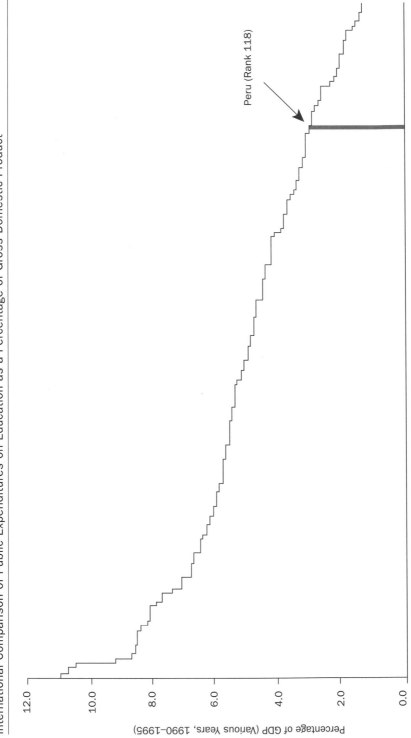

FIGURE 14.2

International Comparison of Public Expenditures on Education as a Percentage of Gross Domestic Product

Peru (Rank 118)

Percentage of GDP (Various Years, 1990–1995)

Source: Edstats Database of the World Bank.

FIGURE **14.3**

Public Spending on Education and GNP per Capita
in Lower-Middle-Income Countries

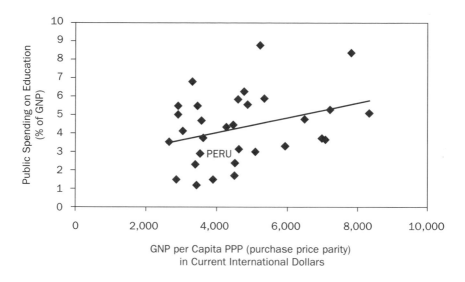

Public Spending on Education
(% of GNP)

GNP per Capita PPP (purchase price parity)
in Current International Dollars

of GDP, falling to 2.2 percent in 1988 at the lowest point, then gradually recovering to 3 percent in 1997.[2] Even though public expenditures on education were increased steadily throughout the 1990s, the level in 1997 was still lower than that of 1972 (see Figure 14.4). The enormous fluctuation of public expenditures on education over time reflected deep-seated instability and unpredictability in resource allocation, which made it difficult for any strategic planning and undermined program continuity (see Figure 14.5).

The trend of public spending in the 1990s showed recovery from the extremely low base in the late 1980s. Between 1990 and 1997, total public expenditures on education increased by 94 percent, while capital investments grew by 980 percent (see Figure 14.6). By contrast, salaries and compensation increased by 74 percent and pensions by 40 percent. Salaries and compensation accounted for only 57 percent of total public expenditures, while pensions accounted for about 22 percent. This level of personnel costs is low by international comparison because, in many countries, salaries often take up over 90 percent of the total education budget. Thus, Peru's ability to contain personnel costs is key to its ability to maintain fiscal discipline, although not without adverse effects on morale and quality of the teaching force.

In 1997, about 6 percent of total public expenditures was spent on initial education, 27 percent on primary education, 19 percent on secondary education, 2 percent on nonuniversity tertiary education, 16 percent on university education, and 21 percent on administration.[3]

Due to relatively slow growth of enrollment in public institutions, expansion of private education, and increased public spending on education between 1990 and 1997, per student recurrent public expenditures increased by 70 percent in initial education,

FIGURE **14.4**

Public Expenditures on Education as a Percentage
of Gross Domestic Product, 1970–1997

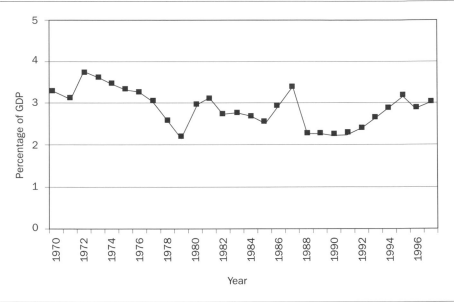

FIGURE **14.5**

Total Recurrent and Capital Expenditures on Education, 1970–1997
(Constant 1997 Soles)

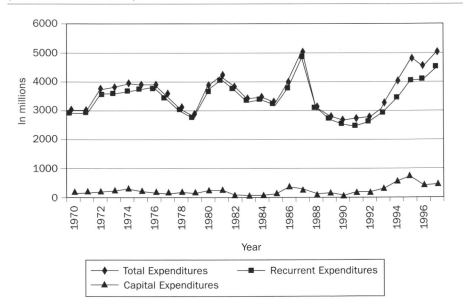

FIGURE 14.6

Composition of Public Expenditures on Education, 1990–1997

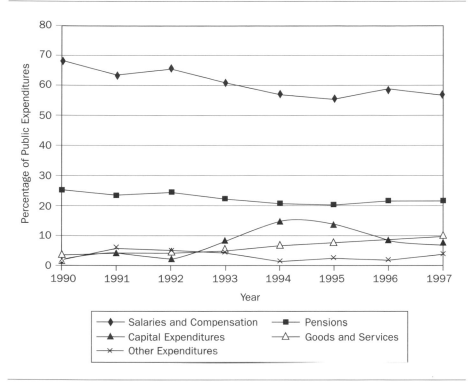

87 percent in primary education, 71 percent in secondary education, 79 percent in nonuniversity tertiary education, and 335 percent in university education (see Figure 14.7). While the percentage increase was impressive, it started from a very low base.

Converted to U.S. dollars,[4] per student public spending (inclusive of pensions) in 1997 was $175 in initial education, $201 in primary education, $260 in secondary education, $324 in nonuniversity tertiary education, and $1,255 in university education. The difference in the unit costs between higher education and primary education in Peru is six times. This is relatively lower than that in many countries of Latin America (which may be as high as twenty times). In many countries in the region, higher education unit costs are often above $2,000. The relative restraint in public spending on higher education is another factor contributing to Peru's ability to contain public expenditures on education.

To assess how equitable public expenditures are distributed among the rich and poor, a Lorenz curve[5] was constructed to reflect the proportion of recurrent expenditures on education which accrue to each consumption quintile. Because of the lack of information on unit cost by consumption quintile, it is not possible to estimate the variation in public spending in schools attended by children from different socioeconomic backgrounds. The Lorenz curves in Figures 14.8 and 14.9 were constructed under the assumption that unit costs are uniform for all quintiles. The Lorenz curve in Figure 14.8

FIGURE 14.7

Per Student Recurrent Public Expenditures on Education by Level, 1990–1997
(Constant 1997 Soles)

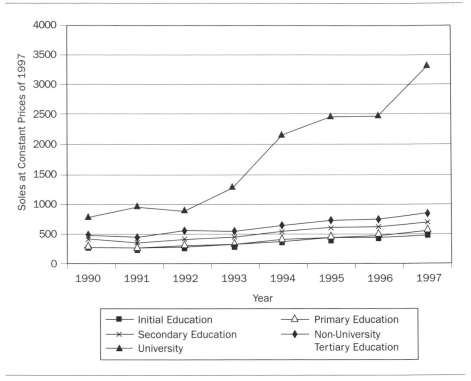

shows that the distribution of public expenditures on education across consumption
quintiles was *relatively* equitable.

Figure 14.9 shows a number of Lorenz curves with recurrent public expenditures
disaggregated by level of education. Public spending on pre-primary and primary education was skewed toward the lowest income quintile (29 percent) because of the universal enrollment in primary education and because families in the top two quintiles
tend to send their children to private schools, leaving the public system to the less well
off. In contrast, public spending on higher education was skewed toward the highest
income quintile because 47 percent of students in higher education were from the top
quintile and only 4 percent were from the bottom quintile.

Given that per student spending varied substantially by department, the assumption
of uniform unit costs across all quintiles may not hold. Therefore, four more simulations were run to test how equitable the distribution of public expenditures would
be under various assumptions (see Figure 14.10). These were compared against the
original in Figure 14.8, which is labeled Simulation 1 in Figure 14.10. Simulation 2
took pensions away from public expenditures. The curve became less equitable than
Simulation 1 but did not differ substantially. Simulation 3 varied the unit costs by
quintile to examine the impact. While the unit costs of the middle quintile were held

FIGURE 14.8

Lorenz Curve for Incidence of Public Expenditures

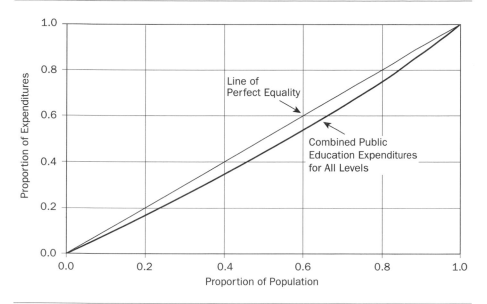

FIGURE 14.9

Lorenz Curves by Education Level

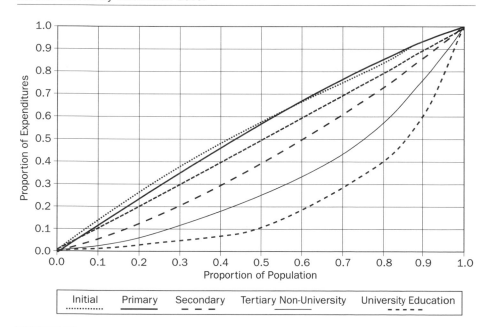

FIGURE 14.10

Lorenz Curves for Incidence with Five Simulations

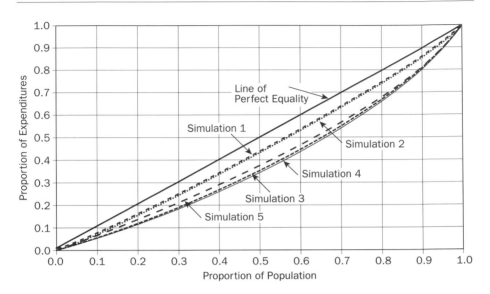

unchanged for all levels of education, that of the second quintile was reduced to 15 percent below that of the middle quintile, and that of the first quintile was reduced to 30 percent lower. Similarly, the unit costs of the fourth quintile were raised 15 percent higher than that of the third quintile, and the top quintile was 30 percent higher. The Lorenz curve of Simulation 3 was dramatically more unequal. Simulation 4 combined the principles of Simulations 2 and 3 and repeated the same experiment after taking out the pensions. Predictably, the distribution was the worst among all simulations.

Simulation 5 tested the hypothesis of how higher unit costs of university education and uniform unit costs for all pre-university education affect the equity of distribution. The Lorenz curve of Simulation 5 was almost as unequal as those in Simulations 3 and 4. This experiment demonstrated that the relatively low unit costs of university education were very important to why the overall Lorenz curve looked equitable in Simulations 1 and 2. However, if school resources were distributed inequitably across quintiles, no matter how high enrollment ratios were in basic education, the Lorenz curve would look worse. The policy implication is that unless public expenditures are increased and targeted to the poor to ensure quality, the system would be unequal even if enrollment in primary education were universal.

HOUSEHOLD EXPENDITURES ON EDUCATION

Peruvian households contribute relatively more to education than their counterparts in many countries, so that total expenditures on education in Peru (public and household) are more in line with the international comparators. Our analysis of Instituto Cuanto's

FIGURE 14.11

Lorenz Curve for Incidence of Private Expenditures, All Levels

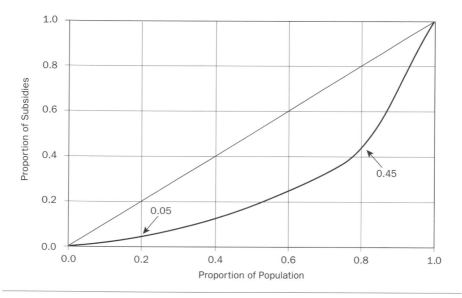

1997 household survey data for this study found that household expenditures on education were about 2 percent of GDP, higher than the 1.3 percent of GDP spent by households in the much richer OECD countries. This was also higher than that of other Latin American upper-middle-income countries such as Argentina (0.75 percent) but lower than Chile (2.5 percent) (OECD 1998).

However, the key question is not whether households in Peru spend too much or too little in international comparison but what the high level of spending by households implies for educational policy in Peru. Are certain groups of Peruvians deprived of educational benefits because they are too poor to afford the necessary expenditures? What variables determine the variation in expenditures across households?

The Lorenz curve for total private expenditures (including spending on both private and public schools) shows the lowest quintile accounting for only about 4 percent of the expenditures and the upper quintile as much as 57 percent (see Figure 14.11). When only examining household expenditures on public schools, the Lorenz curve improves slightly (see Figure 14.12). Peruvian households spent approximately 41 percent for the education of children who were enrolled in public schools to complement the public spending on education. These household expenditures included registration fees and contributions to parents' associations, uniforms, school lunches, and transportation. Figure 14.13 shows the Lorenz curve of household expenditures on public primary schools; the situation was only worse in regard to secondary schooling.

The level of household expenditures on education varied tremendously by income level—the total amount spent on education by the richest quintile in Peru was thirteen times the total amount spent on education by the poorest quintile. Even this figure is

FIGURE 14.12

Lorenz Curve for Incidence of Private Expenditures, Only Public Schools

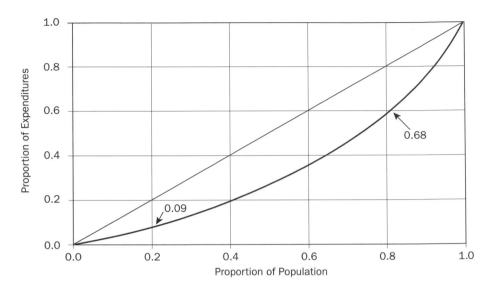

likely to be underestimated because the household survey questionnaire which provided the data for analysis did not include spending on extra tutoring and other school activities such as field trips.

Because recurrent public expenditures cover mostly salaries, household contributions in registration fees and to the parents' associations are often used by schools for repair and maintenance, educational materials and supplies, and water and electricity. The disparity in the ability of parents to pay, therefore, has contributed to the disparity in school resources. Our analysis of the Ministry of Education's 1994 survey of some 400 rural and urban public schools in Lima and Cusco found that the annual parents' contribution to very large urban schools (with an average of over 1,600 students) amounted to 11,735 soles, in contrast to only 279 soles of contribution to small rural schools (with an average of 96 students). Therefore, when taking into account household expenditures, the difference in total expenditures on the education of students from poor and rich households is striking. The very inadequacy in the level of public support makes basic education fall far short of becoming a socially equalizing force.

Nevertheless, Peruvians value education highly and would go to great lengths to make sure that their children have an education. Analysis of the behavioral aspect of household education expenditures (Engel curves) found that the income elasticity of demand was a low 27 percent. This means that education expenditures are considered to be a necessity by Peruvian households and that there is a strong underlying demand for education, by both rich and poor. The income elasticities were lower for the more disadvantaged groups—12 percent for the poorest quintile, 14 percent for rural populations, and 10 percent for indigenous people.

FIGURE 14.13

Lorenz Curve for Incidence of Private Expenditures, Only Primary Schools

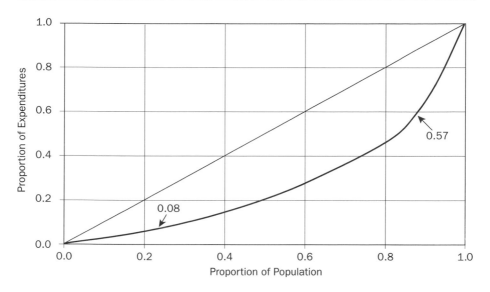

The finding resonated with that of Rodriguez and Alber (1997) for a sample of Peruvian children six to sixteen years old. They found that even if there was a positive relationship between income of the family and the probability of school attendance, the estimated marginal effects were small. Moreover, the magnitude of the negative effect of family income over participating in the labor force was also small. That is why enrollments did not decline, and child labor did not increase, during the time of economic crisis.

From the point of view of educational policy, however, the government cannot rely on general increases in income to bring about greater expenditures on education. For every doubling of household income, the budget share spent on education would go up by only a quarter on average. For the poor, rural people, and indigenous people, their budget share in education would go up by only 10 percent or so. Given that levels of household expenditures on education vary vastly by income level, there is a great need for specific policy instruments to address the inability of poorer households to incur additional expenditures.

INTERNAL EFFICIENCY, QUALITY, AND LABOR MARKET OUTCOMES

The inadequacy of public spending on education, coupled with the inability of the poor to incur additional costs, translates into uneven access, large variability in learning outcomes, disparity in school completion rates, and unequal labor market outcomes. Although enrollment among the six to eleven age group (which corresponds to the age for primary education) has been universal irrespective of socioeconomic status, gender, and urban or rural location, it has not been evenly distributed in other age groups which correspond to early childhood, secondary, and tertiary education. In 1997, in the rural areas only 15 percent of the relevant age cohort enrolled in initial education, 49 percent in secondary education, and 8 percent in tertiary education, in contrast to the urban areas' 16 percent in initial education, 78 percent in secondary education, and 30 percent in tertiary education. The gender and rural/urban differences in net enrollment ratios were striking at the tertiary level even within the same quintile. For example, in the rural areas, only 2 percent of girls and 6 percent of boys of the first quintile enrolled, but in the urban areas, 16 percent of girls and 11 percent of boys of the same quintile were in school.

Rural children tend to enter late into the school system because they often have to walk to school and only older children can endure the journey. Due to the need to help their families and due to vulnerability to climatic factors, absenteeism and repetition are also high among rural students (Montero et al. 1998). The analysis by Saavedra and Felices (1997) of the 1994 Cuanto household survey confirmed the relationship among repetition, income, and rural location—the percentage of repeaters went from 17 in Lima, to 24 in other urban areas, and rose further to 35 in rural areas. Repetition is also much higher in public schools than in private schools. The study also revealed the relationship between income and dropout status (defined as the proportion of individuals in a cohort who have not finished an educational level and are not enrolled in any educational institution). For individuals aged seventeen to twenty-four, the dropout rates were 13 percent in metropolitan Lima, 20 percent in other urban areas, and 54 percent in rural areas.

Analyzing school survival rates using a 1997 household survey, we found that although children from rich and poor families started out the same in the first year of schooling, they rapidly diverged after the fourth grade (see Figure 14.14). Although inequality is not uncommon in developing countries, some countries have done a better job than others. Figure 14.15 provides a contrast with Jamaica (World Bank 1999c). Although the two methods used are different, they both indicate the extent to which the system retains students. In Jamaica, which has a GDP per capita of $1,690, the majority of students in the poorest quintile remain in school up to the ninth grade, in contrast to the rapid dropoff of poor students in Peru toward the end of primary education. Although the small size of Jamaica helps, it should be noted that the commitment of public resources to education is also much higher, reaching 7.6 percent of GDP in 1998.

Uneven school quality has compounded the disadvantages associated with student background and contributed to low internal efficiency and poor achievement. Analysis of the 1996 fourth-grade mathematics assessment test by Goldschmidt for this study found significant differences in the average 1996 fourth-grade mathematics outcomes among gender, school types, language groups, and regions (see Table 14.1). To the extent that the coefficient of variability is large on the country average, and much larger among certain subgroups, the disparity in students' mastery of cognitive skills is a key issue in education.

The between-school variance in achievement (that is, variance accounted for by differences in characteristics among schools, as opposed to differences among students) is an important indicator of inequality in learning outcomes; over 30 percent is normally considered to be serious. In studies done on achievement in primary education in

FIGURE **14.14**

School Survival Rates by Poorest and Richest Consumption Quintiles, 1997

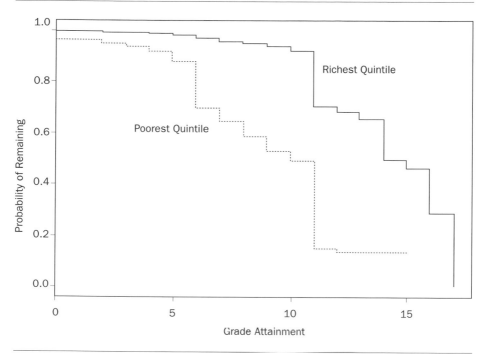

a number of countries, the least between-school variance in primary education was found in the Nordic countries (ranging from 5 to 9 percent in reading), while that in the developing world was found in Thailand (31 percent in third-grade mathematics) and Colombia (29 percent in third-grade Spanish). In Peru, about 54 percent of the variance in fourth-grade mathematics outcomes was between schools.

The indigenous people are the most disadvantaged group (see Table 14.1). Analysis of the determinants of the fourth-grade achievement found that Quechua-speaking students who were attending schools with a predominantly Quechua student population, as well as Quechua-speaking teachers and principals, were associated with lower achievement.[6] If indigenous Quechua-speaking students are already behind in fourth grade, their prospects of advancing through the education pyramid are dim; in turn, this poor outlook negatively affects their opportunity to break out of a cycle of poverty after they grow up.

The labor market consequence of poor quality and low internal efficiency will become even graver in the twenty-first century. The 1990s already showed rapidly increasing wage differentials among workers with various education levels, after Peru opened its economy to international trade and competition. This trend parallels the development in many Latin American economies such as Colombia (Cardenas and Gutiérrez 1997), Costa Rica (Gindling and Robbins 1994), Chile (Robbins 1996), and Argentina (Pessino 1995), where returns to education also increased after structural

FIGURE 14.15

Percentage Remained Enrolled by Quintile in Jamaica, 1998

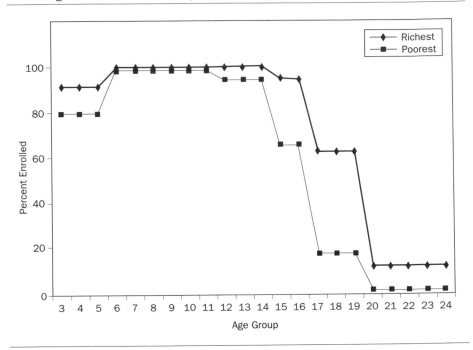

TABLE 14.1

Index of Fourth-Grade Mathematics Outcomes, 1996

	Index of Mathematics Outcomes	Coefficient of Variability
Countrywide average	1.00	0.47
Male	1.04	0.46
Female	0.96	0.48
Public rural*	0.85	0.54
Public urban	0.97	0.46
Private	1.37	0.34
Spanish speakers	1.04	0.46
Quechua speakers	0.73	0.54
Aymara speakers	0.99	0.44
Coast	1.10	0.43
Mountain	1.00	0.47
Jungle	0.83	0.50

* The sample of rural schools excluded single-teacher schools, which accounted for about 29 percent of all schools in the country. The variability of achievement, therefore, is likely to be much greater than what is shown here.

Note: The coefficient of variability is computed by dividing the value of the standard deviation by the corresponding mean of the group. While it is a very standard measure, the coefficients of variability in this table do not have a direct relationship with the index, except in the case of the countrywide average.

reforms. Table 14.2 shows that the earnings differentials in urban areas between workers who had no education and those who had primary education declined drastically from 50 to 33 percent between 1985 and 1996, signaling that the skills of primary school graduates are less and less in demand. Given the unsatisfactory quality of primary education, it is not surprising that the earnings differentials between people with a primary education and people with no education have narrowed.

On the other hand, the premia of secondary education, nonuniversity tertiary education, and university education, after having declined between the mid-1980s and the early 1990s, rapidly bounced back between 1991 and 1996 when the economy stabilized and economic growth resumed (Table 14.2). The magnitude of decline in the 1980s differed among workers of varied education levels—it was less steep for university-educated workers than others. When the premia bounced back, the increase was also steepest for university graduates. In 1996, the university premium was as high as 70 percent. This signals both the poor quality of secondary education and the increasing demand for a higher level of skills in an open economy that faces growing international competition and technological change.

It should be noted that the university premium for women increased much more than that for men, although women's level of earnings was lower than men's (Table 14.2). Given the very low enrollment ratio of women in higher education in the rural area, and among the lower quintiles, the beneficiaries of the rising university premium

TABLE 14.2

Urban Peru: Educational Premia, 1985, 1991, and 1996

	Education Premia			Change in Percentage Points	
	1985 %	1991 %	1996 %	1985–1991 %	1991–1996 %
Earnings differentials					
Primary versus no education	50	40	33	−10	−7
Secondary versus primary	45	7	17	−38	10
Nonuniversity tertiary					
versus secondary	43	13	25	−30	12
University versus secondary	59	47	70	−12	23
Male					
Primary versus no education	3	64	7	61	−57
Secondary versus primary	36	6	18	−30	12
Nonuniversity tertiary					
versus secondary	37	15	30	−22	15
University versus secondary	66	58	71	−4	13
Female					
Primary versus no education	47	25	36	−22	11
Secondary versus primary	57	5	13	−52	8
Nonuniversity tertiary					
versus secondary	54	12	23	−42	11
University versus secondary	39	25	70	−14	45

are women from upper quintiles. However, the increasing education premium will provide strong incentives for urban women in the middle quintiles to seek further education. This is also likely to set into motion a virtuous cycle of higher levels of private investment in education, mostly by women supporting themselves. Rural women, however, are not likely to have access to such opportunities without specific government interventions.

Investment in basic education, both in terms of qualitative improvement and quantitative expansion of secondary education, will have a positive effect on poverty alleviation, although returns to this level are probably lower because the initial general human capital is low. To ensure gender equity, the government needs to proactively institute policies to support women, particularly those in rural areas, to enable those with good academic standing to access higher education.

POLICY IMPLICATIONS

Peru's achievement in attaining universal primary education in spite of its geographical and ethnic diversity and its recent history of macroeconomic instability and civil unrest is undoubtedly remarkable. Its fiscal policy in the 1990s of containing costs while steadily increasing public expenditures on education within overall budget constraints is prudent. But there have been costs. The ability of households to incur schooling expenditures varies across income groups, and constrained public finance entails grave implications regarding the inequity of educational opportunity in Peru. If schooling is to be used as an instrument for poverty alleviation, the instrument clearly needs to be more effective in addressing the basic educational deficits faced by the poor, particularly indigenous students.

Analysis of the determinants of achievement provides a preliminary road map that could be further refined to guide policy. The analysis both identified the key issues and found a message of hope. After controlling for a number of explanatory variables, some departments were doing a better job than others. Aymara students performed as well as Spanish-speaking students. Quechua students could have achieved as much as others if they were not studying in predominantly Quechua schools, thereby indicating the potential for policy to reduce the disparity. Teachers who graduated from universities and from teacher training institutes, teachers who have had longer years of service, and teachers who have had more in-service training courses were positively associated with higher student achievement. The nonavailability of textbooks was associated with lower achievement. Parental expectations helped shape outcomes. Even within the limitations of this first assessment effort, the findings are sufficiently important to warrant attention for the policy possibilities to equalize educational outcomes and improve quality more generally.

Because many indigenous teachers and principals were disadvantaged in their own preparation, in-service and pre-service training can provide special support through compensatory education in subject areas and pedagogical programs to strengthen teaching in bilingual, multicultural, and multigrade settings. Provision of bilingual programs and bilingual textbooks to students could ease the transition from the mother tongue to Spanish. Improvement of facilities and resources (textbooks, library, etc.) of schools attended by the disadvantaged groups, particularly indigenous students and teachers, could provide the necessary infrastructure for teaching and learning to take place.

To finance these interventions, public resources have to be both increased and targeted to the disadvantaged groups, most notably indigenous teachers and students. By increasing public expenditure levels to only the Latin American average of 4.5 percent of GDP, Peru has the opportunity to enhance markedly the intellectual ability and competitiveness of its disadvantaged citizens and alleviate poverty within a generation. No policy challenge is more significant.

NOTES

1. This chapter is condensed and revised from a World Bank sector study on education in Peru (World Bank 1999a). The views and opinions in the chapter do not necessarily reflect the position of either the World Bank or the Peruvian government.
2. The primary source of public expenditures on education comes from the Peruvian Ministry of Finance and Economy. The review of public expenditures for this study was carried out by Silva and Miranda and was built on an earlier study by Saavedra and Felices (1997).
3. Administration includes all the principals, school administrators, and inspectors; disaggregated information is not available by level. Separate accounting of administrative expenses makes spending by each level low and administration rather high.
4. In 1997 the exchange rate was 2.55 soles to $1.
5. The Lorenz curve is an easy diagram to read—the heavy straight black line joining the two corners as shown in Figures 14.8, 14.9, and 14.10 is the line of "perfect equality" or the line that would obtain if each consumption quintile received an equal amount of educational expenditure—for instance, if 20 percent of expenditures accrued to the poorest quintile just as to the richest quintile. The Lorenz curves shown in these figures represent the distribution of expenditures by quintile. The closer the curves are to the diagonal, the more equitable is the distribution of expenditures.
6. However, Quechua students who were not attending predominantly Quechua schools performed as well as Spanish-speaking students. The difference in the performance of Aymara students compared to Spanish-speaking students was not statistically significant. Data are not available to explain the reasons for the differences between the Quechua and the Aymara. It has been hypothesized that Aymara students are exposed more to a Spanish-speaking environment because of the Aymara's commercial activities. Further research on this topic is needed.

REFERENCES

Cárdenas, Mauricio, and Catalina Gutiérrez. 1997. Impacto de las reformas estructurales sobre la eficiencia y la equidad. In *Empleo y Distribución del Ingreso en América Latina: Hemos Avanzado?* ed. Mauricio Cárdenas, 223–262. Bogota: Tercer Mundo Editores.

Díaz, Hugo, Vicente Ramírez Huayte, Francisco Custodio Farro, and José Alvarado Távara. 1995. *La Educación Privada en Lima Metropolitana.* Buenos Aires: Instituto Internacional de Planeamiento de la Educación, UNESCO, Informe de Investigación No. 104.

Gindling, T. H., and Donald Robbins. 1994. Earnings inequality, structural adjustment and trade liberalization in Costa Rica. Mimeograph. Cambridge, Mass.: Harvard University.

Goldschmidt, Pete, and Kin Bing Wu. 2000. Determinants of achievement in Peru. World Bank LCSHD Paper Series, No. 53. Washington, D.C.: World Bank.

Montero, Carmen, Patricia Oliart, Patricia Ames, Zoila Cabrera, and Francesca Uccelli. 1998. *La Escuela Rural: Estudio para Identificar Modalidades y Prioridades de Intervención*. Lima, Peru: Instituto de Estudios Peruanos.

Organization for Economic Cooperation and Development. 1998. *Education at a Glance*. Paris: OECD.

Pessino, Carola. 1995. Labor market consequences of the economic reform in Argentina. In *Social Tensions, Job Creation and Economic Policy,* ed. D. Turnham, C. Foy, and G. Larrain, 293–314. Paris: OECD.

Robbins, Donald. 1996. HOS hits facts: Facts win. Evidence on trade and wages in the developing world. Mimeograph. Cambridge, Mass.: Harvard University.

Rodriguez, José, and David Alber. 1998. Asistencia a la escuela y participacion en el mercado laboral de los menores en el Peru. Draft. University Park, Penn.: Penn State University.

Saavedra, Jaime, and Guillermo Felices. 1997. Inversion la calidad de la educacion pública en el Perú y su efecto sobre la fuerza de trabajo y la pobreza. Documento No. SOC97–104. Departamento de Programas Sociales y Desarrollo Sostenible. Washington, D.C.: Banco Interamericano de Desarrollo.

UNESCO. 1998. *Statistical Yearbook*. Paris: UNESCO.

World Bank. 1998. *World Development Report*. Washington, D.C.: World Bank.

World Bank. 1999a. Peru: Education at a crossroads: Challenges and opportunities for the 21st century. Report No. 19066-PE, Vols. 1 and 2. Washington, D.C.: World Bank.

World Bank. 1999b. Poverty and social developments in Peru, 1994–1997. A World Bank Country Study. Washington, D.C.: World Bank.

World Bank. 1999c. Jamaica: Secondary education: Improving quality and extending access. Report No. 19069, Vols. 1 and 2. Washington, D.C.: World Bank.

Commentary

Richard Murnane, Harvard Graduate School of Education

I enjoyed reading this interesting and thought-provoking chapter. I take the basic theme to be that aggregate trends on school enrollment rates in Peru are deceptive. While school enrollment rates in Peru are remarkably high, a closer look at the numbers shows that family incomes play a large role in determining educational opportunities. At the primary school level, almost all children are in school. But children from poor families and from families living in rural areas start school late and do not progress well. They are underrepresented in secondary education and even more underrepresented in postsecondary education. Kin Bing Wu and her co-authors argue that this pattern is partly due to the level of public expenditures on education—which is low as a percentage of gross domestic product. It is also partly due to the allocation of government educational expenditures—public expenditures per student on university students are six times those the level of public expenditures on primary school students. The basic policy message from the chapter is that the government must find a way to increase public expenditures on primary school education.

I find the basic argument of the chapter convincing. Most of my comments concern possible strategies for implementing the basic recommendations.

I am not sure that it makes sense to argue that the government financing of pensions for retired teachers is simply a drain on the government education budget. My point is not to defend the public pensions. I do not know how important they are in attracting talent to the teaching profession and in retaining talent in teaching. This depends on the structure of the pensions, a topic that the chapter does not cover. However, assume that the pensions are valued by perspective teachers and do act as substitutes for current salaries in attracting talent to teaching. Under this assumption, the pension costs should be seen as part of the cost of delivering educational services, just as teachers' salaries are. This would be more clearcut if Peru fully funded the pension system— that is, put into a trust fund each year sufficient money to cover the future pension costs of today's current teachers. In fact, if the teaching force is growing in size, fully funding pensions would mean more resources devoted to pensions out of the current education budget than is the case under the current funding system.

A basic question that comes out of the chapter's conclusion is: Where should the money come from to increase public funding of primary and secondary education? Without knowing the structure of the tax system, it is not clear that increasing taxes would benefit the poor. It might be that they would pay a disproportionate share of increased taxes. Without knowing a lot about the allocation of public spending, it is not

obvious that cutting public spending in other areas to devote more spending to education unequivocally benefits the poor. It may, but it is not obvious. Given the history of
inflation in Peru, deficit funding of government expenditures on education does not
seem like a good idea. So it may be necessary to think about ways to reallocate government educational expenditures to increase resources devoted to primary education.
One possible strategy for reallocating educational expenditures is to reduce the subsidy
to postsecondary education. The logic underlying this is twofold. First, the information
on relative earnings by education level suggests that the private economic payoff to
postsecondary education is high. In other words, it is a good private investment for students to invest in a university education. Consequently, it is worthwhile to think about
shifting more of the burden of paying for university education to students. Second, the
relatively affluent are much more likely to be students at the university than are young
people from poor families, so not only does cost recovery make sense on efficiency
grounds, it also has attractive equity properties. If this strategy were followed, it is
important that students be able to borrow to pay for university education. Thus some
attention to capital markets makes sense.

Assume that cost recovery at the university level or an increase in government
funding of education does free up public resources to increase funding for primary
school education. How should the money be spent? There are two related issues here.
The first is how to target the money to low-income families. The second is what to
spend the money on. A possible answer to the first question is to allocate a large share
of the money to schools in neighborhoods in which concentrations of poor families
live. This is a strategy that the World Bank recommended for Vietnam.

The low-income elasticities indicate that it is not efficient to give income subsidies
to low-income families or poor communities and expect them to spend it on education. What should be done with it? That is, of course, another study, one that concerns
the determinants of a high-quality primary school education. Kin Bing Wu's chapter
suggests that, as a start, building schools that are closer to the homes of poor families
may be important because young children are more likely to attend school if it is close
to their homes.

A critical, but difficult question concerns how to spend the money to improve the
internal efficiency of education—that is, to promote the timely acquisition of skills.
Donald Winkler's chapter shows how difficult this question is to answer. It is possible
that spreading the money too thinly would be a mistake. It is worthwhile thinking about
an evaluation strategy to learn whether particular investment strategies are effective in
improving the internal efficiency of the education system—that is, in increasing the
timely completion rate of low-income students.

Let me suggest one simple question to keep in mind in designing strategies to improve the education provided to children from low-income families: Does the intervention result in changes in children's day-to-day experiences? If the answer is no,
then it is highly unlikely that the intervention will result in improved achievement.
This may seem obvious, but the point is often neglected. For example, class size
reductions, which are expensive, often do not result in improved student achievement
because teachers teach in the same lecture style with a class of twenty-five that they
did with a class of forty-five. From the perspective of the child's daily experience in
school, the class size reduction made no difference.

A final question that is worth thinking about is whether the government should encourage relatively affluent families to use their own private resources to send their children to private primary schools. The chapter points out that many relatively affluent families do this currently. The advantage of encouraging affluent families to use private primary schools is that it removes the burden from government to fund primary schools for these children. A possible disadvantage is that these families may be the most able to articulate a demand for high-quality education. Moreover, their presence in schools may have positive effects on the education of other, less-privileged children.

In summary, this chapter is thoughtful and interesting. It identifies a critical problem. Inevitably, it leads to tough questions about how to deal with this problem.

A teacher helps two girls with their project at the Summit K–12 Alternative School in Seattle, Washington.

15

Policy and Equity: Lessons of a Third of a Century of Educational Reforms in the United States

Gary Orfield
Harvard Graduate School of Education

This chapter discusses school reform policies in the United States over the past forty years, highlighting the influence that the U.S. experience has abroad in the realm of educational reform but also calling into question the aspects of this experience that international agencies highlight. It is often not obvious that there is significant political debate around the best way to improve low-performing schools, mainly in the most impoverished areas of the country. By tracing the policy trends based on the differing agendas of the political parties and examining the outcomes of these policies, it becomes evident that educational reforms are driven by politics and that the more progressive policies of the 1960s and 1970s were more successful at making schooling more equitable for all students.

Models explicitly or implicitly based on U.S. educational policy and institutions are being widely discussed across the world, largely because of U.S. power and funding of international projects and institutions. Often these discussions take place with no recognition of the intense debates about the basic facts relating to school reform going on within the United States and the evidence that a number of these policies may not work very well. Even less attention is given to a set of more powerful and unusual national policies adopted in the 1960s and early 1970s that grew out of fundamentally different educational assumptions and that actually appear to have had a real impact on educational gains. That experience indicates that it is difficult to make breakthroughs for excluded groups without targeting policies to resolve special problems of the poor and disadvantaged groups in the society. Schools often reflect rather than transform inequality, and reforms intended to upgrade schools may unintentionally expand rather than diminish gaps. When U.S. policy targeted poor children and their schools, in the 1960s and part of the 1970s, major progress was made in high school and college enrollment and completion and in lowering gaps in achievement between various groups in the society. There were also programs that did not produce benefits.

Those successes lost ground and policies were radically altered after a conservative business-dominated coalition took power in the 1980s. Beginning with the Reagan administration and extending through the Clinton administration, the dominant agenda of the past two decades emphasized more tests, more course requirements, and the introduction of market mechanisms. Market and testing reform themes being promoted across the world have little evidence of success in the United States. Apart from small gains in science and math test scores, it has been a period of stagnation in progress. The long-term trend of increasing high school graduation has ended and racial gaps in test scores are no longer diminishing. Attainment of college degrees has become very strongly linked to family economic status. Though the U.S. story is not widely known, it has important implications for reform debates in other nations.

Because of the position of the United States as the world's only superpower in this era, ideas based on U.S. educational policy are being widely disseminated across the world, often through international organizations that are heavily financed by the United States. Sometimes current ideas are presented as the latest scientific discovery about educational efficiency and the dominant U.S. reform ideas of the last generation are presented as the culmination of knowledge about schooling efficiency. It is very important that policymakers and citizens in other countries realize that there is no consensus about many of these issues within the United States and very limited evidence that some of the currently popular policies actually work.

The currently dominant ideas tend to reflect the conservative side of a long and continuing ideological and political debate within the United States. The policies during conservative and progressive eras in U.S. politics tend to set very different goals that result in different consequences. Educational research suggests that the reforms enacted during earlier periods when progressives were in power were actually more effective in terms of extending access and lowering gaps in academic achievement within the society. Most of the policies of the post-1980 period have different and sometimes opposite impacts on those goals.

The United States is a society with a great deal of educational research but also a society in which educational policies are often driven much more by ideological assumptions than by analysis of impacts. The research topics funded and publicized tend to reflect the political climate of the time, though the research community is so large and there are so many privately funded think tanks that there are always dissenting voices. Since the early 1980s the basic goals have been about improving the "quality" of American education and the global competitiveness of U.S. workers in the postindustrial global economy. These reforms, which took shape initially following a 1983 Reagan administration report, *A Nation at Risk,* changed the focus of federal education policy from that of increasing access to one of reaching a higher level of performance.

EDUCATION AS A PRIORITY

Schools occupy a central position in the American dream of social and economic mobility. When U.S. citizens are asked about what government services they think should receive more money, schools are usually at the top of the list, even during very conservative periods.

People typically believe their own children's schools are strong but that others are not. There is a deep consensus that government should support education with substantial resources, though there is an active debate about how to do it and what role different levels of government should play. During the 1996 presidential election, for example, education often came out as the top issue in national and state polls (Pitsch 1996). Both in 1996 and 1998 a conservative Congress added money to education programs because the polls showed they were very popular. A fall 1998 Gallup Poll, for example, showed that 80 percent of people wanted to fix up old schools and an even greater majority wanted to lower class sizes (Rose and Gallup 1998). These are the issues that President Bill Clinton actively pursued. Apart from economic and international crises, nothing so commands the attention of the U.S. public as its system of educational opportunity. Figure 15.1 shows the trends in United States educational spending since 1930.

The strong belief in education does not mean, however, that there is any consensus about substantive education issues. During the past several decades there have been ongoing battles in the United States over the role of schools in social reform, particularly in opening opportunities for racial minorities, the poor, women, students who do not speak English, and the handicapped. There is also a continuing argument about the appropriate division of power among the federal government, the state government, the local school district, the local school, and the parents the school serves. There has been a vast expansion of testing and there are ongoing battles about the way to do it and its consequences. Most of the positive achievement results are in the early grade levels. The major change in the upper grades has been increasing completion of high school, especially for minority students, but that trend has leveled off and may be reversing. Since the early 1980s the emphasis has been on more course requirements, particularly in math and science, more demanding assessments, and the use of market mechanisms. In the past decade there has been an intense discussion about the use of

FIGURE 15.1

U.S. Trends in School Spending

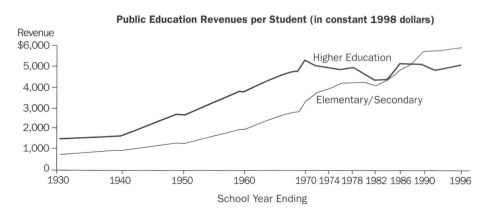

Public Education Revenues per Student (in constant 1998 dollars)

Source: NCES (1999).

public funds to finance private or religious education through vouchers. Many of the issues that are under consideration now in developing countries have been struggled over for decades in the United States.

WHY IS THE U.S. EXPERIENCE IMPORTANT?

Nations exercising great political, military, or economic power are always looked to in educational discussions, as if their power derives from their school system. German schools and universities had great influence early in the century. The Soviet Union's technology education was admired after *Sputnik* in the 1950s. In the United States, there was intense interest in the schools of Japan and the Asian tigers when it seemed like their economies would overtake that of the United States.[1] Now the spread of American ideas, the collapse of the major ideological competition, and the powerful American role in international media, international institutions, and markets all tend to spread examples and claims from the United States. Often, however, the messages are oversimplified.

The U.S. experience may not be relevant to educational policymakers in very different countries and it would be presumptuous to assume that research findings can be easily transplanted. Obviously, the United States is a society with many different traditions and possibilities.

The United States, however, does have characteristics both of the most advanced industrial democracies and of Third World countries. It includes areas with public schools competitive with the best in the world, schools that prepare students well for some of the world's leading universities, and others lagging very far behind (Salganik et al. 1993). The United States is a very large and wealthy society but inside it there is a large underdeveloped country of millions of poor people and isolated groups. With the most unequal income distribution of any industrialized society, the United States has about a fourth of its children growing up in poverty and children living in social crisis dominating many of its city school systems. It has many regions with schools overwhelmingly occupied with residents who are economically marginalized and experiencing the kinds of problems of health, joblessness, family crisis, community decay, and powerlessness that supposedly characterize the Third World. The nation has thousands of schools that operate far below the norm of international competition, schools that usually serve concentrations of poor children, most of whom are members of racial and ethnic minorities. Almost nine-tenths of schools that are 90 to 100 percent black or Latino have concentrated poverty (Orfield et al. 1997). Millions of children do not speak English when they arrive at school. The group of disadvantaged children is larger than the total population of many countries. Figure 15.2 shows the persistence of poverty rates of U.S. children under six over time.

The United States has two other features that are important for comparative purposes. It has tried a very broad range of policies because of deep ideological divisions and extensive decentralization to states and localities that pay more than 90 percent of the cost of public schools. Although many states implement similar programs, states and individual districts have launched widely divergent experiments. Courts also play an unusually important role and have ordered a variety of educational remedies to violations of the rights of groups of students. There are many approaches to study.

FIGURE 15.2

Poverty Rates of U.S. Children under Age Six by Race/Ethnicity, 1975–1997

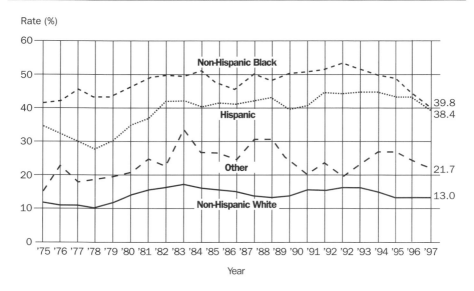

Source: National Center for Children in Poverty (1999).

The second feature is that there is a vast amount of available data about educational trends and outcomes.[2] Since the initiation of a massive increase in testing and reporting systems in the mid-1980s, a great deal of data about school districts and individual schools is available. The existence of many centers of research, the publication of almost all data submitted to Congress, the Freedom of Information laws requiring governments to release information, and the widespread practice of posting data on the Web provide rich resources for analysis. Many important methods for providing equal educational opportunity for poor children, minority children, and children speaking other languages have been tried in the United States. Important lessons have been learned about the impacts and practicality of a variety of approaches.

Countries dealing with suggestions from international institutions to use U.S.-style policy solutions need better information on the actual impacts and limitations of these policies. The strong debates and areas of agreement among U.S. researchers may help other countries evaluate those ideas.

Latin American nations have a special need to understand the U.S. story because many students who start school in Latin America will complete their education in U.S. cities or will return to schools in their home country after being removed from the United States by immigration officials. The U.S. Census Bureau projects a U.S. Latino population of more than 95 million by 2050 and a school-aged population that is about one-third Latino. Figure 15.3 shows the progressively changing demographics of U.S. schools by ethnicity. Latino students, on average, now confront serious problems in U.S. schools, including a rate of failure in high school more than twice the black level. Recent policy changes limiting the rights of immigrants and racial minorities,

FIGURE 15.3

Changing Racial Composition of U.S. Schools

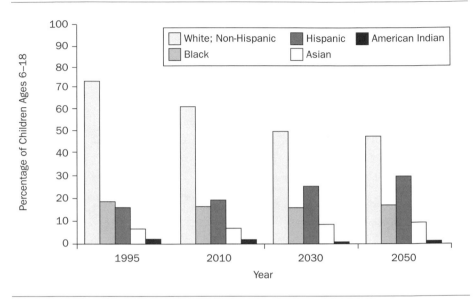

Note: Percents do not add to 100 because the Hispanic population includes members of several races, including blacks and whites.

Source: U.S. Bureau of the Census, cited in United States President's Advisory Commission on Educational Excellence for Hispanic Americans (1996).

particularly in California and Texas, are likely to deepen these problems. Latinos are even more isolated from non-Latino whites than are black students. There is a very rapidly expanding, heavily immigrant, Latino society within U.S. society that is very strongly affected by education. Table 15.1 illustrates the projected ethnic composition of the United States school-aged population by the year 2050.

POLICY TRENDS

There have been two basic policy eras in U.S. educational policy since mid-century: a struggle for access and equity that dominated the period from 1960 to 1980 and a focus on competition and standards that prevailed in the 1980s and 1990s. The first took the public school as a given and attempted to redefine its role to make it a more powerful instrument of opportunity. It was part of a broader movement against poverty and racial discrimination. The second rejected a social role for the schools and re-defined the crisis as one of international economic competition driven by technology and the need for more skilled workers. The dramatically different assumptions and policies within the same society permit some important comparisons of results.

   The first period was basically about access to secondary and higher education for steadily larger portions of the population, inclusion of historically excluded groups in better schools through civil rights laws and special programs, and a variety of strategies

TABLE 15.1

School-Aged Population, 2050 (U.S. Census Bureau Projections for Children 5–19)

Race	Number	Percentage
White	32,952,000	42.9
Black	13,802,000	18.0
Latino	21,111,000	27.5
Asian	7,951,000	10.4
Indian	973,000	1.3
Total non-white	43,817,000	57.1
Total	76,769,000	100.0

Source: U.S. Census Bureau (1993).

to help lower-income people participate fully in education while upgrading educational offerings in low-income communities and addressing other problems related to family poverty.

During the 1800s the battles to create universal elementary education, to develop a common approach to curriculum, to end massive corruption in school politics, and to professionalize teaching and administration were fought largely at the state and local levels across the nation under the leadership of urban reformers in the progressive movement, professional organizations, the press, and universities (Cremin 1988; Peterson 1985).

The federal government played a very small role in education until the 1960s, when massive change occurred under the most activist administration and Congress of the century. When the government did enter, however, its role focused primarily on the goal of equity, and it was a major force for change. Faced with the incentive of massive new federal funds and the threat of lawsuits and fund cutoffs if they broke the law, school districts in seventeen states that had historically practiced educational apartheid began to rapidly change their policies. By 1970, these states had the most integrated schools in the nation. Across the country for the first time, there were new educational programs aimed at schools with concentrations of low-income children, programs that tended to embrace the idea that a powerful intervention for preschool and early elementary children could produce a substantial convergence of educational outcomes.

The 1960s saw huge reforms, largely at the federal level, in both education and social policy. President Lyndon Johnson's War on Poverty led to a series of educational interventions, including preschool education and health programs for poor children and a large program of federal aid known as Title I, which sent money to provide additional educational resources for schools with high concentrations of low-income children. The largest federal interventions in public schools were in the form of aid for schools of poor children, the enforcement of civil rights, research, and the publication of comparative statistics. The government also had an important role in initiating experiments and in putting new issues onto the policy agenda with education decision makers across the United States.

Though the federal funds peaked at about a tenth of public school spending, they were heavily leveraged on equity issues and backed up by the regulatory powers of government. In higher education, where the government plays a larger role in fiscal terms, its budgets are still far behind the state governments and its role is primarily about financial aid to help students afford higher education. In addition, the federal government created the first large program of scholarships, campus jobs, and loans to enable poor children to go to college. It also initiated a set of programs to recruit and help prepare such children for college. The result was a surge of college-going, particularly for previously excluded groups. The equity movement spread to issues of gender discrimination by the early 1970s, and the enactment of laws on that issue greatly accelerated a historic change in the role of women, particularly in higher education. Figure 15.4 shows the percentage of high school completers and those going on to college by race–ethnicity.

The trend during the late 1960s was toward a social-democratic policy, with a special emphasis on minority rights growing out of the civil rights movement, the greatest

FIGURE 15.4

Percentage of 25- to 29-Year-Olds Who Completed High School and Percentage of High School Completers with Some College or a Bachelor's Degree or Higher, by Race–Ethnicity, March 1971–1998

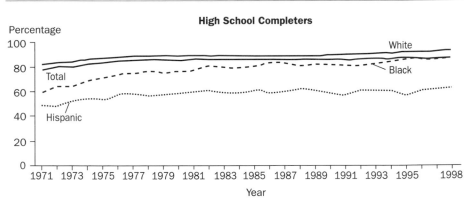

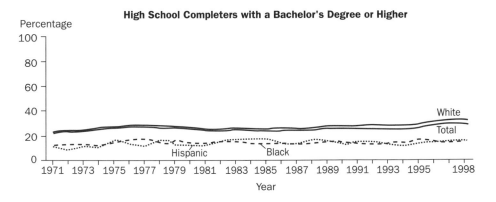

Source: Bureau of the Census, U.S. Department of Commerce cited in NCES (2000).

mobilization for black rights since the Civil War. During this period, strong sanctions were adopted by the government and the courts against racial discrimination and against discrimination on the grounds of language, gender, and handicapped condition. Figure 15.5 illustrates the increasing percentage of black students attending majority white schools in the South between 1960 and 1996. Large sums were invested in training new types of educational experts to deal with these problems and to help local school districts adapt successfully. In addition, the federal government adopted a program of free health care for the poor, the largest subsidized housing program in U.S. history, election of local advisory groups from various poor communities, protection of voting rights for minorities, and many other broad reforms. Large changes in educational outcomes took place during this period. This was a period of major increases of high school completion and college access, particularly for blacks. Southern blacks made the largest educational achievement gains, and the racial gaps in completion and achievement scores narrowed significantly. Figure 15.6 shows the U.S. college-going rates by race and income between 1972 and 1997.

This period of social change gave way to a conservative political movement which won control of the presidency in 1968 and has dominated it since with the exception of two southern governors, Jimmy Carter and Clinton, who were from the more conservative, business-oriented sector of the Democratic party. Between 1968 and 2000, conservatives held the presidency for twenty years and moderate Democrats for twelve years.

FIGURE 15.5

The Percentage of Black Students Attending Majority White Schools in the South, 1954–1996

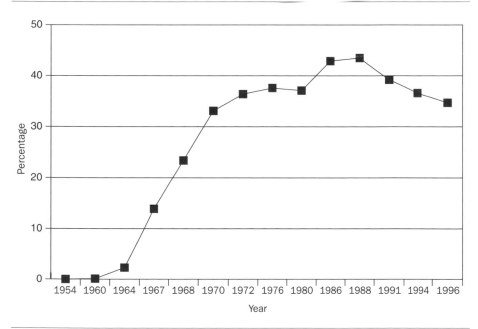

Source: Orfield and Yun (1999).

FIGURE 15.6

Percentage of High School Completers Ages 16–24 Who Were Enrolled in College the October after Completing High School, by Race–Ethnicity and Family Income, October 1972–1997

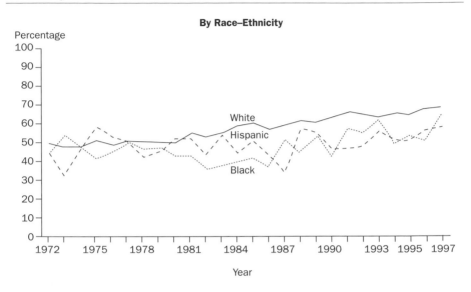

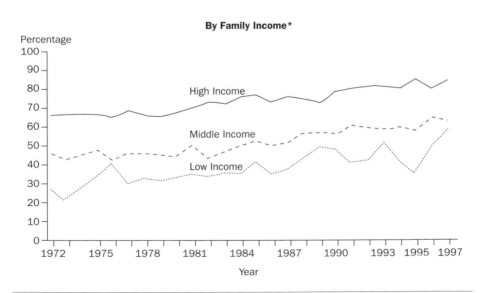

*Low income is the bottom 20 percent of all family incomes; high income is the top 20 percent of all family incomes; and middle income is the 60 percent in between. Data on family income were not available in 1974.

Source: Bureau of the Census, U.S. Department of Commerce cited in NCES (2000).

The election of Richard Nixon and the creation of a powerful new coalition of white southerners and suburban and small-town residents opposed to further social change reshaped national policy. Nixon reduced federal regulation of civil rights and worked to turn more authority over federal education funds to state and local authorities.

The Supreme Court expanded educational rights in decisions between 1954 and the early 1970s, when President Nixon was able to appoint four of the nine justices. By the late 1980s, conservative control over the Supreme Court had been consolidated and educational rights were narrowed significantly in the next decade.

After the 1980 election, the Reagan-Bush team implemented the most conservative policy shifts in more than a half-century during their twelve years in office. This period produced an extraordinarily different educational agenda and a decline in the federal role to about one-sixteenth of the education budget.

Ideas from the Reagan administration dominated policy during the 1980s and 1990s. Policy during that time included sharp cuts in social programs, including welfare payments, housing, and public jobs for the poor, and ending enforcement of many civil rights laws. There was a strong belief that achievement could be increased by insisting on more tests of students and teachers, by requiring more courses, and by introducing competition through various market or competition mechanisms. In the end, forty-seven of the fifty states enacted many elements of the Reagan administration's excellence reforms (Sunderman 1995). President George Bush and then-Governor Bill Clinton negotiated an accord around these ideas between the national and state governments and Clinton continued to press many of the same basic ideas as president.[3] These ideas are being discussed across the world.

POLICY OUTCOMES

Advocates of the current policies claim major benefits, but seldom present concrete results. It is extremely interesting to examine the difference in levels of educational gains, particularly for poor and minority students between the current period and that of the earlier reforms. None of the reforms in either period fundamentally changed achievement outcomes. Test scores are much more strongly linked to family background than to differences in school programs (Coleman et al. 1966). There are, of course, other highly important educational outcomes such as level of attainment of key credentials and the networking opportunities that shape life chances in many ways.

Some reforms do, however, make a significant difference on measured achievement and they appear to make the largest difference for the most disadvantaged students. Following the equity reforms of the 1960s, large gains were made by the most disadvantaged students and the educational achievement gaps by race declined for a generation. The black-white test score gap decreased most substantially in the South (Grissmer et al. 1998).

The biggest differences were in levels of enrollment and graduation in high school and college. The liberal reforms came during a period of increasing enrollment and graduation and that pattern continued through the 1970s. There was a particularly sharp upward trend in high school graduation for black students and for black enrollment in college, particularly in the states that had traditionally excluded black students.

It is, of course, an oversimplification to attribute the positive outcomes to the education policies alone. Related policies against job discrimination and expanding public programs, for example, had much to do with expanding the black middle class by opening up many job categories to blacks. There was a huge migration of blacks from areas with very weak schools in the rural South to areas with better schools. The South was experiencing rapid development and increasing investments in education.

Nothing like the gains of the 1960s and 1970s emerged from the next wave of reforms. The conservative reforms attempted to raise standards through requirements and testing, focusing on science and math, the areas thought to be most critical to international competition. A series of goals for progress by 2000 were negotiated between the governors and President Bush in 1989. In 1999, after sixteen years of implementing the conservative reforms which began in 1983, there was very little evidence of growing educational attainment. In recent years there is evidence of modest overall gains in science and math. On the other hand, reading and writing achievement is flat and, at the highest grade tested, age seventeen, reading shows a decline (NCES 1996).

The trend of completion of high school and college by a growing share of students has ended. High school graduation rates are dropping and more students are obtaining credentials through less adequate alternatives (NCES 1999). The inequality of access to college based on income has grown. Wealthier families now are even more likely to send their children to college, and the gaps by income have been growing. In contrast to the peak of access when the top quartile of families, in terms of income, were six times more likely than the bottom group to have their children graduate from college, the ratio is now ten to one (Mortenson 1998). Postsecondary education has become much more important since the 1960s as income growth has focused overwhelmingly on workers with education beyond high school, but access to college has declined significantly for lower-income families. The maximum federal aid for poor students in 1996 had only 43 percent of the buying power this grant had in 1980 (ETS 1997).

Some of the reforms, particularly those that mandate passing of particular tests for high school completion and college entry, may be causing unanticipated damage. A substantial body of research suggests that such tests lower the graduation rate of lower-income and minority students without a compensating increase in achievement scores (Hauser 1998; Heubert and Hauser 1999; Shepard and Smith 1989). In spite of clear evidence that such policies in the late 1970s and early 1980s increased dropout rates in New York City and Chicago, another strong push for such policies was led in the late 1990s by President Clinton and governors of both parties.

The various reforms are supported as answers to the worry about failure of the U.S. educational system in the nation's big-city schools—mostly schools for minority children, since few whites remain in big cities. Most American families are satisfied with the schools their own children attend and the percentage of U.S. students in public schools rather than private is higher than it was forty years ago, but there is a widespread belief that schools are failing in the nation's concentrated poverty schools, serving the nation's isolated "third world" communities in impoverished city communities.[4]

The policy debate of the 1980s and 1990s has focused attention on the relatively low average scores of U.S. students on international tests as a threat to long-run economic success. On closer examination, however, much of that problem reflects the low performance of low-income and minority students, who make up a growing share of young

Americans. There are many schools, communities, and even entire states that have very strong records by international standards.[5] There are school districts preparing students well for the world's most competitive universities in close proximity to schools preparing students for nothing.

The testing and accountability reforms of the 1980s have produced comparable data on achievement among schools and school districts, in the hope that such data would generate school improvements. (The conservative movement assumes that the failure has not been one of capacity or resources but of laziness, bad values, and poor organization.) The data show, however, that high poverty and minority schools overwhelmingly experience serious educational difficulties in all parts of the country under many kinds of policies and organizations. Increasingly, they and their teachers, teachers' unions, and local administrators are blamed in angry and disparaging terms for the failure. There is virtually no discussion of the possibility that the failure may be rooted in income distribution or poverty concentrations.

In state after state, the schools at the bottom of the achievement list for the entire state tend to be located in high poverty minority areas in big cities. A detailed analysis of test scores in Michigan found, for example, that about 60 percent of the variance in test scores could be explained by family social and economic status (Newman 1998). Some states actually report achievement by poverty levels because of the power of the relationships and the fact that schools are otherwise being rewarded or criticized primarily because of community wealth. Studies of all schools in metropolitan Chicago and metropolitan Los Angeles showed a correlation of 0.8 to 0.9 between the percentage of poor students in a school and the school's test scores and a similar correlation with the percentage of minority students (Orfield and Ashkinaze 1991; Orfield 1992; Orfield 1988). Very high relationships between poverty and test scores were reported statewide in Georgia and South Carolina.[6] Table 15.2 shows that the poorest students are the most segregated by race.

WHAT HAVE WE LEARNED?

If government wishes to invest in improving the outcome of troubled schools, what would be the investments and policies that would make the greatest difference for the education of low-income students and the schools where they are concentrated? Do spending levels matter for educational results? Are there nonmonetary investments that make a clear difference? What kind of impacts should we be most concerned about? Is it true that the only worthwhile investments are those made when children are very young and that those have lasting benefits? How much difference does it make which level of governance decides on policy or whether or not the schools are under public, religious, or secular private control?

U.S. educational policy is largely the product of different and often inconsistent ideas that were written into laws and became part of public beliefs at the height of the liberal movement in the 1960s and at the peak of the conservative movement of the 1980s. The liberal movement reached its greatest influence when research focused on the early years as a time of critical intervention, which became a basic element of U.S. policy in the middle 1960s when the government decided to finance preschool education for poor three- to four-year-olds (Head Start) and elementary instruction in the

TABLE **15.2**

Relationship Between Segregation by Race and by Poverty, 1995–1996

Percentage of Poor in Schools	Percentage of Black and Latino Students in Schools									
	0–10	10–20	20–30	30–40	40–50	50–60	60–70	70–80	80–90	90–100
0–10	31.0	21.2	10.2	6.1	5.9	4.7	5.6	4.7	4.5	3.2
20–25	35.1	37.1	31.1	20.7	11.7	7.1	5.2	3.7	3.2	1.8
25–50	26.2	32.5	43.8	49.0	45.4	38.2	26.3	15.7	11.4	8.3
50–100	7.7	9.1	14.9	24.2	37.0	50.0	62.9	75.8	80.8	86.6
Total	100.0	100.0	100.0	100.0	100.0	100.0	100.0	100.0	100.0	100.0
Percentage of U.S. schools	47.1	10.8	7.7	6.4	5.6	4.5	3.7	3.2	3.2	7.7

Source: Orfield and Yun (1999).

basic skills in high-poverty grade schools (Title I). The basic idea embodied in these key initiatives is that early development is particularly critical and that impacts will be lasting. But research strongly suggests that the impacts of most early interventions fade during the elementary years unless continuously reinforced. Unfortunately, there has been very little focus on either programs or research to improve secondary outcomes, resulting in little progress at that level, so crucial to adult opportunities.

Since the early 1980s, the policy of placing great pressure on testing has been widely accepted as a powerful lever for educational change, but the acceptance has been based far more on ideology than on research evidence. There is significant evidence that much more serious reliance on testing reinforces family background advantages because there is a very strong relationship among income, parent education, and test scores. When tests determine access to further education or flunking, the policies tend to reinforce and intensify differences (Heubert and Hauser 1998).

The outcomes of educational interventions and the efficacy of schools are commonly measured with short-term changes in test scores or the absolute value of test scores. Because test scores are strongly linked to nonschool characteristics and instructional or program changes often take years to be reflected in test scores, the focus on test scores biases the process toward rewarding schools with children from more privileged families and rewarding superficial test preparation over deep reforms.

Although test scores can be important indicators of some outcomes, the outcomes that are most important are success in further levels of education and in obtaining good jobs. These are very imperfectly linked to test scores and are importantly linked to some other outcomes of schooling, such as credentials, networks of information and job contacts, a school's reputation, and acquisition of basic precollegiate skills and orientations.

The focus on achievement scores is curiously out of sync with American culture, which does not view the mission of schools as primarily cognitive but expects college to be the focal point for serious academic training.[7] Employers reflect the same ambivalence about schooling, with most not seriously reviewing academic records but requiring school completion for the great majority of jobs. A 1998 survey shows parents far more worried about school violence, safety, drugs, and other issues than about academic standards (Rose and Gallup 1998). Key policy questions in the United States are usually asked and answered in a manner that is radically oversimplified; the policies adopted, though often presented as if they were research-based, are often based on ideology and do not seriously consider the evidence (Orfield and Debray 1999).

SUPPORT FOR EDUCATION INVESTMENTS, BUT DISAGREEMENT ABOUT PRIORITIES AND GOALS

Money is not the central problem. In contrast to its low social policy expenditures, the United States is internationally competitive in supporting public schools and generous in supporting higher education (OECD 1995). Clearly, there is a desire to invest in education, though there is no consensus about what to invest in. Putting money into schools and getting results requires clear goals, the best evidence about how to achieve them, and the measurement of results.

In recent decades, there has been a tendency to assume that increased test scores are the best, or even the only, way to find out that schools are better. Important goals for schools, however, include a number of factors beyond cognitive development, such as creating skills for lifelong learning and social development. This involves learning skills about functioning successfully with students of many backgrounds (important to future work, communities, and democratic processes), networking into opportunities during and after school, having contact with a positive peer group, acquiring credentials for future education and jobs, and preparing to succeed in college. Placing excessive weight on testing tends to narrow the discussion, reward elite communities, and drive schools, particularly those with low-achieving students, toward whatever is measured on the tests.

The current policies assume that attaching sanctions to tests can force schools to develop strategies to raise scores. The school, under this model, is a big assembly line whose products are students' test scores. Teachers are treated like production workers and the intense focus on tests of basic skills attempts to produce uniformity of the product. These pressures, however, have not produced the desired outcomes. The gains in test scores have, in general, been small in math and science and virtually nonexistent in other subjects, particularly at the secondary level. This has led both to increasingly stringent forms of emphasis on testing and an increasing rejection of public schools altogether. If rising test scores are defined as the only outcome, and one that can be controlled by the schools, then the schools serving disadvantaged students will usually be seen as failures.

DOES MONEY MATTER?

The basic conservative policy about schools in the United States argues that schools can make a very large difference, if only the right accountability or organizational change is imposed, but that resources do not matter. Most of the research about "education production functions" for decades came to the conclusion that there is almost nothing that money spent on schools can do to improve outcomes (Hanusheck 1994). Therefore, there is no reason to spend more or to equalize resources because neither will make significant differences. The U.S. Supreme Court actually cited some research of this type in its 1973 decision against ordering equal funding of public schools (*Rodriguez v. San Antonio Independent School District* 1973).

The principal counter-theory for most of the past thirty years has been that there is a known and critical period for intervention early in educational development that decisively changes the results and that it is in preschool or the earliest grades. This was the central argument for early interventions designed to increase school readiness and the acquisition of basic skills. This was the central theory embodied in Head Start and Title I, the largest federal education program, enacted in 1965. Title I concentrated supplemental funds on additional basic skills instruction, largely in early primary grades. This theory had enough appeal and enough power of educational leadership organized behind it that it has been strong enough to preserve these two programs for more than thirty years, though Title I is now facing what may be its most serious congressional challenge.

Unfortunately, the educational evidence for the permanent cognitive impacts of these early interventions has never been strong. Title I's first major longitudinal study, which produced the *Prospects* (1993) report to Congress, found little evidence of any general benefits and the study has led to a deepening attack on Title I. Among other findings from this longitudinal study was the conclusion that students attending concentrated poverty schools receiving this extra aid performed less well than similar students receiving no programs but attending less isolated schools.

The latest version of the early intervention theory comes in the finding that substantially lowering class size in early grades produces substantial benefits. For years, researchers held that except at the extremes, class size was not significantly related to outcomes. New statistical techniques, as well as a massive scientific experiment in the state of Tennessee, have reversed these conclusions. A series of studies was conducted in the 1990s by University of Chicago statistician Larry Hedges and his associates (1994) and an important study of class size issues was conducted in 1995 by Frederick Mosteller, Richard J. Light, and Jason A. Sachs. Hedge's studies and those of Greenwald and colleagues (Greenwald, Laine, and Hedges 1996) concluded that there were effects of expenditures and that a number of variables including total expenditures, student-teacher ratio, teacher experience, and teacher education were significantly related to student test score outcomes.

The new class size research has had an almost immediate impact on policy, triggering, for example, a massive reduction in early grades in California. This reform was supported by candidates running for governor in at least twelve states in 1998 and by President Clinton (Summary 1998). This reform has considerable impetus because, although it is still controversial in the research community (Shea 1998), it has overwhelming support among the public and among education organizations and does not raise difficult ideological issues.

Another theory that has been explored during the past half-century suggests that the best way to improve educational opportunity for students in isolated, inferior high-poverty schools is to find a way to transfer them to better schools. This was a central justification for desegregation, for choice programs, for the creation of magnet and charter schools, and for vouchers for private schools. By far, the most research has been conducted on desegregation and shows that minority students do commonly obtain access to more competitive schools and do experience small but significant test score gains. The larger effects of desegregation are on success in college and in linkage to networks that lead into the mainstream of society (Stephan 1991). Magnet schools grew out of desegregation efforts and offer specialized curricular opportunities for students who choose to enroll, but they are generally required to be interracial public schools. Their faculties often are there by choice and receive special training and equipment for the specialized curriculum. Magnet schools are available to children from many neighborhoods, often without special admissions requirements. Most are operated under policies that require racial integration. They usually provide free transportation to all interested children and they are part of the regular public school system. Some studies report gains in magnet school programs (Blank et al. 1996).

During the past decade, a number of additional forms of choice and of creating new schools where old schools have been unsuccessful have been implemented. Charter schools are a rapidly expanding innovation under which a private or nonprofit group receives public funds to run a privately controlled school that provides free education, but under different rules and with a different educational program than normal public schools. Small schools are schools that are frequently created by starting up several small schools, often within a building that housed one unsuccessful school. Reconstitution is a policy of removing the entire school staff and creating a new one with the total staff removed and replaced in the old school building to break patterns and expectations of failure. Choice has many forms, but most allow students to depart from their local public school and choose schools elsewhere under a wide variety of rules. Early findings on charter school academic performance show little difference.

Vouchers are public subsidies paid to individuals choosing to send their children to nonpublic, tuition-charging private schools. Since the 1980s these innovations have spread broadly, but there is very little serious research to date on their impacts. There is intense controversy over possible benefits from vouchers, and the issue is far from settled (Lewin 1999).

Great enthusiasm in educational policy in the past fifteen years derives from theories about the impact of choice and market mechanisms on changing the offerings of schools to parents and students to improve educational outcomes. There was a fierce debate in the last presidential campaign over the significance of very limited data on the achievement test results of voucher experiments with studies of a limited number of children in three schools in Milwaukee. Choice mechanisms, if not limited by other policies, tend to have a clear tendency toward stratification along socioeconomic lines. Schools are often popular and sometimes report relatively high test scores. The degree to which this represents selection bias of students and teachers or a net enhancement of educational quality is very difficult to determine since choosing and nonchoosing families may differ in very important ways. Most of the debate has been about issues of comparisons, analytic procedures, and assumptions that have not led to any convergence of findings (Fuller and Elmore 1996).

The small-scale experiments are unlikely to provide answers in any case to the question of the impact of large-scale implementation. Public school systems have found a critical shortage of the kinds of principals and teachers who can sustain a high-quality educational program serving a highly disadvantaged community. Whether or not there is a supply adequate to support large numbers of new or deeply reorganized schools with more autonomy is a very important question. Is there a built-in tendency toward increased stratification with almost any kind of selection and choice mechanism, given the inequality of parental knowledge and connections or are there workable ways to offset those advantages? What happens to the students and teachers who remain in weak schools after the better students and teachers have left?

A faculty seminar at Harvard University commissioned a number of studies of choice and produced a book, *Who Chooses? Who Loses?* which concluded that choice almost always led to stratification of schools, but that there was considerable uncertainty about its net benefits.

The forms of choice that are now being pursued most actively, charter schools and vouchers, are those most in conflict with traditional public schools and those with the fewest protections for equity. They reflect a strong ideological preference for markets and individual choice and a reluctance to consider the way markets work for people with very unequal information, skills, and resources. At this point, there is no convincing evidence of net academic benefits of either charter or voucher schools. Nonetheless, many hundreds of charter schools are being very rapidly formed and the Supreme Court has permitted a voucher plan that includes religious schools to go into operation in the state of Wisconsin. These are very significant changes in U.S. education policy, but it is too soon to speak with any confidence about the long-term consequences.

Probably the best information for thinking about results would come from nations that implemented somewhat similar policies sooner, such as the United Kingdom and New Zealand. The results in those settings suggest that the creation of such mechanisms on a large scale will increase educational stratification. Observers in other countries trying to sort out sweeping claims about markets and privatization in American schools should exercise great caution because of the toxic combination of intense ideological division, very limited experiments that are being given far more attention than they deserve, and no experience at all in the long-term systemic effects of full-blown implementation.

The only parts of the choice experiments that may be far enough along to reach reasonably clear conclusions are the policies of open enrollment, in which students have the right to choose among schools that do not offer specialized curricula, and the policy of magnet schools, in which families may choose very distinctive curricula in particular school sites, usually subject to desegregation requirements. The first policy has been tried in thousands of school districts in the 1960s and a number of states in the recent past. Generally speaking, the transfers are inconsequential, 1 or 2 percent of students. Magnet school programs, on the other hand, are often quite successful in convincing families to choose other schools, though they usually serve a relatively modest share of the school population. They clearly draw above-average students, but they also serve a substantial number of non-white students because of their desegregation requirements and the provision of free transportation. They contribute, at least modestly, to socioeconomic stratification, but they also enhance racial integration and may help hold middle-class families. Some significant research suggests that they have a positive achievement effect that goes beyond the selection effect, perhaps from the combined impact of a new school, a faculty united around a distinctive educational mission, and parents who want that kind of an educational program. Ironically, these schools are now under attack in federal courts by conservatives who object to the desegregation requirements. The magnet school experience, which is a combination of the conservative desire for more parental control with the liberal support for diversity and desegregation, is probably the most interesting and fully developed example of choice in the United States. But the model that is most often conveyed internationally is one in which the U.S. experience is in a very early stage and results are very limited.

The results to date, however, clearly show that simple choice mechanisms maximize options for those who get information about complex choices and know how to work in complex settings and often leaves out those at the other end of the spectrum. Choice that is equitable, or even increases opportunities for those most in need, requires a variety of mechanisms to provide information and to encourage choices by those at the bottom.

We probably cannot assess the possible consequences of a national implementation of vouchers without considering the experience of other nations with fragmented social, religious, and linguistic groups that subsidize private and denominational schools and examining recent experiences in Britain, Chile, New Zealand, and elsewhere. To this information should be added a careful consideration of the likely response of a constituency-oriented political system to the demands of intense and organized constituencies for broad private school subsidies.

The voucher issue, it seems to me, is a clear example of a set of policies where the United States has much more to learn from the experience of other countries with large voucher programs. Many of the key questions are about the capacity to increase the supply of strong school options without causing serious additional damage to the existing troubled schools by recruiting their better students and teachers. As is common in the United States, there is virtually no discussion of the experience of societies that are much farther along this path in the voucher debate.

EVALUATION THROUGH TEST SCORES

Though much can be learned from test scores, particularly when students are followed over time, they are seriously limited measures of policy impacts. They are used so much because they are cheap, readily measurable, and easy to reify into an apparently valid measure of school accomplishment because there is considerable public confidence in them. For example, U.S. Gallup polls from 1978 to 1995 found that between 65 and 75 percent of Americans had enough confidence in testing to favor flunking students who could not pass achievement tests (Elam and Rose 1995). In 1998, 71 percent favored a national testing program advocated by President Clinton (Rose and Gallup 1998).

The basic problems with excessive reliance on test scores, however, are that they largely reflect differences in student background and that the quickest way to change them is to teach about the test. Very few programs are reliably linked to lasting test score changes. Simply relying on scores gives undeserved credit to schools serving children of well-educated and successful families while punishing the schools serving disadvantaged students, a perverse result.

Intense publicity about test scores has been a basic tool of U.S. education reforms since the early 1980s. This is based on a diagnosis of the problem and a motivational theory that may both be wrong in many circumstances. It assumes that ineffective educational techniques and inadequate challenges to students cause poor performance and that public pressure will force schools to improve. Publication of test scores may have perversely negative consequences. Announcing them as proof of low quality encourages families and teachers with choices to go elsewhere, further weakening schools and districts. Test scores from state testing systems are widely used, for example, in marketing real estate.

A second problem is that large investments are now being made in teaching about particular tests. There are also a number of ways in which schools and school districts can manipulate test scores. A very serious problem is that if the tests are imposed as absolute requirements and the preparation of students is not equalized (as it almost never is in the United States) those children and schools that come from the most disadvantaged communities will be punished for what they failed to learn in their inferior schools and the punishment will further demoralize the children and those who are working with them. Use of tests without consideration of educational inequalities also tends to reinforce stereotypes about groups of children. A 1999 study by the National Research Council of the U.S. National Academy of Sciences concluded that such tests were related to higher dropout rates for minority students and that they should never be used as the sole factor in deciding on graduation or admissions (Heubert and Hauser 1999).

None of this implies that good standardized tests are not an appropriate tool. It is very important to know what skills students are acquiring. Test data should be used to identify problems, reward progress, and trigger interventions and tutoring.

Many nations have long employed very high stakes tests, particularly for exit from secondary school. The United States has a number of states that have only recently adopted such tests as well as a vast and sophisticated testing industry, so we can examine the impacts of changes. It offers a good laboratory to examine whether or not such testing is actually linked to increased achievement and whether or not there are serious associated costs of increased stratification and denial of key credentials to students from lower-income, poorly educated families. I believe that we will soon have information that may be of considerable interest to other nations thinking about the linkages between assessment and opportunities for the disadvantaged. Evidence to date shows grounds for deep concern.

BROADER GOALS FOR SCHOOLS

American goals for schools vary according to social and political conditions. One reason that tests on a few subjects have assumed such a great importance in the last generation is that the goals of education have narrowed during that period. Traditionally, U.S. schools had many goals in addition to teaching subjects. Creating a sense of nationhood and bringing many peoples into a common society were long primary goals as was preparing people for participation and leadership in a democratic society. Working out a philosophy of life, learning understanding and tolerance of other points of view, developing the capacity for teaching yourself new things, making friends who enrich life and learning, networking into opportunities, and understanding much more about how civic institutions work are among the basic goals of college education. These goals are given great importance by parents in the United States in surveys. A very important goal in the 1960s and 1970s was to use the schools to repair historical forms of discrimination. These broader goals, however, play virtually no role in the U.S. policy discussion of the past two decades. During this business-dominated period, preparation of more capable and productive workers has been the central goal.

In a world that has many countries trying to create viable modern democracies and that has witnessed the tragic failure of many multiethnic societies, the goals from earlier periods in the United States may be more relevant than the present ones. A society that produces slightly higher test scores but does nothing about deepening social cleavages does not have a model educational system.

NATIONAL LEADERSHIP AND AGENDA SETTING

The U.S. experience shows the importance of national leadership in administering laws intended to produce gains for low-income students since they seldom have significant power in local politics (Citizens Commission on Civil Rights 1998). The level of federal intervention, particularly on equity issues, has declined. Although the 1994 amendments to Title I of the Elementary and Secondary Education Act called on the federal government to emphasize achieving actual gains for poor children and increased accountability, recent research shows that the program has been radically decentralized to the states with extremely little accountability and very little federal leadership or compliance activity (Citizens Commission on Civil Rights 1998). Without enforcing either targeted spending through auditing or accountability, it just becomes general aid and part of the local politics of distributing resources and jobs. The only substantial continuing federal investment and the only substantial research agenda have been about programs to improve learning in preschool and the early grades, which has been going on now for a third of a century.

CONCLUSIONS

Although there have been some recent improvements in science and math scores, these standards-based reforms have not met their goals. In fact, not only is the Goals 2000 agreement between President Bush and the nation's governors falling short of realization, but a number of inequalities are actually becoming worse. Policymakers in other societies should look on any claims that the United States has found the path to major breakthroughs in education with considerable skepticism. The voices of the dominant conservative and centrist American political ideologies are echoing around the world primarily because of the political and economic position now occupied by the United States, not because there is serious evidence that American reforms work.

I believe that those interested in narrowing educational gaps in their societies and increasing educational attainment levels would better focus on an earlier set of reforms built around those goals and begun from a very different diagnosis. Nothing in the American research suggests that education can actually resolve very deep inequalities without changes in other sectors of the society. If high-poverty schools are almost always low performing, if students attending them have much more limited chances, and if the record of hundreds of billions of dollars of special aid has been profoundly disappointing, then the basic problems must be rooted outside the schools. In addition, schools serving primarily low-income children appear to be systematically unequal in many ways even when they get additional money, particularly with regard to the level of competition, the skills of the teachers, the involvement and resources of the parents, and the curriculum.

The absence of a serious level of academic training in too many schools has helped to spur demands for changes, often taking the form of more requirements and more testing. We need a serious and challenging curriculum. We need to select varieties of choice systems that produce school-level change and real educational alternatives and that include key equity measures of parent information, fair selection mechanisms, civil rights requirements to assure access to minorities, free transportation, and authentic educational alternatives. Compensatory education programs should be based on genuinely successful models and be held accountable for actual educational gains on achievement, graduation, college-going, and other critical outcomes. We must acknowledge that we have a very large challenge of linguistic diversity, which is often also ethnic and racial diversity, and that we have done very little in either research or policy to address this critical set of needs. We need experiments to test strong incentives for groups of talented teachers to move into inner-city schools and to keep them there for the years needed to implement deep reforms. We need to figure out what is good assessment and to use testing for diagnosis, tutoring, and other supports, not for sanctions against students.

The U.S. school reform agenda of the past two decades has not been driven by research. It has been driven by politics. These reforms, particularly the market and choice portions, tend to be treated as scientifically valid, particularly by economists, because of their belief that markets work efficiently for the poor and will make things better. This is much more a faith in first principles than a research finding.

The Excellence Movement of the 1980s and 1990s had consistent national leadership for longer than any of the other movements, and its essential aspects were adopted by almost all of the states. This movement, which became known in the 1990s as "standards-based reform," was based almost entirely on the reassertion of tradition. The need for an urgent change, set forth in *A Nation at Risk* (National Commission on Excellence in Education 1983), was based on what turned out to be an inaccurate conclusion that academic achievement had deteriorated seriously in the United States. The solutions adopted—largely more course requirements and more required tests and, in many cases, holding students back on the basis of tests—were asserted in spite of extensive research over time indicating that such tests tended to drive up dropout rates, not raise achievement.

Postsecondary education is as common and as important as secondary education was in the early post–World War II period, but we have almost no serious policy initiatives to increase the success of students from high-poverty schools and communities in the transition to college. Colleges are busily trying to upgrade their performance by raising their standards and expectations and ending remediation. There is very little coordination with high schools. Because postsecondary training is becoming a necessity for middle-class status, it is important to understand that public schools and colleges are part of a continuum that shapes the future stratification of the society. Universities must not pursue "quality" through exclusion in ways that reinforce social divisions.

Educators in other nations interested in the possible lessons of the U.S. experience will often find, if they examine the best evidence, that the United States has far to go and that U.S. research yields no simple model for greater school success. Though the current reforms have had limited and sometimes very disappointing arguments, the voice of their advocates carries across the globe magnified by the dominant power of the United States.

Within the extraordinarily varied experience of American educational reforms, and the massive research on their impacts, however, there are lessons that may be of deep interest to educators who wish to expand educational opportunity in their societies. Now that serious social science research has been around long enough to compare assumptions and outcomes over big political cycles, much can be learned by looking longer and deeper.

NOTES

1. For an interesting discussion of U.S. misunderstandings of Japan, see LeTrendre (1999); an example of the earlier U.S. focus on the Soviet Union can be found in Bronfenbrenner (1970).
2. Among the many Web sites that could lead interested readers to American statistical reports are nces.ed.gov, census.gov, and www.ccsso.org.

3. The basic approach was called "America 2000" under the Bush administration and "Goals 2000" under the Clinton administration.

4. When U.S. data are compared to national data for the major industrial countries, individual states often rank over an extremely wide spectrum, from the very highest levels to among the lowest levels of national performance (NCES [1988]).

5. Only one country in the world, for example, had a higher eighth-grade science score in TIMMS than the U.S. state of Minnesota (*National Educational Goals Report 1997*).

6. National Center for Education Statistics data show that schools that were 90 to 100 percent black and/or Latino in the 1994–1995 school year were sixteen times more likely to have a majority of poor children than schools with 90 to 100 percent white students.

7. See Stevenson and Stigler (1987). The authors found that families in Asian communities focused overwhelmingly on academic achievement, while American families favored balanced development including many nonacademic activities.

REFERENCES

Blank, Rolf, Roger E. Levine, and Lauri Steel. 1996. After 15 years: Magnet schools in urban education. In *Who Chooses? Who Loses?* ed. Bruce Fuller and Richard F. Elmore, 154–172. New York: Teachers College Press.

Bronfenbrenner, Urie. 1970. *Two Worlds of Childhood: U.S. and U.S.S.R.* New York: Basic Books.

Citizens Commission on Civil Rights. 1998. *Title I in Midstream: The Fight to Improve Schools for Poor Kids.* Washington, D.C.: Citizens Commission.

Coleman, James, E. Campbell, C. Hobson, J. McPartland, A. Mood, F. Weinfeld, and R. York. 1966. *Equality of Educational Opportunity.* Washington, D.C.: Government Printing Office.

Council of Chief State School Officers. <ccsso.org>.

Cremin, Lawrence. 1988. *American Education: The Metropolitan Experience, 1876 to 1980.* New York: Harper & Row, 1988.

Educational Testing Service. 1997. The steeper stairs of higher education. ETS Research. *ETS Net*, p. 1.

Elam, Stanley, and Lowell C. Rose. 1995. The 27th annual Phi Delta Kappa/Gallup Poll of the public's attitudes toward the public schools. *Phi Delta Kappan* (September): 47.

Fuller, Bruce, and Richard Elmore, eds. 1996. *Who Chooses? Who Loses?* New York: Teachers College Press.

Greenwald, Rob, Richard D. Laine, and Larry Hedges. 1996. The school funding controversy: Reality bites. *Educational Leadership*, pp. 78–79.

Grissmer, David, Ann Flanagan, and Stephanie Williamson. 1998. Why did the score gap narrow in the 1970s and 1980s? In *The Black-White Score Gap*, eds. Christopher Jencks and Meredith Phillips, 182–226. Washington, D.C.: The Brookings Institution.

Hanusheck, Eric, et al. 1994. *Making Schools Work: Improving Performance and Controlling Costs.* Washington, D.C.: The Brookings Institution.

Hauser, Robert M. 1998. Should we end social promotion? Truth and consequences. Paper presented at the High Stakes K–12 Testing Conference, Teachers College, Columbia University, December 4.

Hedges, Larry V., Richard D. Laine, and Rob Greenwald. 1994. Does money matter? A meta-analysis of studies of the effects of differential school inputs on student outcomes. *Educational Researcher* 23(3): 5–14.

Heubert, Jay, and Robert Hauser, eds. 1998. *High Stakes.* Washington, D.C.: National Academy Press.

Heubert, Jay, and Robert M. Hauser, eds. 1999. *High Stakes Testing for Tracking, Promotion, and Graduation.* Washington, D.C.: National Academy Press.

LeTrendre, Gerald K. 1999. The problem of Japan: Qualitative studies and international educational comparisons. *Educational Researcher* 28(2): 38–48.

Lewin, Tamar. 1999. Few clear lessons from nation's first school-choice program. *New York Times*, March 27.

Mortenson, Thomas G., ed. 1998. Postsecondary education opportunity. The Mortenson Research Seminar on Public Policy Analysis of Opportunity for Postsecondary Education. ERIC document ED 429521.

Mosteller, Frederick. 1995. The Tennessee study of class size in the early school grades. *The Future of Children* 5(2): 113–127.

National Center for Children in Poverty. 1999. *Young Children in Poverty. A Statistical Update.* New York: Columbia University.

National Center for Education Statistics. <nces.ed.gov>.

National Center for Education Statistics. 2000. The condition of education 1999. Washington, D.C.: U.S. Department of Education, Office of Educational Research and Improvement, National Center for Education Statistics, Government Printing Office.

National Center for Education Statistics. 1999. Dropout rates in the United States: 1997. Washington, D.C.: U.S. Department of Education, Office of Educational Research and Improvement, National Center for Education Statistics, Government Printing Office.

National Center for Education Statistics. 1996. NAEP 1996 trends in academic progress. Washington, D.C.: U.S. Department of Education, Office of Educational Research and Improvement, National Center for Education Statistics, Government Printing Office.

National Center for Education Statistics. 1988. Education in states and nations: U.S. states with the OECD countries in 1988. Washington, D.C.: U.S. Department of Education, Office of Educational Research and Improvement, National Center for Education Statistics, Government Printing Office.

National Education Goals Panel. 1997. National education goals report 1997. Washington, D.C.: Government Printing Office.

Newman, Heather. 1998. Test results can be skewed by many outside factors. *Detroit Free Press*, May 7.

OECD. 1995. *Education at a Glance: OECD Indicators.* Paris: OECD.

Orfield, Gary. 1988. Exclusion of the majority: Shrinking college access and public policy in metropolitan Los Angeles. *Urban Review* 20(3): 147–163.

Orfield, Gary. 1992. Urban schooling and the perpetuation of job inequality in metropolitan Chicago. In *Urban Labor Markets and Job Opportunity,* ed. George E. Peterson and Wayne Vroman, 161–191. Washington, D.C.: Urban Institute.

Orfield, Gary, and Carole Ashkinaze. 1991. *The Closing Door: Conservative Policy and Black Opportunity.* Chicago: University of Chicago Press, pp. 123–129.

Orfield, Gary, Mark Bachmeier, David James, and Tamela Eitle. 1997. Deepening segregation in American public schools. *Equity and Excellence in Education* 30(2): 5–24.

Orfield, Gary, and Elizabeth Debray, eds. 1999. Hard work for good schools: Facts not fads in Title I reform. Cambridge, Mass.: Harvard Civil Rights Project.

Orfield, Gary, and John Yun. 2000. Resegregation and American Schools, Harvard Civil Rights Project, June 1999. Reprinted in part, *Primer* 2(4): 1–6.

Peterson, Paul. 1985. The politics of school reform, 1870–1940, part 2. Chicago: University of Chicago Press.

Pitsch, Mark. 1996. Polls confirm the political role for education. *Education Week* (June 19): 1, 30–31.

Rodriguez v. San Antonio Independent School District. 1973. 411 U.S. 1.

Rose, Lowell, and Alec M. Gallup. 1998. The 30th annual Phi Delta Kappa/Gallup Poll of the public's attitudes toward the public schools. *Phi Delta Kappan* (September).

Salganik, Laura H., and associates. 1993. *Education in States and Nations: Indicators Comparing U.S. States with the OECD Countries in 1988.* Washington, D.C.: National Center for Education Statistics.

Shea, Christopher. 1998. Do smaller classes mean better schools? Economists aren't so sure. *Chronicle of Higher Education* (April 3): A18.

Shepard, L. A., and M. L. Smith, eds. 1989. *Flunking Grades: Research and Policies on Retention.* London: Falmer Press.

Stephan, Walter. 1991. School desegregation: Short-term and long-term effects. In *Opening Doors: Perspectives on Race Relations in Contemporary America,* ed. Harry J. Knopke, Robert J. Norrell, and Ronald W. Rogers, 100–118. Tuscaloosa: University of Alabama Press.

Stevenson, Harold W., and James W. Stigler. 1987. *The Learning Gap.* New York: Summit Books.

Summary of gubernatorial candidates' positions on education. 1998. *Education Week* (October 7): 20–21.

Sunderman, Gail. 1995. The politics of school reform: The educational excellence movement and state policy making. Unpublished Ph.D. dissertation, Department of Political Science, University of Chicago.

United States President's Advisory Commission on Educational Excellence for Hispanic Americans. 1996. Our nation on the fault line: Hispanic American education. Washington, D.C.: President's Advisory Commission on Educational Excellence for Hispanic Americans.

U.S. Bureau of the Census. <census.gov>.

U.S. Census Bureau. 1993. Population projections of the United States, by age, sex, race and Hispanic origin: 1993 to 2050. Washington, D.C.: Government Printing Office.

U.S. Department of Education. 1993. *Prospects: The Congressionally Mandated Study of Educational Growth and Opportunity: The Interim Report.* Washington, D.C.: Government Printing Office.

U.S. National Center for Education Statistics. 1988. *Education in States and Nations: U.S. States with the OECD Countries in 1988.* Washington, D.C.: Government Printing Office.

Commentary

Sylvia Schmelkes, Departamento de Investigaciones Educativas, CINVESTAV-IPN, Mexico City

This chapter by Gary Orfield is very relevant to Latin America largely because, as a result of the processes of decentralization under way in many of the countries of the region, local governments are looking outward in search of educational innovations that can help them improve. As Orfield states in this chapter, people tend to emulate powerful countries, under the assumption that their power stems from their educational successes.

A significant conclusion of the chapter concerns the lack of interest on issues of equity in the United States since the 1980s. Counter to the assumption stated in Willie's chapter suggesting that the most effective policies are those that aim to improve both quality and equity, and not one of these two, Orfield states that U.S. education policymakers think of these as opposite goals. Choosing among them is a dilemma; the option is either equity or excellence. Orfield states that federal decision makers have chosen to pursue excellence in education because, in order to maintain the country's standing as a competitive nation, it is enough to educate some children to very high levels. If this is indeed the model of decision making followed in some countries or regions in the hemisphere, it represents a big mistake vis-à-vis the reality of inequality highly documented in this book. This could be one of the most serious mistakes of the educational history of Latin America. The importance of this chapter rests on its value to unveil this potential mistake.

The study by Gary Orfield highlights the importance of taking into account context in assessing the adequacy of education policies. I would think that in some cases taking into account contextual factors of Latin American countries would lead us to conclusions different from Gary Orfield's.

I work in two areas that, from the perspective of progressive researchers in the United States, such as Gary Orfield, are conservative. One of them is the assessment of student academic achievement; the other is values education, or moral education. Both are mentioned in Orfield's work as priorities for the conservative movement in the United States. However, in the Latin American context, I believe the role played by both of these areas is opposite to what Orfield suggests is their role in the United States.

Mexico has a long history of assessing student achievement using sample surveys. These tests are not very good, they have never been comparable over time, and in particular they have never been used to provide feedback in education policy making. They have never been used, until recently, to make decisions about the individuals who take the tests.

Since about ten years ago, a test of academic achievement has been administered in large cities to allocate graduates of primary school to certain secondary schools, and to particular shifts (morning or afternoon) within these schools. Since 1993, primary school teachers have enrolled in a promotion system (Sistema de Carrera Magisterial) and must supply information on a number of indicators, including performance on a test of subject matter knowledge. Since 1997 in the metropolitan area of Mexico City, a curriculum-based test is used to determine which option of upper secondary education each student is eligible to enter.

All these tests can be criticized in several ways. The most serious, from my point of view, is the fact that the information they generate is not used to improve the circumstances that cause the differences between students. Hence, the results of the national examination to enter upper secondary, for instance, have never been used seriously as a diagnosis of secondary education and have therefore not served to improve the quality of the schools where students obtain the lowest scores (which correspond to the schools located in the poorest areas of the city).

But in basic education teachers have always assessed students, and their judgment matters both for the grade students obtain and to determine whether students are promoted or not. The absence of external evaluations, or of a culture to use the few that have been carried out, has simply obscured the large inequalities in the quality of learning results obtained by the schools serving different student populations. As is well known, the measurement of student achievement is a key indicator both for the effectiveness and equity of an education system, particularly in those levels that have been generalized to all of the relevant student population.

In Mexico, particularly, the absence of external evaluation, or of "learning tests," simply hid for years—and still does to a great extent—the dramatic educational inequalities in the results of education. In this context, I believe that the task of conducting student assessments cannot be considered a conservative exercise—even though our own political opposition does see it in precisely those terms—as long as:

- The results of the tests are not used to make decisions about individuals.
- The results of the tests are used to influence schools, but particularly to improve them, never to harm them.
- The results of the tests are publicly disseminated and serve to mobilize officials, teachers, and society against inequality.

As Gary Orfield accurately points out, the tests should be comparable across time and should highlight the value added by teachers and, particularly, by schools. Therefore, I believe a critical analysis of the U.S. experience is very useful. Opposite to the conclusions drawn by Orfield himself, suggesting caution with the use of tests, I would say that in the case of Mexico, we should be cautious about the absence of tests (or about the absence of external mechanisms of evaluation).

Regarding moral education, I would add that, in the same sense in which Orfield addresses it in the chapter, what is important is to educate for democracy, to value diversity, and to create in schools an educational environment that is warm, effective, and full of respect for the child. The goal should be to foster the development of autonomous human beings, able to think, engage in dialogue, and decide their own value priorities and act accordingly. From this perspective, I do not think values education is conservative. Again, context gives policy different meanings.

How can we explain that in the United States, given the ample research base and production of knowledge, education policy making is so "ideological." Politicians seem to complain about the irrelevance of educational research—which is doubtful— as well as about the seeming lack of interest of educational researchers in the process of decision making. It would be useful to understand who processes the enormous amount of information about the performance of the education system and how this knowledge is used. I think that in this area, there is much about the experience of the United States that is useful to Latin America.

Students during break at the Andy Aparicio Fe y Alegria School in the La Vega neighborhood of Caracas, Venezuela.
[Gregorio Marrero]

16

Conclusions: Can Our Knowledge Change What Low-Income Children Learn?

Fernando Reimers
Harvard Graduate School of Education

I started this book discussing the dilemma of a group of education policy reformers trying to improve the educational opportunities of Rosa, a nine-year-old living in a marginalized community in this hemisphere, and of other children like her. This group knows some things about the educational circumstances of children like Rosa and about programs to change those circumstances. Mostly they know how little they know. Does any of it matter? Can their knowledge change Rosa's educational chances? This chapter takes stock of some of the main themes discussed in this book and tries to highlight the broad strokes, the fine lines, and the gaps that emerge in such a composite.

I begin with the kind of recommendations that the team of presidential advisers attempting to influence Rosa's chances might draw from what is already known. I argue that while we still need to learn much about the impact of specific interventions on the learning chances of children like Rosa, and that we need better research to know that, we already know enough about the constraints to equality of opportunity facing Rosa. Some of the research on the factors associated with her learning is suggestive of policies that might work. I use a framework to classify the research extant on this subject and reviewed in this book and to discuss the quality of the evidence emerging from such research. Then I develop a framework to categorize the policy approaches that have been followed to address equality of opportunity in the region. I explain why concentrated efforts to improve the educational conditions of low-income children are the most likely to reduce the opportunity gaps between rich and poor. I sum up the implications of using a stochastic versus a cumulative model to think about educational opportunity and on the basis of this discussion reframe the meaning of compensatory policies. I highlight the issues that still need to be investigated and the kind of research most likely to produce knowledge of use to support policy change.

In a nutshell, this team might draw twelve recommendations to inform a reform strategy. The rest of this chapter develops these recommendations in greater detail.

- Education matters greatly for social opportunity, more so as economies integrate into a global economy. Education should be a priority of the new government strategy.
- Addressing the learning conditions facing poor children is not enough; we need to focus on the distance between the conditions facing the poor and those facing the non-poor. The objective of policy should be to close that distance.
- This kind of educational change is the hardest one can envision; intentional and inertial resistance will make it difficult to implement.
- Education policy matters, as shown by intergenerational education mobility resulting from past policies. The necessary changes must be brought about by deliberate education interventions, not as the byproducts of other kinds of interventions in economic or social policy.
- Education policy needs to address the three core processes that explain the growing education inequalities: (1) inequalities inside the education system (addressed by making the utilization of funds more progressive and reducing segregation), (2) inequalities outside the education system (addressed with supportive social policies to improve the health and nutrition conditions of poor children), and (3) inequalities stemming from the interaction of the school system with the world outside the school (addressed by giving greater voice to school communities, revisiting which skills matter, and reexamining what pedagogy will be most effective). The last point calls into question whether spending more resources on the education of the poor will be enough, a point that will be stressed throughout this chapter.
- Educational opportunity can be thought of as a cumulative process. Policy should support children at all stages of their educational careers; given how little past policies have focused on opportunities to access and complete secondary and higher education, they should be the priority because those are the levels that most matter to social mobility.
- Policy interventions to achieve equity must be conceived as part of a long-term strategy. Education systems evolve in stages, as do schools; policy at each stage should be atuned to the initial conditions of schools and they should support them at the necessary level.
- A possible sequence of policy cycles would be to (1) equalize inputs, (2) make utilization of inputs more progressive, and (3) develop differentiated strategies for the children of the poor.
- Innovation is central to achieve equality. The core questions are: Which methods should help us innovate? What should we innovate in? What should be the extent of the innovation? Methods should look for context-specific knowledge, needs assessments, beneficiary assessments, and studies specifically in schools attended by low-income children. The content of innovation should focus on what kind of skills will matter most to afford social mobility. The extent of innovation should be as much as the existing institutional capacity can manage; in most cases, this calls for gradual and incremental strategies of reform.

- The focus on innovation highlights the limits of what is known to provide a different type of education that will increase the social and cultural capital of the poor to allow them greater freedom. It is necessary to support the generation of more knowledge for this purpose.
- Existing reforms show that it is possible to make policy more progressive and that even modest improvements in infrastructure and the provision of basic materials can have results, particularly in getting more children to complete primary education. These efforts reflect the first stage in the sequence mentioned earlier; they should be sustained and deepened.
- Central to any strategy should be thinking about implementation, which will be challenging. Because the kind of change called for should be sustained over the long term, it is important to obtain broad ownership of this change among the poor, and particularly the non-poor, and to set up systems that will allow ongoing learning from experience.

EDUCATION, POVERTY, AND INEQUALITY

Is there equality of educational opportunity in the Americas? Though the answer to this question depends on how we define educational opportunity, a short and simple answer is no. The educational chances of children are heavily influenced by the social position their parents occupy in the social structure. This refers both to the chances to access different levels of education and to the chances to learn at and complete each level. It also refers to the possibility that what is learned will make a difference in terms of life opportunities.[1] There are fewer poor students excluded from enrolling in school because of the remarkable quantitative expansion in access at all levels which has taken place in the education systems of the hemisphere over the second half of the 1900s, but important inequalities remain in access to the education levels that most matter and in the sheer level of resources going to the education of different groups of children.

The expansion in access of the last half-century resulted in the incorporation of new social groups into the education system and to higher levels of education in the system, with a consequent increase in the average level of schooling of the population in all countries of the region and a decline in inequality in the distribution of schooling around those average levels. At the end of the twentieth century, there was significantly less educational exclusion in the Americas for the children of the poor than there was just fifty years ago. There is less educational inequality in the sense that the distribution of educational attainment, relative to the average number of years of schooling, is lower for younger people than for those who went to school a decade or two ago. This shows that the education system has a degree of autonomy from the larger social structure and that it is not simply an accessory to reproduce the existing pattern of social stratification. Existing evidence indicates also that there is less educational inequality than income inequality. However, disparities in educational attainment continue to be sharp at those levels that currently matter the most to employers for access to the better-paid jobs.

Several chapters in this book provide clear evidence that education expands the choices available to people and families. To several of the contributors, acquiring education is a tool to alleviate poverty; gaining access to education and learning to read, communicate, think, and learn are enhancements of a person's capabilities. The development of basic capabilities provides the foundation for the acquisition of more complex capabilities, and many of these capabilities are acquired in a developmental progression of growing complexity. For example, language development is foundational to acquiring many other abilities. But language acquisition, like the acquisition of all capabilities, is a process, not a discrete event. As discussed by Sen elsewhere (Sen 1992), increased capabilities allow people to increase their functionings, their ability to make choices (functionings), and therefore their ability to be free (Sen 1992). From this perspective, there is compelling evidence that the education systems have provided and are providing opportunities of educational mobility to the children of the poor in the hemisphere. As a result of educational expansion, there has been significant intergenerational educational mobility in the region. The children of the poor have attained higher levels of education and have, therefore, more capabilities than their parents, and they can expect their own children to attain higher levels of education tomorrow. This fundamental social change is a direct result of public policies to universalize access to schooling. In taking stock of education progress in the hemisphere, we must ask not only what has changed, but also what could have changed but has not. It is on this point that conclusions regarding the contributions of education to the reduction of poverty and inequality must become more nuanced.

Inequality matters for poverty in the sense that it indicates the availability of resources that could potentially be mobilized to reduce poverty. Two distinct and somewhat independent processes are involved here. It is possible to observe changes in inequality that have a minimum impact on the incidence of poverty. It is also possible to reduce poverty, in an absolute sense, without influencing inequality. The reduction of social exclusion, however, calls for reductions in poverty *and* inequality. From a narrow perspective interested in reducing the number of people living below the poverty line, the focus would be solely on improving the educational chances of the poor over time. The capabilities of the poor, and arguably their income, would be expanded, even if their relative standing in society did not change because the non-poor also would have increased their education. This approach characterizes most equity-oriented policies in the region: to improve the educational environments of the poor relative to what those environments were in the past. From a broader perspective interested in fostering social inclusion and reducing inequality, the focus should be not just on the absolute educational conditions of the poor but on the social distance between the poor and the most advantaged. It is possible for the poor to stay in the same place, in terms of the gap in their educational attainment, or in terms of income gaps, even as they improve their absolute level of schooling simply because the non-poor improve their levels even more. It is harder to influence this social distance, to narrow the gap, than to improve the conditions of schools for the poor. Reducing the distance, requires that the poor benefit more from educational improvement.

The main emphasis of the chapters in this book is on the social distribution of educational opportunities. One argument supported by several chapters is that it is not possible for the education system to fully equalize opportunities because as coverage in a given level increases, the gaps in access to other levels become the new points of social division. We see that in all countries discussed in the book, as enrollments in primary education reach universalization, access to secondary and higher education increases for some children but not for others. In addition, access to preschool education increases, but not for the poor.

Educational opportunity is not a condition that automatically follows once a child enrolls in school. Rather, it is an ongoing process that facilitates a child's development through many years. Initial opportunities make it possible to move forward in that process, but continued progression is conditioned by opportunities at every stage of a learner's early life. A dynamic understanding of educational opportunity leads to focusing on the barriers to equality in access to secondary and tertiary education and to equality in learning outcomes. Adopting such a dynamic view of educational opportunity matters for how we think of the relationship among education, poverty, and inequality.

In line with this dynamic view of educational opportunity, several chapters in the book have suggested that understanding the dynamic links between education and poverty requires longitudinal information. The chapter by Muñiz suggests that the degree of poverty a person experiences may change during the life cycle of a family. The core factor explaining educational opportunity is how potential students spend their time. How students spend their time reflects how families and teachers structure demands, support, and incentives around them. These are likely to change over time for a given child, reflecting the changes experienced by the family. A child's potential time for study may be constrained by the birth of young siblings who require help. A child's exposure to stimulating educational environments may be increased as a family moves to more urban areas or to different school districts.

GROWING EDUCATION INEQUALITIES

Are the education gaps between different social groups narrowing or growing? This is a difficult question, for we see different patterns at different points in time in different countries. The answer depends in part on the specific indicator of education one uses (access, spending, learning). As mentioned earlier, the gaps, understood as the variation of levels of schooling around the average level for the population, have narrowed. But the same is not true for the gaps in access to higher levels of education. As demonstrated by Orfield, in the United States, between the 1960s and 1980, the gaps in access to higher education narrowed, but progress has stagnated, if not reversed, since. In several countries in Latin America, the speed of educational expansion narrowed the gaps in access. But during the past decade, as the countries of the region have increased their integration into the world economy, families are receiving signals that opportunities in the global economy are for those with higher levels of education.

A very significant level of educational effort is made by families in Latin America. Those who have more resources are contributing more to finance the education of their children. As a result of the high levels of inequality of origin, the gaps in education spending between rich and poor students is widening. Education is a superior good and families with more income will acquire more of it. Because the countries of the region are a long way from achieving universal enrollment in higher education, even for the children of the higher income groups, there is no end in sight to the potential growth of inequality that will result from private efforts to increase the educational opportunities of children.

Several processes explain these growing inequalities. These processes operate inside the school system, outside the school system, and in the interaction between the school system and the larger world.

Three processes inside the school system contribute to inequality. The first is the result of private financing of education. Those children whose parents can best afford it have a greater likelihood of attending quality preschool and therefore more chances of beginning school ready to learn. They are also more likely to attend quality primary and secondary schools and to enroll in higher education. Because educational institutions are highly stratified, a second social process leads to educational inequality: the effect of peers in fostering learning opportunities. Children in schools where their peers receive more support and stimulation at home are likely to learn from them and will have teachers with greater expectations regarding academic potential than children attending schools where most of their peers have poor home education backgrounds. Social and racial segregation is, therefore, another important process that furthers educational inequality. A third and more blatant process results from the disparities in how public educational resources are used. The most obvious manifestation of this inequality is different levels of public expenditures for children attending different types of public schools, or schools in different geographical areas. Related manifestations of inequalities between schools are more low-quality schools for poor children and less experienced and less educated teachers, with fewer materials and support for high-quality instruction.

Outside the school system, the processes that aggravate inequality in educational opportunities stem from the living conditions of poor children. Poor conditions debilitate children's health and make them more vulnerable in physical and psychological ways. A child whose parents have no steady source of income faces daily school tasks at a disadvantage relative to a child who does not know what it is like to go without food. The stresses caused in children by the devastating impact of events outside the control of the heads of household—loss of crops or jobs, abuses of local figures of authority, demands placed by many siblings and insufficient resources, death or abandonment of one of the income contributors to the home—influence whether and how well children can focus on their academic activities. Short-term demands may make regular school attendance a luxury rather than a fact of life. Poor children and their families also are very sensitive to all direct costs associated with attending schools: the costs of uniforms and clothing, fees, notebooks, pencils, and textbooks. These expenses represent a disproportionately larger share of the smaller family budget of low-income children. These social processes reproduce inequality, even if all other things were equal for all children. As we have seen, all other things are not equal.

The third and last set of social processes that contribute to the reproduction of inequality in the schools concerns the interaction between social and educational influences. Direct poverty of the family, particularly as it is expressed in low levels of education in the household, acquires additional meaning as it shapes the ecology of classrooms and schools. The aggregate level of poverty of families influences teacher expectations and practices. Collective cultural and social capital of school communities influences the pressure they can exert to claim or generate resources to support schools. Different aggregates, different constellations of levels of education of parents, lead to different responses of teachers and schools. Teachers are more likely to have high expectations for the academic potential of children when they believe the parents will be able to support the education of the children for many years—a function of the socioeconomic level of the parents. System administrators are more likely to attend to the functioning of a school where parents have the time and understanding to notice malfunctioning and the political voice to complain when things go wrong.

Another way in which these sets of influences interact to shape a distinct process influencing equality of educational opportunity concerns the match between the type of pedagogy used and the various backgrounds of learners. Force-feeding a singular approach to teaching all children, irrespective of their circumstances, will make some groups of children more likely to learn than others. For example, a common school calendar, designed for children in urban areas, and mode of education delivery—all children learning at the same time, on a rigid schedule—will place those children who work occasionally or seasonally at a disadvantage because missing some classes will have a cumulative effect in their ability to master the curriculum.[2] Similarly, a curriculum delivered in a "national" language will place the children who do not speak that language at home at a disadvantage relative to the children for whom this national language is the mother tongue. There are more subtle ways in which pedagogical processes can fail to take into account the social context of origin of the children. For instance, teachers can teach to the fastest learners, or to those who have been to preschool in first grade, placing the rest of the children at a disadvantage. Curricula and textbooks can rely on examples and concrete referents that are more familiar to certain groups of children than to others.

A question that stems from this analysis is whether providing more of the same to poor children is sufficient to overcome inequality. This question is central to making sense of the contradictory conclusions reached by García-Huidobro and the Schiefelbeins with regard to the impact of the reforms in Chile. It also emerges in the analysis of Sarmiento about the effects of Colombia's education policy choices. If the goal of schools is to help graduates acquire the cultural and social capital that will enable them to have more options for a better life, schools should do what communities and families cannot do. The purpose of schools should be to foster the freedom of graduates to have and make choices to improve their lives. The capabilities that make this freedom possible are likely to vary depending on the position of different groups in the social structure.

In addition to cognitive skills developed by academic subjects, poor children must acquire capabilities for collective action, for political efficacy. From this perspective, the dominant view in the hemisphere is inadequate. It equates quality with standards as reflected in curriculum-based tests which measure low-level cognitive skills and the short-term impact of educational programs. Children do need to learn to read and write, and they also need to learn math, science, and social studies. But if the poor are to have a chance to improve their options in life, collectively they need much more than that. For one, they need to stay in school—an objective of more consequence for children at risk of dropping out of school than for children who will almost certainly complete high school and college. They also need to learn to imagine a different future for themselves and their communities than the realities experienced daily in the marginalized village or in the urban ghetto. They need to be able to formulate a strategy to construct that future. They need to be able to access information about occupational options and careers and about the most promising educational avenues. And they need to accumulate financial capital as well as cultural and social capital to be able to reinvest in their communities to generate more opportunities. Getting ahead individually, as opposed to collectively, also calls for more than learning basic skills in a watered-down curriculum.

This is a political view of the purposes of educational change. It aims at changing the position of the poor in the social structure. It calls for changes in the core of the practice of education. As a result, it is arguably the hardest of all forms of educational change—one that is likely to be faced with great intentional and inertial resistance. Few models in the hemisphere have adopted this political view of equity-enhancing policies. The policy by default has been to leave a uniform curriculum fundamentally unquestioned or to make marginal changes around it to make it more stimulating, flexible, or attuned to the cultural background of different children. There are, at the margins of education systems, a few innovations in line with the approach outlined here, such as the Fe y Alegria schools set up by the Jesuits in disadvantaged communities in Latin America (Swope and Latorre 1999), and some efforts to empower marginalized communities inspired by Paulo Freire.

THE COMPLEXITY OF EQUITY POLICIES

To the extent that equity has been a policy priority in the Americas, policies have not reflected a sophisticated understanding of opportunity. In Latin America, for the longest time, opportunity has been understood as expanding access to first grade, as if opportunity for each child would follow naturally from then on. More recent efforts to focus on quality divides between the poor and the non-poor have supported a one-size-fits-all model of instruction. In the United States, the emphasis of compensatory policies has been on closing the financial gap in per pupil expenditures between the poor and the non-poor, on fostering racial integration in schools, on providing supportive services to children at risk, and on experimenting with different programs to improve instructional practice in at-risk schools.

Educational opportunity has been understood as a stochastic process, where initial probabilities condition the net impact of future probabilities. The result of such thinking is to emphasize early interventions and, taken to an extreme, to focus on interventions in health, food, nutrition, and stimulation prior to children enrolling in school. An alternative way to construe opportunity is as a cumulative process, one where opportunity at each stage of development of the learner matters. From this perspective early opportunities are important, prior to enrolling in school and in the early grades, but so are later opportunities, in the upper grades of basic schooling and in secondary education. A cumulative view of opportunity sees later opportunity as enhancing the impact of early opportunity (and vice versa), while a stochastic view leads to neglecting the role of later opportunity. There is no research base to prefer one model over the other; the choice between these perspectives is pragmatic. A cumulative view of opportunity has the most potential to expand the educational chances of poor children to the levels that currently matter the most for social mobility (completion of basic schooling and access to secondary and tertiary education).

Efforts to increase equality of educational opportunity should be construed as a series of long-term and sustained interventions resulting from a series of cycles of policy reform. Each cycle should focus on the particular stage of opportunity that constitutes the main educational divide between rich and poor at a given point in time. Education systems evolve in stages. At an early stage, the system is relatively unorganized and teachers are poorly educated. Gradually, the system becomes more organized and formal, though teachers are still poorly skilled. Later on, as teacher education increases, the quality of the system improves though the goals of the system remain the same. Finally, teachers become professionals, placing an emphasis on meaning and understanding (Beeby 1986, 37–44).[3] Change from one stage to the next is a gradual process. At any given point in time, some schools reflect characteristics of different stages; the modal tendency of schools defines the stage of the system. A strategy to help improve schools needs to allow for differences appropriate to the initial conditions of each school. Some schools require highly structured, prescriptive approaches and infrastructural and technical support to be able to meet the expectation of teaching all children to high standards. Other schools will require help setting the vision and networks to link them with others as they move forward. And some may require very little in the form of external assistance. The current reforms in Latin America reflect a simple-minded understanding of the dynamics of school improvement. This limited understanding is unlikely to yield significant gains in the educational opportunities of poor children attending fragile schools.

A sound strategy needs policies that can support each school at the necessary level.[4] In addition, sequencing these cycles is critical to their long-term success and to effective implementation. For purposes of sequencing policies, we can think of them in three groups, according to the way compensation is interpreted. A first group of compensatory policies includes those that aim to equalize the distribution of publicly financed educational inputs. The objective is to close the input gap between the school environments attended by the poor and the non-poor. These include (1) more equitable formula-based funding of schools, such as the financing reforms implemented in Brazil since 1998; (2) policies that aim to increase access to a given education level by building more schools; and (3) policies that try to provide schools attended by low-income children with minimum instructional resources commonly available to the non-poor such as textbooks, school libraries, and training for teachers. Efforts to expand access for the poor using innovations for the delivery of education also belong in this group. Examples of policies to equalize access include the use of television broadcasting to support the expansion of secondary education in rural areas in Mexico (*telesecundaria*), the use of community-based modalities of education to offer education to multiage groups in remote rural communities (also in Mexico), and the program to expand access to preschool and primary education in rural areas in El Salvador (EDUCO).

A second group of compensatory policies includes those that aim to reorient the utilization of public resources to equalize the distribution of educational opportunities understood as outputs. Some call these policies of positive discrimination. These policies recognize that the outcomes of schools reflect the contributions of school and family resources. Therefore, the purpose of compensation is to balance the greater opportunities some children receive from home resources. Achieving equal opportunity to attain the same levels of schooling requires interventions that appropriately cover children's opportunity costs such as scholarships for low-income students that cover the direct and indirect costs of participation in school. An example of this policy is the scholarship program to support school attendance of low-income children in Mexico (Progresa) or the scholarship program for similar purposes in Brazil (Fundescola). Programs of full-day school sessions for low-income children in Chile, Uruguay, and Venezuela (where the non-poor attend half-day sessions) are examples of positive discrimination focused on increasing the quality of inputs or the intensity of their utilization. Given the stark discrepancies between the conditions of the targeted schools and those attended by the non-poor, and in light of the relatively low level of funding of these policies, much of what are called policies of positive discrimination in Latin America are, in fact, mere attempts to equalize the distribution of inputs. At best, they are designed to close the resource gap—to address the levels of initial input inequality among schools. They are not designed to enable schools of low-income children to add more value to achieve equality of output. For example, the widely documented 900 Schools Program in Chile and the more recent PARE program in Mexico may target resources and attention to schools attended by disadvantaged children, but they are simply trying to redress previous neglect and stark inequalities in resource endowment between these schools and the rest. The same is true of the Escuela Nueva program in Colombia, which attempts to improve the quality of rural multigrade schools through teacher training and provision of materials.

A third group of compensatory policies is those that support differentiated forms of treatment for low-income children in recognition of their unique needs and characteristics. The main objective of these policies is to support opportunities for relevant and meaningful learning for low-income children. The goal is not to achieve equality of learning outputs, but equality of life chances. The assumption is that the school curriculum contributes only a fraction of the cultural and social capital the non-poor acquire in life. The rest is acquired as a result of experiences facilitated by family, neighbors, and community. In order for the poor to have comparable opportunities to live lives consistent with their choices, schools need to provide more cultural and social capital. This means facilitating development of personal efficacy as well as political and negotiation skills. While the first and second approaches mentioned earlier (equality of inputs and equality of outputs) assume the equivalency of the relevance of curricular objectives for all children, this particular group of efforts does not make such assumptions. It attempts instead to support curricular goals and pedagogical approaches that specifically allow low-income children to move out of poverty through individual or collective action. Examples of this approach include various forms of popular education as described by Paulo Freire and his colleagues and followers (Freire 1970), the various modalities of education designed and supported by Fe y Alegria; the network of publicly funded schools managed by the Society of Jesus in thirteen Latin American countries (Swope and Latorre 1999); and the recent modality of community-based postprimary education developed in Mexico.

THE ROLE OF INNOVATION IN FOSTERING EQUALITY OF OPPORTUNITY

The third group of policies outlined above calls for innovation, for experimenting with new ways to organize the instructional process. The chapter by Muñoz Izquierdo and Ahuja asks whether it is reasonable to expect the most fragile part of the education system to do better than the most endowed parts—to innovate in order to use resources in more cost-effective ways.

Innovating to increase educational opportunity calls for three strategic choices. The first must consider which kinds of methodologies are most effective in producing the innovation. The second choice is about the content of the innovations, and the third is about the degree of innovation.

First choice, which methodologies yield innovation? Accepting that we need new knowledge in this area requires looking upon the limits of what we know squarely in the face. In spite of a number of policy initiatives undertaken over the past thirty years to improve the educational chances of low-income children, we do not yet know as much about how to achieve greater equality of educational opportunity as we do about the basic parameters of the human genome, how to treat many of the diseases known to affect humans, and how to launch spaceships. As we discussed in these chapters, none of the programs that have been tried appear to have achieved remarkable results.

This lack of knowledge to guarantee educational opportunity to the poor is probably more an indication of political priorities than of organizational or intellectual inadequacies of governments and research communities. In some cases, it is difficult to find information about the educational chances of the children of the poor. It is almost impossible to compare education statistics for different ethnic and racial groups in Latin America. Few national education statistics and monitoring systems collect information that allows the analysis of educational performance (access, progression, completion, and achievement) of children from different income and ethnic groups. Less common are longitudinal studies of the impact of policies aimed at enhancing these chances.

The research presented and reviewed in this book falls into three groups. The first group of studies provides evidence that low-income children have lower educational opportunities (1) in terms of access to various levels of schooling, (2) in terms of the quality of their schooling, and (3) in terms of how much they learn. Such research identifies a problem that should be central to policy reform efforts in the immediate future. Such research does not, however, suggest what to do about the problem or how to go about solving it. Most chapters in this book provide some of this evidence.

A second group of studies examines the factors associated with the educational conditions of low-income or marginalized children. Most of the research on school effectiveness, when it does address socioeconomic background of the children, is of this kind. This type of research is suggestive of hypotheses about potentially fruitful policy interventions. The main weakness to bear in mind is that understanding how certain variables relate to one another does not explain the causal processes involved and therefore does not tell us much about how to change present circumstances.

Finally, there are evaluations of the specific impact of programs to change the educational circumstances of low-income children. When well done, these can provide information on how much change can be expected from particular programs, in what domains, and at what cost. The problem is that there are few of these, they focus on few outcomes, and most inappropriately control for the potential role of other factors in explaining change. For example, the chapters discussing the reforms in Argentina, Chile, and Colombia present selected educational indicators at various points in time and draw inferences linking those changes to particular equity-enhancing policies. Because other events may have changed during the period in question, we cannot answer to what extent the observed changes would have taken place in the absence of such policies or how much is the result of the interaction of particular education policies and other policies that reinforce the effects of education policies (for example, economic growth generating new jobs that demand higher levels of education, or health policies improving the overall health conditions of students).

The best evaluations of programs try to account for what outcomes we would have observed in the absence of the program. The most common evaluation approach uses multiple regressions as a way to separate the specific contribution of the program from the contribution of other factors, such as is done in the chapters discussing the impact of PARE and Progresa in Mexico. The quality of this evidence is questionable, however, because we do not know whether the children who benefited from the program and those who did not are comparable in relevant dimensions other than those being evaluated in the regression models. Theoretically random assignment of students to programs would provide the best basis on which to evaluate the impact of program interventions, but natural experiments are rare and difficult to produce, and the ethical implications of such social experimentation are questionable. None of the chapters in this book rely on this type of evidence. Should we draw from this that what we know is of little value to improve the education chances of poor children? Existing research and evaluation based knowledge can support much policy reform to expand educational opportunity. As discussed it is necessary to remain aware of the limits of this knowledge as well as to press forward in generating additional research to fill in existing gaps.

A good part of the knowledge that education research has generated in the region is aimed at identifying the factors that improve the quality of education. Most of this research has examined how characteristics of schools and teachers are associated with different levels of learning outcomes. This research might be suggestive of hypotheses of the factors that can explain differences, but doesn't truly explain "learning" as it compares learning outcomes in different children at one point in time, and it does not appropriately account for potential differences between children attending different kinds of schools that may be critical in explaining the observed differences in outcomes. Another weakness of this approach is that it has been driven by the same paradigm that the Schiefelbeins argue undergirds educational pedagogy in the region—a model that assumes all children are equal learners and therefore fosters interventions for an "average" child who does not exist. Recognition of the individuality of all children and of the importance of context as driving a series of intervening processes that mediate the impact of pedagogical influences on learning is very recent. A consequence of this criticism for how to find the most productive approaches to sustaining innovation would be to look, not for practices of effective schools, but for interactions between different practices and different contexts. Such approaches would begin to acknowledge the variation that exists between children, including low-income children, and to collect evidence to build models that simultaneously examine the influence of school policies and poverty conditions on learning. These approaches would lead us to better understand the needs in specific learning contexts attended by low-income children. They would invite the perspectives of key actors in those contexts, such as children, teachers, and parents. Most of the approaches of compensatory education discussed in this book did not originate in this kind of knowledge, but rather reflected the views of central administrators and researchers of what was needed to improve learning opportunity. A mismatch occurred between the approach that was used (targeting efforts to improve learning in specific contexts) and the knowledge and policy used to achieve the objectives (general knowledge and policy prescriptions of a "one size fits all" nature). With the exception of a small component aimed at fostering local innovation in the case of Chile and Argentina, the policies followed in Argentina, Chile, Colombia, and Mexico mobilized resources and solutions with very limited opportunities for local adaptation and innovation.

The second strategic choice is how to innovate in education in terms of contents or pedagogies. It is useful to address this question separately for different grade levels. For those levels and children where the opportunity cost is higher—those where there are more pressures to abandon school in order to work—innovation might be necessary in the form of different educational objectives. This is a point alluded to by the Schiefelbeins when they argue that the second main reason low-income children abandon secondary education is because they get bored and do not find it relevant. Sarmiento brings up the same issue for the case of Colombia as does Bracho to explain the lack of secondary school participation of poor children in Mexico. It is quite possible that children opt to work or to take internships, as opposed to attending high school, when they perceive that the former are more likely to give them skills that will help them get jobs later on. For those levels that are basically preparatory for the upper levels, innovation might be necessary in the form of alternative strategies of delivery, such as Escuela Nueva in Colombia, enabling teachers in rural areas to effectively handle multigrade classrooms.

The third strategic choice involves how much innovation is necessary. The chapters discussing the PARE program in Mexico, the policies toward indigenous children in Mexico, and the Social Education Plan in Argentina show that in terms of the effects of compensatory policies, their implementation is as critical as the soundness of their design. Recognizing that there is limited management capacity in the system serving the poorest children and that these schools are vulnerable, attempting to do less may be the only way to do more. Very innovative models, which have a small likelihood of being implemented, will do little for equity even if under ideal conditions the expected effects should be great. A simple innovation such as providing primers to all children, with an expected effect on achievement of 20 percent increase in reading ability and with an implementation likelihood of 100 percent is a better option than a more complex innovation such as educating teachers to work with a constructivist approach to developing literacy, with a greater expected effect on reading achievement of 30 percent increase in reading ability but with an implementation likelihood of 50 percent. The average net implemented effect in the system of the textbooks will be a 20 percent increase in reading ability, but only 15 percent for the new curriculum. Consequently, attending to the implementability of compensatory policies should be a central consideration in choosing alternatives and not an afterthought.

WHAT HAVE WE LEARNED AND WHAT MUST WE STILL LEARN FROM RECENT EXPERIENCE WITH COMPENSATORY POLICIES?

The chapter by Muñoz and Ahuja highlights how little we have learned from what appears to be a remarkable and massive policy initiative in Mexico. The chapter by Orfield reaches similar conclusions regarding the massive investments in compensatory education in the United States. Documenting program implementation, testing the models embedded in the programs, and discussing and assessing the impact of these programs in a broad range of outcomes have not yet been a central preoccupation of policymakers or of the research community. The few studies that have been conducted appear to have had some impact in reorienting program management (though not program theory).

The chapters by García-Huidobro and the Schiefelbeins on the impact of compensatory policies in Chile reinforce the results available for Mexico; there appears to be improvements in completion rates, but not in learning outcomes, as a result of such policy interventions. Most of the research follows a black box approach, failing to identify significant changes in learning outcomes. There is limited information about program implementation. Only short-term effects are assessed in a narrow set of cognitive domains, as measured by multiple-option tests. The critical perspective offered by the Schiefelbeins' questions the predictive validity of these tests to obtain high-paying jobs in today's labor market. As in the case of Mexico, the greatest challenge in Chile appears to be in documenting changes in teacher capabilities. And, as in Mexico, the existing studies document relatively short-term effects of these policies, spanning over six to seven years.

Chile's recent policies to improve equity in education, like Mexico's, suggest that it is possible to provide inputs to the most disadvantaged schools, hence reducing inequality. In spite of the emphasis of Chilean policy on positive discrimination, and its emphasis on assessing inequality in learning outcomes as a starting point for policy, there are conflicting accounts as to whether the achievement gaps between the poor and the non-poor narrowed. The conflict stems, in part, from the adjustment made to student achievement scores to make them comparable over time. If, in fact, the gap in learning outcomes did close, as suggested by García-Huidobro, this is a significant example of positive discrimination. It should be pointed out that these reforms were implemented in a context where total expenditures in education increased significantly and when other social policies and significant economic growth resulted in reduction of the incidence of overall poverty. The existing studies do not discuss this context nor do they attempt to differentiate the contributions of compensatory policies from the effects of these other policy-induced changes. Judging from differences in raw student achievement scores, the gains over time for all schools are greater than the reduction in the gap between the targeted schools and the nontargeted schools. Therefore, some potentially promising avenues to enhance student learning are left unexplored in this study.

The chapter by Aguerrondo describes the Social Education Plan in Argentina which targeted 3,000 schools with the lowest achievement levels for priority attention similar to the 900 Schools Program in Chile. Studies of the impact of these policies suggest that it is easier to distribute inputs than to educate teachers and that changes in student achievement levels are modest. The chapter by Sarmiento about Colombia focuses on equity policies that emphasized reorienting education expenditures toward rural areas and supporting Escuela Nueva, a program to strengthen the quality of rural schools. The reorientation of expenditures expanded access to different levels. Escuela Nueva has been assessed by various studies documenting that children in rural multigrade schools, where teachers are appropriately trained and where learning materials are available, do significantly better than students in less-endowed rural schools. The basic story of these studies is similar: It is possible to improve the learning conditions of poor children through policies that enhance learning inputs. There are great challenges in implementation, though particularly when the policies involve altering instructional practices. While effects in terms of student achievement and completion rates can be documented, the long-term correlates of those effects have not been assessed. Studies are biased toward short-term effects, probably because sponsors of research are more interested in recent policies than in assessing effects over fairly long periods.

The chapters about Argentina, Chile, Colombia, and Mexico presented in this book highlight the importance of basic school supplies and infrastructural conditions to enable school learning. Children do better when they have textbooks, when their schools are not in disrepair, when they have school libraries, and when their teachers have instructional resources. What the studies do not answer is the question of how far the expansion of such basic provision of school inputs can go. It is reasonable to expect that the effects of these strategies will level off after a point. In fact, the data provided by García-Huidobro suggests that this may indeed be the case. The study by the Schiefelbeins suggests that our concern ought not to be with equalizing outcomes in learning old and dated knowledge, but with developing problem-solving skills and the application of knowledge to new contexts. None of the existing studies in Mexico, Chile, or elsewhere focus on the question of which skills are more relevant to facilitate intergenerational social mobility and the reduction of inequality.

WHAT REMAINS TO BE LEARNED?

The studies of compensatory policies presented and discussed in this book raise as many questions as they answer. What is the practical significance of student achievement in the tests used to measure curriculum coverage? How does performance on these tests relate to life chances? How well does performance on these tests predict performance in higher levels of education? What is the influence of the compensatory programs on other social and attitudinal outcomes? What is the impact of these programs on building social capital in the communities? What are the perspectives of the intended beneficiaries of these programs? What do they think they get out of them? What do they think about how these programs should be run? Existing evaluations document the relatively short term impact of these programs. As the inputs they support consolidate, how do their effects change?

We need to know more about the intensity of additional resources necessary to achieve significant effects in learning outcomes of low-income children. A simple cost accounting of the total level of resources, public and private, spent on the education of children from different income groups would help to set the boundaries of the challenge of closing the equity gap. It should be acknowledged that the stark inequalities among primary schools serving different children occur in contexts of relatively low levels of spending and quality for all children enrolled in public schools in Latin America. In spite of the fact that international organizations and governments have been more prone to emphasize reforms to improve resource utilization (which assumes that there is unutilized or poorly utilized capacity in the system), the public education systems in Latin America spend significantly less per student than the United States or the Caribbean. Expenditures per pupil in primary education, as a percentage of GNP per capita, exceed 25 percent only in Costa Rica and Cuba.[5] In most other countries they are significantly below this level (UNESCO 2000).[6] As a percentage of GNP, public spending on primary education is highest in Cuba (2.5 percent) and Costa Rica (3.3 percent) and significantly lower in most other countries.[7]

We also need to know more about the conditions that foster school improvement and about the social dynamics that explain why some schools targeted by compensatory policies improve to achieve consistently high levels of learning for their students and others do not. That is, future studies need to reveal more about the implementation process at the school level. What are the organizational and cultural factors that facilitate and impede the change of school and classroom processes?

In addition to studies that examine the effects of compensatory policies, our understanding of the alternatives to expand the educational chances of the poor would benefit from two additional forms of research: needs assessments and experimentation. Needs assessments could explicitly investigate which outcomes (social and cultural capital, job skills, social and political skills, and attitudes) are associated with social mobility and with expanding life chances. Identification of these outcomes of education, along with surveys of beneficiaries about what they perceive to be their needs and diagnostic studies of the conditions prevalent in the schools attended by low-income children could inform the development of innovations along the lines suggested earlier in this chapter. Planned variation could be studied in small-scale, radical experiments designed to offer alternative forms to develop those skills and to overcome the constraints identified in the needs assessments. It is especially urgent to design innovative approaches that are not based on deficit theory as explanations for school failure among the poor. These experiments can provide the knowledge base to support restructuring efforts in ways that the assessment of options implemented in the existing system may not.[8]

THE POLITICAL CONTEXT OF RESEARCH UTILIZATION

So far I have argued for more research on ways to enhance the effectiveness of schools serving low-income children. This will yield pedagogical knowledge of value to improve the technical effectiveness and efficiency of schools. But such studies of policy as social experimentation will yield only part of the knowledge necessary to support social change in Latin America. Evaluation designs should reflect multiple ways to value program benefits by different stakeholders in ways that existing studies have not. Poverty policies are contested terrain in which conflict among goals is more likely than consensus among program participants. The implicit assumption of existing studies is that there is a single set of goals and objectives of programs; a constructionist perspective to program evaluation would alter this assumption.

In addition to studies about the pedagogical effectiveness of compensatory policies, we need studies that adopt a political perspective and a cultural perspective of the change process, particularly in the investigation of the micropolitics of school change. To the extent power is an organizing feature of schools and school systems, we need to understand how existing power arrangements are challenged by compensatory programs and how they limit the range of possible options to be considered or implemented.

The generation of more knowledge about the impact of policies to improve the educational chances of children of the poor needs to take place in the context of a critical assessment of the conditions of policy formulation, decision making, and policy implementation. The high levels of social exclusion that characterize Latin America are indicative of politics and history that have produced and maintain such inequities. Compensatory policies are formulated and implemented in a context and through mechanisms that reflect the very inequalities of origin that are at the root of the problem they try to correct. New knowledge to support social change needs to contribute to the formation of an ideology and political frameworks that seek greater social justice. It cannot simply assume that benevolent government officials would do what is right for the poor if they just knew how. The poor themselves and the coalitions of interests to support their options and freedom should be the prime constituency for this knowledge. This knowledge should feed into democratic and public processes of dialogue and debate and not be hijacked by the politics of secrecy and exclusion that have dominated policy formation in the region for most of the last decades.

POLITICS AND IMPLEMENTATION

Different groups in society advance at different paces in their understanding of whether and how the education system should foster equality. In loosely coupled organizations there is much room for policy formulation at the implementation stage. Getting national or federal governments to launch initiatives to foster equal educational opportunity is a long way from changing the social context of schools. Local administrators and leaders, teachers, principals, students, and communities recreate policy in ways that may be counter to intended policy objectives. Perhaps, like no other area of public action, poverty programs and policies are contested terrain. They are, therefore, prime territory for deconstruction, reconstruction, and destruction. It is no accident that the study of implementation in the United States began with the study of federal programs for poverty alleviation (Pressman and Wildavsky 1973). Education systems are arenas for political conflict among opposing interests. Unequal societies have forces that support reproduction of inequality, and they will resist reformed schools that seek greater equality. Where more financial resources are required to fund schools attended by the children of the poor, sustaining progressive reforms will require effective demand from the beneficiaries of these reforms—students or their parents. These efforts might be resisted by those who lose out from the reallocations of public expenditures or by those who will have to pay higher taxes to fund these initiatives. This will make change difficult and slow and its outcomes uncertain.

The chapters in this book show that the social processes that contribute to the reproduction of social inequality in the education system do not operate in a social vacuum. They operate in contexts where some social actors—elected officials, education administrators, teachers and parents, and to an extent, students—try to resist them. The efforts of these actors, individually and collectively, constitute a force that works to overcome the inertial influence of inequality.

Equality of educational opportunity in a given country, at a given point in time, is the point of equilibrium between these opposing forces of social reproduction and resistance. For the same country, this point of equilibrium can shift over time. The point of equilibrium differs across countries. The chapters in this book document several efforts to push the point of equilibrium toward greater equality. The authors document evidence of successes in making it more likely that low-income children learn more. There are, however, important questions remaining regarding these efforts. How many resources are necessary to reach a point of equilibrium of equality? How strong must the forces of resistance be to combat reproduction of inequality? How much should be invested in compensatory and affirmative action programs?

All the resources invested in the programs discussed in this book amount to relatively little in terms of resources per student. The additional financial resources of the boldest compensatory education policy is a modest fraction of per capita income, or particularly of the income of the wealthiest 40 percent of the population. Because families in some countries contribute almost as much as does the state to the education of their children, only the most deliberate and significant efforts to shift public education expenditures toward the children of the poor stand a chance of moving the equilibrium point toward greater equality. None of the efforts discussed in this book is of this magnitude. In this sense, we can conclude the obvious: Educational inequality persists and poverty of education for poor children is so widespread in the hemisphere because eliminating poverty and reducing inequality has not been a sufficiently important priority for governments and the non-poor.

It is remarkable that in all the current discourse about education reform at the hemispheric level there is almost nothing questioning whether enough is being spent on the education of the poor. At the same time, there is an abundance of rhetoric circulating about the need to improve efficiency and to manage what is being spent more wisely. Is all the discourse about the inefficiency in public expenditures on education a cover-up, a distraction, for the real elephant in the middle of the room—the insufficiency of the resources devoted to try to give poor children a real chance to gain an education of value? Are the multiple objectives of the current education reforms in the region (quality, efficiency, relevancy) code language for not making reduction of inequality a central goal of public policy? Some might argue that the economies of the region are too strapped to even consider spending additional funds on education. But how many bailouts of bankrupt banks in the region have been financed by public funds in the past ten years? How much public and private corruption has been swept under the carpet to be picked up as debts owed by future taxpayers? What is the value added to the well-being of the Latin American citizens from the portion of the public budget devoted to military expenditures? These questions are painful reminders that competing interests occupy the agenda of elected officials and that addressing poverty is only one, perhaps not the most important, of the priorities of citizens and governments in the Americas.

Educational improvement takes time, particularly when it involves fundamental changes to what goes on inside schools as opposed to more straightforward initiatives such as getting more children to attend school. This book reminds us that progress is not inevitable and that setbacks in equity gains are possible. The chapter by Orfield suggests that progress in improving equity in education is much slower than decline. Progress can be gauged only over very extended periods of time, but it is possible to see setbacks in shorter periods.

Whether the slow progress in reaching out to new groups reflects the challenges of incorporating the poor into the education system reflects the fact that not enough resources have been allocated to this objective amounts to the same thing: Both express insufficient priority given to incorporating the poor into the education system. It is common in Latin American policy circles, whether in the offices of Ministries of Education, in the corridors of international agencies, or in the meetings and conventions of government officials and even educators, to hear that the main problem to be addressed is quality and that the urgency of this problem is heightened by the requirements of globalization and competitiveness. To the children who will not complete primary school or who will not have a secondary school certificate, policy choices around these distinctions matter greatly. To concentrate on the quality of the education for those students who are already in the system is equivalent to constraining the educational chances of those who are not. It is not clear that all employers in the hemisphere have the capacity to assess different degrees of student achievement, but it is certain that they can all use a credential to screen out applicants for positions when the number of applicants exceeds the number of vacancies. Similarly, there is no chance to progress to higher levels without a credential. To justify excluding children from certain education levels in the name of quality is at best based on the assumption that the curriculum in different education levels is so heavily sequenced and structured that success in higher levels is possible only upon mastery of the contents of lower levels. This assumption is questionable. There is no evidence that performance in primary or even secondary school is a good predictor of college success. As we have seen earlier, there is very little research-based knowledge on which to base any sophisticated argument on the dynamic links between early success in school, success in proceeding to higher levels of education, and the impact of both of these processes in getting children out of poverty.

The fact that investments in support of the education of poor children is so inadequate to the task of achieving results suggests that the non-poor have expectations that are self-fulfilling. Perhaps most people in the Americas believe in an implicit glass ceiling that dictates how much is possible in terms of achieving equity and that, short of a political revolution where achieving equity becomes a fundamental organizing social principle, we really think of equity as a dream or an empty promise. Because we do not think it is seriously possible to counter the sources that reproduce social inequality and stratification, we do not commit the resources to this goal that would make it possible. As a result, policy initiatives in this area serve a primarily symbolic purpose, to signal to the poor an apparent desire to improve their opportunities, perhaps to justify the legitimacy of those elected, but not to seriously affect the functioning of the educational machinery. From this perspective, policy rhetoric on equality of educational opportunity is designed to maintain the dream of equal opportunity— to make the striking social inequalities more acceptable as parents hope that their children will have a better chance—confounding the poor into believing that just because their children achieve higher levels of education than they themselves did, that they will get ahead in life. The rhetoric avoids the issue that what matters is not just whether there is intergenerational educational progression, but whether there are differential rates of progression among income groups, with more gains at the lower levels of the income distribution.

But the chapters in this book also support the view that change is possible—that education systems can, and have, at different times and in different places, expanded educational opportunities for poor children. Educational inequality is thus not an intractable sign of our times, nor is it a necessary price to pay to benefit from global integration of the economy. Rather, it is a human process—the result of collective decisions made about who should be educated, how, and at what cost.

Education poverty is therefore the result of a choice, not just of the poor but also, perhaps primarily, of the non-poor. It is the result of how the non-poor define their interests and responsibilities and about how they influence priorities for public action. Central to studying how to change educational chances for the poor is focusing on the right outcomes. It is not enough to choose options that promise higher levels of results for poor students. The goal should be to close the gap with the non-poor. Quality innovations that improve the achievement of poor students, but improve even more the achievement of the non-poor, will widen, rather than narrow, the education gap between these groups. We need to better understand not just how poor and non-poor students compare in access, promotion, and examination scores, but also which school outcomes matter the most in fostering individual social mobility of some students and greater solidarity and equality. These outcomes must include both the poor and the non-poor.

Because the impact of these reforms is predicated on efforts that must be sustained over long periods of time, it is important that a large number of people in society understand and have ownership of these changes. As education becomes an increasingly important process in social stratification, it is crucial to ensure equal opportunity. To ignore this is to allow education systems to act as the key mechanism for the reproduction and increase of social inequality. That expanding educational opportunity to poor children is possible reminds us of how far we have come in the Americas in understanding that all persons are created equal and have a right to expect from others fair and equal chances. Still, there is much left to learn and do in this long road to help all children develop capabilities that will make them free.

NOTES

1. Obviously, access and quality become inextricably linked as one moves up the education ladder. Access to secondary education is possible only upon completion of primary education, which is possible only upon a strong foundation of early learning, all of which requires quality teaching.
2. Note that an alternative way to organize the curriculum is through individualized or flexible forms of instruction, where it is possible for children to advance at their own pace, or to catch up with their peers, reducing the negative consequences of missing school days or entire school periods. This was done in the Escuela Nueva program in Colombia as discussed in the chapter by Sarmiento.
3. I subscribe to Beeby's view of education systems as proceeding through stages even if the specific characteristics that distinguish one stage from the next may vary across contexts.
4. Defining the necessary level is not something that can be done a priori in typical top-down fashion. It is something that can be done only beginning at the school level, asking what should change in each kind of school to improve the way students spend their time in activities that foster high levels of learning and progressively mapping backward, asking how policy can facilitate these changes (Elmore 1982).
5. Expenditures per pupil in primary education, as a percentage of GNP per capita, in Argentina is 12 percent; Bolivia, 12 percent; Colombia, 12 percent; Chile, 12 percent; Costa Rica, 25 percent; Cuba, 27 percent; Dominican Republic, 6 percent; Ecuador, 9 percent; El Salvador,

7 percent; Guatemala, 5 percent; Mexico, 12 percent; Paraguay, 12 percent; Peru, 7 percent; and Uruguay, 9 percent (UNESCO 2000). It is perhaps no accident that in a recent assessment of student achievement in a sample of schools in several Latin American countries, Cuban students scored significantly higher than their counterparts in other countries (Costa Rica did not participate in the study) (UNESCO 1998).

6. This figure is 26 percent in the United States.

7. This figure is 4.4 percent in the United States. In Argentina it is 1.6 percent; Bolivia, 2.2 percent; Colombia, 1.1 percent; Chile, 1.3 percent; Dominican Republic, 1.1 percent; Ecuador, 1.2 percent; El Salvador, 1.4 percent; Guatemala, 0.8 percent; Mexico, 1.7 percent; Nicaragua, 2.3 percent; Paraguay, 2.1 percent; Peru, 1.4 percent; and Uruguay, 1 percent (UNESCO 2000).

8. The restructuring literature points to the limits to changing the "core" of teaching through control mechanisms, incentives, and learning opportunities in schools where organizational structure, culture, and norms maintain compliance with existing practices. In the United States, restructuring represents the most recent approach to school change, following a journey of four decades that has included innovation and diffusion, organizational development, knowledge utilization and transfer, the creation of new schools, management of local reform, training of change agents, and management of systemic reform (Miles 1998).

REFERENCES

Beeby, C. 1986. The stages of growth in educational systems. In *The Quality of Education and Economic Development,* ed. S. Heyneman and D. White, 37–44. Washington, D.C.: World Bank.

CEPAL/UNESCO. 1992. *Education and Knowledge.* Santiago, Chile: United Nations.

Elmore, R. 1982. Backward mapping: Implementation research and policy decisions. In *Studying Implementation: Methodological and Administrative Issues,* ed. W. Williams et al., 18–35. Chatham, N.J.: Chatham House.

Freire, Paulo. 1970. *Pedagogy of the Oppressed.* New York: Continuum.

Miles, M. 1998. Finding keys to school change: A 40 year odyssey. In *International Handbook of Educational Change,* ed. A. Hargreaves et al., 37–69. Dordrecht, Netherlands: Kluwer Academic.

Pressman, Jeffrey, and Aaron Wildavsky. 1973. *Implementation.* Berkeley, Calif.: University of California Press.

Sen, Amartya. 1992. *Inequality Reexamined.* Cambridge, Mass.: Harvard University Press.

Swope, John, and Marcela Latorre. 1999. *Comunidades Educativas Donde Termina el Asfalto.* Santiago, Chile: CIDE.

UNESCO-OREALC. 2000. Regional report of the Americas: An assessment of the Education for All Program in the year 2000. Mimeograph. Santiago, Chile: UNESCO, Oficina Regional para America Latina y el Caribe.

Index

Ability grouping. *See* Tracking
Access to schooling, 6, 7, 9, 10, 14, 26, 70–71, 74,
    77, 93, 113, 114, 128, 158, 161, 211–216,
    239, 406, 433–434, 434–435, 435, 450n1
  for black students, 53
  and compensatory policy, 135
  and educational demand, 348
  and educational policy, 11
  expansion of, in Argentina, 140–143, 152, 158;
    in Brazil, 67; in Mexico, 67, 312
  and income, 257
  and income inequality, 21
  in Peru, 20
  and poverty, 4, 14
  and PROGRESA (Programa de Educación,
    Salud y Alimentación [Program of Education,
    Health, and Nutrition], Mexico), 18
  of rural children in Mexico, and school factors,
    316
  and social justice, 162
  and socioeconomic level of family, 184–185, 185
  and U.S. educational policy, 406
Achievement
  under PARE, 348–368
  predictors of, 30
  and regional socioeconomic development, 342
  and socioeconomic background, 6, 45, 146
Achievement levels, 6, 86–87
  in Argentina, 159
  assessment of, in Mexico, 427–428
  and education level of parents, 77–78
  in Mexico, 30, 82, 83
  and nutrition, 369
  in Peru, 82, 391
  and poverty, in Argentina, 27; in Brazil, 27; in
    Chile, 27; in Mexico, 27
  and socioeconomic level of family, 369
Achievement test, 22, 27, 234, 329, 333n8, 411.
    See also System of Measurement of Quality
    of Education (SIMCE, Chile)
Achievement-test scores, 44, 46, 354, 355,
    420–421, 444
  and Basic Needs Unmet (NBI, Argentina), 149
  and educational credential, 415
  and educational policy goals, 416, 428
  and family socioeconomic status, 413, 415, 420
  and Indian schools, 329
  international, and U.S. high-poverty schools,
    412–413
  as marketing tool, 420
  and race-contextual schools, 46–47
Affirmative action, 14, 21, 42, 48, 94
  in Chile, 16–17, 183–201
  in Colombia, 17

defined, 198n1
  and remedy, 48
Age
  and educational demand, 348
  at grade level, 347. *See also* Educational delay
  and grade repetition, 91–92
  and school attendance, 293–296, 315
  at start of basic education, 298–300, 316
Aguerrondo, Inés, 15, **136–155,** 157, 444
Ahuja Sánchez, Raquel, 20, **340–373,** 440, 443
ANMEB. *See* National Agreement for the
    Modernization of Basic Education
Argentina
  access to schooling in, 139–147
  achievement levels and poverty in, 27
  country schools in, 155n21
  economic growth in, 59
  educational finance in, 149–150
  educational policy and poverty in, 137–155,
    157–159
  enrollment rates and poverty, 139, 140
  Federal Educational Act, 147–148, 154n9
  primary education in, 9, 15
  Social Education Plan, 148–151, 158
  and universal education, 10
Arregui, Patricia, 20, **376–396**
Assimilationism, in Mexico, 336
Association of Indian Teachers and Professionals
    (Mexico), 320
At-risk students, 96
Authoritarianism, and educational information,
    97

Basic education, 110, 134, 147, 239, 251, 291
  defined, 295
  for Indian populations, 323, 371n9
Basic needs, 205, 206, 250
Basic Needs Unmet (NBI, Argentina), 149, 153
Basic rights, and redistributive policy, 250
Basic skills, 415, 416
Bello, Andres, 133
Bilingual-bicultural education, 321, 322, 323–325,
    347, 371n5
  defined, 320
Black-isolated schools, 45
  achievement-test scores in, 46
  and poverty, 404, 424n6
Blacks
  attending white schools, 409
  in Brazil, 64
  college access, 409–410
  marginalization of, 133
  and U.S. secondary education, 41
Black Wealth/White Wealth, 42